Fighting Prosaic Messages
A Portrait of Family Literacies with Critical Essays on the Causes of School Failure

HENRY C AMOROSO, JR

edited by
JUSTIN AMOROSO

Fighting Prosaic Message: A Portrait of Family Literacies
with Critical Essays on the Causes of School Failure

Printed in the United States of America
ISBN 979-8-89633-038-7 (sc)
ISBN 979-8-89633-039-4 (e)

This book is printed on acid-free paper.

2025.04.10

Page Solutions - Prowriters Network
124 Rock Crystal Ln,
Lakeside Park,
KY 41017A
United States

PAGE
SOLUTIONS
PROWRITERS NETWORK

Fighting Prosaic Messages

A Portrait of Family
Literacies with Critical
Essays on the Causes
of School Failure

HENRY C AMOROSO, JR
Edited by Justin Amoroso

For
Rose and Carmelo Amoroso

A Note to the Reader

Literacy is as much ethereal as it is material. That is because reading and writing are acts of knowing that encompass creativity, choice, and self-expression. To understand literacy is to understand cultural-historical reality. Societies, including our own, do not give the gift of literacy to all. As a former literacy worker in the Caribbean, Africa, and in North America, I can attest to the reality of this statement.

For the past 30 years I have written and spoken about the sorrow that is illiteracy. I have also challenged my students to think of literacy and pedagogy in activist terms. *Fighting Prosaic Messages* gives voice to the millions of poor and working-class Americans, past and present, who struggle to be literate.

I used family literacies to challenge readers to question why so many Americans do not express themselves in reading and in writing. The pattern of literacy across four generations of my relatives has been obstruction. My immigrant grandmother never received fair and just acknowledgment of her literacies from the mill owners she worked for in Lawrence, Massachusetts. My father could read and write yet still failed in school. I turned my back on books until I graduated. Tragically my son's voice was nearly extinguished in school. The real power of literacy, a way to understand experience, was not given freely to us.

This book is about how we can make the gift of literacy more available to all.

—Henry C. Amoroso, Jr.

First Foreword

This was from an email that a former student of Henry's wrote to me after he passed.

—Marilyn Amoroso

Henry was my mentor, not only professionally, but also in life.

I met Henry in the late 1990's when I was a student in his literacy courses at USM. I was a hotheaded new teacher and he was my professor, who listened intently, and helped me see truth and find understanding through his gentle humor and guidance. I was drawn into his stories, by his grassroots efforts and by his genuine respect for all people. He was so clearly intelligent, an intellectual with real world experience and research to his credit, but there was not an ounce of pretense about him. He was approachable, a wonderful listener and always ready to share his insight in a manner that was never haughty, arrogant or assuming. His values were clear, and it was for these reasons that I immediately respected him and grew so fond of him.

Henry's teaching changed the way I saw my role as an educator of young children. Through my exploration of ideas and through considering the thoughtful questions Henry posed in his classes, I grew to understand that my work as an educator was to look less at the big picture, and more into the individual stories, strengths and challenges of the children and families that were in my care. His guidance helped me see my place in the intricate web of people who help children grow and learn, rather than operating as a one-woman show as I had in the past. Whereas I began my career thinking that I knew how to teach, and just wished people would leave me alone to get down to the business of doing so, Henry's influence helped me understand that each child actually taught me about teaching and learning in his or her own unique way. What I learned from Henry humbled me, and helped me become a more effective, more caring teacher and far more in touch with the students and families I served.

His influence did not stop within the confines of my teaching. Henry was a mentor whom I respected because of his enduring love of and commitment to his family. As we began working on projects together at the University, our relationship changed from that of a Professor and student to that of being friends. I feel blessed to have the opportunity to sit with him in his backyard garden and listen to his stories of his grandmother Rose, and his thoughts about family. In our conversations, we shared our similar upbringings, his in a loud Sicilian Italian Catholic family and mine in my loud Franco American Catholic family. We shared a lot of laughs and marveled at how we had similar experiences even though we were a generation apart. On every occasion, we spoke of family, of our grandparents, our parents and of our spouses and children. It was clear that his family was everything to him, and this is one of the greatest reasons I had such respect for him.

Henry was a man who deserved to sit at the head of the table, but would never have placed himself in that position because he desired to raise others into that position. He did that as a teacher, challenging his students to think intellectually through the heart, with respect for all people. He invited us to sit at the head of the table over and over. Most impressive was that this was very natural for Henry, done without any need for restraint or specific planning. His genuine interest in his students' thoughts and feelings was unique, and I appreciated every chance I got to spend time with him.

Henry was a special man, who made an enormous difference not only in his students' lives, but also in the lives of the children who were fortunate enough to have teachers who learned from Henry. He was a great man, who valued and respected people above any material item or fancy title. He lived his life as a model to others, never assuming a pious manner, and because of this his impact was empowering. I am a better teacher and person because I learned from him. For this I will always be thankful.

Jennifer McClure Groover
Department of Education Faculty Member
University of Southern Maine
September 2010

Second Foreword

Henry Amoroso was my teacher, mentor and friend. Henry encouraged me to question the assumptions, most often made without critical analysis, that are behind many educational decisions. He introduced me to critical theory and set me on a path to work for more caring and just educational practices.

Henry was a champion for the underdog, a defender of those whose education had been marginalized. His was not the radical's cry; it wasn't about revolution, and it wasn't about anger. Henry was passionate but, above all, he was a true listener who encouraged his students to *tell their story* and to *find their voice*.

Henry placed personal narrative as the central act of knowing. My story with Henry started with a misunderstanding. This misunderstanding brought us together, which makes sense and fits the narrative of our relationship. The misunderstanding was a result of an assumption I had made which led to our deep and lifelong friendship. Henry knew how important relationships are to teaching and was set on finding ways to connect with his students beyond the academic setting.

My story with Henry, whether as a student in his classes, working with him as an adult educator, teaching a graduate class in his honor, crawling under his 200-year-old house to fix his plumbing, all served to enrich and inform my life. For those who take the time to read and listen to Henry's voice emerge from this publication, a vital connection can be made with this caring and insightful educator.

Bo Hewey
Instructor
Saco-Old Orchard Beach Adult Education
March 2017

Third Foreword

I have a passion for philosophy and I feel blessed that I get to teach it. My dad was the one who introduced philosophy to me, and how he did so illustrates what kind of teacher he was.

Let me back up for a sec and share a little backdrop on my parents. My mother and father were like night and day. They had certain core values in common like education, but they were different. For example, my dad looked so much like Santa Claus that kids would stop him at the Mall during Christmas time to give him their Christmas lists. My mom is a statuesque black woman who, when she was young, looked like she could have sold Christian Dior mascara. An odd-looking couple? Oh, yes.

Here was another difference: my dad got his PhD, and my mother stayed home to raise us kids, unable to complete college. My dad used to say she was smarter than him. She *is* smart. She's one of those who actually listens to her gut and often sees through the B.S. as a result. I'm grateful for their differences as I've learned a lot from both of them.

And where my dad was a recovering Catholic, she was a born-again Baptist. When growing up, I remember one argument they had about the existence of dinosaurs. The Bible didn't mention them, so she told him they didn't exist. My dad was like, "Marilyn are you nuts? There are dinosaur bones!"

Here's my point. As a kid, I was raised as a born-again Christian by my mother. I went to a Baptist Church every Sunday, went to Bible camp in the summer, and thought the world was created in seven 24-hour days. Knowing this about me, here's how my dad introduced Plato (and philosophy) to me. I was in the sixth grade.

Intrigued by the picture on the cover of a book I found in my dad's office on Plato's writings, I asked my dad who this guy "Plato" was. He said Plato had discovered the principles of Christianity 400 years before Christ, by using the power of his mind. Whoa. The mind had that kind of power? Plus, on our car rides to school my dad would ask us kids fun questions to make us think. He captured our imaginations, and I can tell you personally I haven't looked back since.

Now, my dad could have spoken about philosophy like it was accessible only to *those* who went to like "Oxford" or something. No. Instead, he put himself where I was in my sixth-grade life, then spoke about philosophy in terms I could understand, and in a way that sparked my imagination. In the process, he got me to think without my even knowing it. That was the kind of teacher he was. He made learning a joy. This book talks about education of that sort.

You could say this book critiques the kind of education that operates like a business transaction. A "transactional" educator might exchange rewards (or punishments) for performance. They might search for where a student deviates from the rules and correct them, the way a manager might administer employees. Worse, this kind of educator might stress the accumulation of facts and information and give "gold stars" accordingly. Rather than awaken a student's desire to learn, learning would become a chore. In fact, one could argue in this model, what a student might really be learning is how to become a good employee.

This book offers an alternative. Classrooms may need "transactions" to a certain extent, but if they stop there, would students ever be motivated to learn because they want to? And would they grow and "transform" in the process? I mentioned Plato earlier. His allegory of the nature of education gets to the heart of the kind of education my dad was after in this book.

If Plato is right, students begin their education like prisoners trapped in a dark cave, trapped by the puppet show their parents, teachers, priests, friends, and media put on to tell them what is real. Only when the prisoner begins to question those beliefs and seek answers for himself does he free himself from those chains. Once he finds his way out of the cave into the sun and fresh air outside—in reality—his soul is turned to the light and he desires *that* rather than the darkness of the cave. I imagine this experience like those "aha" moments we have that make us feel a shift within. Once his desire has shifted, this ex-prisoner now wants to share his discovery, and so returns to the cave to tell those who still think the puppet show is reality about the fresh air outside. Yes, they resist him—but that's a whole other story.

For Plato, education isn't only about memorizing facts or doing busywork or following the norms to get that stamp of approval. That only keeps us enthralled by the puppet show. True education is about turning the soul beyond the shadows the puppets cast to the sunlight so a student may continue to strive after virtue, wisdom and justice long after school is done. So, my dad preferred instilling in a student a genuine desire to learn. He preferred promoting critical and creative thinking skills, as well as to help students find their voices (even if it meant going against the grain). He preferred Socrates's image of the midwife who helps students give birth to their own ideas so students might become better human beings. This book critiques education as transaction and advocates for education as transformation.

And my dad desired to make education accessible to *all*. That's probably why he was disturbed only a few were truly succeeding in schools. You'll see that in this book he'll argue that if more teachers infused humanity into the "scientific management" of classrooms by bringing heart, care, imagination, and critical thinking into them, more students would *want* to leave "the cave" so to speak. The more intrinsically motivated to learn students would be, the more they could bring that into their lives beyond the classroom, and contribute to their communities.

I can't tell you how much the ideas in this book have helped with my own teaching. This book begins a bit unconventionally—unconventionally for an "academic" piece, that is. It begins like a novel, and then ends with a more traditional analysis of school failure. True to form, my dad thought it was important to speak both to the "mythic" or poetic part of our minds (as we tend to learn best through story) *and* to the more analytic part of our minds. The aim in both methods is the same: to understand why many of us fail in school, and what we can do to help more students succeed.

Plato worried about citizen "ignorance" in a democracy, but let me close with a quote that's often attributed to Thomas Jefferson. I think it gets to what is at stake in this book: "Equal rights for all, special privileges for none." If education is an equalizer, then doing our part in helping more students succeed may help us move closer to a true democracy. And if the measure of a society's health is how many of its citizens are able to grow, then this question is imperative to boosting the health of ours.

On a more local scale, where all change must begin, I hope you gain as much from this book as I myself continue to. Sit back, enjoy, and have fun experimenting with these ideas. They have the power to transform.

Justin Amoroso
Philosophy Instructor
Southern Maine Community College
May 2017

A Note on the Editing

My dad finished the writing of this book before he passed, but there was still a lot of work that needed to be done.

Chapters 8-12 had no references, just last names and a single year for a publication. Sometimes the names were misspelled, sometimes the years were wrong. And the chapters needed citations.

Some philosophy discussions weren't completely accurate, as my dad's background was specific to education (not philosophy). So, I did my best to clean any of those discussions when they were needed.

His historical "clipping" sidebars had no prefatory remarks to help lead the reader into his quoted material. And sometimes the intros to his sidebars called "In Their Own Words" were still in draft form, or had no intro at all. I did my best to polish any intros and to provide any prefatory remarks when they were missing.

My dad also wanted the reader to have a visual experience while reading this book, but many of the pictures he provided would have had copyright issues (and often didn't have the right pixel dimensions). So, I tried to find images like the ones he wanted, but that could be used. Plus, every chapter had pictures except for the one about him. To be consistent, I hunted for the pictures you'll find in chapter 6.

Many footnotes were incorrectly numbered, or referred to nothing. Other references weren't complete or correct. Some statistics had become outdated. No "Developments" for 1970-2015 had been written. Chapters weren't ordered correctly (each had been saved as separate documents). Headings in his Table of Contents didn't always match headings in the text. No index had been created to help navigate a book of this size.

Again, my dad finished the writing and the thinking, but it needed that last polish. I tried my best to pull the book together into a whole, scrub it down, and to honor his vision. Still, I know there are probably oversights. If there are any, please give me the blame rather than my dad. My hope is that, if there are any future corrections of this book, I can include them in a possible future edition and get the book even closer to what he had envisioned.

And without the help of a lot of people, this book would still be "incomplete" (though "complete"). My dad hired an editor before he passed, and Wanda Whitten found subtle inconsistencies that helped me strengthen the text. Westbow also did a superb editing job, which helped tremendously. My brother Tim and my girlfriend Jen helped me find references for chapters 8-12. Rita Molloy generously donated her time and expertise to help my mother send the manuscript to different publishers. Jennifer Groover and Bo Hewey provided excellent forewords. And if it wasn't for my mother's persistence in seeing this book published, this book might be still sitting on a hard drive. A huge thank-you goes out to every one of them.

Justin Amoroso
August 2017

Contents

SECTION II. FATHERS AND SONS

PART II. CRITICAL ESSAYS ON THE CAUSES OF LITERACY FAILURE

Table of Figures

Table of "Developments"

Table of Historical "Clippings"

Table of "In Their Own Words"

Preface

Fighting Prosaic Messages addresses painful issues in American education. The first section of Part I begins the story of Rose, a Sicilian immigrant, and traces the lives of three generations of her family in and out of school (see Figure 1). The first three chapters of the "Rose Speaks" trilogy concerns the conflicts that she faces adjusting to new rules and social institutions. Her responses to the challenges posed by her new country illuminate her critical intelligence and serve as the basis for conversations with activists like Emma Goldman and Elizabeth Gurley Flynn, who fought passionately to give voices to the illiterate. In the second section of Part I, the story shifts from the metaphorical to Rose's son's failings in Depression-era schools and to her grandson's search for self-expression. Part I ends with a detailed account of how schooling not only failed to acknowledge her great-grandson's self-taught literacies but nearly stifled them altogether. The essays in Part II expand the understanding of the human side of failure.

Although the book opens lyrically, it quickly manifests the sense of impending doom that accompanies an industrial metaphor out of control. Characters, however strong-willed, are defenseless. Dialogues with real and imagined characters remind readers that the right to voice one's thoughts is crucial for any viable notion of democracy and should lead to a deeper understanding of what it is to be human. Our stories bear witness to the failure of schools to espouse these goals.

Readers learn the fate of Rose and her family, who struggle with assimilation, poverty, language barriers, and meager parental education. Anyone who has ever suffered injustice will find much with which to sympathize in this book. The issues that the essays address—the political extensities of literacy, conformity vs. self-expression, and understanding literacy as a response to moral crises—are empowering. Even so, the obstructions that Rose and her family face as they seek education—stereotyping, superficiality, fixed answers—persist in schools to this day, hence the need to understand the cultural and historical forces that gave rise to and still perpetuate these barriers.

Despite the fact that *Fighting Prosaic Messages* has many subtexts—immigration, intellectual history, intergenerational contexts—its primary goal is to affirm a vision of literacy as truth telling. I hope that its message will appeal to anyone who educates or seeks education.

—Henry C. Amoroso Jr.

Figure 1
Ancestral Chart with Contemporaries Cited in Text

Key: Names in bold are our cast of characters. Names under "Contemporaries" are figures the book cites.

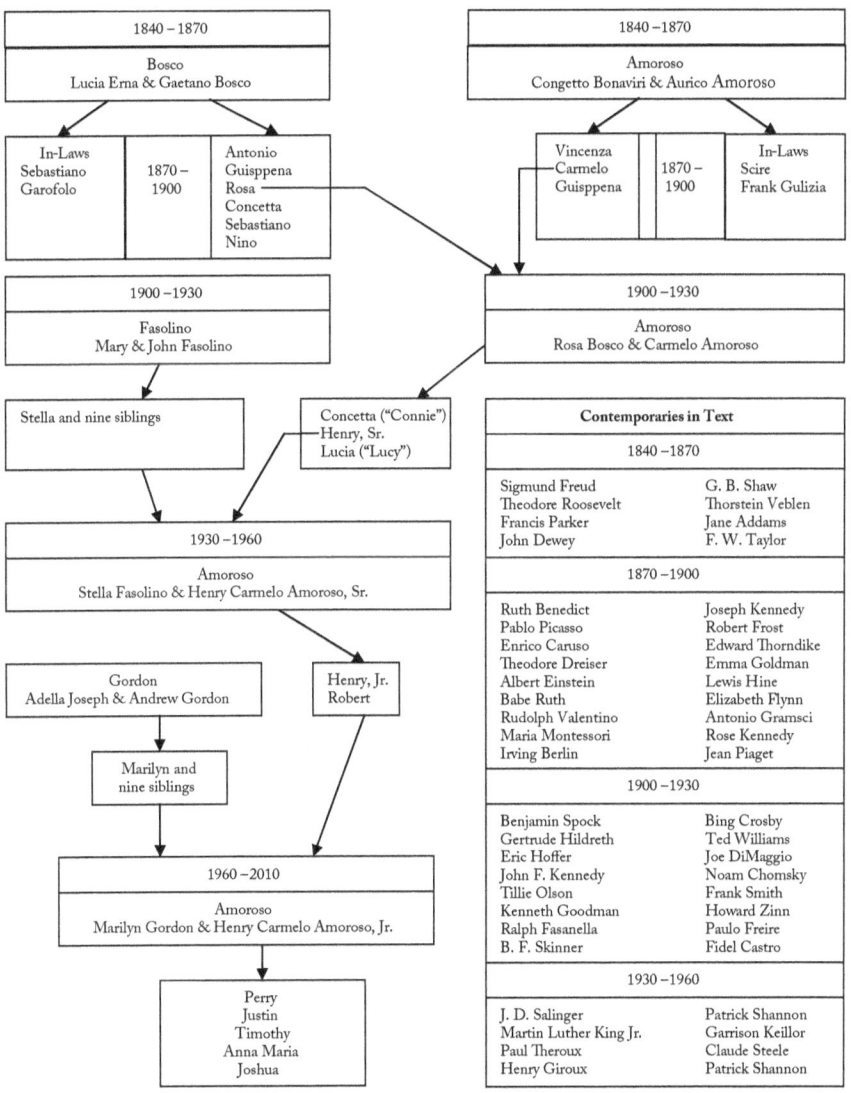

Introduction

A Sober Reader, a vain Tale will slight,
He seeks as well Instruction as Delight
—Horace

Purpose

The purpose of this book is to provide educators, researchers, policymakers, parents, and the general public with ways to understand school failure. I intend it for individuals with little background in educational history or critical theory. My goal is to help readers understand that failure is often rooted in the ethos of schools—the moral fabric and beliefs that govern educational practice.[1] Many ideologies exist in any given school. Some contribute to real learning; others are harmful and, when left unexamined, perpetuate failure.

A special feature of *Fighting Prosaic Messages* is its two-part design. Part I dramatizes the literacy histories of my grandmother, my father, myself, and one of my sons as we searched for our identities as learners. Each story is distinctive and interconnected, embedded in the social and historical contexts that shaped and gave meaning to us, with special attention to the roles of teachers, parents, and community members in our development.

My grandmother came to this country as a single woman with little formal education (see Figure 2). She would need the moral perfection of the saints to survive the harsh realities of American life. My father was a school dropout who never overcame his reluctance to read and write or the feeling that he was a failure because of it. His story unfolds with anecdotes of living on the fringes of respectability. I am his first son, an unwilling reader except for an occasional newspaper article. I chronicle the social interactions that led me to literacies that I had not known existed. My son's story, which completes the narrative section of the book, is a meticulous account of how he taught himself to read and write at an early age. By the time he was five, he had created wonderful texts that expressed his perception of the world. Inexplicably, his teachers did not even notice, much less encourage, his literacies.

These stories are grounded in fact but, in places, read like fiction. There is a reason for this writing style. I entered my grandmother's distant past to find context for the stories that follow. As I researched her life, I was overcome with wonder and amazement at what she accomplished. The mood in her trilogy is poetic and moral, in deference to her heroic nature. My father's narrative is one of pathos grounded in his reaction to school failure. In contrast, the mood in my story is pensive as I chronicle the awakening of my intellect. My son's story is an emotionally wrenching account of how schooling undermined his confidence as a learner.

Figure 2
Rose and Carmelo's Written Literacies

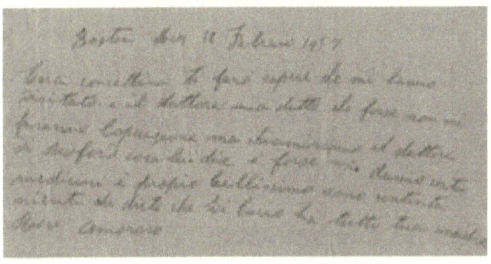

Carmelo's (Rose's husband) signature
from Declaration of Intention, 1917

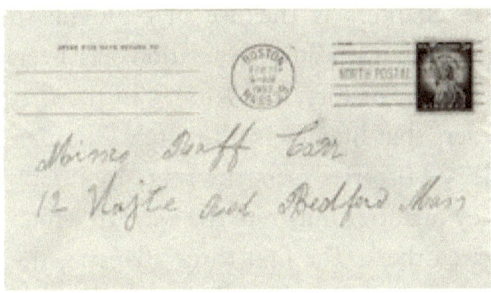

Boston Mass
18 February 1957

Dear Concettina, I want to tell you they have checked me out and the doctor that maybe won't do the operation but they will call the doctor of Bedford to see what he will say and maybe they will give me certain medicine and it's very wonderful and I am contented nothing more to say I kiss all of you, your mother Rose Amoroso.

*Concetta's translation of
Rose's letter to the left*

Envelope addressed to Concetta from Rose

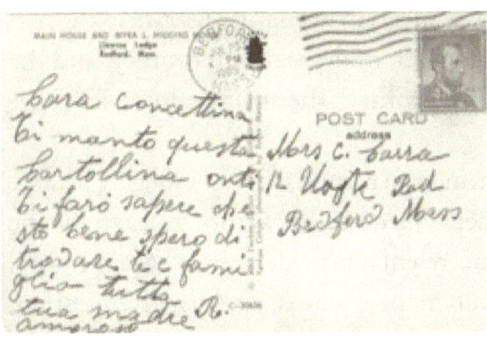

Postcard from Rose to Concetta, 1957

Part II examines our histories in light of various theoretical frameworks. Because learning does not take place in a vacuum, school failure is a psychological and economic problem, and because there are social consequences to failure, it is a social problem. Depressed and alienated children who do not overcome failure will likely have an impact on their communities and the economy. Failure is also an ethical problem that forces us to think about obligations and accountability. For most of us, school failure comes down to the search for a remedy. Although I ask hard questions about schools and the way they work, and I offer instructional remedies, in many cases such solutions are insufficient. Much still depends on caring deeply about children and their success.

Chapter Descriptions and Rationale

Six chapters make up the narrative section of *Fighting Prosaic Messages*. An important feature of these chapters is the use of dialogue to illuminate the meanings of literacy and failure. Narration has been a popular teaching device throughout history, and I use it in the first part of the book to remind readers that literacy is ultimately a human endeavor. "The Power of Literacy Histories" sets the stage by briefly showing how my family's literacy histories illustrate the ways in which schools favor some and subjugate others. The first three chapters, the "Rose Speaks" trilogy, fashion a theory of critical intelligence by looking at history through my grandmother's eyes.[2] The next three chapters explore the contradictions and exigencies of becoming literate in distinct American periods: the Depression era, mid-twentieth century, and the final two decades of the twentieth century. The struggle for voice is the recurring theme.[3]

Rose's story begins in Sicily, an ancient land of long-suffering people. Against the wishes of her father, Gaetano, she wants to leave for the mills of New England. Gaetano relents, provided that she not marry. She agrees and departs without money, status, or formal education, only faintly aware of the moral and emotional crises that await her. She settles in Lawrence, Massachusetts, finds work in the mills, and keeps to herself. Overwhelmed by hostile working conditions, sexual predators, and the painful separation from her parents, she seeks inspiration in the stories of the saints.

Interspersed throughout the plot are real and imagined characters who represent conflict in her life. Durlamo, the local paisano, fantasizes about her. She rooms with Marina, an affectionate and emotional Sicilian seamstress who will do anything to succeed in the country she loves. Rose also befriends Carmelo, who entertains her with songs and stories; later, when her obligation to remain unmarried ends with her father's death, she marries this dreamy idealist. Her struggles reach a climax as Lawrence descends into the chaos of a labor strike. Elizabeth Gurley Flynn, the fiery radical who instills in audiences moral indignation against the rich and powerful, arrives from New York City and enters Rose's life.

"New York City" is a metaphor for Rose's education. She chaperones several hundred children of striking workers to New York with Elizabeth and Marina. On the way, the women talk about historical development, social and economic justice, and the education of children. Rose is particularly straightforward in questioning the tenets of progressivism.

In New York, Elizabeth introduces Rose to some of the greatest activists of the era: the anarchist Emma Goldman; John Dewey and Francis Parker, founders of American progressivism; the social worker Jane Addams; novelist Theodore Dreiser; and activist-photographer Lewis Hine. As in Greek drama, Rose stands opposite a chorus and engages them in dialogue. The activists speak to her about big business, political corruption, freedom, and identity. Scientific observation, not religious belief, they argue, holds the key to the future. Rose wonders if their future will work. Will American schools teach children equitably if they adopt Dewey's principles? Are art and literature the avenues by which to raise the consciousness of the mill owners toward poverty and human suffering? Can people trust Goldman's vision of a just society if personal happiness negates obligation? Whose vision is truest? Rose listens and affirms their ideological passion, but moves on, confident in her simple, principled life.

The dialogues, although fictionalized, are significant; they bring to life the people who charted the course of schools and society in twentieth-century America. Some readers may find the interactions suspicious.

After all, Dreiser was out of the country when Rose and the children arrived in the city, and Parker had been dead for ten years. Moreover, poor people almost never discussed aesthetic, political, or philosophical principles with intellectuals. Ironically, Rose was the perfect witness to her time. In assimilating into American life, she had to choose between sharply divided ideologies: capitalist materialism or social justice, the rights of the individual or obligations to others, scientific progress or faith in the sacred, ethnic isolation or assimilation into the dominant culture. Although she did not study history or political thought, she found her way. These dialogues allow the reader to see her in full voice: smart, serious, and unsparing of her contemporaries. Giving history back to her reminds us that her literacy did not reside in her ability to read and write, but in the way she responded to moral crises.

Rose returns from New York an independent woman determined to continue her education. She and Carmelo settle into a prosaic life in Boston's North End, but they react to their surroundings very differently. Rose's aesthetic sense draws her to the familiar traditions and architecture of the city. Carmelo sees a future filled with brightness. Tender moments give way to tense ones as Rose's sense of sin and Carmelo's whimsy push them apart. In the end, she demands that they move to Quincy to be near her brother and village friends. Carmelo relents and finds work in the shipyard. Seven years later, he is dead.

"The North End" is a story about place and marriage. It is also a testament to immigrants' capacity to respond to a bewildering array of challenges. To reveal the significance of Rose's and Carmelo's assimilation into American culture, I probe ordinary experiences for meaning. A stare becomes an opportunity to examine the roots of bigotry in New England. An imagined encounter with Rose Kennedy, a native of the North End, leads to an analysis of class differences in education and child-rearing. Commonplace moments in church or in an embrace reveal changes in consciousness.

At its deepest level, "The North End" is a critique of literacy and intelligence. Attached to the common definition of literacy as the competence to read and write is the assumption that adults who cannot read are passive, empty vessels, incapable of thinking for themselves. My grandparents' stories expose this belief as an illusion. Rose and Carmelo fully understood the events unfolding around them and knew exactly how to act. They reveal their literacies in how they lived their lives.[4]

"Dad" profiles the life of a school dropout in Depression-era America. Like many other sons of immigrant parents, my father made it through grammar school but left high school as soon as he turned sixteen. Restless and motivated by the need to support his family, he was not interested in school; his only goal in life was to have a few dollars in his pocket. Away from school he built bicycles, walked miles to tend his father's grave, and worked several jobs to support his sisters and mother. Later in life, he became a highly skilled craftsman and responsible parent.

Children continue to fail in school for the same reasons. Unaware of their unique identities in the social world, many people label them irresponsible. The purpose of this story is to remind readers that personalized histories negate harmful stereotypes.

"Henry" chronicles my working-class education. My grandmother shared her memories with me before I went to school, and her unspoken message about perseverance contributed to my success. Yet I graduated from high school unable to express myself in writing. I did not read a book for pleasure until I was in my final year of high school. For me, literacy related only to answers on a test. Fortunately, schoolmates and others helped me find another reason to read. Not only did I gain despite those beginnings, I also discovered that others do not own history.

"Justin" presents my son's literacy history. His story, so full of promise, helps the reader examine the cultural norms that silenced him. This chapter starts with an extensive analysis of how he taught himself to read and write. Numerous in-text samples document his development, which ebbed as schooling demeaned and diminished his literacies. Unable to make sense of an ethos that valued finishing work on time over creativity, he fell into a long period of self-doubt.

By most accounts, schools focus on practice without paying much attention to consequences. Did anyone warn American families at the turn of the twentieth century that intelligence testing would harm children by denying them equal learning opportunities?[5] A hundred years later, are we smart enough or wise enough to know how the push for tougher standards will affect children's learning? Few studies exist, but horror stories abound. Without a critical and historical perspective, sorting out politically mandated imperatives is impossible.

In classical Greek theater, heroes sometimes disregard the limits of their powers. The sin they commit is hubris, and the brightest are usually the most guilty. In a strangely ironic turn, the wisest character in the "Rose Speaks" trilogy is not a philosopher or activist but a simple, pious woman who knows nothing but her own ignorance. My grandmother's literacy symbolizes a stark need in literacy research and instruction: less presumptuous thinking.[6]

Chapter 8 uses Rose's story to argue for a critical interpretation of literacy. Rose represents the tens of thousands of illiterate immigrants who succeeded in America because they had the capacity to think for themselves. I explore the nature of her literacy and competence to learn from experience. I also discuss the value of using literacy histories to examine school practice, advocate the use of literature and biography in teacher training programs, and highlight thinkers who contributed to literacy education.

Chapter 9 connects my father's story to dialogical teaching and responds to the question, "What interventions would have kept him in school?" The chapter revisits old debates about central nervous system disorders and hyperactive deficits that learners can overcome only with systematic instruction and stimulants. This section also outlines an alternative response to failure: centering instruction on knowledge that the student already possesses. If the goal of literacy is the analysis of experience, then dialogue serves as the starting point for instruction. The teacher produces simple poetic texts that elicit strong emotional responses. Students reciprocate by producing stories that matter to them. The roots of a storytelling approach spring from folk traditions and are behind all progressive methodologies. Although simple and inexpensive, the technique never gained widespread acceptance in schools.

Chapter 10 posits that real literacy raises consciousness. It links my story to Paulo Freire's (1974) culture of silence and shows how literacy should emerge through storytelling, which expands and deepens experience. It also makes clear the social and political meaning of literacy by focusing on the link between my story and that of the fictitious child

Felia in the first two chapters. We were both obedient children who behaved according to adult dictates. In school, we were neither moody nor irritable, but merely passive--until friends showed us how literature could free us from the burdens of deception and manipulation.

Chapter 11 finds answers to my son's experience of devaluation in the research on expectations and stigma. His story reflects on the cultural values and behaviors that undermined his achievement. I identify and critique the hidden curriculum that stereotyped him. The conceptual frameworks that I use for this exploration are those of Claude Steele (1992, 1997, 1999) and Henry Giroux and Anthony N. Penna (1979), theorists who argue that schools are settings for more than academic learning. I also find answers in Ray Rist's (1970) seminal study of minority children, Paulo Freire's (1974) pedagogy of communication, and Howard Gardner's (1982) analysis of creativity.

The final chapter of *Fighting Prosaic Messages* argues for the use of literacy histories in debates over medical and cultural models of failure. The past one hundred years has been a dramatic century for American education. Millions of poor and working-class children entered public schools for the first time. For many, learning to read and write came with the needless struggles that I document in the personalized histories of my family. The pattern across our literacies was obstruction. The real power of literacy, a way to understand experience, was not given freely to us.

If we are to fulfill the Jeffersonian ideal of an informed citizenry, we must make changes in how we think about literacy and education. A powerful starting point is to document our own literacy histories. The moral imperative is clear—literacy histories not only broaden our understanding of cultural norms that shape our values but also balance our connections to families and communities (Greene, 2005). Moreover, such histories make clear the level of our consciousness of the world. Some of us are rooted to the core value of competitive individualism, others to social and economic equality. Do we fully understand how our values and rules affect the ways we teach and learn? In the final analysis, engaging the past provides a very powerful basis by which to evaluate our decision making.

Notes

1. *Fighting Prosaic Messages* attempts to answer two important questions: (1) what is the nature of moral behavior in schools and classrooms? and (2) is the essence of teaching an ethical act? Traditional Judeo-Christian religion posits that moral law is personified in the Golden Rule of treating others as you want to be treated. Immanuel Kant (1781/1953) argues that categorical imperatives like altruism apply to all people, regardless of their wants and feelings, but Jean-Jacques Rousseau (1755/1994) warns that private property destroys natural inclinations toward kindness, sympathy, and unselfishness. John Stuart Mill's (1899) utilitarianism posits that one can only judge actions by their consequences. Grounded in the belief that real achievement is the product of individual ability and effort, Ayn Rand's (1961) objectivism finds a laissez-faire approach the most congenial to the exercise of talent. Thus, selfishness is a virtue and altruism a vice.

2. Will Rose's dialogues with progressive thinkers sharpen our appreciation of the strength of mind she needed in order to adapt to a secular society? Was she the type of "organic intellectual" Gramsci had in mind when he wrote that "all people have the capability and the capacity to think" (1971, 9)?

3. Literacy has traditionally referred to the basic skills of reading and writing. Expanding on this definition, the term "literacies" means access to a wide range of information and the ability to critically judge its significance and value (Crowther, Hamilton, & Tett 2001). Defining literacy failure as the loss of voice deepens our understanding of what it means to be illiterate. Children who fail in schools frequently do so in silence. Educators need to free them from disaffection with concern for their unique identities in the world (Freire 1974).

4. The major theme in the "Rose Speaks" trilogy is the competence to learn from experience. Rose was a powerful woman who expressed her agency through her responsiveness, self-discipline, alertness, perseverance, resourcefulness, stamina, and willingness to take risks. Her ability to be on her own shows that she was intentional and goal-oriented. Her multilingualism reveals her intelligence. We see the strength of her mind in the ways that she adapted to her environments. She gained knowledge by attending to detail, evaluating arguments critically, and expanding on new ideas. She was an assertive woman with enough sense of herself to imagine and pursue new possibilities.

5.   See Valencia (1997), *The Evolution of Deficit Thinking: Educational Thought and Practice*; Thorndike (1910), "The Contribution of Psychology to Education"; and Terman (1916), "The Uses of Intelligence Tests."

6.   George Bernard Shaw (1903/1950), Irish Nobel Laureate and arguably the twentieth century's greatest dramatist, examined contemporary moral problems with irony and wit. In *Man and Superman: A Comedy and a Philosophy*, which appeared the year that Rose landed in New York, Shaw took umbrage with sophists, liars, idealists, and other "dangerous intellectuals." His division among idealists, philistines, and realists dominated his thinking and is evident in this anti-establishment snipe:

> But does any man seriously believe that the *chauffeur* who drives a motor car from Paris to Berlin is a more highly evolved man than the charioteer of Achilles, or that a modern Prime Minister is a more enlightened ruler than Cæsar because he rides a tricycle, writes his dispatches by the electric light, and instructs his stockbroker through the telephone? (p. 217).

References

Crowther, J., M. Hamilton, and L. Tett, eds. *Powerful Literacies*. Leicester, UK: National Institute of Adult Continuing Education (NIACE), 2001.

Freire, P. *Education for Critical Consciousness*. Translated by M. B. Ramos. New York: Continuum, 1974.

Gardner, H. *Art, Mind, and Brain: A Cognitive Approach to Creativity*. New York: Basic Books, 1982.

Giroux, H. A. and A. N. Penna. "Social Education in the Classroom: The Dynamics of the Hidden Curriculum." *Theory and Research in Social Education* 7, no. 1 (1979): 21–42.

Gramsci, A. *Selections from the Prison Notebooks*. Edited and translated by Q. Hoare & G. N. Smith. New York: International Publishers, 1971.

Greene, N. P. "Cajun, Creole, and African American Literacy Narratives." *Multicultural Perspectives* 7, no. 4 (2005): 39–45.

Horace, *L'art poétique*. Translated by L. Golden. In *Horace for Students of Literature: The "Ars Poetica" and Its Tradition*, edited by O. B. Hardison Jr. & L. Golden. Gainsville: University Press of Florida, 1995.

Kant, I. *Critique of Pure Reason*. Translated by N. K. Smith. New York: Macmillan, 1781/1953.

Mill, J. S. *Utilitarianism*. Boston: Willard Small, 1899.

Rand, A. *The Virtue of Selfishness: A New Concept of Egoism*. New York: New American Library, 1961.

Rist, R. C. "Student Social Class and Teacher Expectations: The Self-Fulfilling Prophecy in Ghetto Education." *Harvard Educational Review* 70, no. 3 (1970/2000): 257–302.

Rousseau, J. J. *Discourse on the origin of inequality*. Translated by F. Philip. New York: Oxford University Press, 1755/1994.

Shaw, G. B. *Man and Superman: A Comedy and a Philosophy*. New York: Penguin, 1903/1950.

Steele, C. M. "Race and the Schooling of Black Americans." *Atlantic Monthly* 269, no. 4 (1992): 67–78.

Steele, C. M. "A Threat in the Air: How Stereotypes Shape the Intellectual Identities and Performance of Women and African Americans. *American Psychologist* 52, no. 6 (1997): 613–629.

Steele, C. M. "Thin Ice: "Stereotype Threat" and Black College Students." *Atlantic Monthly* 284, no. 2 (1999): 44–52.

Terkel, S. *Working: People Talk about What They Do All Day and How They Feel about What They Do*. New York: Pantheon/Random House, 1974.

Terman, L. M. "The Uses of Intelligence Tests." In *The Measurement of Intelligence: An Explanation of and a Complete Guide for the Use of the Stanford Revision and Extension of the Binet-Simon Intelligence Scale*, chapter 1. Boston: Houghton Mifflin, 1916.

Thorndike, E. L. "The Contribution of Psychology to Education." *Journal of Educational Psychology* 1 (1910): 5–12.

Valencia, R. R., ed. *The Evolution of Deficit Thinking: Educational Thought and Practice*. Abingdon, Oxon UK: Routledge Falmer, 1997.

PART I

LITERACY AND LEARNING
IN THE LIVES OF A
SICILIAN-AMERICAN FAMILY

1

The Power of Literacy Histories: An Essay

History begins in novel and ends in essay.
—Thomas B. Macaulay

Different Ways of Knowing

The story of American education is a great one: an inclusive system open to all, academic and economic successes of countless generations of immigrant children, and an outstanding university system with more Nobel Laureate graduates than the rest of the world combined (WiseGEEK 2010). Hidden from view, however, are the grim statistics of illiteracy and underachievement that afflict millions of Americans. According to the Department of Education's study *Adult Literacy in America* (Kirsch et al. 1993), tens of millions of adult Americans are functionally illiterate. The *National Assessment of Adult Literacy*'s portrait shows that the number of functionally illiterate adults has remained relatively unchanged since 1992 (USDOE 2003). Equally alarming is a 2007 report by the National Endowment for the Arts that found a dramatic decline in the number of adults who read literature. According to the report, the rate of decline has nearly tripled in the last decade.

The realities of school failure have been a subject of inquiry and contention for many years. Sociologists and economists see failure as symptomatic of family disintegration and poverty (Sidel 1990; Harman 1978), whereas critical theorists like Giroux (1990) and McLaren (1998) point to flaws in the political and historical contexts of schools.

1

Conservative scholars like Ravitch (2000) and Finn (1991) blame external factors, such as the erosion of standards, that undermine schools' missions, and interpretative researchers link failure to interactions between students and teachers (Taylor 1991; Haberman 1995; Holt 1964; Alm 1981; and Shavelson 1983). Neuroscientists and human learning specialists (Shaywitz 2003) associate school failure with brain damage, attention deficits, or hyperactivity, but literacy investigators, including Allington and Cunningham (1996) and Harris and Sipay (1990), key in on skill deficits. G. Reid Lyon (1997), a key adviser on the federal Reading First initiative, attributes failure to a lack of research-based teaching practices—evidence-based teaching programs that emphasize phonological word-processing skills and word-reading abilities.

Disagreements about the causes of school failure are rooted in different philosophical concepts about the nature of social, political, moral, and personal life. For many years, progressive theorists have argued that the goals of a democratic society are best advanced by equality of opportunity—everyone in a just society has a chance to succeed (Bruner 1960; Dewey 1916/1997; Hayes 2006; Kohl 1998; Kohn 1999). Given disparities, however, the only genuine way to ensure equality is to treat all children equitably and with compassion, thereby minimizing individual differences that mitigate learning. Conservative theorists scoff at this reasoning; they value a productive society in which competence advances the common good (Ravitch 1988, 2000; Finn 1991). Applied to education, this reasoning posits that standards, accountability, and scientific management provide the best means to manage instruction. Children who do not keep up are defective.

Whereas progressives are concerned with assuring the success of every child, conservatives, such as No Child Left Behind (NCLB) advocates, identify with practices that reward individual effort (Phelps 2005). Little wonder that educators and policymakers endlessly debate who should succeed and who should fail in schools. Educators also cannot agree on what information to teach and how to teach it. The education profession continually swings back and forth between the two views articulated by renowned psychologist Erik Erikson (1963) nearly half a century ago. One extreme considers learning an extension of adulthood. Children learn the skills and knowledge that adults tell them to learn, and they do so through direct instruction. The other extreme encourages children to concentrate on activities that they enjoy. Popularly understood as child-centered, this approach makes learning an extension of children's natural tendency to discover by playing. In this model, learning is not the direct result of teaching but of purposive activity.

The conflict over school failure presents educators with a real dilemma. Progressive arguments can be overwhelming, clouded as they frequently are by the politically strident languages of Marxism, critical theory, and postmodern deconstructivist thinking. Conservative rhetoric can be equally difficult and intimidating, especially when it blames teachers for the drop in the American standard of living. Likewise, critics of pedagogical practices frequently point the finger of blame at each other.

Many teachers try to walk the middle line on matters of pedagogy. Still, it is no small irony to find them vilified as incompetent, old-fashioned, or worse.[1] They must come to terms with competing theories and their influences on practice. If progressives are right, failure to accommodate individual differences is abusive and discriminatory. If conservatives are right, educators are just as wrong to expect too little from children. The problem is to face the issue without succumbing to indifference or, worse, the argument that those who fail deserve nothing more.

Answers are not readily evident, however. Without an adequate understanding of the issues, many people rely on past practices or easy rationalizations. The result is frequent politicization of the question, with undue reliance on quick-fix solutions. The No Child Left Behind legislation is a good example (Paige 2001).

Meanwhile, many intelligent children who come from the same poor and working-class background as I did slip further behind and drop out, never to fully develop their intellectual gifts and talents. Lost in the muddle of statistics and policy, accusations, and blame are the personal stories of individuals who fail in school. What happens to them? Do they overcome their failures, or do these failures influence their lives, identities, experiences, and participation in the social world? How do their teachers, friends, and family relate to them?

Literacy Is a Moral Act of Truth Telling

Thirty years ago, I read Paulo Freire's (1970) *Pedagogy of the Oppressed*. Thirteen years later, I read Jonathan Kozol's (1981) *Children of the Revolution*. Both men wrote about transformative literacy. Their collective premise is simple: the starting and ending point of literacy is liberation from agencies that oppress the human spirit. Because I had often witnessed the oppression of the uneducated in the Caribbean during my years as a literacy worker, I wondered if these authors' social and political analyses of illiteracy were geographic—a perception of reality that emerged from their work in Latin America.

This question was important to me, so I felt obliged to test out their ideas in a North American setting. I began to document the human side of illiteracy by talking with scores of men and women in adult education programs in Nashville, Tennessee, and I developed a way to generate meaningful instructional materials based on the lives of adults. I also set up a prison literacy program in Nashville.

Following a summer of instruction, I asked prison participants to discuss their experiences in the program. Toby, one of the men who struggled as both a reader and writer, was not allowed to participate in regular education classes at the prison; he accepted my invitation to comment on his experience. He came to our meeting with an aura of strength and a smile that was strong and confident. At his elbow was a story he had written. When I asked him to tell me about it, he read to me a story about growing up in rural Mississippi that he had written after his tutor, Lee, had read to him an excerpt from Harry Crews's (1979) *Blood and Grits*. I asked him about his learning experience. His answer follows:

> I asked Dave [his cellmate] what was wrong with me, and he said I just need to learn a little more before I could do anything. So the next day, Dave got me into a reading class, and the teacher didn't mind that I couldn't

read too good. He had me read some lines from a book and told me that I could read good and that it was a pleasure to be teaching me. That made me feel good and made me want to work twice as hard.

This teacher was so good and nice that he didn't seem like a teacher.[2] This man seemed more like a friend that cares about someone that tries to learn. He handed me a book one day, read just a couple of lines aloud, and knew that I liked it. He said that his girlfriend gave him the book and that he hasn't read it yet, but if I like the book I could read it if I wouldn't let anyone have it or lose it. So I left and went back to my unit and started reading it, and a week later, I was finished with the book and gave it back.

The teacher asked me if I liked it and to tell him about it, so I began telling [him] about the book, and how it somehow changed me. Just a little. The teacher then told me that there was a good story inside of me, and he wanted me to write a short story for him, so I wrote a story about prison and what I thought about it. And that story came right out of me. It was the first time I've ever written anything like that. So the next day, I gave it to my teacher, and he liked it and said it was good and that he wanted to read it to the teacher next door. So he did, and she liked it. So then he told me that someday I might be able to write a book and be able to read as good as he can. This is all true. I don't know how to lie on paper, and if I did, I wouldn't.

Thank goodness I met Toby early in my career. Although poor, illiterate, and in prison, he seemed to understand Freire's (1985) assertion that literacy is an "analysis of reality." I had never used this concept as a literacy worker, so I was surprised to hear Toby tell me that *Blood and Grits* had changed him. What did he mean?

He told me that he identified with the main character, who had been victimized his entire life. Toby had felt out of place as well; now he realized that he was no different from others. He had, in fact, become Harry Crews. Toby helped me to understand something else about literacy and education: Becoming literate is not a neutral act. Having read and written his experience, Toby discovered that his life mattered to his teacher. He also simplified another concept for me. He told me that he didn't know "how to lie on paper, and if [he] did, [he] wouldn't." I still remember feeling shallow and Toby wise as I realized what he meant: Literacy is not a codification of skills but a moral act of truth telling. Everything in his literacy was from experience because his teacher, Lee, had not put him through contrived lessons. Toby had bypassed the inane by expressing his perception of the world.

I applied Toby's story to a literacy program that I started in Maine, abandoning the method of instruction that I had modified from the Cuban Literacy Campaign of 1960 (Amoroso 1985). Instead of asking tutors to create *Venceremos*-like primers, I asked them to use Lee's words: "I know that there's a good story inside you. Share it with me." The results were dramatic. Writers produced four books of stories and poems that "affirm[ed] and engage[d] their contexts, histories, and experiences" (H. A. Giroux, personal communication, 1990). As one tutor wrote in her journal, "This man has more than a story inside—he has a book."

Toby had shown me that the secret to literacy lies in storytelling that expands and deepens experience. For him, literacy was as much ethereal as it was material; reading and writing were acts of knowing that encompassed artistry, reflection, and expression. Understanding his literacy meant understanding his cultural-historical reality.

Sadly, schools had not given him what old-fashioned philosophers call knowledge of the human heart. He was not alone. I have seen firsthand the profound loss born from illiteracy. Using Toby's parable, I taught others about the sorrow that is illiteracy and the emancipation that comes from truth telling.

Concerning illiteracy, most accounts focus on education as a commodity, not as an act of freedom. But like Howard Zinn (2003), author of *A People's History of the United States*, I assume that much history draws from too narrow a perspective. To articulate this belief, I decided twelve years ago to write a book based on the proposition that the goal of literacy is to deepen experience.

Fighting Prosaic Messages is a complex cross between auto-ethnography, historical fiction, and literacy theory. I wrote it to address the issue of literacy failure in American schools, using the power of "story" to make literacy theory real while also grounding the story in historical context.

Families Pass Down Literacy

Fighting Prosaic Messages started as a response to an e-mail message from my son during his first year at Fordham University. Having completed *The Republic of Plato* (MacDonald 1967), Justin asked me if I had picked up my habit of asking him questions from Socrates. I wrote back, telling him that, yes, I used the Socratic method in my teaching (and, evidently, in childrearing as well). He replied immediately, asking for the names of others who had influenced my thinking. He wanted to know my reference points to better understand his own.

But I drew a blank. I could not offer him writers, books, or experiences that had shaped my life or imagination. On a professional level, I had a clear idea of who I was at that time: a college teacher with a solid reputation for asking students to think for themselves. I also knew who I was on a personal level: a husband and a dad with five very talented children. But I was unclear about the choices I had made in my life. Why had I become an educator or chosen to focus on literacy? And why had I worked so obsessively to nourish my children's literacies? I had no answers to these questions.

As I thought about my own history, and that of my father and youngest son, I realized that our stories speak to the very nature of who succeeds and who fails in schools. My father was a dropout because he lived in poverty. At ten, he had to work before going to school each morning in order to help support his family. Before long, he had fallen behind his classmates. One retention led to another, and, gradually, he turned his back on learning. Although he became a skilled shipbuilder, he never connected with formal education.

I was raised in a working-class home, where both my father and mother labored to improve our standard of living. I performed well in school, because my parents expected me to be obedient. I studied hard but rarely read anything longer than a sports column. Books meant nothing to me until a friend recommended *The Catcher in the Rye* (Salinger 1960). I picked it up in deference to his academic status at school, but something magical happened: I found myself cheering for the protagonist. Although Holden failed his teachers, he was my kind of hero; he was honest and had convictions. For the first time in my life, I connected reading to something other than passing a test.

Justin's literacies were rare; few children enter school with such well-defined abilities. From an early age, books, drawing, and music stimulated him. He cherished his tiny room, packed with records and paper, where he could express his feelings through drawings and stories. He loved the feel of the pencil as it glided across the paper. Learning was very natural for him. By the age of four, he had discovered the basic rules of reading and writing, music, and drawing. From a child-centered point of view, his literacy and learning came from seeing and thinking (Gardner 1982). He worked tirelessly on certain drawings or stories until he achieved the results that he desired. Spontaneous, playful activity produced dramatic results.

His purpose for and approach to learning, however, were at odds with the ethos of school. His artistic expression, reflected in careful experimentation, did not fit with the rigid demands of the clock. His storytelling shifted to performance measures on a test. His craving to read became less important than quantifying for the teacher the pages he read. School was less about personal expression than it was about the measurement of outcomes. His curiosity, always the impetus for his learning, got in the way. There was simply no room in a fixed curriculum for stories. The rules of school—basic skills and relentless deadlines—were coercive and inflexible. Confused and unable to adjust to what Elkind (1981) calls assembly line learning, my son fell into a long period of self-doubt.[3]

In watching Justin's struggle, the meaning of our literacy histories dawned on me: They dramatize the way that families pass down literacy. My father battled failure, but I graduated. I didn't write, but Justin was expressive and remarkably versatile. For my father and me, education was an escape from poverty. Justin used it as a tool for personal expression. Each of us advanced the dreams of people who were important to us.

I realized too that these stories express something more than the social construction of literacy. They make clear the connection between what teachers value and what students learn. In a conventional sense, my father was a loser. Many people might say that he deserved failure. But surely his portrait is more complex than that. He had no one to help him, yet he helped others. He failed at memorizing the names of the forty-eight states, but he learned the intricacies of shipfitting, welding, and blueprint reading. He gave up in school but rose every day of his life and went to work.

Part of his school failure followed me; I did not read for myself and rarely wrote. My school's curriculum centered on rote learning—teachers frowned on critical thinking. Worse, the past belonged to others. I had no real idea of who I was or from where I had come. Thanks to a friend, I discovered that there is more to reading books than finding the right answers for a test. I was lucky. The statistics on literacy show that most Americans do not read literature or write once they leave school (USDOE 2001).

Each of our literacy histories mirrors the way that many schools work. Real literacy raises awareness. The pattern across each of our stories is incognizance. My father never really understood what happened to him. Neither did I, not until much later in life. Yet our stories offer hope. The answer to many of the problems associated with school failure is neither financial nor technological. It is moral. Paulo Freire (1970), the renowned Brazilian humanist, said it best in defining good teaching as pedagogy of communication. Teachers have to genuinely care about the children they teach. They have to stop using words that control and alienate them. They have to understand how literacy works away from school and how it shapes the way that children think about themselves and others. Finally, they have to give children opportunities to find meaning in their lives. Voice is a very fragile entity; left unattended, it can silence dreams.

Prisoners of Empiricism

Preservice programs in teacher education typically promote instructional approaches, standards, and materials. The assumption behind content and organization is that teachers need to know how to teach. Master's-level programs in reading are no different. Knowledge of instructional tasks dominates the literature, which frequently marginalizes historical content/context and other methods of inquiry (Moore, Monaghan, & Hartman 1997). Of the hundred or so competencies for literacy specialists, the International Reading Association's standards for reading professionals lists one competency related to historical antecedents Alheit, P. (1994): The ' Biographical Question' as a Challenge to Adult Education. International Review of Education, 40(3/5) pp.283-98.

It is enigmatic why the study of literacy, which is part of literature, eschews dialogues with philosophers, historians, or writers. According to Gianturco (1990), one reason may be epistemological:

> We live in a Cartesian world, a world of scientific research, technology and gadgets which invade and condition our lives ... In our milieu, so intensely penetrated on one hand by mathematical intellectualism, by science-worship, and, on the other, by an exacting pragmatic utilitarianism, the inevitable outcome has been the downgrading of the humanist disciplines (p. xxi).

The study of reading and writing became a science in search of proofs during early-twentieth-century progressivism—the dawn of an era in which science promised to subdue humanity in the same way that it had harnessed nature. Mathematical reasoning would unlock universal laws that governed "man" and society, just as Enlightenment scientists discovered the mechanics behind the stars in the heavens. Out were philosophers, historians, and poets with their speculations; in was the business of certitude.

Of course, earlier rationalist pathways to knowledge, elemental to the thinking of René Descartes (1596-1650), had been preceded by the work of Michel de Montaigne (1533-1592) who warned against pretenses of certainty and that we can ever know "absolute truth," as this can lead to dogmatism. Later, the Italian philosopher Giambattista Vico (1668-1744), who reacted against Descartes's "rational method," made a case that reason has its limits and that poetic and imaginative kinds of thinking—though they don't yield mathematical certainty—still get us to important kinds of truth that transcend "scientism," questions that get to our humanity and spirit. Even the French political radical Jean-Jacques Rousseau (1712-1778) placed spirit and feeling at the center of knowing, not cold intellectual thinking.

In the same way, "rehumanizing" (Otto 1990) literacy is a matter of valuing other aspects. Bold attempts to present literacy as a transmitter of morals; efforts to elucidate the meaning of history, culture, and literacy; and autobiographical accounts of literacy learning have been available for some time. Sadly, their usefulness is compromised when they are dry, academically sterile, or out of range of readers with limited backgrounds in social theory, philosophy, or history. As Patrick Shannon (1990) found out early in his teaching career, polemical discourse can hamper student learning.

This line of thought is not to diminish the importance of thinking about issues of agency, struggle, and determination. A promising approach is evangelical narrative (Soskis 2002), wherein people construct and evaluate personal literacy histories for racial, ethnic, religious, and other cultural constructs and identify and evaluate underlying assumptions against democratic notions of self-reflection and consciousness. This position assumes that a critical framework is a more vital method of analysis than a recitation of research facts.

Brown (1999) found that writing personal histories promotes reflective thinking for preservice teachers. Likewise, Roe and Vukelich (1998) have used literacy histories to examine the relationship between teacher candidates' experiential roots and their education to be teachers of literacy. Biographic approaches are also widely prevalent in adult education and are gaining popularity in K–12 settings (Alheit 1994; Winston 1997). Examples in higher education are less evident, but the University of Minnesota sponsored public lectures that focused on literacy histories in various periods, cultures, and fields of knowledge (Jacob, Reynolds, & Choy 2004). As well, the University of Wisconsin–Madison focuses on "a view of literacy that stresses cognitive, social, and cultural factors" (UW–Madison 2004/2009, p. 1; Hammerberg & Grant 2001).

The Power of Narration

The new millennium brought with it the view that literacies are an important political and pedagogical issue. No longer simply skills, they now serve to register history, narrative, and intervention in the world. In that same vein, *Fighting Prosaic Messages* investigates culture, history, and literacy through personal narrative. Each vignette makes a point. For example, as backdrop for Rose's dialogues with John Dewey and Emma Goldman, the Lawrence Strike of 1912 puts literacy in its historical context and speaks to the personal and social nature of competence. I also use extensive documentation to show how my son taught himself to read and write and how his creative literacy went unnoticed in school, thus exposing the moral fallacies about assessment.

Fighting Prosaic Messages reclaims literacy inquiry from the banal with imaginative storytelling and historic anecdotes. Simply stated, I use everyday life to bring forth theory. Readers will meet little-known but important thinkers who speak for themselves. Likewise, illiterate and undereducated characters speak their minds simply and poetically.[4] Their words, not those of the artists, scientists, or philosophers who objectify them, remind us that literacy is about giving voice to those who do not have it. Finally, *Fighting Prosaic Messages* creates dialogue with the real words of Americans interviewed by Federal Writers' Project staff (Library of Congress 1998). Their language permits us to hear those who may have lacked formal education but who nevertheless had much to say. Such use of dialogue to convey meaning mirrors Pask's (1975) view that all learning occurs through conversation. A book that advances dialogic teaching should, de facto, use dialogue as its medium of communication.

Fighting Prosaic Messages records and explains the history of where my family has "passed" (Walcott 1984). Our experience with immigration, assimilation, language, poverty, and racism may garner respect from readers with their own journeys through poverty or language barriers. Alternatively, readers working with children who perform poorly in school or who have lost their will to read and write will embrace the sensible suggestion of treating literacy as a way of knowing, not a codification of skills. This book finds theory in personal testimony. I pull together historical events like screening procedures at Ellis Island and sterilization initiatives in Indiana to show the degradation that scientific thinking forced on the poor. Arrogance of this kind is based on subject/object dualism and sustains passivity. In my father's time, accounts of childhood poverty were common, as were popular films like *Boys Town* (Taurog 1938). But children still failed in school. *Fighting Prosaic Messages* dramatizes how the educational system taught my dad to fail and how he harnessed his anger. His story provides insight into aspirations, shortcomings, and the effect that actions have on others.

I went to school in an industrial city with a progressive legacy in education, yet there was a dark side to my working-class life. I was riddled with guilt in a world defined by rigid rules. I also despised books, believing that they belonged to the wealthy. Thankfully, I worked alongside men similar to Eric Hoffer (1955, 1976) who read poetry and philosophy. They taught me that words matter. My son's educational journey is about stigma. How else can one explain why teachers ignored his literacies? Theft is not always physical; it can also be emotional and psychological.

Great stories are of ordinary people (Coles 1990; Kohl 1996), which is why I use rich contextual tapestries to illuminate such lives. Readers meet historic figures in sections called "In Their Own Words," and illustrative materials are visually engaging, adding texture by illuminating geographic and physical space. Boxed and shaded pages similar to those found in Norton's *In the Devil's Snare: The Salem Witchcraft Crisis* (2003) separate historical analysis from narration and frame excerpts from texts, letters, academic journals, school reports, newspapers, magazines, and letters to the editor by prominent artists, philosophers, and activists who influenced the history of literacy and education but who are little known or rarely read today: Giambattista Vico, Parker, Addams, Flynn, Goldman, Thorndike, Dreiser, Shaw,

Jacob Riis, Hine, Antonio Gramsci, and Eric Hoffer. Likewise, brief profiles of people and events that shaped policy and discourse familiarize readers with historic debate: reporting of the Lawrence strike of 1912, school board disputes over "defective" children, and cases of scientific racism. This historic information deepens the narratives' meanings for readers who do not mind taking brief excursions.

Finally, reference notes that make clear connections between the narratives and larger interpretations of history appear in such a way that readers can skip them without disrupting the storyline. I also alert readers to the fictionalized elements in the "Rose Speaks" trilogy in the opening statements of each chapter and in the reference notes.

Fact or Fiction

Prosaic means ordinary. It also denotes dull, unimaginative, and lacking wit or challenge, terms that people frequently use to stereotype those who fail in school. I use stories about ordinary people to challenge this type of thinking. The title, *Fighting Prosaic Messages*, captures the many messages that adults send to children who struggle to be heard. Conventional textbooks on failure (Tauber 1998) rarely reference underestimation and its corollary, the culture of silence, first articulated by George Bernard Shaw (1942) in his play *Pygmalion* and then examined by Rosenthal and Jacobson (1968) and revisited by Paulo Freire (1985). Hunsburger (2007) has a serious dispute with this omission: "Today in the United States, in the climate of No Child Left Behind, our views of literacy instruction neglect Freire's broader definition" (p. 1). *Fighting Prosaic Messages* redresses the taboo against discussing the complex issue of repressing student voice in classrooms.

This book uses psycholinguistic research to examine the social and anthropological bases of literacy and to critique the processing deficit theories behind current compensatory intervention models and dyslexia programs. Likewise, it employs the power of social theory to examine political issues related to literacy failure and uses history to illustrate how theories of language and learning affect the ways in which educators define and teach literacy. It also turns to the humanities to raise questions about the meaning of literacy and how children experience failure. This mix of various epistemologies sheds light on important questions that prescriptive texts do not address:

- What is scientific literacy? Is the methodology of science the most reliable source of information to use in defining it? Is the ultimate goal of literacy fluency?
- The arts and humanities, especially the study of literature, base decisions on the lessons of history, personal experience, and the application of reason. A humanities approach to problem solving brings what is "hidden" into the open (Fish 2008). What is a humanities-based definition of literacy? Is literacy a neutral skill or a moral act of truth telling?
- Why do definitions of literacy often omit the connection between moral capacity and literacy?
- What are the historic underpinnings of literacy theory and practice? How did formulaic thinking come to be, and who in society benefits from it?
- What is critique and why is it missing from mainstream discourse on the crisis of literacy failure in America?
- Why is literacy theory and practice politicized?
- How does the ethos of schooling (the values and beliefs that teachers hold) help or hinder student learning?
- Does traditional instruction acknowledge the role of desire in learning to read and write? Does dialogic instruction attend to this issue?
- What happens to people who fail in school? What happens to a democratic society when its citizens do not read or write?
- Are answers to the alienation that attends literacy failure available in scientific literacy or in a pedagogy of communication, self-reflection, and consciousness?

As an auto-ethnographic account of literacy failure in American schools, *Fighting Prosaic Messages* features reflexive positioning throughout the histories of family members, the use of biographical and oral testimony as social research data, and a literary tone to engage readers in the analysis of issues. Auto-ethnography is not prevalent in many textbooks, the presumption being that it lacks objectivity and verification. Hackley (2007) counters this argument, however, stating that because "writing constitutes rather than describes reality, neither objectivity nor verification can be relevant ... Its integrity is for readers to judge" (p. 104). An experienced practitioner evidences reader judgment in this reaction to the book:

> [Your] approach enables readers to understand your message about literacy while allowing them to personally relate their own experiences to those of your family. Like Lee sharing *Blood and Grits* with Toby, you are awakening connections in your reader that may speak directly to his or her own experience and personally change him/her in the process.
>
> Furthermore, I believe that your use of the literacy histories to serve as the foundation for further discussion of critical concepts and solutions is important. By engaging your readers on a personal level through narrative first, you are then able to effectively relate theoretical perspectives and arguments to characters and situations they already understand. You have embodied the storytelling/dialogical learning approach by doing exactly what Lee did with Toby—building his comprehension using what he already knows. This is brilliant and should be acknowledged within your book, if it hasn't been already ... to point out to your reader (who is easily absorbing and processing the content) that they are in fact experiencing the very approach that you are advocating ... a storytelling/dialogical methodology.

Blending history with narrative is a unique approach to examining the theme of school failure.[5] The chapters about my father, my son, and me are fact, based on interviews, family stories, self-reflection, and an analysis of school records, reports, and documents. Rose's story is also factually accurate, with the exception of minor characters and her debates with radicals. I invented the latter to show metaphorically her critical intelligence and willingness to confront those who would subjugate her.

My grandmother was part of my education, and, for that reason, I needed to acknowledge her. From an early age, I learned how she worked hard for little money. I also remember her insistence that I speak Sicilian as I sat beside her to watch the evening news. When I began to write her chapter, however, I had little actual knowledge of her life. I did not know the name of her village, details from her childhood, her literacy habits, her motives for leaving, how she ended up in Lawrence, Massachusetts, or how she met my grandfather. She was more mythic—strong, blue eyed, and opinionated—than real because I had never talked with her about her past.

Wanting to see the world through her eyes, I set out to reconstruct her life, much as a playwright or novelist might construct a character. I started with people who knew her. Over the course of several years, I interviewed my father, my aunt, and distant relatives. We talked about Rose's life in Sicily and her personality. We discussed marriage and attitudes toward the government, priests, and teachers. We spoke of day-to-day details, like if she ever laughed aloud in public or where she shopped for groceries. Charming anecdotes emerged from our conversations.

I also researched Sicilian family life in textbooks, newspapers, and magazines and exchanged e-mail with people in Italy with the same surname. In an attempt to determine where she lived, I spent scores of hours at the Lawrence Immigrant Archives, American Textile Museum, Quincy Historical Society, Quincy Public Library, and the Boston Public Library, poring over documents. To better understand her assimilation experience, I read political and social histories, research, newspaper clippings, census reports, genealogical records, and firsthand accounts. To develop a sense of place and setting, I visited the American Family Immigrant History Center at Ellis Island, her point of demarcation, and viewed hundreds of images online from sites such as the Library of Congress. I spent days walking the streets of Lawrence and sketching the textile mills where she worked. I sat in the churches where she prayed and walked the neighborhoods where she lived. I read Verga's (1928) *Little Novels of Sicily* and listened to Sicilian folk songs to pick up cadence and speech patterns. I contacted my grandfather's distant relatives and interviewed old men in the North End who had studied under Gulizia, a relation of Rose's husband.

Many of my discoveries were accidental. For instance, I found out that the Italian Catholic Church was across the street from the historical society in Lawrence, where I went to research my grandfather's time in this city. On a hunch, I walked over to the rectory and asked the priest for the marriage records, circa 1912. Five minutes later, he handed me my grandparents' certificate. On it were the names of their parents and their baptismal locations, details unknown to my father and aunt.

Other stunning discoveries about my grandmother's literacies also emerged: a hospital napkin that she had used to write a lovely message in Italian to her beloved daughter, a long-forgotten postcard that Rose's mother had sent to her soon after the death of Carmelo, and a letter written in Italian from her brother's daughter in Egypt.

The most consequential breakthrough occurred five years ago, as I drove to the North End with my father. Fidgeting in city traffic, he said to me, "I know that building—Ma used to bring me here when I was a kid." He pointed to the Boston Public Library. Shocked, I asked if she had taken him inside. "No," he said, "we just looked at it."

I was stunned. Earlier that year, I had drafted what I thought was an imaginary scene in which Rose had taken him to this very place. The scene had grown out of my intuition about her being the daughter of a skilled mason. Knowing that she used to take my father with her to the North End to buy fresh tuna steaks, I surmised that she would have brought him to see this grand structure in the Italianate tradition as her way of teaching him about his place in the world. My imagination preceded fact. This scene, in the words of Kauffmann (2003), was "generous with paradox." I felt Rose's ambiguity as she stood on the street with my father, staring at this Brahmin likeness of her world, unwelcome in her ordinary dress. Immigrants like her would have to wait a long time to enter.

In these ways, I came to understand my grandmother's literacies. Although I did not find definite answers to all my questions, I understood her better. There was no room in her life for defeat or humiliation. She expressed disappointment with some aspects of American freedom, but she acted ethically and consciously on and in her world.

Despite acquiring an abundance of new information, I still knew little about how my grandmother viewed herself. To capture the problems of identity and survival, I combined known facts with intuitive deductions, creating letter-writing episodes to depict her character and intelligence and devising events to reveal the values and social structures that defined her community. To dramatize the conflict between her Old World ways of knowing and those of modernity, I devoted a full chapter, "New York City," to her involvement in the Bread and Roses Strike of 1912.

Because she had already left Lawrence by 1912, she did not actually participate in the strike. Does this fictionalization weaken her authenticity and that of everything else in the book? I think not. Despite its grounding in ethnic history, I did not intend this chapter to be fact but a dialectic, a battle for choice against insularity. Rose worked in the Lawrence mills and must have known many of the strikers. Moreover, I based the depiction on historic fact—the transporting of striking workers' children to New York City to live with sympathetic families. In my version of the strike, Rose chaperones the children to the city with a leader of the strike, Elizabeth Gurley Flynn. Once there, Elizabeth introduces her to many other progressive leaders in American politics and education who supported the strike.

The dialogues that Rose has with these intellectuals reflect a vision of the times. She represents people from humble origins, present and past, who deal(t) with moral crises decisively and intelligently.[6] I intentionally blur reality to capture the grand epic of her life.[7] Giving history back to her vindicates faith in "organic intellectuals" (Gramsci 1994) to rise above their silence. It also serves as an antidote to the heavy-handed intelligence testing to which this country subjected Rose and other immigrants at Ellis Island.

Will It Work?

Texts that bring theory and critique to literacy educators are becoming more prevalent and include specialized accounts of class and literacy, unacknowledged literacies, family literacy, immigrant literacy, and the history of literacy instruction. Unfortunately, many of these texts place untenable demands on readers with limited backgrounds in social theory, philosophy, or history. References to little-read thinkers like Habermas require an extensive background to understand and appreciate, and arguments are sometimes difficult to follow, especially when they are wordy or unclear. Moreover, politically motivated blaming is intimidating to those who see themselves as working hard to help prepare students for life.

Fighting Prosaic Messages infuses critical theory with family literacy histories. The qualitative and historical research, including oral testimonies from family members and adults in prison, imbue the book with freshness and originality. Its warmth contrasts sharply with what Kanpol (1998) calls the "opaqueness" of texts that address critical theory/pedagogy.

To dismiss *Fighting Prosaic Messages* as unverifiable is to miss the human side of failure. Statistics and rhetoric provide one way to organize thoughts about these matters. Unfortunately, they do not make us care about children who fail, especially those who are ethnically or racially different from the dominant social class. Stories, however, fill us with sympathy and compassion for those who struggle for understanding.[8] Moreover, they show us how easy it is to break a child's will with indifference and how much more satisfying it is to enable him or her with a pedagogy of communication (Freire 1985).

In the twenty-first century, we must confront a staggering moral dilemma: Many schools continue to reduce literacy to a mechanical act. Some readers will find this assertion naive; others will use it to ask difficult questions about the meaning of literacy. By bringing stories of life and learning alive, I hope to guide readers to a better understanding of the issues that contribute to literacy failure and how to address them.

This thought leads me to my final point. Because my family's story spans the twentieth century, readers will see for themselves how schools historically and currently respond to children who fail. From my grandmother's landing on Ellis Island in 1905 to my son's matriculation into college at the end of the century, schools have tried to adapt to waves of poor immigrants, changes in the American economy, and the hegemony of the scientific method in decision making. Despite one hundred years of school expansion and reform, the historical record demonstrates that much has stayed the same. Gertrude Hildreth wrote in 1936 that "no feature of public education is more universal than failure" (p. 789). Seventy-five years later, many Americans continue to fail in school for the same reasons they did in the past: boredom, isolation, alienation, and the irrelevant demands of curricula that favor control over self-expression.

Notes

1. Former US Secretary of Education Ron Paige called the teachers union a "terrorist organization" (Tanner, 2004).

2. Frederick Taylor, a nineteenth-century engineer, brought scientific management techniques to the workplace. This process involved timing all aspects of jobs to make sure that workers accomplished them in the most efficient manner. Taylorism caused a marked loss of autonomy to workers, because supervisors meticulously assessed everything they did. Applied to American education, Taylorisn subordinated student agency through testing, pressure, and regimentation. Such subordination was consistent with Puritan forces embedded in American history and resulted in teaching slogans like *Don't smile until Christmas* (Ryan 1972). It also invoked the ideology of Thomas Hobbs (1651) and contributed to the emotional distance between students and teachers. See Kanigel (1997), *The One Best Way: Frederick W. Taylor and the Enigma of Efficiency*. Callahan's (1962) *Education and the Cult of Efficiency* is also an excellent account of the legacy of Taylorism in schools. In contrast, valuing people for their intrinsic worth, the bedrock of Enlightenment thinking, is reflected in the Constitution of the United States. Derived from Judeo-Christian ethics, it is the philosophy followed by great teachers like Pestalozzi, Froebel, Montessori, Parker, and Dewey, reformers who have tried to awaken America's conscience to the oppression of the human spirit. See Holt (1964), *How Children Fail*; Goodman (1964), *Compulsory Miseducation, and the Community of Scholars*; Illich (1971), *Deschooling Society*; and Postman & Weingartner (1969), *Teaching as a Subversive Activity*. Recent films that comment on student-teacher relations are *Scent of a Woman* (Brest 1992); *Dead Poets Society* (Wier 1989); and *The Prime of Miss Jean Brodie* (Neame 1969).

3. Underachievement is a discrepancy between children's school performance and some index of their ability. If they are not working up to their ability in school, they are underachieving. See Raph, Goldberg, & Passow (1966), *Bright Underachievers: Studies of Scholastic Underachievement Among Intellectually Superior High School Students*; Rimm (1997), "An Underachievement Epidemic"; and Shaughnessy (1999), "An Interview with Sylvia Rimm About 'Underachievers.'" More than sixty years ago, Merton (1948) captured the self-fulfilling prophecy aspect of underachievement:

> So common is the pattern of the self-fulfilling prophecy that each of us has his favorite specimen. Consider the case of the examination neurosis.

Convinced that he is destined to fail, the anxious student devotes more time to worry than to study and then turns in a poor examination (p. 195).

Although full of zeal, Justin was ill tuned to the fixed routine of school.

4. Early in my professional life, I read Studs Terkel's (1975) collections of interviews with everyday people who shared their life stories. The interviews come across as conversations between friends, rather than as tape-recorded interviews that make life an object of analysis. My goal was to mirror such natural conversation in my interviews. Instead of following a script (Geary 2002), my conversations with family members involved hand gestures, interruptions, volunteered answers, contradictions, loss of focus, and frequent stops to eat. Over the course of several years, I collected many powerful memories—paths, defiances, places, and times—that I use to reflect on life experience.

5. *Fighting Prosaic Messages* uses narrative nonfiction—a mix of storytelling and critical analysis—to examine how schools both mirror and shape society. A well-known example of this technique is Gaarder's (1991/1996) *Sophie's World: A Novel about the History of Philosophy*. The genre also includes McCourt's (1996) *Angela's Ashes* and Karr's (1995) *The Liars' Club*. Tomasi (1940) likewise uses fiction to explore her immigrant past in *Deep Grow the Roots*. In the same vein, Canzoneri's (1965) *I Do So Politely: A Voice from the South* is a cross between sociological reporting and fiction, and Viscusi's (1995) *Astoria* is part novel, part cultural criticism. The exploration of family saga is a common theme in Italian American literature. Works include Gambino (1981), *Bread and Roses*; Bonanno (1980), *Ember Days*; and Barolini (1979), *Umbertina*. Tusiani (1965) mixes real and fictionalized characters in *Envoy from Heaven*, as does Doctorow (1976) in *Ragtime*. Writer-comedian Steve Martin (1997) likewise depicts an imaginary meeting between Picasso and Einstein in *Picasso at the Lapin Agile and Other Plays*.

6. Some readers may be offended by witnessing the awkwardness of great thinkers. Thematically, however, the dialogues introduce us to an ethos that threatened Rose's way of life. They show us how unwilling she was to give in to hubris, and how determined she was not to fail, a genius that she offers to the rest of us.

7. The ability of ordinary people to identify with Rose is the key to her story. She was neither blue-blooded nor nihilistic. Her sum and substance were

commonplace. Although critics may see her as a mouthpiece for egalitarian propaganda, most readers will identify with her. As one reader noted:

> [Rose] both captivates my imagination and stimulates my intellect. I find myself anxious to escape to her world, just as I would when reading fiction. Yet the thinking of the intellectuals of the time also challenges me. I did not realize that anarchy was an actual philosophy. I find that I connect with Rose in many ways. This work is helping me realize how today's educational reform fits into a historical perspective. Most of all, I find myself fostering such deep respect for people who endured through so much to give their children a better way. I am inspired to find out more about my ancestors.

For a recent discussion about fostering democratic practices in teacher education, see Fenimore-Smith (2004), "Democratic Practices and Dialogic Frameworks." For a description of teaching critical-thinking skills in undergraduate courses, see Yanchar & Slife (2004), "Teaching Critical Thinking by Examining Assumptions."

8. A reader wondered if my father was thrilled with my "breathing life" into his parents' stories. She also thought that my children must appreciate my documentation of their ancestry. Actually, there has been little hand clapping at home, because the research and writing have taken so much of my time. Except for enjoying the scenes involving Babe Ruth and JKF, my father rarely mentions the book. Part of his silence is due to his anger over the way his mother ruled his life. As for his father, he never talked about him when I was growing up. I think that he never forgave "Pa" for leaving him fatherless. I was inclined to feel the same way. My perception changed, however, as I researched my grandfather's life. Carmelo seemed to be a modern-day Don Quixote caught up in the futilities of the American dream. He lost his job at the shipyard as soon as the war ended. When I told my father about Carmelo's bad luck, he thought about the time that his father was arrested for giving a public speech. As he reflected on the prospect that Carmelo had stood up to wrongdoing, I sensed his delight in making something "luminous with meaning" (Castle, 2004) out of something shameful. To see him deepen his consciousness was an unforgettable moment.

References

Alheit, P. "The 'biographical question' as a challenge to adult education." *International Review of Education* 40, no. 3-5 (1994): 283–298.

Allington, R. L., & P. M. Cunningham. *Schools That Work: Where all children read and write.* New York: Harper Collins, 1996.

Alm, R. S. "The educational causes of reading difficulties." *Journal of Research and Development in Education* 14, no. 4 (1981): 41–49.

Amoroso, H. C., Jr. "Organic primers for basic literacy instruction." *Journal of Reading* 28, no 5 (1985): 398–401.

Barolini, H. *Umbertina: A novel.* New York: Seaview, 1979.

Bonanno, M. W. *Ember Days.* New York: Seaview, 1980.

Brest, M. (Director), & Goldman, B. (Writer). *Scent of a Woman* [Motion picture]. United States: Universal Pictures, 1992.

Brown, D. "Promoting reflective thinking: Preservice teachers' literacy autobiographies as a common text." *Journal of Adolescent & Adult Literacy* 41, no 5 (1999): 402–410.

Bruner, J. *The Process of Education.* New York: Random House, 1960.

Callahan, R. E. *Education and the Cult of Efficiency.* Chicago: University of Chicago Press, 1962.

Castle, T. "High plains drifter." *The Atlantic Monthly* 293, no. 1 (2004): 185–191.

Canzoneri, R. *I Do So Politely: A voice from the South.* Boston: Houghton Mifflin, 1965.

Coles, R. *The Call of Stories: Teaching and the moral imagination.* Boston: Mariner, 1990.

Crews, H. *Blood and Grits.* New York: Harper, 1979.

Dewey, J. *Democracy and Education: An introduction to the philosophy of education.* New York: Simon and Schuster, 1916/1997.

Doctorow, E. L. *Ragtime.* New York: Bantam Books, 1976.

Elkind, D. *The Hurried Child: Growing up too fast too soon.* Boulder, CO: Westview Press, 1981.

Ellis, C. *The Ethnographic I: A methodological novel about autoethnography.* Walnut Creek, CA: Alta Mira, 2005.

Erickson, E. *Childhood and Society.* New York: Norton, 1963.

Fenimore-Smith, J. K. "Democratic practices and dialogic frameworks." *Journal of Teacher Education* 55, no. 3 (2004): 227–239.

Finn, C. E. *We Must Take Charge: Our schools and our future.* New York: The Free Press, 1991.

Fish, S. "Think again." *New York Times,* Aug. 6, 2008. http://fish.blogs.nytimes.com/?scp=1-spot&sq=Think%20Again&st=cse.

Freire, P. *Pedagogy of the Oppressed.* Translated by M. B. Ramos. New York: Continuum, 1970.

Freire, P. *The Politics of Education: Culture, power and liberation.* Translated by D. Macedo. New Haven, CT: Bergin & Garvey, 1985.

Froebel, F. *The Education of Man.* Translated by J. Jarvi. New York: A. Lovell and Co.

Gaarder, J. *Sophie's World: A novel about the history of philosophy.* Translated by P. Møller. New York: Boulevard, 1991/1996.

Gambino, R. *Bread and Roses.* New York: Avon, 1981.

Gardner, H. *Art, Mind, and Brain: A cognitive approach to creativity.* New York: Basic Books, 1982.

Geary, M. L. "Hooked on oral history." *Oral History Review* 29, no. 2 (2002): 33–36.

Gianturco, E. Translator's introduction. In Vico, G. (1698/1990). *On the Study Methods of Our Time.* Ithaca, NY: Cornell University Press, 1990.

Giroux, H. A. "Reading texts, literacy, and textual authority." *Journal of Education* 172, no. 1 (1990): 84–103.

Goodman, P. *Compulsory mis-education, and the community of scholars.* New York: Horizon, 1964.

Gramsci, A. *Pre-Prison Writings.* Edited by R. Bellamy. Translated by V. Cox. New York: Cambridge University Press, 1994.

Greene, N. P. "Cajun, Creole, and African American literacy narratives." *Multicultural Perspectives* 7, no. 4 (2005): 39–45.

Haberman, M. *Star Teachers of Children in Poverty.* Bloomington, IN: Kappa Delta Pi, 1995.

Hackley, C. "Auto-ethnographic consumer research and creative non-fiction: Exploring connections and contrasts from a literary perspective." *Qualitative Market Research: An International Journal* 10, no. 1 (2007): 98–108.

Hammerberg, D. D. & C. Grant. "Multicultural literacy: The power of print, pedagogy, and epistemological blindness." In *Reconceptualizing Literacy in the New Age of Multiculturalism and Pluralism.* Edited by P. B. Mosenthal & P. R. Schmidt. Charlotte, NC: Information Age Publishing, Inc., 2001.

Harman, D. "Illiteracy, poverty and racism: Their interconnexion." *Literacy Work* 7, no. 2 (1978): 11–20.

Harris, A J. & E. R. Sipay. *How to Increase Reading Ability: A guide to developmental and remedial methods* (9th ed.). White Plains, NY: Longman, 1990.

Hayes, W. *The Progressive Education Movement: Is it still a factor in today's schools?* New York: Rowan & Littlefield, 2006.

Hildreth, G. *Learning the Three R's: A modern interpretation.* Minneapolis, MN: Educational Publishers, 1936.

Hobbes, T. Leviathan or the matter, forme and power of a common wealth ecclesiasticall and civil. London: Andrew Crooke, 1651.

27

Hoffer, E. *The Passionate State of Mind, and Other Aphorisms*. New York: Harper, 1955.

Hoffer, E. *In Our Time*. New York: Harper & Row, 1976.

Holt, J. *How Children Fail*. New York: Dell, 1964.

Hunsberger, P. "'Where am I?' A call for 'connectedness' in literacy." *Reading Research Quarterly* 42, no. 3 (2007): 420–424.

Illich, I. *Deschooling Society*. New York: Harper & Row, 1971.

Jacobs, W., T. Reynolds, & G. Choy. "The educational storytelling project: Three approaches to cross-curricular learning." *Journal of College Reading and Learning* 35, no. 1 (2004): 50–66.

Kanigel, R. *The One Best Way: Frederick W. Taylor and the enigma of efficiency*. New York: Viking, 1997.

Kanpol, B. Critical Pedagogy for Beginning Teachers: The movement from despair to hope. http://users.monash.edu.au/~dzyngier/Critical%20Pedagogy%20 For%20Beginning%20Teachers%20Barry%20Kanpol.htm

Karr, M. *The Liars' Club: A memoir*. New York: Viking, 1995.

Kauffman, S. "Riches and rigmaroles." *The New Republic* 229, no. 1/2 (July 7&14, 2003): 22–23.

Kirsch, I. S., A. Jungeblut, L. Jenkins, & A. Kolstad. *Adult Literacy in America*. Washington, DC: US Department of Education Office of Educational Research, 1993.

Kohl, H. *Should We Burn Babar? Essays on children's literature and the power of stories*. New York: New Press, 1996.

Kohl, H. *The Discipline of Hope: Learning from a lifetime of teaching*. New York: Simon & Schuster, 1998.

Kohn, A. *The Schools Our Children Deserve*. New York: Houghton Mifflin, 1999.

Kozol, J. *Children of the Revolution*. New York: Delacorte Press, 1981.

Kraver, J. R. Review of Carolyn Ellis (2004). "The ethnographic I: A methodological novel about autoethnography." *Biography* 28, no. 2 (2005): 316–319.

Library of Congress. American life histories: Manuscripts from the federal writers' project, 1936–1940. http://memory.loc.gov/ammem/wpaintro/wpahome.html.

Lyon, G. R. "Why reading is not a natural process." *Educational Leadership* 55, no. 6 (1997): 14–18.

Macaulay, T. B. "Essay on history." In Macaulay, T. B., & Lady Trevelyan (2004). *Critical and historical essays: The complete writings of Lord Macaulay, Part 1* (pp. 180-238). Whitefish, MT: Kessinger Publishing, 1883.

Martin, S. *Picasso at the Lapin Agile and Other Plays.* New York: Grove Press, 1997.

McCarthy, T. J. *From This Clay: Gifts, surprises, and questions from the spiritual quest.* Lanham, MD: Lexington Books, 2006.

McCourt, F. *Angela's Ashes: A memoir.* New York: Scribner, 1996.

McLaren, P. *Life in Schools: An introduction to critical pedagogy in the foundations of education.* New York: Longman, 1998.

Merton, R. "The self-fulfilling prophecy." *The Antioch Review* 8 (1948): 194–196.

Montaigne, M. *Complete Works of Montaigne: Essays, travel journal, letters.* Translated by D. F. Frame. Stanford, CA: Stanford University Press, 1580/1774/1958.

Montessori, M. *The Montessori Method: Scientific pedagogy as applied to child education in "the children's houses."* Translated by A. E. George. New York: Frederick A. Stokes Company, 1912.

Moore, D. W. E., J. Monaghan, & D. K. Hartman. "The values of literacy history." *Reading Research Quarterly* 32, no. 1 (1997): 90–102.

National Endowment for the Arts. "To read or not to read: A question of national consequence." http://www.arts.gov/research/ResearchReports_chrono.html.

Neame, R. (Director). *The Prime of Miss Jean Brody* [Motion picture]. United States: Twentieth Century-Fox Productions, 1969.

Norton, M. B. *In the Devil's Snare: The Salem witchcraft crisis*. New York: Knopf, 2003.

Otto, W. "Bernie and me." *Journal of Reading* 34, no. 3 (1990): 212–215.

Paige, R. "Back to school, moving forward: What "No Child Left Behind" means for parents, schools and communities." http://www.ed.gov/inits/backtoschool/index.html.

Pask, G. *Conversation, Cognition and Learning: Cybernetic theory and methodology*. New York: Elsevier, 1975.

Phelps, R. P., ed. *Defending Standardized Testing*. Mahwah, NJ: Lawrence Erlbaum Associates, 2005.

Postman, N. & C. Weingartner. *Teaching as a Subversive Activity*. New York: Delta, 1969.

Raph, J. B., M. L. Goldberg,, & A. H. Passow. *Bright Underachievers: Studies of scholastic underachievement among intellectually superior high school students*. New York: Teachers College Press, 1966.

Ravitch, D. *The Great School Wars: A history of the New York public schools*. New York: Basic Books, Inc., 1988.

Ravitch, D. *Left Back: A century of failed school reforms*. New York: Simon & Schuster, 2000.

Rimm, S. B. "An underachievement epidemic." *Educational Leadership* 54, no. 7 (1997): 18–22.

Roe, M. F. & C. Vukelich (1998). "Literacy histories: Categories of influence." *Reading Research and Instruction* 37, no. 4, 281–95.

Rosenthal, R. & L. Jacobson. *Pygmalion in the Classroom: Teacher expectations and student intellectual development*. New York: Holt, Rinehart & Winston, 1968.

Rousseau, J. J. *The Collected Writings of Rousseau*. Edited and translated by R. D. Masters & C. Kelly. Hanover, NH: University Press of New England, 1997.

Ryan, K., ed. *Don't Smile until Christmas: Accounts of the first year of teaching*. University of Chicago Press, 1972.

Salinger, J. D. *The Catcher in the Rye*. New York: Signet, 1960.

Shannon, P. "Re-searching the familiar." *Language Arts* 67, no. 4 (1990): 379–387.

Shaughnessy, M. "An interview with Sylvia Rimm about 'underachievers.'" *The Clearing House* 72, no. 4 (1999): 203–205.

Shavelson, R. J. "Review of research on teachers' pedagogical judgments, plans, and decisions." *The Elementary School Journal* 83, no. 4 (1983): 392–413.

Shaw, G. B. *Pygmalion*. New York, Penguin, 1942.

Shaywitz, S. *Reading the Mind*. New York: Alfred A. Knopf, 2003.

Sidel, R. *On Her Own: Growing up in the shadow of the American dream*. New York: Penguin, 1990.

Soskis, B. "Freedoms and fictions." *The New Republic* 226 (June 2002): 36–40.

Spinoza, B. *The Chief Works of Benedict de Spinoza*. Translated by R. H. M. Elwes. London: George Bell and Sons, 1670/1891.

T*anner, R. "Bush's education secretary calls teachers union 'terrorist organization.'" http://www.commondreams.org/headlines04/0223-08.htm.

Tauber, R. "Good or bad, what teachers expect from students they generally get!" *ERIC Digest*. Washington, DC: ERIC Clearinghouse on Teaching and Teacher Education, ED426985, 1998.

Taurog, N. (Director), & Meehan, J., & Schary, D. (Writers). *Boy's Town* [Motion picture]. United States: Metro-Goldwyn-Mayer, 1938.

Taylor, D. *Learning Denied*. Portsmouth, NH: Heinemann, 1991.

Terkel, S. *Working: People talk about what they do all day and how they feel about what they do.* New York: Avon, 1975.

The Republic of Plato. Translated by C. F. MacDonald. New York: Oxford University Press, 1967.

Tomasi, M. *Deep Grow the Roots.* Philadelphia: J. B. Lippincott, 1940.

Tusiani, J. *Envoy from Heaven.* New York: Obolensky, 1965.

University of Wisconsin-Madison School of Education, Department of Curriculum & Instruction (2004/2009). Foundational principles of the UW-Madison Literacy Program. http://www.education.wisc.edu/ci/graduate_prog/areas/detail.asp?id=14.

US Department of Education Institute of Education Sciences. "National assessment of adult literacy," 2003. http://nces.ed.gov/naal/.

US Department of Education Institute of Educational Science. Section 2: Learner outcomes. In *The condition of education*, 2001. http://nces.ed.gov/pubsearch/pubsinfo.asp?pubid=2001072.

US Department of Education, National Center for Education Statistics. *The Condition of Education 1998.* NCES 98-013. (J. Wirt, T. Snyder, J. Sable, S. P. Choy, Y. Bae, J. Stennett, A. Gruner, & M. Perie, Eds.). Washington, DC: U.S. Government Printing Office, 1998. http://nces.ed.gov/pubs98/98013.pdf.

Verene, D. "Preface." In Vico, G. (1698/1990). *On the study methods of our time.* Translated by E. Giantrurco. Ithaca, NY: Cornell University Press, 1990.

Verga, G. *Little Novels of Sicily.* Translated by D. H. Lawrence. London: Martin Seeker, 1928.

Vico, G. *On the Study Methods of Our Time.* Translated by E. Giantrurco. Ithaca, NY: Cornell University Press, 1698/1990.

Viscusi, R. *Astoria.* Toronto: Guernica, 1995.

Walcott, D. *Midsummer.* New York: Farrar, Straus & Giroux, 1984.

Wier, P. (Director), & Schulman, T. (Writer). (1989). *Dead Poets' Society* [Motion picture]. United States: Touchstone Pictures.

Winston, L. *Keepsakes: Using family stories in elementary classrooms.* Portsmouth, NH: Heinemann, 1997.

WiseGEEK (2010). "What countries have received the most Nobel prizes?" http://www.wisegeek.com/what-countries-have-received-the-most-nobel-prizes.htm.

Yanchar, S. C. & B. D. Slife. "Teaching critical thinking by examining assumptions." *Teaching of Psychology* 31, no. 2 (2004): 85–90.

Zinn, H. *A People's History of the United States.* New York: Harper Collins, 2003.

SECTION I

ROSE SPEAKS

Preface to "Rose Speaks"

History is filled with the sounds of silken slippers going
downstairs and wooden shoes coming up.
Voltaire

Rose came to this country just as science, technology, business, and commerce
were spreading a vast new social order over the landscape. Old boundaries
regarding how people relate to each other were disappearing. This new
world was propelled by motion and change; subways, automobiles, and mass
communication altered the notion of place.

My grandmother stepped into this moment of history and nearly fainted
from the shock. Urban slums with broken windows and a haze of exhaust
fumes replaced her blue sea and ancient ruins. She saw men and women
toiling in factories, clamoring for fair wages and humane working conditions
and dying early. Priests did not speak her language or promote her saints,
but the padrones[1] acted as guides, wrote letters, found lodging, and helped
immigrants send money back to those they left behind. Billboard posters told
her to watch brawny men play a child's game. Other images told her that
romantic love was not wrong. Women marched for moral reform and equal
voting rights.

Rose wanted to escape from this bewildering conflict and change. She
was not alone. Even social institutions like schools faced the ever-growing
problems of the age. New York City schools offered needy children free eyeglasses
and morning baths, even as they tested them for mental retardation. Policy
makers pushed for compulsory attendance, the unionization of teachers, and
special classes for children whom schools judged unmanageable. Men like
Edward Thorndike (1905), John Dewey (1916), and G. Stanley Hall (1911)

37

argued constantly over the best ways to motivate children and measure their progress. Women like Jane Addams (1912) opened settlement homes to meet the social and educational needs of poor working people and their children.

Ethnic history is replete with strong, intelligent women who, like my grandmother, came to this country without privilege or fame but lived their lives with purpose and accomplishment. Like them, she is a heroic figure whose story helps us to understand aspects of the American experience. Her struggles with assimilation, poverty, labor strife, language barriers, and widowhood test her resolve. Her responses acknowledge her independence and reveal her intelligence. Conversations with real and imagined characters, each with his or her own flaws, illuminate the good, the evil, and the wide gray areas between that she had to face to make her place in the world. The same obstructions—materialism, bigotry, deception, and objectivism—persist still. Hence, witnessing a simple, principled woman defy indifference, selfishness, and hubris vindicates faith in the oppressed to rise above their enforced silence.[2]

Rose's voice helps to soften the presumptions of history. We rarely see the poor engrossed in dialogue with artists or intellectuals, because the elite rarely

Rose Amoroso receiving her citizenship papers

socialize with the people they study or about whom they write. In my version of history, however, Rose is not an object of study. She befriends Elizabeth Gurley Flynn and Emma Goldman, with whom she talks, drinks, eats, and exchanges generalizations about race, religion, and class in America. Rose listens and compares her simple core beliefs with theirs. What better way to demonstrate her competence than to let her speak for herself? Like these renowned women, Rose was quick witted, principled, and tough minded. Unlike them, she did not make it into the history books. For this reason alone, her story demands telling.[3]

Developments: 1900-1920[4]

The zipper and vacuum cleaner become realities. Freud publishes Interpretation of Dreams *(1900). The Wright Brothers make the world's first powered flight in 1903. The Great White Fleet, a flotilla of sixteen U.S. warships, embarks on a cruise around the world to demonstrate American naval power. Wireless telegraph transmits speech. Einstein publishes the Special Theory of Relativity in 1905 and the General Theory of Relativity in 1915. People buy comet pills to protect them against the return of Halley's Comet. The New York City Board of Education votes to give free eyeglasses to needy students. Englewood High School establishes a school lunchroom, the first in the city. Babe Ruth wins two World Series games for Boston and sets the record for home runs at fifty-four in one season. The FBI comes into being. Henry Ford introduces the Model T, signaling the Automobile Age. Congress passes child labor laws. Fingerprinting in crime detection becomes widespread. People enjoy peppermint lifesavers. The Titanic sinks. L. L. Bean produces its rubber-soled hunting shoe. New York State law forbids the representation of Jesus Christ on stage. The New York City School Board bans Christmas carols from city schools in an attempt to eliminate sectarianism. The Indiana Legislature passes the first compulsory sterilization law in the world. Progressives support these measures to "reform" society. The Central Powers sign the armistice that ends World War I in 1918. Circulation of Sears' general catalogue increases to three million. The National Education Association condemns the deteriorating behavior of students.*

2

Lawrence

Rose arrives in New England when a woman's place is in the home, leading a quiet, cloistered life. Progressivism frees many women from sexual repression, clerical domination, and subservience to men but also leads to excessive self-indulgence, which runs against Rose's religious upbringing. She reminds some people of the strong-minded, devout Judith from the Old Testament.

An Afternoon in the Lemon Grove

In 1905, Rose Bosco arrived in America with her fifteen-year-old

brother, Sebastiano (Constance B. Carr, personal interview, 1998). The Boscos had been born in Melilli, a small village on the southeastern coast of Sicily. The capital of the province was Siracusa, city of Archimedes, the largest and most powerful rival to Athens in the ancient Greek world. Wealthy landowners lived in the distant hills.

Change came slowly to this part of the world. The poor rarely moved beyond the fields that they tended with broad-bladed hoes. But the Bosco family was different. Their father, Gaetano, was a highly skilled mason who built many

Lucia, Sebastiano, Antonio, and Gaetano Bosco, circa 1898

41

homes in and around Melilli. Like other Sicilian men of his generation, he was a tough taskmaster who had a reputation for severity (H. C. Amoroso, Sr., personal interview, June 14, 1997). Since the death of his youngest son, Nino, he had become wildly impatient. Neighbors who irritated him were defenseless against the stones he pelted.

Rose's eldest sister, Giuseppina, was betrothed to a young man also named Sebastiano. Concetta, their father's favorite, was in the convent. Angered by constant criticism, Antonio, the eldest son, had sailed for Egypt to work on the Suez Canal.[5]

Rose was born in 1883 and graduated with two years of schooling, the endpoint of Italian public education, with the ability to read and write. Serious and intense, she helped around the house and in the fields. She fondly recalled joining her brothers in the harvest of the olive and lemon crops on the Camprini Estate, six miles to the northwest.[6]

At the turn of the century, Sicily was an agrarian economy with limited economic prospects for women. Rose was not alone in believing that she could make something more of herself by leaving. She had read the letters of Giuseppina's betrothed, who was making his way in the New World with his family. Antonio encouraged her to leave as well, sending her enough money to buy a one-way passage on one of the great ships that left Messina and Naples for New York.[7]

Figure 3
Southern Italy and the Nine Provinces of Sicily

Rose Bosco was from Melilli; the man she would meet and marry (in the U.S.), Carmelo Amoroso, was from Mineo--a town within the province of Catania. In separate ships, they would have traveled from Messina to Naples to New York City. Illustration by Justin Amoroso.

When she approached her father with the idea of sailing to America, however, he dismissed her with a flick of his wrist. He loved her very much and was afraid of never seeing her again. He knew from local gossip what horrors might await her. Without a father for protection, strangers might take advantage of her, bringing shame to his name. He would never allow her to leave home.

Gaetano Bosco was a resourceful man, however, and sensible enough to recognize that his daughter was more of an asset than a liability. At twenty-two, headstrong and ambitious, she could take care of herself and might be able to earn enough money to support him. She remembered the walk with him through the pine grove to the overlook, one hundred feet above the long Ionian coastline. Rain had slickened the gravel, so she tried not to look down at the white waves that thundered ashore.

"Rosina," he said, looking straight ahead. "I have changed my mind. I will let you go, providing you keep four promises."

"Yes, Pa."

"First, you must take Sebastiano with you."

A girl in traditional Sicilian dress. Drawing by Justin Amoroso.

"But, Pa, Sonny's like the peretto that grows on the hill. He always has the bitter face. Only a mother could love him!"

"Do not speak that way about your brother. *A matri ama a tutti i so figlioli!* A mother loves every one of her children. Sebastiano is spoiled, but he will be my eyes and ears. I want you to be a good girl in America. You are different from the others. Your skin is pale, and your eyes bite the souls of men. Only God knows where you came from."

Rose shook her head. "I will never marry. Not even with your blessing." If she had her way, she would have gone to the convent with her sister Concetta.

Her father was unconvinced. "Rosina, the world of men will take advantage of you. You must take Sebastiano with you. Return home in ten years, just as you are today (C. Carr, personal interview, 1998). I do not want to have grandchildren running around in filthy rags with wild heads of hair. Go to America with cousin Fontana. She leaves in a month to join her husband. He will help you find work."

Rose sat watching the dust settle on her father's boots. "Pa, we do not get along."

"There is nothing more to say. Pray to St. Sebastiano and send me your savings. Who else can look after your mother and me? Antonio and Sebastiano will soon have their own families. Your mother and I are alone. You are the only one who can care for us in our old age."

When Rose boarded the S. S. Italia that bright morning of June 4, 1905, she came face-to-face with the reality of leaving home.[8] Admittedly, life had been a struggle. Her father and brothers Antonio and Sebastiano had never been able to find steady work for more than three or four months at a time. They frequently had to take whatever jobs they could find, which often meant walking long distances to and from work for a day's wage of thirty-five cents, just enough to buy bread for the family.

The struggle of growing up as a woman was even more difficult. No matter how intelligent she was, the old ways prevented her from developing her abilities. Her life was confined to the domestic work of a late-nineteenth-century Sicilian woman: spinning flax, fetching water, cooking, and cleaning. She could not even take pleasure in walking to church. For one thing, the Sicilian sun was exacting: six months of blazing heat, parched earth, and dust followed by months of rain and mud. Furthermore, centuries of tradition demanded that she have a chaperone wherever she went. Chaste women were never alone with a man.

S. S. Italia, 1904.

As Rose settled into the ship's cramped, foul-smelling steerage, wave after wave of nostalgia engulfed her. She recalled her sister's engagement, the sweet fragrance of jasmine, baby Nino's baptism, holding hands with her mother in their garden of the almond blossoms, the feast day of St. Joseph's. Life had been difficult, but it swept across the landscape in steady and enduring ways. Relatives married and children received baptism rites. Priests said Mass in Latin, a language spoken in Sicily since the time that the Roman armies of General Marcus Claudius Marcellus besieged Siracusa. Every time she walked to her aunt Marchesi's house, she cut across the white, dusty path to the south of the ancient remnants at Thaspos. Even the fall rains drenched the fields every October in time-honored ways, nourishing the almond trees, the citrus groves, the olives, the grapes, and the endless variety of greens that grew wild in the fields behind her house. The fresh soups that her mother made from wild asparagus and fennel were a welcome change from the bread and pasta they ate during the dry season.

Little in her upbringing had prepared her for what she was about to encounter at Ellis Island. The chaos set her head spinning—red brick and steel, noise, congestion, and unintelligible people who were oblivious to her. She found herself in a madhouse of pushing and shoving. The public display of rudeness alarmed her and made her want to cry, but she could not retreat back into her memories. She was here to grow, so she had to learn to break through her fear. Her father had arranged with Cousin Lombardo to have a room ready for her in Middletown, Connecticut, one hundred miles to the northeast. Blocking out the sounds of anguish, she found her way to the train station and left for New England within hours of landing on Manhattan Island.[9]

The Unmarried Sister

Within a year, Rose and her brother Sebastiano went their separate ways. Rose worked in a garment factory, and Sebastiano found work in Florida as a plasterer. When the Miami jobs dried up, he went to Texas looking for work. He liked the warm weather that reminded him of Sicily. Rose prayed mournfully for him.

Their respective parents had arranged Sister Giuseppina's marriage to Mr. Garafolo before Rose and Sebastiano had departed. Young Garafolo, overworked and lonely in America, had asked his parents to find him a wife from Melilli. Sensing his son's passion and pain, the elder Garafolo sent a letter to his friend Gaetano Bosco:

46

Dear Gaetano,

> *This is neighbor Garafolo. My wife and sons are well. Sebastiano carries his tools in the same hand. He is ready to marry. His simple bed will please one of your daughters. I ask for no fine dowry. An ox and two sheep for my ailing father will do. If that is too much, give him what you like. In God's name, who saves us from our sins.*

Garafolo

Gaetano gave the letter to Giuseppina, who tore it up, fearing that he might hear the rush in her heart. Thrilled with the expectation of marrying his daughter to someone he knew, Gaetano calculated the date and time of the wedding. Giuseppina glanced at Rosina in a solicitous way. "It is good," Rosina nodded as she laid out the dishes for supper.

Garafolo returned to claim his bride with nothing but thoughts of lying beside her. He hid his happiness, though, to avoid the envy of the villagers. There was no need. Giuseppina broke his heart when she reminded him that it was a sin to consummate the marriage during the holy season of Advent. "This is the time for repentance," she said slowly and carefully.

As right as she was, young Sebastiano Garafolo decided to obtain a dispensation. "Saint Sebastiano will help me because I do no wrong," he said, fixing his red kerchief. Giuseppina opened her mouth as if to say, "You have reason to do wrong," but gave in to the dreary provincialism that ruled her life. Sebastiano felt the wedding ring rub against his heart as he set foot on the rocky road to the basilica.

The wedding reception took place under the chestnut tree near the ancient Greek temple. Gaetano wore a new shirt and served his guests wine. There was happiness for everyone that day. Gaetano breathed heavily as he passed out jugs of wine, thinking how well off he was.

The newlyweds left for New York with a dispensation in hand (S. Turro, personal communication, October 12, 2001).

Rose was happy to be reunited with her sister. Over fried peppers, Giusepinna shared news of home. Rosina listened contentedly as

47

neighborhood children played under the window. Giuseppena switched the topic to marriage. "Let my husband bring home someone. Jacomo, the skinny boy who lived by the old twisted tree, works with him. He will be faithful."

"The one with the big nose? Leave me alone," Rose said, straightening her apron with the back of her shoulders. "Besides, I am happy in my promise to Pa to return home just as I am."

But talk of marriage returned a month later, when Rose started night school. "Men will seduce you," scolded Giuseppina with wide eyes. "They will snatch your hand and tear out your heart. Then you will be of no use to anyone."

Rose waited for her sister to calm down before she replied, "I can look after myself." Looking for someone to fill her hours was not part of her life. She was happy alone, wanting to be obedient to her father. Giuseppina did not understand. Every day she waited for her husband to throw his arms around her. She was content to wash his clothes, knead bread, and read her mother's postcards. The thought of rebelling against intimacy had never occurred to her.

Rose was less happy to stay at home. Night school uplifted her. She admired the students with their notebooks and kept one of her own, full of dates from American history. To further her learning, she scattered words and phrases over the kitchen table and took the trolley to the library every Saturday to set margins and copy sentences from the newspaper under a portrait of Ralph Waldo Emerson.

Rose knew that it was time to leave her sister's home. On a Sunday, she took out a pen and paper and wrote a letter to her father's friend in Lawrence, Massachusetts. Mr. Durlamo was a musician who had come to America from Melilli in 1899 and had helped many fellow villagers find work in Lawrence. Enormous cotton and woolen mills had made Lawrence the largest worsted center in the world. By 1907, more than ninety percent of Lawrence was first- and second-generation immigrants.[10] They came with hope. Sicilians lived alongside Lebanese, Syrians, and Irish in the heart of the city.

September 2, 1907

Dear Mr. Durlamo,

My name is Rosina Bosco. I am the second daughter of Gaetano and Lucia Bosco. My father built the Visconte villa. I worked in your family's lemon grove when I was a girl. I listened to your music at the festival of St. Joseph. I came to America two years ago. I am a seamstress. It is time to move from my sister's home. My father told me to write you if I needed a job. I am in good health. I attend night school and I go to church. I will pay you for your help.

Rosina Bosco

Certain of his ability to enter a woman's soul, Durlamo wrote back quickly and decisively:

September 23, 1907

Dear Rosina Bosco,

It is a pleasure to write you this morning. I remember you well. You are the one with the pale cheeks and the blue eyes. I am surprised that you are not married. I will speak with the manager at the American Woolen Company. I want to warn you that he prefers to hire young girls who return to their mothers at night.

You are welcome to stay at my house. My wedding dishes have not a single crack or yellow stain to be seen. Students come to my house for music lessons. I hold recitals once a month. My wife makes delicious cakes and serves them with tea. I have a band. We practice at the house every Wednesday night. We play at church festivals and weddings, just like home.

Let me warn you about two good for nothings. Marina is my boarder. She reads the American magazines and puts pictures on her wall. She stays in her room and reads books. Let me tell you a secret. She talks about nothing but men. No man wants her because she has the tired look about her.

The other is a street sweeper who calls himself Don Carmelo. He visits Marina. He wants to throw bombs at the rich. My wife slapped him across the face. She told him, "Forget the whores." Do you know what he did? He threw a shoe at her and ran outside. He came back three days later with a pocket full of pamphlets and a heart swollen for a red-haired Jew.

These gitanos will snatch your soul. Until you can fend for yourself, allow me to look after you.

Durlamo

Rose read the letter with alarm. His audaciousness reminded her of Luigi the soap maker, who kicked his horse in public. His impolite use of secrets to get close to her was the Sicilian way of seduction. She pictured him as a prattling duck in the courtyard.

Besides, Durlamo's warnings about Marina did not distress her. She was most likely reading to better herself. Durlamo must have felt threatened by his lack of control over her, so he insulted her. Rose turned her thoughts to the idealist. He must be young to be infatuated with the Jewish organizer Emma Goldman. Rose's teacher believed that anyone who questioned authority was a traitor. Her example was the fiery anarchist with the red hair.

Rose knew that the street sweeper would not harm her. As far as Durlamo, she would be careful around him. She knew that he would pursue her just as the sun dried the fields. Later that morning, she wrote back to him.

October 23, 1907

Dear Mr. Durlamo,

Thank you for your offer. I am a hard worker and good seamstress. I would like to board with you and your wife. I will attend the recitals. I am not looking for a husband, and I have no interest in politics.

Rosina Bosco

When the letter arrived two weeks later, Durlamo took it to his desk, where he did not allow his wife. He had expected reciprocation; instead, he found rebuke. He reacted badly. Who does she think she is, he thought, staring at the letter. I will ridicule this peasant once she arrives. He took a piece of paper from the desk drawer and wrote:

November 5, 1907

Dear Miss Bosco,

Take the streetcar to Boston. Then switch over to the Boston and Maine. Carry sandwiches. The trip is a long one and you will be hungry. I will meet you at the station. I will be wearing a red jacket and black hat.

Regards,

Durlamo

Them Falling Stars

The next week, Rose left alone for Lawrence in the evening light. The steam engine came into view, and she boarded the train without looking back. Rose was a very smart, perceptive woman but oddly reticent. She did not reveal the caliber of her intellect in dazzling conversation. Nor did books inform her. Her gift was clear-sightedness, which she would need as she headed toward the mills of Lawrence.

Seated across from her was a thickset man who looked to be about her father's age.[12] He was little more than five feet in height, with the same abandoned look that her father had the day she left for America. His rounded shoulders and well-worn clothes gave him the appearance of unimportance. His head was bald, but she could see that he had once had blond hair.

He stared at her for a long while. Rose felt sorry for him one moment and offended the next. When she looked at him, he asked, "Where are you going?" She ignored him as she had been taught. But he was curious, so he said, "I'm from Lawrence, myself. Back from visiting my sister in Springfield. Where do you come from? You sure don't look like a mute."

"Sicily," she said reluctantly.

"Don't know much about that. I refused to go to school when I was young, and no one in my family made me. How do you know English if you're not from here?"

"Night school," Rose replied.

The passenger was not well-educated, but he was talkative. His eyes lit up at her answer. "Let me tell you a story. I went to night school once. I lived near some French people. I went to class one night with my friend Fatty Cyr. It was about ten years ago, and they was having night school over in the French section. Fatty was working at the mill with me. He had been going along for a couple of months, and the teacher decided to find out how much the class knew or had learned. She wrote some names and things on the blackboard. 'What's this word, Mr. Cote?' she says, pointing to the first word.

'That's my name, Cote.'

'Correct. Mr. Moreau, what is this word?'

'M-o-r-e-a-u. That's my name, Moreau.'

'Right.'"

The stranger leaned forward in his seat, his eyes twinkling as he continued: "Then teacher says, 'Mr. Cyr,' pointing to the word cat. 'Tell me what this is.' Fatty looked at the word for about a minute. 'I s'ppose it's my name,' he said finally, 'but I can't seem to make it out.'" The stranger threw back his head and laughed loudly.

Rose rearranged her hat and suddenly realized that she trusted the stranger not to harm her. He continued: "I'm an American, but my father was Irish. He came to Lawrence in '88. That was the year them stars fell. He was sleeping under a tree. The next thing he knowed, big balls of fire dropped all around him. He never went to church much, but he sure prayed a lot that night. Those were the times when there wasn't much work in Lawrence. There was a packinghouse, a brickyard, and things like that. A hotel, too. Belonged to the railroad. Most petered out when they built them mills."

The word mills piqued Rose's interest, so she asked him a question about his father. The storyteller replied, "He went to work for the railroad. I never done much work myself. Odd jobs now and again. My sisters keep me going."

Rose's only contact with Americans had been at Ellis Island, the factory, night school, and the library. Her neighborhood was too segregated to bump into them. This man was the first who had spoken to her in conversation. Unlike Durlamo and her father, he did not expect anything in return. His lack of pretension impressed Rose, so she asked him another question. "You never worked in the mills?"

"Only for a time," he replied. "That's when my mother worked there. She lasted until she got the rheumatism and her hearing went bad. I rode to work on a bicycle. That was before automobiles came in. Sure was handy. They was all the rage, too. Took me 'bout a week to learn to ride. Thought I never would, that week, 'till it come to me sudden how to do it. I got right on then and rode. A lotta the men in the mill rode bicycles to work. Most of 'em that didn't ride the electric cars had 'em, 'less they lived near the place. We'd keep 'em in a shed by the shop. Maybe be a couple, a dozen in that shed."

To many others, this friendly fellow with sweat on his brow, and the listener who faced him were very small and insignificant. But there was a decency about them, and neither was afraid of the other. He shared what was on his mind, and she did not laugh at his bumbling or mock his poverty. Outside, dimly lit houses rose feebly in the night, too weak to hold up for long. Like them, nothing in the storyteller's appearance conveyed substance, yet he had just taught Rose about his America.

When the train pulled into the depot at 8:00 P.M., Durlamo was waiting for her. He was a short man of forty, with an unlined face. He wore a black suit with a red vest and a high-collared white shirt. Atop his head was a black derby that revealed his vanity. He took a cigar from his mouth, bowed, and said deferentially, "So you are Rosina Bosco."

Rose had an urge to ask him why he had told her to look for a man with a red jacket. Instead, she said, "Yes, Mr. Durlamo. Forgive me. I know you would rather be home with your wife."

"My pleasure is in helping others. I insist that you look upon me as a friend." Rose blushed, longing for the memories the storyteller had given her. Durlamo took up too much space.

"Your English is good. How long have you been in America?"

Rose tried not to wince. "Since the time Roosevelt was president."

"So you know politics," Durlamo said, trying to be pleasant.

"Politics are for men, Mr. Durlamo," Rose countered.

"Ah," Durlamo said in a closed-minded manner, as he put his arm around Rose's carrying bag. "We will go to the mill tomorrow. Dress in your Sunday best. Answer yes and no. Take what you are offered."

Rose could not disguise the irritation that she had inherited from her father. Smiling uncomfortably, she replied, "That is the way it is back home."

Her frankness annoyed Durlamo. He had never met an attractive woman who spoke directly to him. She seemed to want to tell him what to do. Humiliated, he tried to put her in her place. "Let me tell you something. I am a life-long musician and businessman. Music is my passion. Anyone can learn to sing, but you need business sense to know how to find work. I am much respected in town. Men seek advice or come to me for financial backing. I am smart like a fox. If I tell you something, you can take it to the bank. I advise the local government on Italian affairs. And I am a leader in the Knights of Columbus."

Refusing to submit to his boastfulness, Rose changed the subject, asking after his wife. He replied, "Mrs. Durlamo is a homemaker. She enjoys knitting and cooking. Enough of this talk. My friend Charles

Anthony loaned me his buggy. Hand me your other bag. We will be home in a few minutes."

A horse-drawn paddy wagon raced by as they climbed into the buggy. "Do not be startled, Miss Bosco. You will get used to the street noise soon enough. The beer halls are close by. The Irish sweat off two gallons of beer a day."

Durlamo's face had the look of unbearable intimacy. Rose was tempted to say something, but she knew better. Her mother had taught her not to give into the temptation of men's small talk. They arrived at the tri-decker a few minutes later. Durlamo opened the door to the first-floor apartment. The furnishings spoke of modest privilege. He did not make enough money to afford a dream house filled with antiques, dark paneling, or library alcoves; instead, the apartment boasted accessories that made him comfortable. There was an old easy chair, a davenport, and a music stand within reach. The floor beside the stand was littered with newspapers and sheet music. Both the writing table and the dining room table overflowed with sheet music as well. An Oriental rug covered the floor.

Rose looked into the kitchen. It was small but spoke of efficiency—well lit and clean. The kitchen sink was open underneath, and off to the side was an ironing board. Rose spotted a device that she had never seen before—an electric toaster. The stove was black and of modest size, with a hot water back and a catch that opened to an ash pit in the cellar.[13]

Pointing to a spot beside the sink, Durlamo said, "Open that door." Rose walked over to it and turned the brass handle. She looked inside, but it was dark. Durlamo walked into the darkness and turned on the light. "This is the bathroom," he said with a broad smile. "We have a toilet, a sink, and a laundry tub. There is good light and ventilation. Very sanitary. I even had the floor tiled and porcelain fixtures put in. Pull this handle." Rose knew that it flushed the toilet, so she declined. "We are very modern. It will not hurt you. Step back." He pulled the cord, and water rushed down from the elevated tank. Marina came out of her bedroom as soon as she heard the sound. She was short, dark, and very attractive. As soon as she saw Rose, she ran over to give her a hug. "I am Marina Copula," she said. "I have heard so much about you. You are so white. You cannot be Sicilian."

Rose smiled as Marina went on, "I cannot believe it. Your hips are so small. Look at mine. You would think I had already had five children. I get so hungry. You will find a man in no time."

Durlamo listened, staring intently at Rose, who changed the subject by saying, "I understand you sew."

Marina replied, "I have sewn all my life. As a young woman, I traveled to Rome with my priest to sew his garment for the Feast of St. Alphonse. My talent is something my mother handed down to me."

"As with me," Rose replied.

Durlamo's wife came and touched his arm. He said, "Ladies. Ladies. Too much complimenting. We must arise early for work. You both have outstanding qualities, and I am sure you will make fine wives. For now, let us show some compassion for this late hour."

The Arlington Cotton Mills, Lawrence, MA from a 1905 postcard.

Marina whispered to Rose, "Do not mind him. We have a lot to talk about."

The next morning, Durlamo and Rose walked to the mill district. Unlike in Melilli, the streets of Lawrence were drab and lonely. Rose said nothing as she watched for danger. The mills came into view as soon she turned onto Essex Street. They stood across the river, strung together at the edge of the dark, churning waters of the Merrimack. Enormous smoke stacks rose among them.

She had seen brick buildings in Sicily, but they did not look like the ones in front of her. In Siracusa, they were yellow and bright, each with character and adornment. These were uniform in shape and color, with rows of geometrically perfect windows that grew smaller with distance.

They walked up the steps next to the clock tower at the rear of the main gate. Durlamo opened the door, just as her father would have if he had been with her. The shine from the hardwood floor startled her; she could not tell if it were wet or slippery. Durlamo sensed her hesitation, so he offered his arm to her and pointed to the office door. They walked into a small, stuffy waiting room. Behind an oak desk, a young woman typed slowly and methodically. Rose stared at her. It seemed that she had just stepped off the cover of the magazine on Marina's bed; she had the same image of feminine beauty: oval face, silky red hair tied above her head, a cotton waist shirt, and a black floor-length skirt. Even her shoes were similar to the ones the magazines advertised. Rose envied her. She worked in a warm place, dressed attractively, and had no boss behind her.

The receptionist looked up and said, "Be seated," pointing in the direction of three young girls with colored head wraps and white frocks who sat impassively with their hands on their chins. Rose turned as a door opened and a tall, physically imposing man with a shock of white hair signaled to Durlamo, who stirred and whispered to her in Sicilian, "Show respect."

"Mr. Durlamo. How are you? Thomas is practicing much more since I spoke with him. I hope that you're seeing the results. What do you have for me today?"

"Rose Bosco, the seamstress. I told you about her."

"Of course. Can she start today?"

Before Durlamo could reply, Rose said, "I am not dressed for work."

Durlamo drew back. "Pardon her manners, Mr. Andrews. She means no disrespect. Of course she can start today. The dress is nothing. She can make another." He smiled at Rose as he turned a huge ring on his finger. Her boss in Connecticut had worn the same kind.

Andrews looked more closely at her. "Have you ever worked in a factory, Miss Bosco?"

Yes."

Tell me about it."

I worked at a large table with three other girls. We cut and sewed corsets. The boss scolded the girls for using too much material."

Mr. Andrews nodded. "We fire workers for inefficiency. You're responsible for a quota. Stand by your machine until you're told to leave. Your supervisor will make sure you don't cheat. Obey him. That will be the key to your success. What do you know about unions?" Andrews had had nothing but trouble from them. His voice became cold, and his words came more quickly. "There's a new one in town that calls itself Wobblies.[14] They're riff raff and communists. They sign up colereds and women—any unskilled worker. The other unions hate them. I don't allow them on my property. I give foreigners a chance to better themselves, and they repay me with strikes. If the IWW had its way, it would destroy every machine in this factory." With his eyes on Durlamo, he said to Rose, "If I find out you've joined them, I will discharge you on the spot. Now please stand up."

Rose complied. As she turned to rest her coat on the chair, she felt his hand brush against her arm. "Skin and bones, hey Durlamo?"

Durlamo chuckled, "She is not spoken for."

Unable to hide behind a polite veneer, Andrews said, as if Rose had worn rags, "I'll start you on machine three. Please don't think of men while the machine is spinning. And cut your hair. I've seen women lose the side of their scalps because they came to work with long hair. Miss Bosco, you look like the type who'll turn a profit for the stockholders of this company."

His words infuriated Rose, and she held her ground. "I am not prepared to work in my Sunday dress."

Smiling at her, he replied, "I'm a God-fearing man, Miss Bosco, so I don't want you to miss Mass on my account. Heaven forbid that your priest condemns me to hell. Missing church is a mortal sin, right Durlamo?"

"Mortal sin. Of course. Of course."

"Start tomorrow if it pleases you. Your rate of pay is five dollars a week. Miss Reynolds will collect your signature. Have a good morning."

The White Stallion

For the next three years, Rose operated a loom under the critical eye of her American bosses. She worked close to sixty hours a week, earning about ten cents an hour. She also followed her father's wishes by keeping to herself and sending him part of her wages. After paying her rent, she sent him about six dollars, equivalent to three weeks wages in Sicily. He was proud of her, but she knew that he had no idea what trials she had to endure to earn that kind of money.

The labor was grueling, dangerous, and monotonous. Workers lost fingers and limbs on the machines. The air was heavy with humidity, dust, and fiber. Summer was unbearably hot and winter numbingly cold. Women and children died from respiratory diseases like pneumonia and tuberculosis.

Marina and Durlamo were right about the men. Rose's slender figure, smooth complexion, blue eyes, and chestnut hair made her irresistible. She was especially attractive to the bosses. They often had their way with immigrant women and expected the same from her, constantly tormenting her with touches and crude humor. She confessed her shame to her priest every Saturday. He told her to attend Mass daily.

These were lonely, hostile times for Rose. Now twenty-six, she did nothing but work and return to her bedroom on Common Street. In Sicily, she could socialize with family at weddings and baptisms. If she wanted company, she could walk to her aunt's home, as long as one of her brothers went along. Here, the harsh winters kept her inside. Rosina talked with Marina and Mrs. Durlamo, but she had little in common with them. Marina enjoyed playing cards with Durlamo's friends and reading her magazines. Mrs. Durlamo stayed in her room a good deal, staring at a photograph taken of her when she was fifteen. She had been very beautiful, with dark hair that fell upon her shoulders. A white lace cap made a most striking frame for her face, with her bright, dark eyes and sweet expression. She was still pretty, but marriage had aged her. She had great difficulty remembering to do simple things, like combing her hair.

Rose's only social outlets were church and night school. Without a brother to accompany her, she rarely went to the church-sponsored dances. Her only fun since arriving a year ago was the Columbus Day celebration. Hundreds of fellow Sicilians and Italians clapped to the band music and danced under colored lanterns. She even allowed herself to dance with the street sweeper, Don Carmelo. (C.B. Carr, 1998).

A week later, she received word of her father's death. Rose made the sign of the cross and cried for her mother. She thought then that she would go home to Sicily to care for her mother. There was nothing to keep her here; her brother and sister had their own lives, and Marina was half crazy.

She did not know about Carmelo's longing for her. For a while, he had overlooked her. As time passed, though, he desired her, finding her attractive and without fault. With a smile on his face, he counted up everything in his favor. Although frail looking, he had a slightly upturned mustache, round black eyes, and a full head of hair. He also dressed neatly and enjoyed wearing a suit and tie to Durlamo's recitals. His outgoing personality, love of music, and easygoing manner made him particularly carefree and happy.

One spring morning, after Mass at Holy Rosary Church, he approached Rose. "I do not think I can live another day without saying your name to your face. May I call you Rosina?"

Carmelo Amoroso, 1912

Rose turned slowly, a slight blush on her cheek. She did not mind his question but was annoyed by his impertinence. Still, he was slim and small, very self-confident, and never in a bad mood. When he talked, his face lit up. Today he looked especially handsome, so she indulged herself. "You speak like a boss but you dress like a tailor. For what reason should you call me Rosina? Do you have something to speak about?"

"Grazie. You know I come from Mineo, where the corn stands high. We are bold that way. I have always admired you. You have the fragrance of my mother's hair. My cousin told me about the death of your father."

He spoke with such sincerity that Rose blushed again as she asked him when he left Mineo.

"A few years ago," he said. "With friends. My brother-in-law told me about Lawrence, so I came here. The others took the train back to New York. Too cold here. Besides, Niccolò could not get a Spaniard out of his mind. He loves women with black hair tied to the back of their heads."

His little face continued to hold her attention. "You are single," she said. "You must write many poems. Perhaps your loneliness drives you to speak my name."

It was his turn to blush. "Yes. I am the new Rodolfo, banished to this awful land. 'When it comes to dreams and visions and castles in the air, I've the soul of a millionaire.'"

"'Che gelida manina,' *La Boheme*," Rose said.

Carmelo lit up, seeing she got him. "'But from time to time two thieves steal all the jewels out of my safe, two pretty eyes.'"

"And, Mr. Poet, do you 'squander rhymes and love songs like a lord?'"

"But 'I live!'"

They shared a laugh.

"I could never figure out why my father hated that song," Rose said. "I love it."

"One of my passions in life is singing. It's not everyday you meet someone who gets you like--" he snapped his fingers. "--that." He paused for a beat. "In fact, you could be my Mimi. My happiness. I would never let you feel the cold. My intentions are as pure as St. Agatha's when she was banished to the den of prostitutes."

Sensing that this poor worker with a presence was pursuing her, she said, "I am on my way home."

"The Madonna in the great church of my childhood reminds me of you," he blurted out. "You both know what you want."

"I want to stand on the top of the hill and look down at the river to watch the children ride their horses." For the past three years, Rose had taken this walk alone, never sharing this secret with another, until now. What had he said that made her want to tell him?

"Rose," he sighed, "your smile awakens a deep sorrow inside me. I must tell you about it. It is about my great uncle Don Tommaso, a man whose passion the winds blowing in from the sea could not contain. As a young man, he was always in the confessional. You see, he loved dearly the daughter of Vicari the fisherman. He noticed her looking at him so long that he could see his own reflection in her eyes. He spent much of his time pining away in the palm grove. Her visage was his secret. Not even fasting for three days took away his longing to touch her lips and breathe in her scent. As he lay awake each night, imagining them as one, he could not comprehend the distance that kept them apart. She could never return his love because she belonged to another."

Rose gave him a distant smile.

"One Saturday, he confessed his mourning to the priest. With tears pouring down, Don Tommaso learned the bitter truth. 'You lust instead

61

of love,' the priest admonished him. 'You cannot have her. Your avarice must end. Do penance because you offend God.' When he returned home, his father beat him across his head. 'What is wrong with you, stupid boy? Do I have to send you to the mines to make you a man? Get over this girl. You will never suck at her breasts. Go back to the priest and ask his forgiveness. He told me about your impiety.'"

Deeply offended by Carmelo's explicit talk, Rose wondered at his power over her. She knew that she had the same power over men. Her mother had told her long ago that men would die to be in her arms. Looking away, she tightened her wrap against the demons who circled her. She would not end up sewing and cleaning for any man.

Carmelo continued. " 'Impiety?' Tommaso thought. He had just been reproached by his priest and now his father, a dark and unforgiving man. He shook his head. His pain at being betrayed by his father was too great to forget. The next morning, he followed his father to the fields but turned at the ovens to ask a favor of Paolo, the boss's son. 'Marti, you know me well. When we were children, I showed you how to catch the brown rabbits in the park. You always said that I could come to you in time of need.'

'Yes, of course. I am your servant. Now tell me, handsome friend, what do you want?'

'I want to ride your white stallion along the beach on Sunday next.'

'Sweet friend. You must have Donna Valentina on your mind. I heard about your infatuation with the fisherman's daughter. Indeed, I have seen her, and her skin glows under her veil. I did not know how strongly you felt about her.'

"Don Tommaso laughed. 'That is right. She draws my breath from me. She will be with her family at the fishermen's village, and, when she sees me ride by, her heart will cry out for the man with the long hair.'"

Carmelo's words were too vivid for the virgin Rose. She annulled them by picturing him as the madman, Don Alberto, who outraged his neighbors every dawn in his dirty nightgown.

"He was lying to Paulo. He would dash along the flat stones next Sunday but then veer inland, cross the Villa Pacini, and head straight to the Church of St. Agata al Carcere. There he would gallop up the steps and into church; among the saints, he would shout to the priest in front of the altar: 'You deceived me and silenced my love. I mock you and your impudence. May you burn in hell, as surely I will.'"

Knowing that God had given her life and could take it away, Rose protested that she did not want to hear any more. "Leave me." Then she hesitated a moment, secretly burning to feel his hands on her.

"Rosina, Rosina. Please let me finish. I mean no disrespect. My uncle's sacrilege was wrong, and he was justly excommunicated and scorned by his friends and family. In the middle of the night, he stole away to America under another name."

"And your point?" she asked, as though it did not matter.

"Longing for a woman is beyond vanity."

Rose made the sign of the cross to hide from this tiny man in his Sunday clothes. "I am a simple woman," she said, meaning that her God had given her no defense against the caresses of his words.

Carmelo waited for her to smile then said, "I am a simple man," meaning that he could not live another day as a victim of her fate.

No one had ever told Rose such an involved story. It complimented her intelligence and aroused her. She could not forget it. Years later, she would tell her daughters that Don Tommaso's feelings were the same that she had for Carmelo. At first she could not admit to them, but, slowly, she realized a constant desire for this man. He gave her something to smile about, so she eventually accepted him and cherished his story without shame. These feelings naturally matched his own. They were married six months after he told her the story of the white stallion.[15]

Tired of dust and squalid-looking women, brother Sebastiano moved to Boston soon after Rose's wedding.[16] For the first time in five years, he could say that he was alive. He later found work in Quincy, twelve miles south of Boston, where he met Frances, who had emigrated from Palermo with her entire family at the age of six. Frances had gone to school in Quincy, spoke English like an American, and supported herself by translating letters sent from Italy for neighbors who did not read or write Italian. She was also as tall as most American women.

Sebastiano wanted to marry this "almost" American. Because her father had died, he approached her brothers to arrange the marriage. They told him that she was in love with another man. Sebastiano threatened to commit suicide by stabbing himself in the abdomen. He also offered them a great deal of money. Sebastiano and Frances were married on April 26, 1913. She never learned to love Sebastiano. She resented him and made him miserable their entire married life.

He brushed it of because he could sit under the shade of trees after work and escape. Over the next fifteen years, he prospered, and his family grew. In less than a generation, he had forgotten about the old ways and the traditions that had oppressed him for so long.

Every time Rose passed the rundown shanty where she had lived in Lawrence, she threw a handful of pennies into the gutter, her way of repaying the misery that this gray, treeless city had given her. In September, she sent Giuseppina a postcard, telling her that she would be arriving at her home—the first that Carmelo had heard about it. "I do not want to be here another minute, Carmelo. I want to be with my family and friends." He agreed and, in the next breath, kissed her. They boarded the locomotive to Middletown, Connecticut a week later in a rainstorm (A. Alosi, personal interview, September 5, 2001).

Bread and Roses

January 10, 1912 was not a typical day. It had snowed the night before for eight straight hours. The crunch of the ox-pulled rollers awoke Rose at 5:00 A.M. She could not get back to sleep, so she put on her robe and went to the kitchen to fix a cup of tea. Soon, the rising sun would illuminate the newly fallen, heavy snow. Rose would not receive Holy Communion when she went to church today, because the snowstorm had prevented her from going to confession the previous day.

She filled the kettle with water and walked over to the water closet. A wall of cold air hit her face when she opened the door. Silly Carmelo must have shut it during the night. The last time he had done that, ice had formed in the toilet bowl. She checked to see if the pipes were frozen. They had not snapped; the dripping faucet had saved them from a costly repair. She lifted the toilet cover to relieve herself. Inside was the dreaded ice, which she cracked open with a yardstick. The closet was clean and dry; she could not stand to use the public privies.

She returned to the kitchen and poured hot water into her cup, added a touch of honey, and sat down in the dim light to cut a pear in half. She cut the halves into quarters and divided the parts again, slowly eating each piece as her mind wandered back to childhood memories.

Rose finished breakfast, washed her cup, and took out a piece of paper to write a letter to Marina:

January 10, 1912

Dear Marina,

> *Last night it snowed. I awoke early to write before I leave for Mass. Nothing has changed. Sister Giuseppina wonders if I will have children. She thinks I am too old. I stay at home to sew. Carmelo works with my brother-in-law. He cannot bear the weight of the sand on his back. He begs me to return to Lawrence.*
>
> *I bought Giuseppina a new white enamel teapot and a new tablecloth. Children play outside in the cold. Before the snow fell, they went to the pond to skate. Now they do nothing but chase after dogs.*

Rosina

Rose heated water then proceeded to wash and powder herself—another of the routines she kept from home. The sweet talcum reminded her of Sunday mornings, when she and her sisters used it to keep dry on their walk to church. She combed her hair and tied it behind her head in a tight bun. Her face was rough from the cold winds that blew off the river. She smoothed the white spots with lotion in long, circular motions then rubbed some into her hands and elbows. She found her Sunday dress and put it on behind the closet door. Although Carmelo was asleep, modesty prevented her from dressing in the open. In fact, Carmelo had never seen his wife naked. She would ready herself for bed in the bedroom, get into bed, turn off the lights, and close her eyes. Carmelo would get ready in the bathroom then slip under the sheets. Good women were not supposed to be seen uncovered.

Rose put on her navy blue coat and woolen hat, which she attached to her hair with a pin, and wrapped her throat with the scarf that she had knitted for herself. It was 6:30 A.M. as she headed into the cold for 7:00 Mass.

The snow had drifted onto the porch; knowing that it hid ice, she stepped carefully until she reached the railing. Then she pulled up the bottom of her coat and stepped into the deep snow that covered the steps, reaching the street without slipping. Once she felt the packed snow, her steps became surer. She walked alone to church, accompanied only by her memories.

Christmas decorations still adorned the bakery window. Rose passed the lunchroom filled with tired men, walking quickly, because the cold air hurt her ears. She met her friend Gabriella at the corner. "How is it? I have not seen your daughter at daily Mass all week. Is she ill?"

"Yes. She caught the cough from the dust. I have decided not to send her back to work. She will go to school. Children die too soon on the machines. Lucia buried her second son last week."

Back in Lawrence, Marina checked into work. At the Pacific Mills complex, Polish weavers did the same. At 11:00 A.M., they lined up to receive their pay. When they opened their envelopes, shrieks of anger rang out. "Mother of God, my pay has been cut! I will not be able to feed my children!" Several workers fainted. Others cried as they returned to the looms. Three men ran through the building yelling, "Stop work! Leave!" Marina saw a long procession of workers pass under her window.[17] At least five thousand women and children were walking home. She did not know why. This was the first time she had seen a strike.

The next day, a sense of foreboding thickened the air. Marina saw it in the eyes of the men and women who walked alongside her on the cobblestones. Mingled with it, however, was a look of determination. Young boys passed out flyers: STRIKE FRIDAY!

Marina and the other workers opened their paychecks. A quick glance confirmed her fear: Her wages had been cut. The cry went out again: "Walk away from the machines!" One thousand women and children stopped work and filed out in an orderly fashion; Marina was among them. Those who stayed back regretted it. They were slapped by angry strikers. Once outside, the group marched to the Almond Mills in hopes of spreading the strike. They walked silently. Marina worried about being shot. She took off her apron and threw it to the ground. Others pelted windows with pieces of coal.

When the marchers reached the mill, they rushed the gates and went to the switchboard to shut off the power. They shouted, "Join us! How can we live on the money they give us? Strike or else our children will starve!" Hundreds walked off their machines and went home.

A week later, Marina would meet Elizabeth Gurley Flynn and three organizers who came to Lawrence. Flynn was one of the most dynamic speakers for the Industrial Workers of the World. She knew about mill towns and dedicated her whole life to the cause of socialism. In fact, she had been speaking to workers since she was fifteen. Marina was excited. She knew that some called Flynn "The East Side Joan of Arc."

Elizabeth Gurley Flynn was born in Concord, New Hampshire, where the mills stretched like prisons along the bank of the Merrimack River. She moved to New York's South Bronx when she was ten years old. Her parents put her in a public school, where she developed a love of reading and writing. She especially loved to study the Constitution and the Bill of Rights.[18]

The strike leaders brought Elizabeth to an organizing meeting. Marina was there. She listened as one of the leaders said, "We have been out for two weeks. Donations are slowing. Mothers worry about their children starving to death. I am afraid they may go back to work."

Rising, Elizabeth held up a newspaper. "Look here. My friend suggests that we send the children out of town for safekeeping. He says that it worked successfully in Europe. We can do it here. The IWW will find families and chaperones. We'll do our part by recruiting the children and sending a few of our own speakers to chaperone. Emma Goldman promised me that she'd organize a mass rally on our behalf. I personally think that if someone from Lawrence speaks to our brothers and sisters about our plan, they'll renew their commitment to the strike."

Someone from the crowd yelled, "Who should go?"

Reno, the operator, spoke slowly, "Obviously Italian children. They are suffering the most, and there are thousands of Italian socialists in the city to take them."

"We'll need women to accompany the children to New York," Elizabeth said. "And help with the language."

Marina had a secret that she was eager to share. "I have a friend who speaks Sicilian, Italian, and English. She writes beautifully and has no children. She is eager to see me. The men knew that she meant Rose. They nodded in approval, remembering Rose's friendship with the sister of Angelo Rocco, a strike leader. Marina rushed home and, in her best handwriting, wrote to her friend.

Several days later, the letter arrived in Middletown. Unshaven, Carmelo brought it to Rose, who was mending his pants. Carmelo was happy to let his wife help his friends. He said to her, "Do not give those miserable bastards another day to oppress us."

Lunch with Mrs. Hutchinson

The next day, Durlamo paid Elizabeth a visit. He said, "An informant tells me that you want the Italians to send their children to strangers in the city. I have alerted the school board. They have very serious concerns about the health and safety of the children. One of the members, Mrs. Royal Hutchinson, wants to meet you. When it comes to children, we can never be too cautious."

Elizabeth's experience in the labor movement had taught her to expect duplicity between business and government. She assumed that if the school board disapproved, the police would prevent the children from leaving. "I would be delighted to meet Mrs. Hutchinson," Elizabeth said, showing no disdain.

Mrs. Hutchinson was waiting for Elizabeth inside the superintendent's office. After exchanging pleasantries, Elizabeth briefed her. "Four hundred families have volunteered to take the children. They will be enrolled in school if space is available. Volunteers will pack sandwiches, and chaperones will accompany them. Translators will be on the train; I am scheduled to interview one this morning."

Convinced of America's might, Mrs. Hutchinson was intolerant of anyone who tried to impinge on it. Moreover, she associated Italians with anarchists. "May I meet your translator?"

Elizabeth reasoned that Mrs. Hutchinson would do anything to break the strike, so she had to find a way to gain her cooperation. "Delighted," she said.

Rose was to meet Elizabeth in front of the Holy Rosary Church, where she and Carmelo had married. She had not felt this excited since that day. She waited on the church steps, staring at the guards outside the Everett Mills. A long black Roadster pulled up. Rose stepped back, studying the tapered look of the passenger who rolled down the window. She was supposed to meet a young woman in a black hat. Instead, she faced a thin-lipped American who studied every detail of her coat. Her hesitancy

Mary Marcy
"Battle for Bread at Lawrence" (excerpt)
The International Socialist Review vol. 12
March 1912

Mary Marcy (1877-1922) was an American socialist author, pamphleteer, poet, and staff writer for *The Internationalist Socialist Review*. In the article from which this excerpt is quoted, she boiled down the causes of the 1912 Lawrence Strike in a nutshell and, quoting IWW (Industrial Workers of the World) leader "Big Bill" Haywoord's speeches at the strike, she linked its struggles with those going on elsewhere.

The classic doors of our oldest colleges have been thrown open to permit youth of "our best families" to join the militia and "insolent, well-fed Harvard men parade up and down, their rifles loaded with ball cartilage, their bayonets glittering, keen and hungry for the blood of the strikers who are fighting the resources of the entire state to secure a wage that will enable them to live in comparative sufficiency and decency" (p. 538).

heightened when the chauffeur got out to open the door. Reluctantly, she entered the car and sat next to the two women who were both dressed in gray.

"Forgive me, Rose. I'm Elizabeth. It's my pleasure to introduce you to Mrs. Royal Hutchinson, head of the Lawrence school board."

Rose nodded, her eyes on Elizabeth. Suddenly she understood the feelings that gripped her. Elizabeth's tone was friendly and noncompetitive, but Mrs. Hutchinson's demeanor put people to their knees. People from humble origins had few happy memories with her kind.

The car stopped at a restaurant, where the women sat at a corner table. This world was new to Rose. Potted palms and rich, polished walnut paneling contrasted nicely with starched white linen tablecloths. Waiters in white jackets and gloves stood stationed at each table. An elegant buffet table packed with fresh fruit, French pastries, meats, cakes, and mounds of bread and cheese edged the far wall. The sight of so much food made Rose queasy. No wonder Americans are so fat, she said to herself. She was out of place, and she knew it. Even the linen and the silverware made her uncomfortable.

Mrs. Hutchinson said flatly, "Rose, what a lovely dress you're wearing. Did you purchase it by mail order?"

"I made it," Rose said, sensing condescension.

Mrs. Hutchinson prodded her with another question. "Where did you learn to sew? At night school, I hope! I've championed classes for aliens since my election to the school board."

Rose replied simply, "My mother taught me to sew." She turned to Elizabeth, more comfortable with her bearing. "You are so pretty. Are you married?" Rose assumed that American women needed a husband to have status.

Elizabeth replied, "My life is my work."[19]

Rose was capable of broadening her own ideas. Having heard Mrs. Hutchinson champion the education of aliens, she asked Elizabeth, "Why are you helping us?"

Elizabeth did not hesitate. "My family has been very active in the socialist cause."

Mrs. Hutchinson knew about Elizabeth's politics. Flynn's father was one of the first organizers for Industrial Workers of the World. When Elizabeth joined the IWW, she spoke in places like Chicago and Iowa. Mrs. Hutchinson could not comprehend why Elizabeth and her family lived in denial of America's greatness.

A fat man entered the café and sat down at the table next to the door. The women watched him squeeze into his chair. The waiter came over and bowed deferentially. "What may I bring you, Mr. Weinstein?"

"Coffee. And bring me the cream and sugar in your finest silver." His legs were wide apart, and his stomach touched the table. He folded his hands across his waist and sat back with his head tilted to the left. Rose noticed his puffy veins and feet. He tapped his left foot twice then looked at his watch. A minute passed, and he tapped and checked his watch again. The waiter brought the coffee and poured it into his cup. The fat man attached the napkin to his vest, picked up the spoon, and placed two teaspoons of sugar into the cup. Then he poured in the cream. Stirring the coffee caused it to overflow. He put the sugar container to his left and placed the creamer next to it. He squared both then squared them again. His foot tapped, and, as before, he checked his watch and sipped the coffee.

A dark-haired youth peered in from the street. Rose recognized him from the old neighborhood. Next to him was a pretty child, not more than twelve. Rose could see that her skin was smooth and unblemished, the color of precious gold. She was dressed plainly, but her cheeks and lips were covered with rouge. The fat man nodded and pushed his chair away from the table. His stomach bumped against the edge, causing the cup and saucer to tip. The waiter rushed over to pick them up.

The two children entered the restaurant through the kitchen door. The fat man met them in the private dining room next to the Employees Only sign. Weinstein pulled open her coat. She blushed and closed her eyes as he touched her. "Open your mouth," he commanded. When she looked confused, Weinstein twisted his own mouth open then put his stubby fingers on her cheeks. She opened wide. Satisfied, he dismissed the boy with a wave of his hand. "Wait outside." Then he signaled the waiter to bring a glass of wine. The child drank it quickly as he reached to shut the curtain. She was not afraid of his ugliness.

The three women were in shock. Ten minutes later, the child ran out the back door. The waiter followed, her coat in his hand. Not seeing her, he tossed it into the garbage can.[20]

The white-haired Hutchinson sniffed, "Disreputable children, the whole lot."

Elizabeth said bitterly, "The child works for food."

Deaf to Elizabeth, the matron replied, "There are office jobs if she stays in school. Nice jobs where she can dress up. It's too bad that her kind does not apply themselves."

Elizabeth knew about the racial clichés perpetuated by American intellectuals like Madison Grant, who preached that melting-pot sentimentalism was dangerous.[21] She had also heard progressive thinkers advocate for the expulsion of the retarded, the insane, and criminals.

Her cause, however, centered on the vicious exploitation of workers by capitalists. "If mill owners didn't exploit the poor, there wouldn't be strikes," she said to Mrs. Hutchinson, her face fixed with certainty.

"Nonsense," Mrs. Hutchinson replied. "Look at what's happening in this city. Violence, confusion, rampage. Hundreds of rioters who'll steal from and kill Americans because we remind them of their own inferiority. They're impelled to obliterate anyone above them, whether the superiority lies in wealth, position, character, beauty, or intellect."

Rose was not sure what she meant, so she asked, "I am less than you?"

"Of course not, my dear," Mrs. Hutchinson responded. "There is a clear distinction between race and nationality. You have the creamy skin and blue eyes of a great Nordic warrior. Dark-skinned people take it for granted that Whites are smarter than they are. They have not the slightest illusion that they could have invented electricity or built skyscrapers. And they recognize that Blacks and Whites differ in moral and psychological characteristics as well."[22]

Elizabeth, a product of a strict moral upbringing that equated bigotry with perversity, was no longer careful with her words. "You are a thief and a parasite, deaf to the uproar of injustice. Rose, this woman is your ruination. Let us leave."

As Rose put on her coat, she offered Mrs. Hutchinson a thought. "I can touch the ice that grips your soul."

"I beg your pardon?" Mrs. Hutchinson replied, confused. Despite Rose's thick accent, she felt the penetrating insult of her remark. It was unusual

---

Madison Grant
The Passing of the Great Race
1916

Madison Grant (1865-1937) was an American lawyer and eugenicist. He published this book on scientific racism in 1916. Below is an excerpt.

Race feeling may be called prejudice by those whose careers are cramped by it, but it is a natural antipathy which serves to maintain the purity of type. The unfortunate face that nearly all species of men interbreed freely leaves us no choice in the matter. Either the races must be kept apart by artificial devices of this sort, or else the ultimately amalgamate, and in the offspring the more generalized or lower type prevails.

---

and unwelcome to be chastised by someone who spoke such poor English.

72

Common Street was a mile away, so Elizabeth and Rose folded their arms together in kinship and began the long walk home. Elizabeth was the first to speak. "What do you hear from Marina?"

"Food is running out, and the children are hungry."

"What do you think about sending the children out of town to volunteers sympathetic to the strike? The children will be safe and well cared for."

"Where?" asked Rose, her heart softening to Elizabeth's patience.

"Cities like New York and Philadelphia. We've received four hundred letters offering to take children."

"Who will be in charge?"[23]

"I will. That's why I asked to meet with you today. I need your help. I don't speak Italian or Sicilian. I need you to help me take applications from families, arrange medical exams for youngsters, and assist me on the trip. Once we arrive in New York, I'll give speeches at two or three rallies that my friends have arranged. You'll sit next to me on the stage."

Rose pictured rooms filled with malodorous men, breathing heavily. "Oh, I could never do that," she said directly.

Elizabeth countered, "Marina speaks highly of you. You'll instill confidence in the children."

Rose answered, "I will accompany you if Marina comes with me."

Notes

1. For a discussion of the padrone system, see Peck (1996), "Reinventing Free Labor: Immigrant Padrones and Contract Laborers in North America, 1885-1925."

2. The "Rose Speaks" trilogy parallels Alfred Young's (1998, 2004) search for the sources of injustice in the past treatment of the weak and poor. Cultural conservatives with New England pedigrees, who once dominated the study of colonial and revolutionary history, considered Young's histories of common people "radical" (Taylor, 2005). In a presidential address to the American Historical Society in 1962, Carl Bridenbaugh wondered whether the ". . . urban-bred . . . products of lower middle class or foreign origins' could understand, or should study, colonial and revolutionary America, which he imagined as overwhelmingly English" (quoted in Taylor, 2005, p. 246). Academic condescension led Young to study "'the outsiders in early America, [those]. . . ignored, marginalized, or patronized by insider historians'" (quoted in Taylor, 2005, p. 246).

3. Given the remarkable stories of immigrants like Rose, why have scholarly biographies not celebrated their lives and times? A major difficulty is the lack of empirical evidence. People of low birth and station usually do not leave behind documents (Taylor, 2005). In Rose's case, I knew little more than her birth and death dates, the names of her two brothers and one sister, her skills as a seamstress, her employment in the mills of Lawrence, her appearance, and her widowhood. To reconstruct her life, I had to search for primary documents and artifacts and collect memories from her descendants. I documented her literacies via a letter and a postcard that she had written to her daughter, and two postcards that she had received from her mother and niece. I then turned to collateral information about the context of her life. Town, church, and immigration records revealed her signature, her parents' names, her place of birth, and details surrounding her departure and arrival. Interviews with descendents revealed the dynamics that led to her emigration, a dramatic story about a white stallion, her time in the North End of Boston and Quincy, Carmelo's gentleness and love of music, his relationship with the Gulizia family, his employment history, his public speech, and details surrounding his death. I also read about Sicilian culture and visited where Rose had lived. Although I had little documentation of her voice and ideas, I had enough to construct a plausible template for her life, which I embellished with fictitious characters and dialogue to illuminate the ways in which she wrestled with impoverishment and bigotry.

4. Events found at *American Chronicle* (Gordon & Gordon, 1999); *New York Times Index* (1973); *American Decades* (Bruccoli, 1996a, 1996b); and *Readers Guide to Periodical Literature* (1915, 1922).

5. Construction of the Suez Canal began in 1859 and ended in 1869. The canal was repaired in 1902. The census of 1907 shows that thirty-five thousand Italians, most born in Sicily and southern Italy, were in Egypt as masons and stonecutters. The Assuam Dam, five hundred miles south of Cairo, was finished at this same time (Colby et al., 1910, p. 220; History.com, 2010).

6. The name of the estate is fictionalized.

7. Foerster (1924) reports that one hundred and twenty-seven thousand Sicilians left Sicily in 1906. He believed that emigration did not originate where misery was greatest; rather, it began ". . . where there was a chance of saving enough money for passage fares and has best maintained itself where wages were at a medium level" (p. 104). Mangione and Morreale (1992) state that of the 3.8 million Italians who immigrated to the United States between 1899 and 1924, 2.1 million returned to Italy. During the peak years of immigration, ninety-seven percent of Italians entered the United States through New York City, giving it the largest Italian population of any city in the country (Foerster, 1924).

8. *The Morton Allan Directory of European Steamship Arrivals for the Years 1890 to 1930* (1998) lists all the arrivals of ships in New York City and other cities. There were virtually no arrivals in cities other than New York until 1909, when the line Navigazione Generale Italiana sent two steamers to Boston. Rosa Bosco, twenty-one, and her fifteen-year-old brother Sebastiano departed Messina, Sicily, June 4, 1905, aboard the S. S. Italia, with Giuseppina Fontana, forty-six, and her son Carmelo Lombardo, sixteen. They arrived at Ellis Island June 23, 1905. Rose declared herself a "servant" who could read and write and had two dollars in her possession. Brother Sebastiano was a laborer, illiterate, with one dollar in his possession. Two-thirds of the passengers were illiterate. This statistic is not surprising; the census of 1901 indicates that sixty-five percent of Sicilian men and seventy-seven percent of women over the age of six were illiterate (Reeder, 1998). Rose stated to the immigrant official that she and Sebastiano intended to stay with their cousin Giuseppi Lombardo, of 8 Elm Street, Middletown, Connecticut (American Family Immigration History Center, n.d.).

9. No one I interviewed knew the date or port of Rose's arrival or where she went after deboarding. My aunt thought that she went to live with her father's

godchild, her sponsor. A review of her ship's original manifest established that her final destination was Middletown, CT, to which she had a ticket. Middletown is Melilli's sister city; more than twenty thousand residents trace their ancestry back to this ancient Sicilian village (The North End Action Team, 2008; Harmon & The Middlesex County Historical Society, n.d.).

10. See the Essex National Heritage Area (n.d.), *Lawrence History Center* and Hirschman & Mogford (2009), "Immigration and the American Industrial Revolution from 1880 to 1920."

11. Fearing that foreigners would corrupt America with their superstitions, city fathers in Middletown required that immigrant mill workers attend assimilation classes. See Wikipedia (2011), *Americanization* and Levinson (2005), *Community Colleges: A Reference Handbook.*

12. Rose did not read books. She gained her information from contact with people, many the brunt of vicious immigrant jokes. Some spoke to her condescendingly; others revealed much, unaware that they were educating her. The Irish American character she meets on the train is similar in temperament to the cartoon character Happy Hooligan. His words come directly from the life histories of O'Neil (Bassett, 1938) and Lavoie (Grady, 1938) at American Life Histories: Manuscripts from the Federal Writers' Project, 1936-1940.

13. A hot-water stove has the capability to heat domestic water in its firebox or through a tank or pipes set at the back of the stove.

14. In 1905, the radical labor organization the Industrial Workers of the World (IWW) formed under the leadership of socialists like William Haywood, Eugene V. Debs, Elizabeth Gurley Flynn, Mary "Mother" Jones, Joseph Ettor, and Arturo Giovannitti. Although many unions refused to accept immigrant workers, such was not true of the IWW. Many of its members were first- and second-generation immigrants. Haywood believed that general strikes, boycotts, and even sabotage were necessary to achieve objectives. Haywood, Gurley Flynn, Ettor, and Giovannitti were involved in the Lawrence Textile Strike of 1912. "In 1914, one of the leaders of the IWW, Joe Haaglund Hill, was accused of the murder of a Salt Lake City businessman. Convicted on circumstantial evidence and despite mass protests, Hill was shot by a firing squad on November 19, 1915" (Spartacus Educational, n.d.). During the First World War, the IWW opposed US participation in the conflict. After the United States entered the war in 1917, IWW leaders, including

William Haywood, were arrested under the Espionage Act. See Spartacus Educational (n.d.), *William Haywood*.

15. My father and aunt had conflicting and imperfect memories about their father. My aunt thought that Carmelo had come to America to escape a neighbor's wrath for throwing a pair of scissors at him. It seems that the neighbor had called Carmelo's sisters "rabbits," because they came out at dusk for a few minutes then quickly went back inside. My father insisted that Carmelo had come to America to escape church persecution after he had ridden a horse into a church. He also thought that Carmelo had been buried in a pauper's grave at the state hospital. He did not know the names of his father's parents, the village from which they came, or their occupations. Nor did he know how his parents met or where they lived. Gulizia, the music store owner whom his mother visited in the North End, equally puzzled him.

16. *The Lawrence Directory, 1907* lists Carmelo Amoroso as an operative living in a boarding house on 306 Common Street, and his future brother-in-law Sebastiano Bosco as an operative who lived at a boarding house on 86 Common Street. Three years later, on August 21, 1910, Carmelo married Rose Bosco at the Holy Rosary Church on 35 Essex Street in Lawrence. *The Lawrence Directory, 1910* lists Carmelo as an operative residing in a house at 35 Valley Street. The same directory does not list Sebastiano, who shows up instead in *The Boston Directory, 1911* as a stonecutter living with twenty other men in a boarding house on 465 Hanover Street, the North End of Boston. In 1912, he moved to 463 Hanover Street and in 1913 to 12 Greenough Lane, North End. The following year, he appears in *The Quincy Directory, 1913* as a mason and machinist living in a private home at 35 Water Street. He worked as a mason and lived at this address through 1918, when he returned to being a machinist. With the war over, he moved to 91 Water Street and opened a fruit stand at 59 Franklin Avenue. Two years later, he moved to 31 Water Street and went back to masonry. Rose does not show up in the Lawrence or Boston directories, because they did not list women. She does, however, appear in *The Quincy Directory, 1914* as living at 2 Wild Court. This timing parallels the birth of her daughter Concetta, whose Record of Birth shows that she was born in Boston on April 24, 1913 but registered in Quincy ten months later. Carmelo appears on Concetta's Record of Birth as an employee of the Boston Gear Works. The same *Quincy Directory* shows that he and Rose moved next to Sebastiano on Quincy Avenue and then to Phipps Street. Carmelo worked at the Boston Gear Works through 1918 then went to the Fore River Shipyard and moved to 2 Cyril Street, closer to his new job. Rose lived at Cyril Street for a year after Carmelo's death in 1923 then returned to Water Street, next door to her brother Sebastiano.

17. See Cameron (1993), *Radicals of the Worst Sort: Laboring Women in Lawrence, Massachusetts, 1860-1912*. For newspaper reporting of the Lawrence Strike, see *The New York Times*: "Strike Riots Close Big Lawrence Mills " (1912); "Strikers Storm Lawrence Mills." (1912); "Twelve Strikers Appeal Sentencing for Rioting" (1912); "Three Thousand Strikers Parading into Town." (1912); "E. G. Flynn to Address Strikers Mass Meeting." (1912); "Haywood on Workers' Reasons for Striking." (1912); "Engineers May Stop Lawrence Wheels" (1912); "IWW and Socialist Federation to Take One Hundred Strikers' Children to New York City." (1912); Fifty Children Taken Arrive in New York City." (1912); Newly Arrived Group of Strikers' Children Parade Down 5th Ave." (1912); and "Halt Strikers' Plan to Ship Children" (1912).

18. See Lewis (2011), *Elizabeth Gurley Flynn: Biography of the Rebel Girl.*

19. By the time of the Lawrence strike, Flynn was already separated from Jack Jones, a miner whom she married in 1908. They divorced in 1920. See Lewis (2011), *Elizabeth Gurley Flynn: Biography of the Rebel Girl.*

20. The hysteria surrounding White bondage was rampant in the early years of the twentieth century. Of the fifteen articles on prostitution cited in the *Reader's Guide to Periodical Literature 1905-1909*, the phrase "White Slavery" appears in thirty percent of the titles. Americans feared that orphans, poor immigrants, or unwanted illegitimate babies would end up as prostitutes. See Goldman (1911), "The Traffic in Women."

21. See Grant (1916), *The Passing of the Great Race*. Nativism refers to a policy or belief that protects or favors the interest of the native population of a country over the interests of immigrants (Scholastic, n.d.). In the United States, nativist sentiment coincided with the great waves of nineteenth-century European immigration on the East Coast and contained a strong anti-Catholic strain, as many of the newly arrived immigrants hailed from predominantly Roman Catholic countries. The most prominent American nativist organization of the nineteenth century was the Know-Nothing party, which flourished in the 1840s, including in Quincy (Tracy, 1988). Samuel P. Huntington (2004), the Albert J. Weatherhead III University Professor at Harvard and president of the American Political Science Association, has tried to rescue nativisn from disparaging overtones. His thesis is that the United States is at great risk of cracking apart due to growing numbers of Hispanics who are unwilling to identify with Anglo–Protestant culture. For historical reading on nativism, see Olmsted (1861), *The Cotton Kingdom: A Traveller's Observations on Cotton and Slavery in the American Slave States*; Archdeacon (1983), *Becoming American: An Ethnic History*; Davis (1970), *The*

Fear of Conspiracy: Images of un-American Subversion from the Revolution to the Present; Dumenil (1995), *The Modern Temper: American Culture and Society in the 1920s;* Higham (1963), *Strangers in the Land: Patterns of American Nativism, 1860-1925*; Levin (1971), *Political Hysteria in America: the Democratic Capacity for Repression*; and Ribuffo (1983), *The Old Christian Right: The Protestant Far Right from the Great Depression to the Cold War.*

22. W. E. B. Du Bois (1868-1963), arguably America's greatest African American intellectual (Harvard-educated sociologist, historian, novelist, and founder of the National Association for the Advancement of Colored People), spent his entire life attacking Black oppression. His prophetic assertion that "the problem of the twentieth century is the problem of the color line" (Du Bois, 1903, p. i), still rings true today. Although Rose knew nothing about race before coming to America, she encountered it in the workplace, in the neighborhood, in church, and in the media. Her America will be segregated for most of her life. At mid century, Benedict and Weltfish (1943) will co-author a government pamphlet entitled *The Races of Mankind* that minimizes racial differences. Conservative congressional representatives will attack it as communist propaganda. Excerpted below is Benedict and Weltfish's (1943) contention:

> The most careful investigations of intelligence have been made in America among Negroes and whites. . . . [Tests show] that Northerners, black and white, had higher scores than Southerners, black and white. Everyone knows that Southerners are inborn equals of Northerners, but in 1917, many southern states' per capita expenditures to schools were only a fraction of those in northern states, and housing and diet and income were far below average too. Since the vast majority of Negroes lived in the South, their score on the intelligence test was a score they got not only as Negroes but as Americans who had grown up in poor conditions in the South. Scientists therefore compared the scores of Southern whites to Northern Negroes.
>
> Median Scores on the AEF Intelligence Tests
>
> Southern Whites:
>
> | | |
> |---|---|
> | Mississippi | 41.25 |
> | Kentucky | 41.50 |
> | Arkansas | 41.55 |

Northern Negroes:

New York	45.02
Illinois	47.35
Ohio	49.50

Negroes with better luck after they were born got higher scores than whites with less luck. The white race did badly where economic conditions were bad, schooling was not provided, and the Negroes living under better conditions surpassed them. *The differences did not arise because people were from the North or the South, or because they were white or black, but because of differences in income, education, cultural advantages, and other opportunities* (pp. 17-18).

23. One way to interpret Rose's life is give her what Maya Angelou (1986) calls Folk Wisdom, poetic insights passed down to her by her peasant culture. Her life narrative, however, shows that her way of knowing was not proverb based but critical, grounded in common sense awareness of everyday life (Gramsci, 2000).

References

Addams, J. (1912). *Twenty years at Hull House with autobiographical notes*. New York: The Macmillan Company.

American Family Immigration History Center. (n.d.). *Original ship manifest, S. S. Italia*. http://www.ellisisland.org/search/shipManifest. asp?MID=10856821470903049536&PID=102420060349.

"Americanization." (2017, July 17). In *Wikipedia, The Free Encyclopedia*. Retrieved July 21, 2017, from https://en.wikipedia.org/w/index. php?title=Americanization&oldid=790954280.

Angelou, M. (1986). *All God's children need traveling shoes*. New York: Random House.

Archdeacon, T. J. (1983). *Becoming American: An ethnic history*. New York: Free Press.

Bassett, L. G. (1938, November). The old Irish mill worker: Edward O'Neil. *American life histories: Manuscripts from the federal writers' project, 1936-1940*.

Benedict, R., A., & Weltfish, G. (1943). *The races of mankind: Public Affairs Pamphlet No. 85*. New York: Public Affairs Committee, 17-24.

Bruccoli, M. J. (1996a). *American Decades, 1900-1909*. (V. Tompkins, R. Layman, V. Bondi, J. Hipp, & J. Baughman, Eds.) Detroit, MI: Gale Research.

Bruccoli, M. J. (1996b). *American Decades, 1910-1919*. (V. Thompkins, V. Tompkins, R. Layman, V. Bondi, & J. Baughman, Eds.) Detroit, MI: Gale Research.

Cameron, A. (1993). *Radicals of the worst sort: Laboring women in Lawrence, Massachusetts, 1860-1912*. Urbana, IL: University of Illinois Press.

Colby, F. M., Churchill, A. L., Wade, H. T., & Vizetelly, F. H. (1910). *The new international yearbook: A compendium of the world's progress for the year 1907*. New York: Dodd, Mead and Company.

Davis, D. B. (1970). *The fear of conspiracy: Images of un-American subversion from the revolution to the present*. Ithaca, NY: Cornell University Press.

Dewey, J. (1916) Democracy *and education: An introduction to the philosophy of education*. New York: Macmillan.

Du Bois, W. E. B. (1903). *The souls of black folk*. New York: Penguin.

Dumenil, L. (1995). *The modern temper: American culture and society in the 1920s*. New York: Hill and Wang.

"E. G. Flynn to address strikers mass meeting" (1912, January 21). *New York Times*, 9:1.

Engineers may stop Lawrence wheels; threatened strike of motor plant would tie up the entire city; other unions in fight; operatives leaving city by hundreds— Haywood pushes plan to send strikers' children here. (1912, February 6). *New York Times*, 2:5.

Essex National Heritage Area (n.d.). *Lawrence history center*. http://www.essexheritage.org/sites/immigrant_city.shtml.

Foerster, R. F. (1924). *The Italian emigration of our times*. Cambridge, MA: Harvard University Press.

"Fifty children taken arrive in New York City; all taken in by Socialist party members." (1912, February 11). *New York Times*, pt. 2, 1:7.

Gans, H. G. (1962). *The urban villagers: Group and class in the life of Italian-Americans*. New York: Free Press.

Goldman, E. (1911). The traffic in women. In E. Goldman, *Anarchism and other Essays*. http://xroads.virginia.edu/~hyper/goldman/traffic.html.

Gordon, L., & Gordon, A. (1999*). American chronicle: Year by year through the twentieth century*. New Haven, CT: Yale University Press.

Grady, R. (1938). The personal history of Alex Lavoie. *American life histories: Manuscripts from the federal writers' project, 1936-1940*. https://www.loc.gov/resource/wpalh1.13150404/?sp=1.

Gramsci, A. (1994). *Letters from prison.* (F. Rosengarten. Ed., & R. Rosenthal, Trans.). New York: Columbia University Press.

Gramsci, A. (2000). *The Antonio Gramsci reader: Selected writings, 1916-1935.* (D. Forgacs, Ed.). New York: New York University Press.

Grant, M. (1916). *The passing of the great race: Or, the racial basis of European history.* New York: Charles Scribner.

Gregorovius, F. (1914*). Siciliana: Sketches of Naples and Sicily in the nineteenth century.* London: G. Bell & Sons, ltd.

Hall, G. S. (1911). *Educational Problems.* 2 vols. New York: Appleton.

Halt strikers' plan to ship children. (1912, February 23). *New York Times,* 8:3.

Harmon, J., & The Middlesex County Historical Society. (n.d.). *The History of Middletown: Part III: 1900-today.* http://www.cityofmiddletown.com/History/history-of-middletown.com.

"Haywood on workers' reasons for striking speech; Carnegie Hall, New York City audience donates over $500.00 for cause. (1912, February 3). *New York Times,* 2:1.

Hirschman, C., & Mogford, E. (2009). Immigration and the American industrial revolution from 1880 to 1920. *Social Science Research, 38*(4), 897-920.

History.com (2010). *This day in history: April 25, 1859, ground broken for Suez Canal.* www.history.com/this-day-in-history/ground-broken-for-Suez-Canal.

Holli, M. G. & Jones, P. (Eds.). (1977). *The ethnic frontier: Essays in the history of group survival in Chicago and the Midwest.* Grand Rapids, MI: William Eerdmans.

Higham, J. (1963). *Strangers in the land: Patterns of American nativism, 1860-1925.* New York: Atheneum.

Huntington, S. P. (2004). *Who are we? The challenges to America's national identity.* New York: Simon and Schuster.

"IWW and Socialist Federation to take one hundred strikers' children to New York City for Adoption during strike." (1912, February 10). *New York Times*, 6:4.

Levin, M. B. (1971). *Political hysteria in America: The democratic capacity for repression*. New York: Basic Books.

Levinson, D. L. (2005). *Community colleges: A reference handbook*. Santa Barbara, CA: ABC-CLIO, Inc.

Lewis, J. J. (2011). *Elizabeth Gurley Flynn: Biography of the Rebel Girl*. http://womenshistory.about.com/od/elizabethgurleyflynn/a/rebel_girl.htm.

Macy, M. S. (1910). The subnormal child in New York City schools. *Journal of Educational Psychology, 1*(3),133-144.

Mallach, A. (2002). *Pietro Mascagni and his operas*. Boston: Northeastern University Press.

Mangione, J., & Morreale, B. (1992). *La Storia: Five centuries of the Italian American experience*. New York: Harper Collins.

Marcy, M. (1912). "Battle for bread at Lawrence." *International Socialist Review, 12*(9), 522-543.

Mertins, L. (1965). *Robert Frost: Life and talks-walking*. Norman: University of Oklahoma Press.

Middleton, W. D. (1985). A century of cable cars. *American Heritage, 36*(3), 90-101.

Mills, R. H. (1996, Spring). Italian immigrant ships. *Steamboat Bill*, number 217, 5-19.

Morton Allan directory of European passenger steamship arrivals for the years 1890 to 1930 at the port of New York and for the years 1904 to 1926 at the ports of New York, Philadelphia, Boston and Baltimore. (1998). Baltimore, MD: Genealogical Publishing Co.

Mulkern, John R. *The Know-Nothing Party in Massachusetts: The Rise and Fall of a People's Movement*. Boston: Northeastern University Press, 1990.

"Newly arrived group of strikers' children parade down 5th Ave. to Union Square with representatives of IWW, Socialists Clubs and Ferrer Association." (1912, February 18). *New York Times*, 4:1.

New York Times index for the published news of 1911. (1973). New York: New York Times Company.

New York Times index for the published news of 1912. (1973). New York: New York Times Company.

North End Action Team. (2008). *History.* http://www.neatmiddletown.org/neighborhood.htm.

Olmsted, F. L. (1861). *The cotton kingdom: A traveller's observations on cotton and slavery in the American slave states.* New York: Mason Brothers.

Paton, W. A. (1897). *Picturesque Sicily.* New York: Harper and Brothers.

Peck, G. (1996). Reinventing free labor: Immigrant padrones and contract laborers in North America, 1885-1925. *Journal of American History, 83*(3), 848-871.

Police clubs keep Lawrence waifs in; heads broken over an order to prevent strikers shipping their children away. (1912, February 25). *New York Times*, 2:1.

Readers guide to periodical literature, 1905-1909. (1910). White Plains, NY: H. W. Wilson.

Readers guide to periodical literature, III 1910-1914. (1915). White Plains, NY: H. W. Wilson.

Readers guide to periodical literature, III 1919. (1922). White Plains, NY: H. W. Wilson.

Reeder, L. (1998, Fall). Women in the classroom: Mass migration, literacy and the nationalization of Sicilian women at the turn of the century. *Journal of Social History, 32*(1), 101-124.

Ribuffo, L. P. (1983). *The old Christian right: The Protestant far right from the great depression to the cold war.* Philadelphia: Temple University Press.

Ricciardi, G. (2007). *Don Bosco in Cairo.* http://www.30giorni.it/us/articolo.asp?id=16463.

Scholastic (n.d.). *Nativism.* http://www2.scholastic.com/browse/search?query=Nativism.

Slater, C. (1997). General Motors and the demise of streetcars. *Transportation Quarterly, 51*(3), 45-56.

Smith, D. M. (1969). *A history of Sicily: Modern Sicily after 1713.* New York: Viking Press.

Spartacus educational (n.d.). *William Haywood.* http://www.spartacus.schoolnet.co.uk/USAhaywood.htm.

Strike riots close big Lawrence mills; angry operators invade woolen plants, attack overseers, and fight police; eleven thousand made idle; feeling over wages cut, due to new 54-hour law; may throw 25,000 hands out of work (1912, January 13). *New York Times,* 7:1.

"Strikers storm Lawrence mills; held back by militia bayonets and threats to shoot; twenty-eight leaders arrested given jail terms; workers now demand fifteen percent pay raise; mills to reopen under guard." (1912, January 16). *New York Times,* 1:3.

Taylor, A. (2005). *Writing Early American History.* Philadelphia: University of Pittsburgh Press.

The Boston directory, 1911. (1912). Boston: George Adams.

The Boston directory, 1913. (1914). Boston: George Adams.

The Lawrence directory, 1907. (1908). Boston: Sampson and Murdock Company.

The Lawrence directory, 1910. (1911). Boston: Sampson and Murdock Company.

The Quincy directory, 1913. (1914). Boston: Green & Prescott.

The Quincy directory, 1914. (1915). Boston: Green & Prescott.

The Quincy directory, 1924. (1925). Boston: Green & Prescott.

Thorndike, E. L. "The Contribution of Psychology to Education." *Journal of Educational Psychology* 1 (1910): 3.

"Three thousand strikers parading into town; strikers plan parade of fifteen thousand." (1912, January 18). *New York Times*, 7:5.

Tolbert, S. (1995). *Reading habits of the nineteenth-century New England mill girls.* http://www.philandsusantolbert.com/research/millgirl.html.

Tracy, J. (1988). The Know-Nothings in Quincy. *Historical Journal of Massachusetts, 16*(1), 1-19.

Twelve strikers appeal sentencing for rioting. (1912, January 17). *New York Times*, 4:3.

Verga, G. (1890). *The House by the Medlar-Tree* (R. Rosenthal, Trans.). New York: Harper & Brothers.

Verga, G. (1925). *Little Novels of Sicily* (D. H. Lawrence, Trans.). London: Martin Seeker.

Verga, G. (1928). *Cavalleria rusticana and other stories* (G. H. McWilliam, Trans.). New York: Dial Press.

Voltaire (1694-1778). "Voltaire and His Wise Quotes" (2011). http://www.buzzle.com/articles/voltaire-and-his-wise-quotes.html.

Young, A. F. (1998). An outsider and the progress of a career in history. *The William and Mary Quarterly, 52*(3), 499-502.

Young, A. F. (2004). *Masquerade: The life and times of Deborah Sampson, Continental soldier.* New York: Alfred A Knopf.

3

New York City

In the early years of the last century, my grandmother, Rose Bosco, left Sicily for the United States, a country that was rapidly industrializing. She tried to make sense of her new world by reminding herself of who she was and from where she had come. In 1912, she joined the most significant labor strike in American history. This chapter takes creative and historic license with her role in it. She befriends one of its leaders, Elizabeth Gurley Flynn, and accompanies her to New York City with children of the striking mill workers. She also meets reformers such as Emma Goldman and John Dewey, who share with her their visions of America. In truth, she never met the writers and activists she encounters in this story. Francis W. Parker, for example, was dead, and Theodore Dreiser was on holiday in France. Yet Rose's imaginative conversations offer glimpses into the lives of great twentieth-century thinkers. The dialogues also act as prisms through which readers can appraise the interplay between these reformers' respect for individuality and their high regard for science, as opposed to the strict moral traditions that many immigrants brought with them.

Innocents on a Yellow Train

In the winter of 1912, over a hundred children, aged four to fourteen, showed up for the train, huddled close to their parents in the cold, damp afternoon. Rose and Marina arrived early, in the company of two men. The committee had sent Angelo and his friend Tony to escort them to the train station. Angelo was one of thirteen children, a charmer who had come to Lawrence ten years earlier and had played football and baseball for the high school. Tony was a short, fiery man with a bad arm. The year before, he had heard a man screaming at children on a playground. He went over to find out what was happening. "Mind your own business," was the reply. Tony and the man exchanged words and a scuffle broke out. He was stabbed in his arm, resulting in severe nerve damage.

Rose was the first to speak up. "We are supposed to meet Elizabeth by the food vendors." Both men were bachelors and had not eaten, so they said, "Let's get something to eat."

Marina frowned. "Didn't your mothers raise you better? You should not eat that food."

"Nonsense," Angelo said. "I buy from them all the time. Who has time to cook?"

The four stopped at the first cart. Tony said, "I think I am going to try one of these. What is it?"

Marina winked at Rose and said, "Roasted chicken."

"Well, all right. That will be good." He took a bite and chewed it slowly. "That ain't no chicken. It has a different taste. Tastes oily."

The vendor said, "It's pigeon, not chicken. It's all dark meat. Dark meat is oily."

Trying to save face, Tony said, "It is very good."

Angelo knew something about bachelor life. "You can buy a whole duck for seventy-five cents, something like that. I shop all the time. Them porkpies are very popular with the French. Come in bright red wrappers. You can get two or three of 'em on a Saturday for a quarter. Put 'em in the oven and heat 'em."

Not to be outdone, Tony answered, "I like the Polish sausage. I take the skin off, though; it's too tough. I have no complaints. The next day I have two or three left over. I love the taste. I bought one of those from the little runt—what they call Stumpy. His are big and round, about twenty cents for six. Sometimes I put 'em right in with beans. Yes sir, throw 'em right in with the beans."

The Apple Cart

Rose and Marina shrugged, thankful that they did not have to eat with them. Both spotted Elizabeth across the walkway, talking with three Salvation Army privates who stood in front of an apple cart.[1] They approached her excitedly but slowed down when they overheard Elizabeth say to one of the privates, "I distrust the Salvation Army. You want poor people to accept their lot in life. The only thing that matters to you is salvation. You want us to forget about exploitation and capitalism, the real causes of poverty. You say, 'Who cares about justice? The poor will always be with us.'"

Marina jumped right in. "What's wrong with passing out apples to the children, Elizabeth? The Bible says that we should feed the hungry. Christ did it with fish and bread. If you cannot trust Christians, who can you trust?"

"Trust yourself, not religion," Elizabeth muttered.

Marina stiffened. "Then how do you explain this? Years ago a woman named Dolores lived in a village by the Gulf of Augusto. Her house was about two miles from the sea and a mile from the river. Winds blew in and stalled over the coast. The sea and the river merged into a single body of water. Her house was flooded. She tried to hold on to her infant son, but the river ripped them apart. She shouted to her husband to grab the other children, but he was dead. She clung to floating branches, debris, and tree roots and drifted out to sea. The corpse of her child floated next to her. She passed the day singing to God. 'God, I am in your arms,' she sang. The next day, she found oranges floating in the water. At night, she stared at the moon and talked to her husband and children. 'Ricardo, I want to run, but there is no place for me to run to. There is no land in sight. Only the sea around me.' Her crying and screaming gradually faded. On the fifth day, she spotted a duck near her raft. 'Little duck. Send a message that I am alive. Take me back to my village. Please take me so that I can fly somewhere with you.' The duck flew off to the north. Hours later, a fisherman rescued her."

Elizabeth sniffed. "That's a fable."

Marina rubbed her fingernails with her thumb and said, "My

mother met Dolores. She came to live with her aunt because she had nothing left. My mother befriended her."

Elizabeth loved to talk religion and politics, so she suggested that they go into the station where the families had gone to get out of the cold. "Marina, no doubt a fisherman saved Dolores. But why do you believe that the fisherman responded to her prayers? He happened to be in the right place. It was luck. Charity doesn't solve poverty or hunger; it merely perpetuates it. Feeding the hungry eases some pain, but it doeswn't eliminate the cause of the pain, which is greed."

Tony pushed back solemnly, blinking several times. "The Salvation Army helped my family when we first came here. Even the government has a store that sells food cheaply. Why are you so full of anger at Americans who want to help the poor?"

People admired Elizabeth's beauty and feared her tongue. She especially disliked those who took advantage of others. She universally disliked the Salvation Army's misdirected charity. "The apples you see being passed out are a sham. They satisfy hunger but are bait to get the poor into church. The real motive behind the Salvation Army is to save souls, not change inequities in society. They don't want to address this cancer called capitalism."

Rose's eyes were focused on Elizabeth. She stood out from the families that milled around. "Why do you feed the children?"

"So that they resist the ravages of capitalism. Once socialism triumphs, the haves will not be able to exploit the have-nots," Elizabeth explained.

Rose wanted to understand. "Doesn't that make socialists the same as Christians? Both want to ease suffering?"

"No. Socialists want to free people from their oppression so that they can feed themselves. The Salvation Army doesn't want to free people. They want them to accept their lot while they pray for salvation. They don't think that happiness can be found in this life. The only reason they pay attention to the poor is out of pity, guilt, or some other reason. They really don't care about human suffering, except as it serves their ends. To them poverty is inevitable."

Rose sounded irritated. "That seems harsh."

1. Elizabeth Gurley Flynn

Elizabeth Gurley Flynn (1890-1964) was born to Irish immigrants in Concord, New Hampshire and they taught her about socialism. When her family moved to the South Bronx in 1900, Flynn's local public school expelled her for her political activities. For example, she gave her first speech, "What Socialism Will Do for Women," when she was only 16 at the Socialist Club in Harlem. By 1907, Flynn became a full-time organizer for the "Industrial Workers of the World" (IWW). She fought for women's rights, birth control, women's suffrage, free speech, and was a founding member of the "American Civial Liberties Union." After an eight-year break from politics following the end of a relationship, Flynn joined the American Communist Party in 1936, and by 1961 became its chairperson. She died in 1964 during a visit to the Soviet Union, where she was given a state funderal. Novel Theodore Dreiser once described her as "an East Side Joan of Arc." ("Elizabeth Gurley Flynn," *Spartacus Educational*, http://spartacus-educational. com/USAflynn.htm, retrieved July 23, 2017.)

Elizabeth Gurley Flynn

In Her Own Words

"Statement at the Smith Act Trial" (Exceprt)
Delivered April 24 1952, New York

I am an American of Irish decent. My father, Thomas Flynn, was born in Maine. My mother, Anne Gurley, was born in Galway, Ireland. I was born in Concord, New Hampshire, 62 years ago. I married in 1908, separated from my husband shortly thereafter, and have always used my own name. My only son, Fred, died in 1940 at the age of 29 from a chest cancer. I reside with my sister, who is a retired school teacher. We have lived in New York City for the past 52 years. My mother was a skilled tailoress; my father a quarry worker who worked his way through the engineering school at Dartmouth College in New Hampshire. My father, grandfather, and all my uncles were members of labor unions.

I come from a family whose day-by-day diet included important social issues of the day, and from this I early learned to question things as they are and to seek improvements. Thus, my mother advocated Women's Suffrage, and my father and mother discussed with their children the campaigns of Debs, the Socialist candidate for President.

My father read aloud to me and to my brother and sisters such books as the Communist Manifesto and other writings of Marx and Engels, which the Government will use as evidence in this trial. I was a serious child, due probably to these childish impressions which are background to my affiliation in my extreme youth with the Socialist movement and in my mature years with the Communist Party.

Times were hard. We were poor. My first experience with discrimination was in Manchester, New Hampshire, when my father ran for city engineer about 1895. I heard it said he was defeated because he was Irish. He was very bitter on this subject and told us of signs on factories when he was a boy, "No Irish need apply."

Our parents opposed all forms of national, religious or color discrimination, which we will prove is identical with the position of the Communist Party today and form the basis of the position I take today in the Communist Party.

My first knowledge of the meaning of imperialism, which will be an issue in this case, was a vivid recollection of my father's opposition to the Spanish-American War and his insistence on the right of the Cuban and Philippine peoples to their independence. He joined an anti-imperialist league to protest against our country embarking on the evil path of imperialism, which we will prove began at that time.

The conditions in the textile towns of New Hampshire and Massachusetts contributed to my later joining the Communist Party, which, as Mr. Lane says, concentrates on the recruiting of workers in industry: huge gray mills, like prisons, barrack-like company boarding houses, long hours, low wages, long periods of slack; the prosperous owner lived in the center of Adams, Massachusetts, and rode around in his fine carriage with its beautiful horses. I saw lard instead of butter on neighbors' tables, children without underwear in cold New England winters, a girl scalped by an unguarded machine in a mill across the street from our school. I saw an old man weeping as they put him in the lock-up as a tramp.

Then we came to live in the drab South Bronx, near the New Haven Railroad's roundhouse, in a cold water, unheated, gas-lit flat. Casualties and accidents were high among the railroad workers. Children were maimed as they gathered coal in the yards in bad times. My mother helped women in the neighborhood who could not afford a doctor when a baby came.

Yes, I was greatly troubled by all this. Why did good hard-working people suffer so? Why were men who were willing, able, and anxious to work, denied jobs? Why was there so much unemployment? Why were there rich people who apparently did little but enjoyed life? I hated poverty. I saw my mother humiliated when unpaid grocery bills could not be met and the landlord stood at the door demanding his rent.

I joined a debating society in P.S. 9 in the lower Bronx. I won a medal in a debate on the subject, "Should the Government own the mines?" I said, "Yes, it should."

This was during the great anthracite coal strike in 1902. I attended [a] Bronx Socialist meeting in 1905; later at the Harlem Socialist Club at 125th Street. My speaking career started in 1906 on the ambitious subject of women under socialism. Naturally, I drew heavily on authors, American women, like Charlotte Petingill and Susan B. Anthony, also on a book written in 1872 by Augustus Bebel, a Socialist member of the German Reichstag, written while he was in prison under Bismarck's anti-Socialist law. It was first published here by the Socialist Labor Party in 1904. I am puzzled to see it on the Government's list of documents. What relation it has to this indictment is hard to fathom, unless to advocate the full political, economic, and social emancipation of women has become a form of advocacy of the overthrow of government by force and violence under the Government's interpretation of the Smith Act. But if this historic and economic study, which is very much out of date today, is to be finely tooth-combed for sentences which torn out of context can distort its meaning, this, we will prove, can be done to any book, no matter what its purpose, even to the Bible, Shakespeare, or Gray's Anatomy.

My youthful ambition, believe it or not, was to be a constitutional lawyer. Instead, I became a labor organizer. Then it was called an agitator, or, by the press, one who stirred up the people. I was determined to do something about the bad conditions under which our family and all around us suffered. I have stuck to that purpose for 46 years. I consider in so doing I have been a good American. I have spent my life among the American workers all over this country, slept in their homes, eaten at their tables. They are the majority of the people who have the inalienable right in our view to govern the country. We mean by workers, all who do useful work of hand or brain. My life work began when I joined the I.W.W., Industrial Workers of the World, in 1906, a pioneer in industrial unions which flashed like a great comet across the horizon of the American labor movement for nearly two decades. I returned as an I.W.W. organizer in 1912 to New England, my birthplace, where the I.W.W. led historical textile strikes in Lawrence, Lowell, and New Bedford, Massachusetts. The strikes were unorganized, largely foreign-born men and women whose wages were cut when their hours were reduced by Massachusetts law.

In 1913 I was a leader in the Paterson, New Jersey silk strike; in 1916, in a strike of the iron ore miners on the Mesaba range in Minnesota, where the mines are owned by the U.S. Street trust, I will attempt to prove to you that it is not the Communists who advocate and use force and violence. I saw it used in all of these labor struggles, not by the workers but by police, company guards and State militia. I saw workers clubbed, beaten and shot down. . . .

My travels as a Communist speaker have taken me all over the country. I saw the fruits of a lawless, aggressive, brutal and ruthless capitalism which garnered profits for a few at the expense of the many.

Our country is a rich and beautiful country, fully capable of producing plenty for all, educating its youth and caring for its aged. We believe it could do this under Socialism. I saw great forests cut down and the denuded land left with blackened stumps; miles of top soil blown and washed away, and fertile fields became like a desert.

I have seen textile workers who wove beautiful woolen fabrics shivering for lack of warm clothing, and coal miners living in cold shacks in company towns, and steel towns that were armed camps. I saw men black-listed, driven from town to town, forced to change their names because they had dared to try to organize a union.

We will prove to you that it is not the Communists who have advocated or practices force and violence but that it is the employing class which has done both throughout the history of my life in the American labor movement, like General Sherman Bell who said in Colorado during a miner's strike "To Hell with habeas corpus; we'll give them post-mortems . . ." (Flynn, 1952).

Flynn, E. G. "Statement at the Smith Act trial." In *Elizabeth Gurley Flynn speaks to the court*. New York: New Century Publishers, 1952. *http://www.americanrhetoric.com/speeches/elizabethgurleyflynn.htm.*

"Rose, we need laws to protect us from our cruelty," Elizabeth said.

"That is not possible," Rose replied. "Poor people do not make the laws. We live by the rules of the rich. If we did not, we would starve. I cannot imagine the poor passing laws."

Socialism and Capitalism

When the train pulled into the station, Elizabeth stood up and briefed the parents. Then she asked the children to line up by age and gender. The IWW had reserved two cars, one for the boys and another for the girls. Each car had three adult chaperones. Elizabeth, Rose, and Marina would supervise the girls. Three chaperones from New York City would be with the boys. Families had been asked to prepare lunches for the children. One parent shouted out, "How long will the trip take?"

Elizabeth replied, "Seven hours. Once we arrive in the city, we'll telegraph the IWW office. Check with them for details."

The adults seated the children. Several of the younger ones cried, but most were excited. Everyone was dressed in his or her Sunday best. Once the train pulled out of the station, Rose, Marina, and Elizabeth continued their discussion. Elizabeth said, "You asked me about laws. Notice how the children behave. They sit looking out the window. They're quiet. We haven't had to stop one fight. These same children are punished in school for misbehavior. Do you know why they are behaving so well? Because we're treating them with respect, and they treat us the same way. We don't have to threaten them with harsh rules or punishment."

Marina said, "They listen to us and support each other because it is in their best interest to do so. I bet their parents told them that if they misbehaved they would be spanked or left in the city."

Elizabeth vehemently disagreed. "They behave because they know it's the right thing to do."

"Elizabeth, you are wrong," replied Marina. "Children will hurt others to get their own way. We cannot allow this to happen. Punishment is what they understand."

"I want them to be good because it is the right thing to do. Laws should follow the same principle—to benefit us."

Rose had another thought. "Bosses do what they want to do."

"That's why capitalism is bad, Rose. It rewards people who take from others. That's why it's wrong," Elizabeth said with conviction.

"Is selfishness a crime?" Marina asked.

"No, but that doesn't make it right. Deep down, people are good. Most people think that craziness is a punishment for past sins. I think that unhappiness is linked to our childhood. Once we realize that, we can change for the better. We need to know ourselves. If we don't know what drives us, we'll stumble. It's the same with nations. Most laws don't help people because they're passed in ignorance. The lawmakers don't have any idea what problem they're trying to solve. They pass the law without asking themselves, 'Why are we doing this?' That's why I despise unjust laws and foolish customs. Nothing is right about them, and I'll work hard to eliminate them. We'll be the better for it."

Rose responded, "You think bad laws are the source of unhappiness? It sounds like you do."

"Yes," Elizabeth said, her hands raised in a theatrical pose. "A good citizen understands where laws come from. Take a grudge. How many times have you seen men forget why they're angry with their wives? They forget. All they know is that they're angry. They need to step back and remember why they feel bad. If they did, they'd realize how silly they've acted. It's the same in politics. Unless we stop to think about our actions, we won't remember why we feel and act as we do."

Rose shook her head and frowned. "I do not think that way."

Elizabeth said, "You left your parents to come here. Are you the better for it?"

"I am less happy," Rose replied. When she spoke those words, she turned to look at Marina.

Elizabeth smiled. "Rose," she said, "you're free to do what you want to do. And yet freedom is very difficult on you?"

Rose knew that Elizabeth was trying to be helpful, not nosy, so she gave her this answer: "I do not boast about my decisions because they are wrong half the time."

Marina knew what she meant. Living under a monarch had its agreeable moments, as when someone fixed your dinner. Being an American involved a large degree of uncertainty. When Rose married and moved away, Rose faced the prospect of running out of food.

Tipping the World Upside Down

"Do you remember our discussion with Mrs. Hutchinson about dark people?" Elizabeth asked Rose.

Rose responded, "Sicilians come in many colors. We call the dark ones 'Mora.' There are light ones too. My priest said I was more serious and intelligent than the others were because I was light. Mrs. Hutchinson said the same thing. So did my father."

"Do you know why many Sicilians are dark?"

"No," said Rose as she looked out the window at the city. Someone needed to put a clean rag to the grime that blurred her view.

"What did you see on your walks?"

"A lot of crumbled ruins. Mountains and hills. Streams filled with fish. A huge volcano to the north. Many groves of white flowering almond trees. Orange trees. Olives. Grapes. Sheep."

"Do you know how the ruins got there?"

"The pagans."

"What's the word you used to describe dark-skinned people?"

"Mora."

Elizabeth could have been reading from a book when she said, "That's short for Moor. Arabs lived in Sicily long ago.[2] Before them, the

Greeks lived in your country. Syracuse was the only city in the ancient Greek world to defeat the Athenians. After the Moors, blue-eyed people from the north invaded Sicily. They built castles and married Sicilian women."

After pausing to comprehend the meaning of these words, Rose asked her friend, "Why did they come? There is nothing there."

Elizabeth offered a serious answer. "In ancient times, Sicily was called the Island Kingdom of the Sun. The warm climate made it the garden of Europe. It was the granary of the Roman Empire. Sicily was important to kings because it was in the center of the Mediterranean and served as a crossroads for migration and invasions between countries in Europe and Africa to the South."

Marina was distracted by the delicious smell of coffee that came from the rear of the car. She excused herself and headed toward the back door. Her expression lit up when she saw an older child sitting alone, holding a brown bag. In her hand was a jelly jar filled with hot coffee. "Smells delicious," Marina said. The child offered her a taste. Marina gulped it down.

Rose and Elizabeth didn't see Marina depart. Rose sat electrified by Elizabeth's history lesson. "I thought I was Sicilian," she said.

"The ancient blood of conquerors from Greece, Africa, Normandy, Spain, and France runs in your veins," Elizabeth answered as she wiped the condensation from her window.

Before Elizabeth could say any more, Rose interrupted innocently, "I know of a castle in the hills, but I never thought about it. Sebastiano used to go there to play. I did not know how it got there. Now I do."

"Rose," Elizabeth said excitedly, "you are a child of history."

"How do you know this if you never lived in my country?"

"I read," Elizabeth said, grateful for the opportunity to fill the gaps in Rose's education. "Beautiful forests once covered Sicily, but the landowners cut them down for profit. They also made the laws and wrote the history books. They didn't want the poor to know the truth. Had they, cries of dissension would have replaced the sound of gold spilling into their coffers."

"I would have heaved the lot of them into the sea," Rose snapped, realizing finally why she had never seen a single tree in Sicily. In night class, she had copied down important dates in American history. In the city library, she copied newspaper headlines with great care. She also studied bookish-looking people in tweed jackets among the bookshelves. One sat next to her, preoccupied with a book about Greek ruins. Rose was eager to tell him that she had passed among them as a child, but he ignored her, preventing her from sharing the truths life had given her. Elizabeth had just shown Rose that knowledge liberates without suffocating. This was exactly what she needed. Rose leaned forward, eager to learn more. "Is history taught to children?" she asked Elizabeth, her voice very serious.

"Let's ask them," replied Elizabeth.

Felia's Literacies

Rose realized that Marina was absent, so she turned to find her, spotting her speaking with a tall, radiant child. "Bring the child here," she said. Marina and the child laughed as they got up. The child had a book in her hand. Rose put her hand to her mouth. This was the child from the restaurant. Elizabeth recognized her too. The child smiled and sat down beside them. Her dress was old but clean. Rose said to her, "What is your name?"

"My friends call me Felia."

Marina said, "Isn't she lovely? She is a golden rose. Felia's mother must be very beautiful."

Felia looked at Marina as she said, "My mother is dead. My stepmother is good to me."

The three women went silent, each hearing cries in their hearts for their own mothers. Rose's sorrow passed in a moment. She touched the arm of the child so that she would continue talking. "What do you study in school, dear child?"

Felia was not apprehensive. The sudden invitation to talk pleased her. "I don't have much time to think about school. I help my family. We are eight girls and two boys. Pa works all day."

"How do you help your family?" Marina asked.

Felia spoke with candor as the train passed over the frozen gravel beneath the rails. "When I came from Sicily, we did not have many

Joe Hill
The Rebel Girl
1915

This song was written in 1911 and published in the *The Little Red Songbook of the Industrial Workers of the World* of 1915. Written for Elizabeth Gurley Flynn, this became a popular ballad in its day.

There are women of many descriptions
In this queer world, as everyone knows.
Some are living in beautiful mansions,
And are wearing the finest of clothes.
There are blue blooded queens and princesses
Who have charms made of diamonds and pearl;
But the only and thoroughbred lady
Is the Rebel Girl.

CHORUS

That's the Rebel Girl, that's the Rebel Girl!
To the working class she's a precious pearl
She brings courage, pride and joy
To the fighting Rebel Boy.
We've had girls before, but we need some more
In the Industrial Workers of the World.
For it's great to fight for freedom
With a Rebel Girl.

Yes, her hands may be hardened from labor,
And her dress may not be very fine;
But a heart in her bosom is beating
That is true to her class and her kind.
And the grafters in terror are trembling
When her spite and defiance she'll hurl;
For the only and thoroughbred lady
Is the Rebel Girl.

things, not even a few good clothes. Our house was dirty. The stove was rusty, and the windows were cracked. We did not even have a garden in the back. I worked in a big mill, but I left."

"Why did you leave?" Elizabeth asked, imagining contemptuous, brutal men shaming female workers.

Felia said, "I asked the foreman if I could change machines. He said sure, if I offered him something."

"Did you know what he meant?" asked Marina, her face tight with irritation.

"No. But I asked my friend Uri."

Marina asked another question, "What did you do?"

"I told the foreman no, so he said he did not want me there. I told my parents I was going to get another job because I wanted to buy some things for the house. I bought my stepmother many things. She stopped me and put me in school. She said I seemed more like a woman than a girl."

Rose knew how she must have felt. She used to go into the street, filled with rage at the abuse heaped on her. She wanted to encourage this child, so fresh in appearance, who deserved more from adults. "Do you like school?" she asked.

"I do not hate it," Felia offered.

Not an unreasonable reply, Elizabeth thought. She felt it important to go further, so she asked her a simple question. "Why do you go?"

The world had been hard on Felia. Nevertheless, she was an intelligent child, glad to share her story with adults who did not mock her. "Last

Joe Hill's Little Red Songbook

summer, a man with long hair stopped me down at the railroad yard. Uri and I were collecting coal. He jumped out of one of the freight cars and asked me if I had something to eat. I gave him a penny and said he could buy bread with it in town. He asked me if I worked at the mill. I said yes. Then he asked me what I wanted to be when I grew up. I said, 'Fed.' He said, 'What else do you want?' I said, 'To live in a big mansion, like my boss.'

"He said, 'Little girl, you should be running the mill.' When I asked him why, he told me that I was very smart and that I spoke my mind. He said girls like me were the best. I said, 'I am nothing.' He said, 'Take this little book of songs I wrote. Learn them, and sing them to anyone who will listen. The next time I pass this way, I will ask you to sing them to me.' I told him I was not too good at reading. He said, 'Find someone who will listen. The words will come easy.'"

Elizabeth knew immediately that Felia had met her dear friend and IWW collaborator Joe Hill, who traveled on freight trains to rallies supporting strikes. His songs "The Preacher and the Slave" and "Casey Jones" were widely popular with laboring men and women all across the country. "Did he tell you his name?" she asked.

Felia said, "I heard a man shout, 'Come on, Joe. We have to get outta town before dark.'"

Rose returned to the subject of school. "What do you do at school?" she asked, interested in what Americans taught their children about history.

"Add and spell," Felia said.

"What about history?"

"No."

Marina added, "Do you like school?"

"It tires me," the child answered.

Elizabeth looked away as Felia spoke these words. She then looked at Marina and Rose and said with an air of certitude, "There are numerous reports about the mental abilities of children. It's possible that Felia has a defect. The poor thing may find it hard to learn."

Recognizing the child's talent, Rose felt that she had to correct Elizabeth. Without blinking, she said, "This child was born with her eyes open. That is what this so-called Joe saw in her." She touched Felia's hand. "Do you go to school every day?"

"I skip a lot," the child replied.

Rose returned with another question, eager to advance Felia's place in the world. "What do you do when you skip school?"

Felia was not frightened by the question. Like children who have been encouraged by a caring adult, she radiated confidence. "I walk across the road and listen to the hum of the mills. One day I took a long walk. I walked until I came to the last house on the road. An old man was on the porch, reading a newspaper. I asked him for a drink of water. He put his paper down and asked me to come in. I said I did not have the time. He went inside for a cup of water. I spied a can of flowers on the porch. I told him I had a garden when I was small. He told me I ought to write a poem about it. He said poems tell the truth. I told him I was not good at spelling. He went back into the house and returned with a small book and a pencil. He said to sit next to him and he would put down on paper how I felt. I told him I wanted my mother to come back and take me away with her. He said that my face told him how much I missed my mother. I asked him if I could have a copy of the poem. He said, 'It's yours,' and that he would be pleased to do this again. I felt warm, thanked him, and hurried home.

"The next day I went back and sat with him at his kitchen table. This time I told him how the rain makes me feel when it hits my window. He told me I was a good poet and wondered where my ideas came from. I told him how the words come right out of me. He asked me to come back tomorrow so that he could read my poems to his wife. I said, 'I thought your wife was dead.' 'No,' he said, 'she is visiting her sister in Maine.' I asked him, 'What is Maine?' He said, 'Rolling green hills, tall trees, yellow fields, and rivers that flow to the sea.' I told him, 'I want to see this Maine and every other place that is beautiful.' He said I could travel whenever I wanted to, but I said I couldn't because I had no money. He said, 'Books can take you places. Yes, books can take you anyplace you want to go.' I asked him. 'How does an old man know so much about books?' He told me he was a teacher long ago. One of his students sold a poem to a magazine.[3] I told him, 'I want to be a teacher just like you. I want to help the children like you are helping me.' He said, 'You'll be a very good teacher, but you ought to be a poet, like my other pupil.'"

Rose noticed that Felia gripped her book as she spoke. "Felia," she said, w is the book you have in your hand?"

"This is the book Mr. Smith gave me. I write my poems in it. Would you like me to read one to you?"

"Yes, dear child."

"Felia," Elizabeth said, "do you write poems in school?"

"We do not write in school," Felia said sadly.

Elizabeth continued. "Have you shared your notebook with your teacher?"

"No. I must learn a great deal before I do that."

"Do you write other things in your book?" Elizabeth asked, allowing a moment to recall the strong feelings she had about her own education.

Felia sat up straight as the conductor checked the children's feet to make sure they were on the floor, not on the back of the seats. "I write letters to my mother. I even made up two songs for my friend with the long hair. I forgot to tell you something. The man I told you about told me to read the newspaper every day."

Rose thought fondly of her own newspaper reading. She had asked Carmelo to attend night school to learn to read English. His reply was always the same: "I don't have the time." Rose found that answer strange; she loved to read news about faraway places. She asked Felia, "I thought you did not like to read."

Felia's memories were fresh, and Rose's invitation to share them turned them into another story. "In school, I am not good at reading. When I am with Mr. Smith, I do very well. I visit him three days a week. He asks me questions. Last week we talked about Catholics. I told him I read a story about priests who teach children. He asked me what the writer of the story wanted me to believe. I told him the writer wanted me to believe that Jesuits work for the pope, and the Jesuits use schools to control children for the pope. The writer thinks the pope doesn't like America because America has religious freedom and the pope wants people to only be Catholic.

"And the writer of the story thinks immigrants will destroy America. Mr. Smith asked me if I agreed. I said I don't know. The pope forced Jewish children, like my friend Uri, to leave the country. Still, the writer wants to force anyone who's not English out of the country. I told Mr. Smith either way isn't right."

"What else do you talk about?" Rose asked her.

Felia's unique insights energized the conversation. With eyes wide, she began, "Last week, he showed me a picture of an amusement park and asked me to find the building called the fun house. I did, but it looked like a church—like the mosque back home. It was decorated with crescents, pictures of fierce-looking bearded men with swords, and dancing women. When Mr. Smith asked what I thought about this fun house, I said I could not believe what I saw. 'That would make my Turkish friends mad,' I said. 'You cannot make fun of religion.'

"I also read a story about a famous Negro writer. He seemed almost white because the writer said he was light-skinned and had straight hair. 'How could he be white?' I asked Mr. Smith. 'One of the writer's grandparents was probably white,' he answered. Then he told me something else. He said that the writer came from a rich family in the West Indies. 'I believe the writer's grandfather was Jewish.'

"'How could you know this?' I asked. He said he reads a lot of history about New England and the West Indies." She sat up straight to recite from memory Mr. Smith's words. "It is a fact that many merchants who migrated to the islands were Jews from Spain and Portugal, so it is likely that the Negro is descended from Jews and Africans." She then smiled at the women, obviously pleased with her recitation.

With defiance in her voice, Rose spoke to her friends. "Felia is not defective. Mr. Smith listened to her. At school, she is ignored."

Marina added, "She's a good talker, that's for sure."

Elizabeth said, "You're right. Felia, tell us what you do when you go home from school."

"I cook. I sew. I make bread. I take care of the children. I wash the clothes. I can cook almost anything."

"Just like me! She is a hard worker," Marina said, slipping the girl a spearmint candy. "School should be teaching her the things she is good at. She's good with her hands."

Frustrated, Rose pressed forward, like the drifting snow pushing against the fence posts in the cornfields as she commented to Elizabeth, "Felia is smart. She can understand and learn. Elizabeth, the books you read about defective children are wrong. I do not find it strange that Mr. Smith got Felia to think."[4]

Building Altars

Elizabeth leaned against her seat and stretched her knee. "There is an Italian doctor I want to tell you about. Her name is Maria Montessori. She's had great success working with the children of the poor by arousing their interest through meaningful games. I heard John Dewey speak about her at Columbia. She set up Children's Houses in the worst slum districts of Rome. The conditions were appalling: crying and pushing, aggressive and impatient behavior. She began by teaching the older children how to help with everyday tasks. She also introduced puzzles. The children delighted in learning practical, everyday living skills that reinforced their independence and self-respect.[5]

2. Maria Montessori

Dr. Montessori (1870–1952) was the first female physician in Italy. Upon her graduation from medical school in 1896, she developed an educational approach based on the simple truth that children teach themselves. She made her first visit to the United States in 1913. According to the Montessori North American Teacher's Association's (NAMTA) website, "Today, Montessori schools are found worldwide, serving children from birth through adolescence. In the United States, there are more than four thousand private Montessori schools and more than two hundred public schools with Montessori-styled programs" ("Introduction to Montessori Education," *Montessori-NAMTA*, 2011, http://www. montessori-namta.org/About-Montessori.)

Maria Montessori, 1913

In Her Own Words

The Montessori Method (Excerpt)

Thus I saw my teachers act in the first days of my practice school in the "Children's Houses." They almost involuntarily recalled the children to immobility without observing and distinguishing the nature of the movements they repressed. There was, for example, a little girl who gathered her companions about her and then, in the midst of them, began to talk and gesticulate. The teacher at once ran to her, took hold of her arms, and told her to be still; but I, observing the child, saw that she was playing at being teacher or mother to the others, and teaching them the morning prayer, the invocation to the saints, and the sign of the cross: she already showed herself as a director.

Another child, who continually made disorganized and misdirected movements, and who was considered abnormal, one day, with an expression of intense attention, set about moving the tables. Instantly they were upon him to make him stand still because he made too much noise. Yet this was one of the first manifestations, in this child, of movements that were co-coordinated and directed toward a useful end, and it was therefore an action that should have been respected. In fact, after this the child began to be quiet and happy like the others whenever he had any small objects to move about and to arrange upon his desk. In fact, after this the child began to be quiet and happy like the others whenever he had any small objects to move about and to arrange upon his desk.

It often happened that while the directress replaced in the boxes various materials that had been used, a child would draw near, picking up the objects, with the evident desire of imitating the teacher. The first impulse was to send the child back to her place with the remark, "Let it alone; go to your seat." Yet the child expressed by this act a desire to be useful; the time, with her, was ripe for a lesson in order.

Montessori, M. *The Montessori Method*. Translated by A. E. George. New York: Frederick A. Stokes Company, 1912

"Dewey tied her ideas to his own. He believes that all children can learn by working on projects that interest them. He calls his ideas progressive out of respect for the Progressive Movement in politics. He agrees with men like President Roosevelt that big industries are ruining our society and that schools need to make things right."

Nothing in Rose's experience could help her understand. "He believes schools can change people?" she asked with a mixture of respect and disbelief.

"He believes that schools can educate children to be good citizens, which means acting responsibly and compassionately. Once children grow up, they'll act for the common good. Of course, this plan will only work if schools themselves become democratic and accepting."

Rose collected her thoughts. "That is fine, but does he think teachers will accept all children? I don't want to argue with him, but I wonder if he thinks all teachers are like Mr. Smith."

An elderly man with a great white beard sat across from them. He had fallen asleep as soon as he sat in his seat. As the train neared Boston, the jarring woke him. He turned to see the car filled with children, which confused him because he did not see parents. Elizabeth smiled at him, so he asked her a question.

"Dear lady, I believe I awoke in a dream—children alone on a train. Are we off to visit Saint Nicholas? How could that be? Christmas is past!"

She laughed. "The children are the sons and daughters of union workers on strike. They're on their way to New York City to live with union families during the strike."

He listened attentively and then said to her, "Allow me to introduce myself. My name is Alton Trombly, and I am ninety-one years old. I am on my way to visit my great-grandchild in Baltimore. I know a bit about children and unions. I was one of twelve children. Left home when I was fourteen and traveled west to cut wheat on the Canadian prairies. The thresher we used was steam-fired. We fueled it with the straw we cut in the field. Got a nasty burn from it one summer. When I was young, I met my wife out there and got married. We came back east to build our own home and have lived in it ever since. Had ten children together. Joined the union in 1871.

"I used to tell my children tales from my youth, about how I worked eighteen hours a day all of my life. Hard physical labor was a way of life in those days. In the summer, I cut wheat; in the winter, I cut timber in the north woods. It was so cold in the woods we carried frozen milk in burlap bags. We couldn't work the horses too hard in those temperatures because they'd get frostbite in their lungs."

"Was the work too much for you?" asked Marina.

"No, madam. What you want in life you have to work for. Besides, hard work never killed anyone. I am physically strong and healthy. A job well done is what life is all about."

Elizabeth remembered something her father had told her. She motioned to Rose as she shared this memory. "Marx believed that the very essence of life is work. That's why he hated machines; he felt that they had taken the charm out of work."

Rose broke in with her own comment. "Mr. Trombly, your story reminds me of the first time I lived in Middletown. I was a dressmaker for an American family. They were a very prosperous family who lived in a three-story house. The children wore fine clothes. In fact, all their clothes came from a store in the city. The children loved to tell me their father was better than the fathers of their friends.

"One afternoon I stopped by to measure Mrs. De Varies for a new dress. The family was having dinner, so I waited in the servants' room next to the kitchen.[6] I overheard them talk about Roosevelt's square deal. They shared a story Roosevelt had read from a magazine called *Collier's*. One of the children said that an unsinkable ship was being built in England. Another son chattered about a man named Babe Ruth. They were successful and confident about the future. They talked like it was a contest to see who knew the most. The mother and father were not listening. The children were talking to themselves. I felt an emptiness in the room."

Mr. Trombly said, "I don't like this modern craze for progress. Something is missing. All this iron and coal and engineering cannot make us happy. No amount of science can replace a job well done. That includes raising children right."

Rose thought aloud. "Elizabeth, you had parents who listened to you. Perhaps Montessori also came from a family of listeners. My mother listened because she loved me. I am sure Dewey can find smart teachers, but he cannot train them to love children. That is why I will never leave my children with strangers. A mother has to put her children's needs before her own."

Elizabeth had wrapped a blanket around her shoulders and was looking outside at a boy sliding down a hill right into a ditch. "I have friends who'll disagree with you. They believe that we need to be concerned about ourselves before others."

"That's ridiculous," Rose said, with fire in her eyes.

Elizabeth wished to elaborate. "The man who wrote it doesn't think so. His books are read in Europe and America."[7]

Maddened, Rose said, "He does not know what he is talking about. I do not want my children to grow up selfish. I will think of them first, not as a boss does about his own profit before the needs of his workers."

Pleased with the way that Rose had just connected selfishness with the profit motive, Elizabeth continued her discussion about John Dewey. "I've visited delightful schools in the city. The teachers love their children and know how to put excitement into learning. Dewey wants to make learning both scientific and pleasurable."

Rose remembered Elizabeth's story about the doctor from Italy. "Are Dr. Montessori's methods scientific?" she asked. The more questions Rose asked, the more she learned. If she could have spoken with her father, she would have told him he was wrong to have called her stupid for asking so many questions.

"Yes, she developed them after watching children very carefully."

"Do the men who write about defective children use the same science?"[8]

"They use tests to measure things like attention, confidence, and love of truth. Their findings are not doubted."

Although Rose was untutored, she knew something was wrong. "Tests remind me of the butcher who marks the lamb for slaughter. He does not change his mind."

Not seeing the potential of testing turning children into commodities, Elizabeth pushed back. "Their business is to find the most effective, economical way to train immigrant children."

Even Marina got angry. "Dear me, Elizabeth; you sound like a boss!"

Elizabeth softened her presumption. "Testing aims to place children in classes that match their abilities."

Rose sensed that testing might take from children what machines had taken from workers. "What about Felia? Will Dewey see the poet in her? Scientists are trained to think in one way. But they cannot teach us to reason about what is good and bad. That truth is in Felia's poetry."

"I share your concern, Rose, but placing students in classes that match their abilities is an improvement over the old ways. A psychologist at Columbia, Edward Thorndike, is constructing tests to identify mental differences in children. He wants to put children who are hard to teach in special classes."

Rose said, "Elizabeth, my brother Antonio was very good at numbers. He wanted to be an engineer when he grew up. Instead, he became a mason. That is because only children of the landowners went to school. I am afraid that Thorndike wants one education for the rich and another for the poor. The children of privilege will test well, while the children of the poor will fail."[9]

Elizabeth said, "He just wants to make it easier on everyone."

Even Trombly understood Rose's concerns. "My dear Miss Flynn," he said with great delight. "Testing is like crafting fine furniture—it takes deep understanding and reverence."

3. Edward Lee Thorndike

Thorndike (1874-1949) was born in Williamsburg, Massachusetts to the son of a Methodist minister and became an American pioneer in comparative psychology. He became interested in the field of psychology after reading William James' *Principles of Psychology*, and he went as far as to enroll in Harvard, after graduating Weslyan University, so he could study under James. But he didn't complete his studies there. He was invited to Columbia University and was awarded a doctorate for his thesis, *Animal Intelligence: An Experimental Study of the Associative Processes in Animals* in 1898. His first employment was at the College for Women of Case Wesern Reserve in Cleveland, Ohio, where he was unhappy. The following year, in 1899, he taught psychology at Teachers College at Columbia University, where he remained for the rest of his career, studying human learning, education, and mental testing. (Erika Reinemeyer, "Edward Lee Thorndike," May 1999, http://www.muskingum. edu/~psych/psycweb/history/thorndike.htm.)

Edward Lee Thorndike

In His Own Words

"The Contributions of Psychology to Education" (Excerpt)

Just as the science and art of agriculture depend upon chemistry and botany, so the art of education depends upon physiology and psychology. A complete science of psychology would tell every fact about every one's intellect and character and behavior, would tell the cause of every change in human nature, would tell the result which every educational force—every act of every person that changed any other or the agent himself—would have. It would aid us to use human beings for the world's welfare with the same surety of the result that we now have when we use falling bodies or chemical elements. In proportion as we get such a science we shall become masters of our own souls as we now are masters of heat and light. Progress toward such a science is being made.

It will, of course, be understood that directly or indirectly, soon or late, every advance in the sciences of human nature will contribute to our success in controlling human nature and changing it to the advantage of the common weal.

The extent to which the intellectual and moral differences found in human beings are consequences of their original nature and determined by the ancestry from which they spring, is a matter of fundamental importance foreducation.

So also is the manner in which ancestral influence operates. Whether such qualities as leadership, the artistic temperament, originality, persistence, mathematical ability, or motor skill are represented in the germs each by one or a few unit characters so that they "Mendelize" in inheritance, or whether they are represented each by the cooperation of so many unit characters that the laws of their inheritance are those of "blending" is a question whose answer will decide in great measure the means to be employed for racial improvement. Obviously both the amount and the mode of operation of ancestral influence upon intellect and character are questions which psychology should and does investigate.

Thorndike, E. "The Contributions of Psychology to Education." *The Journal of Educational Psychology* 1 (1910): 5–12.

Now it was time for Elizabeth to learn. Her companions had rebuked her arguments with ease. She said, "I have a friend who teaches tenement children. She sings to them, reads stories about the past, and has them write about heroes. The children work together writing scripts and making scenery, costumes, and props. They draw, paint, measure, cut, and sew. She speaks to them about their good effort and makes sure that she answers their questions. In February, they put on a huge pageant. Parents took great pleasure watching their children perform, and everyone stayed for a party. By June, the children were reading and writing very well. The following December, her principal asked for her resignation. Several of the senior teachers had complained to him that the children from her class were selfish because they were only energized by things that interested them."

Fletcher B. Dressler
"Fewer Men Teachers: Unwise to Entrust Pupils So Largely to Women, Says Dressler"
American Education, vol. 15, no. 7
March 1912

In this excerpt, Dr. Fletcher B. Dressler of the United States Bureau of Education comments on the decrease of male teachers in public schools from 30% in 1900 to 21% in the next decade. Clearly, he thinks this trend was a bad one.

"There is no doubt," he says, "that it is unwise to entrust so important a matter as the teaching of boys and girls so largely to women; but the facts are known and have been for many years, and yet the hoped-for change does not come."

Rose knew what had happened because Elizabeth had opened her mind. "Your story proves my point. At the mill, no one bothers you if you do what they say. If you ask a question, you are fired. Teachers who follow Dewey's advice are in for trouble. Dewey's children will fatigue teachers with all their questions and interests."

Marina saw another side to this problem. She could not imagine why anyone would want to teach.[10] Elizabeth had an answer. "Teachers are usually young women whose parents started in the mills. As children, they made it through school by following the rules. They expect the same from their children, because they know that conformity is the key to success. Dewey wants teachers to stand apart from all this toeing the line."

Rose wanted to comment, but was absorbed in observing the older girls as they huddled around Felia. They were alive with happiness as she read her poems to them. "I have a friend who asked me to go with her to her daughter's school because her English was not too good. The teacher was lovely—long, braided hair and a big smile. She told us how important it was to read and write. She told us she understood our suffering because her grandparents had worked in the mills. I was surprised to hear her tell us that. She told us about a new way to teach. It did not matter that Infantile had stayed back three years in a row, she told us. She would have her reading in no time. We nodded, because we knew the child was smart. Infantile's mother touched my arm and whispered in Italian, 'Tell her my child needs glasses. He cannot see too well.' If I ever have a daughter, I will want her to become a teacher. I will also tell her not to forget her common sense."

Dialogues with Friends

Grand Central Depot

Five thousand Italian Socialists singing "The Marseillaise" and "The Internationale" greeted the children and their chaperones at Grand Central Depot. The strike had great progressive backing, especially among intellectuals and artists. Many celebrities were in the crowd because the journey had gotten so much publicity. Emma Goldman and her companion Reitman came to meet Elizabeth and the children. Also in the crowd were John Dewey and two guests from Chicago, Jane Addams and Francis Parker. Mill owners were incensed that the media had drawn so much attention to the workers. Elizabeth spied Dewey and waved. She adored him and went to as many of his lectures as time permitted. As he walked over to congratulate her, a reporter from the *New York Times* cut him off and shouted, "What is the significance of this train trip, Miss Flynn?"

She replied, "It is our way of exposing the collusion between government and business. We want to show the country what the mill owners and politicians are doing to these poor workers and their children. They are starving and brutalizing them. The Lawrence strike is worse than the Homestead strike. We will win. We have strength in our solidarity with the hard-working, selfless union families in New York who have agreed to take in the children you see before you. The little ones will be fed and cared for and, when the strike is over, will return to their mothers and fathers, whole and happy."

Reitman[11] nudged Elizabeth and said, "Mario needs you to sign over the children to his care. After you do that, we can head to the village. Friends are waiting for us."

She agreed but first she called out, "Professor Dewey," and rushed over to hug him.

Dewey blushed as he fixed his hat and said, "Elizabeth, you are more beautiful than ever. I wish you would enroll in Teachers College. We need your passion in schools. By the way, what a valuable thing you have done here—I mean bringing these children to New York. I would have helped, but my schedule keeps me away from my apartment too much, and I always have guests showing up at the strangest hours. Speaking of guests, let me introduce you to two dear friends from Chicago, Jane Addams and Francis Parker.[12] They go way back. Miss Addams is here to open another one of her settlement homes. They are very successful, you know. Big things are going to happen to her. As for Francis, I walk in his shadow. He is the real father of progressivism. When I was stumbling along years ago, he had already devised a child-centered curriculum. Actually got it to work. Imagine—thirty years ago!" He shook his head.

Elizabeth had not heard of Parker, but she complimented his Chicago work anyway.

"Oh no," he said with a smile. "John is talking about my superintendent in Quincy, Massachusetts. It is actually close to Lawrence. Quincy is the city of presidents. The Adams presidents were born there. So much history in that city. The little darlings who were under my care are now your age."

Rose heard the word Quincy and looked around because her brother lived in Quincy. She had not been interested in the chitchat because she was a shy person. Her eyes were still on the kids, making sure they were okay. She turned to Marina and said in Sicilian, "Do you know who that tall man is?"

"No, and who cares? He is too old for me."

Rose shook her head at Marina's one-track mind. She was quick to say, "I think he's the man Elizabeth spoke about on the train, the one who works with teachers."

Marina looked at him again and said, "What can he know about children? He's too stiff."

Rose was not listening because she had turned her attention to the other elderly man, Francis Parker. She immediately liked him because he had called children his "little darlings." Rose trusted him more than she trusted Dewey.

Elizabeth excused herself and walked over to Emma and Reitman. "I have an idea. Why don't we invite Mr. Dewey and his friends to supper? They will enjoy themselves."

"Good idea," Emma said. "Ask them along. There will be plenty of food. To tell you the truth, I do not think they will accept—too genteel. Perhaps we will convert them. By the way, Elizabeth, you have not introduced me to your two friends. I must admit that I am attracted to both of them. One is dark and the other light."

"Both are our sisters, Emma. They are mill workers and seamstresses. Marina is the center of attention when men are around. Will Alto be there?"

Emma shrugged. "What about Rose?"

"She is more reserved, more wary and disciplined. Her father wouldn't allow her to come to America unless she promised not to marry."

Dewey, Parker, and Addams accepted the invitation to join the celebration. As the party walked out of the depot to catch a taxi, Rose kept looking at the children. Marina read her mind and said spontaneously in Sicilian, "They'll be fine, Rose."

Brick and Glass Artifacts

Rose looked at the new construction going up around the building they had just exited. The new building was the Grand Central Terminal, a massive structure being built to replace the old one.[13] It was in the

Postcard of Grand Central Terminal, 42nd Street and Park Avenue, New York, circa 1915

form of a Greek temple. A Roman triumphal arch dominated the front, with pairs of Corinthian columns flanking three enormous arched windows. The columns supported an entablature, at the center of which was a dominating sculpture group. A huge clock stood at the center of the group. The terminal had a familiarity to it. Unlike the brick, glass, and wood of Lawrence, this building was full of detail and decoration. It reminded Rose of the train station she walked through the day she boarded the train for Connecticut. She was walking next to Marina and said to her, "I thought I left Italy, but I am wrong. These buildings remind me of Siracusa. When I boarded the train for Middletown, I had to walk through an immense building filed with tall columns and a glass ceiling that opened to the sky. Now I stand beside one adorned with pagan gods."

The *Times* reporter who had tagged along overheard her comment. His name was Jones, and he responded by saying, "Indeed you are looking at the Grand Central Terminal, but I am afraid it won't be in use for another year. It definitely has a European look. Like the other building you mentioned, its purpose is to serve people on the move.

Thousands of Americans will use it to board the trains of Commodore Vanderbilt. He was the first American to invest heavily in the railroads. This great building stands as a monument to his vision."

Emma replied, "It is nothing more than an imperial statement. Its size imposes its will on the masses, just as the good commodore did on his competitors. Grand Central symbolizes unbridled ambition and greed."

"An exaggeration, Miss Goldman," Jones said with a sneer. "Why can't you acknowledge America's magnificence without reducing everything to a political statement? I have been inside, and it is majestic. The entire interior is Tennessean marble that gives off a stately glow. Brilliant shafts of light pass through its massive windows to light the main waiting room. The grandness of the room makes you feel small. The crowning achievement is a blue-green ceiling with twenty-five hundred gold stars etched into the heavens."

Rose listened attentively to both of them and responded, "This sounds like

---

Edwin Arlington Robinson
"Reuben Bright"
Children of the Night
1897

Robinson (1865–1935) grew up in Gardiner, Maine but later moved to New York. He lived there impoverished, in love with a woman his brother married, and had a growing alcohol problem. His fortunes changed when Kermit Roosevelt, president Theodore Roosevelt's son, gave Robinson's second collection of poetry, *The Children of the Night*, to his father. The president admired the poems a lot, and when he found out that Robinson was impoverished, he found him a position in the New York Customs Office. Robinson published more poetry, became more well known, and went on to win the Pulitzer Prize three times. Below is a beloved poem of his.

Because he was a butcher and thereby
Did earn an honest living (and did right),
I would not have you think that Reuben Bright
Was any more a brute than you or I;
For when they told him that his wife must die,
He stared at them, and shook with grief and fright,
And cried like a great baby half that night,
And made the women cry to see him cry.
And after she was dead, and he had paid
The singers and the sexton and the rest,
He packed a lot of things that she had made
Most mournfully away in an old chest
Of hers, and put some chopped-up cedar boughs
In with them, and tore down the slaughter-house.

118

home. When I was young, I used to sit outside at dusk as the clouds disappeared into the sea. As they turned gray and then black, the stars came out. I tried to count them, but there were too many. I miss the night sky. In Lawrence, it is hidden under clouds."

Jones was a progressive thinker, and so he broke in before Emma had a chance to reply. "I agree that nature is picturesque. I admire a brilliant sunset or the sound of falling water, but beauty does not fill the stomach. On the other hand, falling water can be harnessed into electricity and thus sold as a commodity. This is the age of coal, iron, and steel. I presume you are an immigrant. Came to America for a better life, right? You came here because you believed in a better tomorrow. You were right to leave your night sky. You know as well as anyone that nature does not put food on your table. Commerce does. In America, nature serves society. Our industries and the democracy they support fuel progress.[14] We provide jobs for thousands and thousands of Europeans like you. Look around you. New York City symbolizes man's dominion over nature."

Rose did not understand many of his words but detected his presumption. "You erect the future on the backs of the poor."

"How so?" he said, amused by her assertiveness.

More aware than ever, Rose said, "We build your subways and monuments, mine your coal, and weave your shirts and blankets. You take from us as you kiss your wife good night."

This made Jones squirm. "That is progress," he said without hesitation.

"Then there is too much progress."

Jones yawned. "Bright minds and refined tastes are not for everyone. At least that is what science reports. Brain size determines sophistication. Certain immigrants have small brains. Their heads are low and their chins protrude like the muzzle of a monkey; their hands are covered with coarse hair. They are vulgar, beyond education."[15]

"Emma, does this make sense to you?" Rose asked.

"What distinguishes the cultured from the uncultured is privilege. The upper classes make sure the poor do not have access to education. The Irish playwright George Bernard Shaw states this repeatedly. Anyone can be educated."

Rose turned back to Jones. "That is what Elizabeth believes too. As for me, I still do not understand why you call me a brute but steal from me."

Jones replied, "Great Americans like Jefferson believed that antiquity represented the principles of a good life—order, symmetry, and balance. That is why he designed buildings to look like Greek and Roman temples. It also explains why our banks look familiar to you. We respect your past, ma'am, that is why we require school children to study Latin. The study of antiquity shapes the mind. Yet we are modern. Look at the buildings around you."

Rose glanced up. "They touch the sky."

"There is a reason behind this. We decided to build up from the ground, rather than close to it, because congestion forces us to build buildings close together. Second, the mathematics and science your ancestors invented make technology possible. Edison's electricity powers the elevators in these buildings. Carnegie's iron and steel gives form to our designs. However sublime, modern skyscrapers embellish the past. That is because steel and concrete are not art. Everyone here would agree that the Grand Central Terminal symbolizes American enterprise. Why do we build a luxurious hotel next to it? To temper its hard edge. We do the same with libraries and post offices—we balance utility with elegance. Even our commercial buildings follow this dictum. The colossal size and decoration of warehouses and train sheds raise them to the grandeur of Greek temples."

Rose was happy to reply. "The old buildings of my country are in ruins, the builders long forgotten. Your buildings will not last forever."

"Concrete and steel are indestructible."

Rose was silent for a moment and then said, "One afternoon I unpacked my white linen dress to show Marina. I forgot to put it away, and so it lay uncovered on my bed. When I returned home, a fine dust covered it. If this can happen to my linen, what will coal do to these walls and columns?"

Reitman beamed and said, "Well said, Rose. Allow me to make another observation. Railroads are dead. The future of transportation is not in rails but in automobiles. They are a unique American invention. Cars take people where they want to go when they want to go there.

They do not have to depend on schedules or clocks. They are private—the purest form of self-reliance. On the other hand, trains and subways are public. They force you to adapt to arbitrary timetables. You have to stare at people you do not know. Mark my word—once someone finds a way to manufacture automobiles cheaply, the country will be transformed. Whole new industries will evolve—fuel for engines, roads for wheels, bridges to cross, and shops for repair. We will see these changes in our lifetime, my friends. Even the humblest American will own a car. Once this happens, trains will die, and this great terminal will waste away. It will become dirty, unnoticed, and forgotten without a purpose."

Jones was offended and replied sharply to this group of radicals who had come to Grand Central Terminal to cheer the children. "Is that an empirical statement?"

Reitman replied, "The commodore ran sloops. Now they rot at the bottom of the harbor because he replaced them with barges and steamships. He abandoned steamships once he saw that the future was in trains. Do you think he will invest in trains if a cheaper form of transportation is found? Of course not. Greed does not respect tradition. The Exposition in Saint Louis forecasts that automobiles and planes will replace trains shortly. They are cleaner, faster, and less costly to run."[16]

Emma was waiting for her chance to jump in. "It is outrageous that technology runs our lives. The automobile will isolate us from one another. Families will go their separate ways. At least in this station, citizens can mix with others. They can share a common experience, much as the citizens of Rome did in the public baths. Buildings ought to serve civic purposes. They should bring us together. The same case can be made for education. Public schools need to educate the rich and the poor in the same manner so that power and influence does not belong to one class of individuals."

Jones laughed quietly. "Americans won't let this building crumble because we are not a barbaric people. Besides, Vanderbilt will not allow his investment to flounder. It cost him a staggering forty-three million dollars to build it. If the trains stop coming, he will adapt. As we speak, his agents are selling air rights over it."

"What does that mean?" Rose asked.

"He is collecting handsome fees from the buildings that tower over his terminal. For example, the owners of the majestic Waldorf Astoria Hotel have paid him handsomely for the privilege of building next to his edifice. Second, he has plans to cover the terminal with an office tower."

"How ironic!" roared Emma. "Sealing his monument under a tomb of glass and steel."

Legislation and Education

Once inside the taxi, the party crossed Fifth Avenue and passed the mansions of the wealthy. They also passed the tenements and crowded streets of the urban working class. Rubbish was in the street, as was the smell of sewage. Reitman said, "City politicians make a mockery of democracy. Bosses and political machines run the city. Votes can be bought and sold. Politicians do nothing but reap profit through graft and corruption. The city stagnates under filthy air. I do not look to government for answers. They are part of the problem."

Parker asked innocently, "Why do so many people live here?"

"One word," Reitman said. "Excitement. New York pulls people here because there are no constraints. Take entertainment. Baseball, saloons, movie houses, vaudeville, musicals, burlesque, revues, magic shows, minstrels, even female impersonators. For the kids there are wild Indians scalping cowboys. There are picnics in the park and swimming at Coney Island. Education? It is free, tax-supported, including night school and City College. We even offer baths and eyeglasses to the needy. Skyscrapers and subways outline the city. Streetcars connect us to the suburbs. Jobs are plentiful and food is cheap. A dime buys you as much beer and sandwiches as you can swallow. Why would anyone stay away? Sure, it's dirty and corrupt, but there is something here for everyone. Life is unfettered."

The taxi driver tore down Third Street toward the Village. In five minutes the party walked into a middle-brow pub with walls covered in solemn art. Customers were eating and having a great time. Music drowned out the street sounds. Parker collected Marina's and Rose's coats and handed them to the cloakroom attendant. He tipped her a dollar, his usual formality. The attendant straightened her old Arab medallion and dreamed of gaming tables and mysterious lovers. An assistant waiter escorted them to a dark dining room with a high ceiling and a blue Persian rug. He stoked the fire until the room glowed. Rose noticed that the walls were framed with books that no one read. Dewey ordered wine for everyone. Marina moved over to the red sofa between the fireplace and the door to watch famous people eat beef pie.

Addams had not said much all afternoon. Now, she said, "This is a country of laws. We need to reform them, or all will be lost."

Emma jumped in. "There are too many barriers to political solutions, Miss Addams. Too much self-interest to think laws can make a difference."

"I disagree, Miss Goldman," Jane answered. "We are making progress. Writers like Sinclair Lewis are exposing vice and corruption. Citizens are outraged. Calls for prohibition as the prosecution of crooked cops grow louder each day. More state and federal laws will restore competition in the marketplace. Better laws to regulate unscrupulous practices and break the power of business trusts will protect us from greed. Progressive legislators can do that if elected. It is the only way we can stop waste and be more efficient with our resources. And let us not forget about improving the working conditions of women and children."

"A legislative agenda will take forever," Emma said, "because the middling classes have a grip on the country. They want to return us to the old ways. Look at the songs they listen to—pure nostalgia.[17] They want politicians to bring them back to a simpler past, where neighbors knew each other. That type of social order—local and personal—is dead, and they do not know it. I will tell you another thing. They want libraries to be stocked with books that uplift the spirit, not represent reality as it is. Incredibly, they still even love ornamentation on our public buildings. Their beliefs are old and fundamental. That is because they reject science and do not believe in change. They go about trying to legislate us backwards. They are dangerous because they fear the future. Political action is the only thing that will work."

It was Reitman's turn. "The most difficult barriers to progress are the politicians who cling to the idea of rugged individualism—everyone for himself. They are for business. Look what they did to us in Hempstead.

123

They sanctioned repression of labor unions, especially the radical IWW. All we wanted was more cooperation."

"I agree that change is next to impossible," Dewey said. "Too many Americans will not let go of the past. The only way to prepare for the future is to educate the children for it."

Rose admired the thoughtfulness of these well-dressed Americans. Something was missing, however. They did not speak in the way Elizabeth did—with fire in their words. And no one smiled. Rose said nothing, wondering if their tiresome habits and manners had been learned at school. Marina turned back and, breaking into Sicilian, her full bosom attractive to two patrons dickering over a book, said. "I want to hit everyone one of them against their skulls. What bad teeth."

Rose turned coldly to Dewey and said with a bit of cynicism, "You mean the future is about children? What about the suffering all around us? And what about people who hate? Elizabeth, tell him about Mrs. Hutchinson."

Elizabeth touched Rose's hand without bitterness. "Professor Dewey knows about her kind. That is why he has been working hard to end all forms of oppression." Turning to Jane, Elizabeth continued, "Miss Addams, I deeply respect your work. Do you think education is the answer?"

Addams smiled at Rose and Marina. "If by education you mean how we teach, I say no. It is more about what we teach."

"That seems to contradict your work. I thought you show the illiterate how to resist their fate," Emma said.

"We do. We all know that life in the tenements is deplorable. Before I started working with poor people, I thought that they were simple-minded and that their condition was due to failings in their language and culture. I drew up a list of things I thought they could learn and showed it to John. He told me that everyone can learn. He gave me another bit of advice. Respect every learner, even the slow ones.

"I listened and taught. John was right. My students loved to talk about big ideas: politics, America, identity. I showed them how to advocate for more parks, playgrounds, lit streets, and health care. I discovered that they did not know anything about the history of industrial societies, so we talked about that subject. I mean, talk. We added self-expression, arts, dancing, and drama classes. Before long we offered lectures, summer school, Sunday concerts, and even clubs."

"You listen to your students, Jane. That idea interests me greatly." This was Francis Parker speaking. He had been silent for some time, a Yankee from New Hampshire with an honored past. "Jane, you are a Midwesterner. Doesn't matter. We both grew up on farms and went to church. Although I served in the military, I tried teaching. I failed until I watched children closely. Before long, I figured out how they learned."

4. Jane Addams

Addams (1860-1935) is often called the "mother" of social work. In 1889, she co-founded the second "settlement house" in the U.S. called "Hull House," and it became the standard-bearer for all other settlement houses. Hull House had been a rundown mansion that was renovated in Chicago's West Side--a neighborbood populated by recent European immigrants who knew little English. Modeled after "Toynbee Hall," which had opened five years earlier in an east London slum, the goal of a "settlement house" was to get the rich and the poor to live more closely together in an interdependent community. So, "settlement houses" were established in poor urban areas in which middle-class "settlement" volunteers would live. These volunteers would share their knowledge and culture with their low-income neighbors and help alleviate their poverty. For Addams in particular, it was important to her to provide an art program at her house in order to challenge "industrialized education" that merely "fitted" a person to a job. Hull House became a center of research, provided a daycare and healthcare for the poor in the neighborhood, held free concerts and lectures for everyone, and included facilities such as a night school for adults (a forerunner to continuing education classes today), clubs for older children, a girl's club, a public kitchen with

Jane Addams, c. 1916

a lunchroom, a bathhouse, an art gallery, a gym, a book bindery, a library, a music school, a drama group with theater, apartments, a drama group and a theater, apartments, meeting rooms for discussion, and an employment bureau. (Louise Carrol Wade, "Settlement House," *Encyclopedia of Chicago*, Chicago Historical Society, http://www.encyclopedia.chicagohistory.org/pages/1135.html, retrieved July 24, 2017).

Addams was also considered a public philosopher in the pragmatist tradition, she was a prolific writer, was a leader in the women's suffrage movement, and made international efforts towards world peace. In 1931, she became the first American woman to be awarded the Noble Peace Prize. ("Jane Addams," Wikipedia, https://en.wikipedia.org/wiki/Jane_Addams#Primary_sources), retrieved July 24, 2017.)

In Her Own Words

"Foreign-Born children in the Primary Grades" (Excerpt)

Foreign-born children have all the drudgery of learning to listen to, and read and write an alien tongue; and many never get beyond this first drudgery. I have interrogated dozens of these children who have left school from the third, fourth, and fifth grades, and I have met very few who ever read for pleasure

From one point of view the school itself is an epitome of the competitive system, almost of the factory system. Certain standards are held up and worked for; and, even in the school, the child does little work with real joy and spontaneity. The pleasure which comes from creative effort, the thrill of production, is only occasional, and not the sustaining motive which keeps it going. The child in school often contracts the habit of expecting to do his work in certain hours, and to take his pleasure in certain other hours; quite in the same spirit as he later earns his money by ten hours of dull factory work, and spends it in three hours of lurid and unprofitable pleasure in the evening. Both in the school and the factory his work has been dull and growing duller, and his pleasure must constantly grow more stimulating. Only occasionally, in either place, has he had a glimpse of the real joy of doing a thing for its own sake.

Those of us who are working to bring a fuller life to the industrial members of the community, who are looking forward to a time when work shall not be senseless drudgery, but shall contain some self-expression of the worker, sometimes feel the hopelessness of adding evening classes and social entertainments as a mere frill to a day filled with monotonous and deadening drudgery; and we sometimes feel that we have a right to expect more help from the public schools than they now give us.

The isolation of the school from life—its failure to make life of more interest, and show it in its larger aspects—the mere equipping of the children with the tools of reading and writing, without giving them an absorbing interest concerning which they wish to read and write, certainly tends to defeat the very purpose of education.

Addams, J. "Foreign-Born children in the Primary Grades." *National Educational Association Journal of Proceedings and Addresses of the Thirty-Sixth Annual Meeting Held at Milwaukee, Wis., July 6–9, 1897*. Chicago: University of Chicago Press, 189

"That is how I learned to teach too," said Dewey. "When I graduated from college, I taught school. My students did not listen to a thing I said. Nothing worked. I could not get their attention. I was devastated. My philosophy training did not help. So I resigned and went to graduate school. That is where I discovered the writings of this esteemed scholar, Mr. Parker. He wrote that anyone could learn, as long as the subject matter is presented in a meaningful way. I applied his concepts, and they worked."

Reitman wanted to participate. "Does this make sense to you experts on teaching? I read that Baltimore schools are setting up special classes for unmanageable boys."

Addams was the first to reply. "Too much control. Children do not enter school bad. As soon as we force them to learn something they cannot relate to, they fight back. There is something about boys. Some take to learning very easily. Most do not. They see school as a place where they lose their freedom."

Marina had failed to gain the attention of the singing waiter, so she jumped in. "Sounds like boys got it bad in school. If you ask me, boys are more stupid than girls. That is why I beat them at cards all the time."

"Give a cheer for the girls. Marina, you are a true woman," Emma joked. "Let me say something serious about these special classes. The state abhors freedom. Massachusetts has laws that forbid teachers to marry or live wherever they want. Schools are a tool of the state. Their job is to enforce conformity. Does anyone seriously think politicians and businessmen want schools to teach children to think?"

Parker smiled. "It is not easy to teach the sons of men who labor in silence."

Emma said, "That is nonsense, and I will tell you why. Last year I went into the mines to read Ibsen to the workers. They understood it. Jane is right. Workers have the same capacity to think about their history, religion, and cultural heritage as the rich."

"I agree with each of you," said Dewey, "but equality is not a universally held sentiment. We are fighting against history. Plato said it first: only the brightest should be educated. He regarded the education of all others as superfluous. Elitism is an especially dangerous idea in a democracy because each citizen must participate in the running of the government. Horace Mann understood that when he pushed free schools in Massachusetts. Unfortunately, the sheer number of foreign-born children in our schools today are undermining his vision. We cannot teach children who do not speak English or who do not want to be in school. That is why so many schools have adapted scientific procedures to separate deficient children from more capable ones."

Rose needed to make a point. "Elizabeth and I spoke about tests on the train. Just because you can't write your name doesn't mean you are backward."

"That's my point too," Emma said. "The rich and powerful want us to think that way. They do not want workers to think. Does the general want his soldiers to question his authority?"

Dewey smiled sympathetically, for he had written about this subject many times. "Teachers can train children to think."

Parker elaborated by saying, "Teachers need the right tools to do that. Years of observation have convinced me that schools have failed to educate children because they use the wrong materials. Children still read stories about Elsie, Jimmy, and Fannie, who live in homes with fireplaces and spend idle hours popping corn. These children walk along polished wooden floors to their own rooms to play with dolls and teach tricks to their dogs.

"The stories are a lie. Adults sit in rocking chairs, knitting or reading or speaking pleasantly to their children. They serve them snacks and take them on trips to the woods for Saturday afternoon picnics. Mothers also take them on adventures. Days are filled with idyllic walks in clean white aprons, past posted fences, old trees, and flowers. The children play with the farm animals, pick flowers, picnic in meadows, and gaze into clear running brooks. They also take trips to the seashore. Childhood is a time of discovery under the watchful eye of a benevolent mother.

5. Francis W. Parker

1837–1902, Parker was born in New Hampshire. After serving with the Union Army in the Civil War, he returned to teaching. In 1872, he traveled to Germany to study the new methods of pedagogy being developed there, particularly those based on the theories of Johann Herbart. He returned to become superintendent of schools in Quincy, Mass. He originated what came to be called the Quincy movement, emphasizing such elements of progressive education as group activities, the teaching of science, informal methods of instruction, and the elimination of rigid discipline. He extended these practices as a supervisor (1880–83) of schools in Boston, as principal (1883–99) of the Cook County Normal School, Chicago, and as founder and principal (1899–1901) of the Chicago Institute, which became part of the school of education of the University of Chicago. His pioneering work led to improvements in curricula and teacher training.

Francis Wayland Parker

In His Own Words

*Notes of Talks on Teaching at the
Martha's Vineyard Summer Institute* (Excerpt)

I am quite sure that many of you have asked the question, to yourselves at least, while I have been explaining the principles and methods of teaching primary reading as I understand them. What shall we do with children whose teaching has been all wrong from the beginning? Who have been taught by the alphabet, phonic, phonetic, or word methods without the life-giving principle of the thought? Who struggle with each particular word in a painful way, and drawl out the sentences as if there were no beautiful pictures behind them? Who have been led through a dreary waste of empty words in a harsh, unnatural manner? What shall we do with these children? You ask. It is a very difficult question to answer, for two or three weeks' wrong teaching will leave their scars in the child's mind forever: crippling every action, and obstructing every step. The elocutionists, by scores, reap a rich harvest from the bad teaching primary schools. The trouble with the voices generally is, that the natural, easy, pleasant tones of the child are changed to harsh, unnatural utterance. Something may be done indeed for these unfortunate victims.

The active imagination of the child, so strongly marked in his ardent love for stories, may be developed into a still greater love for history. I have spoken briefly, in a former talk, of the use of fairy and mythological stories in mental development. The child's intense desire to use his imagination continually is the foundation of this love. Fairy stories, to the child, are like the parables of the Master: they contain the seeds of truth, that will germinate and fructify in the child's mind, far better than the truth grown to its full stature, and embodied in maxims and precepts. Every teacher should be an excellent storyteller, so as to make the half hour each day given to story telling, a delightful one to the children. As the child gains experience, by contact and communing with his fellows, there comes a time, when the real should take the place of the fictitious, and all the child's love for fancy may be carried over and become more intensified, in his love for the real. Short, carefully selected, and well-told stories make a good beginning for the elementary study of history. It matters not whether these stories be taken from ancient or modern history. They should be brief, simple, well told. Tell the children the story and have them tell it back in their own language. Then let them write it, as I said in my talk upon language: this furnishes one of the best means of talking with the pencil

Parker, F. W. *Notes of talks on teaching at the Martha's Vineyard summer institute, July 17 to August 19,1882*. New York, NY: E.L. Kellogg & Co., 1882,

"I only wish life were this way. Most children live in crowded flats with tired, angry parents, their formative years filled with neglect and boredom. Besides this problem, their books are filled with too many difficult words and too many phonetic markings. It is no wonder the children sink into despair as soon as they open them. The books defeat them. Textbook companies have lost sight of a simple fact—that they are writing for children. Ironically, they hire superintendents to produce them. Most are men without any experience teaching young children. This means they cannot see things as the child does. So what do they do? They create texts filled with words covered with marks and crossed-out vowels in the hope that children will learn how to pronounce them. It is so scientific. So wasted. What they don't realize is that children will only read stories that interest them."

This conversation was easy for Rose to follow because it touched her life. She commented, "I have been listening very closely. You want everyone to go to school." Everyone smiled as they nodded slowly. "You also believe that all children can learn, as long as you separate the bright ones from the defective ones."

"You understand perfectly," Dewey said, trying to avoid being pedantic.

Staring at her water glass, Rose said, "This does not make sense to me."

"Mrs. Amoroso," Parker said, "are we being too extravagant?"

Rose replied, "Did you grow up in clean homes with mothers who read to you in their laps?"

"Yes," Emma said with a hint of irony. "We are bourgeois, inside and out."

Rose continued. "You have a plan to sort children as if they are wool fleeces. Who do you think will be sorted into the dustbin? Children who grow up in dirty rags and are tired from sleeping in crowded beds. You grew up like the children in Mr. Parker's story. It is a wonderful thing to be raised at home by a mother who loves you. Poor children do not have what your mothers gave you. They do not need sorting but uplifting."

Addams knew immediately that Rose was right. That was because she lived in Rose's world. Yet she felt the need to defend the promise of progress embedded in Dewey's thinking. She said, "Rose, you are right to speak about mothers. In fairness to John, it is too soon to know if his plan will work or fail."[18]

Rose did not back off. Instead, she said with certainty, "Oppression does not liberate. The success you want for children comes from mothers, as yours did. If you care about the education of the poor, find a way to keep their mothers at home."

A dark cloud passed over Dewey. "That's what Emma and Elizabeth are trying to do. My job is to make sure all children learn according to their mental powers. Properly trained teachers can do that. I am committed to this goal."

Rose continued. "Let me say another thing, Professor Dewey. Your parents wished you success, but they did not choose what you became. Will you give poor children the same choice, or will you tell them what to study or what they should become?"

Dewey had been thinking about training and education for some time. To him, trade education was immoral. Hearing this untaught woman connect education to democracy surprised him. He had never met an uneducated person act the part of a philosopher. He said politely, "Unfortunately, school boards set the ground rules for what is learned in schools. Many are pressured by businessmen to equip poor children for industry. They rejoice at schools funded by taxes to supply them with efficient workers."

Rose replied, "I hope you stop this because children who are told what to do end up unhappy. I bet Mr. Parker fought against this kind of arrangement too. Is that why he failed in Quincy?"

The question, political in nature, threw Dewey off track. He cleared his throat unsure of his answer. "Change happens slowly," he explained. "It takes powerful personalities and lots of moral arguments to clear the path."

Rose knew something about moral arguments. One of her favorite saints was an ordinary man who cleared many paths. "Have you ever heard of Saint Bosco?" she asked Dewey.

"Can't say that I have," he replied as he moved to the rear of his seat. "Please tell me about him."

Rose used the mysteries of the saints to inspire her. She sensed that Dewey would find the answer to the failure of the Quincy experiment in her simple story, so she spoke in her best English. "I must tell you one thing about him. Saint John Bosco was an Italian priest who dedicated his life to the education of poor boys. Despite their dirt, rags, and foul odor, he never lost sight of their sacredness. That is why he taught them with gentleness, not blows."

"Lord save us," Parker exclaimed. "The same for Pestallozi and Montessori. I told my teachers in Quincy that the greatest gift a teacher can give a child is kindness."

Dewey's voice rose slightly. "There is wisdom in your story, Mrs. Amoroso. I expect teachers to inspire children with love. However, it is dangerous to place emotion over results. Reforming schools will take more than benevolence."

6. John Dewey

Born in Burlington Vermont, Dewey (1859–1952) was an American philosopher, psychologist, and a major educational reformer for the twentieth century. He was a key figure in pragmatist philosophy, writing on a wide array of topics such as metaphysics, epistemology, aesthetics, logic, ethics, and social theory. He's also considered one of the pioneers of functional psychology, a philosophy of psychology that sees mental life as an active adaptation to a person's environment. Arguably, the overarching theme in his work had to do with an unwavering belief in democracy, whether it be in politics, in philosophical ideas, in the arts, in education. As a result, he thought schools and civil society were two critical areas that needed our attention and needed amlerioration. Reconstructing these, he thought, might move us closer to an ethical ideal where everyone could develop themselves, experiment, have a fully informed public opinion, communicate, and where politicians would be held accountable for the policies they adopted.

John Dewey at the University of Chicago in 1902

In His Own Words

"My Pedagogic Creed" (Excerpt)

We are told that the psychological definition of education is barren and formal - that it gives us only the idea of a development of all the mental powers without giving us any idea of the use to which these powers are put. On the other hand, it is urged that the social definition of education, as getting adjusted to civilization makes of it a forced and external process, and results in subordinating the freedom of the individual to a preconceived social and political status.

I believe each of these objections is true when urged against one side isolated from the other. In order to know what a power really is we must know what its end, use, or function is; and this we cannot know save as we conceive of the individual as active in social relationships. But, on the other hand, the only possible adjustment which we can give to the child under existing conditions, is that which arises through putting him in complete possession of all his powers. With the advent of democracy and modern industrial conditions, it is impossible to foretell definitely just what civilization will be twenty years from now.

Hence it is impossible to prepare the child for any precise set of conditions. To prepare him for the future life means to give him command of himself; it means so to train him that he will have the full and ready use of all his capacities; that his eye and ear and hand may be tools ready to command, that his judgment may be capable of grasping the conditions under which it has to work, and the executive forces be train to act economically and efficiently. It is impossible to reach this sort of adjustment save as constant regard is had to the individual's own powers, tastes, and interests—say, that is, as education is continually converted into psychological terms. In sum, I believe that the individual who is to be educated is a social individual and that society is an organic union of individuals. If we eliminate the social factor from the child we are left only with an abstraction; if we eliminate the individual factor from society, we are left only with an inert and lifeless mass. Education, therefore, must begin with a psychological insight into the child's capacities, interests, and habits. It must be controlled at every point by reference to these same considerations. These powers, interests, and habits must be continually interpreted - we must know what they mean. They must be translated into terms of their social equivalents - into terms of what they are capable of in the way of social service.

Dewey, J. "My Pedagogic Creed." *School Journal* 54 (Jan. 1897): 77–80.

Rose's shy demeanor gave way again. "On the train, Elizabeth asked me about Sicily. She listened to every word I said. She asked me more questions. Before I knew it, I learned things. I felt I could learn more. She cared about me, so I cared about myself."[19]

Hearing this, Dewey replied, "Stories are ennobling as long as they do not lead to sentimentalism."

Standing her ground, Rose ended the conversation, saying, "I just do not see how you can succeed. There is too much at stake. Bosses increase their profits when they take away the brains of the poor."

Art as Consciousness

The party ended at nine o'clock. Reitman, sipping his fourth glass of wine, offered to pay the bill. No one protested. Elizabeth, a bit tipsy herself, licked her fingers. She swung her house key playfully as she said good night to everyone. Addams, Parker, and Dewey returned to Dewey's townhouse, five miles away. Rose and Marina walked south with Emma and Reitman to their apartment.

The odor of the river reminded Marina of Lawrence. When they arrived, Reitman kneeled to open the front door of the coal stove. It took him about twenty minutes to get the parlor warmed up. Satisfied, he said, "I leave because I am weary."

Constrained by her corset, Marina replied, "I want to take off this coarse garment."

Reitman teased, "Do you mind if I help you?"

Marina answered, "Why waste your time looking at a woman who is fat as a pig?"

Rose opened her eyes wide, remembering the way Carmelo tempted her with banter.

George Bernard Shaw
Pygmalian (Act V)
1912

George Bernard Shaw (1856-1950) wrote this now classic play *Pygmalion* as a critique of the rigid class system in Britain and arguably as a way to champion women's indepdence. Henry Higgins, a professor of phonetics, "transforms" a poor Cockney flowergirl named Eliza Doolittle into a lady by teaching her how to speak the way the upperclass speaks. In the scene from which this quote is taken, one of the last scenes in the play, Eliza confronts Higgins with a comparison of how he treated her versus how his colleague Colonel Pickering treated her.

ELIZA: "You see, really and truly, apart from the things anyone can pick up (the dressing and the proper way of speaking, and so on), the difference between a lady and a flower girl is not how she behaves, but how she's treated. I shall always be a flower girl to Professor Higgins, because he always treats me as a flower girl, and always will; but I know I can be a lady to you, because you always treat me as a lady, and always will."

Marina returned in her nightgown without anything underneath. Emma was breathless. Unaware of the provocation, Rose asked, "What are our plans for tomorrow?"

"Elizabeth has arranged a breakfast meeting with one of her famous friends," Emma said.

"Is he handsome?" Marina asked.

"Well, he's a bit older than you, but he is very distinguished-looking. He is a much-admired writer."

"He must be high class to be a writer," Marina said as she rubbed her thighs with scented oil. She loved using that expression.

Emma took great pleasure at the spectacle of Marina's fullness. "He's very proletarian," she said in an off-hand manner. "He writes about the struggles of women. His characters come right off the streets of America."

Rose leaned forward and said, "Why does he want to meet us?"

"Speak for yourself," piped in Marina. "I want to know how he knows so much about women."

Emma waited for Marina to stop laughing. "Women know much more about women than you think."

Rose's face took on a pained expression. Alarmed, she covered Marina's shoulders with a blanket. "You must be chilled," she said with a look of censure.

Emma's eyes grew with longing for a night of love with a simple woman. She also sensed Rose's unshakable instincts. Turning to her, she said, "Remember you said something about wanting to meet a person who has lifted himself out of poverty? Dreiser's parents were poor Catholic immigrants."

Satisfied she had blocked Emma's will, Rose spoke frankly, "I have never talked to a writer before."

Emma replied with one of her straightforward answers. "Tell him that. I would be interested in his answer."

***

The next morning, the three friends took the streetcar as far as Forty-Second Street. Emma said, "I have a surprise. For five cents, we will travel under the streets of the city."

"How do we do that?" Marina blurted out.

"It is called a subway. Same as a train only it flies along in the darkness. It can injure your eyes, so do not look at the rows of white columns. And don't try to stick your head out of the window!"

"Do we sit in seats?" Rose asked.

"It depends on the time of day. There are hand straps for overcrowded times."

"How do we breathe down there?"

"There's plenty of fresh air. The stops are beautiful, decorated with exquisite mosaics. Each stop has a different motif. You will see rich oak seats and black iron gates."

Rose and Marina had not taken the Boston subway—the first in the country, built in 1897—so they did not know what Emma was talking about. How could a train travel under buildings? What kept the walls from caving in? They had to see this for themselves. They stepped into the darkness, holding onto Emma's arms. Many people were standing on the platform, silent in their own terror. The walls were clean, but advertising signs spoiled the effect. Rose was scared, but she tried not to show it. She jumped as she heard the rumbling come out of the blackness. Soon, the platform shook, and the light of the train became visible. She winced as the wheels screeched to a halt. The doors opened and out rushed scores of men and women as if possessed by demons. Those on the platform pushed their way into the car. The doors closed tightly, and the train pulled away from the station. Within seconds they were traveling so fast, the outside wall was a blur. Rose's heart burst as the train seemed to fly out of control over the tracks.

Most passengers were sitting with their eyes closed. They were a mix of men and women, with very few children in sight. Two shabbily dressed men, one in need of a shave and haircut, drifted in and out of Italian and English as they spoke about baseball. A few read books. The man next to Marina read a newspaper, whilst she peeked over his shoulder to see what he was reading. He turned around and said to her sarcastically "If you want, I will give you this paper. I wouldn't want you to strain your eyes."

7. Lewis Hine

1874–1940. Born in Oshkosh, Wisconsin, Hine used his camera to expose, in painful images, the social evils of the Industrial Revolution in the United States--he photographed the poverty of newly arrived immigrants and the factory life of working children. His images on their plight helped to bring about the passage of child-protection legislation in 1916.

Self Portrait of Lewis Hine, c. 1930

In His Own Words

"Social Photography; How the Camera May Help in the Social Uplift" (Excerpt)

Perhaps you are weary of child labor pictures. Well, so are the rest of us, but we propose to make you and the whole country so sick and tired of the whole business that when the time for action comes, child labor pictures will be records of the past.

Lewis W. Hine, "Social Photography; How the Camera May Help in the Social Uplift," *Proceedings of the National Conference of Charities and Correction at the Thirty-Sixth Annual Session held in the City of Buffalo, New York, June 9-16, 1909*, ed. Alexander Johnson (Fort Wayne, IN: Press of Fort Wayne, 1909): 357.

Note: The photos below, taken by Lewis Hines, are from the "National Child Labor Committee Collection" at the Library of Congress. Please see http://www.loc.gov/pictures/collection/nclc for more. There are about 5,100 photographic prints and 355 glass negatives along with the NCLC records. They were all given to the Library of Congress by Mrs. Gertrude Folks Zimand in 1954 who was then acting as the chief executive for the NCLC.

Child Laborer, Newberry, S.C. (1908)

Lewis Hine's caption: "A little spinner in the Mollohan Mills, Newberry, S.C. She was tending her 'sides' like a veteran, but after I took the photo, the overseer came up and said in an apologetic tone that was pathetic, 'She just happened in.' Then a moment later he repeated the information. The mills appear to be full of youngsters that 'just happened in,' or 'are helping a sister.' Dec. 3, 08. Witness Sara R. Hine. Location: Newberry, South Carolina"

Child Laborer, 1908

Child coal miners - drivers and mules in a Gary, W. VA. mine.

Lewis Hine's caption: "Drivers and Mules, Gary, W. Va., Mine, Where much of the mining and carrying is done by machinery. Location: Gary, West Virginia."

Caption: Child Coal Miners, 1908

138

Group of children in front of the Old Dominion Glass Co., Alexandra, VA., June 1911

Lewis Hine's caption: "Some of the youngsters on day shift (next week on night shift) at Old Dominion Glass Co., Alexandria, Va. I counted 7 white boys and several colored boys that seemed to be under 14 years old. The youngest ones would not give names, but the following are a few: Frank Ellmore, 913 Gibbon St., apparently ten or eleven. Been there three months. Dannie Powell, 307 Columbus St., Henry O'Donnell, 1923 Duke St. Leslie Mason, 912 Wilke St. Location: Alexandria, Virginia."

Group of Child Laborers, 1911

Family of Mrs. Wm. Fuqua, South Boston, VA, June 1911

Lewis Hine's caption: "Ebb-tide in the industry. Family of Mrs. Wm. Fuqua. On account of slack work in the cotton mill, her husband recently got work up-town. He is the only wage earner. Six in the family. The oldest girl is 14 years old now. She worked last year, but the lint affected her so much they had to take her out. Location: South Boston, Virginia."

Family of Laborers, 1911

African-American School at Anthoston, Kentucky, 1916

Lewis Hine's caption: "Colored School at Anthoston. Census 27, enrollment 12, attendance 7. Teacher expects 19 to be enrolled after work is over. 'Tobacco keeps them out and they are short of hands.' Ages of those present: 13 years = 1, 10 years = 2, 8 years = 2, 7 years = 1, 5 years = 1. Location: Henderson County, Kentucky."

African-American School, 1916

"That's quite all right," Marina said.

"So all right, don't be reading it with me. If you have not two cents to buy a paper for yourself, I am sorry for you. Some nerve. You wouldn't buy your own paper."

Two black-haired women got on at the next stop and sat opposite her.[20] One was slender with nice features but covered under a heavy layer of powder and rouge. Her eyebrows were tweezed to a thin tapering line, and she wore false eyelashes. She wore a black sport hat with a long feather and a plain black box coat. Her friend was short and plump with a slight moustache lightened with peroxide.

They sat down and began to talk about their dates the night before. "Yeah, I had some lousy time last night. I think he's a bore. Where do you think he took me? Yeah, we went to a Broadway show, but was that lousy.

"What was it about?"

"It was so stupid. I didn't even know what it was about myself. It was so dumb. All the time a man was in a tree. If that wasn't dumb, I don' know what is."

"Did he take you out to eat?"

"Sure, we ate. He said he wanted to go to Jimmy's to eat, just for the fun of it. I gave him fun. I'm wise to that baloney. We went to Chin and Lee's. After we ate, he took me home. Yeah, and he lives all the way in the Bronx. Yeah, I think he's boring. What do you think? He didn't even try to kiss me good night."

"It was your first time out."

"So what if it was the first time we went out? Maybe I would not have let him kiss me, but he could have tried."

"Did he ask you out again?"

"No, he didn't ask me for another date. I think he's confused. Say, what about you? Where did you go?"

Her friend replied, "Oh, we just went to the chinks and to the nickelodeon. Yikes, that Barrymore—can he kiss! He can put his shoes under my bed anytime. Saw *Little Rebel* too. That Biograph Girl—what's her name? Florence Lawrence?—was the girl. She looked so pretty. She has a round face. Did you ever notice? Unpleasantly, the way they push around in this train. I had to use my hatpin yesterday. Some wise guy had

140

hand trouble. They ought to have special trains for women. Somebody slit my girlfriend's coat last week with a razor blade or something. She didn't even know it was cut until she got off the train. They ought to catch the louse who does them things. I'm changin' at Utica, Rosalind. Will I see you tonight? Come over to my house. I'll let you do my nails. So long." She turned and pushed through the door.

Rose had just listened to the personal melodramas of two young working women at the social bottom of city life, distant from the bourgeois culture of her companions. Their words brought out the high stakes in contemporary America. Were they victims of a social hierarchy that cast them adrift in lies and blindness? On the other hand, did their vulgarity prove Hobb's point about democracy and freedom? Either way, Dewey and his colleagues faced a heroic struggle to rescue Americans from the free-for-all that was popular culture.

Florence Lawrence (1886-1938) in a Studio Portrait by Frank C. Bangs, c. 1908. A Canadian–American stage player who later became a film actress, Lawrence is often called the "First Movie Star." She was the leading lady in many silent films produced by The Biograph Company, and at the height of her fame in the 1910's was known simply as the "Biograph Girl." She was also the first actor to use her real name to advertise a film. Little Rebel was a 1911 short that took place during the Civil War.

Rose wondered how Emma felt about the folly they had just heard. Before she could ask, Emma turned to her and said, "The day the subway opened, Mrs. Vanderbilt came down to the platform with two of her servants. One set up a chair and the second a table. She sat impassively, watching people enjoy themselves. When she tired, she left unnoticed."

Rose realized that Emma's struggle was with those who abused power. Eliminate authority and purity would follow. Rose could not accept this premise because it negated Satan's malignity. Unfortunately, they were at the Fourth Street stop so there was no time to discuss this aspect of humanity. They exited and walked toward the light at the top of the stairs. They came out of the station, squinting and disoriented. For a second, Emma did not know uptown from downtown, west or east. Others looked as bewildered. She spotted a restaurant and said, "Follow me. I am going to treat you to a breakfast of eggs, ham, toast, fruit, coffee, and juice—all for twenty cents."

They went into a tiny shop on Thirteenth and Fifth near the hotel. The customers were well-dressed Americans. The help was Italian. A tall, handsome teenager came in from the street with his apron on and his hands in his pockets. He went over to the boss to find out what he was supposed to do. The boss pointed to the open grill in front of the counter. He pulled his hands out of his pockets, rubbed them across his face, and began to cook hash-brown potatoes. When he turned around to the counter, he saw Marina looking at him. He stared back, rubbing his arm. Marina turned to Emma and asked for a piece of paper and a pencil. Rose was busy looking at the menu, so she did not notice Marina writing a message to the handsome young boy behind the counter.

Just in case you cannot tell, I think you're swell.

She gestured to the small boy who sat beside the cash register and handed him the note. Her eyes told him what to do with it. He took it and handed it to his brother. The teenager could not read so with his back to Marina, he handed it back to the boy. The boy whispered, "The woman with the red lips likes you."

He told the boy to write her a note. "Tell her how much love I have for her." The boy did as he was told. Satisfied that a pastry roll was distracting the boss, he slipped the note to Marina. She read it and left for the bathroom. The teenager watched her as he put the order on the counter. Marina made gazers out of men with her black luminous hair and a full figure. He went back to meet her. Without saying a word, both embraced. Marina put her hands on his face and pressed. He straightened up. "What are you doing?" he asked impishly.

"Warming my hands." She smiled.

Just then, the boss yelled out, "Pino, Pino! Where are you?"

Pino opened his eyes and said to Marina, "You like me."

As he left, she pressed her hand against his abdomen and said, "Nothing of the sort."

Flynn and a male companion walked in arm in arm. Emma signaled to them and they came over to the table. She stood and hugged the gentleman and then turned to Rose. "Rose, it is my great pleasure to introduce you to Mr. Lewis Hine. Mr. Dreiser is on his way. Mr. Hine is a dear friend and a strong supporter of the Lawrence strike. His photographs have changed public attitudes and contributed to stricter child labor laws.[21] But wait—where is Marina?" As she spoke Marina stepped out of the bathroom and returned to the table. "Oh, Marina! There you are! This is Mr. Hine."

Marina looked back at Pino before she set her eyes on Hine. Distracted, she said, "Sir, you are indeed a handsome man. Emma tells me you are the most famous writer in New York."

Hine blushed, caught off guard by such a free-spirited and mischievous comment. "Thank you, Miss …"

"Maddoza," said Marina. She sat down next to him, and before he could correct her, she said, "I read a lot of magazines, Mr. Hine, but I am afraid I have not read your stories."

"I am a photographer," he said.

"Do you shoot models?"

"I am social photographer. My work is limited to—"

"If that is all you do, what is the point?" Marina asked abruptly.

"It is the only story worth telling," he said.

Taking pleasure in looking at Pino, Marina said to Hine, "Much of the world enjoys cash and lobster parties. I know this because that is what my bosses talk about. If you take more pictures of beautiful women by the moonlight, you will be rich."

"You need to read more than trashy magazines, Marina," Rose said.

"Are you afraid your wife will mock you, Mr. Hine, if you photograph beautiful women?" asked Marina, wondering what Mrs. Hine looked like.

"Not at all," he replied. "I believe that if people see the terrible working conditions children endure in factories and mills, officials will put an end to them. I believe that a greater public awareness will result in corrective social action. Factory owners profit greatly from child labor. That is why I despise this strike. They succeeded in getting the officials in Lawrence to halt any more trips."

"Why do the bosses let you in?" Marina asked. She wanted to know before she dismissed him.

"I trick them," Hine said with a chuckle. "Sometimes I claim to photograph machinery. One time I passed myself off as a Bible salesman."

Emma said, "Lewis has many enemies. So does Dreiser. Anyone who exposes corruption does. Dreiser's enemies mock him because he did not go to college."

Elizabeth said, "The educated cannot stand the thought of the lower classes doing something better than they can.[22] They don't bother Theo because he goes to the public library every day to read. He is educated in more ways than just the street. His education suits him but it is different than theirs. If I might say, it has served him well. His latest novel is—"

"Be truthful, Elizabeth," Hine offered, without sounding dogmatic. "His books did not always show up in bookstores."

"Obviously," Elizabeth said. "He has had to fight to get them published. His publisher thought *Carrie* was too scandalous and unfit for the public. He did not budge. He finally gave in but he did not promote it. Once out, he had to deal with fools like Comstock, who tried to ban it on moral grounds."

"Who is Comstock?" Marina asked.

"He is the head of the New York Society for the Suppression of Vice," Elizabeth said.

"As you might imagine," Hine said, "the book did not do well. He knew it was good so his failure sent him into a depression. Then he lost his job and ran out of money. Thank goodness his brother found him. He recovered and, with his support, he edits the *Delineator,* a very popular women's magazine. *Sister Carrie* was reissued. This time the critics loved it—said it was the best novel of American life."

"I didn't know writers had it so bad," said Marina.

Hine knew that Marina did not know what went into writing, but that did not bother him. He treated all foreigners with dignity and respect. "You are a very handsome woman with subtle thoughts," he told her. Hearing this patronization, the old man at the next table found it impossible to drink his coffee, so he left. Hine continued. "I appreciate your free spirit and sense of the future. I hope I have not been too frank with you."

Marina expressed her thanks but did not waver in love of melodrama. No do-gooders for her. She wanted to be entertained with love and photo reproductions of beautiful women in her copy of *Redbook*. Rose seemed irritated when she said, "I keep telling you to read about uplifting things, not bad characters. You will never advance reading good-for-nothing love stories."

Hine shrugged. "I beg to differ, Mrs. Amoroso. The police reported yesterday that they found a fifteen-year-old heiress from my hometown in Wisconsin working in our city. She had been reported lost. She had disguised herself and had come here to be with a waiter she had fallen in love with. This child had everything, but she gave it up for love. You know what? Americans love to read about love."

Rose responded didactically as she swallowed her lukewarm tea. "Why do writers write about indecent things?"

"Americans love excitement, Rose," Emma said rather glibly.

Elizabeth replied more pedantically, "Dreiser writes about brave people who face hardships. He fights for people who live in a dehumanized world."

Rose replied, "It is wrong to delight in the suffering of others."

Emma went on eating her toast as she said, "Rose, few Americans know how bad it is in this country. Novelists should follow Lewis's example. Use stories[23] to expose the ravages of capitalism. They have a social responsibility to do that."

It was approaching lunchtime. A tall German American of about 180 pounds walked in. It was Theodore Dreiser, the well-dressed cause célèbre of the artistic community in New York City. He had just returned from Europe, doing research for a book titled *A Traveler at Forty*.

Hine walked over to him, flashed a grin, and extended his hand. Both were Midwesterners, making it big in New York City. Dreiser said to the group, "I am impressed with Lewis's Pittsburgh work. He has captured the gap between mill workers and their comfortable bosses."

Despite his regal status, Marina was not afraid of him. "All this talk about factories is boring. I am on vacation," she said to him playfully.

Dreiser laughed, attracted to her lack of pretension. He replied, "Some of the time writing about injustice is a delight. Most of the time, it is very hard work. I prefer to eat, walk, travel, and dream."[24]

Marina gave him a soft look. "Me too. Life is too short to waste on work. So why do you write?"

Dreiser touched Marina's hand, saying in mock seriousness, "Because I am good at it. I can write a book every six months. I am in line to win the Nobel Prize in literature."

Marina giggled. "You must be rich."

Dreiser thought about money all the time. His fear was that there was not enough of it in writing. "Dandy chances to sell books in Europe," he replied.

Elizabeth and Emma sputtered in disbelief at what their champion of disenfranchisement had just said. H. L. Mencken, America's popular political commentator, believed that Dreiser was the only American novelist worth reading. "You can't be serious about charging after money, Theo," Emma retorted. "You seem to be suggesting that you write to move up the social ladder."

Dreiser shot back, "Writing is a game I will quit unless I enjoy a good income from it. I don't care two straws for American books. I prefer Balzac, Flaubert, Tolstoy, and H. G. Wells. I prefer to read history, architecture, and art. I am fascinated by European artistic merit. That is why I want to move to London."

Rose never heard the word dauntless used to describe someone, but she knew it applied to Dreiser. He had just shocked Emma and Elizabeth with an outrageous comment about his motives for writing. Rose knew instinctively, however, he was no different from anyone else who had grown up hungry. Unruffled by his candor, she asked him a question about his trip to Europe.

He smiled again. "I did not care for your noble village of Rome. There was nothing there. It is an eighth-rate city." Bowing his head slightly, he switched the topic. "Elizabeth tells me you are fearless."

8. Theodore Dreiser

Dreiser was a major American novelist (1871–1945) essayist, political writer, playwright, poet, journalist, and editor who battled against censorship and Victorian tastes. His subjects were working-class people striving for economic, emotional, and spiritual fulfillment Growing up Catholic and poor, his principle concern was about the stifling of the sexual appetite. *Sister Carrie* (1900), his first novel, dealt with sexuality, consumption, and class. Provincial and naive, Carrie becomes involved with Hurstwood, a respectable Chicago tavern manager twice her age who alienates himself from his family. Much of Dreiser's work came from his own experiences with poverty. In his own life, he had several affairs at once.

Theodore Dreiser, Published by John Lane Co, NY, 1917

In His Own Words

Sister Carrie, a novel (Excerpt)

When Carrie came Hurstwood had been waiting many minutes. His blood was warm; his nerves wrought up. He was anxious to see the woman who had stirred him so profoundly the night before.

"Here you are," he said, repressedly, feeling a spring in his limbs and an elation which was tragic in itself.

"Yes," said Carrie.

They walked on as if bound for some objective point, while Hurstwood drank in the radiance of her presence. The rustle of her pretty skirt was like music to him.

"Are you satisfied?" he asked, thinking of how well she did the night before.

"Are you?"

He tightened his fingers as he saw the smile she gave him.

"It was wonderful."

Carrie laughed ecstatically.

"That was one of the best things I've seen in a long time," he added.

He was dwelling on her attractiveness as he had felt it the evening before, and mingling it with the feeling her presence inspired now.

Carrie was dwelling in the atmosphere which this man created for her. Already she was enlivened and suffused with a glow. She felt his drawing toward her in every sound of his voice.

"Those were such nice flowers you sent me," she said, after a moment or two. "They were beautiful."

"Glad you liked them," he answered, simply.

He was thinking all the time that the subject of his desire was being delayed. He was anxious to turn the talk to his own feelings. All was ripe for it. His Carrie was beside him. He wanted to plunge in and expostulate with her, and yet he found himself fishing for words and feeling for a way.

"You got home all right," he said, gloomily, of a sudden, his tune modifying itself to one of self-commiseration.

"Yes," said Carrie, easily.

He looked at her steadily for a moment, slowing his pace and fixing her with his eye.

She felt the flood of feeling.

"How about me?" he asked.

This confused Carrie considerably, for she realized the flood- gates were open. She didn't know exactly what to answer. "I don't know," she answered.

He took his lower lip between his teeth for a moment, and then let it go. He stopped by the walk side and kicked the grass with his toe. He searched her face with a tender, appealing glance.

"Won't you come away from him?" he asked, intensely.

"I don't know," returned Carrie, still illogically drifting and finding nothing at which to catch.

As a matter of fact, she was in a most hopeless quandary. Here was a man whom she thoroughly liked, who exercised an influence over her, sufficient almost to delude her into the belief that she was possessed of a lively passion for him. She was still the victim of his keen eyes, his suave manners, his fine clothes. She looked and saw before her a man who was most gracious and sympathetic, who leaned toward her with a feeling that was a delight to observe. She could not resist the glow of his temperament, the light of his eye.

She could hardly keep from feeling what he felt.

And yet she was not without thoughts, which were disturbing. What did he know? What had Drouet told him? Was she a wife in his eyes, or what? Would he marry her? Even while he talked, and she softened, and her eyes were lighted with a tender glow, she was asking herself if Drouet had told him they were not married. There was never anything at all convincing about what Drouet said.

And yet she was not grieved at Hurstwood's love. No strain of bitterness was in it for her, whatever he knew. He was evidently sincere. His passion was real and warm. There was power in what he said. What should she do? She went on thinking this, answering vaguely, languishing affectionately, and altogether drifting, until she was on a borderless sea of speculation.

"Why don't you come away?" he said, tenderly. "I will arrange for you whatever--"

"Oh, don't," said Carrie.

"Don't what?" he asked. "What do you mean?"

There was a look of confusion and pain in her face. She was wondering why that miserable thought must be brought in. She was struck as by a blade with the miserable provision which was outside the pale of marriage.

He himself realized that it was a wretched thing to have dragged in. He wanted to weigh the effects of it, and yet he could not see. He went beating on, flushed by her presence, clearly awakened, intensely enlisted in his plan.

"Won't you come?" he said, beginning over and with a more reverent feeling. "You know I can't do without you–you know it–it can't go on this way–can it?"

"I know," said Carrie.

"I wouldn't ask if I—I wouldn't argue with you if I could help it. Look at me, Carrie. Put yourself in my place. You don't want to stay away from me, do you?"

She shook her head as if in deep thought. "Then why not settle the whole thing, once and for all?"

"I don't know," said Carrie.

"Don't know! Ah, Carrie, what makes you say that? Don't torment me. Be serious."

"I am," said Carrie, softly.

"You can't be, dearest, and say that. Not when you know how I love you."

Dreiser, T. *Sister Carrie*. New York: The Modern Library, 1917.

What better way to be mischievous than to shock an audience with contempt. That is what her brother did all the time. *Artists certainly are full of themselves*, she thought.

Dreiser's attention on Rose angered Marina. To change the subject, she asked him, "Are there women writers in America?"

"I am glad you asked," Dreiser said. "Edith Wharton comes to mind. She writes about the way the rich let social conventions control their behavior."

Marina did not understand, so she said, "Is she poor like you?"

Dreiser replied, "She comes from a wealthy family. But she thinks that the wealthy are emotionally petty."

Marina knew nothing about wealthy people—except that she wanted to be one. "I want you to write about me, Mr. Dreiser. I will tell you a thing or two about suffering. I am not putting you on."

"I am sure you are not, Miss Maddoza. But let me ask Rose a question." He faced Rose and asked politely, "Please tell me about yourself."

No one had ever asked Rose this question. "My English is not good," she said with her head upright.

"We understand you," Emma said.

Marina struck back. "She's spoken for, Mr. Dreiser. Ask me the same question."

Rose was not shy, just cautious. Her mother had always told her to keep her mouth shut. A few seconds passed as she thought about the pleasure she had talking with Elizabeth. Turning to Dreiser, she said, "What do you want to know?"

"Everything about coming to America," he said with a look of earnestness. He had spent his entire life seducing beautiful women. He could not separate his womanizing from his writing.

Proletarian Response

Smiling wistfully Rose looked out the window and recalls that memorable experience. I had awakened early to feed the animals one last time. My father came outside to smoke in the morning air. We did not say much to each other. His friend Stephano arrived with the wagon. We loaded our luggage and set out for Messina. When we reached the port, Sonny saw the steamship far out in the harbor. Stephano said that the only way to get to the ship was in a rowboat. I was scared to death because I had never been in one before. My father sensed my fear and so he made a joke. Turning to my mother, he said proudly, 'At last we will eat.'

"My mother cried. I told her that Pa meant no harm. An Immigrant Aid volunteer walked over to offer us encouragement and to warn us against men who would fill us with false promises but pay us nothing. Everyone in line carried a blanket strapped to their backs and a suitcase in each hand. My father said we looked like a gang of gypsies, and my mother cried again.

"As we entered the rowboats, women put white scarves on their heads. I did not. A dark-skinned man nudged me and said that there was still time to turn back. I ignored him and held on to my rosary beads. We made it to the steamer and were taken below. It smelled of body odor, vomit, and thick smoke. I ran to the open deck and stayed there until it was dark. Sonny made friends with young men his age. I returned to the top deck every day to watch the dancing and listen to the music. During the second week, we were hit by a storm. Everyone got sick. I suffered severe headaches. To comfort myself I looked at my farewell presents. I did not let them out of my sight the whole time. My mother gave me a handmade linen sheet and a bottle of medicine. My priest presented me with a certificate of character. My father's farewell gift was a handmade pair of white socks. I carried a picture of baby Nino in a tiny locket.

"The night before we entered New York Harbor, the captain came by to wish us luck. He told us that immigration officers would inspect first- and second-class passengers on board. Others would have to be checked on Ellis Island. He said that if people were rejected, he was obligated to carry them back to Sicily without cost. No one spoke a word.

"The next morning we climbed topside to view the Statue of Liberty. It was wondrous. I could not believe she was a woman. I compared myself to her, hoping I would be as strong as she was. I saw a bridge off to the right, but I was not interested in it. I could not take my eyes off the statue. She seemed to be telling me to be strong. I kept my eyes on her as the ship dropped anchor. Be strong, Rose. Courage will overcome hardship in this country. Sonny pointed to the platform below the statue and said, 'That is what I will do here, Rose. Cut stone and build statues.'"

"He's a joker like your father," Emma said, laughing.

Rose stared at the tablecloth for a moment, thinking how haughty it was of her father and brother to believe they could do anything. No wonder Sebastiano enjoyed America. All this freedom subtracted from his fear of sin and suffering. He needed a priest to correct him, to show him how to resist temptation.

Dreiser's soothing voice came back to her, so she continued her story. "I was hungry, but I could not eat a thing. The brown water made me sick, and the noise of the engines increased my headache. I swore I would never eat another thing again. We were ferried over to Ellis Island. We were scared because we did not know what was going to happen. The main building was made of red brick and white stones and had a red roof. I studied the towers, and I remember seeing smaller buildings off to the side."

Emma interrupted her again, "Where do you think the city dumped the dirt when they were digging the subway?"

Rose shrugged. "I don't know."

"On Ellis Island. They used it to enlarge the original sandbar."

"The ingenuity of Americans," barked Dreiser. "But let her continue."

"I tried to distract myself by looking at the people around me. I saw blue-eyed, blonde-haired women who had come off another steamer in the harbor. They were much taller than I was. I saw older children minding younger ones. I glanced over at three women who looked like they were my age. I knew they were sisters. They smiled like they were on an adventure. Their hair was extremely straight, red, and uncovered. They had few blemishes on their skin. One noticed me and smiled. She instinctively knew I was one of the few single women in line. We could not communicate so she pulled out a newspaper clipping and showed it to me. I could not read it, but later I learned they were on their way to be married to Americans. They were called 'picture brides' because they had sent their pictures to a marriage broker.

"I glanced over at the men to see how Sonny was doing. Most carried bags and wicker baskets. They were all dressed in black suits and hats. I saw a man with a small round black hat on his skull; he was holding an infant. I wondered if Sonny would have done the same. The languages were strange. Thank goodness the sun was out. It calmed me. A mother fed her baby while her daughters practiced English. I overheard the mother say to them, 'You will get ahead if you speak English.'

"We tried to find others who spoke our language. I heard someone yell out in Sicilian, 'Stop arguing or they will send you back.' Once we entered the main building, I began to shake. We walked in single file under a white brick ceiling to the black stone steps in the corner of the hall. 'Step up!' came the order. We obeyed, holding onto our luggage. Doctors stood at the top watching us. Anyone who panted or who had crooked limbs was pulled out of line. The rest of us were led into a penned area and told to sit. We waited until soldiers came to examine us. We stood and made a line. They examined our eyes with a metal instrument. Then they told us to open our blouses. Several women fainted. 'No!' a young woman cried.

"'We must check your heart and lungs,' came the reply. Many of us had never been to a doctor before. We cried as we bared ourselves in front of strangers. We had no choice. If we did not cooperate, we would have been sent back to the boat. I prayed to the Blessed Virgin as the doctor touched me. I dressed and moved to another section of the great hall to wait. I sat for hours, listening for my name. It was difficult because the Americans mispronounced our names, and their voices echoed off the walls. When I heard Bosco, I jumped up.

"The officer at the desk asked me what country I came from and if I was married. I told him Sicily and shook my head no. He looked at me for a long time and asked me if I'd come with my father. He also asked me what kind of work I did. I did not understand his English so I did not know what to say. He called over a woman and whispered something to her. She looked at me and then spoke in Italian. I told her that I could sew and knit. She told the man I was a 'servant.' She asked me if I could read. I said yes. Then she asked me where I was going and how much money I had. I told the whole truth; I had one dollar, and I was going to my uncle's house in Middletown. She and the officer looked unkindly on me. They called over a third person who handed me a piece of paper and asked me to draw a diamond shape.[25] I did this well and so he said to count backwards from twenty. The woman told me to count in Italian so I did, and she nodded. They still were displeased, and I was near tears. 'What is wrong?' I asked her.

"'The officer does not like it when a young woman comes to America unescorted. He thinks you might become a prostitute.' I blushed. First they'd forced me to undress, and now they called me a prostitute.[26] I wanted to walk back to the ship, but I glimpsed the statue through the window. *Have courage*, I reminded myself. I calmed down and reached inside my blouse for my letter of character. I opened it deliberately and, in my best Italian, read it aloud.

May 13, 1905

Dear sir,

There is no finer woman than Rose Bosco. She is intelligent, hardworking, and saintly. She comes from a respected family and is a devoted Catholic. Her father has

instructed her to remain chaste. I have complete confidence
in her character and in her sound mind.

Sincerely,

Fr. Antonio Beligua

"The officer asked me for the letter, but I held it. A tear dropped on his hand as he grabbed it from me. He studied it for a long minute. Finally, he waved me through. I glanced over to the next line. A young woman was quivering. She was Sicilian too but much younger than me. She was very beautiful. Such a delicate chin. Apparently, the officer had failed her because she was crying for her father. I rushed over to comfort her. She told me she had come alone without money to work as a servant. The woman from the Immigrant Aid Society came over as well. She spoke gently to the girl. The poor thing did not understand Italian. I told her she would be safe. This made her cry even more. The officer was not rude but clearly was impatient. He said he would not allow her to leave Ellis Island without money or an escort. She cried louder. Another women came over to offer assistance. She wore a Red Cross band and told us that she would provide money and an escort for her. She added that the girl would have to sleep in the dorm until the arrangements could be made. I translated the message into Sicilian. The girl pulled at her long hair and, weeping, followed the guard to the rear stairs.

"I walked downstairs to wait for Sonny. He ran to me, waving his admittance card. We exchanged our money for American currency and then purchased train tickets for the trip to Middletown. Sonny bought a big package of sandwiches, bread and cheese, oranges and bananas, and pie for a dollar. When no one was looking, he walked over to a wall. He wanted to write a swear word but didn't know how. I boxed him against his head, but he didn't care. A barge carried us to New York. The place was swarming with baggage helpers, men trying to lead us to boarding homes, and relatives. I didn't pay any attention."

Scientific Racism

Hine said quietly, "I want to assure you, Rose, that your story is of great importance to me. I am especially angered by the treatment of the young girl who was refused entry.[27] One year before you landed at Ellis Island, I went there to photograph the immigrants. I wanted to show people the things that had to be corrected and those that had to be appreciated. There is so much hate in the country against immigrants. My wife convinced me that my pictures would be of great importance. I promised to portray immigrants with dignity and respect. I set up my camera on a tripod and posed many people using gestures. Your story is in my pictures."

Marina was amused. "Rose, a prostitute? How funny. To be a prostitute you have to have sex on your mind. That is what I think. I would not want to be one, but I would not mind being a mistress. What do you think, Mr. Dreiser? I would much rather pleasure myself than be a baby maker. At least a mistress chooses what she wants to do with her body. A wife is a slave to her husband."

Elizabeth smiled as she nodded to Marina. "You have a point. Last week the president of the University of California warned the women on campus not to have the same expectations as men. His point? A woman's role in life is marriage and motherhood."

Rose said, "I am not a slave to my husband. To call me one is a bit extreme."

Although Dreiser had not shown any intellectual curiosity about slavery in his writings, he had no trouble turning the conversation to America's peculiar institution. Over the course of four hundred years, millions of Africans were involuntary immigrants to the United States. He and his breakfast companions were less than two generations removed from the manor house and the slave cottage. Implusively, Dreiser remarked, "I heard rumors that there is a real slave market in the Bronx. According to hearsay, rich white women force poor Negro women to work for them for a few pennies a day.[28]

"I have always been fascinated with exploitation. I heard about the same rumors and wanted to find out for myself, so early one morning I

155

walked up to North 167 Street to do some investigating. I found what I was looking for. Seated on crates and boxes were a dejected gathering of Negro women of various ages and descriptions—youths of seventeen and elderly women of maybe seventy. These women were scantily attired, some still wearing summer clothing. The November wind swept and whistled through them, and they ducked their heads and tried to huddle within themselves. Although properly clothed, I suffered from the bitter cold that made me shift from foot to foot. Immediately, my thoughts strayed to twenty or more unfortunate women who were partly clothed, some with cutout men's shoes.

"A woman with a gold tooth smiled and invited me to share her box. Her face bore cuts over both eyes and the corner of her mouth. She appeared to be as broad as she was tall, but despite all this her face bore a kindly expression. She began to relate her futile struggle of life from past to present into my receptive ears. Her name was Minnie. Minnie was born in the tidewater section of Virginia near Norfolk, a seaport town, in 1885. Her father was a black sailor—brawny of arm and smooth of tongue, or so her mother told her. I interrupted Minnie to question the whereabouts of her father. She stated that he had gone down to sea with his ship. She had been yanked out of school in the third grade at the age of fourteen in order to take her ailing mother's job. Her mother died in a few days.

"I gathered that she had been repeatedly fired from various positions due to lack of experience and youth. She was sixteen but did not have enough endurance and muscle for fifteen to eighteen hours of strenuous laundry and housework. She decided to take a fling at marriage. She married a hard-drinking sailor thrice her age, who gave her fifty dollars for a wedding present and told her to get some pretty clothes for herself.

"Unaccustomed to such a large amount of money, Minnie decided to save it. The next night, her husband returned home, roaring drunk and demanded the money. When she timidly took the roll from under the pillow and peeled off the requested amount, he attacked her insanely, cutting both her eyes and her mouth, knocking out her front teeth and taking all of the money. He stumbled and disappeared into the night. She never saw him again.

"During the next twelve years, Minnie worked steadier, became adjusted to conditions and was now a squat, muscular woman whose endurance was beyond the average, and she could now work unlimited hours without audible protest. At this period, she'd replaced her front teeth with gold ones. 'The scars will be with me until my dying day,' she told me.

"A few years ago, having saved twenty dollars, she decided to migrate to New York. She arrived with about six dollars and paid four for a room, leaving two dollars, and though she was very hungry, she was afraid to spend money for food that night. Early the next morning, Minnie went to an employment agency. They had jobs that paid forty dollars a month. She jumped for joy because that was more money than she could make in Norfolk in two months! This was New York. The employment agent signed her up and then asked her for four dollars.

"When Minnie asked why, the owner said she ran the agency for money, not her health. Minnie said that she had only two dollars but would provide the rest after she began to work. The owner tore up the slip, laughing. Minnie tried agency after agency, but the results were the same. They wanted their money up front. She could not get day or part-time work because the agents had special cliques to whom these choice jobs went. It was rank folly for any outsider to think of getting one of these jobs.

"After many days of trying, with rent due and money gone, a sympathetic girl in one of the agencies told her to stand on one of the corners in the Bronx. Women would come to hire her, she was promised. Minnie paused in her story, squinted her tired eyes, and said that she hated the people she worked for. She said it something like this: 'They are mean, deceitful, but whut I'm gonna do? Ah got to live, got to have a place.'

"A wizened little woman, with aquiline nose, thick glasses, and three big diamonds passed down the line, critically looking at the girls. When she reached Millie, she stopped peering and asked her if she would work hard washing windows from the outside. Minnie told her she could do anything anywhere. The woman offered her twenty-five cents an hour. Minnie wanted thirty-five, but the woman said she could get the young girls for fifteen cents and old women for ten cents. She motioned toward the others who were eagerly crowding around. One

157

girl said, 'I'll go for fifteen cents.' Another one said the same thing. Minnie shot back, 'They can't do the work, but I can.' The old woman finally gave her thirty cents."

"I know women who get beat if they ask their husbands for a few pennies," Marina said. "Minnie is no worse than I am. I work for pennies too. So why are you crying for her and not me?"

"Have you Negroes in your country?" Dreiser asked.

Marina tucked in her blouse and flattened the menu on the table. "No," she said. "But you sure got them here. Black as coal. The ones in Lawrence are a lot lighter. Same kinky hair though. What a bad odor."

"I didn't know you associated with them," Rose said to Marina.

"I don't. My boss, Mr. Doughtery, lives near a whole tribe of them. He told me that their kids make noise in the street and leave a mess under his window. He wants to put up a wall to keep them on their own side of the street."

"Is he serious?" Rose said.

"Sure. He wants the city to seal off the street. Says that is the only way

> W. E. B. Du Bois
> *The Souls of Black Folk: Essays and Sketches*
> 1903
>
> William Edward Burghardt Du Bois (1868-1963), was born in Great Barrington, Massachusetts and became the first African-American to earn a doctorate from Harvard. He then became a professor of history, sociology, and economics at Atlanta University. Du Bois fought for *full* civil rights for African-Americans and thought this could be brought about by the African-American intellectual elite. In 1964, a year after he passed, the U.S. Civil Rights Act, embodying many of the reforms he had fought for all his life, was finally passed. This collection of essays, *The Souls of Black Folk*, from which this excerpt comes, is not only a classic of American literature, but it's a pioneering work in the history of sociology, and of course a linchpin in African-American history. The quote below comes from its first chapter. Du Bois begins what might be called *the* intellectual manisfesto of the black American with a bang: the curse and gift of every black American is to feel marginalized on the one hand, but through the bigotry, hatred, slavery, and suffering he or she experiences, earns a strength of character no average white American can know.

to keep out the noise and garbage," Marina said.

"Seems vulgar to me," said Rose

"You mean Mr. Doughtery? He's not the bad one. He dresses in a clean shirt every day. He obeys the law. The affected are the bad ones," Marina said.

Hine looked at Marina dismayed as he said, "They did not volunteer to be here, Marina. Yet we continue to ill treat them. Millie's story makes that very clear."

After the Egyptian and the Indian, the Greek and Roman, the Teuton and Mongolian, the Negro is a sort of seventh son, born with a veil, and gifted with second-sight in this American world--a world which yields him no true self-consciousness, but only lets him see himself through the revelation of the other world. It is a peculiar sensation, this double consciousness, this sense of always looking at one's self through the eyes of others, of measuring one's soul by the tape of a world that looks on in amused contempt and pity. One ever feels his two-ness,—an American, a Negro; two souls, two thoughts, two unreconciled strivings; two warring ideals in one dark body, whose dogged strength alone keeps it from being torn asunder.

"That's your opinion," Marina said. "Mr. Doughtery says that slaves were happy and well fed. Lincoln freed them and let them take over the government. What did they do? They took their shoes off and put them on their desks, they drank liquor too. They even tried to rape every white woman they could find."

Filled with suspicion, Emma said, "That's a twisted story if I ever heard one. Where'd he get it?"

I don't know said Marina, but. "I read they're going to make a movie of it. Something has to be done about these sex-crazed minorities. I saw a picture of the heavyweight champion of the world. Black as sin, holding a white woman in his arms."[29]

Elizabeth knew she couldn't tell Marina anything, so she sniped, "No need to worry, Marina. The Department of Education in New York routinely transfers black children to schools for the retarded."

Dreiser had more information to share. "Let me offer you another side of the black problem."

Marina was getting restless with all this education. "Don't bother," she said clumsily.

Rose said, "Let him speak."

Elizabeth looked up, remembering Rose's spat with Mrs. Hutchinson.

"Many of the early people in America intermarried," Dreiser began. "I am talking about escaped slaves, white servants, and Indians. A whole tribe of mixed people lived out in Ohio. They got started when a group of runaway slaves and white serfs fled from their masters. They married with Indians and called themselves the Ben Ishmael tribe.[30] They followed the old ways, hunting and fishing and drinking no alcohol. Every winter they returned to their original settlement, where a village had grown.

"Eventually the government opened the territory to settlement, and the whites arrived. Around the Ishmael village, a town began to spring up, called Cincinnati. Soon it was a big city. The Ishmael village was still there, but it was surrounded by white civilization. Now it is a slum. The tribe never tried to adapt to the white ways. They did not bother with property. Everything was owned in common. They earned money by picking up and disposing trash ashes and junk for a fee.

"The whites considered them dirty, dishonorable outcasts who lacked honesty. That's because they flaunted powerful taboos against lasciviousness, savagery, and shiftlessness. If allowed to mix, the thinking went, the white race would be degraded. This fear of intermarriage with minorities and certain European ethnic groups was even shared by President Roosevelt. Politicians and others turned to science for answers. They were told that the white race was superior to others. 'We know,' came the reply. 'We want to

---

Richard C. Phillips with Watson Smith "The Negro of the Congo, West Africa." In *The Year-Book of Facts in Science and the Arts for 1875*.

Under the "Anthropology" section of this "record of scientific progress" is listed the following "scientific fact," which apparently had been collected in 1874.

The Negro is very averse to work, and takes little thought for the future, has little love or hate, is not revengeful, as that would entail trouble or expense, lives unto himself alone. Crafty, cunning, a born swindler, often a confessed rogue, avaricious yet lazy, he generally attaches himself to some one of importance, and does his bidding like a stray cur who follows you home, and of which you take charge. This is not the individual, but the national character.

know how to prevent intermarrying. Since this tribe is biologically degenerate, they must not be allowed to reproduce.' The answer came: 'Castrate them. While you are at it, sterilize chronic offenders, the feeble-minded and sick undesirables. The science of eugenics demands it.'

"The Indiana Legislature agreed and passed a compulsory sterilization law called the Indiana Indian Plan. Prisons performed the operation regularly. The Ben Ishmael was targeted, and their numbers dwindled. The extermination of whole ethnic groups deemed inferior and obnoxious became common. We have a professor here at Columbia who has argued that eugenics should shape our social policies. He is one of the main forces behind the testing that Rose described at Ellis Island. His recommendation is to isolate and expel immigrants with mental deficits."

Rose looked at Elizabeth. There was something in her glance that made Elizabeth drop her eyes. "I have heard about this man before. His thinking is dangerous," Rose said.

"We are in a turmoil, Rose," Elizabeth responded. "Scientists condemn superstition but perpetuate racist ideas with their tests. Writers fight over the purpose of art, unaware that most Americans do not even know how to read and write. Legislators pass laws to protect property but do nothing to safeguard us from exploitation and suffering. Taxpayers support schools but do not send their children to them. We are blind to our folly."

"That is because there is too much freedom in America," Rose said.

"No! No!" said Emma. "It is just the opposite. We are trapped in a web of hypocrisy spun by John Calvin and his adherents.[31] Have you ever wondered why so many women in reform schools are prostitutes? We assume that they are spiritually weak misfits, unable to resist temptation. We punish them. Then we reeducate them with Bible verses. How characteristic of a religious system that believes in punishment. Having a respectable job is what they need."

Hine didn't wait long to jump in. "That is where the artist comes in. We have an obligation to expose this type of immorality."

Rose pushed down on the comb in her full head of hair as she said, "Americans want to test children too much. The child on the train was lifeless when she talked about school. She came to life when she told us about her writing with her friend."

Deepening Culture

Impatient with the conversation, Marina said, "The cook told me about a matinee. Can we go to it?"

"Wonderful. I like that idea," said Emma as she smiled at Rose.

Hine paid the bill, and the group left the restaurant through the newly shined brass door. The theater district was a fifteen-minute walk from the restaurant. As they entered the area, Marina noticed a crowd milling around a car. She cried out, "Goodness! It's Caruso!"

"What is he doing here?" asked Elizabeth incredulously.

Dreiser said, "He sings at the Met, but I don't know why he's here."

"I know why," said Marina. "He does not forget us because he is one of us. Look at him—short and stocky with that clown's face. If he wasn't such a good singer, he'd be working next to me at the mill."

"I thought opera singers had to have enough money to pay for years of lessons," Emma said.

Marina countered, "Not when you are a natural. He has already played the great parts in *Aida*, *Faust*, *Carmen*, *Tosca*, and *La Boheme*, and he is not even thirty. A tenor's voice does not mature until at least age forty." Marina knew these things because her brother idolized Caruso. He had shared the latest news about him every night at supper.

Hine turned to the group. "There is another important person going into the theater—the wife of the great Petrosino, New York City's most famous cop. He fought against the Black Hand."

"Black Hand?" everyone asked in unison.

"A bunch of Italian criminals who extort money from Italian immigrants," Hine explained. "They come to your store and tell you that unless you pay, they will blow it up. Petrosino founded the Bomb Squad and recruited young Italian Americans to work with him as cops. They arrested thousands of members of the Black Hand. The government deported hundreds. He cut crime against Italian Americans by more than half."

"Italian policemen? Can we meet them?" Marina asked.

"I'm afraid not. Petrosino has been dead for about three years. He was shot dead in Palmero. He had gone there to gather information about the Black Hand organization. They flew the body back to New

York for burial. Two hundred thousand people showed up for his funeral. The procession lasted five and a half hours."

As they talked, Hine walked over to an usher to ask him why so many people were in line.

"Everyone has come to hear the young Rosa Ponselle sing," the usher answered. "She was born in Queens. She's a natural—no voice training."

Hine went back to the group and told them about the young soprano. The group agreed to go in to listen to her.

Two actors walked out on the stage and started talking about beaches and bathhouses. It was a farcical comedy called *The Life Saver & Bathing Girl*. The lifeguard had taken a correspondence course in lifesaving. The audience roared when he told the swimmer it was against the law to go in without anything on.

When the comedy ended, a young beautiful girl, no more than fifteen, walked onto the stage. All eyes were on her. She reminded Rose of the beautiful Sicilian she'd tried to help on Ellis Island. The crowd was ecstatic. Caruso jumped on the stage and said to her in Italian, "You are simply the best singer I have ever heard. With your emotionalism and your good looks, you will no doubt become opera's next diva. I insist that you come with me to the Met to sing beside me."

The audience roared. Caruso burst into a rendition of "Won't You Be My Bride?" Men cried. A young American fainted in his seat. Rose laughed, clapped, and even hugged Emma. She was a witness to Italian genius, and it filled her with pride.[32] Here stood Caruso and this angelic singer. Outside. Rose could recognize her architecture, and there also were famous police officers and shop owners who spoke her language. Even Maria Montessori's voice could be heard. This wonderful country had given her opportunity. She could become a citizen and participate in government. She could improve her English or teach others to knit. She could go to the library to read. She could send her children to school at no cost and even to college. They could become politicians or writers, even teachers [see Figure 3]. She could do all these things because Americans like Jane and Elizabeth and Emma cared about her success.

***

When the applause ended, Elizabeth suggested that they go over to her apartment to rest and prepare for Emma's speech. Hine declined, saying he needed to be home for supper. Dreiser asked Marina to accompany him to supper over on Broadway. Emma and Elizabeth were not surprised by his flirtation. They knew of his penchant for chorus girls, not intellectual women.

On the way, Dreiser and Marina stopped at his apartment for pink tea and chocolate bonbons. "There is something common between us, Miss Maddoza," Dreiser said as he glanced at her.

Nodding to the beat of her heart, she asked, "What might that be?"

"We both know what we want," he said, laughing gently.

Marina placed her hands on his. "I have spent too much time alone in my room, standing by the window. I am not tall or thin like American women. My breasts are not small or hard." Clutching his hands tightly, she said, "But I am a woman as real as anyone you have had. I want to hear your stories as we lie beneath the covers."

These words excited Dreiser. He put his lips to her ear. "I have a photographer friend who publishes his work in the most popular magazine in the city. Would you mind posing for him?"

"Of course not! Why do you ask?"

"I thought Italian girls were modest. You are not a streetwalker."

"In my village, the priest was everything. In America, he is nothing. I met a young girl on the train who turned away the lust of a rich man. The priest did not want to forgive her. He knows nothing about a woman's needs."

The church bells began to toll six o'clock. Marina wanted to talk with Rose, so she telephoned her. "Rose, Mr. Dreiser is going to find me work in the city."

"You speak like a madwoman," said Rose, resolved to take Marina's fantasies out of her head.

Marina did not hear her. "He is not dimwitted with grease on his neck and bad teeth. He is a gentleman who wants to help me."

"Where are you?"

"I am … at his office," Marina said, a blush creeping onto her face. "I told him secret things. He wants to smother me with love letters and flowers."

"Elizabeth told me he's married."

"I am not looking for a husband. I hate cooking and taking care of kids. I want to live in a lovely house in the city with plenty of servants. I do not see myself as an old woman with an old man. I want to be told, 'Get packed for Panama.'"

"He will throw you in the trash."

Marina would not accept Rose's reproach. With her present state of mind, she feared no abandonment from Dreiser. "I will not be lonely anymore," she said.

"What does that mean?" Rose said, feeling for the first time Marina's determination to end her solitude.

"Let me tell you what I don't want. I do not want to feel the ice of winter ever again. I do not want to work under the belts of the machines. I do not want to marry someone who will stare at me like a corpse."

"Think about what you are saying," Rose said. She was convinced that something bad was going to happen to Marina in the city.

For the first time in her friendship with Rose, Marina raised her voice. "I want to hear men tell me I am fit for pearls."

Freedom and Obligation

Rose and Elizabeth decided to go to Emma's speech early. Rose was shocked to see so many police standing guard. The stage was set with flowers. Men crowded the room and sang songs. A few women, mostly Italians, were in the audience with their husbands. Rose sat alone, overcome with emotion. She was as strong as any man in this hall.

Emma strode to the front of the stage. A chant began. Rose listened intently as Emma spoke about the strike. Emma caught sight of her. Rose was the only woman who looked interested in her words. When it was over, Emma signaled to her. "Meet me off the stage."

Rose looked at Elizabeth for counsel. "Go ahead. Emma probably wants to introduce you to someone. I am off to dinner with a few friends. I will see you tomorrow."

Rose walked past the crowd and waited for Emma. A score of men and women milled around, waiting for their turn to speak with her, looking like excited children. Emma was radiant in her brown suit.

Rose was overwhelmed by Emma's confidence. Every word she spoke mattered. Emma finished shaking hands with the well-wishers.

"Rose," Emma said, empathetically, "you remind me of myself when I was your age. Let's go to supper. Have you ever eaten a steak?"

"No, I confess that I haven't," Rose admitted.

"Let this be the first time. Men love red meat, so why can't we? We can eat like them and still humor them. I want you by my side when we walk into the café."

Rose had never been to a restaurant at night. It did not matter; she felt alive, so she accepted Emma's invitation. They walked out of the hall together, linking arms. "I enjoyed your story about Ellis Island, Rose. Tell me more about yourself."

"I am a seamstress."

"You understand English very well. What was your favorite part of tonight's address?"

"I liked your ideas about the bosses muttering to themselves about time and seasons. No person deserves to crawl to them on their knees. You calmed me against their conceit."

"Freedom and dignity are universal traits. But tell me about your family. Are they affectionate?"

Upon arrival at the café, Rose stared at the waiters in their long white aprons and clipped mustaches as they sang to the customers. She remembered her husband talking about a young Jewish street singer whose eyes watered when he sang Italian melodies for pennies. "I have a husband who admires you. A brother in Egypt. A sister in Connecticut, and a womanizer for a brother."

Emma laughed at Rose's animation when she spoke about Sebastiano over drinks. It was almost as if she had forgotten her precautions. Emma whispered with curiosity as she raised a glass of black beer to her mouth. "Do you love your husband?"

Rose closed the door before Emma had wiped the foam from her lip. "I have no other."

Staring, Emma said, "My first love was impotent. He lay in bed on our wedding night, quivering. Do you know what I am talking about?" Rose's eyes shone with a sense of sin as Emma continued. "He could not enter me. We went to the doctor. but he could not help. I was disappointed. I had looked forward to lovemaking. I have since found other lovers. I make love when I want to. I am fond of the pleasure of an embrace."

Rose replied, dark and straight, "I do not need a man to make me happy."

Emma could see that Rose was becoming distant, so she changed the subject. "Tell me something else. Do you read the daily newspaper?"

"I read the Italian and English papers at the library."

"It is no wonder that your English is good," Emma replied. She watched as the police captain and his mistress with the dark face and long hair sat next to them. The café was filling with people who had lined up on the street. "What do you do after work?"

"I crochet, and I attend mass. Monday, I go to class. Tuesday, I shop. I do piece work the other nights. On Saturday, I work until three o'clock and then do my laundry. Sundays, I go to church. Sometimes, I go to the recitals."

"What do you do in class?"

"Learn about the Constitution of the United States of America. One time the teacher spoke about you. She said that you were mocking this country. She called you a traitor."

9. Emma Goldman

1869–1940. Emma Goldman was an anarchist known for her radical libertarian and feminist writing and speeches. She was born to a Jewish family in Lithuania, where her family ran a small inn. She immigrated to the United States at sixteen. The hanging of four anarchists after the Haymarket Riot drew her to the anarchist movement, and at age twenty she decided to become a revolutionary. She was deported to Russia in 1917 for conspiring to obstruct the draft.

Emma Goldman, c. 1911. Cropped from the original Library of Congress version.

In Her Own Words[33]

Living My Life: Volume One, her autobiography (Excerpts)

On Anarchy

"You have convicted me, you may pass sentence of imprisonment upon me, but I tell you that I hate your laws; that I hate your 'order,' for I know but one 'order'--it is the highest potency of order--Anarchy."

On The Power of Ideas

I ha[ve] long since become convinced that the modern drama is a fruitful disseminator of new ideas. My first experience in that regard was in 1897, when I had talked to a group of miners on George Bernard Shaw's plays. Their eyes, deep-sunken, looked dull at first, but as I continued speaking, they began glowing with understanding of the social significance of Shaw's works. My well-dressed audience in the luxurious ballroom of the Brown Palace Hotel reacted in the same manner as the miners had. They, too, saw themselves reflected in the dramatic mirror.

On Elizabeth Gurley Flynn

I had known and admired Elizabeth since I had first heard her, years before, at an open-air gathering. She could not have been more than fourteen years of age at the time, with a beautiful face and figure and a voice vibrant with earnestness. She made a strong impression on me. Later I used to see her in the company of her father at my lectures. She was a fascinating picture with her black hair, large blue eyes, and lovely complexion. I often found it hard to take my eyes off her, sitting in the front row at my meetings.

Since she had returned to New York we were often thrown together, in meetings and in more intimate ways. Elizabeth was not an anarchist, but neither was she fanatical or antagonistic, as were some of her comrades who had emerged from the Socialist Labor Party. She was accepted in our circles as one of our own, and I loved her as a friend.

Goldman, E. *Living My Life: Volume One*. New York: Alfred A Knopf, 1931.

"Did she call me an anarchist?" Emma asked, leaning on the table.

The aroma of rich coffee transported Rose back to Middletown. When Carmelo came out of the darkness, Rose's coffee opened his eyes to the morning light. Several seconds passed before she responded to Emma's question. "A bomb-thrower. She said you killed President McKinley."

"Did you believe her?"

"No."

"What do you think an anarchist is?"

Rose was convinced of Emma's interest, so she elaborated. "I listened closely to what you said tonight. You said that the poor suffer needlessly under any form of government. You feel laws protect the strong at the expense of the weak. You believe that the rich use authority to scorn the poor."

"Do you agree?"

"In Sicily we have no government, no police. People steal from my father. In America, we have laws, but the poor still suffer. Suffering is our lot."

Touched by Rose's solemnity, Emma grew serious. "That is not what I believe. There is no proof that suffering cannot be thrown aside. Property turns us into criminals. If we can remove this vice, we will be a lot happier."

Rose was not ready to throw away rules. She reminded Emma of recent crimes in Lawrence. "Marina saw bands of looters destroying machinery. They seemed to want revenge for years of oppression."

Emma replied, "They were taking back what had been stolen from them."

"I don't understand," Rose said, her eyes down. Her father had not stolen from anyone, yet thieves stole from him. The mingling of well-dressed Americans with unwashed, ill-mannered, drunken laborers in this restaurant also confused her. In Sicily, privileged people had not grown up tending goats or farming corn. Likewise, in America, the bourgeoisie did not live in her neighborhood or send their children to the public schools. *Perhaps superiority is overrated*, she thought. *Emma is not stuffy, distant, or competitive. She found time to be with me because she is a fighter on behalf of the underprivileged.*

Emma continued. "Since my earliest recollection of my youth in Russia, I have rebelled against authority in every form. I could never bear witness to harshness, even if I was outraged over the official brutality practiced on the peasants in our neighborhood. I wept bitter tears when the young men were conscripted into the army and torn from homes and hearths. I resented the treatment of our servants, who did the hardest work yet had to put up with wretched sleeping quarters and the leavings from our table. I was indignant when I discovered that love between young people of Jewish and Gentile origin was considered the crime of crimes, and the birth of an illegitimate child was the most depraved immorality.

"On coming to America, I had the same hopes as have most European immigrants and the same disillusionment, though the latter affected me more keenly and more deeply. The immigrant without money and without connections is not permitted to cherish the comforting illusion that America is a benevolent uncle who assumes a tender and impartial guardianship of nephews and nieces. I soon learned that in a republic, there are myriad ways by which the strong, the cunning, and the rich can seize power and hold it. I saw many work for small wages that kept them always on the borderline of want for the few who made huge profits. I saw the courts, the halls of legislation, the press, and the schools—in fact, every avenue of education and protection—effectively used as an instrument for the safeguarding of a minority, while the masses were denied every right.[34] I found that the politicians knew how to befog every issue, how to control public opinion and manipulate votes to their own advantage and to that of their financial and industrial allies. This was the picture of democracy I soon discovered on my arrival in the United States. Fundamentally, there have been few changes since that time."

"What is your answer?" Rose asked, electrified by the conversation.

"Anarchism. It is a most beautiful philosophy.[35] We all want to be free from laws, right? It is our human right to feel this way. Anarchism stresses the importance of the individual—his possibilities and needs in a free society. Instead of telling him that he must fall down and worship before institutions, live and die for abstractions, break his heart, and stunt his life for taboos, anarchism insists that the center of gravity in society is the individual, that he must think for himself, act freely, and live fully. The aim of anarchism is that every individual in the world shall be able to do so. If he is to develop freely and fully, he must be relieved from the interference and oppression of others. Freedom is, therefore, the cornerstone of the anarchist philosophy."

"The families who took in the children are socialists, not anarchists."

"Socialists are silly. There is no such thing as good laws."

Rose detected a bit of high-mindedness against Elizabeth. In response, she said, "You cannot rid the country of laws."

"Man made them, and he can destroy them. I told you what I am doing about it. Now it is my turn to ask you what you want to do about bad laws."

"What can I do?"

"Speak out against them."

"I am uneducated."

"Listen, Rose. I was once a seamstress like you. I asked for a raise but was turned down. I heard a speaker say how unfair things were. I volunteered at meetings. I listened to speeches. And I read everything I could get my hands on."

Rose was an intuitive person, not an intellectual, but like intellectuals, her answers to life's questions could be glib, dogmatic, and even prickly. Resistance to hubris, though, came from her faith, not overstuffed books. Her questions made intellectuals nervous because she did not seem to reason as they did. In search of Emma's meaning, she asked, "Did you go to school in Russia?"

"Yes."

"Did you read books when you were a young child?"

"Yes, of course. I loved my books and my friends. One of the things that angered me about my father was his telling me to stop reading. He said it was a waste of time."

"Where did you get the books?"

"My father bought them for me."

Rose deduced a lesson from Emma's answers. "I loved school when I was small. That is all we have in common. I had no one to talk with about books, and I had no books at home. I cannot make up for that."

Emma disagreed. "You have ability and talent. You refused to be subservient. You can think for yourself. You can strip people of their foolishness."

Emma's words were comforting. They communicated intimacy, as had Elizabeth's affirmations. This time, however, praise could not change Rose's consciousness. "I am too old to start on a new journey. School is for the young. My children will study hard and get goods jobs."

Emma responded, "Jobs at what? Owning their own business so

that they might exploit others? Look at your mill owner. He started out with nothing. Now he is rich, and he hates the untutored. That is wrong. A good job does not make men good."

Rose explained, "We still have to eat."

Having spoken for two hours, Emma had come down with a headache. Rose was tired too, having struggled with Emma's teacherlike ways. Each did not know how the other felt. Emma turned to the small corner of the café to order more coffee. While gazing, she saw someone slumped on her table. It was a patron whose face was as white as a ghost. The woman's hair was dirty, in need of a clean wash. Emma was fascinated by the vulgarity of her beauty. She was not sure if the woman was a prostitute with painted lips or an office worker ready for sleep. Rose failed to notice her.

Emma connected this scene to exploitation and offered Rose this thought: "The scientist and artist are not primarily moved by the consideration of gain or profit. The urge to create is the first and most impelling force in their lives. If this urge is lacking in the mass of workers, it is not at all surprising, for their occupation is deadly routine. Without any relation to their lives or needs, their work is done in the most appalling surroundings at the behest of those who have the power of life or death over the masses. Why, then, should they be impelled to give of themselves more than is absolutely necessary to eke out their miserable existence?

"The examples are sickening. I bet the governor of Massachusetts owns stock in your mill. He gets rich off you. No wonder he sent out the troops. He wanted to protect his property. More important, he does not care about you. You are a cog in a wheel meant to make him rich. He wants to keep you in your place. It is the same with the president of Harvard.

"Rose you have an obligation to fight against abuse. Leave your past. Join our cause. We need women like you. Together we can end our enslavement. The Constitution guarantees us this right."

Emma was charming and sincere, but Rose did not like what she had just heard. "Emma, I am deeply honored that you think me capable," she acknowledged after drinking her coffee. "It seems, though, that you have not listened to a single word I have said. The best I can do is stay put. That is my fate."

"You have your own life. You need to free yourself from your religion, Rose. Your church teaches you to sacrifice. Reject that thinking. You have to do what is right for you, not what others want you to do. That fosters dependency. You supported your parents in their old age. Look what it did to you. You are weary. Once you cut away, your energies will be released."

"I am obligated to my husband and family."

Emma remained silent for a moment and then said, "It is not right. You give but never receive. Your suffering is not of your own doing. You are caught in a trap laid by others."

"Nonsense," said Rose. "Carmelo is important to me. My family is important to me. My parents loved and protected me. My mother taught me to look to the church for solace. She used much intelligence and skill to raise us. It is not easy to raise a family of six when money is scarce. The least I can do is return their love."

"There is a higher virtue than duty. It is called freedom. Think of yourself as a woman who has the right to become her own person."

"I know who I am. I know what is right and wrong."

"You are not free."

Rose had not come to America in search of freedom but to work. She accepted her setbacks as part of God's plan. She expressed this faith by saying, "My happiness is in my salvation. I will be rewarded in the next life."

Armed with her distaste of the artificial, Emma replied, "Look at it this way: in Sicily you were unhappy, but you left. Don't you see? Your craving for liberty is a very fundamental and dominant trait. Unfortunately, your development stopped for a while. Take the case of love. When is the last time you felt Carmelo in your arms?"

"Men cannot make me happy."

"Your father is dead. Enjoy Carmelo."

"That is wrong to say that, Emma."

"Put yourself first. Promise me that you do this. And for God's sake make love to your husband before the machines wear him down."

"I cannot make such a promise."[36]

173

"Then go to the library. Many women write to me. They tell me how empty their lives are. I tell them the same thing as I am telling you—change!"

Rose turned and looked wonderingly at Emma and asked, "Emma, what do you think is success? I know you do not favor money and fame."

"That is correct. I consider them most dismal failures. I am devoted to the triumph of anarchism in my lifetime."

Rose could not match Emma's messianic spirit, but she was her equal in shaking loose folly. "This is a mistake, Emma. It is better to submit to the church than to take refuge in a lie."

Figure 4
Notable Italian-Americans of the 20th Century

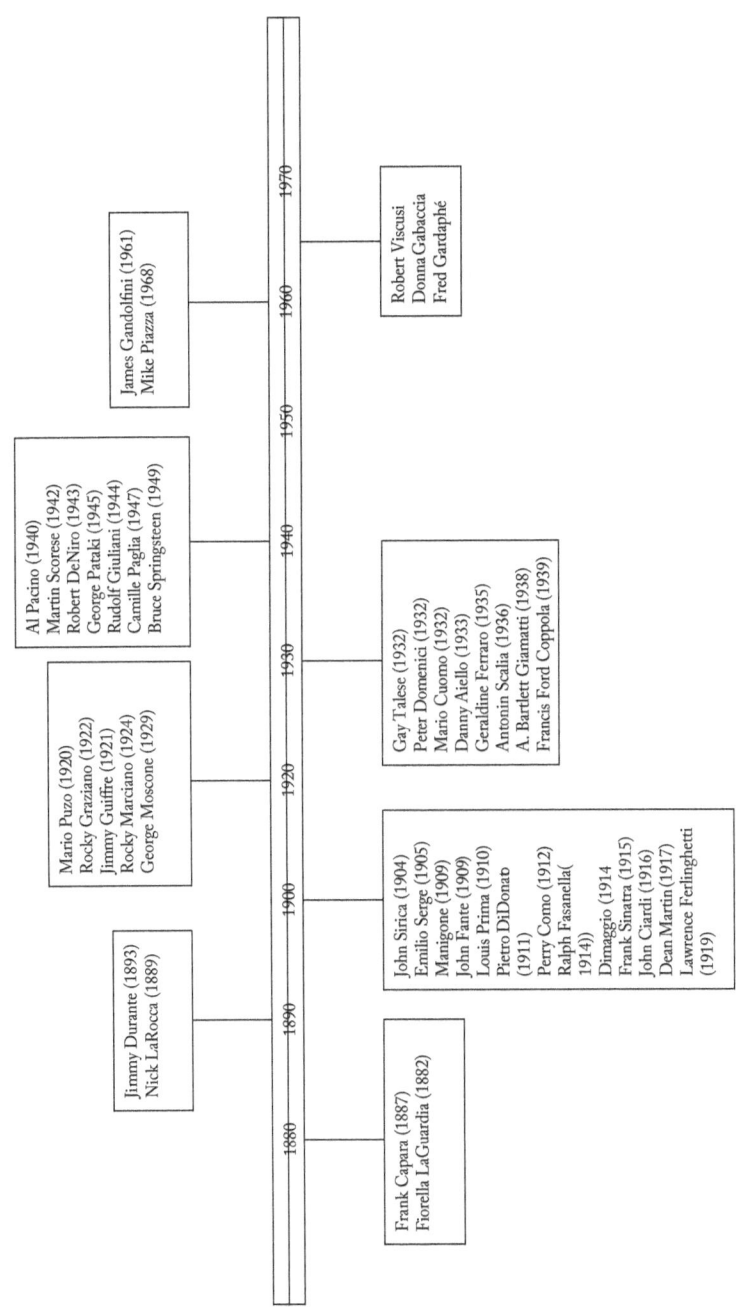

Notes

1. The Salvation Army, an evangelical organization founded in 1852 in London by William Booth, preached the gospel of salvation to the poor, the homeless, the hungry, and the destitute. The word "army" connotes a fighting force at war with the powers of evil. Early followers called Booth "General." His converts were soldiers of Christ called "Salvationists." Excerpted from *Salvation Army* (n.d.).

2. With the barbarian invasions of AD 440, Sicily came under Vandal control and later Byzantine rule. Byzantine culture was a unique mix of Hellenic, Roman and Oriental. North African Muslims (Saracens) starting raiding Sicily in the seventh century. One of the first villages they overran was Mineo, a day's march from Syaracua (Ahmad 1975). By 902, Muslims had spread across Sicily, dominating in the west. They allowed Sicilians to stay Christian. Many of the slaves who worked in the fields converted to Islam. Muslims introduced lemons, oranges, dates, pistachios, eggplants, figs, cotton, sugar cane, rice, and cannoli, a deep-fried pastry filled with cheese (Schacht 1974). Their legacy extended to social relations, including patriarchal control of daughters and the wearing of the black shawl. For an overview of Islamic Sicily, see Stowasser (1976).

3. Poet Robert Frost (1874–1963) was one of America's leading twentieth-century poets and a four-time winner of the Pulitzer Prize who pioneered the use of everyday speech in poetry. Frost's paternal grandfather was a mill supervisor in Lawrence, Massachusetts. When Frost's father died, his mother returned to Lawrence. Frost graduated from Lawrence High School, taught school, and worked in a mill and as a newspaper reporter. In 1894, he sold his first poem. Over the next ten years he wrote more poems, operated a farm purchased for him by his paternal grandfather, and taught school. During the year of the Lawrence Strike (1912), he sold his farm and went to England. He returned to New England three years later and bought another farm.

4. Dialogue in teaching is as old as Socrates (Burbules and Bruce 2001). Some view it as speech that facilitates the discovery of insight. Others define it as vigorous debate, dialectical processes, or back-and-forth forms of thinking. Still others stress the role of the teacher as a partner in inquiry with a student, learning together as they explore a problem through reciprocal questions and answers. Paulo Freire used dialogic teaching to teach Brazilian peasants to read and write (deMarrrais and Le Compte 1995). His goal was to use texts from the daily lives of people to show them their role in the world. Discussing

the familiar gave them the courage to speak up against the government, the police and the church. Speaking up led to efforts to transform their conditions. Dialogic teaching has attracted less scholarly interest than gender, race, class, and sexual orientation. The *Reading Research Quarterly*, a key journal in literacy studies, has not devoted a single article to it in thirty years, yet critical theorists express high interest in it.

5. Montessori's method spread rapidly. Jean Piaget (1896–1980) was director of the modified Montessori school in Geneva and served as head of the Swiss Montessori society.(Enright and Cox 1997). By 1915, over 100 Montessori schools were operating in the United States. However, progressive advocates of John Dewey considered her materials outdated and restrictive and disliked her individualistic view of the child. Montessori was also out of line with the behavioral learning theories of E. L. Thorndike and later B. F. Skinner. She was largely ignored until David Elkind and other child development researchers replaced outdated psychometric paradigms with developmentally appropriate ones. For a historical analysis of the legacies of Thorndike and Dewey on early childhood education, see Elkind (1989, 1999). Selected books by Maria Montessori: (1967) *The Absorbent Mind*; (1970) *The Child in the Family*; (1975, c1955) *Childhood Education*; (1969,c 1948) *The Discovery of the Child*; (1988, c1964) *The Montessori Method*; (1964) *The Montessori Method: Scientific Pedagogy as Applied to Child Education in the Children's Houses, with Additions and Revisions by the Author*; (1966, 1972) *The Secret of Childhood*; (1971,c1917) *Spontaneous Activity in Education*.

6. Rose arrived at the height of the Edwardian era (1901–1911) when woman began working outside the home. Unlike Europe, where peasants wore colorful costumes to distinguish themselves from the rich, everyone in America wore the same clothes (Olian 1995). With the advent of rural free delivery in 1902 and parcel post in 1913, women were able to buy the latest fashions from catalogues. Fashionable women, however, continued to hire dressmakers to make costumes for every occasion—visiting costumes, pedestrian costumes, morning gowns (Elite fashion 1994). The goal was to present oneself with grace and femininity. To emphasize curves, women wore S-shaped corsets that pushed the bust forward and the hips back. Clothes were lavish, with layers of decoration and ornamentation. White was the color of choice. High collars were used for daytime, low décolletage for eveningwear. Skirts were long and sweeping.

7. German philosopher Friedrich Wilhelm Nietzsche (1844–1900) rejected Western bourgeois civilization and regarded God as dead and Christian civilization as decadent. He maintained that freedom means living a life

without the artificial limits of moral obligation. With the translation of *Beyond Good and Evil* (1907), *Thus Spake Zarathustra* (1909), and *The Birth of Tragedy* (1910), his influence on American intellectuals became great. Excerpted from Friedrich Nietzsche (n.d.) and Nietzsche: beyond morality (n.d.).

8. The following quotations from Macy (1910) reflect the negative and disparaging attitudes many turn-of-the-century educators had toward children who failed in school. "Subnormal" children, she stated emphatically, are found among the inefficient, parasitic, petty criminal classes, psychical and mentally defective children called aments. It is "altruistic contagion" to think laggards can be educated. Since they are a menace to the public weal, they need to be educated for competition with their peers. It is a well-known fact that the true ament is incapable of education up to the normal standard. Their reaction to sensory stimuli is weak, lethargic or absent due to dull, stunted or sensory mechanism. They have to be taught to feel, taste, smell, hear, and see. Their psychic processes are also inefficient and inaccurate. They grasp with difficulty concrete facts. Abstraction for them, in large measure, is an idle and impractical dream of the optimist. Their education must be essentially practical. Facts and muscular coordination cannot be transferred. Relearning has to be done. Training needs to focus on industrial work: mat weaving basketry, chair caning, sewing, dressmaking, carpentry, and brasswork with minimal training in reading, spelling and writing.

New York City started to care for subnormal children in 1900. By 1906, a department of ungraded classes was formed to take care of the more than seven thousand children who had been "found" to be mentally defective. Macy's analysis of subnormal children foreshadowed a century of restrictive labeling based on IQ testing. It took many court cases to protect children from discriminatory labeling and placement. These included the integration of students in public schools (Brown vs. Board of Education 1954); free appropriate education for all children (PARC vs. Commonwealth of Pennsylvania 1972); the unconstitutionality of IQ placement testing (Hobson vs. Hansen 1967–68).

9. Rose's intuition about labeling was not far off. Howard Gardner (1999) verified the inherent bias in intelligence tests: "Tests in general, and intelligence tests in particular, are inherently conservative instruments—tools of the establishment." It is therefore worth noting that many testing pioneers thought of themselves as progressives in the social sphere. They were devising instruments that could reveal people of talent even if those people came from "remote and apparently inferior backgrounds," to quote from a college

catalogue of the 1950s. And occasionally the tests did discover intellectual diamonds in the rough. More often, however, they picked out the privileged.

The belief that income reflects intelligence was perpetuated by early twentieth=century psychologists like Kornhauser (1918) who baldly asserted in *The Journal of Educational Psychology* that wealthy parents produce smart children. He based this claim on a study that divided one thousand children in Pittsburgh public schools into three groups: Retarded, defined as one or more years below expected grade level; Normal, defined as expected grade level; Advanced, one or more years above expected grade level. He separated the rich and poor students based on family telephone ownership. Then he identified the types of schools the children attended. Poor schools were populated by laborers, day workers, and street venders; the average schools were populated by artisans, small shopkeepers and boarding house properties; and Wealthy schools by professionals. Children with the highest retention rates came from the poorest schools. The advanced children came from families whose parents owned telephones. Claiming a causal relationship, he committed the logical fallacy known as "cum hoc ergo propter hoc," by concluding that "parents having telephones are inherently of good enough stock to have succeeded and hence naturally their off spring are also of superior native ability." Not satisfied with bestowing good genes on the wealthy, he impugned the integrity of social workers and teachers who worked with the poor by declaring they " fail to acknowledge the fundamental premise that wealthier parents have children that are more intelligent." The relationship between IQ and social privilege is still unresolved.

10.   The early years of the twentieth century were riddled with unresolved issues in the teaching profession. In 1910, the *New York Times* reported that Elizabeth, New Jersey, parents resented the appointment of a "Negro" woman to teach white primary grades (Name Negro, 1910). Although teaching was becoming the dominant profession for women (Graduates 1912) in early January 1911, the New York City Board of Education rejected a resolution to allow appointment of married female teachers as principals (Stormy Education 1911). Later that year, the *New York Times* took issue in an editorial with the board's decision to grant equal pay to women because it deprived the Police department of needed men to protect the city against crime (Police 1911). A few months later the *New York Times* reported that Dr. Flirter Dressler of the US Bureau of Education deplored the steady drop in numbers of male teachers holding it unwise to entrust the education of children to women (Fewer Men 1912).

Other themes were discussed in teacher training textbooks and professional journals. A major focus was on individual differences. Ruediger (1910) wanted teachers to pick out those who were not fitted to acquire certain types of knowledge. Researchers in the 1910 *Journal of Educational Psychology* argued that the best way to identify bright children from subnormal ones was with statistical measures. Smith (1923) wanted policy makers to eliminate uniform curriculum and train children's hands. Reed (1927) felt that the best way to motivate children was to publish their test scores. O'Shea (1924) believed that the parents of intellectually inferior foreign children did not keep their children in school because they had rebellious and defiant attitudes. Childhood Education (1924) wanted the state to give parents guidance in child raising techniques.

11. Ben Reitman (1879–1942), a physician who rode the rails, lived in hobo jungles, and spoke hobo dialect, was keenly aware of the injustices of the homeless. In 1907, he opened a Hobo College in Chicago. At the age of twenty-eight, he became Emma Goldman's lover and manager. He published two books: *The Second Oldest Profession* in 1932 and *Sister of the Road: The Autobiography of Boxcar Bertha* in 1937. For his daughter's insights into his life, see Reitman-Carpenter (1999).

12. I took license with placing Francis W. Parker in this chapter. A friend of Jane Addams and John Dewey, this most innovative thinker in elementary education and teacher training before1900, had died in 1902.

13. Grand Central Terminal (1903–1913) was one of two railway stations built in New York City during the first decade of the twentieth century. Penn Station (1902–1911) was the other. In 1863, Cornelius Vanderbilt built the largest railway station in the world on 42nd Avenue. By 1900, a larger station was needed to compensate for the electrification of trains. In 1903, a competition was held for its design. The project included not just the new railway station but a whole complex with office buildings and apartments, which became known as "Terminal City." Developers were allowed to construct buildings beside it but had to pay an extra sum to the Railway Company for so-called air rights. Construction cost eighty million dollars. One hundred eighty buildings between 42nd and 50th Streets, including hospitals and churches, were demolished. The new facade on 42nd Street was beaux-arts in design, combining ancient Greek and Roman forms with Renaissance ideas. A large sculpture group topped large arches flanked by Corinthian columns. The 50-foot high group depicted Mercury (the god of commerce) supported by Minerva and Hercules representing mental and moral strength. The main concourse was 470 feet long, 160 feet wide, and 150 feet high. The ceiling

design with zodiac constellations was taken from a medieval manuscript. Light entered the main concourse through three 75-foot arched windows. The western double staircase in Botticino marble was designed after the large staircase in the former Opera Building in Paris. It connected the main concourse with the entrance on Vanderbilt Avenue. The floor of the concourse was made from Tennessee marble, the walls of Caen stone. Excerpted from Grand Central Terminal (n.d.). For a history of Grand Central Terminal, see Schlichting (2001).

14. The essential elements of the Protestant ethic are diligence, punctuality, deferment of gratification, and primacy of the work domain (Rose 1985).

15. Scientific-sounding books with statistical curves and tables proliferated by Ivy League and other prestigious professors of psychology, sociology, and eugenics warned Americans that Jewish, Polish, Italian, and other non-Nordic immigrants risked lowering the American gene pool (Chasse 1997). Ellwood P. Cubberley (1934), dean of Stanford University School of Education, author of close to twenty texts on education, reflected the racist sentiments of the times when he wrote in his widely used text, *Public Education in the United States.* "[Original immigrants] came from countries which embraced the Protestant reformation where general education prevailed ... All were from race stocks not very different from our own, and all possessed courage, initiative, intelligence, adaptability, and self-reliance to a great degree. After about 1882 the character of our immigration changed in a very remarkable manner...Southern and Eastern Europeans [were] largely illiterate, docile, often lacking in initiative, and almost wholly without the Anglo-Saxon conceptions of righteousness, liberty, law, order, public decency, and government [.] [Their] coming has served to dilute tremendously our national stock and to weaken and corrupt our political life."

16. Thorstein Veblen (1899) reasoned that people acquire wealth not to satisfy needs but to prove their superiority over others. Reflecting on Veblen's theory of conspicuous consumption, Woodrow Wilson, president of Princeton University, told the North Carolina Society, "Nothing has spread Socialistic feelings in this country more than the use of automobiles [because] they are the picture of arrogance and wealth with all its independence and carelessness." (Motorists 1906)

17. Popular songs between 1900 and1912 were nostalgic in nature. They included "In the Good Ole Summer Time" (1902); "Yankee Doodle Boy" (1904); "In the Shade of the Old Apple Tree" (1905); "School Days" (1907); "Shine on Harvest Moon" (1908); "Take Me Out to the Ball Game" (1909); "Down

by the Old Mill Stream" (1910); and "I Want a Girl Just Like the Girl that Married Dear Old Dad" (1911). Excerpted from Tompkins (1996) *American Decades 1900–1909* and *1910–1919*.

18. More is known about Dewey than is possible to read. His legacy in education ranges from educational purposes to pedagogical practices, teacher training, and theories about the emotions and imagination. According to Cohen (n.d.), "unlike many of his academic colleagues then or now, [Dewey] worked prodigiously hard to make his ideas count for ordinary Americans. In addition to writing about issues that did count, he was active in the social and political causes that he thought important, including tests, vocational schools that tracked workers' children away from brighter futures, and civil liberties/ civil rights. He fiercely opposed Communist and other totalitarian regimes, and spoke out strongly against them at a time when such independence was quite unfashionable." Representative books by John Dewey: (1997*) Democracy and Education: An introduction to the Philosophy of Education*; (1958*) Experience and Nature*; (1991) *How We Think*. Sample articles: (1895) The theory of emotion. (2) The significance of emotions; (1886). Psychology as philosophic method; (1903) Logical conditions of a scientific treatment of morality. Works about Dewey include Boisvert (1988); Bullert (1983); Dykhuizen (1973); Rockefeller (1991); Welchman (1995).

19. Elizabeth modeled Rousseauian principles of self-expression, not authoritarian tactics.

20. These dialogues were constructed from life histories found at the Folklore Project of the Federal Writers' Project for the US Works Progress Administration (WPA) from 1936 to 1940, at American Life Histories.

21. According to Zwick (n.d.), *Political Cartoons*, close to two million children, ages ten to fifteen were working in factories, fields, mills, mines, tenement houses, and on city streets across the country at the turn of the twentieth century. In 1904, the National Child Labor Committee was founded to work for effective national legislation to end child labor. In 1908, they hired photographer Lewis Hine to document the extent of child labor throughout the country and the children's working conditions in various industries. His photographs are the most enduring images from the crusade against child labor that began in the United States in the early 1900s.

22. Snobbery is the trait of condescending to those of lower social status. A snob is someone who affects to be better, richer, or more fashionable than he really is. Noted essayist and former *American Scholar* editor Joseph Epstein

(2002) posits that snobs are insecure people who have latched onto arbitrary measures of status to prove they're worthier than those around them. It is natural fallout, he says, in a world where complete fairness is nonexistent. John Carey (1992) argues that post-modernism and literary theory grew out of the turn-of-the-century snobbery against the common person who was catching up in sophistication, thanks to the educational reforms. To protect themselves from the new reading public, modernist writers invented an esoteric body of knowledge without human or narrative content to which the masses could not relate (Geerinck 2004). "Smart" people like D. H. Lawrence, Ezra Pound, W. B. Yeats, Knut Hamsun, George Gissing, and Wyndham Lewis scorned "the masses" as vulgar and trivial while exalting the artist as a natural aristocrat and transmitter of timeless values. Gissing concluded that the masses were uneducable, while T. S. Eliot predicted that the spread of education would lead to barbarism. Wells considered common people manifestations of a "biological catastrophe" and proposed measures to restrict parenthood as a means to curb the black and brown races. Charles Baudelaire condemned photography as a distraction for the "vile multitude," while other intellectuals expressed contempt for newspapers and popular entertainment. E. M. Forster went so far as to advocate the elimination of "superfluous" people. Much of the hubris against poor people and democracy, argues Carey, derives from Nietzsche's philosophy. See Ekstein (1990), *Rites of Spring*, for a cultural history of the early twentieth century. Kabaservice (2004) documents the contempt for public school graduates to elite universities like Yale in the 1960s.

23. Two American artists who took up Emma's call were Paul Robeson (1898–1976) and Carl Sandburg (1878–1967). Robeson was an African American athlete, singer, actor, and advocate for civil rights who rose to prominence when segregation was legal in America. He attended Rutgers University on a scholarship, earning All-American honors in football. In 1919 he graduated valedictorian of his class and attended law school but switched to theater to promote African and African American history and culture. He had leading roles in *Othello* and *Showboat*. His friends included anarchist Emma Goldman and writers James Joyce and Ernest Hemingway. In 1950, the US government revoked Robeson's passport, leading to an eight-year battle to secure it and to travel again. Carl Sandburg, born to a working-class family, quit school in the eighth grade to deliver milk, harvest ice, lay bricks, thresh wheat, and shine shoes. Traveling as a hobo, he saw firsthand the sharp contrast between rich and poor, a dichotomy that instilled in him a distrust of capitalism. Sandburg grew increasingly concerned with the plight of the American worker. In 1907, he worked as an organizer for the Wisconsin Social Democratic party, writing and distributing political pamphlets and literature. For several years

he worked as a reporter for the *Chicago Daily News*, covering mostly labor issues and later writing his own feature. Sandburg wrote the Pulitzer Prize-winning *Abraham Lincoln: The Prairie Years* in 1926. Excerpted respectably from Paul Robeson (n.d.) Carl Sandburg.

24. In late February 1912, Dreiser was on his first tour of Europe. He had just completed a stay on the Riviera and was now at the Grand Continental Hotel in Rome. His trips abroad foreshadowed the "Lost Generation" a group of American writers including Ernest Hemingway, F. Scott Fitzgerald, and John Dos Passos, who rebelled against American materialism by living in Europe. Dreiser's failure to renounce wealth upset Goldman and Flynn. A half a century later Podhoretz's (1967) bourgeois confessions had the same effect on intellectuals. For an overview of the social life and customs of American elites, see Veblen (1899) *Theory of the Leisure Class*; Baltzell (1964) *The Protestant Establishment*; Packard (1959) *The Status Seekers*; and Fussell (1984) *Class*. David Brooks (2000) describes the status drive of contemporary intellectuals in, *Bobos in Paradise*. To read Dreiser's comments about writing, talent, reading habits, and Europe, see *Letters of Theodore Dreiser* (Elias 1959).

25. At the time of these dialogues, Americans suspected that most immigrants were mentally defective. In 1882, the United States Congress passed a law prohibiting mentally defective people from passing through the Ellis Island checkpoint. Enforcing this law proved to be difficult because as many as 5,000 immigrants arrived each day. Goddard developed a procedure to expedite the process. He had immigrants visually screened for mental defects and then tested with a variety of performance measures from the Binet scales. The number of immigrants who were deported increased exponentially because of these screening measures. For discussion of bias in intelligence testing, see Zenderland (1998), Pearson (1991), and Brown (1992).

26. Many Americans worried over the importation of white women as slaves. A little more than a year after Rose arrived in the United States, President Roosevelt designated the secretary at the American embassy in Paris to represent the United State at the European Congress for the Suppression of the White Slave Trade (White Slave 1906). Soon after, Secretary of Commerce Frank P. Sargent proposed that any immigrant woman brought to the county illegally be deported (Will Deport 1907).

27. To learn about the indignities suffered by immigrants at Ellis Island, see, Sherard (1902) *At the Closed Door*.

28. The following narrative was excerpted from Vivian Morris "Bronx Slave Market" (1938), *Library of Congress, Manuscript Division, WPA Federal Writers' Project Collection, 1936–1940*.

29. See Johnson (1977), *Jack Johnson in the Ring and Out*.

30. See Leaming (1984*), Hidden Americans: Maroons of Virginia and the Carolinas* and Leaming (1977), *The Ben Ishmael Tribe*.

31. John Calvin (1509–1564) is second to Martin Luther (1483-1546) in influence in the Protestant Reformation. His primary tenets included a belief in the primacy of the scripture as an authority for doctrinal decisions, a belief in predestination, a belief in salvation wholly accomplished by grace with no influence from works, and a rejection of the episcopacy. Calvinism became the religion of the majority in Scotland, the Netherlands, and parts of Germany. Most settlers in the mid-Atlantic and New England were Calvinists including the Puritans. Transcendentalism was a reaction against the Calvinistic doctrine of the depravity of man. See Robinson (1998), *The Death of Adam* and Starkey (1966), *The Congregational Way*.

32. The myth of Italian and Sicilian inferiority collapsed as second- and third-generation Italian Americans became doctors, lawyers, scientists, teachers, priests, pharmacists, architects, sculptors, and businesspersons and leaders in national politics and local government. Examples: Manigone, di Donato, Ferlengeti, Talese, Fante, Puzo, Martin, Sinatra, DeNiro, Scorsese, Coppola, La Guardia, Cuomo, Dommenci, Giuliani, Ferraro, Paterno, Lombardi, Marchiano, and DiMaggio.

33. Emma's words were excerpted from the electronic version of Living My Life at *Anarchy Archives*. Additional Goldman electronic documents, images, speeches, and newspaper accounts can be retrieved from *The Emma Goldman Papers* (n.d.) and *The Jewish Women Archives* (n.d.). Related electronic sites are *Eugene V. Debs Foundation* (n.d.); *Samuel Gompers Papers* (n.d.); and *Elizabeth Gurley Flynn's Memories of the IWW* (n.d.).

34. During the Thirty Years War (1618-1648)--Europe's deadliest religious war that resulted in 8 million casualties--Descartes sought a universal method to provide a certainty that would transcend religious oppositions. Descartes found a solution in the mind's ability to think rationally. In fact, he saw mind and body as so distinct from each other that he had trouble explaining how the two could even interact—a problem that bedevils philosophy to this day. Influenced by this ideal of universal rationality, many European intellectuals

began to organize themselves along rationalist (and often bureaucratic) lines. In the social realm, this may have translated into a dualism where that which lacked rationality (natural phenomena, women, non-European cultures or "races," emotion, sexuality, the arts, humanities, lower classes) was seen as "inferior" to that which was "rational" (humans, men, European culture and their "race," rationality, the sciences, mathematics, the "respectable" classes). See Toulmin (1990), *Cosmopolis: The Hidden Agenda of Modernity*, for example 96-100, 107-115. In late nineteenth-century America, the ideology of keeping inferior people in their place lead to unmitigated subordination of the poor. A half century later, conservative political scientist Edward Banfield (1958) reintroduced the nativist stereotype of the amoral Sicilian.

35. Emma knew that the central premise in western philosophy was the belief first articulated by Socrates: the examined life is the key to the life well lived. The Enlightenment had produced moral philosophers like Kant who argued that moral truths were universal. They believed that tolerance, basic rights, rule of law, fairness, rightness, and sincerity applied to everyone. Truth was discovered and validated through discussion, argument and mutual understanding. They believed governments should be just. Postmodernists took another track to moral philosophy. One of the precursors of postmodernism, Nietzsche, rejected the universality of truth, claiming that God was dead and we must free ourselves from Christian herd moralism. Emma's anarchism, atheism, and feminism were grounded in a desire for fairness on one hand, and in her distaste for a "timeless" status quo on the other.

36. Rose worked for women who were caught up in the call for gender equality and independence. Some marched in suffragist parades and at labor demonstrations. Others attended football games at Harvard, visiting the Squantum airfield to cheer pilots, showing up at car and horse races at the Brockton Fair and swimming in contests in the Charles River (Halpert and Halpert 1973). Rose heard Carmelo speak about a young woman named Evelyn Nesbith, whose lover murdered her husband. Rose squirmed when Carmelo joked about dancing gypsies and women horse thieves. Rose's feminism was directed at the patriarchal culture of her past. She made her way in a hostile environment, thanks to her self-reliance and her independence. She also set high expectations for her children. Authors who treat parenthood from a feminist perspective include Buchi (1979), *The joys of motherhood*; Carter (1981), *Neighbour Rosicky*; Olson (1961), "I stand here ironing," in *Tell Me a Riddle*.

References

Addams, J. *Foreign-born children in the primary grades. National Educational Association journal of proceedings and addresses of the thirty-sixth annual meeting held at Milwaukee, Wis., July 6–9, 1897.* Chicago, Ill: University of Chicago Press, 1897.

Ahmad, A. *History of Islamic Sicily.* Edinburgh: Edinburgh University Press, 1975.

Ascher, S. *Subway Stuff: Folktalk.* Library of Congress, Manuscript Division, WPA Federal Writers' Project Collection, 1938. Retrieved March 04, 2004, http://memory.loc.gov.

Asimov, I. *The foundation trilogy: three classics of science fiction.* Garden City: Doubleday. 1951.

Bagley, W. C. *Classroom management: Its principles and technique.* New York: Macmillan, 1915.

Baltzell, E. D. *The Protestant establishment: aristocracy & caste in America.* New York: Random House, 1964.

Baltzell, E. D. *Puritan Boston and Quaker Philadelphia: two Protestant ethics and the spirit of class authority and leadership.* Boston: Beacon Press, 1982.

Banfield, E. C. *The moral basis of a backward society.* New York: Free Press, 1967.

"Biography." *Carl Sandburg.* http://carl-sandburg.com/biography.htm. Retrieved June 3, 2004.

Boisvert, R. D. *Dewey's metaphysics.* New York: Fordham University Press, 1988.

Boynton, P. H. *Some contemporary Americans; the personal equation in literature.* New York: Biblo and Tannen, 1966.

Brooks, D. *Bobos in paradise: the new upper class and how they got there.* New York: Simon & Schuster, 2000.

Brown, J. *The definition of a profession: the authority of metaphor in the history of intelligence testing, 1890–1930.* Princeton, NJ: Princeton University Press, 1992.

Buchi, E. *The joys of motherhood*. New York: George Braziller, 1979.

Bullert, G. *The politics of John Dewey*. Buffalo, NY: Prometheus, 1983.

Burbules, N.C. and B. C. Bruce. "Theory and research on teaching as dialogue." In *Handbook of Research on Teaching*, 4th edition. Edited by V. Richardson. Washington, DC: American Educational Research Association, 2001.

Carey, J. *The intellectuals and the masses: pride and prejudice among the literary intelligentsia, 1880–1939*. New York: Saint Martin's Press, 1992.

Carter, W. "Neighbour Rosicky." In *The treasury of American short stories*. Garden City, NY: Doubleday, 1981.

Chapman, P. D. *Schools as sorters: Lewis M. Terman, applied psychology, and the intelligence testing movement, 1890–1930*. New York: New York University Press, 1988.

Chasse, A. *The Legacy of Malthus: the social costs of the new scientific racism*. New York, NY: Knopf, 1997.

Cubberley, E. P. *Public education in the United States*. Boston: Houghton Mifflin, 1934.

DeMarrais, K. B. and M. D. LeCompte. *The way schools work: A sociological analysis of education*. White Plans, NY: Longman, 1995.

Dewey, J. "Psychology as philosophic method." *Mind* 1 (1886): 153–173.

Dewey, J. "The theory of emotion. (2) The significance of emotions." *Psychological Review* 2 (1895): 13–32.

Dewey, J. "My pedagogic creed." *School Journal* 54 (Jan. 1897): 77–80.

Dewey, J. Logical conditions of a scientific treatment of morality. *Decennial Publications of the University of Chicago*, First Series, 3 (1903): 115–139.

Dewey, J. *Experience and nature*. New York: Dover, 1958.

Dewey, J. *How we think*. Buffalo, NY: Prometheus, 1991.

Dewey, J. *Democracy and education: An introduction to the philosophy of education.* New York: Simon and Schuster, 1997.

Dreiser, T. *Sister Carrie.* New York: The Modern Library, 1917.

Dressler, F. B. As quoted in "Educational News and Comment" by *American Education,* vol. 15, no. 7 March 1912: 318.

Du Bois, W. E. B. *The souls of black folk: Essays and sketches.* New York: Vintage, 1990.

Dykhuizen, G. *The life and mind of John Dewey.* Carbondale, IL: Southern Illinois University Press, 1973.

Emma Goldman Papers. http://sunsite.berkeley.edu/Goldman/Writings/index.html. Retrieved April 2, 2004.

Eugene V. Debs foundation. http//www.eugenevdebs.com/index.htm. Retrieved April 5, 2004.

Ekstein, M. *Rites of spring: The Great War and the birth of the modern age.* New York: Anchor Books, 1990.

Elias, R. H., ed. *Letters of Theodore Dreiser: A selection.* Philadelphia: University of Pennsylvania Press, 1959.

Elkind, D. "Developmentally appropriate practice: Philosophical and practical implications." *Phi Delta Kappan* 71 (Oct. 1989): 113–116.

Elkind, D. "Educational research and the science of education." *Educational Psychology Review* 11 (Sept. 1999): 271–286.

"Elizabeth Gurley Flynn." *Spartacus Educational.* http://spartacus-educational.com/USAflynn.htm. Retrieved July 23, 2017.

Elite fashion catalogue, 1904. Mineola, NY: Dover Publications, Inc, 1994.

Emma Goldman people and events. *PBS.* http://www.pbs.org/wgbh/amex/goldman/peopleevents/p_reitman.html. Retrieved May 25, 2004.

Enright, M. F., & D. Cox. "Foundations study guide: Montessori education." *The Objectivist Center.* http://www.objectivistcenter.org/articles/foundations_montessori-education.asp. Retrieved July 8, 2004.

Epstein. J. *Snobbery: the American Version.* Boston: Houghton Mifflin, 2002.

"Fewer men teachers." *New York Times,* January 7, 1912.

Flynn, E. G. (n.d.). *Memories of the IWW.* http://www.geocities.com/Capitol Hill/5202/rebelgirl.html. Retrieved April 3, 2004.

--------. (1952, April). *Statement at the Smith act trail.* http://www.americanrhetoric. com/speeches/elizabethgurleyflynn.htm. Retrieved February 5, 2004.

Foer, F. "Closing of the presidential mind." *The New Republic* 5 (July 7, 2004): 17–21.

"Friedrich Nietzsche" (n.d.). *The Stanford Encyclopedia of Philosophy.* http://plato. stanford.edu/entries/nietzsche. Retrieved February 23, 2004.

Fussell, P. *Class.* New York: Ballantine, 1984.

Gardner, H. "Who owns intelligence?" *Atlantic Monthly* 283 (Feb. 1999): 67–76.

Goldman. E. *Living my life: Volume one.* New York: Alfred A Knopf, 1931.

"Graduates like teaching." *New York Times,* September 22, 1912.

Grand central terminal (n.d.). *New York.* http://www.aviewoncities.com/nyc/grandcentralterminal.htm. Retrieved July 2, 2004

Halpert, S. and Halpert, B. *Brahmins & bullyboys: G. Frank Radway's Boston album.* Boston: Houghton Mifflin, 1973.

Hill, J. "Rebel girl." *Socialist Music,* 1914. http://www.newyouth.com/archives/music/joehill.asp#Casey Jones. Retrieved February 5, 2004.

Hine. L. W. "Social Photography; How the Camera May Help in the Social Uplift." *Proceedings of the National Conference of Charities and Correction at the Thirty-Sixth Annual Session held in the City of Buffalo, New York, June 9-16,*

1909. Edited by Alexander Johnson. Fort Wayne, IN: Press of Fort Wayne, 1909: 355-59.

"History of the Salvation of Army." (n.d.) *Salvation Army*. http://www.salvationarmyusa.org/. Retrieved March 10, 2004.

"Introduction to Montessori Education." *Montessori-NAMTA*, 2011. http://www.montessori-namta.org/About-Montessori.

"Jane Addams." *Wikipedia*. https://en.wikipedia.org/wiki/Jane_Addams#Primary _sources. Retrieved July 24, 2017.

Jewish women archives. http://www.jwa.org/exhibits/wov/goldman/index.html. Retrieved April 6, 2004

Johnson, J. *Jack Johnson in the ring and out: the classic autobiography by the first black champion*. New York: Two Continents Publishing Group, 1977.

Kabaservice, G. M. *The Guardians: Kingman Brewster, His Circle, and the Rise of the Liberal Establishment*. New York: Holt, 2004.

Kornhauser, A. W. (1918). The economic standing of parents and the intelligence of their children. *The Journal of Educational Psychology* 9 (1918): 159–166.

Leaming, H. P. The Ben Ishmael Tribe: A fugitive nation of the Old Northwest. In *The Ethnic Frontier*. Edited by M. G. Holli & P. d'A Jones. Grand Rapids: MI: William B. Eerdmans, 1977.

Leaming, H. P. *Hidden Americans: Maroons of Virginia and the Carolinas*. Ann Arbor, MI: University Microfilms International, 1984.

Macy, M. S. "The subnormal child in New York City schools." *Journal of Educational Psychology* 1 (1910): 132–144.

Marcuse, H. *Reason and revolution; Hegel and the rise of social theory*. New York: Humanities Press, 1968.

Montessori, M. *The Montessori method*. Translated by Anne Everett George. New York: Frederick A. Stokes Company, 1912.

Montessori, M. *The Montessori method: scientific pedagogy as applied to child education in the Children's Houses, with additions and revisions by the author.* Cambridge: R. Bentley, 1964.

Montessori, M. *The Absorbent Mind.* New York: Holt, Rinehart, and Winston, 1967.

Montessori, M. *The Discovery of the Child.* Madras: Kalakshetra Publications, 1969.

Montessori, M. *The Child in the Family.* Chicago, Ill: Regnery, 1970.

Montessori, M. *Spontaneous activity in education.* Cambridge, MA: Bentley, 1971.

Montessori, M. *The secret of childhood.* New York: Ballantine Books, 1972.

Montessori, M. *Childhood Education.* New York: New American Library, 1975, c1955.

Montessori, M. *The Montessori Method.* New York: Schocken Books, 1988.

Morris, Vivian. "Bronx Slave Market." *Library of Congress, Manuscript Division, WPA Federal Writers' Project Collection, 1936–1940* (December 1938). Retrieved June 12, 1998, http://memory.gov.

"Motorists don't make socialists, they say." *New York Times*, March 4, 1906.

"Name Negro teacher for white pupils." *New York Times*, July 17, 1910.

"National Child Labor Committee Collection." *Library of Congress.* http://www.loc.gov/pictures/collection/nclc. Retrieved July 25, 2017.

Nietzsche, F. W. *Beyond Good and Evil.* South Bend, IN: Gateway Editions, 1955.

Nietzsche, F. W. *Thus Spoke Zarathustra.* New York: Heritage Press, 1967.

Nietzsche, F. W. *The Birth of Ttragedy.* Oxford: Oxford University Press, 2000.

"Nietzche: Beyond morality" (n.d.). *Nietzsche.* http://www.philosophypages.com/hy/5v.htm. Retrieved February 23, 2004.

Olian, J., ed. *Everyday fashions, 1909-1920*. New York: Dover, 1995.

Olson, T. "I stand here ironing." In *Tell me a riddle*, New York: Delacorte, 1961.

O'Shea, M. V. *The child: his nature and his needs*. New York: Arno Press, 1975, c1924.

Packard, V. *The status seekers; an exploration of class behavior in America and the hidden barriers that affect you, your community, your future*. New York: D. McKay Co., 1959.

Parker, F. W. *Notes Of talks on teaching at the Martha's Vineyard summer institute, July 17 to August 19, 1882*. New York: E. L. Kellogg & Co., 1882.

Pearson. R. *Race, intelligence and bias in academe*. Washington, DC: Scott-Townsend Publishers, 1991.

Phillips, R. C. with Smith, W. "The Negro of the Congo, West Aftica." In *The Year-Book of Facts in Science and the Arts for 1875*. Edited by Charles W. Vincent. London: Warwick House, 1876.

Podhoretz, N. *Making it*. New York: Random House, 1967.

Police, and "equal" pay. *New York Times*, November 2, 1911.

Porter, T. M. *The rise of statistical thinking, 1820–1900*. Princeton: Princeton University Press, 1986.

Reed, H. B. *Psychology of elementary school subjects*. Boston: Ginn and Company, 1927.

Reinemeyer, E. "Edward Lee Thorndike." May 1999. http://www.muskingum. edu/~psych/psycweb/history/thorndike.htm.

Reitman, B. L. *The second oldest profession: a study of the prostitute's "business manager."* New York: The Vanguard Press, 1931.

Reitman, B. L. *Sister of the road: The autobiography of boxcar Bertha*. San Francisco, CA: Last Gasp, 2002.

Reitman-Carpenter, M. *No regrets: Dr. Ben Reitman and the women who loved him*. Lexington, MA: SouthSide Press, 1999.

Robeson, P. *American Masters*. http://www.pbs.org/wnet/americanmasters/database/robeson_p.html. Retrieved June 5, 2004.

Robinson, E.A. *Children of the night*. New York: Charles Scribner's Sons, 1897.

Robinson, M. *The Death of Adam: essays on modern thought*. Boston: Houghton Mifflin, 1998.

Rockefeller, S. C. *John Dewey: Religious faith and democratic humanism*. New York: Columbia University Press, 1991.

Rose, M. *Reworking the work ethic: Economic values and socio-cultural politics*. London: Schocken, 1985.

Ruediger, W. C. *The principles of education*. Boston: Houghton Mifflin, 1910.

Samuel Gompers papers at University of Maryland. http://www.history.umd.edu/Gompers/web1.html. Retrieved April 3, 2004.

Schacht, J. *The legacy of Islam*. Oxford: Clarendon Press, 1974.

Schlichting, K. C. *Grand central terminal: Railroads, engineering, and architecture in New York City*. Baltimore: Johns Hopkins University Press, 2001.

Shaw, G. B. *Pygmalion, and other plays*. New York: Dodd, Mead, 1967.

Sherard, R. H. *At the closed door: being the true and faithful account of an experiment in propria persona of the treatment accorded of the pauper emigrants in New York Harbour by the officials of the American democracy*. London: Digby, Long & Co., 1902.

Skoulas, G. E. The theoretical dimensions of authoritarian rule in our time. *Democracy & Nature: The International Journal of Inclusive Democracy* 9 (July 2003): 263–283.

Smith, W. H. *All the children of all the people*. New York: Macmillan, 1923.

Social sciences. http://www.fact-index.com/s/so/social_sciences.html. Retrieved June 23, 2004.

Starkey, M. L. The *Congregational way: The role of the Pilgrims and their heirs in shaping America*. Garden City, NY: Doubleday, 1966.

"Stormy education meeting." *New York Times*, January 5, 1911.

Stowasser, K. Review: A history of Islamic Sicily. *American Historical Review* 81 (1976): 570.

Thompkins, V., ed. *American Decades 1900–1909*. Detroit, MI: Gale Research, 1996.

Thompkins, V., ed. *American Decades 1910–1919*. Detroit, MI: Gale Research, 1996.

Thorndike, E. L. "The contributions of psychology to education." *The Journal of Educational Psychology* 1 (1910): 5–12.

Toulmin, S. *Cosmopolis: The Hidden Agenda of Modernity*. Chicago: University of Chicago Press, 1990.

Veblen, T. *Theory of leisure class*. New York: Macmillan, 1899.

Wade, L. C. "Settlement House." *Encyclopedia of Chicago*. Chicago Historical Society. http://www.encyclopedia.chicagohistory.org/pages/1135.html. Retrieved July 24, 2017

Welchman, J. *Dewey's Ethical Thought*. Ithaca, NY: Cornell University Press, 1995.

"White slave congress." *New York Times*, October 24, 1906.

"Will deport white slaves." *New York Times*, October 5, 1907.

Zenderland, L. *Measuring minds: Henry Herbert Goddard and the origins of American intelligence testing*. Cambridge, MA: Cambridge University Press, 1998.

Zwick, J., ed. (n.d.) Political cartoons and cartoonists. *Child labor cartoons*. http://www.boondocksnet.com/gallery/child_labor_intro.html. Retrieved February 7, 2004.

4

The North End

Rose's Consciousness

Reaching an Agreement

The images of women and children being beaten by police officers on horses aroused the conscience of the nation to the inhumane treatment the strikers received. Zinn (1980) captures dramatically the significance of the children's exodus to New York City:

> The following week, another hundred children came to New York, and thirty-five to Barre, Vermont. It was becoming clear: if the children were taken care of, the strikers could stay out, for their spirit was high. The city officials in Lawrence, citing a statute on child neglect, said no more children would be permitted to leave Lawrence.
>
> Despite the city edict, a group of forty children assembled on February 24th to go to Philadelphia. The railroad station was filled with police, and the scene that followed was described to Congressmen by a member of the Women's Committee of Philadelphia:
>
> "When the time approached to depart, the children arranged in a long line, two by two, in orderly procession, with their parents near at hand, were about to make

their way to the train when the police closed in on us with their clubs, beating right and left, with no thought of children, who were in the most desperate danger of being trampled to death. The mothers and children were thus hurled in a mass and bodily dragged to a military truck, and even then clubbed, irrespective of the cries of the panic-stricken women and children ..."

A week after that, women returning from a meeting were surrounded by police and clubbed; one pregnant woman was carried unconscious to a hospital and gave birth to a dead child.

Still, the strikers held out. "They are always marching and singing," reporter Mary Heaton Vorse wrote. "The tired, gray crowds ebbing and flowing perpetually into the mills had waked and opened their mouths to sing."

The American Woolen Company decided to give in. It offered raises of 5 to 11 percent (the strikers insisted that the largest increases go to the lowest paid), time and a quarter for overtime, and no discrimination against those who had struck. On March 14, 1912, ten thousand strikers gathered on the Lawrence Common and, with Bill Haywood presiding, voted to end the strike.

Ettor and Giovanitti went on trial. Support for them had been mounting all over the country. There were parades in New York and Boston; on September 30, fifteen thousand Lawrence workers struck for twenty-four hours to show their support for the two men. After that, two thousand of the most active strikers were fired, but the IWW threatened to call another strike, and they were put back. A jury found Ettor and Giovanitti not guilty, and that afternoon, ten thousand people assembled in Lawrence to celebrate (pp. 336–337 of Howard Zinn's *A People's History of the United States*, in the "Socialist Challenge" chapter).

Certainty with Rules

After the strike, Rose returned to New England by herself. It was nice to be alone. Opening her bag, she took out the picture of her mother and father, staring at them before falling asleep and filled with ambiguity about her husband. She had been gone for several days and felt different. She wondered how it would feel to try to fit into her old life. Three hours later, she was in her sister's kitchen in Middletown. They spoke in dialect; Giuseppina still did not speak English.

"Where did you go?" Giuseppina asked, shutting the broom closet door. She stood back, resting from morning chores, and studied her sister's serious face. Outside, the snow was piled high against the window.

"I took children to New York on a train."

"What?"

"Families in New York agreed to take the children of striking workers."

"Rose. "I felt good doing it."

"Where did you stay? Don't tell me you slept in the back of a church."

Rose answered candidly, "I slept with Americans, and I sat down with them to eat."

Giuseppina sat down too. Feeling the loss of honor, she snapped back, "Carmelo will have a fit."

"Carmelo gave me his blessing," Rose said officiously "I am surprised he did not tell you."

Still angry, Giuseppina did not soften her news. "He stays out after dark. Carmelo is not cut out to be a plasterer. Sebastiano replaced him with a new boy from Melilli."

Rose barely recognized Carmelo when he arrived home later that day. The poor man could not stand on his feet. The exertion of carrying sand and water for ten hours a day staggered him. Rose unbuttoned his shirt, put his belt on the chair, and lay beside him.

"I am struck with paralysis," he said to her. "Bring me back to life." Rose held his fingers tightly, glad to be needed on this windy evening.

The next morning she awoke at five o'clock to prepare breakfast for her husband and brother-in-law. She fixed black coffee and cut meat into small pieces. Sebastiano Garafolo was a kind, serious man. "I am sorry I did not see you last night," he said to her.

"What are you working on?" Rose asked as she passed him a piece of sheep's cheese.

"The library at the university. Rain threatens the books."

"I want to see your work. Pa always liked you. That is why he gave you a good wedding."

Garafolo was glad to have Rose take interest in him, so he gave her directions to his site. Later that morning, Rose left without telling Giuseppina where she was going. She arrived at the university at noon. Snow covered the grounds and the slate roofs of the red brick and brownstone buildings. Doric columns and white steeples contrasted sharply with the fragile houses in the Sicilian neighborhood across the street. So did the prominent men and women who passed her in long, warm coats.

Bells chimed. She spied Carmelo sorting planks beside a steep incline. Garafolo stood nearby, talking to a well-dressed man who was taking notes. Rose watched her husband for a moment, cringing at his stooped shoulders and tired arms. Beside him, her brother-in-law laughed suddenly with the stranger, gesturing toward the place where the new library would stand. She wondered if this man was Henry Bacon. Garafolo had told her that the Wesleyan trustees had hired the New York architect to design three new buildings, one of which would be the new library. Garafolo had also heard that this American would soon design a memorial to Abraham Lincoln in Washington, DC.[1]

Garafolo did not look tired, as Carmelo did. Her sister's husband had chosen this work—a craft, not just a paycheck. The sun broke through the clouds, but the day was still cold. Rose shivered, pulled her thin coat more tightly around her neck, and stepped toward the men.

Carmelo smiled. "Mr. Bacon, please excuse me. I have just noticed my sister-in-law."

Bacon wrote in his notebook: *Marble and granite. Good idea.* Then he looked up at the immigrant woman walking toward them. Puzzled for a moment, he gave her a closer look, recalling where he had seen her. "Of course," he mumbled. "Is this your sister-in-law, Mr. Garafolo"

"Yes. That is Rose. Mrs. Carmelo Amoroso."

"I know her. I mean, I saw her picture in the newspaper. She accompanied Italian children to New York. I also saw her in a restaurant with a close friend of mine."

"You must be mistaken, Mr. Bacon." Rose had reached them and now stood apart, listening. "Rose, can this be true?" Garafolo asked.

Rose nodded silently. Bacon bowed and said that he was honored to meet her. "I saw your picture in the paper. You were in front of the Grand Central Terminal with a group of famous people. Did you read what the reporter said about you?"

"No."

"That the immigrant woman was as unyielding as the anarchists."

Bacon's remark pleased Rose, but Garafolo, feeling a bit impotent, said that he had to get back to work, so he showed Rose where to go and told her to be careful when she entered the library. Then he excused himself and walked away, shaking his head slightly. Rose's conversation with a distinguished American was impossible to comprehend.

"Did you come to Wesleyan in search of work, Mrs. Amoroso? I will need a servant when I move here in a few months."

Rose looked straight at him. She could sense her husband's sudden quiet. "I came to see the books," she replied. "My children will read them some day." Behind her, Carmelo began whistling softly as he worked—a man who would someday have children.

Bacon smiled at her presumption as he stared across the lawns. "I'm afraid that your daughters, at least, won't do that here, Mrs. Amoroso. The trustees voted to bar women from the university."

"Then they will learn elsewhere."

On June 1, 1912, the Amorosos departed for Boston's North End. The decision to move had been an easy one. Brother Sebastiano lived there; besides, Carmelo's brother-in-law Frank Gulizia told him that his brother Salvatore would help him secure a job.

Uncle and Aunt Gulizia are in the back row.

Rose and Carmelo stepped off the train and headed to the grocery store to buy bread and fruit for supper. Three men in black shirts stood outside the door, shouting slogans. No one recognized her. She was anonymous again. The strike and all that it had meant to her was suddenly in her past. During the thirty-minute walk to Gulizia's house, they passed the grammar school and the library where she planned to read about the Normans.

The lights were out, and Gulizia and his woman friend were gone when they arrived at the apartment and slowly climbed the steps. Once inside, Rose found a telegram addressed to her from New York City on the table. Thinking that it was from Emma or Elizabeth, she opened it.

Dear Mrs. Amoroso,

I write you with a heavy heart. Marina passed away May 20 in the New York State Mental Asylum. She died strapped to her bed. You were her best friend. I hope you can forgive her shame because there is no way I can.

Best regards,

Theodore Dreiser

Rose did not see her husband pacing as she collapsed in a chair. "Dear God," she prayed in the darkness, "have mercy on her soul."

The North End, the oldest neighborhood in Boston, was home to thousands of Italian and Sicilian immigrants. They had come in such great numbers that nearly every Irish and Jewish American or Yankee who had lived there had been displaced. Over the past two hundred years, development had changed this hilly pasture into an urban village crammed with odd-angled buildings and narrow streets and alleys. There were no zoning restrictions and manicured lawns here; in fact, no one who lived there could remember seeing trees or grass in the North End; by 1900, black iron lampposts and cobblestone streets had replaced them. This was now an Italian community with grocery stores, specialty shops, schools, and churches.[2]

Only a keen eye could tell that this place had once been of historic importance. Mere traces of its colonial past were in a few buildings, like

Paul Revere's wood-framed house, or the Old North Church and the Old North Meeting House. The names of the patriots who had lived here and their heroic deeds were long forgotten, their homes torn down and replaced at mid-century with rows of four-story brick Greek Revival dwellings and other popular styles, such as Italianate and the French-inspired Mansard. In turn, many of these buildings had been replaced with plain four-story brick tenement structures with little external ornamentation.

Although remnants of the past survived, they were of little interest to Carmelo. On the other hand, he admired the elegant row house with the copper-sheathed, curved front that stood across from Rose's church. An Irish merchant had built it years ago; now his descendants lived in it.

Rose and Carmelo lived in a tiny flat above a short, narrow, bent alley. Most streets in the North End broke sharply to the left or right rather than curving or bending. Buildings abutted the street, leaving little room to pass. Shops occupied the ground floor, with apartments above. Before long, Carmelo knew most of the merchants by name. He was especially fond of Nunzio's daughter, who smiled at him when he passed by her in the store. He hoped his own daughters would glow with her confidence.

The older women of the North End made their own dough at home but had it baked over wood coals at the baker's. Carmelo's job back home in Mineo had been to bring the loaves to the baker, and he loved doing the same thing for his wife now, especially at Easter, when Rose made large circular loaves with boiled eggs set on top. He also loved the rectangular breads that she dusted with light brown flour. She would use leftover dough to make angel hair cookies dipped in honey. The aromas of his childhood—anisette, olives in oaken barrels, warm ricotta pies—delighted him. He had even acquired a taste for American baked beans.

The North End, which sloped down to the polluted waters of Boston Harbor, was a place where Italians could confess their sins to a priest in dialect or pin money on holy statues during religious feasts. Women pushed baby carriages and shopped every day in small grocery stores. Boys carried home large, round, freshly baked loaves of bread, uncovered and steaming. Children played in the streets, while uncles sat outside, watching a marching band on its way to play traditional Italian tunes at a religious society meeting. Women visited each other after church or walked to the harbor on a warm Friday evening to see their men unload cod from boats named in their honor. Young boys raced to the decaying waterfront to throw stones at the ancient three-masted fighting ship *Old Ironsides*, which was berthed across the harbor at Charleston. The North End was crowded and noisy, a vibrant place where Italians followed the old ways.

Carmelo and Rose lived well during their year in the North End. Ten cents bought a month's worth of pasta and beans. Pennies bought enough meat to last a week. A tailor made a suit for three dollars. Rent was ten dollars a month. Rose knew how to stretch Carmelo's wage of fifty dollars a month, and Carmelo appreciated her frugality.[3]

Each Friday he brought her a bouquet of fresh flowers from Polaccio, the bachelor with the drooping eyebrows. Open-air vendors called to Carmelo as he rushed by with his flowers, but he ignored them. He knew exactly what he wanted—freshly picked Caribbean lemons, tangerines, bananas, and oranges from the United Fruit Company ship. His routine was to buy three pieces and place them in the salad bowl before Rose came back from her errands. When she opened the door, he would shout out in mock anger, "Why do we eat the same old thing every night?" They would kiss, knowing that they would not starve in this country. Their diet was simple but so very healthy.

The North End felt like home. Even Sacred Heart Church, a red brick structure that Boston Methodists originally used as the "Seamen's Bethel" so-called because sailors and whalers visited it before setting sail (in fact, Herman Melville often visited it and modeled his character Rev. Mapple from *Moby Dick* off of the famous sailor-preacher Edward Thompson Taylor who preached here) was purchased in 1884 by a group of Italian immigrants in order to minister to the social and spiritual needs of other new Italian immigrants.[4] Rose Amoroso was one of the most pious and devout parishioners. The church was her spiritual lifeblood during this difficult period. Without a mother or sister or aunt to talk with, she suffered inwardly.

Each day before sunrise she walked to the small devotional chapel to pray to her saints. The smell of burning candles reassured her. Kneeling in front of Saint Rosalia, she prayed silently. "Dear sister, have I done the right thing? Carmelo stirs something deep inside of me. I know you are mortified. I will fast and I will pray to you every day. Dear Rosalia, watch over me."

Then she turned to her Redeemer and the other patron saints. Beneath thick oak beams, she became transfixed on the white marble altar and its gold crucifix, finding meaning in life. She prayed to the virgin martyr Saint Lucy, majestic with her black hair and blue eyes, holding a set of eyeballs in her hand. Rose knew her story well. Lucy's mother had tried to arrange her marriage. The beauty of her eyes infatuated the suitor. "Do not look on my eyes," she said. "I am dedicated to Christ." He persisted, so she blinded herself, saying to him, "Now you have no cause to covet me." After he ran off, Christ restored her eyes, more beautiful than ever.[5]

Rose kept praying. "Saint Lucy, you suffered greatly for the love of Jesus. I suffer too but not as much as you. Give me the courage to remain faithful to the Lord every moment of every day."

Saint Rita, the nun who had devoted her life to Christ crucified, and Saint Rosario, who clutched rosary beads, comforted her as well. They were strong Italian women who had dedicated their lives to God. She adored them because they showed her how to live.

Her mother's voice came back to her during these meditations. "Rose, I named you after Saint Rosalia. She was very beautiful, like you. A rich, handsome prince wanted to marry her, but she refused because she was committed to Christ. Her father insisted she marry him, so she hid in a mountain cave with little more than grass to eat for the remaining days of her life. Devote yourself to Christ as Rosalia did. Do hard penance like her."[6]

Rose had replied, "Yes, dear Mother, I will follow her example, even if I have to live in a cave." The sin that plagued Rose was her physical relationship with Carmelo. Nothing filled Rose as completely as Carmelo's manic love for her. Why, then, was she disgusted by her trembling excitement? She could not stand the way he came to her at night. "I do not want you," she would say softly.

And he would look at her sadly and say, "I do not understand."

Carmelo's Consciousness

The Stroke of the Clock

Carmelo worked part-time around the neighborhood, assembling black iron fire escapes and tending to the newer tenement buildings made from yellow or white brick. The older ones were usually red brick. He also worked occasionally for Goldman, the Jew, who sold paper and iron products out of his 1727 wooden building. Most recently, Carmelo had worked on the Christ Church project.[7]

One night before heading home, Carmelo walked over to Copp's Hill for a smoke. A stiff breeze amplified the excited cries of neighborhood children jumping off the pier. He smiled as he lit his small pipe. Across the street, a steel-framed destroyer eased out of its berth to the sound of a Sousa march. Sailors in white military caps stood at attention. The music stiffened him, its cadence making him feel vulnerable. Across the harbor was the Bunker Hill monument, fashioned from massive blocks of Quincy granite. To his right was the USS *Constitution*, still rigged for maneuvers. Both were icons of Boston's military past.

The city had a gloomy and heartless look about it, sheathed in gray light and dark stone. Unlike his beloved Mineo, there were no white and yellow flowers, orange blossoms, or wild mint to lure people outside to laugh or talk. Bostonians passed their time behind closed doors, watching the strokes of the clock with crooked frowns. In Mineo, neighbors sat outside to watch the last rays of sun give way to bright moonlight. When Bostonians ventured outside, they did so alone, with a look of determination, their hands over their eyes so as not to see the old churches. Year-round in Mineo, Carmelo and his friends came to the grand square to listen to the larks whistle in the shadows of the magnificent Baroque structure and distant mountains.

Two women passed by. "I boil mine and cover them with melted butter," one said to the other. Carmelo shook his head, wondering how Americans derived pleasure from eating dull food. He picked up his hat and gloves and started home, thinking of Rose crumbling fresh bay leaves for his simmering sauce. He smiled, strengthened by thoughts of eating well tonight.

Sicilian masons were busily covering up a granite cemetery wall with red brick. A dog barking startled him as he passed in the shadows of tenement houses that Irish masons had built from the same brick. Ahead of him stood a helpless-looking colonial dwelling that neighborhood boys used as a clubhouse. Fearful of their mothers' eyes, they came here to smoke and play cards. At the top of the hill, he paused a moment to stare at the tall, elegant spire atop the old church, unaware that two lanterns hung by Robert Newman in its belfry on the night of April 18, 1775, had set off the war for American independence.

Carmelo had worked on the restoration of the Old North Church for the past two months. It was he who had found an old hymnbook behind a boarded-up window. He had given it to his supervisor, the Italian heretic who called himself a Waldensian.[8] As he walked down the center of the narrow street, a tiny woman peered out at him, her white head barely visible. Carmelo shrugged, puzzled by the weeds in her yard growing without sunlight. A fruit vendor had told him that she was one of the last Bostonians in the North End and that her father and grandfather had been shipbuilders. He had said that she sometimes talked about the clipper launchings down at the harbor and the wealthy Anglicans who had worshiped at the Old North Church, but she had stopped attending soon after the Irish immigrants arrived.

The rest of the old Yankees had departed years before.[9] Many resettled in the luxury townhouses built on top of reclaimed land in Back Bay. Before long, their colonial churches and elegant homes decayed and were torn down to make way for four-story tenements. Local officials were alarmed by the influx of so many illiterate immigrants. Horace Mann, head of the State Board of Education, urged the Commonwealth to act quickly to educate the children of the new Americans. Free public education, he pointed out, was the only way to preserve the republic from the "giant vices, which now invade and torment [us]."[10] Politicians reluctantly agreed and funded the common school movement.

Children enrolled in the new schools, but many dropped out. Mann advised his teachers to adapt their teaching to the interests of the students. They tried, but the children still failed.

By the time Carmelo arrived in the North End, the colonial texture of the neighborhood had disappeared, but, unknown to him, old Puritan beliefs, customs, and laws had not vanished and would make his assimilation difficult. The phantoms of discrimination and intolerance were especially dangerous to the achievement of the neighborhood children. Mindful that the North End had become an immigrant enclave, the Boston School Committee built a new school next to Copp's Cemetery, hallowed ground where Cotton Mather and many of Boston's original settlers were buried. The school was big, and it was named after an Italian.[11] Local politicians were pleased, but the school did little to slow school failure. Success was still outside the grasp of most children.

Roots of Discrimination and Democracy in Boston

The first inhabitants of the North End were Puritans who came in search of religious liberty. They believed that the Bible revealed all truth, that human nature was flawed by original sin, and that the only way to avoid evil was to live a life in strict accordance with the scriptures. They combined this belief with the doctrine of predestination, seeing themselves as elected spirits chosen by God to revolutionize history, a sense of righteousness that fostered intolerance of others.

Puritan orthodoxy controlled life in the North End for one hundred years,[11] although it eventually gave way to an intellectual movement that glorified the self. Men like Ben Franklin and Paul Revere—descendants of the original inhabitants— longed for a morality that supported their worldly pursuits. This age signalled the dawn of the eighteenth century, a time of commercial expansion and the mass production of books. Thanks to the Puritan proviso that all citizens of the Commonwealth needed to read the Bible, North Enders had become a highly literate people.

Puritan righteousness was no match for the high optimism of the Enlightenment. With inhabitants free to pursue individual interests, Boston exploded in a frenzy of capital and income. Before long, it was leading the world in the production of wool, leather, footwear, seafood, and coffee grinding. Bankers and financiers like Peabody and Morgan fueled industrial expansion throughout the colonies. Freed from duty and tradition, artists and intellectuals applied the classical qualities of discipline, balance, and restraint to art and architecture. Overnight, Boston became the Athens of America.

By the end of the eighteenth century, Enlightenment thinking was losing favor among intellectuals and average citizens. The popular view was that a few laws ran the world, so the goal in life was to use reason in pursuit of these laws. But as Bostonians prospered, they realized that they were more than the sum of their deductive powers. Feelings and aesthetic sensibilities made life worth living. Why ignore the charm and wonder of the natural environment? It was benevolent and blessed, and it tied truth to beauty. Aesthetic experiences were divinely inspired.

Middle-class American mothers were quick to accept views that reason oppressed the spirit of children and that effortless learning came through the use of the senses.[12] Clarke's *The Boy's Own Book* (1829) portrayed childhood as a time of play, and Mrs. Child's self-help text *The Mothers' Book* (1831) borrowed for its cover Wordsworth's notion that "The Child is Father of the Man." Such works encouraged readers to observe all aspects of child behavior and use accidental remarks to teach because these techniques were better than direct maxims or memorization.

For all its celebration of spontaneity, romanticism was less successful as a political philosophy in the North End, where life was harsh. Improving the environment would not rehabilitate the poor. Moreover, sentimentality did not square with Darwin's discoveries about the origins of life. People felt helpless, at the mercy of invisible and arbitrary forces. By the 1850s, the melancholy and disillusionment that had dominated life two hundred years earlier returned. The best one could do was use science and technology to control the environment as efficiently as possible.

Brahmins and Bullies

Carmelo did not understand the context behind the indifference that met him in Boston. He did not feel welcomed here. Bosses pitted one nationality against the other and fired men on the spot for making a mistake. Name-calling was common. In Mineo, the wealthy had treated the poor like dirt. To see the same oppression in America, a religious country with the motto "In God We Trust," was disheartening.[13] American banners flew inside churches; why, then, did greed and indifference obscure the ideals of the revolution? Carmelo worked for bosses who fasted for days to gorge at banquets. These same men collected tithes on Sunday but beat women and children for stealing bread.

The Enlightenment had thrown out God's will and replaced it with American materialism. Life was about wealth and privilege, not benevolence or justice. The Constitution afforded rights to landowners, not workers. Carmelo was unaware that academics were in league with capitalists or that his bosses relied on Adam Smith's *Wealth of Nations* (1776/1904) to condone their practices and policies. President of Harvard University Abbott Lawrence Lowell was a mill owner, and he had no idea that learned men wrote of how the poor were at the bottom of the food chain, that they had lost out in the battle of life, or that poverty was their own fault, and giving them charity only perpetuated their parasitic impulses. It seemed to Carmelo that the high-status men of Boston were filled with self-aggrandizement, not moral principle. In his mind, they laughed to themselves when they read stories about the squalor in which mill workers lived.

Capitalism had made his life easier—he wore fine suits, enjoyed the movies, and rode the subway—but it had also crushed his soul. He knew that something was wrong when the militia sent to keep the workers in check at Lawrence were Harvard students from the best families.[14] Did they not sense that their rifle butts kept the poor from feeding their children? Why did the enlightened not fight for him? This was not progress; it was the same abuse he'd known in Sicily.

One day at lunch, a friend handed Carmelo an advertisement for a free lecture by Professor Leo Max from Harvard College. A fish morphing into a man was on the cover. Carmelo chuckled as he thought about his friend Vito, the one with the nostrils of a pig. "Is this what you think about me?" Carmelo joked, crumbling the paper. He could not read it because it was in English.

If he had been able to read it, he would have learned that some people claimed the ability to classify races according to physical characteristics, such as hairline, nose, and chin size. He would have read that the top race is the Anglo-Saxon, with their aquiline noses and "high brows," and that the lowest are the Irish, with their jutting chins. Although phrenology had been discredited years before, it still had a powerful hold on public opinion in Boston.[15]

Discrimination became an instrument of control. In response to the waves of Irish immigrants fleeing the potato famine, many job posters and "newspaper ads for employment ended with 'No Irish need apply,' and restaurants and hotels would display signs reading 'No Irish permitted in this establishment.'"

In 1851–1852, railroad contractors in New York advertised for workers and promised good pay. When mostly Irish applied, the pay was lowered to fifty-five cents a day. When the workers protested, the militia was called in to force the men to accept.[16]

The Irish fought back. In Ireland, their oppressors had been wealthy landowners. In America, it was the Brahmin, a term coined by Oliver Wendell Holmes, Harvard graduate, descendent of Ann Bradstreet, and poet and professor of anatomy and physiology at Harvard Medical School. He thought of his kind, the Brahmin, as "Americanized Englishmen, proud squires unmellowed, and antheticized by change of climate."[17]

Life for Holmes and his Harvard-educated Unitarian and

Episcopalian Yankee peers was filled with confidence, affluence, and refinement. Their writers were blue bloods. Their businessmen, bankers, and financiers were shrewd. They put their wealth to work building the First Baptist Church, the Museum of Fine Arts, the Boston Public Library, Trinity Church, and the Boston Symphony Orchestra. By the 1870s, they had turned Back Bay into a mecca of intellectual activity. Boston was the "Hub of the Solar System."[18]

"By 1855, more than a third of Boston's population was Irish."[19] By 1880, Irish immigrants were in the majority. The city teemed with poverty, slums, religious discrimination, and unemployment. The Irish fought discrimination in a number of ways. Some changed their accents, names, and even religion. Others sent their children to parochial schools. A few second-generation Irish attended the new Jesuit university, Boston College.

By the time Rose and Carmelo moved to the North End, Italians were the new Irish. Hostility against them in the North End was so intense that Irish and Italians could not attend mass together. Before long, the Italians bought their own church two blocks away and renamed it Sacred Heart Church.

Writings by American intellectuals did not help the Italians' cause. The highly credentialed Francis Walker, fearing the loss of the American standard of living, submitted an essay to the *Atlantic Monthly* that called for the total elimination of immigration. The new immigrants, he felt, posed a far graver threat than the Irish had.

By 1900, Sicily had become one of the chief emigration regions in the world. More than a million Sicilians left for America before the First World War.[21] Few Bostonians realized that Sicilians like Carmelo were some of the most oppressed peasants in Europe. Slavery was deeply entrenched in their psyches. In the Middle Ages, the plague had created a shortage of agricultural workers, so Italian merchants bought slaves from the Balkans to work in the vineyards and on sugar plantations. The nobility looked down on them as uncivilized and immoral, treating them with the same degree of contempt, cruelty, and possessiveness as their Roman ancestors had treated the ancient slaves of Sicily.[22]

The new North Enders had come from a feudal society where freedom of speech and the press meant nothing. They came with no tradition of voting, because literacy tests excluded them from the vote. Young men had run to the hills to escape military service. Allegiance was to family, not government. There were few educated Sicilians among the arrivals; most were illiterate dialect speakers. In Sicily, even bourgeoisie families did not teach their children to read and write. Illiteracy was particularly high among women.

In America, local and state government did little to help the new arrivals. They had few political rights and were victims of ethnic slurs and police violence.[23] Other indignities made everyday life insufferable. Apartments lacked plumbing, so families had to use public bathhouses. There was no recreation for the children, so they swam in the foul harbor.[24]

Many of the women who stayed home to raise children refused to speak English. Others left childcare to church and volunteer associations. Still others recognized that education was the only way out of poverty, so they pushed American ways on their children. A few allied themselves with the socialists in the belief that government- and business-sanctioned discrimination could only be broken by force.

Poetry Lessons

Carmelo kept to his kind and minded his own business, often citing his favorite expression, "Don't tell anybody anything." When time permitted, he walked past Saint Stephen's to watch the old men play Bocci near the harbor. He recalled having sung at a christening in this church before he had moved to the North End. It had been his first time in an austere white Catholic church. Pewter chandeliers and elegant columns had merit, but everything else was bland.[25] He needed images to think about God. That was why he liked Saint Leonard's—ceiling frescoes in dark colors framed by off whites covered every space.

The effect pulled the eyes upward to meditate. Symbols abounded: crowns, thorns, snakes, praying women, and crucifixes. Saint Leonard's made Carmelo feel small and insignificant, ready to ask forgiveness from an all-powerful God.[26]

It was Friday afternoon when he walked to *Banco Italiano* to deposit his money. After completing his business, he sat on the curb stone to talk with friends.

Tito said, "I am going to buy my wife a new rosary. She wore out the one she brought with her.

"Do you know how to say the rosary?" asked Carmelo.

"I tried it as a boy, but I could not remember when to say the Our Father or how many Hail Marys to recite. Besides, what is the point?"

Carmelo was happy with his life in the North End. He loved the look and feel of the old cobblestone streets. He gazed at the man who sat alone in the evening chill, smoking a long cigar. He nodded to the pair of older men who passed by, hands in their pockets, bent and bowlegged with age. Across the street, two friends dressed in suits, vests, and hats sat outside the Jewish restaurant, dunking small round rolls with holes into mugs of hot coffee.

Also in a suit, young Gino walked by, holding his father's hand. "Tony, it's not Sunday," joked Carmelo.

"Getting our picture taken," Tony replied. He had just received a letter from his mother, instructing him to spend Easter with her. She wanted to see him before she died.

But Tony could not leave because his son was in school. In Sicily, few cared if children missed school. Neighbors said to each other, "Teachers like it that way; it lets them work with the deserving ones."

Gino, who attended Saint John's Catholic School, read the newspaper to his uncle every evening. In return, the uncle told him Sicilian stories. The youngster put them to good use. Carmelo had heard him tell one at the Esposito wedding. "Hey, Tony, let Gino tell me the story about the wolf boy. Here is a penny for him."

The boy looked up, and Tony nodded. Gino put his arm around Carmelo's shoulder and began to speak softly. "Long ago, a young boy from Calia walked the hills in search of wheat for his mother. It was late, so he took a shortcut past the Trinka crypt. The warm autumn sunshine bounced off the heavy brass door. The boy noticed that it was open. 'I am going to look inside,' he said to himself. An old coffin lay atop a white marble table in the center of the room. He walked over to it. His touch opened it. Inside was a tiny skeleton with a gold crown atop the skull. The boy knew he would be a hero at school if he wore the crown, so he grabbed it and ran home.

"Dusk fell over the fields as he neared the church. He did not notice the priest standing in the path, saying his vespers. The crown fell to the ground as he bumped into him. The priest saw the crown and blessed himself. He marched the boy home without saying a word. The boy's father was outside, shaving. The priest ordered the boy to tell his father where he got the crown. The father was so ashamed that he whipped his son until the crying stopped.

The next day he took his son to the hills. 'Sleep in this cave,' he commanded. 'Drink water, but do not eat anything. I will come back tomorrow night.' The boy cried quietly as he lay down to sleep.

"The following evening, a shepherd approached the cave in search of the wolf who had eaten three of his newborn lambs. He spied a small

---

Pietro di Donato
Christ in Concrete
1939

Son of Italian immigrants, di Donato (1911–1992) was a bricklayer when he published *Christ in Concrete* (1939), a critically acclaimed novel about the injustices that Italian immigrants encountered in America. Although it was chosen as the Book of the Month Club's selection for 1939, di Donato was subsequently ignored by the literary establishment and so returned to bricklaying. *Christ in Concrete* represents one of the first Italian American voices to be heard in this country (Gardaphé 1993).

The great building of the Compensation Bureau was a thick-walled, forbidding, ten-storied structure. It had the discouraging semblance and overwhelming morgue aspect of Institution. Head-of-Pig got down from the wagon, tied the reins to a telephone pole, and went into the building. From the third story of the building projected a flagpole and from it hung a huge blue flag. On it in soiled white letters was the State emblem and the words: "Workmen's State Compensation Bureau."

People, poor people. And their faces pulled at Paul's heart. Their eyes and lips said, we are the battered poor, poor stupid poor, we are the maimed and crippled and bandaged and blind workers who can not speak and are led and pushed through these corridors like subway corridors and into chambers where we understand nothing (p. 25).

---

figure on all fours by the creek. It was the boy, kneeling down to drink the water. The shepherd took aim and fired. The boy staggered to his feet before falling to the ground. Just then, his father came over the hill with a basket of food in his hand, anxious to see his son. He was sorry he had punished him so harshly. It was too late. His son lay at his feet, lifeless, never to hear his father beg for mercy."

Carmelo cried whenever he heard stories of misfortune. He would never be mean to his own children. Wiping a tear, he told Gino that he was a smart boy. Gino replied that his uncle was the smart one. "He works in the library, polishing big tables. A professor writes down his stories."

"Will you tell stories when you grow up?" Carmelo asked gently as he winked at Tony.[27]

The Wages of Sin

The North End streets were always bustling with excitement. In the gathering dusk, an elderly woman sat by her kitchen window, high above the noise, hand on her chin, listening to a loud argument in the alley below. The driver of a horse-drawn wagon and a young mother on her way to confession with her daughter were arguing about the right-of-way. "Back up," she said, head bobbing. "There's no room to pass. I will have my husband come after you! You are Folgia's cousin, the one who married Madelena Mascoli."

"Relax. Here, catch this," he said, throwing a penny to the child. "Go buy a rose for your beautiful mother."

Carmelo's joy was great this evening. He decided to stop off at church to pray. Sacred Heart was close by, so he walked over and entered the basement chapel. The lifelike statue of Saint Rosalia greeted him, with her crucifix, rosary beads, and skull in hand. Carmelo compared her long, dark hair; small mouth; thin nose; and sad, blue eyes to his wife's. Opposite was Mary with her dead son, the Christ. The depiction of his death was very realistic, with bloodied wounds and glowing chest. He found twelve more statues inside; most were of Mary—one in rich brown and green robes, holding the Infant Redeemer in her arms. Two children stood beside her outstretched arms. At her feet, sinners from hell grasped at her rosary beads. Each figure was blue-eyed.

Carmelo again thought of his wife. This closed space of marble floors, sweet smells, and female heroines offered intimacy to Rose. He had told her last week, "Sacred Heart is a woman's church, full of blue-eyed women. That must be why you go there. You are a martyr with suffering on your mind."

He turned and walked over to Saint Leonard's, a block away. Masculine saints, mythic beasts, avenging angels, and clashing cosmic forces adorned the walls. Saint Francis, not Mary, was the center of attention here. He looked up to the ceiling frescos, where Christ and his twelve apostles gazed down at him.

Carmelo did not accept the resurrection story, just as he found it ridiculous to think a man could live inside the belly of a fish for three days. Also, rising from the dead was impossible. *When you are dead, you are dead.* His mother had told him to believe the stories. "God can do anything," she'd said to him.

"It is a lie, an exaggeration. Can you not see, Ma? The stories keep us in fear. Everyone is afraid of Jesus. The priests work for the rich. They spit on us."

He remembered his promise to Rose, so he left his pew in search of religion, stopping to examine the frescoes on the back wall. One was of a chariot pulled by a bull and a lion. A woman stood inside it. He did not know what it meant, so he meditated on the snakes. Then he walked over to the statues, making sure to keep his eyes off beautiful Saint Lucy.

He was not making a good start. A beautiful young woman who knelt at the feet of Saint Francis tempted him. Another woman about his age walked in the side door and sat beside him. Her hair was luxuriant, deeply dark and clean. Her full figure appealed to him. She was dressed in a white blouse and skirt, white shoes, and a shawl. She whispered aloud to Jesus: "Why did you make me marry Partini, the merchant? He is so much older than me and does not speak Gaelic. I told you I should have married my own kind. He took me to Italy to see his dying mother. She's eighty-four. He told me that she kept money under her mattress. He wanted to get it before his father gave it to the poor.

"She was lying in bed on top of soiled sheets that had not been washed in a year. An old man sat outside and rocked. I tried to lift the mattress, but she grabbed my hair and pulled me to her. 'I know what you want, and you are not going to get it.' I vomited as the smell of death covered me."

She spoke so rapidly that Carmelo understood little of what she said. It did not matter, though, because he watched her red mouth move, fascinated by tiny scars on her upper lip. Unknown to him, Rose stood behind him. She had come to help him pray. Without saying a word, she left through the side door.

Carmelo was a fierce lover with an endless imagination. Unable to stop his desire for women, he prayed in rage. "Dear God, you even tempt me in your house." As he turned away from the woman in disgust, she let her shawl fall into his lap as she left. He held it to his nose. The door closed before he reached it, but the smell of her hair transfixed him. She walked quickly toward Commercial Street and then turned north onto Baker Street and entered a three-story bay apartment. He walked behind her and up to her door. She opened it without saying a word. Carmelo spoke first. "Madam, I believe this is your shawl."

"It is, but how did you come to find it?" She looked genuinely puzzled.

"You sat next to me at Saint Leonard's. It fell into my hands when you rose to leave."

"That is impossible; I have been home all day. However, come in. The March wind is picking up. You look like you could use a cup of tea." She showed him to the parlor and left. He sat alone, with his hands on his lap, examining the expensive African mahogany furniture, the ornate marble sideboard, Victorian palms, and deeply combed oriental carpet. He closed his eyes for a moment, trying to slow the pace of his heart. When he opened his eyes, she stood in front of him, her full figure barely visible as the sun changed position. "Would you go into the basement to fetch my cat? She is crying in the dark."

Carmelo fumbled for words, remembering what Frenchie had told him about American women: "You can't love them in the night," he had said. "Oh my." He sighed and got up to open the basement door. As he reached the bottom step, he heard the door lock. He did not react at first. Five minutes passed without a sound. A brown Norwegian rat scurried across his foot. He knew at that moment he was in trouble. Sweat broke out under his arms and on his forehead. He renounced all past sin, but it was too late. "I am going to die with an ax blow to my head, like Saint Jude," he blurted.

As he quivered in the dark, heavy footsteps sounded from above, and then the door opened slowly. The woman with the blood-colored hair stood at the top of the stairs, covered in nothing more than a black shawl and holding a wooden crucifix in her left hand. She came down the steps slowly, her eyes fixed on the passage of time. Standing before this Mora, she sobbed quietly as she raised the crucifix above her head and said, "You gaze upon me in a blasphemous way."

Carmelo screamed so loudly that two more rats darted past him. Pushing her aside, he raced up the steps and into the parlor. Sitting next to the fireplace was a huge black man. Carmelo tripped over his feet. The giant, who smelled of the sea, held a small package wrapped in brown paper and tied with red string. He stared at Carmelo and broke into a high-pitched giggle. "Te-he-he. How many time I see dis sight?"

Carmelo turned ashen as the giant stood, waving his hands above Carmelo's head. The box slipped out of his hand, scattering fishy scented shellfish and fishy scented ice about the carpet. "I see dat Miss Molly went crazy. She feeling bad, little man, when she alone to grieve." Racing out the door, Carmelo crashed into a Portuguese sailor from the Azores locked in the arms of Carmelita, the prostitute. She spit on Carmelo, but he did not care; he ran all the way to his apartment. "Rosina, Rosina," he implored, "do not force me to sleep on the pavement."

Rose was not in the apartment, nor did she ever ask Carmelo why he never left her alone again. She assumed that her prayers had been answered.

Legacies

Public Amusements

Late one Saturday afternoon, Carmelo surprised Rose. "Let's walk to Scollay Square. We can shop for fresh fruit and go to an American restaurant. The owner promised me a free meal."

"Where is Scollay Square?" she asked.

He called her to the window. "Near the tall building with the pointed roof."

"How do you know about it?" she asked as she watched her neighbor, who looked up at her.

219

"Several friends from the club worked on a skyscraper there. They invited me to sing at a party and told me the great Babe Ruth was going to be there. I rushed over from work, and there he was, with a mug of beer and a mouthful of sausage. I laughed so hard at his puffy cheeks that he turned around to see what was the matter. Looking down at me, he said, 'By God, you are the tiniest ironworker I ever seen. Where'd they find you? In a circus?' Everyone laughed. I tried to smile without showing my teeth."

Rose was frowning but continued to give him her attention.

"Babe said, 'For a little man, you sure have a big smile. Where'd you get it, for crying out loud?' Everyone roared again. Brusca, the painter, piped up, 'Hey, Babe, ask Carmelo to sing like a bird.' The Babe loves a good tune and fancies himself an opera lover, so he says to me, 'Say, little man … Goodness. I don't even know your name. What did your friend call you—Carol? Impossible. That's a girl's name.'

"I stood there politely, not moving. 'No, sir, my name is Carmelo.'

"'Sure. Sure. Carmen—hey, that's still a girl's name.'

"'Just call him Don Carmelo!' shouted my friend Butrini."

Rose froze. The title *don* meant that his friends expected Carmelo to return their respect with invitations to his table.

"'Whatever,' the Babe retorted. 'Sing me a song.' Everyone clapped. Before I knew it, the Babe hoisted me up to the top of the bar with his free hand. I bowed and, fixing my tie, sang 'Marie from Sunny Italy.'

Oh, Marie, 'neath the window I'm waiting
Oh, Marie, please don't be so aggravating
Can't you see my heart just yearns for you, dear
With fond affection.

"Babe was in tears. He whispered to the bartender, 'Drinks for everyone. Shockingly, this little Dago sings as good as my Jew friend in New York.[28] Perfect pitch. Carmen, if you can bring tears to the Babe, I wonder what you do to women!'

"I smiled and said to him, proudly, 'Mr. Babe, I have a baby on the way.'

"'What a shame! If I had those pipes, I'd sing to every blonde from here to Cleveland. You're a real gentleman, Don Carmen.' Hugging me like a bear, he continued. 'Take this gift, and buy your wife a good meal. Tell her it's on the Babe.' When I opened my hand, I saw a hundred-dollar bill."

"My goodness!" shrieked Rose, who wanted to kiss him. "Get me a glass of water. A hundred dollars is more than you make in a year! Where is it?"

Carmelo stayed still, pulling at his black hair. "I couldn't accept it, not when there are poor orphans roaming the city. I told him to give it to Saint Joseph's. I figured the little angels could use a nice meal and new baseball equipment."

"Husband," she said, her voice rising, "we have a baby on the way."

"Do not worry. The saloon owner invited us to come over for New England pot roast."

Rose was too angry to answer. Thank goodness God had given her other emotions. Slowly, Carmelo's benevolence sank in. Laughing, he grabbed her and twirled her around the kitchen, as if dancing to a Sousa march. She kissed his forehead again and again as she said, "You will bring us down to nothing."

In a little while, they walked down Hanover Street, arm in arm, past the fruit stand and Carmine's Bakery. Carmelo wore his everyday suit and hat; Rose wore her green skirt, pleated white blouse, and new straw hat. They passed familiar faces. Most were Italian, but a few were Jewish or Irish. When they reached the vacant corner store facing the alley, they turned and walked briskly past mounds of garbage. They chose not to see the garbage, concentrating instead on the scent of onions and garlic simmering in olive oil and hot bread baking in stone ovens.

Within minutes, they were in a different world. Brick residential buildings gave way to rows of commercial buildings and warehouses covered with colored advertisements and posters. The streets narrowed as they wound through three- and five-story buildings packed with retail shops, bookstores, office space, restaurants, and pubs. This was the market district of Boston, where workers prepared meats and produce for shipment. Many of the painted storefronts were the same dark color as the house across from Rose's church.

The similarities ended there. The shops had odd names like New England Oyster House and Durgin Park and were crowded with busy men who ate boiled meat and drank dark beer. Men in bloodied aprons jostled for space with shoppers, horse-drawn carriages, and trucks with bright red spokes. Quickly moving pedestrians clutched baskets of fresh carrots and cabbage. People were here to buy and sell, not socialize.

Straight ahead, the crowd dispersed, and the dense street pattern ended. Peering around numerous signs painted in black with gold letters, Rose spied a beautiful building in the center of a cobblestone plaza. She had reached Faneuil Hall, Boston's main market, with its ample space and open-air stalls. She felt connected to this place and stopped to take in the mélange of color and sound. A beefy pedestrian bumped her off the sidewalk in his haste to reach the trolley. Carmelo reached out to smack him but was too late. He tried to make light of it by saying, "Do not stop for nothing." Then he remembered the baby and asked, "Rose, is the baby okay? Did he move? That's all I need—more bad luck. I forgot to tell you that O'Brien is going up on the rent next month. Gulizia is interested in buying the property."

Although her ankle throbbed slightly, Rose was more embarrassed than angry or hurt and replied, "Americans will never starve. They have everything under the sun. I wish I could say the same for us. You are not bringing home enough money, husband. I thought you were going to ask Gulizia for a job."

"Ah, he's a big windbag. Says I cannot add fast enough."

"Ask my brother to find you a job," Rose countered, pushing her hair behind her ears.

The thought of moving again made Carmelo sweat. "I do not want to leave Boston. All my friends are here."

Rose answered, "We have to think about the baby. You need a steady job. You cannot expect me to work when I am nursing."

"All right. All right. I will speak to Gulizia when we get back."

As she picked up her hat, she noticed a long, massive building that looked like a Roman temple: Quincy Market, with its centered dome. It had the same name as the town in which her brother lived. The same ugly stone as the base of the Statue of Liberty gave this building, blackened with dirt and grime, a cold, impersonal look. "Carmelo, what is the name of that stone?" Rose asked.

"Granite. They quarry it in Quincy. Sebastiano says Americans use it for gravestones. He says lots of Italians work in Quincy, mining and polishing it—I guess it shines like glass."

"Did he say anything about other jobs up there?"

"I told you; I will talk with Gulizia again. A pack of horses couldn't drag me out of the North End."

Rose grumbled, and Carmelo turned dark. She knew that she was mistress of the house and much cleverer than her husband. For his part, Carmelo hated squabbles; Rose always turned around his words, so he just never said anything she didn't like to hear. His refusal to move showed a new resolve.

Ever the observer, Rose turned her attention to a red brick building among the drab granite warehouses: the Old State House building, the original house of the British governor and the colonial legislature. It was very old and historic, almost feminine in appearance, with a lion and a unicorn above its front door. The Declaration of Independence was first read here. "Carmelo, what is that building? It looks out of place."

"I don't know, and I don't care. I hope they tear it down because that will mean a job for me."

"Nonsense."

"It's an old building that is taking up space. You see those tall buildings that block the sun? Count the windows. Behind each are a hundred secretaries. New buildings mean jobs. That is what buildings are all about—jobs. Good, clean jobs, not the dirty ones I do."

As he spoke, Rose studied the skyline. Her father had taught her to remember the past. The classical gray-tan structures in Italianate detailing and the edifices calmed her soul. Why replace art with absurd skyscrapers that sucked the soul from the city?

Carmelo spoke up. "I know a shortcut to the sun." Just then, a blast of white steam shot up from the sidewalk, making both of them jump back. A passing policeman laughed; so did the butcher who was carrying a fresh side of beef. Carmelo laughed too, joking, "Satan is on his way to catch me."

Rose said what was on her mind. "Boston's skyscrapers are tiny compared to the ones in New York. They are so tall you get dizzy looking up at them. They make you fall over if you stare at them." Carmelo looked at her suspiciously, so she said playfully, "Come here and stand next to me. When I say look up, look up." He twitched his cheek and waited for her command. "Now," she said. He looked up and lost his balance.

A decisive moment had arrived for Carmelo. "Rosina! You are

strangling me. You always find ways to humiliate me. You came back from New York, bossing me around."

"Carmelo," Rose said, "stop being a crybaby and listen. The oldest buildings are wood. We live in an old brick building. We just passed one made from stone. Now, skyscrapers. My father built homes the same way his grandfather did. I wore the same clothes my aunts wore when they were my age. This is not a place where time stands still."

Carmelo agreed. "Yes, in Sicily, the poor stay poor. Here, the humble become noble."

"Exactly," Rose said. "Anyone can make it to the top floor of that building with an education."

A deep longing flashed in Carmelo's eyes. "I want America to bring out the best in my son."

Rose thought of her sister Concetta in the convent. "He will pray too. What will it matter if he is rich but stops going to church? I want him to be successful, not a fool. Did you see the look of the man who pushed me? He was too busy to say excuse me or may I help you. I do not want my son to forget the saints. That is what I want for you too. Make something of yourself at night school and pray to Saint Anthony."

Carmelo replied, "I do not want my son to smell of oregano. I want him to be like the Babe, a ballplayer who makes women tear at their hair. My friends will shake my hand."

Rose listened to Carmelo closely and wondered if he heard himself. "I am fond of you, husband, but I say this for your own good—*Falloccu!*"

A man waiting on the street corner for a shoeshine laughed. Visibly hurt at being called a fool, Carmelo struck back. "Do you know why Italian priests followed us to America? To keep us in the dark. And why do they admonish you to adore the Virgin Mother? To chase me out of the bedroom."

Rose had never wanted to marry, but she did, and it was to a cannibal. "Look at me," she said with enough anger to cast out devils. "Jesus and Satan cannot exist together."

Carmelo hated dichotomies. Watching her closely, he said, "Last night you were quiet at first, covered up. You tilted your head and, with that coy look on your face, squeezed your legs around me. I lost my breath."

"If you try to sleep by me tonight, I will drive you to the street."

Husband and wife grew silent as they passed the elegant American House, one of the largest hotels in New England. Getting out of a taxi on Hanover Street was a heavyset man who waved to Carmelo. Carmelo tried to ignore the salute, but it was too late. "Carmelo!" the man called out. "Where have you been?"

Carmelo reddened and touched his moustache nervously.

"Who is this classy lady on your arm? Durlamo told me you had an eye for the delicious ones."

Rose was not in the mood for flattery, and she knew this man's face. Mothers whispered when he walked by that he came to the North End only to shop for pretty little girls. This defiler of children knew her husband. Carmelo put his hand on Rose's shoulder and, with his head bent, mumbled, "I am a married man, Mr. Weinstein. This is my wife, Rose."

Weinstein was vast, and so was his laugh. Crushing his cigar into his hand, he said, "Married at last. Who would have thought that? May you make beautiful children."

Rose was enraged. Who was he, and how did he know her husband? "Carmelo," she said, once the rotund man had lumbered away, "who is that man? You know what I will do to you if you tell me a lie."

Carmelo knew her fury. In mock piety, he said, "He works at the Old Howard Theater. My friends took me there as a wedding present. See that restaurant?" He pointed past Stoddard Street. "We went there for a hot dog."

Rose scowled. "Don't play the fool." She knew exactly what he had done. Marina had told her about wild-eyed men shouting obscenities at girls who were kicking up their legs. "The night before our wedding you came down here? I feel like poking your eyes out."

"How could I know where my friends were taking me? I could not disappoint them when we got here, not after the cost of the train trip."

"Husbands are for the arms of their wives," Rose countered. "You are not telling me everything. This man you call your friend takes children into the back room of a restaurant, and they come out crying."

Rose was sickened by Carmelo's talk. He was the one who gazed upon her nightly as she combed out her hair beside the flickering candle. He was the one who draped her hair back across her shoulders, causing her to blush. The man who stirred so much passion in her was vile.

Carmelo glanced at the children who played in the street. "Mr. Weinstein searches for new talent all over Massachusetts. It is a real honor to work for him. All the biggest names in Boston patronize his business. Even the police commissioner is a regular customer. The young children must have been beauties. Mr. Weinstein selects only the prettiest girls for his review."

What he did not tell her was that Weinstein also ran the largest brothel in the city. After the regular crowds went home, his steady customers walked through the secret green door at the rear of the stage to release their solitude amid loud laughter and open arms.

She yelled, "You do not understand, do you? What does it matter that he is a businessman? His money is tainted. If I had known he was your friend, I would have thrown my wedding band into the river."

No Time to Cry

It had been a miserable afternoon. Rose had twisted her ankle, argued with her husband, and seen a totally despicable man—too much for a thirty-year-old woman who was six months pregnant. "Take me home. I feel faint," she said.

When she entered the apartment, Rose sat in the dark, sobbing with rage. Her life had been poisoned by tribulation. For the past eight years she had been a model citizen at work and in the community. She had been a quiet, dependable, and responsible worker at the mill. She had stayed in good health by watching her diet, and she had learned English and American history in night school. She honored her parents by sending them her earnings every week. She had not given herself to a man until she married Carmelo. She had lived by a strict moral code, conforming to every expectation set by others. In return, she had earned the respect of coworkers and American intellectuals during a critical labor strike. She had also found a husband in America, a fellow Sicilian who enriched her life. Why, then, was she so unhappy? Could Carmelo be patronizing prostitute houses?

Her success had come with conditions. The mills created wealth but were dangerous places, filled with discrimination and exploitation. Now Carmelo's faithfulness proved empty. Faith and conscientiousness were not enough. After she prepared bean and macaroni soup for Carmelo, she sat down at the kitchen table to take matters into her own hands.

March 19, 1913

Dear Brother,

> *Today I took a fall. I have no one to help me. What happens if I take ill when the baby comes? We will run out of food. Carmelo is too small to sweat at work. Is there a workshop for him in Quincy?*

Rosa

Sebastiano saw the letter on the kitchen table when he returned home from work. In his mid-twenties, short but lithe, and given to quick movements, he was one of the top plasterers in the state. Married for three years, he owned his house and had a bank account. Sebastiano missed the citrus, grapes, raisins, and wheat of Mineo, but he did not miss the religious fears that held back so many of his friends. Like many men, he ridiculed women who associated the red socialist flag with the devil. Like other artisans who traveled in search of work, he knew something of the world and acted on his knowledge.[41] The last time he had spoken with his sister was at her wedding. He had given her away and then disappeared into night with one of the guests. He had run into Carmelo at a wedding in Somerville a little while ago.

Unable to read or write, he asked his wife to read the letter as he enjoyed a cold glass of beer. When she finished, he threw the envelope in the stove. The next day his wife wrote to Rose.

March 25, 1913

Dear Rosa,

> *You are welcome to live with us. Sebastiano will find Carmelo a job in one of the factories. We live on the second*

floor and rent out the first floor to a bachelor. It does not look like much from the outside, but I keep it spotless. Sebastiano bought me a player piano for my birthday.

There is a big field behind our house. It is filled with rye grass and black beetles. A brook runs through it. I sit near it as I mend. The church is a short walk from my house. The Italian grocery and meat shop are at the corner.

To cheer you up, here is a tale from my childhood. A count lived alone in a gold castle deep in the forest. His cries of loneliness were heard in the village. The widow Carina and her daughter Gema walked hand in hand to visit him. "Don Certo," they cried out, "we come to mend your heart." He appeared on the steps in his slippers. Feeling weakness in his heart, he threw himself into their arms. In all his glory, he had never felt the love of a woman.

Love,

Fannie

Sebastiano and Fannie walked to the Quincy Adams depot. She carried a small box filled with a dozen cakes that she had prepared for dessert. This was Fannie's first visit to the North End. Her husband, however, was a seasoned traveler with a wide reputation in the Italian community; his American friends called him Sonny. Like his sister, he was not an emotional person. Responsibility at an early age had hardened him. His father had taught him that there is no excuse for a poor job. He used to watch his father and Antonio work on a job until it was right; neither ever complained how long it took or how much they earned. They were artists, intent on expression. Before he left for America, Sebastiano had told his parents that he would be as good a plasterer as his father. His father had shot back, "Not until you sleep in marble dust."

They got off at South Station and hopped onto the Union Wharf trolley. Fannie was overwhelmed by the congestion. Carmelo was waiting for them at the stop. Rose was preparing the meal. Fannie was filled with excitement, but she knew her place. Men talked to men, and women talked with women. Her turn to talk would come after lunch, when she and Rose sat down away from the men.

They arrived at the apartment and immediately sat down to eat. Rose had prepared calamari over pasta. The flesh was tender and succulent, flavored with just the right touch of fresh onion, red pepper, olive oil, bay leaf, and garlic. She had even made her own pasta for this special occasion. Their mother had set a table just this way for family, and she knew that Sonny would love it. Fannie congratulated Rose on keeping such a spotless kitchen. Rose accepted the compliment; keeping domestic order was important to her. They gossiped as sisters as they set the table and cut the bread. Carmelo and Sonny sat at the other end of the table, talking about Florida over homemade wine.

During lunch, the men shared stories about their parents' birthplaces and their favorite songs and then quickly moved on to the poor flavor of imported cheeses, fat politicians, and the dreams of unmarried cousins. Fannie filled them in on her newest paper player roll, "Lights and Shadows." Carmelo kept still until he mentioned the latest movie he had seen—*The Stampede for Gold*. Rose got up to wash the dishes and start the coffee boiling, while Fannie set out the delicious orange cakes she had brought along. The men continued to talk about America.

Sonny took a sip of wine and blinked at Carmelo. "Rose, you never told me you married a good singer. I heard him at a wedding a few weeks ago. The crowd would not let him sit down."

She turned around as she took off her white apron and said in a tired voice, "He tells me that all the time. He comes home with a big smile on his face but nothing in his pocket."

"He lives for applause, sister."

Frustrated, Rose countered, "God is not blessing us because Carmelo does not go to church."

Sonny replied, "Ma did the praying in our family, and Pa went to work. We did not have new clothes, and we certainly did not have chicken soup every day. Give to your husband thankfulness. He needs more than a crack on his head." He then turned to Carmelo. "Rose tells me she wants to move by us."

Carmelo grew moody. "I have nothing against Quincy. It is the way

Rosina is forcing me into it. She knocks me down. Everyone respects me except her."

Sebastiano knew the answer. He told him about the big field behind his house and the Sicilians who were moving into the neighborhood. "Young families arrive every day. The shipyard draws them here. There is enough work for a lifetime."

Carmelo's face suddenly changed, and he shot up before Rose could reply. "My son is going to play baseball in Quincy!"

Venduto Per un di Canzone

In October 1913, two months after Connie was born, Carmelo and Rose moved to Quincy and found an apartment on Water Street, two houses down from Sonny and Fannie. A few weeks later, Carmelo landed a job in a machine shop at Norfolk Downs.

As a steady income came in, they looked for a bigger apartment in the neighborhood. Rose wanted an extra room to rent out. A year later, baby Enrico was born, so they moved into an even larger duplex. Shortly after, Carmelo came home with wonderful news—he had found a bungalow to rent on Cyril Street, next to Silberman's junkyard, near the shipyard. With the war on, he reasoned, he could count on steady work.

Rose was skeptical about moving, especially away from her sister-in-law. She had found friendship with Fannie, and having family close by was the Sicilian way. Since leaving home, she had lived among strangers.

Carmelo persisted, but Rose screamed, "Are you crazy? Why raise children next to a rat-infested junkyard? Don't you love them?"

He replied calmly, "Of course I do. More than you will ever know." Carmelo was a good listener, so he perceived where the conversation was headed. "Rosina," he said, "you will be able to spend more on food, because we will save on the rent." He was right. Since the start of the war, milk had jumped from nine cents to fifteen cents a quart and fresh eggs from thirty-four to sixty-one cents a dozen. Prices for other commodities had risen an average of 55 percent. He reminded her how difficult it was making ends meet on his weekly earnings of five dollars.

He also reminded her how miserable it had been for him to get to work in the winter. Even though he was used to walking great distances in Melilli, the long treks he now had to endure on bitterly cold days were killing him. He detested the icy winds that blew off the harbor and the desolate skies. He had no intention of pushing and dragging his legs through snowdrifts three feet high, only to spend the rest of the day wet inside a frigid ship. She saw the melancholy in his eyes and gave in to his wishes.

Those years were untroubled and filled with tender moments. Many times, Carmelo called out *"Rigu. Vendeci comare*—come for a song."

With his tiny hand resting on his father's shoulder, little Enrico listened to melodies distinctively Sicilian (H. C. Amoroso, 1997, April 5, personal interview with author):

Si comm'a nu sciorillo,
tu tiene na vucchella
nu poco pocorillo
appassuliatella.
Meh, dammillo, dammillo,
—e comm'a na rusella—
dammillo nu vasillo,
dammillo, Cannetella!

You are like a little flower,
You have a little mouth,
A little, tiny
Passion.
Meh, give it to me, give it to me,
--and like a little rose—
give it to me a little flower pot,
give it to me, Cannetella.

Many generations later, after Carmelo had long past away, Enrico's sister Concetta (or "Connie") would recall her father as a gentle, loving man who took care of his children and set a good table for his friends. She remembered acquaintances called him "Don Carmelo" in deference to his charm, friendliness, and generosity (Carr, C. B., 1998, May 23, personal interview with author).

Pictures of Enrico and Concetta during this time reveal a healthy, plump boy of two dressed in shorts and framed in shoulder-length black curls. His sister, Connie, was just as angelic in white, with a huge ribbon in her hair. They were healthy and happy, unfettered by the suffering common to other immigrant children. They were blessed with two loving parents who made them the center of their lives. America was giving them a chance to grow up strong. As a measure of her intelligence, Connie quickly became the brightest child in her class. She came home one day to find a new baby sister in her mother's arms.

Concetta and Enrico Amoroso, 1918

Carmelo moved his family to Cyril Street in the sixth year of his employment at the Boston Gear Works, where he spent his days sweeping twisted metal off the floor. It gave him enough money to pay rent, place food on the table, and buy white cream for Rose's alabaster skin. On one occasion, a bookish-looking machinist stayed after work to show Carmelo how to operate a lathe. His coworkers were angry because they were fiercely anti-foreigner. Smacking Carmelo across the head, one cried out, "This serves you notice, you alien. Touch the machines, and I'll punch you in the jaw." Carmelo swung his broom at him. That was the day he was fired from the Gear Works.

One Saturday afternoon, after Carmelo had finished making a batch of red wine, Rose handed him a postcard from the music teacher Gulizia.

Carmelo

Sister Josephine and niece Giuseppina walked off the hill. They are in Lawrence with Brother Frank. She desires to see you and your family.

Regards,

Salvi

Carmelo had always felt awful about his brother in-law sitting alone among books. *A night of love will do him good*, he thought, smiling. "Concetta, get out your best dress. We go to see your cousin."

Connie was perplexed; she had never been with cousins. "Pa," she asked, "what cousin?"

Rose never made an effort to talk or ask about Carmelo's family, but his daughter's question gave him reason to remember in detail the life he had left so long ago. "Cousin Giuseppina comes from a village that rests atop a large hill. She is my sister Josephine's child. Your aunt Josephine was very beautiful. She lived with our brother, your uncle, on the estate of a wealthy landowner. Uncle was a very good-looking man. His children passed for opera stars. He wanted me to become a priest.

"His foreman's name was Frank. My sister stared at him from behind drawn curtains as he made his daily rounds atop a horse, a book of poetry in his hand. She thought about him from dawn to dusk. Frank fell in love with her as well and gave her the wedding ring that had belonged to his great-grandmother. The wedding celebration ran out of food after the third day. That was when she moved in with Frank's sisters. I was about thirteen years old. She scolded me whenever she caught me watching her kiss Frank in the courtyard."

"Tell me about when you were a boy, Pa," Connie asked, feeling his glee.

Carmelo patted her little neck and continued. "The rich owned all the land. They lived in great palaces with walls covered in silk and sent their children to church schools far away. My parents never took me on a trip, even when the heat of summer scorched the air. I had to say hello to our neighbors and mind my own business. Your grandmother punished me severely if I ate with my mouth open.

"I went to school, as did my father. Others in the village worked in the fields. At night they slept in the same room as their animals. That is why they became priests and nuns. My mother told me stories about the great Girabaldi, who freed Sicily from the Bourbons. Musicians came to my house to sing songs about love and honor. I sat straight up when they came."

Rose picked up little Enrico, who was coughing sharply. She dreaded seeing her in-laws; she knew that they were her betters. In Sicily, Rose had scrubbed walls and dragged dirty laundry outside to wash. She had been little more than a household servant with a single black dress. She murmured, "I need to give the baby medicine. I also need to iron Concetta's Sunday dress and polish her shoes. Be sure to wrap a pie in white paper for your sister."

After mass, Carmelo and Concetta took the subway to North Station and the train to Lawrence. Carmelo was dressed for the occasion, derby included. The conductor, who was dressed in a black hat and coat, was much taller than Carmelo. He admired the lovely child beside him, self-assured in her love. "What a little princess of Persia," he whispered as he punched the ticket of her slight parent.

The Lawrence depot approached; Connie caught sight of the mills, one overlapping the other. Father and daughter walked hand in hand over the bridge to Valley Street. Carmelo had been back a few times to visit Frank but had never taken his daughter along. A friend from the socialist club whistled to him.

Hugs, kisses, and tears greeted them at Frank's apartment. Josephine was still beautiful, her hair straight and black, and little Giuseppina was stunning. She had inherited the fine features of the Amoroso clan, along with the smooth complexion that comes from a diet of grain and fruit. Only nine, she could read fluently.

Josephine was putting the parlor in order, and Giuseppina was peeling eggplant when Carmelo and Concetta arrived. The scents of prickly pears, cactus plants, figs, cherries, and fruit trees filled him with memories and cleared his head. Frank mentioned offhandedly that he had helped a man find work in the Quincy shipyard.

Away from the adults, Giuseppina handed Concetta a gift—Etna candy from Uncle Enrico. Connie hugged her and started to clean the spinach. Knowing that everyone was watching her, she washed it three times. The cousins conversed in Sicilian. They were having so much fun that they forget to put the macaroni into the boiling water, which earned them a rebuff from Josephine.

Five minutes later, the bell rang. It was Frank's brother Salvatore—Salvi—with one of his pupils, a native of Naples with the voice of a sparrow. Salvi had brought along an accordion and flutes for the girls. He was the older, outgoing, take-charge brother who had convinced Frank to come to America many years ago. He called himself "a bird of passage," whose singular goal had been to stay for a few years, save money, and return home a rich man. Salvi had left behind his wife and son, Mario, whom he adored. Frank had left his wife and daughters, Concetta and Giuseppina.

Salvi had prospered as a music teacher and store owner, a completely Americanized Sicilian. Frank worked in the mills. At the end of the day, he read Italian newspapers and wrote letters for others. His and Josephine's eldest daughter, Concetta, had married the Nolfo boy when she turned sixteen and had immigrated to America the year before, at the height of World War I, when immigration was closing down. Salvi convinced Frank to send for his wife and other daughter.

"How was the crossing?" Carmelo asked his sister.

"It was terrible. Nineteen Frenchmen threw themselves into the ocean to escape the suffering. The ship will never sail again. We stayed in New York for eight days, forced to eat white bread. Officials were about to deport us when someone recognized us and took us to Lawrence."

Frank sat disinterested, alternately reading the paper and picking hair fibers from his coat. Not long ago, he had lost two fingers in a mill accident, which had pushed him into a deeper depression. Now, he rarely left the apartment.

Josephine suffered in a different way. Like most Sicilian women of her generation, she had no literacy and refused to learn English. The extreme poverty and coldness of tenement life disheartened her. Every day she cried for her summer sky. Concetta sensed her loneliness.

A short time after everyone sat down to eat, Josephine started berating Carmelo. "You crowed to Frank and Salvi about America. They followed you, but look what happened to Frank."

Served with a summons, he could not reveal his joy with women's delicate hands or nights filled with mirth. "There is something here for everyone. Myself, I love to watch the Bambino hit home runs."

His silliness set his sister off, and she launched into the dialect of their childhood.[31] "Uncle Enrico could have made you an archbishop. What did you do? Went to brothels, not the seminary. Now you have a wife who smashes dishes off your head. You disgust me."

There was no compassion in her voice. Before today, Rose's assertiveness had dulled Carmelo's senses. Now, his own flesh and blood taunted him. Without a witness to vouch for his spirit, he cracked and faded. All eyes appeared above him. Josephine's condescension made tears come down. Putting his arm around Concetta, he barely managed to sigh, "I will be a machinist one day."

Salvi stared at him and replied, "You are from a good family, but you sweep floors."

Defeated, Carmelo made the sign of the cross and touched his daughter's cheek. "My future is with this pure angel. Men beg to adopt her." Concetta closed her eyes, hoping to go to a church school like the well born in Mineo.[32]

Dreams Interrupted

With the war over, Carmelo found himself unemployed once more.[33] With three children to feed, he brooded day and night about their well-being and spent every moment searching for work. He was told the same story: "Don Carmelo, you are too pale and used up. Go home and get well."

With all of his savings expended and no work in sight, he turned to collecting rags for Mr. Silberman. In the end, he lost his mind. As the attendants placed him in a straightjacket, he talked to himself, his face twitching and blushing. He pushed his head back, lay on the seat with a smile on his face, and went to sleep. The jerky movements of the van made small drops of sweat fall onto his pale lips. One step removed from reality, he heard the cobbler tapping as he tacked new soles onto to his wedding shoes. Gold lettering appeared above him. He was within sight of the blue sea and white roads of his beloved Catania when an Albanian-speaking guard pulled him to the ground. Disorientated and delusional, he staggered beneath the imposing façade of the state hospital. Wasted and heartbroken, he died a year later, alone, at the age of thirty-seven.

Rose was in a state of shock. Penniless and with three children to feed, there was no time to grieve. Friends talked of marriage, but she shut out their words for the sake of the children. Her mother sent words of encouragement on a postcard of Saint Sebastiano, reminding Rose of her saints. "There is little hope, but do not despair," she told herself.

The Marcheses, an elderly couple who were friends of her parents, paid for Don Carmelo's burial lot. After the funeral, Fannie helped Rose move back to Water Street.

Life was not easy for Rose and her three young children. She applied for city relief—the five cents an hour she earned for home sewing did not pay the rent, buy clothes, or feed her children. In those days, people had to earn nearly seven dollars a week to support a family of four.

The children faced their own problems. Lucy, three years old when Carmelo died, came down with pneumonia. Concetta, intent on honoring her father's memory, was unable to study because she had too many chores. Little Enrico, seven, did not have time to be a boy; he was the man of the house. The family had entered a new and very uncertain era.

Notes

1. For more information on Bacon's life and work, see North Carolina Architects & Builders (2009), *Bacon, Henry (1866–1924)*.

2. For further readings on Italian Sicilian culture, immigration, and assimilation, see Caico (1910), *Sicilian Ways and Days*; Chapman (1971), *Milocca, a Sicilian Village*; Corsi (1935), *In the Shadow of Liberty: The Chronicle of Ellis Island*; Dolci (1981), *Sicilian Lives*; Gabaccia (1984), *From Sicily to Elizabeth Street: Housing and Social Change Among Italian Immigrants 1880–1930*; Gambino (1974), *Blood of My Blood: The dilemma of the Italian-Americans*; Mangoine (1943), *Mount Allegro: A Memoir of Italian American Life*; Mangione & Morreale (1992), *La Storia: Five Centuries of the Italian American Experience*; Moroso (1923), *The Stumbling Herd*; and Panunzio (1921), *The Soul of an Immigrant*. For a discussion about the historical background of aristocratic families in Sicily, see Sorlin (1995), "The Leopard." See Friedenberg (2000), "Early Jewish History in Italy" for a review of Sicilian peasant life.

3. See Geoff Williams' article in *U.S. & World News*, "A Glimpse of Your Expenses 100 Years Ago." The average salary was about $687 per year in 1915--if you were a man (a woman would make about half that). According to an inflation calculator on the Bureau of Labor Statistic's website, $687 would be comparable to about $16,063 a year today. Source: https://money.usnews.com/money/personal-finance/articles/2015/01/02/a-glimpse-at-your-expenses-100-years-ago.

4. Today, Sacred Heart Italian Church is part of the Saint Leonard Parish, which also encompasses Saint Mary's Chapel and Saint Stephen Church. The Saint Leonard Parish website can be found at: http://saintleonardchurchboston.org. A good site that discusses the Sacred Heart Church in particular can be found at: https://www.northendboston.com/churches.

5. For Saint Lucy's story and those of other saints, see Catholic.Org. (2011). *Catholic Online: Saints and Angels*.

6. Like most Sicilian women of her time, Rose did not marry young, nor did she engage in premarital sex, factors that contributed to her sense of self-reliance and independence. She departed, however, from the unwritten rules by marrying without permission, a dowry, or a family to provide for her security. All she had was her faith in God. In his "Introduction" to di Donato's *Christ in Concrete,* Fred L. Gardaphe (1939/1993) states that

American Catholicism failed to protect Italian immigrants from the injustices of American capitalism. He also opines that Christian repression led di Donato toward a socialistic vision of the world. To learn about the role of the church in the Italian immigrant experience, see Tomasi (1975), *Piety and Power: The Role of the Italian Parishes in the New York Metropolitan Area, 1880–1930*; Tomasi (1972), *The Italian American Family: The Southern Italian Family's Process of Adjustment to an Urban America*; Orsi (1985), *The Madonna Of 115th Street: Faith and Community in Italian Harlem*; and Malpezzi & Clements (1992), *Italian American Folklore*. For information on individual saints and their legends, see Catholic.Org. (2011), *Catholic Online: Saints and Angels*.

7. For information about the renovations to the Old North Church ordered by Rt. Rev. William Lawrence, bishop of Massachusetts, and the church's history in general, see Massachusetts Historical Society (2011), *Old North Church (Christ Church in the City of Boston) Records: 1569–1997*.

8. For information about the Waldensian Church and its history, see Waldensian. Org., *The American Waldensian Society*.

9. Native Bostonians in the nineteenth century had to come to terms with the rapidly changing ethnic, cultural, and religious composition of their city. By 1860, 10 percent of the population in Boston held 95 percent of the wealth. Ninety percent of the population was poor, unskilled laborers (citation 29).

10. The quoted material is from Mann (1848), *Report No. 12 of the Massachusetts School Board*, para. 2. Raised in poverty, Horace Mann graduated from Brown University and went into politics, becoming the first great American advocate of public education.

> His Education Bill of 1837 mandated a powerful state board of education and secretary ... In his new position as the first secretary of the ... State Board of Education ... Horace Mann instituted a minimum school year of six months, a doubling of educational appropriations, 50 additional schools, increased public support, higher teacher salaries, new curricula, new teaching methods based upon European models, professional training of teachers, and professional standards overseen by one central authority (Bakersfield City School District, *Horace Mann Elementary: Who Was Horace Mann?* 2011, paras. 1–2).

For more information about Mann and nineteenth-century education, see Ensign (1921), *Compulsory School Attendance and Child Labor*; Linscott (1948),

State of Mind: A Boston Reader; and Caldwell (1925), "The Boston Public Schools in the Days of Horace Mann." For information regarding Mann's work as secretary, see Mann (1849), *Tenth Annual Report of the First Secretary of the Massachusetts Board of Education*.

11. For example, Puritan orthodoxy in New England Congregational churches mandated that parishioners be seated accorded to class, gender, and race. See McLellan (1903/1992), *The History of Gorham, Maine*.

12. Although they may not have been conscious of the fact, these parents were following concepts that Jean-Jacques Rousseau put forth over one hundred years before their time. See, for example, Rousseau (1762/1979), *Emile or On Education*.

13. See Riall (1998), *Sicily and the Unification of Italy: Liberal Policy and Local Power, 1859–1866* for an excellent analysis of nineteenth-century feudalism and peasant struggles against landowners. Cook (1997) examines the restrictions Sicilian men placed on women during the same period.

14. See Marcy (1912), "The Battle for Bread at Lawrence."

15. Phrenology, a theory of personality typology that originated in Europe in the late 1700s, assumes that mental traits and aptitudes are located in specific regions of the brain. One can ascertain, therefore, which traits are strongest in an individual by examining the shape of the cranium. Phrenology appealed to social reformers, who thought that the knowledge it provided could help people. It also provided an easy explanation of mental illness and criminal behavior. Others viewed it as unscientific and fatalistic, believing that it allowed people to deny moral responsibility for their actions. Interest in phrenology ebbed in Britain by the early1850s but found popularity in the United States, especially with "professors" of phrenology, who read heads for profit. During its heyday in the 1820s–1840s, many employers demanded a character reference from a local phrenologist to ensure that a prospective employee was honest and hardworking. Horace Greeley reputedly published phrenology lectures in the *New Yorker* and suggested that trainmen be selected on the shape of their heads (Combe, 1833). Late nineteenth- and early twentieth-century racial anthropologists used phrenology to confirm their belief that Europeans were superior to other humans. See van Wyhe (2009), *The History of Phrenology on the Web* and Davies (1955/1971), *Phrenology: Fad and Science: A 19th Century American Crusade*.

16. This material is quoted from Miller (1985), *Emigrants and Exiles*, p. 319–322.

17. Holmes (1860, 1861) first used the term "Brahmin" to describe the "upper crust" of nineteenth-century Boston society in a series of articles published by *Atlantic Monthly* under the title "The Professor's Story" (1860). This series was republished in 1861 as the novel *Elsie Venner*. "Allied by marriages, education, and church affiliations against Boston's swelling foreign-born population" (Perk, 2001), the Brahmin were very careful about who could join their select social circle. To be a Brahmin, one had to trace back four or five generations to ancestors who had either served on the king's council or had been a governor, doctor of divinity, or member of Congress. Brahmins used words like "plebeian" to describe others and had no interest in building parks or recreational facilities for commoners; their own children attended private academies. They were conservative humanists who protected their class interests. Although a number of Brahmins were abolitionists, many more were aloof about slavery. Nathan Lord (1855), president of Dartmouth, wrote that slavery was a divine institution, according to natural and revealed religion. During the Civil War, mill supervisors, like Robert Frost's father, supported the Confederacy because their livelihood depended on cotton. Others encouraged their sons to find Irish immigrants to stand in for them in the draft.

18. Another phrase coined by Holmes (1858), "the Hub of the Solar System" or "the Hub of the Universe," originally referred to the Massachusetts State House. See Celebrate Boston (2011), *Hub of the Universe Origin*.

19. Many studies exist on the history of Irish immigration to Boston. See, for example, the National Park Service (n.d.). *Setting the Stage*.

20. Walker (1896) also argued that technology minimized the need for unskilled labor and, worse, made it easy for foreigners to arrive in horrifying numbers.

21. For this statistic and other information on the topic of emigration, see Verso (2011), "Risorgimento's Class Character: Poets and Scholars—Lampedusa and Denis Mack Smith." As Linda Rudolph (2011) notes:

> The first significant wave of Sicilian immigrants to the United States began in the late 1880s. Before 1880 less than 1,000 Sicilians immigrated to America per year. But by 1906 over 100,000 Sicilians left for the States in that year alone. Ultimately, out of the 4.5 million Italians that immigrated to the United States between the years 1880 and 1930, one out of every four was a Sicilian. The immigrants represented virtually every area in Sicily. The numbers would have been higher but for the passage of the U.S. Immigration Act of 1924. The Act reduced the

number of persons allowed to immigrate to the United States from Italy to 3,845.

22. According to the Encyclopedia Britannica (1995):

> The Etruscans in Tuscany and Umbria and the Greeks in the south preceded the Romans, who "Latinized" the whole country and maintained unity until the fifth century ... With the collapse of the Roman Empire in the West, Italy suffered invasions and colonization, which inevitably affected its ethnic composition. With some exceptions, the north was penetrated by Germanic tribes crossing the Alps, while the south was colonized by Mediterranean peoples arriving by sea ("The People: Ethnic Composition"). After 1347, Balkan slaves replaced agricultural workers killed by the plague (McKay, Hill, & Buckler, 1996).

> > [A more recent] analysis of Italy's cultural assets carried out by the presidency of the Council of Ministers shows that the cultural wealth of the nation is unevenly divided between the northern, central, and southern regions ... Almost one-half of the nation's libraries are situated in the north ... The south houses just over a quarter of the country's libraries but has 36 percent of the national population ("Cultural Institutions: North and South").

> The major economic problem of modern Italy is the "underdeveloped" south, with little industry. The Italian political party Lega Nord, founded in 1989, wants to divide Northern Italy from the rest of the country, believing that the Northern Italian culture and economy is more "European" than the rest of Italy (Montanelli, 2003). For further reading on Sicilian history, see Ahmad (1975), *A History of Islamic Sicily*; Schneider (1976), *Culture and Political Economy in Western Sicily*; Browne (1873), "Sicily and the Sicilians"; Amari (1850), *History of the War of the Sicilian Vespers*; Cipolla (1994), "The Jews in Sicily"; and Smith (1968), *A History of Sicily: Volume III, Modern Sicily after 1713*. Books on contemporary Sicilian life include Maggio (2002, 2001, 2000), *The Stone Boudoir: Travels Through the Hidden Villages of Sicily*; *Mattanza: The Ancient Sicilian Ritual of Bluefin Tuna Fishing*; and *Mattanza: Love and Death in the Sea of Sicily* respectively. See also Simeti (1986), *On Persephone's Island: A Sicilian Journal*. Classics in Sicilian literature include Sciascia (1985/2000), *The Wine Dark Sea*; di Lampedusa (1960/1991), *The Leopard*; Verga (1883/1925), *Little Novels of Sicily*; Vittorini (1951/1973), *A Vittorini Omnibus: In Sicily and Other Novels*. Works on Italian and Sicilian literature include Ragusa (1993), "A Study of Literary Relations:

France and Italy in the Late Nineteenth Century"; D'Aquino (1998), "Successful Sicilian Storyteller: Sicilian Author Andrea Camilleri"; and Dolci (1968), *The Man Who Plays Alone: The Story of One Man's Fight Against the Sicilian Mafia.*

23. Sicilians encountered persistent acts of prejudice, severe injuries, loss of livelihood, and evictions from their homes. For example, "Between 1886 and 1910, southern lynch mobs murdered 27 Sicilians" (Webb 2002, 1).

24. According to Boynton (1923):

> Boston society mirrored Dreiser's analysis of city life. At the top were the privileged; then came the bohemians, the world of artist, actor, author, and dilettante; then the makers of money, builders of fine houses, buyers of libraries and pictures, manipulators of law ... and, finally, a substratum of the millions in factory, railroad, and shipyard upholding all the rest.

See also De Marco (1981), *Ethnic Enclaves: Boston's Italian North End.*

25. Saint Stephen's had an Italian Renaissance exterior designed by Charles Bullfinch, "The first American to practice architecture as a profession." The interior was federalist, the North End Congregational Society having commissioned it years before. (PBS, n.d.).

26. The second oldest Italian church in the country and "the first Roman Catholic Church in New England built by Italian immigrants," the Franciscans of the Immaculate Conception Province built Saint Leonard's Church soon after the Civil War (Catholic Church.Org, n.d.).

27. Themes in Italian American literature range from becoming American and coming of age to the struggle for survival. Works that trace development over four generations include Gambino (1981), *Bread and Roses*, and Bonanno (1980), *Ember Days*. Works that portray the lives of Italian American women include Ets (1970), *Rosa: The Life of an Italian Immigrant*; Sferra (1989), *Virgilia*; and Puzo (1964), *The Fortunate Pilgrim*. Memoirs that mix narrative with criticism are Barolini (1979), *Umbertina: A Novel*; De Rosa (1986/2003), *Paper Fish*; Viscusi (1995), *Astoria*; and Tusiani (1965), *Envoy From Heaven*. Books on education include Torgovnick (1994), *Crossing Ocean Parkway: Readings by an Italian American Daughter*; Martone (1988), *Safety Patrol: Short Stories by Michael Martone*; Picano (1985), *Ambidextrous: The Secret Life of Children*; and Marzini (1992), *The Education of a Reluctant Radical:*

Book 2, Growing Up American. Books on the Sicilian American experience are Mangione (1943), *Mount Allegro: A Memoir of Italian American Life,* and Napoli (1986), *A Dying Cadence: Memories of a Sicilian Childhood.*

28. Irving Berlin (1888–1989), America's most famous composer and lyricist, emigrated from Russia in 1893 with his Jewish family and settled in the tenements of New York's Lower East Side. When his father died in 1896, he supported his family by selling newspapers and singing in Bowery saloons. By nineteen, he was working as a singing waiter in Chinatown and as a staff lyricist on Tin Pan Alley. In 1907, he published his first song, "Marie from Sunny Italy" and, in 1911, had his first hit, "Alexander's Ragtime Band." He wrote more than one thousand songs and Broadway musicals, including "White Christmas," "God Bless America," "Puttin' on the Ritz," "Easter Parade," and "There's No Business Like Show Business." See Whiting (2004), *The Life and Times of Irving Berlin.*

29. For more information about rural Sicilians in the New World, see Gabaccia (1988), *Militants and Migrants: Rural Sicilians Become American Workers.*

30. Their Quincy settlement date appears on Concetta's birth certificate.

31. Agora Hostel describes Sicilian as

> a unique blend of Greek, Latin, Aragonese, Arabic, Longobardic, and Norman-French elements . . . Rarely written, [it] has regional forms: the dialect of Agrigento is different from that of Messina. Sicilian gradually fell into disuse among the aristocratic and literate classes, becoming the vernacular tongue of the "popolino," as the masses were called by the nobility. By the seventeenth century … Sicily's aristocratic classes learned Tuscan, though some nobles necessarily spoke Sicilian in communication with the employees who managed their country estates. Italy's royals spoke Tuscan Italian and formal French … The Savoys spoke Piedmontese within their family at their court at Turin, while the Bourbons of Naples spoke Neapolitan as their mother tongue … Despite attempts by the national government to suppress it after 1860, Sicilian remained the native language of most Sicilians until the twentieth century. In 1922, Mussolini banned the use of all languages other than Italian and forbade all Sicilian language publishing. Even today, there is no Sicilian language newspaper in Sicily (Agora Hostel, n.d.).

32. Salvatore Gulizia returned to Sicily and died there in 1967.

33. The Great War ran from 1914 until 1919. Before the outbreak of hostilities, the Fore River Shipyard in Quincy produced eight submarines for the US Navy. Between 1914 and 1918, the number escalated to thirty-four. By 1919, the year that Carmelo went to work at the shipyard, production peaked at thirteen R-class submarines. Several months later, the war ended, and submarine production dropped to three over the next two years (Toppan 2000).

References

Accel Team Development. *Historical perspective on productivity improvement: Scientific management and Frederick Winslow Taylor.* http://www.accelteam. com/scientific/scientific_02.html. Accessed 2/5/2007.

Agora Hostel. *A history of Sicily.* http://www.agorahostel.com/main/4sicily/ SicilyUnica.htm. Accessed 2/5/2007.

Ahmad, A. *A history of Islamic Sicily.* Edinburgh: Edinburgh University Press, 1975.

Amari, M. *History of the war of the Sicilian vespers.* Edited by F. E. Ellesmere. London: R. Bentley, 1850.

American Waldesian Society. *History.* http://www.waldensian.org.

Bakersfield City School District. *Horace Mann elementary: Who was Horace Mann?* http://www.horacemann.bcsd.com.

Barolini, H. *Umbertina: A novel.* New York: Seaview, 1979.

Bergin, T. G. *Giovanni Verga.* Westport, CT: Greenwood Press, 1931/1969.

Berlin, I. & M. Nicholson. "Marie from Sunny Italy." New York: Joseph W. Stern & Co., 1907.

Bonanno, M. W. *Ember Days.* New York: Seaview, 1980.

Boynton, P. H. "American authors of today: VII. Theodore Dreiser." *The English Journal* 12, no. 3 (1923).

Boynton, P. H. *Some Contemporary Americans: The Personal Equation in Literature.* New York: Biblio and Tannen, 1924/1966.

Browne, J. H. "Sicily and the Sicilians." *Harper's New Monthly Magazine* 47, no. 278 (1873): 183–202.

Caldwell, O. W. The Boston public schools in the days of Horace Mann. In *Then and now in education:1845–1923.* New York: World Book Company, 1925.

Caico, L. *Sicilian Ways and Days*. New York: D. Appleton and Company, 1910.

Cannato, V. J. Immigration and the Brahmins. *Humanities* 30, no. 3. http://www. neh.gov/news/humanities/2009-05/Immigration.html.

Catholic.Org. *Catholic online: Saints and angels*. http://www.catholic.org/saints.

Celebrate Boston. *Athens of America origin*. http://celebrateboston.com/culture/ athens-of-america-origin.htm.

Celebrate Boston. *Hub of the universe origin*. http://www.celebrateboston.com/ culture/the-hub-origin.htm.

Chapman, C. G. *Milocca, a Sicilian village*. Cambridge, MA: Schenkman, 1971.

Chase, A. *The legacy of Malthus: The Social Costs of the New Scientific Racism*. New York: Knopf, 1977.

Child, L. M. *The mother's book*. Boston: Carter, Hendee and Babcock, 1831.

Cipolla, G. "The Jews in Sicily." *Arba Sicula* 15, no. 1 & 2 (1994): 56.

Clark, F. *Hats (Costume Accessories Series)*. New York: Drama Book Publishers, 1982.

Clarke, W. *The boy's own book*. Boston: Munroe and Francis, 1829.

Cook, B. "Sicilian women peasants in the nineteenth century." In *Consortium on revolutionary Europe 1750–1850: Selected papers*. Edited by K. O. Eidahl, D. D. Horwood, & J. Severn. Tallahassee: Florida State University Institute on Napoleon and the French Revolution, 1999.

Combe, G. "Lectures on phrenology and its applications." *The New Yorker* (1883). http://www.lostmuseum.cuny.edu/archivesphrenpast7.htm.

Corsi, E. *In the shadow of liberty: The chronicle of Ellis Island*. New York: Macmillan, 1935.

D'Aquino, N. "Successful Sicilian storyteller: Sicilian author Andrea Camilleri." *Europe* 380 (October 1998), 38.

Davies, J. *Phrenology: Fad and science: A 19th Century American Crusade*. New Haven, CT: Yale University Press, 1955/1971.

DeMarco, W. W. *Ethnic enclaves: Boston's Italian North End*. Ann Arbor, MI: UMI Research Press, 1981.

De Rosa, T. *Paper Fish*. New York: The Feminist Press at CUNY, 1986/2003.

di Donato, P. *Christ in Concrete*. New York: Signet, 1939/1993.

di Lampedusa, G. T. *The Leopard*. Translated by A. Colquhoun. New York: Pantheon Books, 1960/1991.

Dolci, D. *The man who plays alone: The story of one man's fight against the Sicilian mafia*. Translated by A. Cowen. New York: Pantheon, 1968.

Dolci, D. *Sicilian Lives*. Translated by J. Vitiello & M. Polidoro. New York: Pantheon, 1981.

Doray, B. *From Taylorism to Fordism: A rational madness*. London: Free Association Books, 1988.

Encyclopedia Britannica, Inc. *Italy*. http://www.uves/EBRIT/macro/macro_5003_35_7.html#0019.

Ensign, F. C. *Compulsory school attendance and child labor; A study of the historical development of regulation compelling attendance and limiting the labor of children in selected group of states*. Iowa City: The Athens Press, 1921.

Ets, M. H. *Rosa: The life of an Italian immigrant*. Minneapolis: University of Minnesota Press, 1970.

Foerster, R. F. *The Italian Emigration of Our Times*. New York: Russell & Russell, 1968.

Friedenberg, D. M. "Early Jewish history in Italy." *Judaism: A Quarterly Journal of Jewish Life and Thought* 193, (Winter 2000): 3–13.

Gabaccia, D. R. *From Sicily to Elizabeth Street: Housing and social change among Italian Immigrants, 1880–1930*. Albany: State University of New York, 1984.

Gabaccia, D. R. *Militants and Migrants: Rural Sicilians become American workers.* New Brunswick, NJ: Rutgers University Press, 1988.

Gambino, R. *Blood of My Blood: The dilemma of the Italian-Americans.* New York: Doubleday, 1974.

Gambino, R. *Bread and roses.* New York: Avon, 1981.

Gardaphe, F. L. "Introduction." In *Christ in Concrete.* New York: Signet Classic, 1939/1993.

Goodwin, D. K. *The Fitzgeralds and the Kennedys: An American Saga.* New York: Saint Martin's Press, 1987/1991.

Holmes, O. W., Sr. "The autocrat of the breakfast table." *The Atlantic Monthly* 1, no. 6 (1858).

Holmes, O. W., Sr. "The professor's story—Chapter 1: The Brahmin Caste of New England." *The AtlanticMonthly* 5, no. 27 (1860).

Holmes, O. W., Sr. *Elsie Venner.* Charleston, SC: Biblio Bazaar, 1861/2007. The full text of this novel is available from Project Gutenberg at http://www.gutenberg.org/dirs/2/6/9/2696/2696.txt.

Hoopes, J. *False Prophets: The Gurus Who Created Modern Management and Why Their Ideas Are Bad for Business Today.* Cambridge, MA: Perseus, 2003.

Hume, D. *An Inquiry Concerning Human Understanding: With a supplement, an abstract of a treatise of human nature.* Edited by C. W. Hendel. New York: The Liberal Arts Press, 1748/1955.

Lagier, J. *Second-Class Citizen.* West Lafayette, IN: Bordighera Press, 2000.

Linscott, R. N., ed. *State of Mind: A Boston Reader.* New York: Farrar and Straus, 1948.

Lord, N. *A northern presbyter's second letter to ministers of the gospel of all denominations on slavery.* Boston: Little, Brown, and Company, 1855.

Maggio, T. *Mattanza: Love and Death in the Sea of Sicily.* Cambridge, MA: Perseus, 2000.

Maggio, T. *Mattanza: The ancient Sicilian ritual of Bluefin tuna fishing*. New York: Penguin, 2001.

Maggio, T. *The Stone Boudoir: Travels through the hidden villages of Sicily*. Cambridge, MA: Perseus, 2002.

Maier, T. *The Kennedys: America's emerald kings: A five-generation history of the ultimate Irish-catholic family*. New York: Basic Books, 2003.

Malpezzi, F. M. & W. M. Clements. *Italian American Folklore*. Little Rock, AR: August House, 1992.

Mancuso, J. C. *Italy's art in the United States: Tracing the immigrants' influence in the upstate New York region*. http://www.sersale.org/mancuso/itamarts.html. Accessed February 5, 2007.

Mangione, J. *Mount Allegro: A memoir of Italian American life*. New York: Harper and Row, 1943.

Mangione, J. & B. Morreale. *La Storia: Five centuries of the Italian American experience*. New York: Perennial, 1992.

Mann, H. *Report No. 12 of the Massachusetts school board*. http://patriotpost.us/document/report-no-12-of-the-massachusetts-school-board.

Mann, H. *Tenth annual report of the first secretary of the Massachusetts board of education*. Boston: Dutton and Wentworth, State Printers, 1849. http://www.archive.org/stream/massachusettssy00educgoog#page/n12/mode/1up.

Marchione, W. P. *Italian-Americans of Greater Boston: A proud tradition*. Charleston, SC: Arcadia Tempus Publishing Group, Inc., 1999.

Marcy, M. The battle for bread at Lawrence. *International Socialist Review* 12, no. 9 (1912): 522–523.

Martone, M. *Safety Patrol: Short stories by Michael Martone*. Baltimore, MD: Johns Hopkins University Press, 1988.

Marzini, C. *The Education of a Reluctant Radical: Book 2, growing up American*. New York: Topical Books, 1992.

Massachusetts Historical Society. *Old North Church (Christ Church in the city of Boston) records: 1569–1997.* http://www.masshist.org/findingaids.doc. cfm?fa=fa0290.

McLellan, H. D. *The History of Gorham, Maine.* Edited by K. B. Lewis. Camden, ME: Picton Press, 1903/1992.

McKay, J. P., B. D. Hill, & J. Buckler. *A history of world societies, to 1715, Vol. 1* (4th ed.). Boston: Houghton Mifflin, 1996.

Middleton, W. D. "A century of cable cars." *American Heritage* 36, no. 3 (1985): 90–101.

Miller, K. A. *Emigrants and Exiles.* New York: Oxford University Press, 1985.

Montanelli, P. *Origin of Padania.* http://flagspot.net/flags/it-pad.html#ori.

Moroso, J. A. *The Stumbling Herd.* New York: The Macaulay Company, 1923.

Napoli, J. *A Dying Cadence: Memories of a Sicilian childhood.* Bethesda, MD: Marna Press, 1986.

National Park Service (NPS). *Setting the stage.* http://www.nps.gov/nr/twhp/wwwtps/lessons/33jfk/33setting.htm.

North Carolina Architects & Builders: A Biographical Dictionary. *Bacon, Henry (1866–1924).* http://ncarchitects.lib.ncsu.edu/people/p000028.

O'Conner, T. H. *The Boston Irish: A political history.* Boston: Northeastern University Press, 1995.

Orsi, R. A. *The Madonna of 115th Street: Faith and community in Italian Harlem* (2nd ed.). New Haven, CT: Yale University Press, 1988.

Panunzio, C. M. *The soul of an immigrant.* New York: Macmillan, 1921.

Paton, W. A. *Picturesque Sicily.* New York: Harper & Brothers Publishers, 1898.

Perk, J. "The story of Boston." In *The Boston Handbook.* Emeryville, CA: Avalon Travel Publishing, 2001.

Picano. F. *Ambidextrous: The secret lives of children*. New York: Gay Presses, 1985.

Public Broadcasting System (PBS). *City guide to sacred spaces—Boston & Cambridge, MA*. http://www.pbs.org/godinamerica/art/bos_cityguide2.pdf.

Puzo, M. *The Fortunate Pilgrim*. New York: Atheneum, 1964.

Ragusa, O. "A study of literary relations: France and Italy in the late nineteenth century." *Symposium* 47, no. 2 (1993): 147–155.

Reed, H. B. *The Psychology of Elementary School Subjects*. Boston: Ginn and Company, 1927.

Reitman, B. *Sister of the Road: The Autobiography of Boxcar Bertha*. New York: Macaulay Company, 1937.

Riall, L. *Sicily and the Unification of Italy: Liberal policy and local power, 1859–1866*. Oxford, UK: Clarendon Press, 1998.

Riis, J. A. *How the other half lives: Studies among the tenements of New York*. http://www.bartleby.com/208.

Rousseau, J. *Emile or on education*. Translater by A. Bloom. New York: Basic Books,1762/1979.http://www.questia.com/PM.get?a=o&d=9964951.

Rudolph, L. C. (2011). *Sicilian Americans*. http://www.everyculture.com/multi/Pa-Sp/sicilianamerican.html.

Ruediger, W. C. *The Principles of Education*. Boston: Houghton Mifflin, 1910.

"Saint Leonard of Port Maurice." CatholicChurch.Org. http://www.catholic-church.org/stleonard/churchwebsite/index.html.

Schneider, J. *Culture and Political Economy in Western Sicily*. New York: Academic Press, 1976.

Sciascia, L. *The Wine Dark Sea*. Translated by A. Bardoni. New York: New York Review of Books, 1985/2000.

Sferra, G. C. *Virgilia*. New York: Vantage Press, 1989.

Simeti, M. T. *On Persephone's Island: A Sicilian journal.* New York: Knopf, 1986.

Slater, C. "General Motors and the decline of streetcars." *Transportation Quarterly* 51, no. 3 (1997): 45–66.

Smith, A. *An inquiry into the nature and causes of the wealth of nations* (5th ed.). Edited by E. Cannan. London: Methuen & Co.,1776/1904.

Smith, D. M., with M. Finley. *A History of Sicily: Volume III, modern Sicily after 1713.* New York: Viking Press, 1968.

Smith W. H. (1912). *All the children of all the people: A study of the attempt to educate everybody.* New York: Macmillan.

Sorlin, P. "The leopard" [Review of the film *The Leopard* by L. Visconti]. *History Today* 45, no. 9 (1995): 44–49.

Synott, M. G. *The Half-Opened Door: Discrimination and admissions at Harvard, Yale, and Princeton 1900–1970.* Westport, CT: Greenwood Press, 1979.

Talese, G. "Where are the Italian-American novelists?" *New York Times Book Review* 1 (March 14, 1993).

The Best of Sicily (2004/2009). *The Sicilian Language.* http://www.bestofsicily. com/ history3.htm#dialect.

The History Place. *Child labor in America 1908–1912: Photographs of Lewis W. Hine.* http://www.historyplace.com/unitedstates/childlabor.

Tomasi, L. F. *The Italian American Family: The Southern Italian family's process of adjustment to an urban America.* Staten Island, NY: Center for Migration Studies, 1972.

Tomasi, S. M. *Piety and Power: The role of the Italian parishes in the New York metropolitan area, 1880–1930.* Staten Island, NY: Center for Migration Studies, 1975.

Toppan, A. *Fore River production record (1884–1924).* http://www.hazegray.org/ shipbuilding/quincy/fore1.htm.

Torgovnick, M. (1994). *Crossing Ocean Parkway: Readings by an Italian American daughter.* Chicago: University of Chicago Press, 1994.

Toulmin, S. E. *Cosmopolis: The hidden agenda of modernity.* Chicago: University of Chicago Press, 1990.

Tusiani, J. *Envoy from Heaven.* New York: Obolensky, 1965.

Van Wyhe, J. *The history of phrenology on the web.* http://www.historyofphrenology. org.uk/.

Verga, G. *The House by the Medlar-Tree.* Translated by M. Craig. New York: Harper and Brothers, 1890.

Verga, G. *Little Novels of Sicily.* Translated by D. H. Lawrence. New York: T. Seltzer, 1883/1925.

Verga, G. *Mastro-Don Gesualdo.* Translated by D.H. Lawrence. Westport: Greenwood Press, 1889/1976.

Verso, T. *Risorgimento's class character: Poets and scholars—Lampedusa and Denis Mack Smith. Italian American digital project i-Italy.* http://www.i-italy. org/bloggers/16396/risorgimento-s-class-character-poets-and-scholars-lampedusa-and-denis-mack-smith.

Viscusi, R. *Astoria.* Edited by A. D'Alfonso. Toronto: Guernica, 1995.

Vittorini, E. *A Vittorini omnibus.* In *Sicily and other novels.* Translated by F. Keene & W. David. New York: New Directions, 1951/1973.

Voltaire. *The Philosophical Dictionary.* Translated by H. I. Woolf. New York: Knopf, 1759/1924.

Voltaire *Candide.* Translated by D. Gordon. New York: Grosset & Dunlap, 1759/1930.

Walker, F. "Restriction of Immigration." *The Atlantic Monthly* 77, no. 464 (1896): 822–829. http://www.faculty.fairfield.edu/faculty/hodgson/courses/city/ walker/walker.htm.

Wallace, J. M. "The feminization of teaching in Massachusetts: A reconsideration." In *Women of the Commonwealth: Work, family, and social change in nineteenth-century Massachusetts*. Edited by S. L. Porter. Amherst: University of Massachusetts Press, 1996.

Webb, C. "The lynching of Sicilian immigrants in the American South, 1886–1910." *American Nineteenth Century History* 3, no. 1 (2002): 45–76.

Whalen, R. J. *The Founding Father: The Story of Joseph P. Kennedy*. Washington, DC: Regnery, 1993.

Whiting, J. *The Life and Times of Irving Berlin*. Hockessin, DE: Mitchell Lane, 2004.

Wilson, B. *Sisters of the Road*. Seattle, WA: Seal Press, 1986.

Wohl, A. S. *Race and Class Overview: Parallels in racism and class prejudice*. http://www.victorianweb.org/history/race/rcov.html.

Wordsworth, W. "My heart leaps up when I behold." In *The Complete Poetical Works of William Wordsworth*. London: MacMillan, 1888. http://www.bartleby.com/145/ww194.html.

Zinn, H. "The Socialist Challenge." In *A People's History of the United States: 1492–Present*. New York: HarperCollins, 1980. http://www.historyisaweapon.com/zinnapeopleshistory.html.

SECTION II

FATHERS AND SONS

Preface to "Fathers and Sons"

Realism is in the work when idealism is in the soul
—Bergson

The previous chapters draw attention to the commonplace by mixing sociological reporting with fiction writing to depict an ordinary person's resilience in a society based on money, prestige, and power. This story reflects the notion that history is the struggle between the powerful and those they try to silence. Although undereducated, Rose had enough of a sense of herself to evaluate experience critically and express her agency through self-discipline, acute perception, and perseverance. She was, in the parlance of Antonio Gramsci (1929-1935/1971), an "organic intellectual" with the capability and capacity to think for herself. Defining her competence as a vision of reality (Bergson 1912) deepens our understanding of what it means to be literate. She resisted silence because she was conscious of her surroundings.

Rose's life parallels the historic development of schools in the United States. Her dialogues with progressives reveal how conventional thinking and practice came to be and who in society benefited from them (Oakes & Lipton 2001). The dialogues also help us examine the principles underlying teaching and learning in a democratic society. Good teachers not only question the status quo or the givens of daily life in the classroom but also understand the importance of their students being able to do the same. In addition, good teaching requires the personal qualities of integrity, decency, and the capacity to work very hard for children.

The next section extends the social and historical analysis of lives and literacies. It picks up with Rose's son as he assimilates into American society and ends with her great-grandson's fight for his unique identity in the world. These stories shed light on the obstacles that mask school failure, including the hidden agendas of class, race, and political ideology. When Rose arrived in Boston, a small percentage of the population held most of the wealth. Most citizens were poor, uneducated laborers whose children endlessly repeated grades in school. Her son also failed in school and repeated grades until he dropped out. A generation later, I became literate, but as a child I chose not to read and write, only becoming passionate about literacy when I was nearly an adult. Paradoxically, my son was a prolific reader and writer but suffered greatly under the regimentation of school.

Our stories reflect the values that schools hold. At a time when political ideology dominates educational discourse, we need to evaluate how schools think about children who are different; ideas are the basis of action. We also need to understand how good teachers help children convert their disaffection into success.

The first three chapters poetic tone captures Rose's heroic nature and Carmelo's lyricism. Chapter four through six uses different writing styles to capture the unique joys and sorrows in our histories. Dialogue brings readers into my father's bewildering world. Chronicles set a pensive mood to characterize my search for meaning in books. Analytical exposition duplicates the impersonal discourse that characterized much of my son Justin's school experience.

Developments: 1920–1945[1]

The Nineteenth Amendment to the U.S. Constitution is ratified in 1920, giving women the right to vote. Al Jolson's "California, Here I Come" and "A Tisket, a Tasket" by Ella Fitzgerald and Al Feldman are popular songs. The Jazz Singer, starring Al Jolson, is the first "talkie." Walt Disney introduces the first sound cartoon synchronized with sound, along with Mickey Mouse, in 1928 with "Steamboat Willy." Prohibition bans the drinking of any type of alcohol. On October 24, 1929, the stock market crashes, creating panic on Wall Street. Unemployment reaches four million. The US Supreme Court upholds the principle of a minimum wage for women. The Empire State Building, begun in 1930, stands completed. The Hoover Dam, in the Black Canyon on the Colorado River, is completed, making Lake Mead the world's largest reservoir. Werner Heisenberg formulates the quantum uncertainity principle in 1927. F. Scott Fitzgerald's The Great Gatsby *and John Steinbeck's* The Grapes of Wrath *are popular books. Women's hems range from ankle- to calf-length and then to knee-length. Men's suits with two pair of pants become popular. Construction begins on Rockefeller Center, a proposed complex of modern high-rises in New York City. Graham Greene's* The Power and the Glory *is published. The forty-hour workweek begins as a result of the Fair Labor Standards Act. Colorfast textiles are improved. Weekly movie attendance reaches eighty million. John Atanasoff invents the first "official" electronic computer in 1939. RCA exhibits a television at the 1939 New York World's Fair. Bing Crosby records "White Christmas." Disney's feature-length animation film* Fantasia *(1940) opens. Sugar Ray Robinson loses a ten-round decision to Jake LaMotta on February 5, 1943. The Atomic Bomb is dropped on Hiroshima and Nagasaki in 1945, officially ending World War II. "The Races of Mankind," a pamphlet attacking Nazi racial doctrines, is deemed controversial by many people because it opposes racism. W. L. Warner, R. J. Havighurst, and M. B. Loeb report research they conducted at schools in the Midwest, the South, and New England that shows middle-class white children performing better in school because tests are biased in their favor.*

5

The Education of an Immigrant's Son

Like many other sons of immigrant parents, Rose's son made it through grammar school but stopped attending high school as soon as he turned sixteen. Restless and motivated by the need to support his family, he was not interested in school; his only goal in life was to have a few dollars in his pocket. Away from school, he built bicycles, walked miles to tend his father's grave, and worked several jobs to support his sisters and mother. Later in life, he became a highly skilled craftsman and responsible parent.

It is easy to stereotype men like him. Many would say that he failed in school because he lacked the will to succeed. What he lacked, however, was a chance. Aside from his mother, he had no adults in his life who encouraged him, who cared that he received an education. Behind every successful American is a teacher, an uncle, a minister—a reference point—someone who communicates confidence and expectation. We call this love, and it is, even today, appallingly absent from the lives of many who fail in school. Without it, talent easily hides from view.

Practical Lessons

Tiny Feet

Rose awoke upset over the name-calling. Very few Sicilian American children went to Saint John's Parochial School. In fact, Concetta was the only one in her class. One classmate teased her constantly, calling her the "Welfare Kid." Henry did not escape the teasing either; every day at recess a gang of boys sat up on the rocks, shouting "Guinea" at him.[2]

Rose knew these words from her early days in America, although she had never paid any attention to them. Now, there was much to consider. How could her children learn to love themselves under such conditions? She remembered the time she told Carmelo that she wanted her children to know themselves and their history. This was not happening on Water Street. Instead of doing his schoolwork, Henry ran off with his friends to play ball. Sports were his passion. Connie's spirit was elsewhere too. She hardly spoke Sicilian anymore. The world of school and name-calling pressed on Rose's conscience.

She sighed, knowing deep down that her children needed to be around Sicilians who were successful and other children who were performing well in school. She decided to take them to the North End when she returned her piecework. They would meet accomplished people like Gulizia, the music teacher, and perhaps one of her union friends. She would also show them the Old-World heritage of the architecture that reminded her of home.

"Get ready," she said fretfully to Henry one morning. "I need to bring back my homework"—her term for the linens she sewed for wealthy Americans.

"Ma, please," he begged. He had three games that day.

Henry's whining irritated her. All he wanted to do was play with friends. He was just like his father—all the wrong cares. She spoke sharply to cover her disappointment. "We have fish to buy, so get ready."

Crowds rocked the South Station platform. Only age seven, Henry had never seen so much commotion. As they approached Salem Street, he saw a sign painted in Italian. He had never seen one before, so he asked his mother what it said.

"That is a shoe store for men with tiny feet," she said.

He smiled at the thought of little men happily walking up and down the street in new shoes. He stood at the curb, ready to cross.

"Not yet," she said. "I want you to meet someone."

It was early June, but the heat was unbearable. Shirtless boys were playing ball in the street. Henry knew their faces but not their names. He caught a glimpse of a boy crying. All around him were spilled strawberries. The storeowner stood before the boy with a strap in his hand. Henry could see the fury in the man's face and hear the crack of the strap on the boy's arm. He turned away, smelling the sweat of the street. Boys were supposed to play baseball in green fields surrounded by trees that touched the sky and play cards on flat boulders beside a brook. Boston's streets were unforgiving.

The door to the music store was open, so Rose and Henry entered. The professor motioned Rose to his back room. She told Henry to sit on a chair in the corner. He obeyed, not wanting to be smacked. As he passed the glass case, he caught sight of a bright silver harmonica.

Rose and Gulizia exchanged pleasantries. This was the first time that she had seen him since the funeral. She was grateful that he had come; his presence had lent an air of dignity to the solemn occasion. For a moment, she saw the image of Carmelo buried in a pauper's casket in his Sunday suit.

Rose had aged in the past year, her blue eyes drained of emotion. Before Gulizia could say another word, she asked him to teach Henry to sing. He frowned at the boy sitting in the corner, dark and melancholy. Too skinny—no depth in the eyes—too distracted. An American customer entered the store. Gulizia opened the book and motioned to Henry. Standing before him, he said, "You have a good mother. I told her not to marry your father, but she did not listen. Now you are the man of the house. Do not be afraid to use your back."

The words meant nothing to Henry, but he smelled the inside of Gulizia's mouth and stepped back. Gulizia grabbed his arm and brought him closer. "It is time to put food on the table." He turned to Rose and said, "He lacks determination."

His comment made Rose move across the floorboards slowly. She understood that it had to be this way. Gulizia had rent to pay, and she had no money. It was time to leave, so she took her son's hand and wished the professor good-bye. Gulizia, still looking at Rose, slipped something into Henry's pocket as he passed by. A silver harmonica.

Parlor Games

"Can we get the tuna now, Ma?"

"No, not yet. We are going to visit your father's cousin. He has a bakery shop. His daughter won a prize for science."

Henry hated smart girls. They had their hands raised all the time. He would rather stand in the hall than sit next to one at school. His thoughts turned to the harbor vista, gray and windy.

"We have to take the ferry to East Boston," Rose told him. The North Ferry left Battery Wharf on Commercial Street, so they walked over to catch it. Ten minutes later, they docked at Border Street. Henry did not know that his father had stared out onto these waters the day he decided to move to Quincy. He knew little about his father; his mother hid her thoughts from him. In a few minutes, they were in the living room of his father's cousin. He saw his mother smile as she caught up on people's lives.

Saldana came out of her room as soon as she heard the chatter. She stood in front of Henry and pushed back her black curly hair. She was twelve, with breasts beginning to push against her blouse. Henry turned to look at his mother, beaming as he heard Saldana say, "I didn't know I had such a handsome cousin." Grabbing his hand, she said, "Let's go meet my friends."

Rose shook her head. "It's too cold over here."

Henry had the sense to say feebly, "It's much warmer in the city."

Saldana giggled and answered, "That's because the buildings block out the wind."

Rose was glad to see that Henry was learning something. He needed to be around a higher class of people. "Listen to her. You will learn something."

Henry blushed. Rose motioned with her hand for him to sit between her and Carmino's wife, Carlena. His mother spoke rapidly in Sicilian, so he was not sure what she said. Saldana stood behind him and whispered, "Three men want Pa to pay them protection money. Your mother told Pa to watch out or they'll shoot him."

Henry sat transfixed, staring at his uncle's long black mustache. Lifting his hand, the man spoke in a serious tone. Henry understood his mixture of English and Sicilian. "I carry a gun on my shoulder. It is worth more than the images of the saints." He cut the air again with his long finger. "Besides, big dogs quarrel over a good bone. I have no bones to give these scoundrels."

Henry stirred with the image of his uncle shooting good-for-nothing rats in a hole. This man could build castles. He wished he slept here. Whenever he got into a scrap, he would say to himself, "Uncle Carmino will come for you."

It was a mortal sin to speak about sex in front of children, but Saldana's mother, Carlena, had a reputation for speaking the forbidden. Rose recalled her discussing the subject the night before she married Carmelo. "Take notice of my words," she had advised her. "Sex depends on your priest. If you like it too much, tell him that you will send your firstborn to the seminary. He will forgive you." Now Carlena knew that Rose needed a husband. "Rose, you look lost. There are so many men to care for you. Remember the man who led the band? He is a good man. Open your heart to him. You have paid your debt to Carmelo."

Rose was not thinking of marrying anyone. "I do not want a stepfather to beat my children."

Everyone fell silent. Wrapped up in himself, Henry jumped up and said, "Ma slammed the door in the priest's face." This could be a time of unforeseen temptations, at least in the imagination of the Irish priest who had officiated at Carmelo's funeral.

Angered by her son's impertinence, she said, "This boy has no fear."

Saldana sat watching him as he and his mother stood to leave. "Please come back to visit us soon," Carlena said.

Child Rearing for the Rich and Poor

Rose and her son went straight to the fish market when they returned to the North End. It was past noon, and the best tuna steaks were gone. Rose sensed Henry's disappointment, so she said, "I have a mouth to feed. Your father took me to a restaurant nearby. Today you will eat like an American, so wash that sad face away."

Despite his size, Henry felt like he could touch the tower atop the Custom House. He was the apple of his mother's eye, a real Prince Charming.

After lunch, they walked over to Lambert Street to deliver the linens. When Lipman saw Rose, he clapped his hands and said, "Mrs. Amoroso, your patron is here. She has wanted to meet you for the longest time." Standing in his office was a beautifully dressed woman of about Rose's age with her two boys.

Meet Rose Kennedy

The life stories of the Kennedys symbolize how the Irish fought back against discrimination.[3] The first Kennedy to immigrate to Boston died in poverty, as did his son. One of his grandchildren, however, started a neighborhood bar. Within a few years, he expanded into coal; wholesale liquor; and, finally, banking. By the 1880s, he had become a business and political force in the East End, controlling the group who selected candidates for political office. He sent his son Joseph to Boston Latin School and Harvard. Two years later, Joseph became the youngest bank president in America. By thirty, he was a millionaire. Roosevelt appointed him as head of the Securities and Exchange Commission and later as ambassador to Great Britain.[4]

Rose and Joseph Kennedy arrive for dinner at the Colony Restaurant *in New York in 1940. Joseph Kennedy Sr. here was the* U.S. ambassador to Great Britain.

Across the harbor in the North End lived another group of Irish. In 1863, John Francis Fitzgerald lived in a tenement. He attended public grammar school, graduated from the Boston Latin School, and secured entrance into Harvard Medical School.

Known for his intelligence and political skill, he gravitated toward politics, starting out in the Boston Common House and becoming a member of the Boston Common Council. By 1893, he was a member of the state Senate and was elected to Congress, later becoming mayor of Boston. As mayor, he built the Franklin Park Zoo and, ever the populist, declared Columbus Day a legal holiday. He was also in the insurance and investment business and owned a weekly newspaper.

Unlike merchant-class candidates like Storrow, he was full of life and vitality, an extrovert who greeted immigrants and associated with popular athletes. Known to jump up onto tables to sing "Sweet Adeline," newspapers dubbed him "Honey" because women in the audience swooned.[5]

In 1911, his favorite daughter, Rose, came out as a debutante. One of the guests at her ball was the tall, handsome Harvard undergraduate Joseph Kennedy. During a summer vacation to Old Orchard Beach in Maine, the popular vacation spot of Boston's Irish politicians, Rose and Joseph met formally. Honey disapproved.[6] "Kennedy attended Harvard and graduated in 1912. He was first a bank examiner and active in real estate and at 25 became president of the Columbia Trust Company." He bought a five-year-old, three-story house in Brookline, a middle-class suburb, and married Rose in 1914. "They chose the neighborhood for its spaciousness, good schools, and proximity to the trolley lines to Boston, [as] Joseph Kennedy did not own a car when the family first moved there."[7]

Joseph knew that the Brahmin class would not give up its power without a fight. At Harvard, he had seen how its members prepped for their privilege on the playing fields in a world where the strongest succeeded. He prepared his children for battle in the same manner, requiring them to read the paper daily and talk politics at the dinner table. He also encouraged them to play football and sent them to the best private schools. Rose tempered her husband's drive with stories about her father's compassion for the poor. She also made sure that the children went to mass every Sunday.[8]

About the time that Carmelo and Rose moved into the North End, Joseph Kennedy and Rose Fitzgerald became engaged. Rose Fitzgerald was a faithful Catholic and loved to attend mass in her old neighborhood. She even wanted to be married there, although Joseph disapproved, "believing the North End to be a slum." Rose prevailed; they were wed at Saint Stephan's.[9]

The eldest boy kicked his feet under his chair, reading a book. The other stared at Henry's Salvation Army shoes. The two boys reminded Henry of his classmates—fit, nicely dressed, and well fed.

Suddenly, the younger one flashed a smile and said, "Want to see something?"

"Sure," Henry replied. He knew that it was time to have some real fun. They tiptoed past the older boy, still immersed in his book.

"Ma'am, this is your seamstress, Mrs. Amoroso," Lipman said, knowing that Rose's lack of status did not offend his patron—a gracious woman who had asked after Rose before.

"Your work is exquisite," said the remarkably beautiful, radiant, and confident woman. Rose Amoroso's beauty was hidden beneath the grief of the past year. She felt suddenly plain and untidy. The wealthy woman asked her what all American women asked her: "How did you learn to sew so magnificently?" Many Americans did not realize that numerous poor foreigners had rare sensibilities.[10]

"My mother." Rose smiled.

"My mother taught me things too. I learned more from my father, though—opera and geography."

Rose replied, "My father took me to the opera when I was a young girl."

The other woman wiped her cheek with her white silk handkerchief and said, "I have visited your country. Indeed, all of Europe. I hung copies of famous paintings I brought back. The pictures over my sons' beds are copies of Italian paintings of the Madonna and Child. They give me great pleasure."[11]

"I have a statue of the Madonna in my bedroom," Rose said. The other woman nodded, wondering where her youngest had gone.

Rose noticed that the older boy was still reading his book, so she said, "My daughter is very smart. She reads all the time. I cannot get her out of her room to help me."

"Let her read, Mrs. Amoroso. We spend a lot of time with books in the living room in the evening. Mr. Kennedy is president of a bank, and this is his one opportunity to read the newspaper or his favorite detective stories. He sits in his chair, reading the *Boston Transcript*. I sit opposite him. When the children are ready for bed and have said their prayers, they come to the living room and play for a little while before we put them to bed. I spend a good deal of time reading to my children. I make no engagements outside in the evening so that I can help them with their schoolwork, doctor their colds, or find out what activities had interested them during the day. Books are a favorite pastime."

Rose was intrigued. "Do you share your husband's love of detective stories?"

"I use a smaller room as a study, where I do my correspondence and keep a card file on the children's health. That is a most helpful system. I purchased a card file from the stationers near here and record all the important information about each of the children. It helps so much to be able to check back on symptoms of illness, weight, diet, and all the important information, such as vaccinations, Schick tests, confirmation dates, et cetera. I recommend this idea to any mother."

Rose envied this woman who did not have to work outside the home. Widowed with three children, Rose lived on welfare and spent long hours washing clothes, cooking, and sewing for strangers. Her brother's family lived nearby but did not help with babysitting, groceries, or repairs around her apartment. She worked hard for little pay. In recent months, her son had become disruptive in school. She found herself yelling at him, even threatening him with the frying pan. The long hours at work and tensions at home were wearing on her. The more she worked, the less time she had to educate her children, adding to her shame and guilt. She tried to imagine what it would be like to have this wealthy woman's life. She asked, "Do you select your children's books?"

The lady smiled again, her beautiful teeth impressing Rose. "Probably Jack's favorite book is *King Arthur and His Knights.* I am very careful to select books that are recommended at school or by a children's bookshop. My children, however, are indifferent to these edifying selections, for one of Jack's book treasures is *Billy Whiskers,* a story about a goat, which my mother bought in a department store. The illustrations seem to me to be crude and the colors harsh, but the boys adore the stories and delight in the whole series, pictures and all."

Rose stared, feeling helpless. These children seem to have received a wonderful gift, one that she was too poor to give. Their mother bought them books, read to them, and kept track of every detail in their lives. They also had a father who sat with them, a book in his hand. No wonder they owned the universe.[12] Carmelo was dead, and that changed life for her children. "When my husband was alive," she mused, "he sang to the children."

The other woman's face registered surprise. Tentatively, she reached over to touch the sleeve of Rose's blouse. They had been speaking for some time, and it had never occurred to her that her seamstress was a widow. With a timid smile, she said, "Please accept my condolences, Mrs. Amoroso. Was it from the fever?"

"No. His lungs collapsed from the weight of the dust in the ships."

There was a short silence as the other woman struggled with some new thoughts, but before she could speak the two little boys returned under Mr. Lipman's arms. He had caught them playing cards on the loading dock. Henry had a handful of pennies in his handkerchief and the admiration of his new friend. The mothers gave a collective sigh and told them to go to confession that afternoon. The boys looked at each other and winked.

Restoration Work

Outside, Henry asked his mother a question: "Ma, have you ever lied?"

Rose, unable to contain her anger, said, "I should slap your face."

"Then why did you tell that lady you were going to kill me when we got home?"

271

This boy is killing me, she thought. *If only he would pay attention to his teachers.* This thought reminded her that she had one more stop to make. They boarded the trolley; within minutes, Henry was fast asleep. When he awoke, he spotted the grandest sight he had ever seen—the majestic Boston Public Library.[13]

"Who do you think built this building?" Rose asked him aggressively.

"Uncle Bosco?" he answered hopefully, watching the ants hurry along the sidewalk.

Rose softened and reached over to touch his cheek. "I lived near ancient ruins when I was a girl and passed them on my way to school. In the evening, I danced with friends among the ruins. Your grandfather was a great builder who designed palaces. My brothers learned from him. Uncle Sebastiano shows the Americans how to build in the old way, and Uncle Antonio does the same thing in Egypt. Your uncles Erna and Garafalo are skilled plasterers who create beautiful libraries like this one."[14] A tear spilled under her cheekbone as she continued. "You are small like your father, so you have no chance to become a builder. You also play too much. Forget about this crazy baseball. Pay attention to your schoolwork. I do not want you to beg for bread when you become a man."

"I hate getting whacked by Sister Clara Ann, Ma. Besides, I want to watch after you. I'll never leave you."

She held his face in her hands. "Remember our trip to this place." Then she kissed him and drew him close, something she had not done in a long time.

1909 Postcard of the Boston Public Library

Dewey Was Right

The Paper Route

As soon as he turned ten, the legal age to sell papers, Henry hawked the news at the Quincy Adams train station every morning at six. To be on time, he had to wake at dawn. Many mornings he overslept, missing his eggnog breakfast as he dashed to the station. He would set up his stall at the far end of the depot because an older boy always took the best spot. The selling price for a paper was two cents.[15] When the last train for the morning had left, he would cross the tracks and head over to Center Street to hawk papers to the mechanics and tradesmen who worked in the garages and machine shops along Water Street. One of his customers, an Irishman by the name of McDonald, gave him a forty-cent tip every Friday.

Once he had sold the last paper, he walked about a mile to school with his earnings and a jackknife stuffed in his pocket. Some days, the urge to stop at the candy shop was too great to resist. More times than he cared to remember, he spent every penny on devil dogs and candy and then found himself in trouble with his mother for not being able to pay his paper bill at the end of the week.

On another occasion, his paper business caused him trouble with his sixth-grade teacher. One morning, the knife he carried to cut the string that held together his stack of papers fell out of his back pocket. Sister James Agnes spotted it on the floor and demanded to know who had dropped it. Henry raised his hand. She stared at him for a long time. With contempt in her voice, she finally said, "You would know that an Italian would have a knife." He blushed with shame. It was one thing for classmates to poke fun of his oversized boots from the welfare department, but it was humiliating to be ridiculed for being the son of Sicilian immigrants.

This altercation would not be his only exposure to the church-sanctioned bias against immigrant children.[16] A year later, Connie completed the eighth grade with the highest grades in her class, but the school did not recognize her achievements. At the graduation ceremony, the top prize went to the daughter of a merchant who had donated handsomely to the church coffers.[17]

273

In addition to selling papers, Henry found many other jobs. He delivered bread for the baker on Saturday mornings and helped deliver milk—it was demanding work in the winter when the streets were not plowed. He often had to crawl over deep snowbanks to make his deliveries. Other times, he had to help his mother carry home groceries and run various errands, like fetching ice for the icebox.

One trip to the icehouse turned into such a disaster that Henry did not have to go there again. Rose was always thinking of ways to stretch her budget and one day had a brainstorm. She assumed that buying ice directly from the icehouse would most assuredly reduce the overall cost—a savings, she reasoned, that would result in a larger piece of ice. It was a great plan, so she sent Henry off with his wagon and fifteen cents in his pocket. The icehouse was about a mile away, and the quickest route there was to cut through the ball field. On his way to the store, no one was at the field. On his return trip, though, some of his friends had arrived and started a pick-up game. The temptation was too great for a right-hand throwing, lefty-batting center fielder. Sure enough, by the time he returned home, the bonus-sized block had melted. That was the first and the last time Rose sent Henry to buy ice.

The Red Wagon

Henry did a lot of walking in those days. When he was seven, he used to walk over to the train yards behind Lincoln's Department Store to pack his gunnysack full of cast-off coal that he found alongside the railroad tracks. He disliked this job; it was dangerous, with trains coming and going all the time, so that year his mother bought him a wagon to fetch firewood. To find suitable wood, he went to Quincy Square, behind Kincade's furniture store, to ask for packing crate scraps. Once home, he unloaded the wood and watched his mother chop it up into firewood. It pained him to see her doing such strenuous work, and it angered him that his uncle and other men on the street never came by to help her. The situation taught him a good lesson, though. He realized that he and his family were on their own. He made up his mind to make life a little easier for her, so, with his new wagon, he walked once a week to Door's Market, by the Strand Theater, to wait in line for the packing crates that Florida farmers used to ship produce to markets in the Northeast. The wood was much lighter than the oak planks he brought home from Kincade's. Usually five or six other kids were waiting for crates too. A worker used the street elevator to hoist up dozens of them for the kids to haul away. Henry put three side by side, three the opposite way, and topped off the pile with three more. Then he tied them down with rope and headed home. One time, he tripped and watched them cascade onto the street. To solve the problem, Rose traded in the wagon for one with removable sideboards, so that Henry could make a flat surface for the boxes. She also decided that he needed some help, so the next time he went for boxes he brought along Lucy to steady the load.

He and Lucy spent a great deal of time together because Connie was either at work or reading at the library. When he was in sixth grade, Connie was in ninth, and Lucy was in third. They walked home for lunch and returned for afternoon classes. Their mother wasn't home because she worked as a seamstress at Cosgrove's in West Quincy, but she prepared sandwiches and fresh custard before she left for work. After school, he walked his sister home. Rose didn't allow them to play outside after school.[18]

By the time he was thirteen, Henry was responsible for walking Connie home from her work at a dry cleaner's shop near the shipyard. He left South Junior High after school every day and walked to Quincy Point to accompany her home. The distance from the school to Quincy Point was five miles, and the trip home was another four. Later, Connie got a job at the Enterprise store in Quincy Square. By the time she graduated from Quincy High School in 1931, she had saved up enough money and had won a scholarship to pay for college.

Growing up in America certainly kept Henry in shape. Aside from his duty-driven treks, during the summer he spent most of his time with friends. Most of them were Sicilian Americans, although he played with a few Irish kids with nicknames like Spud Murphy. Their favorite pastime was baseball. Actually, there was little else to do because none of them owned a bike. Only the rich kids were able to purchase two-wheelers. If one of the boys wanted a bike, he had to enlist the rest in a three- or four-day project. First, the troupe walked to the dump, scavenged for parts, and carried them home. Then they begged and borrowed tools to disassemble and reassemble the parts. Before long, they erected a masterpiece in mechanical ingenuity.

Besides engaging their imaginations, bike building kept them out of trouble—it took a lot of time to put together one these beauties. The projects also afforded them continuing benefits.[19] Building a bike from discarded parts required aptitude in problem solving; moreover, by working on a product that mattered, their mechanical skills developed free from the pressures of more formal learning.[20]

Yet another bit of good fortune brought Henry great happiness. Every summer, the Salvation Army selected the neediest children on the South Shore to attend a one-week summer camp at Nantasket Beach. This opportunity was very exciting; the boys got to swim every day, play baseball, buy ice cream, and sleep over in the barracks. Those selected to go took the train into South Station, trollied to Mariner's Wharf, and crammed aboard the excursion boat. With great fanfare, the captain signaled the departure of the boat with a loud blast from his steam-generated horn, the sound resonating across the harbor for what seemed a lifetime. It was a very special adventure—a leisurely cruise out of Boston Harbor to the sandy beaches of Hull, fifteen miles down the coast.

The drama was too much for Henry. He was so caught up in the excitement of waving his handkerchief to his mother that the pennies she had tied in it loosened and fell into the water. Another time, he didn't receive an invitation to go to the camp and moped around the neighborhood for days. One sunny afternoon, as he trudged to the cemetery to water the flowers that decorated his father's grave, a man stopped to ask him why he looked so sad. Henry told him that he was not going to summer camp at Nantasket Beach. Two days later, he received a letter in the mail from the Salvation Army: an invitation to camp.

Henry learned a good lesson that day. The man who stopped him wasn't Italian, Irish, or Jewish. He was what the kids called an "American." There weren't many opportunities for immigrant children to interact with "real" Americans, as the latter didn't live in the same neighborhoods or attend the Catholic school. The only time that immigrant children ran into them was at the train station or perhaps as storeowners in the larger shops downtown, so they based their images of Americans on the horrible stories that their parents told them about harsh immigration officials or the mill bosses who tried to be fresh with the young girls. Americans were mean to immigrants, who should fear and distrust them. But the American stranger who stopped to talk with Henry was different. He was a good man who helped him without expecting anything in return. His good deed shattered Henry's views about growing up in America. He had met an American who treated him kindly.

As he matured, Henry reflected on another important lesson he had learned about people.[21] The Salvation Army had helped him and his family for many years. His childhood was filled with fond memories of trips to the beach, summer camp, baskets of fruit, and scrumptious turkeys at Thanksgiving.[22]

The family moved often in those days, as Rose sought to improve their living conditions. After Carmelo's death, they moved back to Water Street and rented three different houses over a four-year period. From there, they moved to the other end of Water Street, so that Connie could be closer to her new school, South Junior High School. A year later, they moved back to the Quincy Square area, on School Street. Soon, they moved next door, across from the Robert Burns statue on Franklin Street. The final two moves were to Richie Road and, finally, to Kendrick Avenue.

One of the better rentals Rose found was on South Street, a five-room apartment with a skylight over the bathroom. Connie and Henry had their own bedrooms. In fact, during his childhood, he and Connie had their own rooms. Being the youngest, Lucy had to share a bed with their mother. There was no furnace in the house, so they had to rely on heat from the oil stove in the kitchen. Connie had a small potbellied stove in her bedroom, which was at the opposite end to the kitchen. Nevertheless, she couldn't sleep in that room during the winter months, as they couldn't afford to purchase coal.

Henry helped during all the moves with his newly varnished wagon with the removable sides. One time, he helped his mother move across the street to the apartment next to her brother's house. Henry had just carried a heavy chair up a flight of stairs. The day was hot, so he decided to get a cool drink of water from the kitchen tap. The next thing he knew, the faucet wouldn't turn off. His heart sank as the sink filled with water and began to spill onto the floor. Unknown to him, the occupants in the apartment below were admiring their newly plastered ceiling. Crash! It collapsed on them, soaked with cold tap water from upstairs. Screaming obscenities, they rushed upstairs to find young Henry cowering in the corner, panic-stricken.

"What's the meaning of this, you crackpot?" they shrieked at him.

"I couldn't shut off the faucet," he cried, tears welling.

They knew he was Rose Amoroso's son, so they grabbed him by the ear and, cursing, dragged him down the stairs and across the street. When she found out what had happened, she lashed him across the back as she pleaded to the Holy Mother to straighten out this hopeless boy.[23]

Trouble had a knack for finding Henry. Once, he begged his mother to let him take the family Victrola to the neighborhood clubhouse. He wanted his friends to listen to his mother's Caruso records. She hedged, knowing that some of kids were what she called "crackpots." Eventually, though, she gave in; two days later, Ralphie Primavera, a youngster who lived by himself in the attic above the train depot, chopped it up for firewood.

Despite Henry's pranks, his mother adored him. She knew that he was a good boy who was always willing to help and share his pennies with his sisters. One way she tried to reward him was to purchase top-of-the-line clothes for him on special occasions. Most of his clothes were rugged but ordinary, made to last. A store-bought item made him feel like a million dollars. One Good Friday, his mother asked him to walk with her to Baker's, a famous men's and women's store in Quincy. He was suspicious; perhaps the storeowner had told her that he had done something wrong. She could read his mind and told him to stop worrying. When they arrived at the store, she presented him with a genuine black-leather jacket with snap buttons. She had bought him, on credit, an expensive, snazzy jacket that was in style and just the right size.

She repaid him in other ways too and wasn't afraid to ask people for work. For example, her uncle Erna was a plasterer, and she knew that workers could make good money in this profession, so she asked if he would make Henry his helper. He declined, saying that the boy was not strong enough to carry the heavy plaster up the staging to the work area. Later, she did succeed in putting her son into the apprenticeship program at the shipyard.

Retaliation

By the time Henry graduated from Saint John's, he was a real tough guy, small but rugged in manner and appearance. Growing up without a father or male role model had forced him to use his wits. He was a wise guy who could bluster his way out of any jam. Responsibilities had also hardened him. Selling papers to adults, making deliveries in the dead of winter, outmaneuvering kids for wooden crates, and combating mean-spirited teachers taught him how to survive in an often cruel world. Behind the wise-guy veneer, though, were deep feelings for his mother and sisters. He would do anything to please them because he knew how unfair life had been. He also feared his mother's temper, so he obeyed her. When he graduated from Saint John's, he wore boys' knickers to the graduation just to please her, although he immediately ran home to change into adult long pants so that he wouldn't have to take his graduation picture dressed like a sissy.

Despite unrelenting poverty and the trauma of widowhood, Rose raised her children carefully and lovingly.[24] Her greatest fear was their susceptibility to pneumonia and tuberculosis, infectious diseases that afflicted poor children. To keep her children strong and healthy, she fed them well. Breakfast was simple: toast or fried bread and cocoa or eggnog. Lunch usually consisted of American sandwiches and fruit. Evening meals were light; there was no husband to eat a large meal, and the girls didn't like to eat heavy Italian food. Consequently, traditional dishes like pasta with meatballs were rare. A more common meal consisted of elbow macaroni with green peas and sauce, or rice and milk, chicken soup, or bean soup with macaroni pieces. Italian bread was the mainstay of every meal, and she would buy fresh fish whenever she went to the North End to pick up her piecework. The children especially loved the tuna she brought back wrapped in paper. She prepared it the Sicilian way, with plenty of sauce, preserving leftovers in jars. Other fish dishes included squid and salted cod. On Sundays, she cooked all day. For lunch, she served dishes like ravioli or baked pork with potatoes. In the evening, she prepared another favorite meal, usually veal cutlets. As the children grew and prospered, more American items—pork shoulder with stuffed apples, steak, and roast beef—showed up at dinnertime.

The Amoroso diet was modest but satisfying. Besides soup and pasta, Rose served desserts on a regular basis—cakes, pies, and even homemade root beer. The kids bought doughnuts at local specialty bakery shops like Sander and Guay's. Henry even went to the Quincy Market to purchase day-old cookies for ten cents a bag. His favorite Sunday dessert was crushed peanut brittle and pineapple over the heavy whipped cream that he brought home every Sunday after delivering milk. Holidays were a special time for sweets. Rose's specialty was *fattduci* cookies soaked in honey. Occasionally, she allowed the children to dip peach slices into wine.

Rose kept her family together with remarkable determination and restraint, a feat that she accomplished through intelligence and independence. As a measure of her commitment to her children, she declined to remarry, fearing that a stepfather would treat them poorly. She had no semblance of an active social life. She was too tired and busy even to visit her brother for more than an occasional cup of coffee. The only social outlet she had was membership in the Torrie De Pasi Italian Club and, occasionally, her sister Josephine and her family would visit for a day or two. When they did, they would bring along a feast of roasted chickens from the bakery and take Henry and his sisters over to Remick's to buy them new clothes.

Rose's goal in life was to give her children the best lives she could, walking many miles to and from work, taking odd jobs washing floors on her hands and knees and sewing piecework.[25] She made and mended their clothes, washed and ironed their laundry, found and moved them to better dwellings, secured jobs for them and herself, and did all the shopping and cooking. Every Wednesday, she humbled herself at Quincy City Hall in order to pick up her assistance check. She was a resolute woman who refused to feel sorry for herself. Her favorite saying mirrored the reason she came to this county: "You gotta get an education and get a job in an office."

Becoming American

Concetta's Story

Rose's message about education took hold of Connie, who did very well in school. Her eighth-grade teacher, Sister Culbert, told her, "Connie, you're a smart girl. Go to college to further your education."[26]

Those words of encouragement meant a great deal to Connie. She only wished that her father could have heard them. He had adored his little Concetta with the blue eyes. As he lay dying in the hospital, he would manage to sit up and wave to her as she sat outside his window. She dedicated herself to his memory and set her goals on becoming a teacher. She read constantly, completed her homework, and studied for tests. Her favorite books were historical romances. She did so well in school that the Italian American Club awarded her a scholarship to attend college. She was a model citizen for all the sons and daughters of Italian immigrants in Quincy—a girl who had overcome much to graduate at the top of her class. Despite being the firstborn to parents who hardly spoke English, the loss of her beloved father, constant moving, and persistent poverty, she glowed with intelligence, dignity, and life. She had striven to honor her father's name and had succeeded. She also received the personal encouragement to achieve, which is so essential. She had adults in her life who told her that she was smart, precisely what Henry did not have.

SCHOLARSHIP AWARD MADE BY L'ECO CLUB

Bizzozero Makes Presentation to Conceda Amorosa, Quincy High Graduate

Newspaper clipping of the college scholarship Concetta had been given in 1931. (The newspaper misspelled her name.)

Concetta's graduation photo from Quincy High School, 1931

Connie's assimilation into mainstream American life was not without consequence, however. The changes that she incorporated caused trouble in the family. Rose was set in her ways; there was a right way and a wrong way of doing everything. In the case of church attendance, she expected her children to go to 8:30 mass every Sunday. Connie ran into trouble with this rule when she started college. In addition to attending classes, she worked nightly until nine o'clock, including Saturdays. On Sunday mornings, she liked to stay in bed and read the paper.

Sleeping late drove Rose to distraction. Banging on the door, she would shout, "Connie, get out of bed! What are you doing in there?"

Her daughter would shout back, "Ma, I want to read the paper. I'll go to eleven o'clock mass." To Connie, it didn't matter when she went to church, as long as she went, but to Rose, Concetta was putting her own needs ahead of God's. Rose also reasoned that America had given Connie a chance to make something of herself. As her parent, she needed to make sure that her daughter did not become too self-absorbed.

As the old Sicilian proverb warned, *"Non essiri duci sinno to mancianu, non essiri amaru sinno ti ffutanu,"* or "All things in moderation."

Her mother was not the only one to chastise Connie. Henry played the role of a social critic all the time. Connie liked to experiment with American manners, like putting candles on the dinner table. She saw it as adding a touch of class to the house. Her brother saw it differently. "Connie," he cracked, "you better marry someone with a lot of money." In his mind, only wealthy people decorated their homes with frivolous things, and he saw Connie being pulled into that other world.[27]

Rose told him to be quiet. She was very proud of Connie and enjoyed the refinements that she brought to the family. She even encouraged her to invite friends over for Sunday dinner. One time, Mary Sweeney, Concetta's best friend, dropped by for one of Rose's famous Sunday feasts. The wise guy was there and, as usual, had to add his two cents' worth. Mary had just complimented Rose on the elegance of the meal. The sauce was light, the homemade pasta fresh, and the meatballs flavorful. She had never experienced food this delicious. So what did Henry say to ruin the ambience? "Did you enjoy the garlic?" He would never allow his sister to forget who she was. Peasants are meant to be peasants forever.

Charitable Functions

From the start, Henry had trouble finding his way in school. Grieving for her husband, Rose kept her son home and let his hair grow long.[28] His friends came by and said, "Look at his hair. He looks like Saint Joseph." Naturally shy around adults, the six-year-old ran to the basement to sit alone with his chin in his hands.

Connie knew better than her mother, so she asked, "Do you want me to take Henry to school tomorrow?" Rose shrugged, knowing that she had no money to pay the tuition bill. The nuns knew about Carmelo's death and had told Connie that they would go easy on the family. They liked Henry because he was quiet.

Henry sat alone the first day in school, his head swirling in pandemonium. Although he was bright, he had trouble grasping what the teacher said. "If you carry a quarter to the store, what can you buy?"

He had never seen a quarter, and his mother had certainly never let him go to the store alone.

He did better with the alphabet and by December could read his primer. His difficulty was in opening his mouth too little. He also forgot what he read. His most difficult subject was handwriting. The nuns taught the Palmer method; Henry's letters were crooked, and he substituted i's for e's. One day, he looked at his friend's perfect paper and said aloud, "I wish I could write like you." Because he didn't, he started to believe that he was a bad writer and fell into a great silence. He wanted to please his mother, but rushing through his work prevented him from doing that. He didn't take his time because, in his mind, being smart meant that he had to complete the work quickly.

Only his memories put him at ease. He couldn't forget the time that he ate peanuts with his father in the attic before the doctors took him away. There was something dreary in his father's voice when he said, "Your mother will kill me if she finds the peanuts. Do not tell her." Carmelo was worn out from carrying the great sack of peanuts up the stairs. With his son beside him, he drifted back to his childhood. He saw his mother praying to the beautiful patron saint of his hometown, Saint Agrippina. He smelled the delicious salted peanuts she bought for him at the festival. Suddenly, a terrified look came over his face. He was not out of danger. Saint Agrippina had not freed him from his illness. He cried at his ruin as the sound of a marching band played in the distance.[29]

Henry also could not forget his uncle Garafolo. Last spring, on a visit to Quincy, he had overheard his uncle say, "It is important to keep my car off the street." Henry told him to park his new Packard next to the Firestone building. Uncle winked as he put a coin in Henry's hand.

Uncle Garafolo brought Henry back to Connecticut to swim and fish at his cottage, and before they went to the camp, he took his nephew to the Sicilian social club,[30] where only Sicilians from Melilli were members. When they entered, the men in the sparsely furnished room stopped playing cards and put their hands on the table. Each face mirrored the hardness of life. A tall, lean man in a vest stood at the stove, frying sausages. "Everyone," Uncle Garafolo said, "this is my nephew, Enrico. He is a little big shot." They nodded.

"Come here," a fat man nicknamed Pasta King said in a gravelly voice, leaning back in his chair. "Try this," he said, gesturing to the cigar in his hand. Uncle Garafolo waved him off. Someone else named Creiddi took off his hat and passed it around. When it came back, it was stuffed with dollar bills, which Creiddi handed to Henry. These silent, gruff men knew what it was like to be without a father.

Later in the week, he took Henry to a woman's house. She opened the table and placed a huge bowl of sausages in front of him. Then she went into the living room, speaking to no one. Uncle asked Henry, "You want to talk about your father?"

"No," the boy said. He was still angry with Carmelo for dying. He wanted to eat and sleep in a warm bed, not talk about his father.

Uncle took out a picture taken in this very kitchen many years ago. "This is your father. He was a handsome man. The two small children at his feet are you and Concetta. He came to me to find work. He was a clever man, but he was weak. The woman in the other room knew him. He told her to stay close to you if he died."

Henry was deep in memories when a classmate poked him. "Why are you daydreaming?" she asked, annoyed by his differentness. She didn't live near Sicilians. She wondered why Henry wore ill-fitting clothes and sat with his eyes down and his hands in his pockets. Her parents told her to pay attention in school. "If you do, you will attract a man with a lot of money." When the teacher asked a question, she raised her hand with lips pressed together, eyes rolling. The only one who didn't share in her glory was Henry, who just sat there like a fish out of water.[31]

By the third grade, school had twisted his perceptions. The worst time came in May, when he took final exams. He was so nervous that he never finished. Although he failed each time, he passed to the next grade.[32] He wondered if his teachers felt sorry for him because he had no father. Did they figure that he would be okay because he was Connie's brother?

The nuns at Saint John's cared for the children. The eight children in the Nigro family had just lost their mother. The youngest, Francis, was in Henry's class. Each day, Sister brought him into the coatroom and handed him an apple or banana. She was a good person. Whatever the reason, the nuns didn't help Henry with his learning problems, and he received scant encouragement at home.

He was going downhill fast. By grade five, he thought of himself as dense. Rose was beside herself; she knew he was intelligent. "What is wrong with you?" she shouted in frustration. He didn't know why he struggled. His sister sat relaxed for hours and read. When he tried to read, he got so ahead of himself that he didn't finish the sentence. Then panic set in. Compelled to keep moving forward, he failed to understand anything he read.[33]

Those were the years when Rose and the children moved from one house to another to improve their lot. It was also when Henry became obsessively concerned about his mother. When other boys were in bed, reading, he was down by the railroad tracks, collecting wood and coal, delivering bread and milk in the dark, and selling papers at the train station.

His mother's yelling didn't help. Haunted by her suffering, she disappeared into the morning darkness to work.[34] Besides, school failure had made him self-conscious around books. His teachers suspected nothing as they went about giving lessons on citizenship, conjunctions, and sin. When he failed, they said, "He's the son of misfortune."

Blackie

Meanwhile, Henry washed floors for a dime so that he could go to the movies at Merchant's Theater. A nickel got him in; a dime got him a ticket and a loaf of bread to bring home. When his mother didn't have

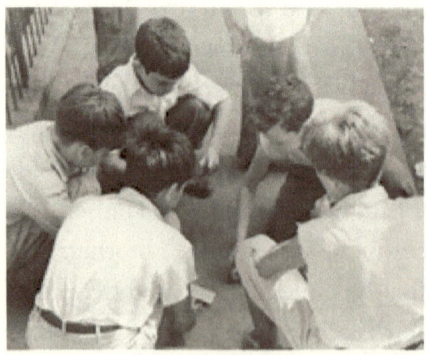

a nickel, he bummed pennies in the neighborhood. He sat alone in the back to watch the serials and westerns. Hoot Gibson, Tom Mix, and Buck Jones were his heroes. Mr. Campbell's wife played the piano and cleaned the ladies' bathroom. Movies took his mind off his worries.[35]

Boys playing cards in the street in 1935. Photograph by Carl Mydans. Part of the "Farm Security Administration – Office of War Information Photograph Collection" at the Library of Congress.

In the summer, he played outside from dawn to dusk. There was no traffic on the street in those days. Mothers stayed outside, minding sons and gossiping with neighbors. Daughters stayed inside until they were grown up and went to work as clerks in stores or baked pastries for sale. Most waited to be married.

Water Street was Quincy's Little Italy. Aside from Galubbrio's, which delivered bread from the North End, family-run businesses met every need. Chester Raniri, who owned a bakery and a grocery store, paid Henry a dime to deliver bread on Saturday mornings. Mr. Macurio was a barber. Babe Marini owned the pharmacy on Franklin Street and always gave the kids big portions of soda and sandwiches. Mr. Palara was a laborer who kept a winepress in his basement. Mr. Whalen worked for the city, and Mr. Venna was a supervisor for the highway department. Mr. Cacheei had a truck business, and Mr. Calabro owned a wrestling gym. Bill Demore peddled fruit and vegetables from a horse-drawn cart.

Rose knew all the families. Years before, when her neighbors found out about Henry's curls, they pleaded with her to cut them off. Rose found it hard to do, so Mrs. Tantillo volunteered. "I am no barber. I do not know the first thing about it. But I am bound to do it. Poor neighbor Amoroso, the time for mourning has passed."

Rose replied. "Yes, I know. Oh, blessed son, this will make two daughters."

Hearing this from the window, Henry began to cry. Mrs. Tantillo looked up and said, "Don't cry, child. Your mama will be next to you."

Afterward, when he walked downstairs and came outside, the neighbors gasped. Mrs. Tantillo wiped a tear with her fist. She had cut his curls, wrapped them in clean linen, and handed them to Rose. "Blow on this," she said to Henry, handing him her frock.

Boys never spoke to him about his hair because he was almost an orphan. "Take this," Vinnie said, handing Henry a chrome tire rim, and the boys set off rolling their rims down the street. Guy Perfetto was about sixteen and lived near Cottage Street. The rim-rollers passed down Water Street, turned onto Quincy Avenue, and headed straight to Ash Avenue. Guy heard them coming and ran outside, screaming, "Go home before you get hurt!"

The boys' favorite game was Peg. Someone drew a circle in the road with chalk and one of the boys tapered both ends of a five-inch stick with his jackknife. Each one took turns pitching the peg toward the circle. If the peg landed inside, you were out. The kids with the closest throws to the edge took turns hitting the peg with a long stick. The winner was the one who hit the peg the farthest.

Another game was Buck. Two or three boys bent over in a row. Another boy took a running start and tried to leap over them. When they got bored with jumping, hitting, and running, they played marbles, cards, or went for a swim up at Patches, the local Pond.

Boys boxing after school in the 1920s.

Blackie Macurio always won at Peg. He was the biggest and oldest kid on the street. His dad, a barber, treated the kids nicely. His brother-in-law, Salvo Palara, lived next door. Old man Palara was a wise guy who always told the kids what to do. His son Sal took after him; if the other kids didn't do things his way, he would beat them up. Mr. Palara had a powerful whistle, and when Sal didn't respond to it, his father kicked him in the behind. He kept his two daughters, Lena and Mary, in the house.

Another neighborhood kid, Sammy Cacheeci was a 118-pound boxer who worked out at Colabros' gym. Rose was his godmother. Twice a week, the gang boxed behind the school. Henry was small but fearless, so he did all right against bigger guys like Philly Iavanna, although one day, Sal was beating him up pretty badly. Sammy said, "Okay, stop." He put on Henry's gloves and beat the hell out of Sal. Sammy was good; no one could knock him down. Sal grew up to be quite a dancer. Like the rest of his family, he was short, dark, and stocky. His mother was of the Granizzi clan, a group from western Sicily who were as dark as Africans.

Sal and Henry were the only kids from the neighborhood who went to Saint John's School. The rest went to the Adams School. In the winter, Henry stopped by Sal's house to pick him up but usually pinched his nose to block out the fish smell.

When they got to school, Primo, the furnace guy, sometimes

invited them inside to keep warm. They were all terrified to hear the coals crackle and spit when he turned them over. Primo had been the caretaker of a vineyard in Sicily. He had no wife, so he and his watchdog had kept away trouble for the vineyard's owner. A fire destroyed all but an acre; now he sat in front of the furnace, handing boys bowls of macaroni.

Lifetime Friendships

When Henry turned twelve, the family moved next to the ballpark near the new junior high school into a mixed neighborhood close to quarry sheds; small, family-owned businesses; the old Jewish synagogue; and the city jail. He knew the neighborhood because he and his friends used to sneak around the jail after school to see what was happening.

Mr. Pavin, who was Jewish, owned the flat that they rented. His cousin, Mr. Scola, owned a clothing store around the corner on Brooks Avenue. Mr. Labasky's printing shop and Mr. Shemgo's junk business were also close by, as were Mr. Gamino's barbershop and Mr. McGantry's floral shop.

The sons of immigrants came to Smith's Field to play baseball in the summer and football in the fall. Quincy was a different place than their parents had known at the turn of century. For one thing, Lewis Hine's photographs for the National Child Labor Committee (NCLC) between 1906-1918 had convinced legislators to pass laws preventing children from working long hours in mills and factories. Gone too were the days when their fathers were a step away from begging for food. Nowadays, children went to school, ate well, and played ball.

Although the Puritans had hated sports, America became a nation in love with athletics and competition.[36] Sports spoke directly to immigrants. Their heroes were men like Jim Thorpe, the "world's greatest athlete" and a Native American. They adored Jack Dempsey, the most feared boxer alive, who had climbed out of the copper mines of Colorado, hard as nails. Then there was Babe Ruth, the most famous baseball player in the world, who was orphaned at 7 years old but eventually signed with the Baltimore Orioles in 1914 when he was 18. Sports heroes inspired the boys to work harder, throw longer, and kick farther. Being on a team like the South Quincy Tigers also bestowed status and a sense of belonging. Smith's Field was about striving and loyalty.

The oldest boy in the neighborhood was Dom Grazio, the son of a bootlegger and Italian grocer. They made him coach because he let them use his dad's shed as a clubhouse. Hollis, the infielder, was a joker who called everyone "Ta Ta Tomato." Herb Spago played second. Al Parker, the third baseman, was part Scottish and part Irish. His half-brother Louie walked with a severe limp. Henry liked Louie the best. "There's something about him," he told Al. Labasky's son Henry was big and fat but still a good catcher. On his way to work at Grossman's Lumber Yard one morning, his older brother saw him trip as he ran to catch a foul tip. The brother yelled out, "Atta boy, Ifsky Sisky." The name stuck. Abbey Kotzen was a good ballplayer but preferred to umpire. Harry McGantry pitched, even though every time he did someone hit a ball through his father's greenhouse. He drowned in the quarries at sixteen. Honey Drupus, little and nice-looking, was an excellent shortstop. His father ran a fruit stand on Hancock Street and told him every day, "I am going to turn you into a doctor." Henry took turns with Barney Shemgo; Tony Abrade, a dark kid from Spain; and Phil Gamino in the outfield. Schola, the redhead, rarely played, because his dad always said, "It is too hot to play ball. Come home."

Days were filled with action. The team walked miles to play games against boys from other wards and towns. When they returned, they headed to their clubhouse to smoke and talk—unless it was too hot; then they stood outside Peachy Regina's store. Henry smoked a Turkish brand that his uncle had once left at his house. The others smoked Lucky Strikes as they shared stories about Babe Ruth, Al Jolson, Bob Steele, and Ken Maynard. Later in life, they idolized Joe DiMaggio and Bing Crosby, handsome men who dined with beautiful women.

Although they laughed at each other's grammar, they tolerated their accents, backgrounds, and differences. They despised old-fashioned celebrities like Rudolf Valentino or Enrico Caruso—men with moustaches and accents who reminded them of their parents. Instead, they looked to American actors and athletes for inspiration. Men like Charlie Lindbergh taught them to say clever things and dream of success. All too soon they would turn their summer fun into productive lives as shop owners, state troopers, craftsman, physicians, and parents.

Laughter and Fear

In August, the gang switched to football. Henry could catch the fastest runner, so he played tackle. At 112 pounds, though, he took a real beating. He was unconscious so many times that the kids just disregarded his "Where am I?" plea. One day, Rose spotted him walking home, pale and disorientated. "That is it," she said. "No more football." The next day she sent him in search of farm work.

He returned without a job offer. As luck would have it, though, one of his friends asked him if he wanted to usher at the Merchant's Theater. Henry jumped at the chance; movies were his passion. For the next three years, he worked summers and weekends on eleven-hour shifts, polishing brass door handles and sweeping floors.

The assistant manager, Bob Farrell, was an ex-marine who required the boys to wear a military-type outfit, pinned at the neck with two clips. The uniform made it too difficult to work. Henry saw clearly that the attire had to change.

Boldly, he went to the manager's office to complain. The following week, the boys donned their new uniforms: white shirts, open at the collar; matching slacks; black sashes; and gray jackets. They complimented Henry with questions like, "What did you tell him?" and "So what do you think?" He felt important; to his mind, this was the first time he had done something right.

With its grand entrance and magnificent stage, Merchant's Theater had been the cultural center of the city for many years. Before silent movies, more than a hundred vaudeville and variety shows had been produced inside its opulent walls. Mrs. Campbell's musical accompaniment during silent movies added glamour. With advent of talkies, the live venue disappeared. Still, the theater served as a cultural experience for the surrounding region.

During the past year, Mr. Hollis had replaced Mr. Farrell as the assistant manager. Hollis loved to sit at the top of the stairs to collect tickets. One evening, Henry noticed that he put several dozen tickets into his pocket rather than tearing and placing them in the ticket bin. "Hey, Eileen," he said to the ticket seller, "what's Hollis up to?"

"He gives me the tickets, and I give him money."

"Like, if he gives you ten tickets that cost fifteen cents each, you give him $1.50?"

"Ya."

Henry smiled at the scam. "You getting nothing out of it?"

"No."

Sensing that he could make an extra two or three dollars a week this way, he said to her, "Do it with me, or I'll squawk." He may have been a lousy math student in school, but he had money in his pocket.

That fall, he entered South Junior High School. His teachers were dedicated progressives who had studied John Dewey at schools like Boston University. Miss Fernand was his homeroom and English teacher; Miss Keaveny, the well-dressed history teacher. Ray Sterling taught mathematics and coached the ninth-grade baseball team. Eager to decrease the dropout rate among Quincy's poor, they tried to motivate their students by tracking them and pushing personal expression.[37]

Good-natured and able to tell jokes, Henry made many friends. Every time the star football player answered a question correctly, Henry clapped and called out, "Good answer, Pip." Before long, he was elected president of his homeroom class.

Although he liked business courses, typing was uncomfortable. He was the only male in the class, to the delight of his friends. Nevertheless, he dressed sharply and, in May, went to the prom with Anne Monti, a friendly girl from West Quincy who had a father with a car.

He graduated from South and spent the summer ushering at Merchant's. His ticket scheme worked so well that he became a regular at the ice cream shop. Using lines from movies, he also became a skilled flirt. Girls waited for him to ask them out. He felt more than ever that he understood and learned from pictures.

Mrs. Campbell, the piano player, turned nasty on him the day that she caught him in the balcony with her granddaughter. Growing anxious at not seeing the girl, she had asked the manager to locate Henry. When he hadn't come, they'd gone looking and found the teens in the last row, kissing. This circumstance stuck badly in Mrs. Campbell's throat. "Who are you to be kissing my granddaughter?" she demanded. Preston fired him on the spot but rehired him a week later. She and Henry continued to meet behind the theater every Saturday night. He liked this moody girl who stared wistfully into his eyes.

When he started high school, he told himself that no one was going to make a fool out of him. Within weeks, Mr. Mitchell heard him talking about a teacher in a fresh way and grabbed Henry's arm so forcibly that he ripped the boy's jacket. Henry knew the part he had to play. "I'm going to sue you," he said angrily.

"Think you're a tough guy, huh?" Mitchell replied.

"Hey, don't bother me," Henry said, pointing his finger in the man's face.

When he got home, Rose was waiting in the dark. She had heard about the rip and recognized the look on his face. "Tell me." When he stopped, she blamed him for speaking rudely to the teacher. He knew her mood, so he was careful what he said next: "I bet Uncle Bosco would have done the same thing, Ma." He lost his pretension when she raised her hand to slap him.

To take his mind off school, he ran outside to smoke. He knew that high school was going to be difficult. Connie had told him to be careful. "They don't fool around." She'd been right. Teachers didn't seem interested in him; in his mind, they wanted to throw him in jail.

Unlike the teachers at South Junior High School, Quincy High School faculty followed the old ways. School was about order and discipline, not the love of learning.[38] Students learned by drill and took tests. If they passed, they went to the next grade. If they didn't, they stayed put. This approach supposedly motivated the best students for the real world of competition. It also provoked hostility from those who failed. As the progressives liked to say, cream will always rise to the top; the rest will learn to destroy.

The following week, a teacher pulled Henry aside. "Why are you smoking? You're small enough."[39] Her tone cut his soul. He knew that she didn't care about his health. If she did, she wouldn't have been so sarcastic.

Put-downs seemed to be the way that teachers responded to him.

Take football tryouts: although only 112 pounds, he was fast and tough. Coach McClarin, a Wollaston native, looked at him and said, "What are you doing here? I suppose you want to play tackle?" The varsity players laughed loudly. Many knew Henry from the theater and envied his success with girls.

Henry smiled and replied, "Why not?"

"Are you joking?" coach shot back. "Go home and put on some weight."

There were days when Henry didn't want to get out of bed. Test days were the hardest. Deep down, though, he didn't want to disappoint his mother, so he kept up the ritual. Thank goodness he still wanted to please her. Several of his friends were already in jail. Charlie Camelli drank on school nights and stole cartons of cigarettes on weekends. Now he was doing time. The same thing happened to his buddy Sam Rainey. He shot a storeowner in a failed robbery attempt in New Hampshire.

Henry had met Sam in September. He was a tiny Scottish kid who lived on Quincy Street, next to the Presbyterian church. He and Henry were in the lowest division classes; both wanted to look like the body builder in the *Boston American*.

Sam suggested that they skip class to work out at Beston's Gym above Bargain Center. "Let's go watch Ivy work out. Then we can too."

Ivy was a local middleweight fighter. Henry agreed but turned back when he had to pay. Rainey had forgotten to tell him that it cost to work out. To avoid going back to school, Rainey said, "I got a sister over at Charleston. Let's take the train to drink with her."

Henry looked at him; he didn't drink. Yet the agony of failing week after week told him to go. Smiling, he pulled out his favorite line, "Why not?"

Meet Jimmy Monti

Gradually, Henry stopped doing his homework and began to cut classes on a regular basis. After school, he went into Charleston or hung out with the guys who drank beer. His report cards were so bad that he forged his mother's signature. He repeated his sophomore year twice. At the start of the third year, he was expelled for insubordination.

He walked home, dejected and fearful. What would he tell his mother this time? He had let her down so many times, but she had always given him another chance. This time, he had run out of luck. He didn't know what to expect.

He didn't have to wait long to find out. As soon as he opened the door, a frying pan came sailing across the room. He ducked, turned to his right, and fled down the steps. Rose knew that something was wrong; she had seen him walking through the square that morning when he should have been in class.

He had been kicked out of school, and now he was out on the street, running away from a small, thin woman with an awful temper. Without thinking, he decided to bum a ride to Lawrence. He had heard Connie talk about family up there. With ten cents in his pocket and wearing nothing but slacks and a short-sleeved shirt, he set out for a city he had never visited. Within five minutes, a middle-aged man picked him up. "Where ya goin'?" he asked.

"Lawrence," Henry responded. But can ya drop me off at Neponset Circle?"

"Sure, kid, but it's a long way to Lawrence, and it's already after two. Why don't ya get a fresh start tomorrow morning—early? I can sure use a nice-looking kid like you to caddy for me this afternoon. Hey, I'll pay you fifty cents and even buy you a hot dog. Ya sure look like you could use some lunch."

Henry thought for a second. Something was fishy. No one had ever acted this nice to him. What was this guy up to? "Sorry, mister, I gotta get to Lawrence tonight," he said, mimicking the man's crude speech. "Some other time. But say, can I bum a cigarette?"

Henry thought that changing the subject would keep the man's questions at bay. It always worked when anyone pressed him too hard for answers. Sure enough, the driver reached into his glove compartment and pulled out a new pack of Chesterfields. As he handed the pack to Henry, he said, "I like you, kid. You got a lot of moxie, turning me down. Say, do you know who I am? Frank Provonovitch. My friends call me Flat Top. I work for Mr. Giriopolis. He owns the Sunset Diner over on Southern Artery. Here, take the whole pack. By the way, what's your name"?

"Jimmy Monti," Henry said, lighting up his tenth cigarette of the day. He always told strangers that was his name. He liked the way it sounded. It made him feel like he was in the movies.

His own name was too long with too many vowels, and people were always asking him the same question: "Rico Amoroso? Don't that come from a song, kid? Sure. 'Tio Amore.' 'My Love.' Hey, you must have quite a reputation with the ladies. Ha-ha."

As they approached Neponset Circle, Henry asked Flat Top to drop him off at the corner of Allen Avenue so that he wouldn't have to cross all the traffic to get back on Route One. Flat Top downshifted into second and then put the car into neutral as he came to a stop. "Nice meetin' ya, Jimmy. If ya ever want a job, come on over to the Sunset Diner. Mr. Giriopolis can always use a smart kid like you in the business."

"Thanks for the offer. I'm not too smart when it comes to book learning, though. That's not my cuppa tea."

"Mine neither, kid. Let's just say you and me got a way with people that fits Mr. Giriopolis's line of work. He likes guys who can think on their feet."

"Like, knowing how to get out of a jam?"

"That's it, Jimmy. Just like you done with me. You sure are sharp."

"I got a feeling I might drop by after I get back from Lawrence. See ya 'round."

With that, Henry jumped out of the car and headed up past the stop light to where cars could more easily pull over to pick him up. Three cars later, he had a new ride and by five o'clock was in downtown Lawrence, sitting at a trolley stop, cold, hungry, and confused. It finally dawned on him that he was alone in a strange city with a dime in his pocket. He was smart, all right. How was he going to find his relatives without knowing their names?

It was getting dark, and the temperature was dropping steadily. He had to get out of the cold spring air. He looked across the street and spied a dance hall. Of course, he would pay his nickel to get in and dance all night. Genius! By nine, he pulled himself out of the marathon. The nonstop jitterbugging had exhausted him. After all, he hadn't eaten all day. Besides, he was the youngest person on the floor.

Kids his age were home doing homework. The older men gave him dirty looks because the ladies were lining up to dance with him. This place was dangerous. What if one of these hoods decided to kill him? Anything was possible away from home. For the first time in his life, he was afraid. A song lyric flashed in his mind: "The grass is always greener in the other fellow's yard." He now knew what those lyrics meant. He would rather be hit over the head with a frying pan than kicked to death in an alley behind a dance hall.

Fearing for his life, he went out into the night again to catch a ride back to Quincy. He would play his luck one more time. A truck driver picked him up an hour later. Half frozen, he climbed into the rig and told his entire story without any prompting. As soon as the driver reached Haymarket Square in Boston, he parked his truck and took Henry to breakfast. Next, he dropped him off at South Station and told him to go inside to sleep on one of the benches, assuring him that it would be safe. Henry trusted this kind man and was soon fast asleep.

Three hours later, he was awakened by the sound of the first train pulling into the station. With his nickel, he bought a one-way ticket on the 7:00 a.m. train to the South Shore. The nickel brought him as far as North Quincy. He got off and walked four miles to Merrymount before he needed to take another nap. He was hungry, but he couldn't go on until he slept for a while on a park bench. When he awoke, he was famished, so he walked the last three miles. His mother and sisters were about to lose their minds when they heard his footsteps. "Henry! Where have you been?" they screamed. "Are you all right? Why didn't you tell us where you were going?"

When he told them the whole story, they didn't know whether to laugh or cry. "We have no one in Lawrence anymore," Connie said. "Years ago, Pa had a sister who lived up there, but she moved to East Boston. Promise us you'll never do anything stupid like this again. Tomorrow we'll find you a job. We'll start with Cousin Erna, the plasterer. It's a good business."

Rose commented, "My only worry is that you are small like your father. He will tell me you are too weak to carry the wet plaster to him. Henry, you should really be working in an office. You are too small to work as a plasterer. God only knows why you had a hard time with school. Now you will never get a good job."

She was right. His friends were impatient young men with cheapened dreams and underestimated abilities. During the day, they worked at odd jobs, like setting up pins in bowling alleys or passing out flyers in tenement buildings. After work, they stole cigarettes, drank beer, and sat in their clubhouse, singing tunes from sheet music. They also played cards in Jerry the Barber's basement. The chief of police and his younger brother often came by to play with them. Angelo was older than Henry and wore a pencil-thin mustache. He liked Henry's lines and stole his "I'm gonna become a doctor."

Rose didn't like him. "Why are you hanging around with someone older than you?" she asked. Henry ignored her; he and Angelo picked up girls.

One evening, as they parked with two girls on a hill overlooking the sea, a light shone on them. "Let me see your license," the police officer demanded.

"For what?" Angelo replied.

"Don't be a wise guy," the cop said. When he saw the name on the license, the cop apologized and said to the girls, "Don't let them holler."

Angelo and Henry also hung around Jerry's son, Al. With his blondish hair and dapper dress, he thought he was King Tut. Like Angelo, he didn't work. His father had thrown him out of the house because he didn't have a job. Al came to the back door late at night to eat. Henry's advice was, "Marry an Italian girl—she'll straighten you out."

The George Raft Look

Although Henry still had his Merchant's Theater job, it was becoming more difficult to buy groceries for his mother and two sisters. Believing that his future was in the theater business, he asked Hollis, the manager of the Alhambra, for a part-time job. Desiring a George Raft look-a-like to keep the young hoodlums in line, he said, "Great. Can you start yesterday?"

"Delighted," Henry said.

On the way home, he laughed out loud at the thought of being paid five dollars a week to watch movies. Preston hadn't blinked when Henry had told him that he was going to work for his competitor. He would continue to employ this skinny kid with the big mouth, unaware that Henry would eventually contribute to his downfall.

Preston was an ugly man with a broad nose and a thrusting chin. He had been in the entertainment business for years. His roots went back to the days when he produced variety shows at Merchant's Theater. Ten years ago, the new owner had asked him to improve business. Preston had accepted with one thought in mind: turn a profit for himself, his wife, and his daughter.

Quincy had two other theaters, both of which offered first-run features and expensive advertisements. Preston gasped at the thought of spending money on such things. His savvy was a spectacle in itself, and he used it to lure people back to his theater. He hated the rapid changes that had come to daily life. Gone were the days of horse-and-wagon deliveries and oxen pulling granite slabs to the harbor. Now, sleek trucks delivered goods and congested the square. Before the war, lovers had paddled the bays and rivers, and families had gone on carefree picnics. Now, young people in tank tops rode around in search of adventure.

The past glamour of Merchant's Theater was not enough to get patrons out of their cars long enough to see a movie, but a two-cent copy of the *Quincy Patriot Ledger* gave him an idea: promise patrons something for nothing. After all, other businesses knocked them over the head with this promise every day. Buy a two-pants Palm Beach suit. Buy labor-saving devices such gas stoves, which allowed mothers more time to parent. Buy eight-piece walnut suites on credit. This generation equated life with goods. Nothing else mattered.

The *Ledger's* motto was "America for Americans," but Preston knew that this slogan meant something else. If America stood for business, why did the paper advise readers to stay away from peddlers, who also offered consumers a product? Of course—they didn't pay for advertisements. Preston knew that "America for Americans" really meant "Say one thing but do another." He also read the editorials that passed as objective news, such as the story about the 1907 Bell telephone strike in Toronto. The female operators were threatening a work stoppage for better pay and shorter hours. Rather than present the issues objectively, the editors cast them as "a class of girls well paid and taken care of ... [who] threaten the public."[40]

As a manager, Preston admired how the editors demonized employees under the guise of the public good. He also chuckled at the paper's obsession with school rankings. Each May, it conferred special status on the highest achievers by publishing their photos on the front page as proof that competition improves society. He knew too that these high achievers were the sons and daughters of Quincy's well-connected families. The kids who stayed back three or more years and dropped out were the ones in search of happiness, a circumstance especially true of the Italian American kids who flooded his office every day, willing to work for pennies.

Sensing that most people in Quincy desperately wanted to keep up with "progress," he would promise them instant happiness. On Mondays, Wednesdays, and Fridays, he raffled off free merchandise from local merchants like Kay Jewelers. On Tuesdays and Thursdays, he auctioned off a stage full of furniture and clothes from the Federal Clothing Store. Once a month, he put on a wedding. Like actors waiting on cue, people would come to his theater to participate in a love story. The wedding script that placed his friend Bob Ellis and his bride on a stage filled with furniture instead of potted plants and religious objects proved his point. People would attend his theater as long as they could fill their lives with gadgets.

Preston's view of the American dream was about private economic gain. In simpler terms, he was a thief. He billed the theater for the hours his ushers spent working on his yard. He rigged the raffles so that his friends won. Worse, he pocketed 40 percent of his employees' earnings each week.

Steinburg, the owner, never showed up. Curiously, though, he did surmise that money was being lost, so he sent his nephew to become the Merchant's new assistant manager. Henry became friendly with him. One afternoon, Tony and Bud said to Henry, "Herbie's nice. You get along good with him. Ask him for a raise."

Henry didn't need any prodding. On the way out, he stopped to speak with him. "How much you making?" Herb asked.

"Three dollars a week."

That night, Herb recommended to his uncle that he increase their pay to five dollars a week. "What do you mean?" Mr. Steinburg asked. "That's what I pay them now. Check the expense sheet."

Herb couldn't believe his eyes. "That despicable Preston is paying the kids three dollars and pocketing the difference! He's even robbing George, the projectionist!"

Henry had never liked that Preston made him clean the windows at his house on Furnace Brook Parkway. He hated him for never calling him by his name. ("Hey, you, bring this to Mr. Farrell.") He also detested that Preston had fired him for the balcony incident. "Do you know how much money I make? Get the hell out of here before I have you pinched."

When Henry found out about the salary scam, he told the Steinbergs about the garden work and the fixed raffles. Preston was fired on the spot. Three months later, Preston pulled into Dulimpio's gas station on the corner of Water and Franklin Streets. The teenagers who hung out there stopped to stare at his long, beautiful car. Henry went over to pump the gas. "Hey, you got me fired!" Preston blurted out.

"That's not a crime," Henry replied. More than ever, he had a voice, and he was not afraid to use it. Preston's avarice had pushed him over the edge, and he would never let it happen again. Henry would never be fat, dumb, and slow. He would take care of himself, wear clothes that fit, and speak his mind. Whenever he spoke, he wanted others to listen.

Henry's recent experience taught him that people are not nice. Preston was covetous, his greed insatiable. The nuns at Saint John's School were fickle and false, too cowardly to name his sister as the top graduate in her class. His uncle disgraced his mother by not helping her. Palara was mean and hostile. Henry's high school teachers harped about moral rules that they didn't apply to their own conduct. Life was a fight for survival.[41] To win, he had to be strong like a lion and cunning like a fox.

This law-of-the-jungle mentality went heart and hand with the gangster movies that Henry loved to watch.[42] Having outgrown virtuous cowboys like Bill Steele, he drew inspiration from tough guys like Edward G. Robinson and James Cagney, who sneered and bullied their way to fame and women. Both were creditable role models who mirrored his life experience. In 1930, at the age of fourteen, he saw Robinson portray the life of the real Sicilian gangster Al Capone in *Little Caesar*. Although the movie taught him that criminal ambitions lead to inevitable downfall, he loved Robinson's ruthlessness. *Doorway to Hell* (1930) taught him that people could be bought. The following summer, his first as an usher, he went to the Alhambra to see Cagney in *The Public Enemy*. The sound and the realism gripped him—like Cagney, he had once been a mischievous and misunderstood boy. Now he was a sexually magnetic and cocky gangster in the making. Fortunately, he had time to save himself from a gruesome death. His tough-as-nails attitude and his smarts would keep him out of trouble. When he saw *Smart Money* (1931) with Robinson and Cagney, he learned about blackmail and how to cheat crooks. All through the movie, he thought of how to make greedy executives lose their jobs. *Winner Takes All* (1932) reminded him that even your best friends can turn against you.

Henry's favorite movies didn't imitate the respectable lives of teens portrayed by illustrators like Norman Rockwell in *Boy's Life* or *Look* magazines or writers like Edward Stratemeyer of *The Hardy Boys* fame. His pop culture icons didn't ride horses, play tennis, vacation in the mountains, or dream of medical school. They certainly didn't solve mysteries with flashlights. They were tough men from lousy environments who trusted no one, intimidated their enemies, and stayed on the winning side. Henry vowed that he would do the same.

Turning Point

Landing an Apprenticeship

Mr. Hollis had always admired Henry's ironic wit and movie-star persona and one day pulled him aside after hearing Henry complain about walking up seven flights of stairs to deliver flyers. "Come here, wise guy," he said. "What's going to become of you?"

"Who wants to know?" Henry said, looking down at his nails.

"Don't be wise. How old are you?"

"Sixteen."

"What's going to happen to you?"

"I don't know."

"Your mother is on welfare, right? Tell her to go to City Hall. Ask the welfare people to get you a job at the shipyard. Tell her to ask for Mr. Broberg."

Henry looked at him suspiciously, shifting slowly from one foot to another. Hollis was, after all, a petty thief like him. Still, he told his mother about his conversation when he arrived home. "Go up to City Hall and ask for a Swedish guy named Broberg.[43] Mr. Hollis says he'll get me a job."

Rose hesitated a moment, thinking about the time that Durlamo had found her a job at the American Woolen Company in Lawrence. This sounded like the same story—a stranger helping another for unknown reasons. "Who is Hollis?" she asked him.

"My boss."

"Does he bother you?"

"No."

Rose remained suspicious of this man's intentions because they did not bear any relation to her reality. In such circumstances, she knew what to do—ask a credible person. Tony Venna, who lived across the street, was the only Italian boss in the yard. She knew that he got Italians jobs all the time. He had even found an entry-level position for Sal Palara. She had not asked Tony to help Henry because he favored men with families. Venna told her it was a good idea.

The next day, Rose walked to City Hall alone. Mr. Broberg came out to meet the grim-faced woman, who said without preamble, "My son needs a job as an apprentice."[44]

Broberg knew that she'd be coming; Hollis had told him at Sunday service. Always a perfectionist, he had done his homework. "I read in the paper that your daughter is doing well at college. My daughter graduated with her. I wish that she had as much ambition as Concetta."

His comment changed Rose's mood. "Thank you," she said. She normally did not hear compliments from Americans.

"Tell me about your son."

"He is a good boy. There is no future for him in the theater business. He needs a real job."

"Mr. Hollis told me that Henry is the best usher he's ever had. Dependable, funny, and—dare I say— fearless. He doesn't back down from anybody. Not even football players. One time a gang of six athletes tried to carry bags of food into the theater. Your son told them he would fight every one of them unless they ate the fruit outside. Mr. Hollis said that he's afraid of nothing." As legends go, this one was monumental. In truth, Henry had said to the players that he would lose his job if he let them in with the fruit.

Rose was not impressed so she did not smile.

Broberg continued. "My brother is a boss in the shipyard. He told me that they're hiring apprentices. Let me put in a good word for Henry. The class starts in a few months. In the meantime, I'll put him to work with the WPA. They're building a stone wall around Faxon Park." [45]

Two weeks later, Henry received a letter from Bethlehem Steel, inviting him to apply to the apprenticeship program.[46] Mr. Broberg's recommendation allowed him entrance without a high school diploma. He was beside himself with happiness. Lugging stones up a hill was not his idea of making a living.

The next day, he walked to the shipyard and introduced himself to the receptionist as Mr. Amoroso. She poked at her hair and turned away. "There are two openings: inside as a machinist or outside as a shipfitter. Take your pick."

Feeling like he had to impress her, he put on his tough guy mask and said, "Shipfitter." Little did he know that he had just condemned himself to forty winters of ice-sharp winds.

He went to work the following Monday in dress slacks and a sweater. He was the only shipfitter in the history of Bethlehem Steel to fit freshly painted trusses to horizontal plates in formal wear. Within minutes, he looked like a bleeding gangster. On the way home, he bowed his head to cover his shame. He would face many more embarrassing moments like this one in the weeks ahead.

The following day, he showed up for work in new coveralls. In his nervousness, he'd forgotten to read the schedule. Tuesday was math class; in fact, apprentices attended classes three days a week—math in the morning and blueprint reading in the afternoon. His instructor was a balding man who stared at him for a long time. "Where's your notebook?" he snapped.

"I'm Italian; I don't need one" came the reply. The class went wild. Who was this wisecracking guy who took the edge off his fellow students' tension? Everyone wanted to be his friend. Math came hard to the apprentices, most of whom schools had tracked out of academic courses like geometry or algebra. Nevertheless, they plugged away and asked questions. Their instructors didn't question their desire to learn. No matter how many mistakes they made, Henry found a way to make them laugh.

Adept at visualizing three-dimensional objects, everyone did better in blueprint class. Most had put in a great deal of rehearsal time, drawing pictures and hitting baseballs. The first assignment was to make a model of a bulkhead using cardboard and glue. The trick was to make it to scale, which meant converting blueprint numbers with proportion and ratio formulas. Henry went home confident. Although he had never read a blueprint before or passed a math test, he knew that his mother made dresses from patterns, and this assignment called for the same type of thinking. She would help him succeed. So would Connie; she had plenty of materials in her desk.

The apprentices were put to work building a fishing trawler. The lead instructor was a hard-driving Scot who had been recruited by Bethlehem Steel to turn these kids into skilled mechanics. He assigned each one to a first-class shipfitter. Henry worked with Henry DeGust, fitting the shaft and rudder into place. De Gust liked the young man's easy demeanor and curiosity. Before long, he taught him to visualize complex structures and then assemble and tack them. Three years later, Henry could perform any job on his own. His aptitudes were mathematical, spatial, and cognitive. His greatest strengths, however, were organizational and interpersonal. A shipfitter laid out a job for others to complete; in order to remain on or ahead of schedule, the shipfitter had to plan, schedule, and negotiate the work of many others. This part of the job required good oral communication skills, a high degree of stress tolerance, personal motivation, good judgment, a sense of timing, and, most important, good human relationships. A shipfitter who was not sensitive to a welder's needs or who acted unfairly to a chipper or a grinder was in for misery.

The whole family attended Henry's graduation ceremony. Six years earlier, Rose had swelled with pride when the citizens of Quincy had given Connie an ovation for her accomplishments. Last year, she'd seen Lucy graduate. Now it was Henry's turn. She had nearly given up; thank goodness there were Americans who had believed in him.

She looked over at the graduates. There were two Sicilian boys; the rest were what she called American. Rose stared at the program, certain that Henry's name was first. She turned to the stage as his name was called. There he was, the first in line to receive his ring and diploma. She stared for a moment and then burst out of her chair, cheering, "Thatsa my boy! Thatsa my boy! He is the smartest!" Years of slight and humiliation overwhelmed her sense of decorum.

Lucy pulled her back. "Ma, be quiet. They're calling names in alphabetical order." It did not matter to Rose; she knew that her son was the best.

Turning Failure Around

Henry began working with "the tools"—the term describing the third-class mechanics. He rose rapidly to second-class mechanic and then to first-class shipfitter. His engaging personality and responsiveness made him a favorite with his peers. His superiors noticed him as well. They were so impressed with his positive attitude that they chose him to break in the recent college graduates in their management program.

One day in early August 1946, Henry's old mentor saw him. DeGust had risen to senior quarterman in charge of scores of shipfitters. "Where you been? Not a boss yet?"

"I got into a little trouble with Horace."

"What happened?"

"It was lunchtime, and I was freezing my ass off, so I put on this long coat and asked the burner to toast my bread. Mayo saw me in the coat and figured I wasn't working. Horace, the uncaring farmer from Maine threw me off his ship. Andy saw me walking toward the gate, so he asked me what happened. When I told him, he told me to get right back to work. The next day, Mayo handed me a jackknife and walked off. Andy must have set him straight."

"So do you want to be a boss?"

"Of course."

"I'll break you in as my special rater. That'll give you more pay; in two weeks I'll promote you."

When Mayo found out, he sent Henry back to DeGust to decline the offer. DeGust went to headman Dave Jackson and told him, "Maybe Henry's wild, but he knows his job, and he knows what he's doing. I think he'll do a good job."

Jackson told Mayo to give him a trial run. Mayo fumed at the thought of a high school dropout leading his men but reluctantly assigned Henry a minimum of four men. Henry turned Mayo's negativity into a positive. His sense of humor and sound decisions made it easy for the mechanics to work for him. They also appreciated how he got the burners and welders to work without quarreling. He eased their demands so much that they finished the job ahead of schedule. As a reward, each one made bonus money. Tommy Donlon, head of the Structural Department—all welders, burners, shipfitters, and grinders in the yard—took notice of Henry's leadership skills. An MIT graduate, Donlon had shadowed Henry when he came to the yard in 1943. Now he needed to send someone to the Sparrows Point Shipyard in Baltimore to learn their assembling techniques. He polled his senior quartermen at a cookout held at Mayo's house. The old Yankee from Maine stood up and said, "As you know, Mr. Donlon, Henry's been known to embarrass and madden me, but his foundations are the best. He does a wonderful job. For that reason alone, you should send him."

It took Henry only ten years to become the best shipfitter in the yard. When he was close to retirement, his superiors made him an instructor in the apprenticeship program. Throughout his career, they thought highly of how he encouraged employees to work to the best of their abilities.[47] Henry took great pride in his accomplishments and always introduced himself as a graduate apprentice of the Fore River Shipyard. His learning in a hands-on environment was more meaningful than the tiresome academic learning that bestowed little dignity on him.

*Henry and Rose celebrate his graduation from the Graduate
Apprentice Program at the Bethlehem Steel Shipyard, 1937.*

Instincts

Friendships meant a great deal to Henry. There was Alex Mitchelson,
the son of Scottish immigrants, and Ferra Di Bonna, the son of a
Finnish mother and Italian father. Duke Di Limpio, another first-
generation Sicilian, owned a gas station. Buddy Maranelli played in
a jazz band. George Foley was Irish, and George Defoe was French.
They worked at different jobs but after supper hung out down at Doble's
Corner. Both Georges also came around Henry's home because they
wanted to go out with Lucy—a problem for Henry, who knew what
they were like.

Always looking for excitement, the group would occasionally walk
over to Quincy Station to catch the train to the Essex Street Station and
go into Boston for some action. One trip was especially memorable.
They first stopped at the Playland Cafe for a few beers, but nothing was

happening there, so they headed over to the Silver Dollar. As soon as they walked in, they knew that something was different. Men were dancing with men and women were dancing with women. Mortified, they left without finishing their drinks.

Mr. Tough Guy

George Defoe was the first to get a car, and the gang started to drive down to Brockton, an industrial city ten miles south of Quincy with great dance halls and safe barrooms. Alex and Buddy met the women there who would become their wives. One of Henry's favorite hangouts was a place called the Bungalow, a small club on the Brockton/Avon line that had a nice three-piece band. Duke was a singer and friends with the owner, Tommy Hallorin. Tom liked Duke's musical style, so he asked him to sing when things were slow. Duke's performances were always well received, and Tommy showed his gratitude with free beer for the guys.

Defoe usually drank too much when they went to Brockton. One night, after a dozen beers, he was in no shape to drive home, which worried Henry because it was past midnight, and tomorrow was a workday. He didn't know how to drive, though, so there was no choice but to see if De Foe could make it to Randolph Square. If not, Henry would have him pull over to sleep it off. A cop stopped them before they got to the rest stop. "Get out" came the command.

Defoe got out and weaved right into the paddy wagon. Henry was sober, so the cop told him to leave.

"What did you say?" Henry asked in confusion. "How am I supposed to get home?"

The reply was sarcastic. "Walk."

"I live ten miles from here, and I have to get up for work at six. By the time I get home, it'll be time to go to work."

"Get moving, you ugly Wop! If you ask me one more question, I'll put you bodily in the wagon with your friend."

Off he started to Quincy, disgusted with Defoe for being such a lush. That's why Lucy refused to go out with him. His so-called pal was never going to amount to anything. All he cared about was himself. Lucy had told Henry a hundred times to stop hanging with him. "His boozing is going to get you into trouble, brother," she'd predicted.

The cop galled him too. No one called him a Wop and got away with it. He'd inherited his mother's temper, and hearing that word made him crazy. Like the time Shaughnessy had called him a "dumb crazy Wop" for filling up the boys' bathroom on the third floor with cigarette smoke. Henry had kicked him solidly in the groin and smashed his chin with a razor-sharp uppercut without missing a drag. Duke had been speechless. Shaughnessy, a six-foot, 200-pound starting right tackle, had just been KO'd by a short, scrawny freshman who tipped the scales at 115, tops.

But Henry had to cool his rage this time. He knew enough about odds to ignore an ignorant cop's wisecrack at two o'clock in the morning. He'd collect his dues later. A nose that big would be an easy target when he least expected it.

What really upset him, though, was the cemetery. He knew that he had to walk past the old burying ground in the pitch-black, and nothing terrified him more than graveyards with rusting wrought-iron fences. In a brawl, you could see the next punch coming, but whatever was in a graveyard cloaked in midnight mist was imperceptible. He couldn't laugh this one off, so as he neared the entrance of the cemetery, he crossed the street and ran past it, wide-eyed but determined not to stop until he reached the safety of the blinking yellow light at the intersection of Routes 124 and 37.

A year later, Duke got his own car. One night in late September 1937, the gang took two cars down to Brockton to go dancing: Duke, Harry, and Henry in Duke's car, and Larson and Alex in Defoe's. Nothing was happening at the dance, so they headed to the nearest gin mill. Defoe met a girl and asked her if she wanted to go to the diner for a coffee. Henry overheard the line and knew what it meant. He excused himself, saying he had to go to the bathroom. On the way, he nodded to Harry.

"What's up, Rico?" Harry asked playfully. He knew that Henry was good for at least one practical joke a night.

310

"Are you up for doing some research?" Henry asked with a slightly crooked grin.

Harry was confused. He hadn't heard that word since tenth-grade history class. "What the dickens is that supposed to mean, Rico?"

"Defoe's putting the move on that pig"—a reference to all women they sought to dominate—"He's been with her since we got here. Let's hide in the backseat to see what happens. Besides, I owe him one for making me walk home last year."

"Rico, that's brilliant," Harry said. "But what if he sees us? You know he's crazy."

"Nah. Listen, all we say is that we were broke so we came to dig some change out of the backseat. We'll say that when we saw him coming, we got scared 'cause he told us not to be in the car without his permission."

Harry liked the joke, so they both walked out, making sure that no one saw them leave. They got into the back and lay on the floor. Defoe and the woman came out shortly, and he immediately started to unbutton her top. He had a reputation for being able to talk the blouse off just about any woman.

She said, "Hold on. I want to eat first. I'm starving. I worked late tonight and didn't get a chance to eat supper. So hold your horses. You know the old saying: 'First things first.'"

Henry and Harry squeezed their eyes and mouths shut as tightly as they could to keep from laughing and waited for the next line.

Defoe was on tonight. "Listen, sweetheart, I'm hungry too. But my needs are different. I love a woman to run her hands through my hair. So how about it? Gabbies' is open all night, but I can't wait that long to taste your sweet kiss."

That did it. The guys couldn't keep it in any longer. From the rear floor came a tremendous roar that filled the car. Defoe slammed his head against the fogged window. Half-undressed and nearly hysterical, the girl screamed, "Who are these guys? Is this your idea of a joke? You sicko! Unlock the door before I tear your eyes out, you crazy freak."

Defoe, sweating profusely, tried to calm her. "I swear, babe, I don't know what's going on. Come on; I can make it up to ya. See? I got a pint with me." He grabbed her by the arm and pulled her close, at which point she elbowed him in the chest, broke away, and ran back to the tavern. Defoe had to admit defeat. He wasn't going to score tonight.

Slouching back in the seat, he began to moan, "Why me? You wise guy, Rico. Wait until I tell Lucy. She'll come after you with a batch of frying oil."

Henry bought his first car in 1939 for five hundred dollars, even though he didn't yet know how to drive and didn't have a license. He told a friend at the shipyard about his predicament. The guy said, "Don't worry, Rico. My father works for the Registry of Motor Vehicles. Meet him at noon at the Hollow Restaurant with a pint of whiskey. He'll have a license for you."

Henry got someone to drive him to the restaurant. There was the man in the parking lot, leaning against his car. "You got the whiskey?" he asked.

"Yeah, here it is," Henry said, trying to look the part of George Raft.

The man reached into his glove compartment and pulled out a tan envelope, which Henry took and walked back to his friend's car.

Once back home and behind the wheel of his own car, Henry engaged the clutch, turned on the ignition, and headed out onto the street, jerking the vehicle for the next two miles. That didn't bother him, though. He was a big deal with his own car and a license to prove that he could drive. With his armed cocked out the window, he squealed and stalled his way through the neighborhood in his '38 Chevy.

Two months later, George Nenna from the Chevy dealership pulled up in front of Henry's house, driving a new two-tone Chevy. "Rico, I have something for you. Have you heard about automatic shift?"

"No."

"Well, I've got one to show you. It is a demo. Not a scratch on it. And how about that paint job? Two-tone, Piasan. I bet you don't know anyone with a two-tone. Do you? Of course not. This is the first one in Quincy. How about that radio? It even has an umbrella for those April showers. Talk about May flowers and June brides, Stella's gonna love that heater right under her legs. And how about them fog lights? Goodness gracious me, Rico, you'll never be lost again. Why she's even got directional signals! How can you go wrong? All this for only a grand!"

*Stella Fasolino, the woman
Henry would marry.*

Henry was speechless. He could see himself and Stella, the woman he would eventually marry, zooming down Route 138 to the Roseland Ballroom in his new two-tone Chevy. Nothing else crossed his mind. George asked him how much he brought home at the end of the week. Henry told him forty dollars, a first-class mechanic's wage.

George tapped the tire with his loafer. "No sweat," he said. "I'll get you a monthly payment plan that won't bust your nuts."

Henry couldn't resist the temptation to own such an impressive automobile. As he signed on the dotted line, the thought of buying a car that cost an entire year's wages crossed his mind. He dismissed it, however, as soon as he got into the driver's seat. Newly promoted and wrapped in luxury for the first time in his life, the sky was the limit for this Sicilian American street kid.

When he got home, Rose and Stella brought him swiftly back to reality. Both went into fits and nearly passed out when he showed them the bill of sale.

Rose was the first to speak. "Henry, you cannot buy a new car. Take it right back to George."

Stella found it hilarious to see Rose pushing around her tough guy. She understood his mother's concern, however, and pulled him out the screen door and into the car. When they got to Parker's, she waited in the car. Henry went inside, wondering what he was going to say. He thought, *What would Raft do in this situation?* "George," he snarled, "I want my money back."

But George had heard this line a hundred times before and knew exactly how to respond. "Too bad, Rico. You signed on the dotted line."

For the next ten years, Henry made monthly payments to the Parker dealership for that 1940 demo with the umbrella and fog lights.

313

Love and Prosperity

Vices and Virtues

As the family prospered, they moved up the hill to a better section of the neighborhood. In Henry's words, "We moved to Richie Road, where a different class of people lived." Two years later, they made their final move. The spinster Miller sisters owned the house on Kendrick Avenue and lived on the first floor. Kermondy, the iceman, and his wife lived on the second floor. The Miller sisters wanted to move and offered the house to Rose for five thousand dollars. She declined, so the sisters sold it to the McClouds. The new owners were very strict. They didn't allow ball playing on the sidewalk on Sundays. Concetta and Lucy shared the back bedroom with Rose, and Henry had the front bedroom to himself.

Rose continued to struggle with Henry, who had never been able to resist the world's temptations. In Sicily, young men his age worked from dawn to dusk under the stern supervision of their fathers. In America, Rose's son stayed out every night of the week with losers. "Stay home," she said.

"You're too pious," he replied. Rose frowned, unable to keep him away from bad influences. Every night she said a rosary for him, her hands lifted in front of her. She also went to church daily to pray to Saint Sebastian. She was rewarded by a visit from her brother. Knowing that Henry needed positive influences in his life, she said, "Take Henry to the Sons of Italy Club."

"Why?" he snapped.

"He doesn't have a father."

"I'm always on his back, keeping him straight," said Sebastiano. "I come up to the house to keep an eye on him."

She despised her brother's refusal to help her. She was relieved the day that Henry brought Alex Mitchelson home to meet her. Alex was a good boy, someone who went to church. "Take my son with you," she said.

"Yes," he replied encouragingly and every Sunday stopped by to pick up Henry. After mass, they returned for a hearty meal and a game of Italian Lotto or the Bingo that Rose had bought in the North End.

She believed that Henry was changing. As a boy, he had always liked to listen to radio dramas. After she bought the big Philco console, he stayed around after Sunday lunch and listened to her favorite show in Italian. Following supper, he listened to his shows.[48] Knowing that he liked to sing, she got out Carmelo's old Italian records. Henry especially liked the tune "Yes, We Have No Bananas."

A month later, he returned to the streets. Rose could not understand why he wanted to be out so much. She had created a stable world for him after the death of his father. Now he abandoned her.

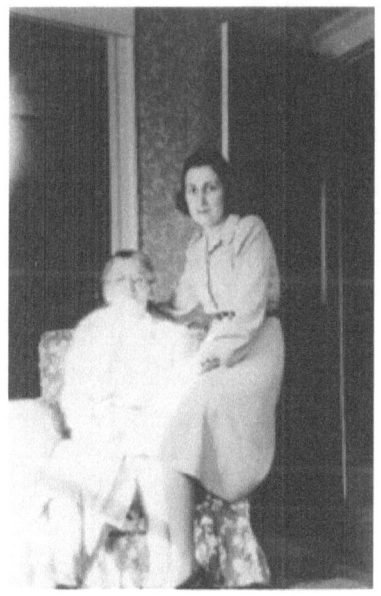

Youngest child Lucy with Mama Rose, 1940

Experience had taught her that men were unfaithful, which is why she did not want her daughters to go out with them. When the girls were small, it had been easy to enforce the old ways—"Do not let any boy kiss or touch you." But the Roaring Twenties shook loose her hold on them. In this free-spirited age, popular culture preached an anything-goes attitude. Inventions like the automobile, the airplane, and the telephone freed youth from the past. Woman's suffrage and unionization diminished social taboos and the boredom of work. Popular music and talking movies celebrated fun and whimsy. Even literature assaulted restraint. Authors like Theodore Dreiser and Eugene O'Neill exposed young people to a new morality.

It was in this spirit that Lucy begged Henry to take her to a dance hall called the Riverview over by Neponset.

His reply was right out of a Jimmy Cagney movie: "Why do that? I want to make out."

Lucy was an attractive young woman with a pleasant smile. Boys liked the way she held her cigarette and called them "sucker." Determined to keep her chaste, Rose turned to the Marchesies, the family who had bought Carmelo's gravestone, for help. They still lived in Braintree and were wise in the old ways. Mary was hard of hearing and bent with arthritis. The old man, however, was still robust. He had worked as a plasterer for sixty years; now, he sat out back alone, tending to his memories and grapevines.

Years before, his best friend, Gaetano Bosco, had asked his friend to treat his Rosina as his own. He agreed; that was what friends did in his world. In the following years, he encouraged his first son, Mike, to move from Middletown to board with Rose and Carmelo when they arrived in Quincy. He had also told his youngest daughter, Teresa, to spend time with Rose before the young girl's marriage to the newly arrived mason from Melilli, Alosi.

Alosi was lean and muscular, someone other men envied. Every time women heard him play his guitar, their shyness evaporated. Unfortunately, this handsome man with the sharp nose and thick mustache had seen his first wife die on the boat from Sicily. For the past two years, he had not felt the tender caress of a woman.

He had seen Teresa Marchesi when she had brought ripened fruit to her father. Alosi had gazed on the elegance of her fingers as she had passed the fruit to her father. Turning to Mr. Marchesi, Alosi had said, "I will build your daughter a stone house if you let me marry her."

"Teresa doesn't know anything."

"Can't someone teach her?" Alosi said.

Turning to his daughter, he said, "Watch Rose. Learn how he comes and goes."

Rose remembered these things. And she knew Teresa and Alosi later had a son who took after Alsoi, named Antonio. Antonio was the independent one who had thumbed the New York's World's Fair in 1939.

Rose told Mr. Marchesi, now an old man, about her daughter Lucy. He put his glass down and scratched the stubble on his chin. Remembering his

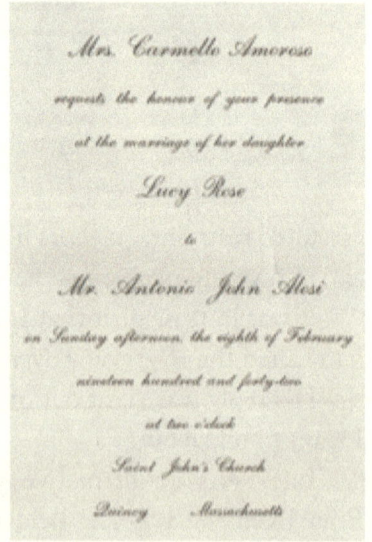

Rose's wedding invitation for Lucy and Antonio Alosi's wedding in 1942.

316

vow to Bosco, he said, "Ask Teresa to arrange a marriage between Lucy and my grandson Tony."

Rose told the old man about Lucy. He put his glass down and scratched the stubble on his chin. Remembering his vow to Bosco, he said, "Ask Teresa to arrange a marriage between Lucy and my grandson."

This was a matter of honor, and Rose bowed to him, saying, "I am grateful."

Teresa agreed to the arrangement. On April 12, Lucy and Tony were married at Saint John's Church. An expensive reception followed in Wollaston. Three months later, Tony left for the Pacific Theater.

Concetta's Calm

Rose's control of Connie was different. One afternoon, she overheard Connie mention to Lucy that a boy named Scotty was going to come to her rehearsal at the Strand. Rose told Lucy to wait across the street. When Connie came out, Scotty was holding her hand. Lucy reported it to her mother.

On another occasion, Rose saw Connie walking home from work with a boy who held her umbrella. She ran out to meet them. Grabbing the umbrella away, she said to the boy, "I will take her home now."

After that encounter, Connie followed her mother's example—no contact with boys. Only once did she break the rule—when she went to her senior prom. Her date, a good-looking guy from North Quincy named Byron, came from a wealthy family whose roots traced back several generations. Servants ironed his clothes and turned down his bed. Guests to his parents' dinner parties at their summer home in Cohasset were some of the most powerful people in Boston.

Rose did not care if he had grown up in privilege or in poverty. She was going to make Connie a beautiful white gown that accentuated her chaste blue eyes. When the boy came for her, he smiled. Rose read his secret thoughts and moved her hand to guard her daughter's perfect skin. Connie was the only girl he knew whose eyes lit up any room. She was also very famous. The Quincy papers had reported, "Concetta Amoroso, daughter of Mrs. Rose Amoroso, received the largest scholarship in the graduating class." Yet she was not consumed by her ego.[49]

The following week, he invited her to go flying at Squantum. He had earned his pilot's license the year before. Connie was giddy. She had seen pictures of Wellesley and Radcliff female students waving at the camera as they entered the cockpit of a plane. Of course, Rose nearly passed out when Connie told her about the amusement. She looked at her daughter for a moment and then quickly walked away.

As he helped Connie into her seat, he said, "You're not like any other girl I know. You're not preoccupied with yourself. Tell me the truth. Do you think you can like me?"

Connie pressed her hand in his and said, "I can't have a boyfriend."[50]

Byron buckled himself in and primed the choke. "I adore you."

"I promised my mother that I wouldn't have a boyfriend when I go to college. I wouldn't dare waste her time supporting me by having a boyfriend." Connie said nothing more. She had vision and motivation. Unlike her brother, she saw life the way it could be.

Henry vilified her for wanting to be high class. "You think you're top shelf," he said defiantly.

Four years later, Concetta earned a bachelor's degree and became the first Italian American teacher to work in the Quincy Public Schools. She taught for ten years, first at Atherton Hough School in Hough's Neck and later at Coddington School in the square. In the early years, she took a trolley to work. Later, she took driving lessons in Braintree and bought herself a black coupe. Every summer, she and her friends drove to have outings at Salisbury Beach, where she met her future husband, Ralph.

Later in the year, Henry drove Rose and Connie to New Hampshire to meet Ralph's family. It was early winter, and the ponds were iced over. As they approached his house, Connie shrieked, "Ma, look! There's Ralph!" Rose looked out her window; on the ice was her future son-in-law, sliding back and forth with some other men. She had never seen anyone skate. "What is he doing?"

"It's called hockey, Ma. It's a form of exercise."

Rose noticed everything. She knew that Connie was happy inside. The meeting also went well, with Ralph's mother agreeing with her son's decision to convert to Catholicism.

Rose gave her blessing, and the couple set a wedding date. They were married four months later in Connecticut. Unlike Lucy's wedding, the reception was small and held in a local restaurant. Stella and Henry were maid of honor and best man.

The Yale football team happened to be in the restaurant, and a bunch of players came over to congratulate the bride and groom. One of them saw Rose staring out the window. He went to her and politely introduced himself. With intense pride, she pointed to Connie and said, "My daughter graduated from college ten years ago."

They spoke a bit more about his plans to join the navy upon graduation.

After he rejoined his friends, she edged herself down in the chair and absorbed herself in thoughts about Carmelo. Then she edged herself down in the chair and absorbed herself in thoughts about Carmelo.

With the war raging on two fronts, Ralph shipped out immediately. At the time, Connie lived on Kendrick Avenue with Rose and Henry. Lucy was alone and pregnant in a small duplex two streets away, so Connie moved in with her. The following week, she received a letter of termination from the superintendent of schools. In his best administrative language, he told her that she was in violation of the Commonwealth's marriage policy.[51]

Connie couldn't accept this action. The next day, she marched into his office with a picture of her husband in uniform. A strand of her hair touched her cheek. "I am married to a man who is fighting for this country. Do you mean to tell me that I cannot teach?" She said nothing more. He couldn't bring himself to disagree; he rehired her and made her assistant principal of Coddington School.

When Ralph returned from duty, he and Connie moved to his home in Concord, New Hampshire. A short time later, he found a job in Boston and rented a tiny bungalow nestled in the woods of Braintree. By this time, Connie was pregnant, so Rose visited her often. In the spring and summer, Rose took long walks in the woods to pick blueberries and lady slippers. She saw white birch trees for the first time and especially loved the scent of the pine needles and the earth beneath her feet.

On these walks, her thoughts deepened. She had left behind her mother and father for the New World. Although they lived thousands of miles away, she had maintained ties with them, as she also had with

Antonio.[52] Thank God he had written on a regular basis; his letters of support had helped her put her struggles aside. Likewise, her friends from the old country had helped her face social and economic difficulties in this culture. Of equal importance was the support from the welfare office in Quincy. She was indebted to many people who had helped her keep her family together.

Although Connie had absorbed the dominant culture, she too had not forgotten her past. When she graduated from college, she visited her father's relatives in New York. She stayed with Frank and Jenny Gulizia the first week and with the Sira family the second week. She wanted to know everything about her father. Her aunts told her that Uncle Enrico had offered to send Carmelo to the seminary; instead, he fled to America. They also told her the story about the white stallion and showed her a letter that Carmelo had sent them on his deathbed. "I die because I did not keep my promise to my wife ... do not blame her."

Aunt Sira offered Connie a picture of Carmelo when he was a young man. In return, Connie recollected the times that her father had sung with his Venetian friend with the musical voice and her trip to Lawrence to visit cousin Josephine. She also showed them Carmelo's expense book, which she had found in his room. He had been a fastidious recorder of details. She said proudly, "My memories of Pa will never disappear. I'm proud of him. I like to be proud of him." Both sisters nodded as Connie held Carmelo's record book to her chest.

The Amoroso sisters had not attended Carmelo's funeral. Connie knew that they disliked her mother's bossiness. As the afternoon wore on, they felt comfortable asking Connie intimate questions.

"Tell us what you remember about the funeral, dear niece?"

Connie replied, "After the funeral, Ma took us into Pa's rag room and said to us, 'How am I going to raise you?' Right then, I grew up."

Aunt Sira asked Connie if Rose was angry at Carmelo for dying. "My mother was too busy to feel sorry for herself. She prayed to Saint Lucia and Saint Sebastiano for strength. Her mother sent her a postcard of Saint Sebastiano."

"Did she stay to herself?"

"Many friends in the neighborhood advised her to remarry. She asked me about it once. I told her that I didn't want another father."

Connie also stayed in touch with her uncle Antonio and his family in Egypt and insisted that Ralph visit him when he was stationed in Cairo. She encouraged her cousin and her family in Cairo to immigrate to the States after the war. Instead, they settled in Montreal; the following year, she and Ralph took Rose to visit them.

Jimmy Monti Redux

Unlike his sister, Henry excluded family history from his life. When Connie told him about the trip, he said, "Good riddance with that."

One Friday afternoon, on the way out the South Street gate of the shipyard, a big welder with a car asked him, "Wanna go to Old Timers' Night at the Roseland?"

"What's that?"

"A dance hall in Boston. Next to Symphony Hall. The broads are a dime a dozen."

"I like them dressed up," Henry replied

"They're all young. Some are fancy numbers."

At this point in his life, sex was the only thing on Henry's mind. That evening, he met Stella on the dance floor. She was beautiful and only twenty. It was a fast number, a jitterbug. Ever the manipulator, he asked her, "How am I doing?"

"Fine." They danced three more numbers. Now it was her turn to ask him a question. "Where you from?"

"Who'd you come with?" Henry asked in an almost defensive way.

"My girlfriend, Josephine," she said. They didn't have much of a dialogue. Neither wanted to show too much at first; in fact, Henry used his alias when she asked his name. Several weeks passed before they met again at the Roseland. Stella came over eagerly to ask him a question. "Hey, Jimmy, you know a guy named Finn?" she asked innocently.

He knew Finn all right. He was a wild guy. If a girl didn't come across, Finn made her walk home. Growling, he replied, "You fooling around with him?" Although they hadn't said much the first time they'd met, he knew that she was different from the women he dated. Stella was innocent.

"No, no. Take my word," she said. She was attracted to this guy

321

who spoke like a gangster. He was gruff but had a way of making his brusque manner and obsessive scowl lovable. For the next year, they met on Friday nights in front of Jordan Marsh's Department Store. The routine varied. Some nights, they ate at the Waldorf and then went to dance and have a few drinks. Other times, they caught a movie and then went to the deli on Essex Street for pastrami and coffee, with pie a la mode for dessert.

Henry didn't own a car yet, so he took the train home. Stella did the same, returning to Roxbury alone. Her employer, Mrs. Silverman, disapproved. "What kind of fellow you dating, making you come late at night by yourself?" Stella was the Silverman's live-in nanny.

"It's okay, Mrs. Silverman. He has a long way to return home."

Henry and Stella loved to tease her sister Jenny and her husband, Tony. One day at work, Tony came up to Henry. "Too bad about Stella not hearing."

Angered, Henry shot back, "She never told me."

"She reads lips," Tony said.

When Henry confronted Stella, she said, "I thought you'd drop me."

Rose was even more upset when she found out. "There are plenty of nice girls around. Why this one?"

"She has some hearing, Ma. I know because she's a very good dancer."

The following year, Henry bought a car and visited Stella's parents. As soon as he walked into the kitchen, his prospective father-in-law derided his Sicilian background. Italians looked down on all dark-skinned Sicilians. Dropping his charmer façade, Henry shot back, "Be thankful, old man, that I want to take your daughter off your hands. She's deaf."

"Before you do that," Mr. Fasolino replied, "I will throw you out of my house, you good-for-nothing dirt-eater."

"It's time to settle down with a good woman," Henry answered back.

"One day I caught Stella in the bathroom, smoking. I threw her out of the house."

Henry responded sharply, "My sisters smoke."

"Girls who smoke are no good," the old man retorted.

In tears, Stella said, "I'm going to marry Henry, Pa. Look what he brought for you." Lost in the argument were a dozen carnations for Mrs. Fasolino and a coffee with milk for him. Henry had also picked up a napkin that had fallen on the floor. *"Marry him, Stella,"* her mother said with her eyes.

Henry and Stella dated for four years before they married. When they finally did wed, her father offered them a tiny bungalow he owned. Stella was happy; she wanted to be near her parents. But Henry didn't want to leave his mother, so he told her that they had to live in Quincy.[53]

After honeymooning in New York City, Henry told Rose a story. "I told Stella I was going out for a walk. When I came back, I rang the bell, but there was no answer. I rushed down to the manager to tell him my wife was hard of hearing. He said that he wasn't supposed to let anyone into the rooms. I yelled at him, and he finally let me in. I knocked on the bathroom door. Stella was taking a bath but heard the banging. Ma, she screamed so loud that the security officer pulled out his gun."

"Take her to Dr. Harkin," Rose said, knowing the tragedy that threatened his peace of mind.

The doctor told them that she must have picked up an infection when she was young. "Nothing can be done, so get her a hearing aid," he advised.

Henry knew that the doctor's suggestion was the only way that he could handle his wife's disability. Stella was willing to attach batteries to her bra and wrap a big one around her leg. When she turned on the hearing aid, she smiled. For the first time in years, she heard birds sing.

Henry and Stella were proud of their heritage. Like most Sicilian and Italian Americans, they were especially crazy about Italian food. Stella had cooked with her mother since the age of six. She had a passion for cooking and loved to create new dishes. Henry loved the traditional dishes, where tomatoes tasted like tomatoes. "Keep it simple," he told her.

On Saturdays, they were like two chefs on a mission. First, they purchased staples at the Mohegan Market on Grand Street. Then they walked over to Quincy Market for sugared pastries. Then, because the secret to Italian cooking lay in fresh and simple ingredients, they headed to the North End to purchase everything from imported cheeses to roots and meats.

The visit to the North End was the highlight of their week. It was their second home. They especially loved to hear the old people speak Italian. Stella made sure to visit the Abruzzi Meat Market. Her family came from that region of Italy, and the owner knew her from the days when she had come there with her father. He always mixed pork and beef together for her meatballs.

One afternoon, late in August, Henry was leaning against his car when Ted Williams and the DiMaggio brothers, Joe and Dom, walked by. Henry flicked his cigarette into the gutter and said ironically, "The chapel is the other way."[54]

Joe turned around and smiled. "Know where we can get a good pizza?"

Henry didn't know, so he bluffed. "Can't get a Sicilian pizza here. Ya have to go to the Adams Tavern in Quincy. They got this woman who makes two kinds—one with sauce and cheese and the other with the anchovies embedded in the crust."

As fellow Sicilian Americans, the DiMaggios knew what Henry meant. They'd grown up eating anchovy pizza without sauce every Sunday night. "Next time we're in town, pal."

Williams's eyes were on the pastry shop across the street. Like other Americans, he was turning Italian cuisine into the country's favorite. In fact, he and Dom had talked about opening a restaurant in the North End at the end of the season. "Small and classy," said Ted.

"Friendly, like the old neighborhood," replied Dom. Joe wanted white linen, mirrored walls, and very fresh seafood all day. "It won't last," Dom said. "You gotta keep it simple."

Henry started playing the numbers in 1934, when he went to work at the shipyard.[55] Two "big wheels" ran the show. One came from Brockton; the other was out of Boston. Each had a lieutenant and several bookies to take the bets. Most were chasers who ran all over the yard looking for materials. Coco was a welder and the only one who booked at his job. Guys came to him with their numbers.

Five cents was the minimum bet for a thirty-dollar payoff on three numbers. Boxing three numbers—any order won—cost a quarter a day or $1.50 a week. Payment was due Monday morning. Henry bet 313 for fifty cents a day over the course of forty years. The number came in three times.[56]

Hot numbers were birthdays, weddings, and anniversaries. Henry changed to 313 because Stella told him to one morning. Henry picked up his lunch pail, kissed her, and went to work. When Red came by, Henry said, "Play three one three, boxed."

"Is it hot?"

"Stella dreamed it last night."

"Could be a bad sign."

"She's not in mortal sin, so it can't kill me."

The Burden of Conscience

The early years of Henry and Stella's marriage were difficult on everyone. Rose had spent the previous twenty years as a defiant and independent woman. She had chosen the apartments, bought the furniture, made the clothes, shopped, cooked, and washed. She had taken the children on trips to Boston and to the pier near the shipyard to picnic. Now her daughters were gone, and Henry gave his check to Stella every Friday. Henry's friends stayed too late, sister-in-law Jenny's kids jumped on her couch, and Stella spent too much time talking with Lucy on the telephone.

Stella sensed Rose's unhappiness, so she asked her to share in the cooking. She also invited her to shop with her and accompany them to the beach on hot days. Rose was especially happy when Lucy and Tony came down to sit on the porch and play rummy. Still, Stella had no relief from Rose's criticism and Henry's outbursts. One evening, she said to him, "Ma never smiles at me."

Henry assumed that Stella liked Rose because she called her "Ma." Then he thought for a moment and said, "She doesn't like you. She doesn't like your family, either. There are too many of you to feed."

Stella was dumbfounded. She was caught between a strong-minded woman and her volatile son. Both of them yelled a lot and were impatient and insensitive to her feelings. They rarely smiled at or hugged each other. Both insisted that she cook more meat. Worse, they had to have everything their way. Their nitpicking drove her crazy; they both took life too seriously.

Her father had warned her, "Sicilians are worse than dirt and criminals to boot." His belief reflected how Hollywood portrayed gangsters and fit perfectly with newspapers that still printed nativist rhetoric.

Stella didn't buy the stereotype. She knew that Rose had a sharp mind, but life had robbed her of emotion. Henry's failure in school had made him insecure. No wonder he was cranky and nervous; the yard was a menacing place to work. Repeatedly, he told her that his boss said to him, "If you can't get the job done, I'll find someone who can." Men in permanently dirty clothes screamed and hollered all day: "Who cares?" or "Your wife is a prostitute." Air-compressed machinery, dust, and unwashed windows added to the misery of the place. Like his father before him, Henry left Fore River tired and worn out every day, with desperation etched across his face. Stella knew too that he worried about being laid off. Rose constantly reminded them, "Don't spend all the money; it will go fast when nothing is coming in."

When Henry lost his temper or shouted at her, she calmed herself with thoughts of summer, when her brother Francis used to take her to the ocean. He was taller than Henry and wore his shirt collar open, revealing the hair on his chest. He spoke eagerly and passionately about playing football for Holy Cross on a scholarship. He used words like industrialization, democracy, and revolution when he spoke about their uncle, a communist organizer in Rhode Island.

Henry didn't speak like Scara about the Jazz Age, Broadway, Harlem, or the New Deal. He never took Stella to museums or discussed the significance of architecture or military operations. He couldn't care less about culture. In many ways, though, he was no different from more educated Americans who had concluded that this country was not a nice place. He knew that the rich got that way by robbing the poor. His classmates at Saint John's had graduated from high school; his Water Street friends were dropouts. The graduates cut their lawns and spoke about stock options; his friends lived in crowded apartments and stepped onto the sidewalk from their front doors. Although his sister had won the largest scholarship, the newspaper put her at the end of the story and didn't refer to her as "Miss" as they had with the other recipients. Now she had a high-status position and lived in a prestigious neighborhood. He had seen Preston shake the mayor's hand as he robbed the theater's owner with the other. Even sports were fixed. America exploited the weak, with the support of the schools. Unlike Scara, he trusted no one, especially newspaper writers, politicians, and teachers.[57]

Henry's skepticism was as deep as that of writers like the white-haired Robert Frost, who had revolted against established tastes and privilege. Like Nietzsche and Heidegger, his father distrusted words, which he knew people could use to mask indifference, hostility, and conflict. Still, he went to work and paid his taxes. Although impatient and irascible, Rose had raised him to be a responsible citizen, husband, and father.

Notes

1. Events found at *American Chronicle* (Gordon & Gordon 1999); *New York Times Index* (1973); *American Decades* (Bruccoli 1996a, 1996b); and *Readers Guide to Periodical Literature* (1915, 1922).

2. With the exception of the Kennedy exchange, the characters and events in this chapter are factual, with dialogues drawn from interviews with Henry. C. Amoroso, Sr (2005-2008) and Concetta B. Carr (2006-2008). With respect to the name-calling episode, Rose landed in America at a time of great racial, ethnic, and religious strife. The Immigration Restriction League (1894–1917), initiated by "three Harvard College graduates, Charles Warren, Robert DeCourcy Ward, and Prescott Farnsworth Hall," had urged Congress to pass a literacy test as a way to keep out "inferior" immigrants from southern and eastern Europe (Immigration Restriction League 2002/2011). People blamed most social ills on immigrants ("Infected Immigrants," "No Immigrant Plague," and "Immigrants and Insanity" 1980). According to Vecchio (1997), Italians and Sicilians faced more prejudice than other ethnic groups, with the popular press portraying the men as smelly organ grinders and the women as earthy, buxom, childlike, and superstitious. Americans called them "smarmy," due to their dark skin. In Louisiana, they were "black dagoes" (Laurino 2000). Hollywood profited from perpetuating racist stereotypes of Italians. Of all the films about Italian Americans produced since 1928, 69 percent are negative. For a study of prejudice behind New England immigration restrictions, see Solomon (1956), *Ancestors and Immigrants: A Changing New England Tradition*.

3. See O'Connor (1995), *The Boston Irish: A Political History*. Suggested readings on the Kennedy and Fitzgerald families and the Irish diaspora are Goodwin (1991), *The Fitzgeralds and the Kennedys: An American Saga*; Maier (2003), *The Kennedys: America's Emerald Kings*; and Whalen (1993), *The Founding Father: The Story of Joseph P. Kennedy: A Study in Power, Wealth and Family Ambition*. In 1912, when Joseph Kennedy graduated from Harvard, the university was changing, accepting more students from middle-class families. Sixty percent of the men in his class had gone to public high schools; only 25 percent had college-educated parents. But acceptance into Harvard did not necessarily translate into social acceptance. There was different housing for wealthy and middle-class students, and although Joseph was socially successful, he always sensed that he was outside the exclusive "Gold Coast" set. See Synnott (1979), *The Half-Opened Door: Discrimination and Admission at Harvard, Yale, and Princeton, 1900–1970*, and Whalen (1993), *The Founding Father*.

"From the Civil War through the 1920s," academic requirements at Harvard were modest; "students of good character who could pay the tuition were usually admitted" (Synnott, 1979) the early 1900s, however, increasing numbers of foreign students and immigrants were applying. In 1904, Harvard joined the College Entrance Examination Board, which created a uniform test for college applicants. In 1911, the school adopted the New Plan Applicant, which required applicants to submit high school records and satisfactory results on four comprehensive exams. President Eliot was very committed to diversifying the student body, including students from around the country and foreign and immigrant students. Scholarships played a large role in bringing these students to Harvard, with funds coming from state legislatures and wealthy benefactors. See Synnott (1979a), "The Admission and Assimilation of Minority Students at Harvard, Yale, and Princeton, 1900–1970" and Synnott (1979b), *The Half-Opened Door: Discrimination and Admission at Harvard, Yale, and Princeton, 1900–1970*.

Irish Catholics first started attending Harvard in the 1870s. Although there was definite tension and controversy surrounding their presence, overall, the belief that Irish Catholics were capable of total cultural assimilation presided. This attitude did not, however, extend to Jews or Italians. Much of the controversy had to do with Eliot's public statement about standards at Catholic schools and colleges. By 1911, several hundred Catholics attended Harvard. See Synnott (1979).

[4.] See "Reading 1: The Kennedy Family Background" of "Birthplace of John F. Kennedy: Home of the Boy Who Would Be President," *National Park Service: U.S. Department of the Interior*, retrieved 6/12/17, https://www.nps.gov/nr/twhp/wwwlps/lessons/33jfk/33facts1.htm.

[5.] See Doris Kearns Goodwin's excellent book *The Fitzgeralds and the Kennedys: An American Saga*. New York: Saint Martin's Press, 1991. It's an unsurpassed look at the family backgrounds of Rose and Joseph Kennedy.

[6.] Ibid.

[7.] Quoted portion is from "Reading 1: The Kennedy Family Background," from *National Park Service*.

[8.] Goodwin.

[9.] Goodwin.

10. The majority of Sicilians who immigrated to the United States were hardworking, frugal individuals who left in search of higher wages in America. Some were skilled tailors and shoemakers. Most were agricultural workers who joined relatives and village friends. The trip to America lasted two weeks. Many travelers became sick from the filth in steerage and the horrible food. Once in America, men favored outdoor work with the railroad or building trades, considering factory work disgraceful and embarrassing. A common laborer received $1.50 for a ten-hour day. More than half received less than four hundred dollars a year. Single men usually lived in boarding houses, where they slept, dressed and washed without privacy. Many became lonely and went to brothels. Small by nature, hard work used them up and made them susceptible to pneumonia and tuberculosis.

The work situation for women was as bad. Girls were at the mercy of bosses and timekeepers. They married as young as thirteen and had children by fifteen. Women who sewed at home for others earned about five cents an hour. In Lawrence, loom operators worked fifty-six hours a week for ten cents an hour. They lived in crowded conditions most always with no heat other than that from the kitchen stove. They ate little in order to save money. Fathers were in the superior position as breadwinners, and strict authoritarian relationships kept children under control. A mother's love often tempered the severe rules of the father.

Many families needed their children to go to work instead of school. Seventy-five percent of boys ages fifteen to nineteen and 20 percent of girls worked and submitted their wages to the family budget. Legislation passed in 1903 prevented boys under ten from selling newspapers. In order to curb truancy, those ten to fourteen had to have permits to sell after school.

11. Quoted portions of this material are from the National Park Service (1969–2004), *Reading Two: Daily Life at 83 Beals Street.*

12. A tenet of American education is that parents are the most important teachers of their children. With respect to Mrs. Kennedy's education and parenting skills, she attended public schools in Concord and Dorchester—somewhat surprising, given that most Catholic children attended parochial schools. Her family had moved out of the North End to a WASPish enclave, but when her father decided to run for mayor, the family moved back to Boston. The North End was a slum, so they settled in Dorchester. Feeling that she was in a conspicuous role as the mayor's daughter, Rose Kennedy was highly motivated and planned to attend Wellesley College in 1907. People described her as having the world by the tail and possessing tremendous confidence about her

intellectual future, a trait that diminished somewhat when her father forbade her to go to Wellesley.

Instead, he sent her to the Academy of the Convent of the Sacred Heart, which had chains of schools in Europe and North America for daughters of the Catholic aristocracy. These schools trained young women to be wives, mothers, and social figures. The curriculum emphasized the fine arts, religion, and domestic science. Rose Kennedy reflected that the education she received there was not in keeping with her high school education, which was secular and college preparatory. After her first year of attendance, she and her family went on a two-month tour of Europe. At the end of the trip, Rose entered an academy in the Netherlands. The school was austere and rigid, prescribing every minute of the day. There were periods of seclusion and religious contemplation, which she took very seriously. Overall, this experience deepened her faith. She returned home and completed her education at an academy in New York in 1910, after which she spent much time traveling with her father.

Rose Kennedy read frequently to her children, especially to JFK when he was ill. Father Joe emphasized the importance of winning and being the best. The children matured in an atmosphere of intense competition, which they often played out in sports. Joe Jr. and JFK always competed. They started out in public schools but soon moved to Dexter School, a country day-type academy. When the family moved to Riverdale in New York, they went to Choate. Joe Jr. struggled at first with his grades but was incredibly disciplined and soon met the high expectations that his family set for him. He was also an athletic star. JFK lacked his brother's discipline and was often reprimanded by his father for his lack of focus and application. JFK had difficulty following in brother Joe's footsteps. Once Joe Jr. graduated, JFK's performance improved.

13. "Founded in 1848, by an act of the Great and General Court of Massachusetts, the Boston Public Library (BPL) was the first large free municipal library in the United States." Designed by European-trained Americans, it is a dazzling monument, equal to any work produced in ancient Rome. The style is Renaissance Revival, and it is decorated with motifs and the names of famous philosophers, scientists, and poets. "Bates Hall, acknowledged by many to be architecturally one of the most important rooms in the world, features a majestic barrel-arched ceiling enclosed by half domes on each end, English oak bookcases, busts of eminent authors and Bostonians, and a richly carved limestone balcony" See Boston Public Library (n.d.). *A Brief History and Description.*

14. Most scholars of the Italian American experience believe that second-generation children turned away from their parents' traditions in favor of American styles and values. Orsi (1990) found, however, that many immigrant parents told stories about the places they had left to teach their children their values and understanding of the world.

15. The price of a newspaper in the 1920s-1930s was about 2-5 cents. Today, if a single copy were bought in the local gas station or grocery store it would cost a $1 or more.

16. See Mangione (1943), *Mount Allegro: A Memoir of Italian-American Life* for an account of the Italian and Sicilian immigrant struggle with the Irish Catholic Church. See also Dolan (2002), *In Search of an American Catholicism: A History of Religion and Culture in Tension;* Fisher (2002), *Communion of Immigrants: A History of Catholics in America;* and Fisher (2000), *Catholics in America.*

17. My father did not forget this injustice and was extremely reluctant to send me to parochial school when I was a youngster.

18. My father doesn't even remember playing with his cousins, although they lived close by.

19. America's preeminent philosopher John Dewey wrote that projects like these prepared children for the world of work. A moral idealism imbued Dewey's thoughts about work. He envisioned students voluntarily developing work skills that served both them and society. He also envisioned cooperative employment in the workplace. In contrast, anti-labor films in the first two decades of the century often portrayed workers as dynamiters and killers, and scabs as social heroes. See Ross (1991), "Struggles for the Screen: Workers, Radicals, and the Political Uses of Silent Films"; Bodnar (2003), *Blue-Collar Hollywood: Liberalism, Democracy, and Working People in American Film*; and Foner (1983), "A Martyr to His Cause: The Scenario of the First Labor Film in the United States."

20. It's no wonder that so many men like my dad dropped out of high school. Textbook learning was irrelevant to their lives. Their real talents, hidden under a veil of school failure, surfaced later in their work as highly skilled electricians, mechanics, shipfitters, and machine operators.

21. In *Slaughterhouse-Five* (1969), Kurt Vonnegut, recounting his experience as an American soldier during the bombing of Dresden, Germany, concluded that people are needlessly cruel and careless. *Fighting Prosaic Messages* chronicles

the unrelenting disdain for people who are different but also draws attention to acts of kindness.

22. My father didn't need anyone to tell him what challenges he faced, and he certainly didn't need to be burdened with the stigma of being a "charity case." As best as I can tell, the Salvation Army must have shown a great deal of respect to the people it helped, and it offered assistance that was unpretentious and heartfelt.

23. As father and mother, Rose needed to be the source of authority (Child 1943), which meant being extremely strict in the Sicilian tradition of her father. She taught her children to behave in "ways that pleased adults" (Gans 1962). She spoke to them in an adult tone and expected them to assist her as soon as they could. Although she gave more freedom to my father than to my aunts, she disciplined son and daughters with a strong hand. I have wondered about the impact of her sternness on her children because, as Greven (1991) states in *Spare the Child*, "Being assaulted violently in the name of discipline invariably produces anger and often rage in children, as it does in most adults. Anger is the key to understanding the long-term consequences of corporal punishment" (p.44).

24. Rose faced difficulties similar to those experienced by parents today, with the added stress of being uneducated, a non-native speaker of English, widowed, and poor. She came to terms with her children's needs by giving them a sense of security and stability. She fed them, sewed and cleaned their clothes, and kept them warm during harsh New England winters. She sent them to church, school, Scouts, playgrounds, and camps. She monitored their social lives and took them via streetcars to the beach and on picnics. As they grew, she moved them to better housing. She reinforced family memories and cultural ties to her past. She even brought them to the Boston Public Library, the Museum of Art, and the Harvard Dental Clinic.

25. Rose's key concern was to keep her family together. In one interview that I conducted with my father, he said, "[Ma] didn't want us to get married. Just stay together." Given all the distress and anxiety that she experienced, with leaving her parents and losing her husband, it's no wonder that her attachment to her children was so great.

26. One of the most important tasks teachers have is to nurture the aspirations of children in need. Why, then, as Murray (2002) notes, is the subject of teacher apathy taboo? Cook (2001) also posits that there is a "hiddeness" to teacher attitudes. He asked seventy classroom teachers to nominate students to whom

they were close and those to whom they were not. Students with either severe or obvious disabilities were significantly overrepresented in the latter category, as were those with mild or hidden disabilities. Rizza and Morrison (2003) also uncovered stereotypical thinking in characteristic identification of students with EBD, and Richey and Petretti (2002) report on teacher apathy and student discouragement in an inner-city school. Likewise, Murray (2002) discusses a teaching assistant who professed not to care that over 30 percent of her students had failed her class.

27. Rose left Sicily knowing that her primary role was to support her mother and father. She defined herself in terms of self-sacrifice, not personal ambition. In sharp contrast, American culture embraced the tenets of individualism, without consideration of family values. These contrasting value systems of family obligation versus individualism played out in how Rose socialized her children. Her anger with Connie's reading in bed instead of attending early mass was a clash between self-expression and adherence to group norms. My father's long walks to the cemetery and work experiences represent self-sacrifice and group helpfulness. The power of family literacy histories lies in their ability to question and identify the social expectations and ethical values that were and are at work in our families. Tropman (1995) and others have hypothesized the existence of a distinctively Catholic ethic, centered on the values of community and sharing with others, in contrast to a Weberian Protestant ethic, emphasizing individual achievement and self-reliance. For a study that corroborates the existence of the Catholic ethic, see Rigney, Matz, and Abney (2004), "Is there a Catholic sharing ethic?" For further reading about families in the American experience, see Faulkner (1929/1946), *The Sound and the Fury*; Steinbeck (1939/1989), *The Grapes of Wrath*; Cather (1913), *O Pioneers!*; and O'Neill (1946) *The Iceman Cometh*. For a conceptual framework with respect to the socialization of immigrant children, see Kim and Choi (1994), "Individualism, Collectivism, and Child Development," and Harkness, Raeff, and Super (2000), *Variability in the Social Construction of the Child*.

28. There is no family memory of Rose's bereavement for Carmelo. No one remembers her crying or blaming God for his death. She went about the business of keeping her family together, never giving herself to another man. She went to night school to become a citizen, corresponded with family members in Sicily and Egypt, and saw her daughter graduate from college. What was the source of her power and strength? Pagalia (1996) provides an explanation, paraphrased here: Italians view death in simple, pragmatic terms, as a physical process to be efficiently planned and managed. They rarely allow extreme emotion. Rose's culture had taught her to dread incapacity

and dependency, not death. Her acceptance of Carmelo's death was part of her approach to life. For further readings on resiliency, see Henderson & Milstein (2003), *Resiliency in Schools: Making it Happen for Students and Teachers*, and McCubbin, Thompson, Thompson, and Futrell (1999), *The Dynamics of Resilient Families*.

29. As Carmelo became more disoriented, the glow of his intelligence gave way to a pale and tattered look. Rose hospitalized him on April 20, 1922. The asylum was an imposing structure, its classical facades resembling a university. It was designed to arouse feelings of grandeur and importance in its therapeutic mission. To my grandfather, it was a prison. Once gregarious and affectionate, he died alone, his body and mind used up. For details on asylums during this period, see Dwyer (1987), *Homes for the Mad: Life Inside Two Nineteenth-Century Asylums*.

Treating the mentally ill in asylums is a recent development in the history of psychiatry. In ancient Greece and Rome, treatment ranged from turning to religion to exorcism, music, abstinence, exercise, and entertaining stories. For much of history, the insane were subjected to bloodletting, purging, induced vomiting, underwater submersion, violent spinning in revolving chairs, sudden splashes of ice water over their naked bodies, burning of their scalps with scalding water, and sudden plunges into a lake from a room with a trap door (Sills 1968). Chemical remedies included mercury, phosphorous, copper, iron, salts of silver iodine, or lead. Some hospitals treated insanity with opium and whiskey (Harvey 1979). By the eighteenth century, facilities controlled many patients with whips and chains for long periods, making no differentiation between the mentally ill and criminally insane; all were packed together in dark cells. Some women were committed for the "crime" of attempting to leave their husbands or at their husbands' insistence in order to gain control of their assets. Poorer individuals were jailed or placed in publicly funded almshouses.

Thanks to the work of Dix (1843) and other social reformers, mid-1800s asylums instituted a humanitarian approach. Although these institutions were intended to be compassionate respites for the mentally disabled, treatments were still crude (Zainaldin & Tyor 1979). Following WWI, theories about insanity shifted from moral premises to medical conditions that caused mild to severe disturbances in thinking, perception, and behavior. Classifications such as schizophrenia, bipolar affective disorder, and clinical depression were popularized, as were radical treatments. For example, paresis victims were deliberately infected with malaria in hopes that the ensuing fever would destroy the germs that affected brain cells. Psychosurgery treatments

335

involved applying salvarsan, a compound of arsenic, through holes bored in the skull (Serum Applied). Patients, many of whom suffered from anxiety and depression, also received shock therapy and lobotomies. With the advent of tranquilizers in the 1950s, psychiatric care underwent a revolution. Today, more than 54 million Americans are affected by one or more mental disorders, anxiety being the most common.

30. See Trillin (1990), "The Italian Thing," for a discussion about social clubs in the Italian Sicilian experience.

31. Conventional wisdom posits that schools favor boys over girls. Sommors (2000), however, says that the very opposite is true. By virtually every measure, girls thrive in school to a greater degree than boys.

32. For decades, repeating grades was the norm in schools. Hildreth in *Learning the 3 R's* (1936) reports that thirty-six children in a third-grade class in a large urban school had repeated seventy-nine half years of school. It was common, years ago, to group children aged eleven, twelve, and thirteen with eight- and nine-year-olds. In a typical school, 30 percent of children took more than a year to complete a year's work. In the first grade alone, 20 percent of the population was retained. By the seventh grade, that number rose to more than 32 percent. Mindful of the consequences, Hildreth hypothesizes, "We can infer from these data the broken morale, maladjustment, inferiority feeling, negative attitude toward school activities, the rebellious attitude developing and unpreparedness for after-school recreation ad future working years" (p. 65). The fear of emotional harm to children retained in school led reformers to promote children regardless of their abilities. In the past twenty years, retention practices have been on the rise. Brooks (2002) estimates that schools retain more than 2.4 million students every year, more boys than girls, and more minority students than whites. In a review of the research literature, Jimerson and Kaufman (2003) note that grade retention does not improve educational success. Likewise, Sherwood (1993) found that retention impacts negatively on not only the academic progress of at-risk students but also on their self-image and motivation.

33. Anxiety, a reaction to an imagined threat, is characterized by powerlessness, apprehension, and doubt (Campbell 1996). Anxiety differs from fear, which is a reaction to a real threat or danger. Anxiety neurosis, characterized by irritability and pains of conscience can impede learning (Günter, Holtkamp, Jolles, Herpertz-Dahlmann, & Konrad 2004). In fact, one of the greatest obstacles to learning is doubt in the minds of either or both learner and teacher. Due to the influence of behaviorism, which had little interest in

noncognitive aspects of learning, researchers ignored the associations among anxiety, stress, and learning. In the late '60s, sociolinguists corrected the imbalance (Kling 1971).

34. Teachers and classmates thought that my father was slow-witted. Rose disciplined him for laziness, but he reacted with sarcasm, determined to travel his own path. Knowing that he needed a role model, Rose told him stories about men who were smart and hardworking. She prayed for him at the foot of her crucifix, with her rosary beads. On Sundays, she cooked two meals to please him. He saw her stand tall every Wednesday at Quincy City Hall as Mrs. Waddle handed her a weekly welfare check. He wasn't ashamed; he knew what she was going through. He worked numerous jobs instead of sleeping late or reading books. Although his own father's death ate away at my father, as he grew older, he gave up on looking for a father figure and caring about other people's opinions of him. By then, the only thing that mattered was having a good time.

35. Although debate occurred regarding the cultural importance of amusements, due to increased immigration and a shifting population, they developed on a relatively large basis. One view is that mass entertainment—amusement parks, movies, and radio—was a tool of the elite to manipulate passive audiences. Others posit that ordinary people were creative receivers of these cultural products. For a discussion about the influence of mass media on 1930s youth, see Springhall (1998), "Censoring Hollywood: Youth, Moral Panic and Crime/Gangster Movies of the 1930s." Cawelti (1975) shows how Hollywood heroes reflect American individualism in "The Gunfighter and the Hard-boiled Dick: Some Ruminations of the American Fantasies of Heroism." See also Rubin (2002), "Gangster Generation: Crime, Jews, and the Problem of Assimilation."

36. In the early years, Blue Laws suppressed the playing of sports on Sundays (Jable 1974). By the early 1800s, however, strictures against amusements and sports diminished. Sports became recreational, and hero worship reinforced the Western core values of superiority and hierarchy (Morrow 1992). Mandelbaum (2004) argues that the evolution of sports mirrors the industrial development of the country. Baseball appealed to our pure, agrarian roots at a time when most people lived in rural areas. Specialized factory work supported the development of football, with its assigned roles. Basketball, a post-Industrial Age invention, required athletes to bring little equipment to the court. School sports became institutionalized in the late-nineteenth century, predicated on the values of unassailable rules, teamwork, trust, and excellence (Swift 1991). In contrast, the commercialization of sports has

undermined the importance of sportsmanship and team loyalty (Lumpkin 1983). For further reading, see Riess (1989), *City Games: The Evolution of American Urban Society and the Rise of Sports*; Betts (1974), *America's Sporting Heritage, 1850–1950*; Hardy (1982), *How Boston Played: Sport, Recreation and Community 1865–1915*; and *The Journal of Sport History*.

37. For much of the nineteenth century, secondary schools conceptualized the aims of education as mental discipline, not cultural refinement or life adjustment. Such discipline occurred through the study of Latin and Greek, with mathematics added about 1850. The study of science and foreign languages was ridiculed as being too simplistic, shallow, and poorly organized for inclusion in the curriculum. In response, chemistry and physics were toughened up with more memorization and theoretical work. Schools used grammar drills universally in the study of Latin and Greek. Foreign languages and English literature followed suit.

In 1898, there were three hundred public high schools in America. By 1932, the list had grown to 2,500. Universal education was becoming a reality. Schools shifted radically from educating the elite to the moral enculturation of the masses (Kaestle 1973; Schultz 1973). Curriculum and instruction did not spring from the tenets of Pestalozzi, Herbert, Froebel, or psychology, as they had in the transformation of American elementary schools. Instead, decisions arose out of compromises over the aims of education. Conservatives wanted every student to take the same courses. Progressives wanted differentiation based on utilitarian norms. Compromises occurred following the 1912 Commissions on the Reorganization of Secondary Education, which defined educational aims in a democracy. Excerpted from Noble (1938), *A History of American Education*.

In the mid- to late 1920s, students who enrolled in teacher training programs for young children learned that (1) children who were taught in an intimidating manner developed anxieties; (2) children are not machines that absorb the three R's; (3) teachers need to be guides rather than dictators; (4) children who actively participate in their learning develop good citizenship skills; and (5) parents should not ignore their children's questions or provide them with information without direct experience. Educators who read professional journals such as *Childhood Education* and/or attended professional conferences knew about the need for unity in progressive education, the meaning of education in a democracy, and ways to distance themselves from traditionalism. Progressive philosophy continued to shape educational research and practice. For example, *The Elementary School Journal* (1970) published Dean of the School of Education at the University of Michigan J.

D. Edmonson's critique of proposals to limit secondary education to those who could pay for it as class biased and antidemocratic. Street (1934) linked student insecurity to behavioral and academic problems. *Progressive Education* (1969) railed against the conservative belief that the arts were merely an optional luxury. It also chastised educators for being too preoccupied with trivial details, such as the distribution of time in methods of learning, instead of addressing the problem of student motivation.

38. The greatest nineteenth-century popularizer of the myth of the American dream was Horatio Alger (1874), whose rags-to-riches stories gave Americans a moral blueprint with which to achieve financial and personal success. In the twentieth century, Ayn Rand (1943, 1957) reinforced this myth in her celebration of individualism and capitalism. Why did the American educational system fail so many students and embitter them with a dream that they couldn't attain? Part of the problem resided in values. Quincy schools reinforced the free-enterprise, self-reliance, and self-improvement norms preached from New England pulpits and political platforms. Modern industrial societies demanded winners and losers. The norms of competitive individualism permeated all facets of school. City newspapers furthered competition each June by publishing the names of students who received school merit awards. Those who failed never made it to the graduation list; schools had already ejected them.

Literary criticism of individualism and materialism ranges from Dewey to Twain, who parodied the Horatio Alger myth (Scott 2000). Literary critiques of wealth, success, individualism, and the American dream include Dickens (1854/1965), *Hard Times*; Sinclair (1906/1984), *The Jungle*; Orwell (1946), *Animal Farm*; Miller (1949), *Death of a Salesman*; Fitzgerald (1925/1986), *The Great Gatsby*; West (1933/1969), *Miss Lonely-hearts*; and Rand (1943, 1957), *The Fountainhead* and *Atlas Shrugged*. For a primer on capitalism, see Marx (1867/1990), *Das Kapital* and Weber (1905/2001) *The Protestant Ethic and the Spirit of Capitalism*.

39. Dago, spick, mick, kike, kraut, polack, peckerwood, and redneck are examples of derogatory stereotypes (Henderson 2003). Name-calling or slurs, the most direct expressions of prejudice in language, have been common throughout history to disparage others (Mullen 2001). Slurs link a person to negative symbols in the hope that listeners reject the person or idea based on the symbol instead of evidence. The experimental literature on physical attractiveness supports the reality of height and attractive stereotypes. Tall, slender people are generally considered more elegant and moral than short people (Korda 1975; Jackson & Ervin 1992). Stereotypical behaviors also

exist in schools. White authority figures, for example, tend to dismiss name-calling as singular incidents, although minority students feel that they occur often enough to negatively affect their schoolwork. Attractive children receive better personality ratings than do unattractive ones (Buck & Tiene 1989; Rich 1975; Dusek & Joseph 1983). College-age students tend to be more accepting of authoritarian teachers if they are attractive and female.

40. By 1900, Bell Telephone began hiring only women because they found boys to be less patient, less polite, more rude and hard to discipline. They expected women to be tall enough to reach the top wires, have good hearing and eyesight, not have a disruptive couth, and be of good moral character. On top of that, the company offered them lower wages. In February 1907, 400 female operators walked off their jobs. The strike aroused public interest and sympathy. For more, see Joan Sangster's excellent article "The 1907 Bell Telephone Strike: Organizing Women Work," which appeared in volume 3 of the journal *Labour / Le Travail*, pp. 109-130.

41. Darwin's "survival of the fittest" captures the biological conception of human nature and society. Herbert Spencer (1850) believed that human progress would take place once the culture eliminated the unfit. Until the nineteenth century, society looked after the poor. Increasingly, however, the population thought that poverty arose from idleness or personality defects. New laws forced people to work and learn the error of their ways. With the rise of immigration in the United States, many feared engulfment by defective people. Moral obligations to help the mentally ill and the poor gave way to political and economic arguments aimed at eliminating them. Members of the Joint Committee on Appropriations in Connecticut supported a law that would have put to death persons who were "hopelessly" insane. As early as 1889, the Indiana State Reformatory used vasectomies to control the spread of mental defectives. Several states declared that the feeble-minded and insane could not marry and made sex between them illegal. In 1909, California passed a law that permitted the sterilization of certain types of insane and mentally deficient individuals. A 1926 study in North Carolina that predicted large birthrates of feeble-minded infants led to the establishment of a Eugenics Board charged with eradicating social ills through sterilization. Twenty-seven other states adopted similar procedures (Davis 1948). Between 1929 and 1974, more than 7,600 sterilizations took place in North Carolina (Damico [2003]; Begos et al. [n.d.]). Although sterilization procedures have ceased, the hunt for the fittest has not. Unraveling the human genome has opened the possibility of producing the mentally superior individuals for whom Spencer hoped more than 150 years ago.

42. It is easy to view my father with sympathy or condescension. He had a great deal of pressure on him to be a man. Tests made him despise school. Without a father, he turned to smoking, drinking, and movies—impelled toward and distracted by characters who lived outside the law. His heroes were stars like James Cagney, who got ahead with street smarts, fine clothes, and big hearts. They showed him how to smooth-talk girls and gave him confidence at work. Concetta suffered the same hardships but overcame them by living in reality. She succeeded as Rose had. Dad's path, like his father's, took him on a different journey.

43. Rose underwent social and psychological traumas that were accelerated by the death of her husband, but throughout her ordeal, she remained resourceful and resilient. Her character went unnoticed, however, except for individuals like Mr. Broberg. In the same way, children who suffer in school need education to affirm not ignore them. In recent years, over two dozen books on the subject of resiliency have appeared. To learn more about resiliency in single parents, see Stretch (1999). Ramsey and Blieszner (1999) discuss *Spiritual Resiliency in Older Women*. Books and articles about resiliency in children include Ashcroft (2004), "Preventing School Failure by Enhancing Reading and Social Skills"; Thomsen (2002), *Building Resilient Students: Integrating Resiliency into What You Already Know and Do*; and Dugan & Coles (1989), *The Child in Our Times: Studies in the Development of Resiliency*.

44. Stereotypes of Sicilian mothers range from the powerful, overprotective Teresa in Ermelino's (2001) *The Black Madonna* to the prayerful Annunziata in di Donato's (1993) *Christ in Concrete*. In between are the old-fashioned neighborhood caricatures who gesticulate, suffer, and cook their way into our hearts. None of these images defined Rose. When her son needed to find employment, she broke barriers by speaking with others about opportunities. For a look at today's Italian American mothers, see Desalvo & Giunta (2003), *The Milk of Almonds: Italian American Women Writers on Food and Culture*.

45. Details about Faxon Park wall emerged via interview and library research.

46. For historical thinking about child labor and apprenticeships, see the American Academy of Political and Social Science, *Child Labor* (1907); Copeland (1995), *Memoirs of an Apprentice: A Saint John Shipbuilding Experience*; Seybolt (1917), *Apprenticeship and Apprenticeship Education in Colonial New England and New York*; and Veum & Weiss (1993), "Education and the Work Histories of Young Adults."

47. Psychologists assess intelligence with paper-and-pencil tests of cognitive tasks. Others favor the measurement of reaction times, brain waves, and other physiological measures. Some associate intelligence with a person's ethics and values, traits that no intelligence test can capture. Social and cultural constructions of intelligence have also been around for years. Thorndike (1920) defined social intelligence as the ability to manage the work of others. Wechsler (1958), one of the most influential researchers in the area of intelligence, defined it as "the global capacity of a person to act purposefully, think rationally, and deal effectively with his/her environment" (p. 7). Yale psychologist Robert J. Sternberg (2000) combines these two viewpoints into the following definition: "Intelligence is the cognitive ability of an individual to learn from experience, reason well, remember important information, and cope with the demands of daily living" My father's success mirrors Thorndike's and Sternberg's views on social intelligence. See also Gardner (1983), *Frames of Mind: The Theory of Multiple Intelligences*; Gardner (1993), *Multiple Intelligences: The Theory in Practice*; Gardner (1999), "Who Owns Intelligence?" Kihlstrom & Cantor (2000), "Social Intelligence"; Kincheloe (2004), *Multiple Intelligences Reconsidered*; and Sternberg (2000), *Handbook of Intelligence*.

48. Rose loved to listen to radio dramas and the comedies of Jack Benny and Eddie Cantor. Her favorite tune was "Ma, He's making Eyes at Me" (S. Claire & C. Conrad (1960). Dad liked Al Jolson tunes and, especially, Cab Calloway's "Minnie the Moocher" (C. Calloway & I. Mills 1931), whom he saw in person the night that Hubbie DeCosta paid for his ticket in return for a date with Connie. Dad also loved to listen to Glenn Miller on his car radio with my mother at his side. He saw his first movie at the Nantasket Beach Salvation Army camp—Lon Chaney in *Phantom of the Opera* (Laemmle & Julian 1925). He also liked *The Champ* with Wallace Beery and Jackie Cooper (Marion, Praskins, Tuchock, & Vidor 1931).

49. Although Concetta received the largest award, she was listed last in the *Quincy Patriot Ledger* article, which referred to her as "Concetta" Amoroso but recognized other recipients as either Mr. or Miss. Perhaps she understood the highly subjective nature of awards. School prizes are usually based on popularity rather than what a person actually earns. They also can serve as political tools, thereby further reducing their significance.

50. Rose was decisive, strong-minded, and smart. She was also suspicious of her daughters. The Victorian morality code she followed was common in Sicilian households and was the subject of Lara Cardella's (1994), *Good Girls Don't Wear Trousers*.

51. From roughly the 1920s to the 1950s, a "marriage bar" had restricted the employment of married women, especially in teaching jobs. In fact, if a married woman worked a lower paying job, she was less affected. This lowered the incentive for a woman to get an education. In addition, sometimes a state would apply the marriage bar to a woman who was widowed with children--she was still considered "married." See "Marriage Bar," *Wikipedia*, https://en.wikipedia.org/wiki/Marriage_bar, retrieved 6/13/17.

52. Rose exchanged mail regularly with Antonio, who had left Melilli at sixteen. His daughter Giovanna sent Rose a picture postcard of her father around 1938. Translated from Italian, it reads, in part, "Papa sends you this photograph. He prays to the saints for you. Love and kisses from my mother to you." Rose's mother, Lucia, expressed the same tenderness to her on a postcard following Carmelo's death. Years of family separation had not diminished the depth of feeling that these family members had for each other.

53. In the tradition of *Mammismo*, my father sided with Rose in disputes with my mother. His attachment to his mother is a common Sicilian and Arab tradition.

54. This incident is based on a chance meeting between Ted Williams, the DiMaggio brothers, and my father on a street corner in Boston's North End. Ted Williams (1918–2002) played for the Boston Red Sox for nineteen years and is widely considered the best pure hitter who ever played the game. His 1941 batting average of .406 still stands and is only overshadowed by Joe DiMaggio's (1914–1999) 56-game hitting streak. Many consider DiMaggio to be the best all-round ballplayer of all time. Brother Dominic (1917–2009) was an all-star seven times for the Boston Red Sox. They were American heroes at a time when career expectations were extremely limited. For the definitive biography on Ted Williams, see Montville (2004), *Ted Williams: The Biography of an American Hero*. For a poignant travelogue of Dom DiMaggio's trip to see the dying Williams, see Halberstam (2003), *The Teammates: A Portrait of Friendship*. Halberstam (1989) also captures the ethos between the DiMaggo brothers and Williams in summer of '49.

55. Numbers is a form of illegal gambling in which a person places small bets by choosing three numbers between 000 and 999 and then receives a receipt from a bookie. The bookie passes a receipt to a "pickup," who carries it to the "bank," or the accounting room of the numbers operation. If the customer wins, he/she gets a multiple almost one hundred times the amount of the bet. Winning is based on the last three digits of the total amount of money a particular racetrack handles on a specific day. In those days, bookies made

343

a 10 percent commission on their receipts, besides tips. Numbers and other forms of low-stakes gambling became popular after the Great Depression with people who were unable to make a decent living (excerpted from Organized Crime [2004]).

Playing the numbers was as simple as playing the lottery, with two minor exceptions. Instead of numbers drawn out of a drum, winning numbers were the first digits of the daily mutual at Suffolk Downs Race Track listed on the *Record American* sports page, 7:00 p.m. edition. Second, today's lotteries are state-sanctioned and taxed. Playing the numbers in my father's time was illegal and tax-free. The only added expense was a 10 percent payoff to the bookie who had placed the winning bet.

For a historical perspective on gambling, see Asbury (1938/2003), *Sucker's Progress: An Informal History of Gambling in America* and Sasuly (1982), *Bookies and Bettors: Two Hundred Years of Gambling*. For a description of how the numbers racket works, see Stapinski (2001) *Five-Finger Discount: Crooked Family History*.

56. Fifteen years later, my brother's friend was accidentally shot to death on March 13. One afternoon, my parents drove up to visit his grave. Mom spied a beautiful oak tree in the distance. "I want to be buried under that tree," she said. Three years later, she died of cancer. Dad remembered her wish and went to the cemetery office to purchase a lot under the tree. The lot was taken. He noticed that the salesperson's name was Sliverman. He was the boy for whom my mother was a nanny years before. He arranged to have my mother buried under her tree. When Dad walked over to examine the lot, a lump raised in his throat. On one side was a marker named Monti; on the other was the stone of a woman who had died on 3-13. My father stopped playing numbers that day. Two weeks later, three one three came in.

57. My father's story isn't about nostalgia but assimilation and consequence. Although he didn't read books, he didn't succumb to self-hatred or blaming others for his condition (Sennett & Cobb 1993). Dad understood clearly the obscured agendas of class that worked against him. He seems to be the person Freud (1930) had in mind when he wrote, "Anyone who has been through the misery of poverty in his youth and has endured the indifference and arrogance of those who have possessions, should be exempt from the suspicion that he has no understanding of … the economic inequality of men and all that it leads to" (p. 140). For insight and analysis into enculturation and socialization, see Child (1943), *Italian or American: The Second Generation in Conflict*.

344

References

Alger, H. *Risen from the ranks; or, Harry Walton's success.* Boston: Loring, 1874.

"Alien influx increasing; Class of emigrants less desirable than formerly, inspectors say" *New York Times,* June 17, 1905.

American Academy of Political and Social Science. Child Labor. Philadelphia: Author, 1907.

Annual reports city of Quincy for the year 1919. Cambridge, MA: Cosmos, 1920.

Asbury, H. *Sucker's progress: An informal history of gambling in America.* New York: Dodd, Mead and Company, Ltd., 1938/2003.

Ashcroft, L. "Preventing school failure by enhancing reading and social skills." *Preventing School Failure* 48, no. 2 (2004): 19–22.

Bachin, R. F. "At the nexus of labor and leisure: baseball, nativism, and the 1919 Black Sox Scandal." *Journal of Social History* 36, no. 4 (2003): 941–962.

Barry, J. M. *The great influenza: The epic story of the deadliest plague in history.* New York: Viking, 2004.

Begos, K., D. Deaver, J. Railey, T. Richardson, & S. Sexton, S. "Against Their Will: North Carolina's Sterilization Program." A special report from the *Winston-Salem Journal* and *Journalnow.com* http://againsttheirwill.journalnow.com. Retrieved May 2, 2009.

Bergson, H. *Laughter: An essay on the meaning of the comic.* Translated by C. Cloudesley & F. Rothwell. New York: Macmillan, 1911).

Bergson, H. *An introduction to metaphysics.* Translated by I. E. Hulme. New York: G. P. Putnam's Sons, 1912.

Bettelheim, B. *A Home for the Heart.* New York: Knopf, 1974.

Betts, J. R. *America's Sporting Heritage, 1850–1950.* Reading, MA: Addison-Wesley, 1974.

Bodnar, J. E. *Blue-collar Hollywood: Liberalism, democracy, and working people in American film*. Baltimore, MD: John Hopkins University Press, 2003.

Boston Public Library. "A brief history and description." http://www.bpl.org/general/history.htm.

Brooks, R. *School retention: A common practice but is it effective?* http://www.drrobertbrooks.com/writings/articles/0211.html.

Bruccoli, M. J. *American Decades, 1910–1919*. Edited by V. Thompkins, V. Tompkins, R. Layman, V. Bondi, & J. Baughman. Detroit, MI: Gale Research, 1996.

Buck. S., & Tiene, D. (1989). The impact of physical attractiveness, gender, and teaching philosophy on teacher evaluations. *Journal of Educational Research*, *82*(3), 172-177.

Campbell, R. J., ed. *Psychiatric Dictionary*. New York: Oxford University Press, 1996.

Cardella, L. *Good Girls Don't Wear Trousers*. New York: Arcade, 1994.

Cather, W. *O Pioneers!* Boston: Houghton Mifflin Company, 1913.

Cawelti, J. G. "The gunfighter and the hard-boiled Dick: Some ruminations on the American fantasies of heroism." *American Studies* 16, no. 2 (1975): 49–64.

"Census of insane persons and defectives in institutions." *New York Times*, July 8, 1917.

Child, I. L. *Italian or American: The second generation in conflict*. New Haven, CT: Yale University Press, 1943.

Cook, B. G. "A comparison of teachers' attitudes toward their included students with mild and severe disabilities." *Journal of Special Education*, 34, no. 4 (2001): 203–213.

Copeland, G. L. *Memoirs of an apprentice: A Saint John shipbuilding experience*. St. Stephen, NB: Data 1 Ltd., 1995.

Damico, D. "Law that lets judges order sterilizations facing repeal: Womble says 1975 measure 'atrocious, ungodly'." *Winston-Salem Journal* (February 19, 2003). http://extras.journalnow.com/againsttheirwill/parts/epilogue/story12.html.

DeSalvo, L., & Giunta, E., eds. *The Milk of Almonds: Italian American women writers on food and culture.* New York: Feminist Press, 2002.

Dickens, C. *Hard times.* New York: Harper and Row, 1854/1965.

Dickerson, G. E. *The Cinema of Baseball: Images of America, 1929–1989.* Westport, CT: Mecklermedia, 1991.

DiDonato, P. *Christ in Concrete.* New York: Signet, 1939/1993.

Dix, D. "Plea for humane treatment of the insane." *Annals of American History* (1843). http://www.america.eb.com/america/article?eu=411507.

Davis, C. S. "The case for sterilization: Quality versus quantity public: North Carolina law, little used, makes small dent in problem." Winston-Salem Journal and Sentinel. (March 7, 1948). http://extras.journalnow.com/againsttheirwill/background/documentsbody17a.html.

Dolan, J. P. *In Search of an American Catholicism: A history of religion and culture in tension.* New York: Oxford University Press, 2002.

Dusek, J. B., & G. Joseph. "The bases of teacher expectancies: A meta-analysis." *Journal of Educational Psychology* 75, no. 3 (1983): 327–346.

Dugan, T. F., & R. Coles, eds. *The Child in Our Times: Studies in the development of resiliency.* New York : Brunner/Mazel, 1989.

Dwyer, E. *Homes for the Mad: Life inside two nineteenth-century asylums.* New Brunswick, NJ: Rutgers University Press, 1987.

Ermelino, L. *The Black Madonna.* New York: Simon & Schuster, 2001.

Faulkner, W. *The Sound and the Fury.* New York: Modern Library, 1929/1946.

Fisher, J. T. *Catholics in America.* New York: Oxford University Press, 2000.

Fisher, J. T. *Communion of immigrants: A history of Catholics in America*. New York: Oxford University Press, 2002.

Fitzgerald, F. S. *The Great Gatsby*. New York: Collier Books, 1925/1986.

Foner, P. S. "A martyr to his cause: The scenario of the first labor film in the United States." *Labor History*, 24, no. 1 (1983): 103–111.

Fox, J. W. "Irish immigrants, pauperism, and insanity in 1854 Massachusetts." *Social Science History* 15 (1991): 315–336.

Freud, S. *Civilization and Its Discontents*. Translated by J. Riviere. London: Hogarth Press, 1930/1955.

Gans, H. J. *The Urban Villagers: Group and class in the life of Italian-Americans*. New York: The Free Press, 1962.

Gardner, H. *Frames of Mind: The theory of multiple intelligences*. New York: Basic Books, 1983.

Gardner, H. *Multiple Intelligences: The theory in practice*. New York: Basic Books, 1993.

Gardner, H. "Who owns intelligence?" *The Atlantic Monthly* 283, no. 2 (1999): 67–76. http://www.theatlantic.com/issues/99feb/intel.htm.

Goodwin, D. K. *The Fitzgeralds and the Kennedys: An American Saga*. New York: Saint Martin's Press, 1991.

Gordon, L., & A. Gordon. *American Chronicle: Year by year through the twentieth century*. New Haven, CT: Yale University Press, 1999.

Gramsci, A. *Selections from the Prison Notebooks*. Translated and edited by Q. Hoare & G. N. Smith. London: Lawrence & Wishart, 1971.

Greven, P. J. *Spare the Child: The religious roots of punishment and the psychological impact of physical abuse*. New York: Alfred A. Knopf, 1991.

Günther T., Holtkamp K., Jolles J., Herpertz-Dahlmann B., & Konrad K. "Verbal memory and aspects of attentional control in children and adolescents with anxiety disorders or depressive disorders." *Journal of Affective Disorders* 82, no. 2 (2004): 265–269.

Halberstam, D. *Summer of '49.* New York: Avon, 1989.

Halberstam, D. *The Teammates: A portrait of friendship.* New York: Hyperion Press, 2003.

Halpert, S., & B. Halpert, eds. *Brahmins and Bullyboys: G. Frank Radway's Boston album.* Boston: Houghton Mifflin, 1973.

Harms, M. M. *Orphan train.* http://www.iagenweb.org/iaorphans.

Hardy, S. *How Boston Played: Sport, recreation and community 1865–1915.* Boston: Northeastern University Press, 1982.

Harkness, S., C. Raeff, & C. M. Super, eds. *Variability in the social construction of the child: New directions for child and adolescent development.* San Francisco: Jossey-Bass, 2000.

Harvey, K. A. "Practicing medicine at the Baltimore almshouse, 1828–1850." *Maryland Historical Magazine* 74, no. 3 (1979): 223–237.

Henderson, A. "What's in a slur?" *American Speech* 78, no. 1 (2003): 52–74.

Henderson, N., & M. Milstein. *Resiliency in Schools: Making it happen for students and educators.* Thousand Oaks, CA: Corwin Press, 2002.

Hildreth, G. *Learning the Three R's: A modern interpretation.* Minneapolis, MN: Educators Publishing, Inc., 1936.

Hochschild, A. R., with A. Machung. *The Second Shift.* New York: Viking, 1989.

Immigration Restriction League. *Immigration Restriction League (U.S.) records: Guide.* http://oasis.lib.harvard.edu/oasis/deliver/~hou00163.

Jable, J. T. "Pennsylvania's early blue laws: A Quaker experiment in the suppression of sports and amusements, 1682–1740." *Journal of Sport History* 1, no. 2 (1974): 107–122.

Jackson, L. A. & K. S. Ervin. "Height stereotypes of women and men: The liabilities of shortness for both sexes." *Journal of Social Psychology*, 132, no. 44 (1992): 433–445.

Jimenez, M. A. "Psychiatric Conceptions of Mental Disorder among Immigrants and African Americans in Nineteenth and Early Twentieth Century American History." *Research in Social Movements, Conflicts and Change* 16 (1993): 1–33.

Jimerson, S. R. & A. M. Kaufman. "Reading, writing, and retention: A primer on grade retention research." *Reading Teacher* 56, no. 7 (2003): 622–635.

Journal of Sport History. http://www.aafla.org/5va/history_frmst.htm.

Kaestle, C. F. *The education of an urban school system: New York City, 1750–1850*. Cambridge, MA: Harvard University Press, 1973.

Kihlstrom, J. F. & N. Cantor. "Social intelligence." In *Handbook of Intelligence*. Edited by R. J. Sternberg. Cambridge, UK: Cambridge University Press, 2000.

Kim, U. & S-H Choi. "Individualism, collectivism, and child development: A Korean perspective." In *Cross-Cultural Roots of Minority Child Development*. Edited by P. M. Greenfield & R. R. Cocking. Hillsdale, NJ: Lawrence Erlbaum Associates, 1994.

Kincheloe, J. L., ed. *Multiple Intelligences Reconsidered*. New York: Peter Lang Publishing, 2004.

Kling, M. "Quest for synthesis." In *The Literature of Research in Reading with an Emphasis on Model*s. Edited by F. B. Davis. New Brunswick, NJ: Rutgers University Press, 1971.

Korda, M. *Power: How to get it, how to use it*. New York: Random House, 1975.

Laemmle, C., (Producer), & Julian, R. (Director). *Phantom of the Opera* [Motion picture]. United States: Universal, 1925.

Laurino, M. *Were You Always an Italian? Ancestors and other icons of Italian America*. New York: W.W. Norton & Company, 2000.

Lumpkin, A. "Sport and human values." *Journal of Popular Culture* 16, no. 4 (1983): 4–10.

Maier, T. *The Kennedys: America's Emerald Kings: A five-generation history of the ultimate Irish-Catholic family.* New York: Basic Books, 2003.

Marion, F., L. Praskins, & W. Tuchock (Writers), & Vidor, K. (Director). *The Champ* [Motion picture]. United States: Metro-Goldwyn-Mayer, 1931.

Marx, K. *Capital: A critique of political economy* (B. Fowkes, Trans.). New York: Penguin Books, 1867/1990.

Mandelbaum, M. *The Meaning of Sports: Why Americans watch baseball, football, and basketball and what they see when they do.* New York: Public Affairs, 2004.

Mangione, J. *Mount Allegro: A memoir of Italian American life.* New York: Harper and Row, 1943.

McCubbin, H. I., E. A. Thompson, A. L. Thompson & J. A. Futrell, eds. *The dynamics of Resilient Families.* Thousand Oaks, CA: Sage Publication, 1999.

Mental Health America. "Mental illness and the family: Part I recognizing warning signs and how to cope." http://www.nmha.org/go/information/get-info/mi-and-the-family/recognizing-warning-signs-and-how-to-cope.

Miller, A. *Death of a Salesman.* New York: Viking Penguin, 1949.

Montville, L. *Ted Williams: The biography of an American hero.* New York: Doubleday, 2004.

Morrow, D. "The myth of the hero in Canadian sport history." *Canadian Journal of History of Sport* 23, no. 2 (1992): 72–83.

Mullen, B. "Ethnophaulisms for ethnic immigrant groups." *Journal of Social Issues* 57, no. 3 (2001): 457–475.

Murray, P. "When we could care less: The taboo subject of teacher apathy." Paper presented at the 53rd Annual Meeting of the Conference on College Composition and Communication, Chicago, March 20–23, 2002.

National Park Service. "Birthplace of John F. Kennedy: Home of the boy who would be president: Reading 2: Daily life at 83 Beals Street." http://www.cr.nps.gov/nr/twhp/wwwlps/lessons/33jfk/33facts2.htm.

National Park Service. "Birthplace of John F. Kennedy: Home of the boy who would be president: Reading One: The Kennedy family background." http://www.nps.gov/nr/twhp/wwwlps/lessons/33jfk/33facts1.htm.

Oakes, J. & M. Lipton. *Teaching to Change the World*. Boston: McGraw Hill, 2001.

O'Connor, T. "Organized crime investigation." http://www.apsu.edu/oconnort/3220/3220lect07a.htm.

O'Connor, T. H. *The Boston Irish: A political history*. Boston: Northeastern University Press, 1995.

O'Neill, E. *The Iceman Cometh*. New York: Random House, 1940/1946.

Orsi, R. A. "The fault of memory: "Southern Italy" in the imagination of immigrants and the lives of their children in Italian Harlem, 1920–1945." *Journal of Family History* 15, no. 1 (1990): 133–147.

Orwell, G. *Animal Farm*. New York: Harcourt, Brace and Company, 1946.

Pagalia, C. "The Italian way of death." http://www.salon.com/weekly/paglia960805.html.

"Pictures of baseball players." *Quincy Patriot Ledger*, August 12, 1929.

Public Broadcasting System (PBS). "A scientific odyssey, people and discoveries: Moniz develops lobotomy for mental illness." http://www.pbs.org/wgbh/aso/databank/entries/ dh35lo.html.

Public Broadcasting Service (PBS). "American experience: The orphan trains" (J. Graham & E. Gray, directors & producers). http://www. pbs.org/wgbh/amex/orphan/.

Public Broadcasting System (PBS). "American experience: Influenza 1918: 'The worst epidemic the United States has ever known.'" Retrieved May 9, 2009 from http://www.pbs.org/wgbh/amex/influenza.

Rabe, M. Albert and the animals. *The Atlantic Monthly*, 277, no. 2 (1996): 66–73. http://www.theatlantic.com/issues/96feb/albert/albert.htm.

Ramsey, J. L. & R. Blieszner. *Spiritual Resiliency in Older Women: Models of strength for challenges through the life span*. Thousand Oaks, CA: Sage Publications, 1999.

Rand, A. *The Fountainhead*. New York: Bobbs-Merrill, 1943.

Rand, A. *Atlas Shrugged*. New York: The New American Library, 1957.

Sherwood, E. J. & E. E. Painter. *Readers' Guide To Periodical Literature, IV, 1915–1918,* (1919). White Plains, NY: H. W. Wilson, 1919.

Readers' Guide to Periodical Literature, III 1913–1922. White Plains, NY: H. W. Wilson, 1922.

Rich, J. "Effects of children's physical attractiveness on teachers' evaluations." *Journal of Educational Psychology* 67, no. 5 (1975): 599–609.

Richey, A. & D. Petretti. "What can I do about teacher apathy?" *English Journal* 92, no. 2 (2002): 20–23.

Riess, S. A. *City Games: The evolution of American urban society and the rise of sports*. Urbana: University of Illinois Press, 1989.

Rigney, D., J. Matz, J. & A. Abney. "Is there a Catholic sharing ethic? A research note." *Sociology of Religion* 65 (Summer 2004):155–165.

Rizza, M. G. & W. F. Morrison. "Uncovering stereotypes and identifying characteristics of gifted students with emotional/behavioral disabilities." *Roeper Review* 25, no. 2 (2003): 73–77.

Ross, S. J. "Struggles for the screen: Workers, radicals, and the political uses of silent film." *American Historical Review* 96, no. 2 (1991): 333–367.

Rubin, R. "Gangster generation: Crime, Jews and the problem of assimilation." *Shofar: An Interdisciplinary Journal of Jewish Studies* 20, no. 4 (2002): 1–17.

Sasuly, R. *Bookies and Bettors: Two hundred years of gambling*. New York: Holt, Rinehart, and Winston, 1982.

"Scholarship and prize awards prove feature." *Quincy Patriot Ledger*, June 13, 1931.

Schultz, S. K. *The Culture Factory: Boston public schools, 1789–1860*. New York: Oxford University Press, 1973.

Scott, H. "The Mark Twain they didn't teach us about in school." *International Socialist Review* 10 (2000): 61–65. http://www.marxist.de/culture/twain/noteach.htm.

Sennet, R. & J. Cobb. *The Hidden Injuries of Class*. New York: W. W. Norton, 1993.

Seybolt, R. F. *Apprenticeship and apprenticeship education in colonial New England and New York*. New York: Teachers College, Columbia University, 1917.

Sherwood, C. *Retention in grade: Lethal lessons*. Available at: http://files.eric.ed.gov/fulltext/ED361122.pdf. (ERIC Document Reproduction Service No. ED361122), 1993.

Shapiro, J., K. Douglas, O. Rocha, S. Radecki, C. Vu, & T. Dinh. "Generational differences in psychosocial adaptation and predictors of psychological distress in a population of recent Vietnamese immigrants." *Journal of Community Health* 24, no. 2 (1999): 95–113.

Silver, F. & I. Cohn. (1928). *Yes! We have no bananas* [Recorded by E. Cantor]. Columbia Phonograph Company, 1922.

Sinclair, U. *The Jungle*. Cutchogue, NY: Buccaneer Books, 1906/1984.

Solomon, B. M. *Ancestors and Immigrants: A changing New England tradition*. Cambridge, MA: Harvard University Press, 1956.

Sommors, C. H. "The war against boys." *The Atlantic Monthly* 285 (May 2000): 59–74.

Spencer, H. *Social statics: The conditions essential to human happiness specified, and the first of them developed*. London: J. Chapman, 1850.

Springhall, J. "Censoring Hollywood: Youth, moral panic and crime/gangster movies of the 1930s." *Journal of Popular Culture* 32, no. 3 (1998): 135–154.

Stapinski, H. *Five-Finger Discount: Crooked Family History*. New York: Random House, 2001.

Steinbeck, J. *The Grapes of Wrath*. New York: Viking, 1939/1989.

Sternberg, R. J. *The Triarchic Mind: A new theory of human intelligence* New York: Viking, 1988.

Swift, E. M. "Sports in a school curriculum: Four postulates to play by." *Teachers College Record* 92, no. 3 (1991): 425–432.

Synnott, M. G. "The admission and assimilation of minority students at Harvard, Yale, and Princeton, 1900–1970." *History of Education Quarterly* 19, no. 3 (1979): 285.

Synnott, M. G. *The Half-Opened Door: Discrimination and admission at Harvard, Yale, and Princeton, 1900–1970*. Westport, CT: Greenwood Press, 1979.

The fisherman's feast: A cultural tradition in Boston's North End." *90 Annual Fisherman*, August 19, 2000.

The proceedings of the second annual meeting of the National Child Labor Committee, Washington, D.C., December 8-10, 1905. *Annals of the American Academy of Political and Social Science* 27, no. 2 (1906). Retrieved from http://pds.lib.harvard.edu/pds/view/2575317?n=1&s=4.

Thomsen, K. *Building resilient students: Integrating resiliency into what you already know and do*. Thousand Oaks, CA: Corwin Press, 2002.

"Thousands of sane locked up he says; Former Justice Hoffman charges the temporarily deranged often are railroaded and go mad in asylums, urges special institutions to provide for those who can be cured." *New York Times*, May 7, 1922.

Thorndike, E. L. "Intelligence and its uses." *Harper's Magazine* 140 (January 1920): 27–235.

Torrey, E. F. & J. Miller. *The Invisible Plague: The rise of mental illness from 1750 to the present*. New Brunswick, NJ: Rutgers University Press, 2001.

Toulmin, S. E. *Cosmopolis. The Hidden Agenda of Modernity.* Chicago, Ill: The University of Chicago Press, 1990.

Trillin, C. "The Italian thing." *New Yorker* 66 (Nov. 1990): 107–118.

Tropman, J. E. *The Catholic Ethic in American Society: An exploration of values.* San Francisco, CA: Jossey-Bass, 1995.

Varma-Joshi, M., C. J. Baker, & C. Tanaka. "Names will never hurt me?" *Harvard Educational Review* 74 (Summer 2004): 175–208.

Vecchio, D. C. "Italians." In *American Immigrant Cultures: Builders of a nation*, vol. 2. Edited by D. Levinson and M. Ember. New York: Macmillan, 1997.

Veum, J. R. & A. B. Weiss. "Education and the work histories of young adults." *Monthly Labor Review* 116, no. 4 (1993): 11–20.

Vonnegut, K., Jr. *Slaughterhouse Five.* New York: Dell Publishing, 1969.

Weber, M. *The Protestant Ethic and the Spirit of Capitalism.* Translated by S. Kalberg. Chicago: Fitzroy Dearborn, 1905/2001.

Wechsler, D. *The Measurement and Appraisal of Adult Intelligence* (4th ed.). Baltimore, MD: Williams & Wilkins, 1958.

West, L. *Miss Lonelyhearts & the Day of the Locust.* New York: New Directions, 1933/1969.

Whalen, R. J. *The Founding Father: The story of Joseph P. Kennedy: A study in power, wealth and family ambition.* Washington, DC: Regnery, 1993.

Zainaldin, J. S. & P. L. Tyor. "Asylum and society: An approach to institutional change." *Journal of Social History* 13, no. 1 (1979): 23–48.

Developments: 1945–1970[1]

Gandhi is assassinated. Jackie Robinson wins the National League Rookie of the Year in 1947. Harry Truman issues Executive Order 9981 on July 26, 1948 abolishing racial segregation in the U.S. military. "Dick" and "Mac" McDonald open the first world's fast food restaurant in 1948. George Orwell *publishes* Nineteen Eighty-Four *(1949). Memphis bans the musical* Annie Get Your Gun *because the cast is integrated. Charlie Parker and Miles Davis invent a new form of jazz. Colorfast textiles improve. Padded, broad-shouldered dresses give women an air of strength and authority. Dr. Spock publishes* The Common Sense Book of Baby and Child Care *(1946). Work on an artificial kidney begins. North Korea invades South Korea. Dwight D. Eisenhower wins the U. S. presidency. "Rocket '88," the first rock and roll record, is released in 1951. James Watson and Francis Crick discover that the DNA structure is a double helix in 1953. William Golding publishes* Lord of the Flies *(1954). "If I Knew You Were Coming I'd've Baked a Cake" is a popular song. Ralph Ellison publishes* The Invisible Man *(1953). On the Waterfront* (1954) *with Marlon Brando wins an Academy Award for best picture.* American Bandstand *begins. Marilyn Monroe marries playwright Arthur Miller. Jack Kerouac publishes* On the Road *in 1957. The Supreme Court rules that schools can bar "subversives" from teaching. A 1952 study shows that 90 percent of research funds are earmarked for physical and biological sciences. John Dewey dies in 1952. Progressive education is the driving force in American public schools. A 1951 study of eleven thousand high school juniors finds that 18 percent do not know the number of months in a year. The National Defense Education Act of 1955 prohibits federal control over school curriculum. The Davy Crockett craze peaks in 1955. Rosa Parks refuses to give up her bus seat to a white man, also in 1955. The* Great Books Foundation, *originated by Robert Hutchins, president of the University of Chicago, provides a means for general liberal education for all adults. The* Today Show *premieres on NBC. Warhol's first pop paintings are displayed in 1961. Kinsey publishes two surveys on sexual behavior in 1948 and 1953,* Playboy *is founded in 1953, the FDA approves the first birth control pills in 1960, and Warhol directs* Blue Movie *in 1969. In 1963, Martin Luther King, Jr. delivers the "I Have Dream" speech and John F. Kennedy proposes*

357

the Civil Rights Act--the bill is signed into law the next year. Some 1,000 students gather in New York City and burn their draft cards in 1964. By 1969, Neil Armstrong becomes the first man to walk the moon. And for three days in the same year, half a million people live in peace without security, and cooperate to share shelter, food (and drugs) during Woodstock.

6

A Working-Class Education

I considered myself a failure. Granted, that appraisal may be too critical, given that I achieved much in school. Still, I didn't read for my own pleasure until I was sixteen, and I rarely wrote. My schools' curricula emphasized rote learning; teachers frowned upon students questioning the material or its presentation. Worse, the past belonged to others. I had no real idea of who I was or where I was going. Thanks to a friend, I discovered that there is more to books than finding the right answer for a test. I was lucky. The statistics on literacy show that most Americans don't read and write once they leave school.[2]

Social Education[3]

Daily Routines

I recall my childhood as a time with little to occupy me. I had no real identity, aside from my reputation as a quiet kid who did what he was told. With the exception of a Jackie Gleason impersonation in a talent show, my early life was rather uneventful, organized as it was around Scouts, Sunday school, TV, family, and friends. I rarely read books, worked at a hobby, or played on an athletic team. I was always cut from Little League. I took lessons on the trumpet but quit after two weeks. Summer evenings I spent on the porch, watching cars pass by.

Family time in 1949. From left to right: Henry Sr (my dad), me in the cowboy hat, Robert (my brother), Connie (my aunt), Ralph III (my cousin, Connie's son), Rose (my grandmother), Stella (my mom)

Actually, I did have a hobby of sorts. I must have watched thirty hours of TV a week in those days. There was *The Abbott and Costello Show*, *Beat the Clock*, *Boston Blackie*, and countless B westerns with white-hat heroes like Hopalong Cassidy who faced down the bad guys. TV fueled my fantasies about girls. Like most boys in my neighborhood, I was madly in love with Annette Funicello, star of *The Mickey Mouse Club*. The girls we knew were plain, but Annette was a good-looking Italian American, like our cousins.

Much of our family time revolved around food.[4] We ate supper every night at six. Everyone sat in the same place. We came to the table when our parents called; if we didn't, we were slapped. The women prepared all the meals in the traditional way, flattening veal cutlets by hand, simmering sauces for hours, or running mashed potatoes through a strainer twice. Even waffles were from scratch. We drank milk and ate plenty of fresh Italian bread (Grandmother Rose called white bread American bread). All meals ended with fruit.

We talked a great deal during supper. Instead of discussing religion, politics, or current events, however, we spoke about work or family. Aunt Lucy just bought a new bedroom set for Jackie and Billie. Tony Intella was in the hospital. Mr. Taddio's father passed away. Occasionally, Dad would sneak in a wisecrack about his favorite bums, the Red Sox. After supper, we watched TV until bedtime. I would change into my pajamas and head for the kitchen, where I sat alone to munch on a snack of milk and cookies. Right before I fell asleep, one of my parents came in to remind me to say my prayers and to wish me good night.

Life was predictable. Thursdays were for grocery shopping. Saturday nights we prepared for church the next morning, taking a weekly bath, cutting nails, and polishing shoes. Sundays started out with a twenty-minute walk alone to church. Mom stayed home to prepare the afternoon meal, which worried me. I feared that God was going to punish her for missing mass—at least that's what Sister had diagrammed on the chalkboard during one of my First Communion classes—a large circle representing mortal sin with the words "Missing Mass" inside it. I asked Mom about her sinful ways one Sunday.

"Mommy, why don't you go to church? You know it's a mortal sin, don't you?"

"Well, God knows that I can't hear too well. Besides, I honor him by preparing Sunday dinner for you."

Of course, I thought, feeling considerably relieved.

I took the Franklin Avenue route to church, keeping to my side of the street. The top half was residential, with old, well-kept, turn-of-the-century shingle or clapboard homes on either side. Three new brick apartment buildings stood on high ground next to the large colonial by the ancient elm tree. My side consisted of shaded duplexes with open porches. During the summer, I passed owners cutting their lawns. My father told me that he knew the families who lived in these homes from his childhood.

I passed Vincent's Barbershop and Dr. Eno's house at the bottom of the hill. Both men were friendly and outgoing. Dr. Eno was very popular because he sent his kids to public school. I never had difficulty answering his question, "How's school, Henry?"

"Fine."

"And your grandmother? I haven't seen her in some time. How is she? Does she still go shopping downtown?"

"Yes, but she sends me for pears."

Many shops congregated at the intersection of Franklin and Quincy Avenues. Herb's Drugstore, Quincy Shoe Repair, Dr. Moran the dentist, and Bonfigulo's Funeral Parlor were on my side of the street. The Shop and Save market, with its basement bowling alley; Sweeny's Funeral Home; the Swedish doughnut shop; and the Adams Historic Homestead were across the street. First-generation Italians had their funerals at Bonfigulo's; everyone else went to Sweeny's. My father reminded me—on more than one occasion—that he wanted to be waked at Sweeny's.

Herbie, the druggist, spoke with an accent and knew my teacher's name. "So, Henry, how are you doing in school? Doing long division yet?"

"Yes, but my cousin can divide by three numbers."

"What grade is he in?"

"Fifth."

"Is his teacher Mr. Stefanie?"

"No. He goes to parochial school."

"You be sure to study just as hard."

I walked to the drugstore in the summer to buy an ice cream cone or a nickel candy bar. Later, as a teenager, I bought my first paperback there. In all the years I lived in Quincy, I never sat at the counter to order a hot fudge sundae or banana split—in my view, an extravagant waste of money. I could buy three ice cream cones for the price of one sundae.

Franklin Avenue was busy with traffic, even on Sundays, when all the stores but Herb's were closed for the Lord's Day. The Scottish meat market was two blocks away. The building was sandy brown and tiny, set off by a large green door that faced the street at an angle. I used to peek in on my way to confession to smell the sawdust on the floor. My family never shopped there, and I knew why. The customers were better dressed than we were.

The neighborhood changed as I passed the meat market. Trees and lawns gave way to fruit stands and taverns. This area is where Italians lived and shopped for imported tomatoes, flat-leaf parsley, and eggplant. John's Fruit Stand and Baldicui's Variety Store were open on Sundays. Arguments over the best ingredients for soup were inevitable. I never stopped to listen, though. I was an American.[5]

Scott's, which overshadowed the other buildings, is where I saw my first magic show and attended my first record hop. If late for church, I would cut behind Scott's and through the ragweed to the church parking lot. Most kids didn't use this shortcut; they were too afraid of the Italian kids who lived nearby. I usually took a deep breath and walked as fast as I could with my head down to avoid the torn underwear and discarded shoes that pockmarked the ground. I took my chances because I was more afraid of being late for mass than being choked or beaten up. When I wasn't late, I continued on Franklin Street, past the Robert Burns statue and the Episcopalian cemetery. This route took a few minutes longer but didn't smell like rancid urine.

Once I got to church, I knew what to do. The kids had their own mass in the basement. Each grade sat in its own section, boys on one side, girls on the other. Once mass ended, Sister Superior took out her wooden clappers. The first clap was the signal to stand up. The next clap meant to file out silently in pairs. Once outside, we walked in columns to our classes in the parish school. Few kids dared talk or break ranks. The nuns segregated the classes by gender and ran them in a fixed, regimented way. Sister expected us to recite the answers to the catechism questions that she had assigned the previous week. In turn, kids stood up beside their desks to repeat what they'd memorized. Those who said the right answers got a star in their catechism book.

Classes ended at eleven. My dad waited outside to drive across town to buy Sicilian bread at the Sumner Street Bakery and pick up the Sunday paper. We went all the way to Quincy Point because our market didn't carry the crusty bread we liked for sandwiches. Later, I discovered that Quincy Point was Grandfather Carmelo's last neighborhood.

Once home, I changed into my regular clothes and sprawled out on the living room carpet to read the funnies and browse through *Parade* magazine. Lunch was around noon. It was the biggest, most elaborate meal of the week. My parents spared no expense. Dad was fond of saying, "I wonder what the poor people are eating today." This quip meant that we need not be ashamed. There were always ample servings of roast beef, lasagna with brasciole, or fried chicken. Mom would send me to Herb's to buy a quart of tonic, the name for soft drinks in my neighborhood. Sunday was the only time our parents allowed us to have it.

Even though family dinners could be miserable for an adolescent, they were worth it. Top row, far left: My dad, Henry, Sr. Bottom row, far left and center: Me and my mother Stella.

We set aside afternoons and evenings to watch the New York Giants football game, *You Are There* with Walter Cronkite, and *The Jimmy Durante Show*. Once a month we drove to my maternal grandparents' house in Hyde Park, an old, drab section of Boston. I dreaded those visits and longed for the day when I wouldn't have to go. I got nervous just thinking about the chatter, the hello/good-bye kisses, and the other formalities that awaited me. I also felt silly when they referred to me as "Little Henry" and my father as "Big Henry." Besides, there was nothing to do except watch TV because my cousins were younger. Even dinner was a chore. I squirmed through comments like "Little Henry is such a picky eater." There was no chance for a shy kid to be himself at my grandparents' house.

All in all, though, the visits were worth the adolescent misery. My grandmother always made homemade ravioli or pasta, Italian meats roasted with potatoes, and a delicious salad. Occasionally, she made thick pizza as a fourth course. No restaurant pizza, then or now, tasted as good. This was Napoli pizza, prepared in long black pans, not the thin round ones used in taverns like the Roman Gardens. It was square, thick, and golden brown, with a hint of faraway places.

She made her dough by hand, pulling it down the sides of a bowl and tucking it under. I watched her intently as she rolled the balls under her palms until they were smooth and firm. She then put them in another bowl, covered the top with a damp towel, and placed it on top of the stove. Next, she and my aunts chopped fresh herbs and grated plenty of mozzarella and fontina cheeses. When the dough had risen, my grandmother placed it on the table to press into large shapes, which she then spread into the pans, making sure that the corners were thick. She brushed them lightly with extra virgin olive oil and covered them with a simple sauce, topping off each one with cheese, green peppers, and pieces of garlic and onion.

As we waited for the pizza to bake, my grandfather pulled out his homemade wine from the cabinet next to his chair and poured a tiny amount into glasses filled with orange soda. This concoction was for the grandchildren; the adults' glasses received only the wine. By four o'clock, my grandfather was reminiscing about past romantic liaisons.

Even in his elderly state, he terrified me. I'd overheard stories, whispered when he went to the bathroom or the basement, about his razor strap, which he was known to use on any daughter who disobeyed him. I had even heard whispers about his disapproval of my parents' marriage, but by this time he saw my father in a whole new light.

Once or twice a year, his brother-in-law Sammy stopped by to pay his respects. Sammy was a florist with a small, round face sporting wire-rimmed glasses. Like all the others, he was diminutive. Sammy lived in Boston but worked in a wealthy suburb. My relatives called him an "oddball" because he never married. His visits gave me a chance to fantasize. His favorite companion was a slightly overweight blonde woman who wore thick red lipstick and dressed in tight skirts. She worked as a secretary in an office and didn't look like the rest of us. My aunts said that she was an American who drank a lot. Sammy and his girlfriend thrilled me. He dressed in suits, talked without an accent, and flipped quarters to the kids. His girlfriend wore hats pinned to her hair, smelled of perfume, and never laughed loudly or bothered me. I imagined that she was the famous Mrs. Calabash to whom Jimmy Durante said good night at the end of his show. In my mind, Sammy had stolen Mrs. Calabash away from Jimmy and was living with her next to the subway station, a flight of fancy nourished by my parents' reluctance to answer my questions.

"Where does Sammy live?"

"In the city."

"What does he do?"

"He's a florist."

"Why isn't he married?"

"He can't."

"Why?"

"That's enough."

Such uninformative exchanges backfired. Instead of forgetting Sammy, I wondered why he wore a flower on his lapel and what it must be like to ride the subway home. Sammy became larger than life. He was different from the others; he lived by his own set of rules.

Later in the day, everyone left to play penny poker at my aunt Jenny's. Before departing, my grandmother squeezed a dollar bill into my hand, gave me three or four loud kisses, and said, "You be a gooda boy in school, Henery." She always added an extra E to my name. I would blush and say, "Thank you, Grammy," making sure to pronounce my words very slowly and carefully so that she could understand me.

Once at my aunt's house, about seven houses down the street, the laughter became louder, and the talk and attention less obtrusive. My aunts still feared my grandfather. Memories die hard, so I figured that they didn't want to provoke him with "American" behavior. For instance, I never remember seeing anyone except him smoke in his home. He favored those foul-smelling Pardoni cigars.

Once my aunts arrived at Jenny's, though, everyone lit up and didn't stop until the last card was played. There must have been fifteen cigarettes going at any one time. The men smoked Chesterfields; the women favored Pall Malls. Smoke filled the entire apartment so thickly that my eyes burned. After ten minutes or so, I escaped to the living room to watch TV. My Sunday school training had taught me that it was wrong to gamble, so I felt uncomfortable joining the game. My cousin Anthony always played, though. He was three years older than I, an avid drummer who was comfortable with grown-ups. I felt remote from everyone, so I stayed in the background. Like my grandmother, my aunt put out a big spread of Italian cold-cut sandwiches, pastries, and freshly brewed coffee. We kids got more orange soda.

We spent summers playing ball, riding bikes, building forts, picking blueberries, and swimming at Nantasket Beach, where Dad had gone to camp. We didn't go to the beach often, so when we did it was a big deal. One trip that brings back fond memories happened the day that the shipyard closed due to the heat. My father told us to pack for the beach. Mom prepared an eye-popping lunch. No peanut butter and jelly sandwiches, mind you, but an all-out Italian feast of macaroni and meatballs, fried chicken, and salad. Like all previous trips to the beach, we ate after our first swim and then sat out for twenty minutes to prevent cramps. We took the wait quite seriously; no one wanted to drown from an undigested meatball.

Body surfing was the sport at Nantasket Beach. Cousin Anthony knew exactly when to catch the waves for the longest ride. He was good at everything.

In those days, we didn't have fans or air conditioning, so we cooled off the natural way, by going shirtless. My bedroom was unbearably hot, so I slept by the window. But forget trying to sleep with a sunburn—it was next to impossible, even smothered in lotion. The only consolation was that the redness would soon turn to bronze, the color of a tough guy.

My parents put very few demands on my brother and me during those innocent days. They expected us to make our beds, clean off the dinner table, and wash the dishes. Otherwise, we had it easy—no homework, music lessons, ski trips, or sleep-overs to organize; grass to cut; siblings to baby sit; or pets to mind. Nor did we have to wash or iron our clothes, put them away, or collect wood. Dad must have been proud to give us that freedom to be children. We didn't even have to shovel snow. Mom did the shopping, cooking, cleaning, and laundry. Dad went to work, ran errands, and took naps.

When it came to religion, we attended mass on Sundays and Holy Days of Obligation. We didn't eat meat on Fridays. A crucifix hung over my parents' bed and on my bedroom wall. We displayed palms on Palm Sunday, tipped our heads whenever we rode past a Catholic church, and said our bedtime prayers. Unlike devout Catholics, we didn't put out advent wreaths at Christmas, sing religious carols, pray before meals, or conduct family devotions.

My parents left religious instruction to the nuns. The only home instruction I received was on Sunday school lessons. Every week I needed someone to test me on the assigned material in the Baltimore catechism manual. Mom was very good at quizzing. She also taught me my prayers and helped me prepare for my First Communion.

More Family Ways

Connie marries Ralph, Jr., a New Hampshire Yankee. Neither exactly looked (nor acted) Italian.

A college education separated Aunt Connie from my father and Aunt Lucy. Connie had married a New Hampshire Yankee, a Northeastern University graduate with a degree in civil engineering. She neither looked Italian nor acted like one. She lived in a fairytale bungalow deep inside the Braintree woods, drove a car, worked as a teacher-administrator, and hired a housekeeper. She asked questions and called everyone "honey." Her husband smoked a pipe and cracked ethnic jokes about Italians.

Aunt Lucy was frank and opinionated. You didn't talk to or with her; you listened. She lived in a black-and-white world of indisputable fact. My father never yelled at her because she could—and would—give it right back to him. Like my mother, she was a homemaker who didn't drive. She spent her life keeping her home spotless, putting everything in its place, and raising four children. She was a hugger too, very generous with affection.

She had married a fellow Sicilian, an extremely good-looking and highly intelligent man. Uncle Tony was one of my role models. Lean and athletic, a real Robert De Niro lookalike, he spent most of his time in his basement workshop. I spent hours in his den, thumbing through back issues of *Popular Mechanics*.

My aunts had a strong impact on me. Both had successfully adapted to American life. They owned new homes with modern

Lucy and Antonio Alosi. A Robert De Niro lookalike, he was one of my role models.

conveniences, dressed their children in dungarees, prepared roast beef dinners on Sunday, and vacationed on Cape Cod. They also had family dentists and personal physicians. I wanted to be like them.

My family had not fully assimilated. Like my mother's family, we lived on a busy street in an old, treeless neighborhood, ate Italian food four nights a week, and never took vacations. Our furniture was old and dark, our floors covered with linoleum. When we socialized with my mother's family, the hugging, kissing, cheek pinching, and eating never ended. My father felt comfortable around his in-laws because they were like him.

My mother's sisters spoiled me with adoration. "Little Henry! Oh, you're getting so big! God bless you. How's school?"

"Fine, Aunt Josephine."

"You take after your mother. We're so proud of you. Keep up the good work."

"Thank you."

"Do you want something to eat? How about a piece of chicken? You want some more pizza? How about something to drink? Oh, I just want to hug you to death!"

I was uncomfortable with so much affection, having grown up under Grandmother Rose's stern eye. She and I shared a bedroom until I was five. She told me stories of her hardships and taught me to tie my shoes. She spoke to me in Sicilian, cooked Sicilian pastries and soups, and had me pray to her saints. She took me on shopping trips to the square, knitted all my socks and mittens, and sent me for Italian bread. She even took me to the Sicilian doctor and had me watch entertainers like Perry Como and Don Ameche.

My Neapolitan education was less rigid, as I didn't see my mother's parents as often. My maternal grandmother was small but exuberant, with lots of love to share. My grandfather was a skilled artisan who never spoke to his grandchildren. When he was single, Grandpa had worked as a laborer on the railroad and lived in the worker's dorm inside the train yard. As soon as he saved enough money, he returned to Italy to claim his bride, Maria. He and my grandmother spent their wedding night aboard the Providence-bound train and later set up living space in the dorm. After my mother was born, Grandma covered her head with a red handkerchief and hoed cabbages on an urban farm. Grandpa found skilled work in a piano factory. Eventually, they bought a car, purchased a three-family house, and sent their ten children to parochial school.

My mother had helped to raise her siblings. Those were the days when the eldest daughter carried as much responsibility as possible. It was also a time when children of the poor received the rare treat of an orange for Christmas. I loved to listen to my mother's stories about nuns and penmanship tablets. I also liked her to reminisce about the injured squirrel that scratched her when she tried to pick it up. This story taught me how loving and thoughtful she was. My father just shook his head every time he heard it.

Brothers

I took after my aunt Concetta, solitary and withdrawn by nature. My brother, Robert, however, was wild. I studied all the time. Robert read for a minute then went off to socialize. My grades were good. He failed. I was cast as the Madonna in a Cub Scout play. Robert was the pirate. I was thin and athletic. He was round and slow. Like my father, I was nervous before tests. Robert was fearless, willing to go on any ride at Nantasket Beach.

My father compared us all the time. I was the good student. Robert was the troublemaker who clogged up the toilet or played with matches. He countered, "You care about Henry more than me!" Whenever we fought, I caught my father's belt because I "should have known better."

Robert and I drifted apart in high school. I focused on homework and sports. Robert had a paper route, built and flew model planes, and talked endlessly on the CB radio. We attended the same parochial school until he got expelled for smoking. When he came home, he said, "The nuns threw me out. They told me, 'We don't want you here. You're trouble.'"

Me and my younger brother Robert.

When he got older, Robert switched to black leather and slicked down his thinning hair with water. Married women called him "Bobby." Worried that his son was heading down the wrong path, Dad phoned an Irish American named Daley. "You don't know me," he said, "but I went to school with your sister. Can you get my son into a trade?" Daley headed the trade school, so he put my brother into mechanics. Dad spoke against it, though, because it was dirty work, so Daley switched Robert to electronics.

Robert used Dad's car to drive to work at the Stop and Shop on Southern Artery. One Friday night, his friends waited for him outside the bowling alley. They'd been rude, so the owner told them never to come back. Robert gave the owner a hard time when he found out. The cops arrested him because he refused to leave. My father grimaced when he saw his son behind bars. "Robert," he said to himself, "has taken after me."

The arresting officer released him because he knew Dad but warned, "Don't let him do this again."

Three months later, Robert befriended a kid from Italy who had his own car. One night he said to my brother, "I know two girls who like to fool around. Let's go to Curtis Farms to get some liquor." Robert had no trouble purchasing a six-pack. Within minutes, two officers locked him up for underage drinking. "Who sold you the booze?" they asked. Robert refused to answer because he was afraid of getting beaten up. Grabbing him by his jacket, my father growled, "Tell them where you got the booze." Robert wouldn't budge. Satisfied that my brother would be worse off with my dad than in jail, the cop let Robert go. On the drive home, Robert told Dad that the girl in the car was the cop's daughter.

My brother was uninhibited and expansive. By sixteen, he had made Eagle Scout, learned to sail, bowled a perfect 300, rode a motorcycle, and finished vocational school. After a hitch in the navy, he built and raced cars and became a master millwright and crane operator. He was the ultimate can-do American, afraid of nothing. By twenty-five, until his untimely death at fifty, he was an imposing union leader who kept bosses honest.

Accidental Literacies

When I was growing up, my mother's sisters used to say, "Henry, you're a good boy. God bless you." I never knew what they meant. I supposed that they liked my schoolwork. I was certainly a good student. My teachers generally had nice things to say about me. I was the kind of pupil they liked to have in their classrooms—I did everything they asked and never talked back.

They thought of me as a conscientious child. Dad used to return home from PTA meetings very proud of what he heard. Yet he managed to use the reports against me. His favorite put down was, "Stop fighting with Robert, or I'll tell your teacher what you're really like."

I was a serious kid who longed to be in the top group. I paid attention, completed my work, and came straight home. My neighbor Mrs. Andrews had given me a copy of *Peter Rabbit* for my First Communion, but when I sat down to read it, I couldn't pronounce the unfamiliar words. I put the book down, feeling stupid, and never opened it again. Avoidance of books plagued me for the rest of my life.[6]

In school, I dreaded oral reading because I made mistakes. If I hadn't seen a word before, I couldn't pronounce it. I can still feel the blood rushing to my face with every mispronunciation. Eventually, I learned to read, but books never really appealed to me. I read in school because I had to. Without incentives at home, I watched TV instead.

I started to read for my own enjoyment when I turned ten. The event that turned me around occurred on our annual subway trip to Boston to buy school clothes. I noticed that my cousin Jackie wasn't staring out the window as the subway car sped toward the Park Street station, deep below the city. We always had a contest to see who could count the most windows on the cars that rushed past us in the opposite direction. This time, though, he was busy reading a comic book he'd bought at Ashmont Station. It was the *Walt Disney Annual Fall Edition*. Disney put out the comics of choice in my neighborhood, and the *Fall Edition* was the most coveted because it was packed with extra stories, characters, and puzzles.

As we hopped onto the platform, I asked Jackie if I could borrow it. He gave it to me reluctantly but also said to check out the Scrooge McDuck story. Scrooge was one of my favorite Disney characters, so I was immediately drawn into the fascinating tale about treasure hidden in an intricate underground maze. A creature that was half bull and half monster guarded it. Scrooge's nephew, Donald, was smart enough to elude the Minotaur and return with the treasure by following a string he had laid down.

I became so absorbed in the story that I asked my cousin to loan it to me. He said that he would trade it for baseball cards. We cut a deal and, as the saying goes, the rest is history. I never let that comic book out of my sight. I must have read it cover to cover a dozen times. I memorized every panel and started to draw pictures of the labyrinth. I became so wrapped up in the tale that I bought other Scrooge McDuck issues, hoping to find more great stories. I wasn't disappointed. Over the next year or two, Scrooge introduced me to epic adventures of the past. Comics connected me to the adventure of reading that other kids already knew.

I discovered biography at about the same time, when the True sisters gave me a book about sports heroes. I loved the stories and reread them many times. Each highlighted the life of a great athlete, like Jim Thorpe, who had to overcome adversity to make it to the top. Never having made a Little League team, I identified with their setbacks.

Another event that helped me to develop an interest in reading was joining the Boy Scouts. I asked my parents for a subscription to *Boys' Life*, the official magazine of Scouting. When the magazine came, I turned immediately to the comics and jokes section. The following year, I used my own money to subscribe to *Sport* and *Life* magazines. Although I didn't read them cover to cover, I treasured them because they were mine.

My literacy career took a detour in seventh grade. South Junior High School was about a mile away. To get there, I had to pass the Adamses' houses; cross the railroad tracks, where my father had sold papers as a youngster; walk down Water Street; and cut through Kincade Park. The trip usually took about twenty-five minutes. The change in neighborhoods was very evident. As soon as I crossed Franklin Street, the single-family and duplex homes with trimmed lawns and elm trees gave way to three- and four-story duplexes, light industrial buildings, garages, barrooms, and shops.

My parents thought that it might be unsafe for me to walk to school alone, so they encouraged me to go with my friend Richard. He and I liked the idea of walking to school together, so he used to call for me every morning at 7:45. We were good friends and both popular with our teachers. The similarities ended there. My father worked in the open, whereas Dick's dad worked as clerk in an office. My mom worked in a factory; Dick's mom was a florist. Dick was a talented achiever, an all-American boy whose family had been in this country for several generations. He lived in a single-family home on a quiet street next to Faxon Park. He played the clarinet, was active in Scouts, swam at the YMCA, and excelled in sports. I was a third-generation Sicilian American whose family rented an apartment on a busy street. Dick went to the Bethany Congregational Church in the square. I went Saint John's Catholic Church, next to Morrill's Corner. He had a popular older brother. I had a younger brother who annoyed me. Dick had a train set permanently set up in his basement. I stored mine in a box under my bed. He always finished first in school. I always finished second.

Dick told me that football players who won school letters had them sewn onto school sweaters that the prettiest girls in class then asked if they could wear. That notion appealed to me because I was greedy to touch every inch of a girl's skin. I tried out for the team and went from being a Little League reject to a football hero. I was the star and center of attention, a quick and elusive runner. I was so good that the eighth-grade coach promoted me to his team. An opposing player complained to the referee about my age when he saw my stubble. I told the referee I was Italian.

HEN

67

I started to go steady with an Annette lookalike as olive-skinned as me. In those days, my nickname was Blackie. The name caught me by surprise; I didn't consider myself different from anyone else.

My football career was going fine until Mrs. Faye blew the whistle on me. She wanted the coach to suspend me from the team because I hadn't passed in a single book report. I told her that I liked to browse through magazines instead of reading boring books.

From Little League reject to a football hero. It's amazing how inspiring the promise of a pretty girl will take you.

She was the same teacher who forced me to wear a tie in the school play. When the time came to don costumes, she told me to wear a shirt, tie, and jacket because I was playing the father. I said that I was going to wear a sports shirt, just like my dad did at home. Being dressed up at home didn't make sense to me.

Despite making the honor roll and being elected class president, I had no high concept of myself as a scholar. I dressed in black and pink and never wore a hat or overshoes in the rain. I rolled up my sleeves, wore my belt buckle on the side, sported snapjack shoes, and bought Elvis records. I went alone to the Friday night dances at the Armory, hung out downtown on Saturdays, and took the train to Boston to attend Celtics and Bruins games.

During the eighth grade, I applied to and was accepted at the local Catholic high school. I wanted to go there because they had a great football team. I got off to a fast start, making varsity and captaining the ninth-grade team. I was again elected class president and performed well in my classes. One day after practice, the assistant coach told my dad that I was going to be the team's next star. The current one was another Italian American kid who played three sports, got all A's, and dated a Marilyn Monroe copycat. I was packed with fury but lacked the requisite poise of a superstar.

Socially, I was friendly and unassuming, everyone's pal. Below the surface, my emotions were in turmoil. Since summer, the captain of the football team had joked about my "five o'clock shadow." Fewer than six boys in my class of 250 were Italian American. Most had names like McKenna, Ryan, and Fitzgerald, all John Kennedy imitators—peach-fuzzed with full heads of hair.

HENRY AMOROSO
215 Kendrick Ave.
Quincy
Senior Council President.
"Hank"..."Oh wicked"... quiet but friendly . . . the Harvard look . . . football's whiz kid . . . goes all out for a buddy . . . Williams own matador . . .
OX 8-5376?
Homeroom Officer 1, 2; Science Fair 2; Sodality 3, 4; Spanish Club 4; Student Council 3, 4; Secretary 3; Varsity Club 3, 4; Football 1, 2, 3, 4; Track 3, 4.

Senior yearbook picture, Archbishop High School, 1962. I may have been everyone's pal socially, but below the surface my emotions were in turmoil.

Another source of shame, this one hidden, was my difficulty with language. Although I was in the top fourth of my class, I couldn't parse a sentence or translate Latin. When my SATs came back, and I had performed only slightly better than average, I felt betrayed. I had been a conscientious student—read my texts, did my homework, and studied for tests. I thought that conformity produced results.

In hindsight, I became aware that no subject excited me. I don't remember debating a single issue, writing an essay, or researching a topic of personal interest. Students with the best grades had the best study habits, and I tried to emulate them. Grandmother Rose had taught me that if I kept plugging away, I could succeed at anything. I spent a great deal of time memorizing facts. My teachers called me "determined."

Despite passing through adolescence without knowing how to write, I wanted to go to college. My dad had warned me that he would "break my back" if I went to work in the shipyard. He knew too well the dreadful winter wind that gusted off the water. I flirted with becoming a naval architect or a physician, but my test scores negated both. Besides, none of my friends thought about prestigious jobs. We were working-class kids who aspired to be teachers.

Reading started to matter at Saint Michael's College. The humanities curriculum was a three-year sequence centered on the works of Plutarch, Plato, Dante, Montaigne, Milton, Mills, and Joyce. The program's premise was simple: studying political, religious, artistic, and literary accomplishments in their historical contexts increases awareness of the human experience.[7]

The classics connected me to intense emotions that I had never felt before. These writers spoke to me with grace and depth. I found comfort in learning about the passions of the heart, everyday life, and cultures far from my home. Peers came to me to discuss the meaning of Dante's *Inferno* or Melville's *Moby Dick*. I no longer felt inferior.

My father believed that the United States had fought WWII to climb out of the Great Depression. I knew no one else who thought that way. His radicalism frustrated me because I didn't know what to say to him. College gave me a way to respond. I explored the past, read primary sources, and argued for hours with dorm mates over the meaning(s) of history. We played off each other's opinions, never knowing where the conversation would lead. One comment led to another and to eventual insight. On and on we debated, fearlessly constructing theories, offering proofs, revising conclusions.

To offset abstract theory, I read novelists like Hemingway and Dos Passos, who wrote with nostalgia about ordinary men and women who played guitars and danced into the night. Their introspections gave me completely different ways to see myself. I started to sense that life is connected to art.

Actually, I had started to think about "big questions" three months before I left for college. One day at the beach, I shared my SAT scores with Jon, a top-notch student and friend. He told me that he read all the time. When I told him that I didn't read, he suggested *The Catcher in the Rye*.

His advice seemed too facile. How could fiction improve my language deficiencies? I thought that vocabulary came from flash cards. At least that's what a large pile of self-help materials had led me to believe. Still, how could I deny the bottom line? Jon had scored higher than I, and his room housed shelves upon shelves of paperbacks. Never had the thought occurred to me that I should have spent more time reading than watching TV.

I don't blame my parents for this oversight.[8] They returned home too tired after a grueling day in the shipyard and factory to relax with books. We rented an apartment, drove an older car, and didn't take vacations. My parents' income went primarily to feed and clothe us. Christmas and birthdays were the only times we received gifts, and the closest library was thirty minutes away.

Although I could pick out a simile on a test, I had never heard one at home or in school. I finally came across one when Holden Caulfield said, "cold as a witch's tit." This phrase had a cathartic effect on me; it was apart from my experience. Nuns had scared me into avoiding all thoughts about sex.

Everything in my upbringing primed me for Holden. Both my home and school environments forbade any form of rebellion. Those rebels who did strike back against the status quo ended up with long greasy hair, black clothes, leather boots, and motorcycle jackets. I had nothing to do with them, and authority, precedent, and law detested them.

Yet Holden had taken a stand for his own belief that it took more courage to quit school than it did to capitulate to the hypocrisy that surrounded him. He had acted on principle, but the payoff was a visit to the mental hospital. He failed because he was depressed. No one asked him why he lost his motivation to learn. No one acknowledged the roots of his anger and sadness, his loneliness. Instead, his English teacher offered him an insignificant lens into his condition: "Life is a game, boy. Life is a game that one plays according to the rules" (p. 20).

Students have lives outside of school, and events in their lives can offer reasons for distractions in their studies. Unfortunately, in today's society, everyone looks for a quick fix for the "troubled" or "distracted" child in school. If the school had known about the passing of Holden's brother and had offered some type of counseling, the sorrow might not have eaten away at him. Perhaps he still wouldn't have passed his classes, but the grieving process would have been easier. Holden had the abilities to succeed, what he lacked were genuine opportunities to use them.

I craved to be inspired by free spirits like Holden, which is how I discovered Socrates. An unlikely candidate for adoration, he dressed poorly, rarely worked at his trade, didn't provide financially for his family, and never wrote anything. He was utterly unlike the men in my life. Like Holden, however, he destroyed prejudice. Truth mattered to him more than how he dressed or what his contemporaries thought about him.

His rejection of wealth, fame, and power appealed to me, as did his pursuit of virtue, defined as knowledge. He challenged presumptions through careful reasoning. If someone asked him a question, he replied with a question. If the individual answered, Socrates countered with another question aimed at sorting out the essential points of the answer. In this way, the speaker discovered his own inconsistencies.

Their peers scorned Socrates and Holden. In Socrates's case, one of his contemporaries disliked him so much that he brought charges against him. Athenian society found him guilty of corrupting the youth and sentenced him to death. Although a friend offered him a plan of escape, he rejected it as a morally incongruous act.

Socrates's rejection of hypocrisy spoke to me. Although my secondary teachers lectured on history and philosophy, they kept a lid on classroom discussions and rarely asked us to write. My college teachers were no different. I sat passively in airless rooms, took notes, and studied their words. Although a few were brilliant, they never felt easy speaking with students. When one did, it was through written comments like, "Your poetry lacks depth" or "Your moral reasoning is imprecise." We meant nothing to them; we added nothing to their lives.

My doctoral mentors at the University of Wisconsin, however, were at the top of the academic ladder, accomplished scholars who worked long hours, wrote prolifically, and served on national committees. Yet they were neither smug nor conceited. Their singular goal was communication, not detachment. Having believed for so long that teachers owned education, I was enthralled to learn that my thoughts mattered too.[9]

Out-of-School Learning

Neighborhood Stories

I had little choice in how I turned out. Family taught me diligence and responsibility. Neighbors infused me with tolerance. School rewarded conformity, and church guilted me into pay my bills on time. I obeyed all the rules.[10]

My parents didn't shame me into becoming a conformist, nor did I have cousins my age who were scholars. I don't remember feeling pressure to be like the other kids in the neighborhood. My parents certainly didn't resort to bribing me with gifts or money, and I don't recall their filling my head with stories about great Americans who had achieved success. They spoke about relatives and friends—about Red Rand, who supported ten kids on the same salary that my dad earned. I heard about my uncle Tony, who designed and built his own home and created elegant furniture but never graduated from the eighth grade. I listened to my parents talk about our next-door neighbor, Gus, who cared for his invalid wife without complaint. I admired these people.

My parents were wonderful teachers. Rather than bribe or pressure, they told us kids stories about ordinary people defying the odds. And I wanted to be like the "heroes" in those stories. Back row, left to right: Stella and Henry, Sr. Front row, left to right: Robert and Henry, Jr.

As I look back on my childhood, I realize that my parents were wonderful teachers. Their stories about ordinary people defying steep odds taught me to do the same. I also learned to be tolerant of others, as nearby residents were Scottish, Dutch, English, Italian, and Irish. It didn't matter to us what their names were or if they owned property. We respected everyone who earned such regard through their actions.

Although my friends came from different backgrounds, we went to the same public school, a short walk up the hill from where we lived. Our school had been the site of Francis W. Parker's experiment during the latter part of the nineteenth century.[11] At Adams School, teachers brought us together. My parents' decision to send me there was easy. The nuns and priests at Saint John's were as fierce as they had been in my father's time, and he figured that one day a week of browbeating Italians was more than enough.

In child-rearing, there are two basic modes for passing down rules and norms to children. The first is through books.[12] The second is through oral storytelling, a tradition that dates back hundreds of years. I was raised in a family that followed neither tradition. There were no fairy tale episodes or bedtime stories in my childhood. I grew up learning right and wrong from listening to my parents talk about people they knew. I listened attentively, figuring out who was good and who was bad. Before long, I knew who I wanted to emulate.[13]

There was Leo, from Dad's old neighborhood, who wore dark glasses to hide the hot oil scars his mother inflicted on him the day he talked back to her. This story taught me the value of obedience, particularly given that my father had a bad temper. Then there was the story of Sonny Vitale, another character from my father's childhood. Sonny was a first-generation Italian American who had been wild in his youth. Later, he tamed down and became a cop. Sonny taught me about succeeding. If he could rise from being a hood to being a cop, anything was possible in America.

Other stories mattered too. Most were about my grandmother Rose chopping wood and washing floors. I knew about my father selling papers to train commuters early in the morning. I knew about the family moving and how the Salvation Army delivered a turkey every Thanksgiving. I heard stories about my aunt's mistreatment, but I also knew about the kindnesses that people had shown her.

These were my favorite stories; they made me proud to be part of a family that had overcome adversity. I didn't know of any other kid whose dad had grown up without a father or who had a grandmother who loved her children so much that she sacrificed her own happiness to raise them correctly. My history set me apart from others. My role models taught me to see humor and opportunity in the ordinary and to overcome any challenge with effort and persistence. After all, my grandmother had successfully raised three children on next to nothing. The least I could do was strive to be as diligent.

Tenants

The house in which I grew up was a handsome, turn-of-the-century, well-constructed multifamily residence with a slate roof, hardwood floors, and thick granite walls in the basement. We lived on the first floor; the owners, the McClouds, lived on the second floor; and a rotating array of other tenants occupied the third floor. The McClouds had three sons who were older than I. Each was a good student. Mr. McCloud was in the contracting business and built another home up on Penn's Hill. He offered to sell the multifamily house to my parents, but my dad declined.

I remember the first time I met our new landlord. I had just returned from an Easter shopping trip to Woolworth's in Quincy Square, a new toy gun in hand. I was in the living room, watching TV, when a loud voice in the dining room broke my concentration. When I turned to see who was making all the noise, I saw a woman towering over my mother, monopolizing the conversation. I had never been around such an overbearing person.

My mother asked me to leave what I was doing. "Henry, this is our new landlord. She has two children about your age." I nodded as I fidgeted with my rifle, thinking about what I was missing on TV.

The new landlord said, "You will like Wayne. I understand that you are a good student. He is a top student too. He is in Scouts as well. He just completed a scrapbook on fighter planes. And he catches for his team."

I hated baseball. Citywide tryouts to choose fifty replacements for the older kids who moved up to Pony League had just ended. The rest were sent home with the advice to try again next year.

My father had brought me to the tryouts behind the new YMCA, across the street from the Quincy Police Station, although I don't know why; I wasn't a good ballplayer, so I was self-conscious at the tryouts. The adults in charge were unfriendly and spoke in monosyllables: "Go." "Wait." "Next." The surroundings were strange too. I had played baseball in a grassy field next to homes and trees. This place was fenced in, cold, gray, and somber. After checking in and taking a number, a man told me to get in line in the outfield. I jogged across the hard-packed gravel surface, dodging puddles left over from the evening rain. Spring dampness hung in the air, and the gusts off the bay were brisk.

Someone called my number, and the man hit me a long, high fly ball. I was supposed to catch it and throw it back to the kid standing beside him. I just stood there as the ball sailed over my head and then went back in line to wait for another turn. Ten minutes later, standing alone, waiting to catch a ball that had just left the batter's hand a hundred feet away, I could only think about one thing—hiding. Sure enough, I didn't catch it.

Next, we went to the hitting station. I hated that walk; there was a constant roar from the infield. It seemed like everyone was chanting, "Hum batter. Hum batter." When someone called my number, I walked to the plate, looking serious; all eyes turned toward me. The pitcher was wearing a Boston Red Sox warm-up jacket. He must have been one of the coaches because he wore a Clark's baseball cap. My dad stood behind the screen and told me to swing if the ball came across the plate between my chest and my knees. I listened obediently, waiting for the next pitch. It came in high. The one after it was outside. So were the next ten. I stared straight ahead and kept thinking, "Over the plate, between the chest and knees." The next ball was right down the middle. I didn't even see it. Two more pitches sped past. Finally, my dad yelled, "Swing the bat for heaven's sake!" He frightened me so much that I lost my concentration and could hear Jackie starting to complain about waiting too long for his turn. The next thing I remember was riding home in silence. I'm convinced that my fear of failure started that day.

A few weeks after the new landlords moved in, Wayne asked me to go with him to his old neighborhood in West Quincy. It was a long walk, but I was excited by the prospect of playing with sixth-graders. When we got to the field, his friends asked him who I was. "Homer," he said. Everyone repeated my new name. When the players picked sides, I was left out. Wayne looked back at me and said, "Go home, Homer."

Wayne's dad was a northern Italian who spoke with an accent, raced cars, and adored his son. Wayne was an extremely confident and competitive kid—athletic, popular, and smart. I know, because Wayne used to tell me all the time how intelligent he was. He even told my mother and me how many biographies he had read the year before. I was very impressed; I hadn't read any. His death from leukemia was sudden. His parents grieved for years; his father's eyes watered whenever he saw me. He must have thought that Wayne and I were good friends.

Three teachers from Maine moved into the vacant apartment—the

True sisters, Bertha and Blanch, and their friend Edith. They were very good neighbors who cared about us. My mother even felt comfortable enough to invite them down for coffee.

The True sisters were quiet and unassuming. They looked like they came from Maine. Both had plain, iron-rimmed glasses and dressed in brown and gray suits. Their speech was equally unadorned. Edith was more flamboyant. She favored earth-tone sweaters, matching red and yellow scarves, and pleated wool skirts. Occasionally, she wore lipstick to school.

At about this time, I became acutely aware of how much my dad's yelling embarrassed me. He lost his temper over the slightest thing, like coming to dinner late, and once he lost control, rage enveloped him. We never spoke during his outbursts; we just sat with eyes downcast and ate. If we opened our mouths, we might be slapped or, worse, whipped with his belt.

In summer, his voice carried through the open kitchen windows, which Mom instinctively closed when he began a tirade. More difficult was quashing the noise inside the house. Although our walls and ceilings were solid, his voice echoed through a vent pipe in the pantry, a fact that I discovered when I went upstairs to borrow eggs one time.

I was humiliated when I discovered the opening in the pantry ceiling. The True sisters must have heard everything we said. Mom accepted this invasion of privacy as inevitable. Still, she reminded my father about his loudness. "Henry, calm down. The people upstairs will hear you." He looked puzzled, as if he couldn't fathom what she was talking about. I did my part by stuffing the hole with rags but to no avail. The True sisters' body language told me that they knew about his latest diatribe.

Years later, in Maine, the True sisters caught up with me, in a sense. One afternoon a colleague stopped by to ask me how my house hunting was progressing. I told him that I hadn't yet found one I could afford. He suggested that I speak with a newly retired professor who lived in the village, which is how we became owners of an antique Yankee homestead.

In cleaning out the basement, I came across a box full of dissertation notes written by none other than the sisters True. I excitedly told my retired colleague about the three Maine teachers who had lived above us in Quincy. Without blinking, he replied in typical Down East fashion, "They were former students of mine who accompanied me and my wife to Boston for my residency." This discovery was very unnerving, because all spring long I had doubted my decision to return to New England. Discovering a connection between my new house and my childhood home was frighteningly prescient. I also feared that the True sisters had told him about my family.

The sisters moved out after Edith married a real estate agent from Waterville. A young, outgoing couple from Braintree moved in. Paul was a firefighter. Carol still wore his varsity football jacket. We sat on the porch during warm summer evenings, talking about the latest episode of *Route 66*.

I remember the day that Carol brought me upstairs to see her new canopy bed. Paul Junior was two at the time; David wasn't yet a month old. He was much darker than Paul, with a head of curly chestnut hair. Carol made me blush when she winked in mock seriousness and said, "Hey, Henry, you might be David's 'real' father."

Carol and Paul brought great joy into my life. They lived without the rancor or hostility I witnessed every day. They kissed a lot. It was novel to see people express so much love so openly. Moreover, Carol praised me every day—no one else ever had. Five years later, when I started to think about law school—most English majors at my college went to law school—I remembered her comments about my easy way around her children. Some of my fondest memories involved umping pickup baseball games, tutoring my cousin's child, and befriending an emotionally disturbed child in Burlington.

The more I thought, the more I realized that my future was in education. After all, one of the most important people in my life had been my seventh-grade guidance counselor. Her advocacy of working people influenced how I thought about myself. "Children," she'd said, arms outstretched, voice smooth and sincere, "you must not look down on those who work with their hands. There's dignity in work, even if it is picking up someone's garbage. It doesn't matter what you do, as long as you do it well." My parents were utterly shocked when I told them about Miss Wood's speech. Having worked with their hands their entire lives, they expected me to do something more with mine.

I abandoned the idea of law school completely after a chance meeting with my boyhood friend Dick. I asked him about his older brother. "Dave's working as a reading specialist with young children," he told me. "Really loves it." Hearing about his profession legitimized my decision to teach.

The last family to live upstairs was a skilled German machinist, with whom I worked, and his wife. Hans was a family man who knew a great deal about American politics. Soon after I arrived home from undergraduate school for summer vacation, he invited me up for an evening of conversation. Being an English major with a humanities background, I jumped at the chance to show off. Besides, his wife was very attractive.

We talked about Goethe and Nieztsche and drank Johnny Walker Black. The talk and the scotch nearly killed me. Although he had a technical school certificate, he also had a surprising breadth and depth of knowledge about philosophy. At the time, I still had neither a trade nor a love of books, which I treated as trophies to impress others.

Although my father was proud of me—as in, "This is my son Henry. He goes to college"—deep down he was suspicious of learned people. In his world, an expensive tailored suit and a college degree were of dubious merit. Educated people might speak brilliantly, but they were no different than hustlers. He had seen friends with children fired because they refused to work around cancer-causing chemicals. He had seen grown men cry after losing their pensions due to a protracted strike. He had seen glib lawyers and management types shrug their shoulders at the injustices that working people endured. Their modus operandi was not to think twice about cheating workers out of heath care, sick pay, or retirement provisions. Instead of looking for answers in a book, Dad's education came from witnessing the stoic grief of others.

Hans was different. He hadn't subordinated his roots to his literacy and learning, a demeanor in sharp contrast to my earlier role model, my college proctor. Jim was a well-bred kid from New York City who had a famous dad. He wrote a column for the college newspaper and edited our literary magazine. He was the only student to ace the advanced poetry class.

I heard him typing late at night and smelled the smoke from his cigarettes. His first drafts were his final drafts. He wore pin-striped, button-down shirts; cuffed charcoal-gray slacks, and a sports jacket without a tie. He read the *New York Times* and talked about art, foreign movies, contemporary fiction, and Broadway musicals. Coming from the Upper West Side, he knew how to dine in a four-star restaurant. He had been to Europe twice, had interned at his father's newspaper, and spent summers at Flying Head Point.

He also had a liberal-chic side: uncombed hair, a distinct body odor, and penny loafers without socks. He reminded me of my contemporary fiction professor, a recent graduate of the Iowa Writer's Workshop. Like him, Jim spoke in long sighs without direct eye contact, code for WASP-like superiority. Although he was afraid to get his hands dirty, he was most willing to pick apart my grammar. I took a deep breath whenever I spoke to him. He especially talked down to those of us who came to college lacking a background in books.

College buddies, ca. 1964-5

That was my group. We wore sweat pants to class and ate at the Dairy Queen—when we could afford it. We rarely read for enjoyment or put in long hours at the library. Our idea of current events was the latest box score. We hunted in the fall, went to Sunday mass, marched every Tuesday at ROTC, and cut classes whenever we could. We went to college to please our overworked parents.

Although I had nothing in common with Jim, I wanted to be just as witty, sophisticated, and urbane. I subscribed to a literary magazine called the *Saturday Review*. I read the *New York Times Review of Books*. I even joined the Book of the Month Club. I began to drink coffee, display my books, and experiment with smoking.

Yet I derived no pleasure from literary criticism or contemporary fiction. More important, Jim's lifestyle was costly. Best sellers were expensive, as were the latest Charlie Parker records, movie tickets, trips to Montreal, dry cleaning, and five-ounce hamburgers at Charlie's. Who was I kidding? I couldn't afford his brand of culture.

I needed a more down-to-earth role model. Although I admired my father's distrust of authority, I found his closed-mindedness difficult to accept. Jim's sophistication was appealing, but his narcissism offended me. Hans was unassuming about his joy in history. He was also happy to share his passions with me. I wanted to be like him.

My admiration of Hans was not the first time I had found direction in the workplace. Two summers earlier, I had worked with an elderly Scottish mechanic in the shipyard. My job was to grind out faulty welds from huge rings with a twenty-pound hand-held hydraulic grinder. It was numbing work, made dangerous by deafening noises and the foul smells of abrasives that could scorch black steel. Mr. Cameron made sure that I held my machine away from my body. Otherwise, I would have sliced off my leg, or worse.

At lunchtime, I left, exhausted, to rest outside in the clean air. Mr. Cameron never joined me. Instead, he went off by himself to eat and read. One day, as I passed him on my return to the work area, he asked me if I enjoyed poetry. His question caught me off guard. My only focus in this place was the 3:30 blast to pack away my tools. "Um ... of course ... I like the romantic poets ... John Keats ... bought a new biography about him last fall."

"Do you know who Robert Burns is?" he asked.

"He's a Scottish poet, isn't he? There's a statue of him near my church."

"That's right. Do you know any of his poems?"

"My bonnie lives over the ocean?"

"Oh, you mean ..." He recited that poem verbatim and added two more of his favorites. He said proudly, "I know them all by heart. I eat with Bobby Burns every day. I carry his verses in my pocket. You see this book?" He took a small leather-bound volume from his rear pocket. "I've had this book since I was a child. I take it every place I go. Bobby Burns takes me home."

Both Hans and Mr. Cameron influenced my moral and literacy development. They were skilled artisans who read philosophy, poetry, and history. Their literacies were not expressions of privilege but ways to humanize their experience. Jim's literacy wasn't. He was a kid, worried about impressing and living up to his father. Literacy was a tool he used to make himself "special."

Solitary Places

Although we were renters, I never considered myself inferior to friends who lived in their own homes. Our floors were maple and accented with scatter rugs. The woodwork was dark-stained pine, as were the doors. The wood had a rich patina that glowed warmly against darkened brass fixtures. The rooms were average size, with eight-foot ceilings. A long corridor connected the front door entrance to the kitchen. Upon entering the house, you either headed straight to the kitchen or turned into the living room, which was connected to the dining room by a ten-foot opening. Another door opened to the kitchen, with its maple wainscoting. If you walked toward the kitchen and turned right, you would see the bathroom and my parents' bedroom. My bedroom was off the kitchen. Opposite my door was the entrance to the back porch and the basement. The walk-in pantry door was located in the far corner.

Grandmother Rose continued to live with us until my brother turned three and was too big to sleep in our parents' room. Robert is sitting on my lap on the right side of the front row. Grandmother Rose is standing above us.

Grandmother Rose shared her room with me. I still remember the smell of her age. Our beds were metal. A long oak writing table, stained lustrous brown, separated them. The table was the kind that one would find in libraries, ringed with books. My grandmother continued to live with us until my brother turned three and was too big to sleep in our parents' room. That year she moved in with Aunt Lucy.

My parents replaced her polished wood with chrome and Formica. Other changes followed. Gone were the soapstone sink and the old cast-iron stove with its compartment for baking potatoes. We traded the old wooden refrigerator for a modern one. The water heater remained another five years. I was vaguely aware that we were rejecting the life that she had provided for her children.

When Aunt Lucy moved to California we inherited her maple bedroom set and mahogany dining room table. Out went more metal and oak. Fortunately, the old painting of two women in Victorian day dresses—one fair-haired, the other dark—escaped the trash heap. These ladies pulled me in opposite directions. Hollywood expected me to fancy the blonde, blue-eyed lass, but I preferred the exotic look of the woman with the black hair.

The final change came when my parents replaced my grandmother's Persian rugs with wall-to-wall carpeting and linoleum. They also purchased store-bought paintings and new lamps, completing our break with the past.

The basement, a special place to me, remained relatively unscathed by the mad rush into modernity. Each family had a separate storage space and furnace. A five-foot-high partition of amber-colored two-by-tens divided the sections. Our space was small, about twenty by twenty, very dark and dusty. When I was in the seventh grade, Gus helped Dad and I build a long, sturdy tool bench along the outside wall, under the coal window. It was my treasured space in which to build things and listen to the radio.

A coal bin, brimming with black, shiny nuggets the size of my fist, sat next to the workbench. We were the only family in the house to heat with coal. The others had converted to natural gas in 1954. The furnace was circular and rust colored, framed by a huge iron door. A separate door allowed access to the ashes.

My father lit the furnace in October and kept it going until April. The coal-truck driver would park on the street, about thirty feet from the house, and assemble the long, black chute that shuttled the coal from the truck to our bin. Then he opened the latch on the truck and out flew a ton of coal in a cloud of black dust.

Stoking the furnace was a real adventure. My father had to stir up the cinders and shovel in new coal before he went to work every morning and again when he came home at four o'clock. On cold nights, he returned a third time before going to bed. I went down to watch him keep us warm. First, he turned the grate to loosen the charred embers. Then he shoveled them into a heavy metal barrel, about three feet high. When it was full, he rolled it onto its side and under the porch outdoors. Every Thursday, he hoisted the barrels above the steps to the curb for city pickup.

Behind the furnace lived an elegantly framed picture of a man dressed in a suit and upturned bow tie. I knew from his appearance that he had to have lived long ago because he reminded me of the men in the silent movies. "Dad, who's that?" I asked.

"My father."

"Where is he?"

"He's dead. I grew up without a father."

"Did he die in the war?"

"No."

"How old was he when he died?"

"Aunt Connie knows those things."

My grandfather's portrait whetted my appetite for the family's history. Having one day spied a dozen or so boxes covered with spider webs, my imagination ran wild—even more so when my father said that he didn't know what was in them. "They're Nana's junk," he told me. The next day, I went into the basement with lights blazing. I found an old root beer stand before I dashed upstairs.

Later, I explored a safer section of the cellar, where I found a tennis racket on top of a trunk beneath the stairs. I was perplexed; Italians didn't play tennis. My father told me that it belonged to my Aunt Connie, but that's all he said. My questions annoyed him, so I asked my grandmother. "Nana, why did Aunt Connie have a tennis racket?"

"Concetta went to college. She took the trolley to get there every day. She was a very smart girl and even won a scholarship. She played tennis with her American friends at college. I made her a white tennis outfit."

I felt my grandmother's pride in her daughter's accomplishments. I was proud too and decided to be just like my aunt and go to college when I grew up.

I wanted to ask about my grandfather but was too fearful because she stiffened when I referred to the picture in the basement. I asked her instead to tell me about the "old country." She seemed to enjoy my curiosity and brought me into the dining room, where she opened the mahogany sideboard. She took out a silk flag trimmed in yellow tassels. It was a map of Italy and Sicily. Beside it, she placed a faded picture of a man with a mustache. She said, "Italy is shaped like a woman's boot. See the heel and the toe?" I did. She continued in a tone I had never heard before, "Italy is kicking Sicily like a ball." She sounded as if she had been slapped in the face. Looking at the pointed toe, I experienced her pain.

It was the first time that I made a connection to metaphor. Fixing her glasses, she pushed the picture in front of me. The paper was gray and old. I remember her hand on my head as she smoothed my hair. "This is my brother. He was a famous engineer. He lived in Egypt." I didn't know where that was, but I sensed that she saw something of him in me.

The True sisters stored boxes of books in neat rows on their side of the cellar. I looked through them now and again, especially the pictures of athletes in their old yearbooks. They were so ancient-looking in those baggy outfits.

In junior high, I used my carpentry skills to turn their section of the basement into a weight-training room, an idea from a friend who had parties in his pine-walled basement. I wanted a hangout too, so I organized a work crew to help me clean out the dust and cobwebs. First, we washed down the granite walls and painted them white. Next, we scrubbed the concrete floor and built a platform over it, putting our shop-class skills to good use. We hung a cheap mirror on one side and plastered cutouts of our favorite athletes on the other.

I also remodeled the coal bin after my dad replaced the furnace. The bin had been empty for some time, and I needed privacy. He thought I was nuts when I told him about my plan. I, however, remained undaunted. As I rubbed off fifty years of coal dust, old wide-pine boards glowed amber-pumpkin. I washed the floor, put in a rug, and ran an extension cord over the front wall. I even found an old maple chair and table under a canvas cover. I finally had a place to call my own.

Alone in the cellar, I would stare at my grandfather's portrait. His debonair appearance made me respect him, and I wondered why he had been relegated to a coal bin. Was it because he had left my father a near-orphan and my grandmother a widow? My grievance against him was less admirable—being named after him made me feel poles apart from my American friends.

One day, I was so engrossed in thought that I didn't hear the True sisters come down the steps. I slipped behind the partition as Bertha scribbled something on a notepad in a very efficient manner. Blanche looked uncomfortable. Reaching into a box, she pulled out an old handkerchief and wiped off her shoes, saying," I'd love to ball this up and put it in Henry's mouth. I can't take his yelling anymore."

Bertha replied, "Stella says his growl keeps people from pushing him around at the shipyard."

"I'm not buying that," Blanch responded. "She told me that Mrs. Amoroso took out her fury on him. She wanted him to be a girl. Seems his father had done something awful to her."

I had always pictured my grandmother as holy and pure, not an avenging angel. I thought again about my father's temper. Perhaps there was a reason behind it.

On the Street

The houses on our side of the street were well-kept, multifamily units. One neighbor was an elderly Italian man who fertilized his tomatoes with chicken droppings. Like other Italian men in the neighborhood, he also cultivated Concord grapes. His vines turned and twisted over a wooden and wire-mesh shell that measured six feet high by twenty feet wide and thirty feet deep. On summer evenings and Sunday afternoons, he sat at a wooden table under this pale green canopy and sipped a glass of homemade wine.

Each August, the sweet scent of his grapes tempted every boy in the neighborhood. Although we had tired of baseball, we found our gloves and marched down the driveway to my backyard. What better excuse to climb under his fence than to search for an errant pitch that just happened to roll under his vines? We never got past the third row of tomato plants, though. Mrs. Descere would spy us from her kitchen window, where she sat in her white apron, ready to scare us off. We lost more than a dozen baseballs that way.

Her youngest son, Joe, a recently discharged sailor, lived in the second-floor apartment with his new wife and stepdaughter. Joe caused quite a scandal in the neighborhood when he married a divorced Southern woman. She was very young and attractive. Our houses were close enough that we could hear each other's conversations. One morning, I overheard him complaining about her sitting in front of the mirror instead of keeping house. He also hated her wearing jeans to Shop n' Save. She demanded that he not leave after supper every evening. "You're never home. Play softball tonight, and I'll lock you out." This threat angered him even more, as he was one of the best fastball pitchers in Quincy. She moved back to Virginia a few months later. I overheard my parents say that Joe never should have married a divorced woman.

Gus Sanford and his invalid wife lived on our other side. They were the first residents on the street to own a TV. I used to go to his house to watch westerns. When I was older, I saw the same ones at the theater for fourteen cents. After Gus's wife died, he took in a boarder, Steve. Gus and Steve played catch every night on the sidewalk; sometimes Dad and I joined them after supper. I enjoyed their stories about great ballplayers like Walter Johnson and Babe Ruth. Their tales gave the impression that they had played with them when they were young men.

I adored Gus. He knew how to fix things, hunt in the north woods, and play baseball. Although he had a semi-nude calendar in his basement, he never used profanities around me. I remember him singing songs like "Summer Time in the Rockies" and "Cruising Down the River on Sunday Afternoon." On Sundays, when I went to mass with my dad, Gus and Steve packed an old laundry tub with ice and Narragansett beer and headed to Milton to play baseball. Gus used a size forty-one bat with a fat handle that I couldn't swing without hitting the ground. I could hardly wait to grow up.

Across the street were single-family homes with hedges, trees, and bigger yards. To our right lived a middle-aged couple who never spoke to me. Next to them lived the Andrews family, another elderly couple whose children had grown up and moved away. They were considerate; Mrs. Andrews always asked me about my schoolwork.

The Mazzetti family, Italian Americans with five children, lived next to the Andrewses. Janet was the eldest and my first love. Her brother Johnny was my brother's age. We played together in a large field behind their home. Their dad liked us to call him Johnny. He owned a bowling alley and billiards parlor. Like Joe next door, there was something mysterious about him. He always wore dark blue tailored suits, kept his hair well trimmed, and drove a late-model Mercury. His kids dressed in hand-me-downs and didn't mind asking us for something to eat. He was rarely home; when he was, he slept. The family didn't go on trips, but Johnny flew frequently to Cuba to gamble. His kids went with us to get ice cream cones. My father's favorite complaint was, "Johnny doesn't do anything for his kids, but they adore him. I kill myself for you and your brother, yet you show me no respect."

Kendrick Avenue was a main route between Braintree and the Bethlehem Steel Shipyard, the largest employer on South Shore. We lived at the bottom of the street, where the steady noise of cars accelerating or downshifting never stopped. At the top of the street stood the Adams School, where I learned to read, write, and compare myself to others. No matter how hard I tried, someone else always finished ahead of me. I did, however, accomplish something that no other student had—I befriended Mr. Mills, the principal. In fact, I had an open invitation to stop by his office whenever I wanted. This arrangement was shockingly unique; he never even spoke to students.

Mr. Mills was overweight and menacing. He wore baggy three-piece suits, never smiled, and pulled kids aside for tongue lashings or paddle spankings. Whenever he walked into our classroom, we froze and folded our hands, each of us earnestly praying not to be his latest victim. His reputation for disciplining troublemakers was so legendary that we ran when we spotted his old gray coupe turning into the schoolyard. The first kid to spot him screamed, "Head for the hills—here comes Mills!"

One day he stopped me in the corridor and said, "Henry, please come with me to my office." I was surprised but unafraid because he had asked me kindly. This was the first time I had been to his office. It was very small and dark. He sat next to a large walnut-stained antique roll-top desk. I sat beside him in a matching bow chair. The highly glossed

395

light maple floor contrasted nicely with the dark luster of the furniture and the trim. Our conversation went something like the following:

"I usually don't ask pupils here unless they've done something wrong, but I asked you here to tell you that you're a fine young man. Your parents must be very proud of you."

I blushed. "Thank you."

"I wish that all the other children were as well mannered." I sat with perfect posture. He continued, "Henry, I've selected you to be my special helper. Whenever I need a message or a letter delivered to one of my teachers, I'll ask you to take it."

I had never been anyone's special helper. In the months ahead, he still snapped at the other children but kept his promise to me. I must have gone on a dozen errands. Every time he came for me, I levitated out of my seat. His friendship gave me confidence as I entered junior high across town. He believed in me.

Faxon Park served as the eastern boundary of my neighborhood. Aside from two duplexes on the street that abutted it, the rest were 1920s-style single-family dwellings with neatly trimmed yards. No Italian American or Catholic families resided here, but my good friend Richard did. During the war, my aunts Lucy and Connie had shared an apartment in the corner duplex. My best friend lived there now. His mom was my Cub Scout den leader. Each week, we worked on projects that advanced our skills as she told us wonderful stories about Scouts who helped less fortunate people—stories about courage, obedience, and courteousness, values with which I was familiar.

As the meetings ended, she passed out fresh homemade cookies for us to eat on the way home. One Scout was unwashed and messy, out of place. He made us fearful. One night, as I wrapped my cookies in a napkin, he marched over to me. "Want to see a rabbit?" he asked. I looked back at Mrs. Flaven, but she had left the room. My instincts told me to say no; he looked like he was going to get me into trouble, but I decided to go with him. We were, after all, fellow den members. "Sure," I said.

"Follow me."

We entered the park where the brook passed under the street. I knew exactly where to step, having walked this way many times. As soon as we were on the other side of the brook, he said, "Bend down and look under the old trunk." I knelt down and stretched out to see the hole. Just then, I felt a heavy blow to my neck. I cringed in pain, and my cookies dropped to the ground. Laughing, the bully picked them up, saying, "You're so stupid." He'd kept his word about a rabbit, except it was a rabbit punch with his open hand. Terribly embarrassed, I forced back the tears. As I walked home, I wondered why he had picked on me.

The humiliation of this incident didn't keep me out of Faxon Park, a vast wooded area donated to the city in 1885 by Henry Harwick Faxon. A stone wall, too long to follow from start to finish, encircled it. Thick, knotty oaks—many wrapped in vines—and massive rocks gave the illusion of being in the Wild West or the jungles of Africa. Several trails crisscrossed the park. One led to the picnic area and baseball field; another headed to Lover's Lane, where young couples sat on stone benches, inhaling the scent of the distant sea.

We were always thrilled to run through the woods, on the lookout for an ambush. Our only worry was the poison ivy that grew along the rocky trails or the occasional teenager who spied us. I also enjoyed taking long walks to my private lookout to sit and think.

The most expensive homes in the neighborhood were those built opposite the park in the late forties and early fifties. They were spacious, contemporary in style, and landscaped with big green lawns and older trees. A number of families put in swimming pools. Kids from my neighborhood rarely received invitations to these homes. One time, however, a classmate asked three of us over to swim and play croquet. After the fun, I walked home full of self-importance. Knowing where I had been, my father growled, "Come off your high horse."

Phipps Street, north of the park's entrance, was an extension of the eastern boundary of the neighborhood. It was a steep, narrow street, crowded with box-shaped homes, paved yards, and chain-link fences. Second-generation Italians set out statues of the Blessed Virgin on tiny lawns. Their children roughed up outsiders and received whippings from Mr. Mills. They knew that I was related to Frankie Colabro, so they left me alone. This was my father's first neighborhood and the one to which my grandmother returned at the end of her life.

Our western boundary was Franklin Street, a wide route that

descended gradually from Penn's Hill to Quincy Square. An orchard and two dairy farms stood sentry at the top of the hill. The Adamses' houses were at its base. Abigail Adams had taken her son, John Quincy Adams, to the top of Penn's Hill to watch the Battle of Bunker Hill, twelve miles to the north. In early May, pink dogwoods stretched from the top of Franklin Street to the bottom.

Grandmother Rose had moved to a side street off Franklin in 1940, and I was born there four years later. In 1951, my uncle built Aunt Lucy a brick home atop Penn's Hill on land owned by an old Yankee family who had no heirs. I longed for the same seclusion, away from pavement, congestion, and noise.

The Ethics of Caring

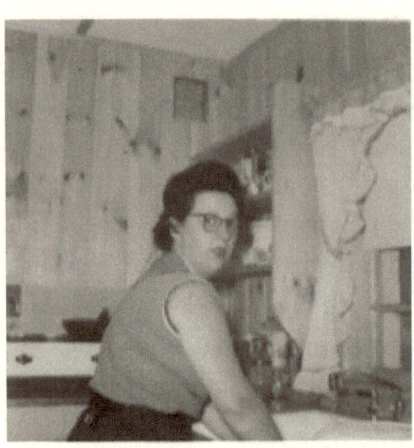

My mother began to lose her hearing at sixteen but this would have an advantage later in life. When my father snapped, she'd simply shut off her hearing aid.

My mother had lost her hearing at sixteen, a fact that at least afforded her some peace when my father snapped; she simply shut off her hearing aid. She could easily have been frustrated by his abuse and taken it out on us, but she was a very even-tempered person. She knew about his pent-up anger and didn't judge him.

Instead of reprimanding, scolding, or lecturing, she listened. One day, a friend and I were making a model when he accidentally spilled the bottle of paint thinner onto our new mahogany table. It ran through the newspaper and the tablecloth and left an ugly blotch on the finish. Instead of exploding or demanding compensation, Mom asked us what had happened. When we told her that it had been an accident, she merely said that she was sorry we had used the dining room table instead of the kitchen table. Her manner was calm and respectful. She didn't punish us but chose instead to teach us about prevention.

All parents want to protect their children from danger, and my mother was no different. She had rules but also wanted me to think for myself. When I was a young boy, the most feared place to swim was Echo Lake, an abandoned quarry deep inside Faxon Park. We knew about the undertow at Nantasket Beach and the floating excrement at Avalon Beach. We even knew about the sinkholes up at Houghton's Pond. The quarry was much more menacing. At the beach, you could touch the sandy bottom if you got a cramp. At the quarry, you sank into a black, bottomless pit, never to be seen again. Drownings occurred regularly.

Only the really tough guys dared to jump in feet first. No one went there to have a good time or to catch a tan. You went there, heart in hand, to prove your manhood. As soon as you hit the water, you pulled yourself out. Rumor had it that if sunken debris didn't knock you unconscious, huge flesh-eating fish lurking in the deep would tear you apart. I can vouch for the latter rumor. One hot summer afternoon, my friend and I spied a four-foot beast sunning near the surface.

Quincy was dotted with more than fifty abandoned quarries like the one in my neighborhood. Between 1750 and 1962, Swedish, Finnish, Scottish, and Irish immigrant workers mined Quincy granite. Cranes, gin poles, and other rigging lifted the monstrous stones out of deep holes, hundreds of feet below the surface. Several of the sites had long been filled in as a precaution against drowning. Not so with our quarry. Located in the southern corner of the park, right across the Braintree line, it served as a magnet for every teenage boy who dared test his courage.

The quarry, cut into a hill more than a hundred years before, released about three hundred feet of pure spring water. The southerly side was level and open to the water. About twenty feet on each side of the opening, rust-colored granite walls rose in a circular loop until the sides merged more than a hundred feet above the water. The eastern side was too slanted for jumping. The western side, where the jump spots were located, shot up in jagged ledges. To get to them, jumpers had to crawl down from the top of the rim. Each spot had a name. The lowest, Betsy, was fifteen feet above the water. The next one was Lowery, twenty-five feet up. The third was about forty feet high. The highest peak, Suicide, was so high that kids got dizzy from peering down into the icy, dark water below.

As the name suggests, jumping off Suicide wasn't easy. Tree limbs and sharp outcroppings shot out from the ragged wall. To clear the obstacles, jumpers had to take a running start. Only a handful of people ever made it. The legendary Frankie Colabro was one of them. He did it the summer of '56, his first day back from reform school. They called him Brickhead because he hit the water headfirst rather than feet first. Word was that a sailor stationed at the shipyard tried it when he was drunk. He was ripped apart by the trees before he made it to the water. Part of his underwear could be seen dangling from a snapped birch limb that summer.

One July afternoon, soon after I turned thirteen, Norman McCloud asked me if I wanted to swim at the quarry. Two years older, he was a good kid and a good student—the only person I knew who took Latin in junior high. Although he didn't play organized sports, he was a good athlete and a reliable first baseman and lead-off hitter who played every day at Faxon Park.

He could see my uncertainty about joining him. On the one hand, I imagined a horrible death, slipping during takeoff and smashing into the side of the ledge before I made the water. On the other hand, I was the only kid left on the block who hadn't tested his courage at the quarry. My cowardice embarrassed me; after all, I was the star running back on the school's football team.

Sensing my fear, Norman said, "Henry, my brother Roger will be with us. He's home from summer camp. He's a sophomore at Norwich University and knows a lot about swimming. Just tell your mother that Roger will be there."

I walked confidently into the kitchen to ask permission to go to the quarry. Mom was sitting at the table, peeling the blackened skins off roasted peppers. "Mom, Norman's out on the front porch. He wants to know if I can go swimming at the quarry."

She looked at me with the wisdom of Solomon. "Isn't that dangerous?"

"I'll be okay," I replied. "Roger is going to be with us. He goes to a military college in Vermont."

She knew that I could be courting trouble, but she also knew that transitions were essential. She looked up and said confidently, "Be careful."

At that very moment, I grew up. I ran into the bathroom, grabbed a towel, and shot out the door. I didn't bother hunting for my bathing suit; no one wore one at the quarry. Norman and I walked up to the entrance of Faxon Park and took the shortcut next to Mrs. Licone's house. Five minutes later, we passed the ball field and headed for the water fountain near the parking area. The quarry path started near the gravel pile. I turned around to see if my brother had followed me. I didn't want him along. If word got back to my father about my adventure, both my mother and I would be in big trouble.

We pushed back the briars carefully and eased our way over moss-covered rocks to solid ground. Enormous granite boulders, worn with age, stood opposite each other along the path. Their rounded, somnolent shadows mixed with those from the old oak trees to block out the afternoon sun. The trail sloped down to the right for about three hundred feet before it ran into the old stone wall that cut through the park. For the most part, the wall was in good shape, about three feet high and as thick. As a member of the Youth Corps Workers, my father had helped build it in 1933 with rust-colored rocks from another quarry in the park. They had rounded its top to prevent rain erosion and capped it with a thin layer of spicy brown cement. Unfortunately, the design had not protected the stones from vandals. One of the games we used to play was leaping over the smashed sections until we could go no farther.

Norman and I straddled the loose rocks that spotted the trail. An occasional sock, empty bag of Wise Potato Chips, or a Coke bottle littered the ground. Sharp prickers and dandy grass mixed with the trash. Tiny green berries also grew along the trail. In another month, we would return to snack on ripened blueberries. Using our caps as pails, we would pick just enough for our mothers to make sweet muffins and pancakes for breakfast.

The earth smelled clean, and the woods were still. We were by ourselves with our thoughts. The trail continued its descent to the right.

After walking briskly for five minutes, we spied the enormous black girders of the shipyard just above the tree line. We stopped to look at the latest destroyer being built in the second bay, but the shipyard was too far off to see my dad. We turned to the right and ceremoniously raised our middle fingers to the owners of the white-tiled house that was just visible above the western tree line. We shook our heads in disgust at the violation of our domain.

The quiet was broken only by a squirrel that scampered across dried oak leaves or an occasional hawk that circled overhead. Massive outcroppings of pale-green rock surrounded us. We paused at the latest graffiti—*Buddy '53*. I wondered who he was. As if reading my thoughts, Norman said, "He's Tommie Marino's cousin. Went into the navy 'cause he was kicked out of school."

We too fell silent as we neared the quarry. We slowed and walked carefully, not wanting anyone to know we were there. Older teenagers were known to ambush kids and throw them into the quarry. Before long, we reached the clearing next to Suicide. Roger was already swimming without fear and yelled up to us. We waved and backed off slowly onto the trail, following it around the rim until we reached the far side. The last fifty feet were a blur as we dashed across loose gravel not five feet from the edge of the precipice. We crawled down to Betsy, stripped off our clothes, grabbed our crotches, and—shrieking obscenities—jumped into the cold, deep water below.

School Learning

Home and School Literacies

Like my father, my mother had left school before she graduated. She was a wife and a parent, not a child psychologist or behavior specialist. I don't think that she ever read Dr. Spock or other self-help books. Yet she raised us with love. Martin Luther King Jr. described people like her:

> Everybody can be great because anybody can serve. You don't have to have a college degree to serve. You don't have to make your subject and your verb agree to

serve. You don't have to know about Plato and Aristotle to serve. You don't have to know Einstein's theory of relativity to serve. You do not have to know the second theory of thermodynamics to serve. You only need a heart full of grace. A soul generated by love (From "The Drum Major Instinct," a sermon by Rev. Martin Luther King, Jr., 1968).

My mother learned her parenting skills intuitively from her mother. It was as natural for her to forgive as it was for me to be afraid of the dark. She had genuine love for my brother and me. Her goal was to give us space to grow.

Like my father, my mother left school before she graduated. She was no child psychologist or behavior specialist. She simply raised my brother and me with love, and gave us space to grow.

I recall an outing to the branch library on Franklin Street, about a mile from our house. I must have been five, because she pushed Robert in a carriage. The library was windowless and small. I couldn't find any books that I wanted and started to complain about the heat. Mom chose a few books, and we departed. I was happy just to be with her.

I don't remember going to the library with her again, nor do I recall hearing bedtime stories. The one experience that sticks in my mind took place about the time she went to work. I had come home for lunch, expecting an empty house. To my surprise, Mom was there, having become ill at work. I had a book with me, and she asked what I was reading. I told her a poem about the sun. She recognized it from her childhood. Smiling, she read it aloud as we sat together at the kitchen table. Mr. Sun visited the children in the summer to warm them with his golden rays. Old Man Winter chased him away, and annoying clouds blocked him out sometimes. But Mr. Sun smiled, knowing that he would return to nurture the children.

I cherished this quiet moment alone with her and didn't want it to end. Like Mr. Sun, Mom calmed me with affection. I could count on her to return every evening to take care of me. Just her presence encouraged me to do well in school, and her love became the foundation for all my learning. I wanted to please her as she pleased me.[14]

Although my mom didn't provide instructional or managerial support—she wasn't comfortable due to a lack of formal education—she was still the driving force behind my motivation to succeed in school. As I grew up, my impetus shifted to argument. Aristotle believed that the human soul naturally seeks harmony through knowledge (see Chapter 4 of his *Poetics* or the very first sentence of his *Metaphysics*), a curiosity that he called *periérgeia*. I definitely had *periérgeia*, and it was about the past. I used to go into my grandmother's old chest to look at her American flag and pictures of her family. The few books I read were about historical athletes and inventors. Television shows about medieval castles or pirates fascinated me. A sixth-grade unit on ancient Egypt led me to purchase a book called *The Epic of Man*. Ancient times inspired me.

Stories like *A Christmas Carol*, *Treasure Island*, and *Tom Sawyer* fed my interest in the past. The melodies in Paine's *Common Sense* and Longfellow's *Evangeline* filled me with music. By the time I was fourteen, one of my favorite places to go was the Thomas Crane Public Library in Quincy Square. Built in 1885 from local granite and brownstone, this impressive Romanesque structure—with its grand turrets, eyebrow windows, and red tile roof—was my hideout. The interior included an ornamental fireplace, finely crafted woodwork, and stained-glass windows. I would sit in the reading room for hours, browsing through old books. I found great joy in holding the leather-bound volumes, but I could never make myself read one. Instead, I studied the illustrations and skimmed through chapters, perhaps stopping to read a paragraph or two. Long, impenetrable sentences made too many demands on me.

Paul Theroux (1996) captures my frustration: "[G]reat writers inspire me by first proving me stupid and then making me feel wise" (p.95 of *My Other Life*) oks made me feel stupid. When I started one, I felt dumb; if I stuck with it, though, I felt smart. The dangerous time was at the beginning. If the information captured my imagination, I would engage, but dry, pedantic prose bored me.

School also contributed to my reluctance to stay with a story. We had to read brief stories out of common textbooks called basal readers, which were full of words like "walk," "see," and "there," words that reading experts had decided were important to learn. Writers introduced these words in a story and then repeated them several times so that students could easily memorize them. Teachers drilled and questioned us about characters who owned pets, lived in pleasant homes on tidy streets, and went fishing in the country with pipe-smoking granddads. My grandfather was short, round, and bald and never spent time with me alone, so I couldn't relate to the stories emotionally.[15]

Little changed in the upper grades. Instruction emphasized spelling, grammar, penmanship, and reading. Lessons were brief, self-contained, and centered on finding answers to specific questions, remembering one's place while reading aloud, following directions, staying within margins, and copying sentences neatly. Little space existed for creativity, excitement, or stimulation. We worked alone at our desks, reading from schoolbooks or completing exercises from the chalkboard or worksheets.

Francis Parker and the Quincy Experiment

My school experiences were ironic, given the fact that seventy-five years earlier the Adams School had been the site of Francis W. Parker's famous Quincy Experiment, America's first attempt to reform public education. The city had also been one of the first in the country to establish common schools. In fact, Horace Mann, the father of the common school movement, served as supervisor in Quincy for five years. The city allowed children from all classes to attend elementary and secondary education at taxpayers' expense. [16] Quincy was a historic city whose foundations went back to the English settlers of 1692, who came to farm its rocky soil. John and John Quincy Adams, both legislators and presidents, and John Hancock, the first signer of the Declaration of Independence, were born here. Many families prospered and were able to send their sons to any one of several private academies in the area.

Like other communities during the second half of the nineteenth century, Quincy's agrarian character was in transition. Fishing, quarrying, and commercial endeavors had taken hold. Immigrants from Ireland, Scotland, and Scandinavia satisfied the labor needs of the new industries, constructing new roads, office buildings, housing, churches, and other infrastructures needed to support the expanding economy. The children of these new Americans went to tax-supported public schools. Many were the sons and daughters of men who worked at punishing jobs in the quarry pits of West Quincy and women who worked as domestic servants for the wealthy.

As recorded by Partridge (1883), in 1875, the Quincy School Committee, caught up in the rhetoric of assessment, determined that "after eight years of attendance in the public schools, 'the children could neither write with facility nor read fluently; nor could they speak or spell their own language perfectly.'" It went on to say that "'the whole existing system was wrong—a system from which the life had gone out. The school year had become one long period of diffusion and cram, and smatter had become the order of the day'" (xvii).

The high rate of failure did not sit well with city leaders. Schools, they felt, had failed to carry out their civic mandate because teachers taught the wrong things in the wrong ways. They taught literacy by rote, reduced history to slogans, and limited numeracy to endless drill. No wonder parents complained that their children arrived home weary. Quincy's curriculum—with its emphasis on memorization, mental training, and examinations—had failed to educate the mass of new Americans from working- and lower-class families.

A drastic change had to occur. The committee invited Francis W. Parker—a professional educator and administrator who had just returned to the United States from two years of advanced study in history, philosophy, and pedagogics at King William's University in Berlin—to become Superintendent of Schools. His credentials were impressive: family ties to New England educators, successful grammar school teaching throughout New England, varied school administrative duties in the Midwest, and a distinguished military record with the Union Army.

Prior to his studies in Germany, Parker had developed instructional techniques based on his observations of children's learning. He had his teachers try them out, first in Manchester, New Hampshire, and then in Dayton, Ohio. Many teachers resisted the methods, which contradicted time-honored practices. For years, traditionalists had assumed that the mind was a muscle, with separate facilities like memory and perception, that learners needed to exercise. Thus, the study of Latin, with its rigid demands on drill and recitation, improved a learner's mental toughness.

Disheartened by teacher resistance to his ideas, Parker left for Germany to consult with recognized scholars in pedagogy. He first familiarized himself with the writings of great teachers and thinkers of the past. In Comenius (1649/1967), he found justification for having children learn actively rather than memorizing information. Pestalozzi (1894, 1951) reinforced this point by arguing that learners understood truths better via discovery than memorization. Both theorists solidified Parker's commitment to active learning.

He then turned his attention to the central question about education. Froebel's (1826/2005) assertion that the aim of education is the harmonious growth of the individual connected nicely with Parker's belief that learning is the natural unfolding of inner tendencies. Herbart's (1892) concept about the moral development of children appealed to him as well. Good character, illustrated through the history of literature, provides the best life preparation.

When he arrived in Quincy, Parker set out to free children from learning that focused completely on silence and industriousness. Teachers covered pages of text and then tested students on facts. They also tested children in May to determine promotion and retention.

Parker praised teachers who worked toward change and criticized those who used techniques that did not require much preparation.

He argued that ideals like the love of truth and humility, not skill and knowledge, are the primary aims of education. All subjects are simply means by which to develop character and can be "beautifully taught" if grounded in respect for the learner. He referred to children as "little ones" and forbade teachers from scolding them when they made mistakes.

Parker assumed that learning occurred when children were unconscious of a subject's inherent difficulties. He banned fear tactics for gaining their attention. Instead, he taught teachers how to exploit the natural power of the child's imagination and curiosity for learning and problem solving. He expected teachers to be good storytellers and artists to stimulate learning. He referred to phonics as harsh and unnatural and replaced it with literature and writing. He advocated the simultaneous teaching of reading and writing and believed that children developed vocabulary better from writing than reading. He even had students read each other's compositions. He knew firsthand that children have different capacities, so he divided classes into instructional groups according to mental abilities. He called the memorization of historical generalizations "useless rubbish" and replaced the practice with histories adapted for children. Finally, he believed that the greatest obstacle to real teaching was the standard examination, which he replaced with assessments of real work over time.

The results of his innovations were dramatic. Partridge (1882) proudly reported that 80 percent of tested students showed satisfactory to excellent results. The study lacked modern statistical controls, but objectivity was not the point. Word spread rapidly about the positive results. Thousands of educators rushed to Quincy to learn about Parker's remarkable teaching methods. The Boston School Committee offered him the highly prestigious position of Supervisor of Boston Public Schools.

Soon after his departure, however, the reforms that he had put in place crumbled. Patrick Shannon (1990) believes that this failure occurred because Parker had not bothered to have his teachers fully embrace his plan. Without his charismatic leadership to keep them focused on change, they returned to the tried-and-true when he left.

Shannon concludes that Parker's ideology of child centeredness died because it lacked moral and political leadership.

Remarkable in itself is the school committee's mandate to overhaul the curriculum so thoroughly. In accepting this charge, Parker had to confront teachers, many of whom must have reacted poorly to his heavy-handed tactics. To adjust curriculum for individual children takes a great deal of work, so little wonder that some teachers were relieved when he left. Had he been coercive? Inflexible? Had he offended their underlying beliefs about the nature of childhood? Many of Quincy's teachers grew up in churches that preached the doctrine of original sin and its corollary: breaking children's will to save them from destroying themselves.

By the time I entered the Adams School, Quincy had completed its transformation into an urban-industrial city. In 1896, Thomas Watson, an associate of Alexander Graham Bell's, tried farming on the shores of the Fore River on the Quincy/Braintree line. He failed, so he turned his attention to what he knew: the technology of engines. Within a few years, he received huge government contracts to build warships. There were not enough men to fill the jobs, so he sent his lieutenants overseas to find cheap labor.

They found thousands of willing workers in Italy and other southern European countries. Many were illiterate and unfamiliar with industrial shops and Anglo-Protestant values. Even more arrived in Quincy sick from the voyage and the train trip from New York City. Others wanted to be left alone or return home as soon as they earned enough money. Those who stayed found rooms with other families in hastily constructed and unkempt wooden houses.

The men went to work not knowing the grief they faced: air filled with dust and dangerous fumes, machines that cut off fingers, and bosses who stood over them all day. Still, they went to their jobs and returned at night, tired and haggard, their faces and clothes black with soot, grease, and dust. Ultimately, despair would push them to strike for better working conditions.

In the meantime, they resigned themselves to the sicknesses that stole their lives. They knew that their lungs were filling with poison, but they accepted the fact as an inevitable consequence of the job that fed their families. When sickness hit, it usually lasted a long time. When they died, wives—who simply had no inkling that their husbands were in danger—quickly did the same. Others were left with their children to struggle the best they could. Life was hard for immigrant widows in Quincy. Some went door to door, often with a baby in tow, trying to find cleaning jobs. Others found work in sweatshops or stayed at home to crochet piecework for rich people.

Their children enrolled in the public schools unable to speak English. Coming from overcrowded homes with little privacy and no protection from frustrated adults, they were tired, hungry, and cold. Others were mature beyond their years, having helped their mothers raise younger siblings. Many became completely paralyzed by the names that others called them.

These immigrant children must have overwhelmed their teachers, most of whom were young women who earned less than five hundred dollars a year.[17] Children came to school with linguistic and cultural differences, emotional needs, and little academic preparation. Along with having to learn basic educational principles, they needed to embrace American political and civic virtues so as to assimilate rapidly into American society. Finally, they had to acquire the discipline and conforming attitudes of the workplace to replace their fathers and uncles when their time came, all too soon.

Teachers had little about which to cheer. They were undertrained, underpaid workers themselves, who faced disorder and chaos in their classrooms. They needed a solution, so leadership looked to the corporate world for answers, which they found in business concepts like productivity. If school personnel scientifically managed their resources, school efficiency experts argued, output would increase. Teachers were not to think of students as special persons sanctified with goodness but as objects to measure and quantify. In his book *Classroom Management*, William Bagley (1907) went so far as to state that classrooms should be run like a business operation, and Spencer's (1857) social Darwinism justified such a move. Inevitably, some children would be productive and others not. Those who interfered with output did not belong in school. If they became criminals, so be it. Their intellects were subnormal, so schools could not be accountable for them. Rather, schools had to produce the best-qualified workers possible. Goals like self-fulfillment and personal development were quaint, irrelevant, antiquated notions.

Such thinking reduced Parker's legacy at the Adams School to grouping practices and graded texts. Lost in the intervening decades were the interests of the child. Parker had based his child-centered ideology on the belief that children are essentially good—an assumption in stark contrast to the reality of exploited immigrant children. Many seemed dysfunctional, as numerous psychological studies "proved." Moreover, child-centered beliefs used mystical concepts that professors of psychology and education could neither measure nor quantify. To them, reality was measurable. Spiritual abstractions did not exist, because they could not be seen, felt, or quantified. Philosophical concepts about self-fulfillment were vestiges of romantics long dead.

Adapting the curriculum to the child seemed as ludicrous. The practice of making special teaching materials to explain abstractions was good. It worked. Extrapolating it across the entire curriculum proved impossible, however, unless teachers were willing to stay up all night creating materials. Not even Parker was able to motivate teachers to such an extent. Moreover, times had changed, and it was difficult to justify a commitment to teacher-made materials when so many children didn't come to class, or those who did spent their time disturbing others or gazing out the window.

Treating education as a means to harmonious development was not in tune with the profit motive. The bottom line on the factory floor was obeying the bosses. In less than a generation, Quincy cast off the advice of idealistic philosophers, replacing individual worth and joy with methods to regulate behavior. The child as learner became the child as object. History as critical inquiry morphed into facts for students to absorb through habit and association. Schools returned to the role of transmitting skills and knowledge to those who could learn them. The rest were damned.

Despite changes in teaching and curriculum, failure rates continued to escalate, even as psychology became synonymous with education. In 1905, the average American student skipped fifty days out of one hundred fifty. Less than 11 percent of children, aged fourteen to seventeen, attended high school. Of these, only 63 percent graduated.[18]

Scientific studies showed that without compulsory attendance laws many students stayed away. The new science of heredity, pioneered by Francis Galton's 1869 book *Hereditary Genius* (Galton also coined the term "eugenics"—see page 24 of his 1883 book *Inquiries into Human Faculty and its Development*), postulated that intelligence differences between races explained school failure.[19] Some people simply did not have the mental capacity to learn, and if schools held them to strict standards, they would fail. Racial and ethnic differences were laws of nature about which appeals to democratic principles of equality could do nothing. Only one inescapable conclusion made sense: only the best and the brightest were educable. The rest belonged elsewhere.

Battle lines were drawn. Those who found statistical differences in student ability argued for separation. By 1928, schools established tracks for bright, average, and slow students and vocational tracks and special classes for the mentally impaired.[20] Critics argued that eliminating a single common curriculum undermined the school's role to arbitrate a common culture for all. Others were incensed by the inherent injustice of segregating children based on mental abilities, believing that tracks perpetuated a class society, with children from the lower classes invariably ending up in the lowest tracks.

Tensions rose as the debate over education became polemical. Business knew what it wanted and found plenty of support from politicians and psychologists. Yet their "vision" did not touch the hearts of teachers who met children every day. The person who did that was a philosopher from Vermont, an admirer of Francis W. Parker. John Dewey knew exactly what education ought to be in an industrialized society and had the energy and intelligence to articulate his thoughts successfully to American educators.

Using philosophy and psychology, he constructed a vision for schools that answered the question, "How should we live in a democracy?" All matters of pedagogy (how we should teach) and curriculum (what should we teach) had to pass through this filter. Given that America stood for freedom, Dewey argued, children (and teachers) should experience freedom in school. This stance meant throwing out traditional organization and replacing mandated content with individualized experiences.[21]

By 1935, Dewey's ideas dominated teacher colleges in Massachusetts and across the nation. His impact was also evident at the Adams School, which again became a friendlier place where teachers considered children's interests and needs. Adams practiced direct experience in subjects like science and again offered projects of study. Even literacy returned to the "Look Say" method that Parker had advocated a generation earlier.

When I entered the Adams School in 1950, the progressive renaissance was over. Critics claimed that child-centered teaching smacked of improvisation. Too many teachers, they argued, taught what students wanted to learn, and literacy was too important to consider in such a haphazard fashion. Educators replaced project learning with separate subjects. Ability grouping and music, art, and history as subjects of study survived, however. So did narrative-based report cards and social-promotion policies.

Filling in the Cracks

Bookmarks

Textbook learning emphasized the science of instruction, wherein my teachers followed scripted questions to obtain authorized answers. I didn't flourish in this cold world of right and wrong. I was an intuitive learner who thought in shades of gray. Asking me if Dick liked his pet dog, Spot, might elicit, "Well, yes, but I'm not sure he always felt that way." No one asked my opinion about motives, character reactions, or personal connections. I was tripped up on easy questions because I read too much into them.

Still, I plugged away. Unlike the young Parker, who had told his teacher, "[You] don't know how to teach," my upbringing prevented such bluntness. I also feared punishment if I complained. Besides, too much was riding on me to be insolent. My aunts and uncles used me as a role model for their children. Consequently, I blamed myself for my difficulties and avoided whatever tasks made me uncomfortable. This tenet was especially true with books. My other tactic was procrastination. No one asked me any questions, so my failures became secret.

I was on my own to succeed or fail. Luckily, we purchased a TV when I entered school. TV shows and movie reruns substituted for my lack of knowledge in printed matter. Groucho Marx drove me batty. Mae West got her way via double entendres. James Cagney and George Raft played tough guys and spoke like Dad. I loved the potpourri of entertainment on variety shows. I related to Jackie Gleason, Art Carney, Sid Caesar, and Freddie the Freeloader. Heroes like Flash Gordon faced villains with tact and courage. I loved Betty Davis, who was so smart and always solved her problems intelligently. I escaped into *The Grapes of Wrath*, *Mutiny on the Bounty*, and *Cleopatra*. I developed values through *Captains Courageous*, *Wuthering Heights*, *The Old Curiosity Shop*, and *Frankenstein*. War movies like *Yankee Doodle Dandy* filled me with patriotism; films like *The Last of the Mohicans* and *Mr. Smith Goes to Washington* changed my views. *King Kong* challenged my ideas about good and evil. Race movies introduced me to dignified actors like Paul Roberson and Lena Horne. Even commercials added value to my life. Hearing Dinah Shore sing "See the USA in a Chevrolet … America's the greatest land of all" made me want to travel across the country.

Television served a valuable function in my education.[22] It stimulated my imagination, introduced me to the past, showed me how to act, and even forced me to think. It also offered a respite from the alienating control of church, school, and family. These institutions seemed to take pleasure in keeping me locked in a box. All expected me to behave as they dictated. If I acted or said something contrary to them, I received punishments or reprimands. I had no freedom to think my own thoughts.

When I sat down in front of the TV, however, I chose what show I wanted to watch. If I didn't like it, I switched the station or turned off the television. I was the boss. TV didn't force me to do anything, and it never scolded or tested me. This literacy was different from school literacy, which insisted that I read required stories whether I wanted to or not. I also had no say about when and where I read. Reading was always at the same time and always took place at my desk. If I were confused or distracted, I might lose points on a test. TV was more accommodating and allowed me construct my own meaning.

Relying on small snippets of information for knowledge made perfect sense to me, and the cliché "A picture is worth a thousand words" became my password. When I sat down to watch a show, I did so alone, which reinforced my social isolation, a stance that I wouldn't outgrow with books, given that reading is equally antisocial.

I spent years trying to overcome my reluctance to read. I didn't read novels because they demanded commitment. My home literacy—newspapers, magazines, comics— and junior high school signaled my first steps toward breaking my avoidance of books. I was amazed at my progress. I read for longer periods without falling asleep. I started to count the pages. I became less concerned with illustrations and the thickness of the book and started to judge books by their content and language. My aversion to reading gradually decreased as I increasingly received valuable ideas from books.

I had much ground to make up, though. I continued to rely on magazine articles as my primary source of information because they were cheaper than books and, oddly, I wanted to own every book I read. Opening one was like starting a new relationship. The author and the characters became part of me; I wanted to mark favorite passages and return to them whenever I wanted. For this reason, I was reluctant to use the library. Not only did I have to read those books in a prescribed amount of time but also had to return them unmarked so that others could enjoy them. Not liking these restrictions and hating the separation from new friends, I never developed the habit of borrowing books.

Joining a book club helped, but my real breakthrough came the day that I discovered the Goodwill store. Imagine buying twenty-five-dollar books for twenty-five cents! I made up for years of print deprivation by returning home with piles of paperbacks and hardbound books. A good friend in Nashville taught me how to use flea markets for books and furniture. Bob always ended up bringing back dozens of books to hand out to his students. He was widely versed in policy studies, philosophical and historical foundations, and literature instruction—an avid reader with a vast understanding of American and British literature. His grand view of life allowed him to put any problem into its proper context. I not only learned something about antiques from Bob but also how to approach life.

Until twenty years ago, I still read opportunistically. I had great difficulty casting off years of complaisance. I needed an emotional jolt to push me to the next level. Mario Puzo provided that impetus. I had read about Don Vito Corleone years before I saw *The Godfather* (1972). This well-written story gave me insights into my heritage. I could relate to the authentic characters and their familiar words. I couldn't put down the book. My life unfolded on every page.

The Godfather became my template as I looked for entertaining, well-written, instructional stories. The characters had to express real feelings and allow me to live inside their skins. The plots had to be understandable yet complex enough to satisfy my curiosity. Finally, stories had to have themes that pulled me toward a higher moral plane. Authors like James Michener; Jean Auel, with her series of novels *Earth's Children* (1980-2011); as well as John Grisham mysteries (1989) started me in that direction. I later discovered Paul Theroux (1996), William Kennedy (1983), David Guterson (1994), Toni Morrison (2007), Robertson Daveis (1983) and Joyce Carol Oates (1992).

I read daily. Like others who connect to literature, I cherished every nuance of plot, never wanting the stories to end. I rose early in the morning to read and frequently stayed up with a story late into the night. I even read in public places. Not surprisingly, my TV viewing diminished.

Writing: More than Thinking

Along with my early aversion to reading, I also had serious difficulties with writing. I could generate ideas but rarely was able to articulate them clearly. Lacking confidence and expertise, I avoided writing.

My study of language began in the third grade with penmanship exercises, finding words in the dictionary, and drawing neat margins. We used real ink from inkwells in those days. Teachers passed out blotters and pens so that we wouldn't make a mess. I was left-handed, so my writing was frequently smudged. I remember practicing language exercises that involved using words correctly. Words like *let* and *leave* and *lie* and *lay* confused me; I couldn't figure out why Johnny had *lain* in bed all day but *laid* the book on the desk.

I never won a prize for penmanship; in fact, it was the only subject I ever failed in school. I didn't have to write a report until the seventh grade, and even then teachers still concentrated on improving handwriting, spelling, and punctuation marks. Before that time, I wrote only letters. I became very good at knowing the parts of a letter, especially the appropriate business greetings. The only other assigned writing before high school was a creative story in eighth grade—a mystery about the Russians stealing blueprints from the shipyard. I had a good time writing it; the tale just flowed from me painlessly.

I first realized that I had a writing problem in high school. The assignment was to analyze *The Rime of the Ancient Mariner* (Coleridge 1798). No matter how many times I wrote my name and title on the paper, nothing followed. I rewrote the first sentence numerous times, hoping that the second would emerge. Eventually, I wrote a few sentences, but they were garbled and ungraceful. My word choice was juvenile and transitions were nonexistent. After several hours of rewriting, I produced a grammatically correct but unpolished paper. I didn't know how to develop an idea.

I rarely wrote in school. English consisted of grammar drills and tests on figures of speech. Teachers neither taught nor used composition as a learning tool. My first insight into writing came at home. I finally connected reading to writing on a visit to my aunt Connie's. Sandra, my second cousin from Middletown and a recent college graduate with a degree in classics, happened to be there. My aunt had built me up as her studious nephew because I studied Latin. As they talked about family, I browsed through an encyclopedia. To my astonishment, I enjoyed the experience. In a solitary way, I reflected on this nascent link between home and school. If I had a set of encyclopedias, I could catch up to my more knowledgeable peers, whose bedrooms boasted books, maps, globes, typewriters, and encyclopedia sets.

A few weeks later, I asked my mother about buying a set. She replied, "Dad doesn't make enough money to buy one. I think they cost six hundred dollars."

Looking for someone to blame, I responded with a melodramatic cliché that I must have heard from a TV character: "Life is so unfair. I didn't ask to be born."

Shocked by my betrayal, my mother replied, "Henry, that's a terrible thing to say. Your father loves you very much. He works very hard to support us." She was right. My father didn't shirk his duties, use profanity around us, gamble, or drink. He led a responsible life, as his mother had while raising him.

Unlike in high school, I couldn't duck out of writing assignments in college. My freshman English course required several papers, and two of my English courses assigned research papers. Despite my weaknesses, I worked hard at writing. I conducted thorough research and took extensive notes. I bought a typewriter and tried to teach myself to type. I had no choice; I couldn't afford to pay someone to type my papers.

When I returned to school my sophomore year, I was relieved to learn that none of my classes required written papers. The same held true for the next two years. During all my years in college as an English major, I wrote fewer than five papers. I graduated with honors, unable to write.

Eight years later, I began my doctoral work and quickly sought aid through self-help manuals and a writing clinic. When those proved useless, I broke down articles to examine their construction. Most followed a predictable formula: short, direct sentences with plenty of citations and jargon. The writing was unadorned and boasted words and phrases such as "In addition to," "shortcomings," or "Smith (1986) provides further evidence."

I learned tricks like cutting and pasting typewritten passages. By the end of the semester, I had written several good papers and was confident when I took my department's three-hour writing examination. My confidence dissipated, however, when I learned that my professors found it nearly impossible to read, due to illegible handwriting and many spelling errors. I retook the exam six months later.

Learning to write took a great deal of hard work. Changes were slow and painful, but a major breakthrough came with the invention of personal computers. The built-in thesaurus and spelling/grammar checker took care of word selections, spelling errors, and awkward syntax. The more I wrote, the better I became at it. The biggest demon I had to overcome was attitude. I had long avoided the difficult, lonely work of writing. Now, however, I sensed that competence was within my grasp, and my willingness to concentrate increased. I even started to ask questions. Before long, I figured out which steps I had to take to become a better writer:

My first mission was to *learn from others*, and my first lesson happened the day that I asked my advisor to tell me the secret of his success. I had come to the university an accomplished teacher, a community organizer, a Vista volunteer worker, and the director of the Right to Read program. I had even designed and built my own home. But my record paled in comparison to his academic and linguistic achievements: full professor, prolific writer, senior investigator of Wisconsin Design for Instructional Improvement, and the chairperson of the Curriculum and Instruction Department. The fact that one person had gained so much intelligence and learning was inconceivable to me. I figured that he was either a god or a speed-reader like President Kennedy.

He smiled and said, "I'm a good listener." He sounded flippant, but I assumed that he "sucked" up information from a variety of sources, including his observations of others (Murray 1981). I found this circumstance a bit ironic, given that he was a reading expert, but I didn't quibble. I left his office with a path to follow: pay greater attention to the stuff of life, especially how others communicate. Listen to the structure of their arguments and how they connect ideas. What words do they use? What phrases and slogans carry the most meaning? Also, ask questions about print. Pay attention not only to meaning but also to the specific craft that writers use to create meaning—introductions, organizational structures, documentation, vocabulary, and even sentence and word choices. My plan was to improve my own writing by examining that of others.

My second mission was to *write from experience*. I never understood why I wrote letters so effortlessly but became tongue-tied over essays or memos. I had never figured out that I couldn't write about what I didn't understand. When I tried to write formally, my syntax became crude and ineffective. Consequently, I procrastinated whenever I had to write because the experience was so painful. Moreover, I never had enough time to rewrite in a casual manner. A colleague at Peabody College tipped me off to an answer about writing. She knew that I was searching for a writing topic, so she suggested the literacy method that I had developed for Peace Corps trainees. I hadn't considered my "organic primers," because they weren't scholarly. I had assumed that my writing had to be empirical or at least grand in theme. In searching for a subject, I had overlooked a topic that I knew well. I took her advice and, sure enough, I didn't have to labor on the article.

A colleague at the University of Southern Maine (USM) gave me another push in the right direction. Having never learned how to write in school, I had no insights into my writing, and not knowing how to think about the act of writing aggravated me. Few college professors will admit to having writing problems, and I was one of them, at least until Miriam Clasby, a former editor of the *Harvard Educational Review*, joined our faculty. I immediately sensed her integrity and asked for her help. I found the confidence to share my work because I trusted her and knew that she wouldn't associate my deficiencies with flaws in my character. Her help was invaluable and resulted in numerous insights into areas that needed work.

Mission number three was to *experiment*. My writing-related struggles had kept me from engaging in the experimentation that seasoned writers consider crucial. I worked with a grant writer who composed elegant sentences effortlessly, his fingers gliding across the keyboard, knowing exactly where he wanted them to land. I stumbled over my first sentence. He drew upon abundant words and an outline that never varied. My first attempts were primitive, full of fragments and without direction. Then I discovered the computer. It allowed me to revise my language instantly in a give-and-take manner. I was so excited to realize that my ideas would gain focus as I reread and reworked them. And if I needed additional information, I could find and place it with the cut-and-paste option.

The computer was a remarkable discovery. I had never been able to visualize my ideas, but now I was free to create and control the process. Donald Murray's 1982 paperback *Learning by Teaching* supported my inductive approach, as did James Michener's (1993) article relating how he returned to earlier drafts to fill in details. Paul Theroux's (1997) analysis of his own writing was also helpful—sometimes he doesn't know where the work is leading him; other times he's clear, and his words flow.

Theroux's description of writing as hard work boosted my ego and led to my willingness to invest more time and effort in the craft. I realized for the first time in my life that the nature of the writing process is to revise. His words freed me from the grip of self-doubt. I had always assumed that bad writing reflected laziness. Now I write to learn and to inform because I know that others can understand my words.

The Legacy of a Working-Class Education

My working-class family valued tradition and obligation. Together, we ate, went to church, and socialized with relatives. We didn't think of ourselves as poor—there was always enough to eat. Although neither of my parents graduated from high school, the social climate at home and in my neighborhood encouraged me to do well in school. The only aspect missing from my education was a critical perspective. I didn't really think for myself until I entered college.

Letting others think for me wasn't all bad. One lesson my father taught me was to live within my means. Credit cards, bank loans, and checking accounts were not part of my world growing up. We didn't have disposable cash to eat out or take in a movie. If I wanted something, I worked for it. I didn't complain; everyone else did the same. We had few books or magazines at home, but I didn't feel disadvantaged—I had learned to read and was one of the best students in my class. I did pay a price, however; I took longer to engage in behavior that Jones and Jones (1998) call "taking charge of my own mind." Eventually, as I became self-reliant, I purchased books.

The first poem I learned was about a bum who sat by the railroad all day, chewing a piece of gum. This character's actions—or general lack thereof—stood in stark contrast to my father's view on the topic of idleness: People who didn't support themselves were worthless. His stories about selling papers before school and searching for coal in the train yards strengthened my resolve to achieve, just as he had. I understood that hard work would overcome any disadvantage.

I followed my father's sense of identity uncritically. As I grew up, however, I began to resent his control and closed-mindedness. I wanted to talk with him but couldn't, so I looked elsewhere for answers about forming one's place in the world. Books that celebrated history, politics, and relationships tipped me in the opposite direction from my father and started my education. I learned that I could take charge of my life and accomplish whatever I wanted. This power to understand my experiences came through books. They freed me from trying to please others.

I needed to learn how to ask difficult questions so that I could make good decisions. My sense of history told me that if I didn't think for myself, others would do so for me. My education was more social than academic: Family members, friends, and neighbors taught me to value the past. The popular culture of the '50's taught me to live in the present. Institutions like the church and Scouts made me responsible to others. Literature taught me how to think.

Stories about my grandmother Rose fostered my need to understand the past. I wanted to know about the difficulties she faced adjusting to a strange culture. Did she conform by renouncing her past, her ideals and values? Did schools teach her children that American culture was superior to hers? If so, did they use coercion, condescension, and suppression to Americanize them? Did she resent their actions? What did my father and aunts think about assimilation? Did their education teach them that certain psychological tests showed that Italians had far lower IQs than other groups? Did they challenge those results? And finally, what factors determine success or failure? Why did my father and Aunt Lucy fail in school but Aunt Concetta succeed? What is the meaning of her story?

My neighborhood was home to old Yankee families, Germans, Irish, Swedes, Finns, Scots, and Italians, and we all got along because we minded our own business. We didn't criticize each other over the cars we drove or the churches we attended. The values I learned in my neighborhood incubated my interest in issues of social and racial justice, including questions about the exploitation of different peoples and the appeal of genetic theories that correlate ethnicity to innate endowments such as intellect and moral capacity. These interests clearly connect to my upbringing—I never heard my neighbors condemn others.

My school experiences also influenced me. Mrs. Faye, who lived in my neighborhood and had attended school with my aunt, was right to expect more of me. I needed someone to stimulate me. She wanted me to succeed and therefore didn't tolerate my dislike of reading. She could have more easily let me slide, but she wouldn't; she knew that books held answers for me.

Church shaped my values as well. The social gospel led me to a join Vista and to study language and culture in graduate school. The church taught me to value hope, learn from my mistakes, and serve others.

My mother never blamed my father for his meager paycheck or ridiculed his dislike of books. And rather than set goals for me, she let me choose my own. When I turned eight, she went to work. My dad, who felt that supporting the family was his responsibility, was very upset. I remember picking her up at the factory. She worked in an abandoned shipyard about ten miles from our home. The building was old and rusted, pockmarked with rows of cracked and broken windows. Weeds covered the road circling around the entryway. I drew ships as I waited for her. I was very proud of her every time she stepped out from the building's darkness. It was a huge, damp space filled with massive assembly tables. She worked long, tiring hours for minimum wage, breathing dangerous fumes from the glue she used to attach mattress covers. When she returned home at night, she started her second job of the day—feeding, cleaning, ironing, and washing. She gave us a neat home, freshly laundered and ironed clothes, and home-cooked meals seven days a week. She also gave me the freedom to think and encouraged me to be creative like my maternal grandfather, a highly skilled artisan.[23]

I succeeded because I had opportunity. I also had a great deal of luck. One cannot find a formula for success in my story; the real message is in how easily I could have failed. Many Americans my age never realized their dreams: They didn't have the same breaks or find a mentor or have a friend suggest a book to them. As Thoreau (1854) reminds us, too many people lead lives of quiet desperation.

Some will argue that in any society there must be winners and losers. I disagree, and I certainly don't want schools to sort my children by those standards. I would much rather they prepare them for an uncertain future. Real power emerges through self-expression. Children who develop confidence by having others listen to them won't be afraid to make choices or express themselves. The scenario sounds simple, but in the final analysis, one must have real courage both to speak and to hear. The good news is that children inevitably find their voices when adults allow them to discover meaning in their experiences.

If we don't empower them with the drive to write, many children will fail, a circumstance that we cannot allow in this time of cultural conflict, shrinking economies, and changing demographics.[24] We need citizens who can stand up against the erosion of core values and be flexible as the workplace changes. So much of our world's success depends on our children's abilities to think and act critically.

If we leave too many behind, society will erode. We cannot afford to waste a single soul if we are to prosper in the next millennium. The clock is running, and the number of uneducated Americans is on the rise.[25]

We are at a critical crossroads in the history of our great country. As Kaplan (1998) points out, too many Americans have already given up their civic responsibilities by condemning instead of voting. We have to make a better effort to understand how schools can remedy our social problems. All children need a voice and a listener. Vico (1732/1979) wrote more than four hundred years ago that people are blessed with heroic minds capable of learning and caring for others. That message transcends place and time and—now more than ever—needs reaffirmation in our schools.

Notes

1. Events found at *American Chronicle* (Gordon & Gordon 1999); *New York Times Index* (1973); *American Decades* (Bruccoli 1996a, 1996b); and *Readers Guide to Periodical Literature* (1915, 1922).

2. The National Endowment for the Arts reported in July 2004 that only 14 percent of adults with a grade-school education had read literature in 2002.

3. *Fighting Prosaic Messages* is a story about struggle, assimilation, and morality. It is also about how families pass down codes of conduct and routines that influence literacies and learning. The premise behind *Fighting Prosaic Messages* is that literacy is thought, wonder, and analysis, not simply reading and writing. Most educators want students to understand and act within their worlds through the lenses of authors; thus, education fails when students reject books as venues to learning. This story, depicting great turmoil, presents many norms that made me suspicious of words. I learned how to deal with them randomly, not smoothly as in a plot, where everything unrolls easily. The sections "Solitary Places" and "On the Street" emphasize the fact that my passion for words developed away from school.

4. Why is there such an emphasis on food in Italian American families? Peri (1997) believes that one of the few acceptable places where old-neighborhood Italian and Italian American women showed off their skills was in the kitchen. Poe (2001) posits that in rural Italian communities, food was the basis of economic and social exchange. Di Donato (1939/1993) captures the religious significance of food in his novel *Christ in Concrete*: "Christ is happy when the poor table weeps red in the laughter of wine."

5. According to Macias (2003), a common theme in the literature on the enculturation of third-generation ethnic Americans is the social pressure to conform to the expectations of the dominant culture.

6. Aliterates (people who can read but choose not to) far outnumber illiterates in society and encounter many of the same problems (Beers 1996). My indifference to books compromised my learning because literacy is the primary ability for all school-based learning. The causes of my choice not to read are diverse. Advocates of developmental learning believe that the dislike of books derives from the lack of literacy experiences before children enter formal schooling. Researchers such as Lyon (2003) and Orton (1967), from medicine and psychology, respectively, believe that aversion occurs when

children take far too long to read words, leaving little energy for remembering and comprehending what they read. A tradition of research in anthropology and sociology that stretches back into the 1930s suggests that instructional factors such as misdirected emphasis in the curriculum, lack of attention to individual differences, or unsatisfactory pupil-teacher relationships (Bond & Tinker 1957) contribute to the reluctance to read. Beers (1996) found that aliterates define reading as a skill rather than a pleasurable activity. Mackey and Johnston (1996) believe that reluctant readers don't know that reading can be enjoyable, because they don't know how to find books that they like.

7. In an article for the Spring 2004 issue of *Saint Michael's College Magazine*, Tarnacki describes the Saint Michael's curriculum as "Thomist thinking with a Great Books core." A distribution requirement model replaced it in 1971. For an analysis of liberal arts models in higher education, see Keller (1982), *Getting at the Core: Curricular Reform at Harvard* and Gaff, Ratcliff, & Associates (1997), *Handbook of the Undergraduate Curriculum: A Comprehensive Guide to Purposes, Structures, Practices, and Change.* For an analysis of the secularization of Catholic education, see Mahoney (2003), *Catholic Higher Education in Protestant America: The Jesuits and Harvard in the Age of the University* and O'Brien (2002), *The Idea of a Catholic University.*

8. What factors contribute to the high academic achievement of people who come from families with little formal education? From a sample of fifty Mexican Americans who had come from backgrounds of poverty but had completed doctoral-level education, Gandara (1995) found that their parents had instilled in them the motivation to achieve. For the most part, parents supported their children's educational goals, set high performance standards, and helped in any way they could. They also modeled a good work ethic.

9. Taylorism is behind the authoritarian pedagogy that turns the fear of being wrong into helplessness (Elkind 2001) and procrastination (Spache 1976). Schroeder (1992) claims that coercive learning inhibits children's independent thinking; likewise, Fielding & Fielding (2001) argue that authoritarian instruction obstructs the desire to learn and is in conflict with humanistic traditions, including dialogue and reciprocation.

10. Education is the act of advancing learning. Schools promote skill and knowledge acquisition via planned, managed methods. Learning, however, takes place informally, in families, at work, and at play. For a coherent analysis of community-based learning, see Brookfield (1983), *Adult Learners, Adult Education, and the Community.* Likewise, Harrison (2003) discusses the nature of informal learning and teaching in "A Case for the Underestimated,

Informal Side of Lifelong Learning," and Hull & Schultz (2001) offer a comprehensive review of out-of-school literacy and learning in "Literacy and Learning Out of School: A Review of Theory and Research."

11. See, for example, Columbia University Press (2004), *Francis Wayland Parker*, and L. E. Partridge (1883), *Notes of Talks on Teaching Given by Francis W. Parker at the Martha's Vineyard Summer Institute, July 17 to August 19, 1882.*

12. One example is Bennett's (1993) *The Book of Virtues*, a contemporary version of the didactic stories that Americans told in earlier times.

13. Heroes instruct and inspire. Children grow up to be like the heroes who give them vision.

14. Support is an odd thing. We know from studies of Japanese mothers that parents play a central role in their children's school success. They support them with encouragement, homework assistance, and even special care in lunch preparation. Their goal is to make learning as distraction-free as possible. Parents of successful American students tend to manage their children's schedules; help them set goals; bring them to the library; buy them computers; and provide direct instruction on assignments, including brainstorming topics, editing papers, testing children, monitoring their work, and tutoring them in subject matter when warranted.

15. See Graves & Dykstra (1997), "Contextualizing the First-grade Studies: What is the Best Way to Teach Children to Read" for a history of basal reading instruction. See Shannon & Crawford (1997), "Manufacturing Descent: Basal Readers and the Creation of Reading Failures" for a discussion about how basal readers obstruct the reading development of students from less privileged economic and social backgrounds.

16. For more on Francis Parker and the Quincy Experiment, see Columbia University Press (2004), *Francis Wayland Parker*, and L. E. Partridge (1883), *Notes of Talks on Teaching Given by Francis W. Parker at the Martha's Vineyard Summer Institute, July 17 to August 19, 1882.* For Horace Mann's work on the Common School movement, see Bakersfield City School District (2011), *Horace Mann Elementary: Who was Horace Mann?* and O. W. Caldwell (1925), "The Boston public schools in the days of Horace Mann."

17. The national annual average for female teachers in 1901 was $381.50. The national annual average for male teachers in the same year was $452. See for

example, "Salaries in 1901" *Doing the Pan…* http://www.panam1901.org/visiting/salaries, retrieved 6/13/17.

18. See Caldwell's "The Boston Public Schools in the days of Horace Mann," found in his classic book *Then and Now in Education: 1845-1923*, New York: World Book Company, 1925. Other references: Jeffrey Mirel, "The Traditional High School," *Education Next*, winter 2006 vol. 6, no. 1, http://www.educationnext.org/the-traditional-high-school, retrieved 6/13/17, or Susan J. Bodilly and Megan Beckett, *Making Out-of-School Time Matter: Evidence for an Action Agenda*, Santa Monica: RAND Corporation, 2005, p. 13.

19. Francis Galton pioneered the "science" of racial intelligence in his 1869 book *Hereditary Genius*. He wanted to see whether intellectual abilities were genetic or not. In fact, he coined the term eugenics in his 1883 book *Inquisitions into Human Faculties and its Development*. Others who followed suit to use "science" to prove a "race" was superior to others included, R. Meade (1895), Frank Bruner (1912), George O. Ferguson (1916), and Robert Yerkes & Henry Goddard (1916). They often used an intelligence test that Alfred Binet (1857-1911) had invented in order to put forth their arguments. See "History of the race and intelligence controversy," *Wikipedia*, https://en.wikipedia.org/wiki/History_of_the_race_and_intelligence_controversy, last modified April 17, 2017, for an overview of this history.

20. See Anne Wheelock's book *Crossing the Tracks: How "Untracking Can Save America's Schools*. New York: New Press, 1992.

21. John Dewey's (1859-1952) five major educational writings are: *My Pedagogic Creed* (1897), *School and Society* (1899), *The Child and the Curriculum* (1902), *How We Think* (1910), and *Democracy and Education* (1916).

22. My dislike of books was in sharp contrast to Italian writers such as Mario Puzo (1920-1999) and Guaresci (1908-1968) who read all the time. Instead, I escaped into television for at least five hours per day, more on weekends. My parents set no rules regarding what I could watch or when I had to turn off the TV. Not surprisingly, I gained role models (Chombart de Lauwe 1981) and positive social behavior (Paulo, Afonso, Magalhães, & Pereira 2003) via television programming. I especially identified with bashful historic figures (Merritt 1975) who followed an egalitarian philosophy. Although Heathorn (1996) critiques schools for using historical heroes to indoctrinate working-class students into the principles of "virtuous masculinity," my TV heroes broadened my horizons.

23. Because my mother encouraged my creativity, I designed and built my own home in the Virgin Islands and remodeled two others. I especially love to refinish antique furniture. My own children are accomplished artists, actors, and musicians. When I spoke with my son Justin about his grandmother's own creativity, he reminded me that the attic shelters two of her oil paintings. She had a creative soul that she expressed in beautiful sewing, cooking, and painting.

24. The works of Dreiser (1871-1945), di Donato (1939/1993), and Olsen (1978) dispel the myth that the poor and working class cannot capture artistically the universality of experience. Why, then, do many nonprivileged children continue to face writing difficulties and frustrations? Do they have sufficient space and encouragement to write? Do cynicism and uninformed criticism silence their drive to write? Was Hoffer (1954) right when he said, "Pedants drain achievement of life and turn it into an orthodoxy which stifles all stirrings of originality"? See Hoffer, *Between the Devil and the Dragon: The best essays and aphorisms of Eric Hoffer* (1954). We need to encourage, not stifle, a child's willingness to tell stories. See Olsen (1978), *Silences*.

25. See Paul Krugman's *New York Times* Op Ed piece "The Uneducated American," *New York Times*, October 8, 2009, http://www.nytimes.com/2009/10/09/opinion/09krugman.html.

References

Allington, R. L. & P. M. Cunningham. *Schools That Work: Where all children read and write.* New York: Harper Collins, 1996.

Auel, J. M. *Earth's Children: The Clan of the Cave Bear.* New York: Crown Publishing Group, 1980.

Bagley, W. C. *Classroom Management: Its principles and techniques.* New York: The Macmillan Company, 1907.

Bakersfield City School District. *Horace Mann elementary: Who was Horace Mann?* http://www.horacemann.bcsd.com.

Barnett, L. The epic of man series part I: Man inherits the Earth. *Life Magazine* (November 7, 1955): 74–99.

Berlin, I. *Against the Current: Essays in the history of ideas.* New York: Viking Press, 1979/1995.

Beers, G. K. "No time, no interest, no way! The 3 voices of aliteracy." *School Library Journal* 42, no. 2 (1996): 30–33.

Bennett, W. J., ed. *The Book of Virtues: A treasury of great moral stories.* New York: Simon & Schuster, 1993.

Best, J. H., & R. T. Sidwell, eds. *The American Legacy of Learning: Readings in the history of education.* Philadelphia: J. B. Lippincott Company, 1967.

Bobinski, G. S. *Carnegie Libraries.* Chicago: American Library Association, 1969.

Bond, G. L. & M. A, *Tinker Reading Difficulties: Their diagnosis and correction.* New York: Appleton-Century-Crofts, 1957.

Boorstin, D. J. *The Seekers.* New York: Vintage, 1999.

Boyer, E. *College: The undergraduate experience in America.* New York: Harper & Row, 1987.

Brookfield, S. D. *Adult Learners, Adult Education and the Community.* Buckingham, UK: Open University Press, 1983.

Brophy, J. E. "Classroom organization and management." *The Elementary School Journal, Research on Teaching* 83, no. 4 (1983): 265–285.

Caldwell, O. W. "The Boston public schools in the days of Horace Mann." In *Then and Now in Education:1845–1923.* New York: World Book Company, 1925.

Cameron, A. *Radicals of the Worst Sort: Laboring women in Lawrence,* Massachusetts, 1860–1912. Urbana, IL: University of Illinois Press, 1993.

Coleridge, S. T. *The Rime of the Ancient Mariner.* New York: Dover Publications, 1970.

Columbia University Press. Francis Wayland Parker. *Columbia Encyclopedia* (6th ed.). New York: Author, 2004.

Comenius, J. A. *Didactica Magna (Great Didactic).* Translated by M. W. Keating. New York: Russell & Russell, 1649/1967. http://core.roehampton.ac.uk/digital/froarc/comgre.

Commins, S. & R. N. Linscott, eds. *Man and Spirit: The speculative philosophers.* New York: Random House, 1947.

Chombart de Lauwe, M. J. "The interaction between television and children." *Montrouge Neuropsychiatrie de l'enfance et de l'adolescence* 29 (March 1981): 157–168.

Dante, *Inferno.* Translated by John Ciardi. New York: Modern Library, 1996.

Daveis, R. *The Deptford Trilogy.* London: Penguin Books, 1983.

Dewey, J. & J. H. Tufts. *Ethics.* New York: Henry Holt and Company, 1909.

Dickens, C. *A Christmas Carol.* London: Chapman & Hall, 1843.

Di Donato, P. *Christ in Concrete.* New York: Signet, 1939/1993.

Disney, W. (producer) & James Algar (director). *Fantasia* [motion picture]. United States: Walt Disney Productions, 1940.

Dreiser, T. *Sister Carrie*. New York: The Modern Library, 1917.

Dupuis, A. M. *Philosophy of Education in Historical Perspective*. Chicago: Rand McNally & Co., 1966.

Elkind, D. *The Hurried Child: Growing up too fast too soon*. Cambridge, MA: Perseus, 2001.

Ellison, R. *Invisible Man*. New York: Vintage Books, 1952/1995.

Fielding, P. & R. Fielding. "Like mother like daughter: Two stories from a Upattinas family." *Paths of Learning: Options for Families and Communities* 10 (Autumn 2001): 17–19.

Froebel, F. *The Education of Man*. Translated by W. N. Hailmann. New York: Dover Publications, 1826/2005.

Gaff, J. G., J. L. Ratcliff & Associates, eds. *Handbook of the Undergraduate Curriculum: A comprehensive guide to purposes, structures, practices, and change*. San Francisco: Jossey-Bass Publishers, 1997.

Gandara, P. "Choosing higher education: Educationally ambitious Chicanos and the path to social mobility." *Education Policy Analysis Archives* 2, no. 8 (1995. http://epaa.asu.edu/ojs/article/viewFile/671/793.

Golding, W. *Lord of the Flies*. New York: Perigee Books, Berkeley Publishing Group, 1954.

Graves, M. F. & R. Dykstra. "Contextualizing the first-grade studies: What is the best way to teach children to read?" *Reading Research Quarterly* 32, no. 4 (1997): 342–344.

Grisham, J. *A Time to Kill*. New York: Dell, 1989.

Guareschi, G. *The Little World of Don Camillo*. Translated by Una Vincenzo Troubridge. New York: Doubleday, 1986.

Gutek, G. L. *Historical and Philosophical Foundations of Education*. Upper Saddle River, NJ: Merrill, 2001.

Guterson, D. *Snow Falling on Cedars*. New York: Vintage Books, 1995.

Harrison, L. "A case for the underestimated, informal side of lifelong learning." *Australian Journal of Adult Learning* 43, no. 1 (2003): 23–42.

Heathorn, S. "For home, country and race: The gendered ideals of citizenship in English elementary and evening continuation schools, 1885–1914." *Journal of the Canadian Historical Association* 7, no. 1 (1996): 105–124.

Herbart, J. F. *The Science of Education: Its general principles deduced from its aim, and the aesthetic revelation of the world.* Translated by H. M. Felkin & E. Felkin. London: Swan Sonnenschein & Co., 1892.

Hoffer, E. *Between the Devil and the Dragon: The best essays and aphorisms of Eric Hoffer.* New York: Harper & Row, 1954/1982.

Hijuelos, O. *The Mambo Kings Play Songs of Love.* New York: Farrar, Straus and Giroux, 1989.

Hull, G. & K. Schultz. "Literacy and Learning Out of School: a review of theory and research." *Review of Educational Research* 71, no. 4 (2001): 575–611.

Jones, B., & G. Jones. *Earth Dance Drum: A celebration of life.* Center City, MN: Hazelden, 1998.

Kaplan, R. D. "Was Democracy Just a Moment?" in *Atlantic Monthly*, December 1997.

Keller, P. *Getting at the Core: Curricular reform at Harvard.* Cambridge, MA: Harvard University Press, 1982.

Kennedy, W. *An Albany Trio.* New York: Penguin Books, 1996.

Kerouac, J. *On the Road.* New York: The Viking Press, 1957.

King, M. L., Jr. *The Words of Martin Luther King, Jr.: Selected and with an introduction by Coretta Scott King.* New York: Newmarket Press, 1958/1987.

Lasker, H., J. Moore, E. L. Simpson, & National Institute of Education. *Adult Development and Approaches to Learning.* Washington, D.C.: US Department of Education, Office of Educational Research and Improvement, U.S. Government Printing Office, 1980.

Longfellow, H. W. *Evangeline: A tale of Acadie*. Boston: William D. Ticknor & Company, 1847.

Lyon, G. R. "Reading disabilities: Why do some children have difficulty learning to read? What can be done about it?" *Perspectives* 29, no. 2 (2003): 17-19.

Mackey, M. & I. Johnston. "The book resisters: Ways of approaching reluctant teenage readers." *School Libraries Worldwide* 2, no. 1 (1996): 25–38.

Macias, T. "The changing structure of structural assimilation: White-collar Mexican ethnicity and the significance of ethnic identity professional organizations." *Social Science Quarterly* 84, no. 4 (2003): 946–957.

Mahoney, K. A. *Catholic Higher Education in Protestant America: The Jesuits and Harvard in the age of the university*. Baltimore, MD: The Johns Hopkins University Press, 2003.

Márquez, G. G. *One Hundred Years of Solitude*. New York: Harper and Row, 1970.

McCroskey, J. C. *Quiet Children and the Classroom Teacher*. Urbana, IL: ERIC Clearinghouse on Reading and Communication Skills, 1977.

McQuillan, J. *The Literacy Crisis: False claims, real solutions*. Portsmouth, NH: Heinemann, 1998.

Melville, H. *Moby-Dick; or, The Whale*. New York: Harper & Brothers Publishers. London: Richard Bentley, 1851.

Merritt, R. L. "The bashful hero in American film of the nineteen forties." *Quarterly Journal of Speech* 61, no. 2 (1975): 129–139.

Meyer, R. J., ed. *Stories from the Heart: Teachers and students researching their literacy lives*. Mahwah, NJ: Lawrence Erlbaum Associates, 1996.

Michener, J. A. *Literary Reflections: Michener on Michener, Hemingway, Capote & others*. Austin, TX: State House Press, 1993.

Morrison, T. *Beloved*. New York: Alfred A. Knopf, 1987.

Moustafa, M. *Beyond Traditional Phonics: Research discoveries and reading instruction*. Portsmouth, NH: Heinemann, 1997.

Murray, D. *Learning by Teaching: Selected articles on writing and teaching.* Montclair, NJ: Boynton/Cook, 1982.

National Endowment for the Arts. *Reading at risk: A survey of literary reading in America.* Washington, DC: Author, Research Division Report #46, 2004.

Noll, J. W., ed. *Taking Sides: Clashing views on controversial educational issues.* Guilford, CT: The Dushkin Publishing Group, 1991.

Oates, J. C. *Where Are You Going, Where Have You Been?: Stories of Young America.* Ontario: Ontario Review Press, 1994.

O'Brien, G. D. *The Idea of a Catholic University.* Chicago: University of Chicago Press, 2002.

Olsen, T. *Silences.* New York: Delacorte Press/Seymour Lawrence, 1978.

Orton, J. L. "The Orton-Gillingham approach." In *The Disabled Reader: Education of the Dyslexic Child.* Edited by J. Money, Baltimore, MD: The Johns Hopkins Press, 1967.

Orwell, G. *Nineteen Eighty-Four.* New York: Harcourt Brace and Company, 1949.

Paine, T. *Common Sense; Addressed to the inhabitants of America on the following interesting subjects...* Philadelphia: R. Bell, 1776.

Partridge, L. E. *Notes of talks on teaching given by Francis W. Parker at the Martha's Vineyard summer institute, July 17 to August 19, 1882.* New York: E. L. Kellogg & Co, 1883.

Paulo, J. C., Afonso, J. A., & Magalhães, Pereira, J. P. "That seductive thing: Representing the illiterate as readers." *Paedagogica Historica*, 37, no. 1 (2003): 347–371.

Peri, C. "My grandmother, the godfather: She who stirs the pot wears the pants." *Salon.* http://archive.salon.com/july97/mothers/godfather970728.html.

Perry, W. G., Jr. *Forms of Intellectual and Ethical Development in the College Years: A scheme.* New York: Holt, Rhinehart, & Winston, 1968.

Pestalozzi, J. H. *How Gertrude Teaches Her Children*. Translated by L. E. Holland & F. C. Turner. London: Swan Sonnenschein, 1894.

Pestalozzi, J. H. *The Education of Man—Aphorisms*. Translated by H. Norden & R. Norden. London: Greenwood Press, 1951.

Poe, T. N. "The labour and leisure of food production as a mode of ethnic identity building among Italians in Chicago, 1890-1940." *Rethinking History* 5, no. 1 (2001): 131–148.

Puzo, M. *The Godfather*. New York: Penguin, 1978.

Salinger, J. D. *The Catcher in the Rye*. New York: Little, Brown and Company, 1951/1991.

Schroeder, K. "Authoritarian teaching." *Education Digest* 58, no. 1 (1992): 74–75.

Shannon, P. *Reading Poverty*. Portsmouth: Heinemann Publishing, 1998.

Shannon, P. & P. Crawford. "Manufacturing descent: Basal readers and the creation of reading failures." *Reading & Writing Quarterly* 13, no. 33 (1997): 227–243.

Spache, G. D. *Investigating the Issues of Reading Disabilities*. Boston: Allyn and Bacon, Inc., 1976.

Spencer, H. "Progress: Its laws and causes." *The Westminster Review* 67 (1857). http://www.fordham.edu/halsall/mod/spencer-darwin.html.

Spock, B. *The Common Sense Book of Baby and Child Care*. New York: Duell, Sloan and Pearce, 1946.

Stevenson, R. L. *Treasure Island*. London: Cassell and Company, 1853.

Tarnacki, M. "The foundation of a liberal arts education." *Saint Michael's College Magazine* 4 (Spring 2004): 20–25.

Theroux, P. *My Other Life*. Boston: Houghton Mifflin, 1996.

Theroux, P. *Sir Vidia's Shadow: A friendship across five continents*. Boston: Houghton Mifflin, 2001.

Thoreau, H. D. "Economy." In *Walden; or, life in the woods*. Boston: Ticknor & Fields, 1854.

Twain, M. *The Adventures of Tom Sawyer*. Chicago: American Publishing Company, 1876.

Van Loon, H. W. *The Story of Mankind*. New York: Garden City Publishing Company, 1921/1959.

Vico, G. "On the heroic mind: An Oration." In *Vico and Contemporary Thought*. Edited by G. Tagliacozzo, M. Monney, & D. P. Verene. Translated by E. Sewell & A. C. Sirignano. Atlantic Hightlands, N.J.: Humanities Press, 1732/1979.

Vincent, C. W., ed. *The year book of facts in science and the arts for 1875*. London: Ward, Lock, and Tyler, 1876.

Yebry, J., N. Buerkel-Rothfuss, & A. P. Bochner. *Understanding Family Communication*. Scottsdale, AZ: Gorsuch Scarisbrick Publishers, 1995.

Developments: 1970-2015

The Beatles breakup in 1970. Walt Disney World opens in Orlando, Florida in 1971. Congress votes to withdraw troops from Vietnam. Nixon takes the dollar off the gold standard in 1971, and becomes the first president to resign amidst the Watergate scandal in 1974. Hip hop and rap develop during '70s Bronx block parties. The United Nations Conference on the Human Environment is held in Stockholm in 1972. ALTAIR, the first microcomputer is introduced in 1975. The PTL Club is launched nationally the same year. In 1977, Star Wars is released and is a cultural unifier. The attempt to free seven U. S. hostages held in Lebanon leads to the Iran-Contra affair. In 1981, the U.S. Centers for Disease Control and Prevention announce an epidemic called AIDS. IBM releases their PC in 1981, and four years later Microsoft releases Windows to be run on those PCs. MTV launches at 12:01 am on August 1, 1981 with the words "Ladies and gentleman, rock n roll" over footage of the first man on the moon. In the next year Michael Jackson releases Thriller, *which remains to this day the world's best-selling album. Apple introduces the Macintosh PC in 1984. The journal* Nature *publishes a paper in 1985 announcing the annual depletion of the ozone layer. East and West Germans begin tearing down the Berlin Wall in 1989, signaling the end of a "Cold War" that had been heating up since the Truman Doctrine of 1947. Nelson Mandela is released from 27 years of prison in 1990--South Africa's apartheid is abolished the next year. Researchers at CERN introduce the World Wide Web in 1990. The Persian Gulf War begins and ends swiftly in 1991 under George H. W. Bush, but its "unfinished business" leads to the larger Iraq War in 2003 under his son, George W. Bush. MTV comes out with a show called "The Real World" in 1992, introducing a new way of telling stories. Michael Jordan wins 3 NBA Championships in a row, 1991, 1992, and 1993, retires to play baseball then returns to basketball to lead his team to 3 more NBA Championships in a row, 1996, 1997, and 1998.* Harry Potter and the Philosopher's Stone *is released in 1997. On September 11, 2001, Islamic extremists carry out suicide attacks against the World Trade Center in New York City and the Pentagon in Washington, D.C., shattering the U.S.'s sense of safety. Congress passes the standards-based "No Child Left Behind" education reform Act in 2001. Facebook is created for Harvard students in*

2004. The Boston Red Sox win the World Series for the first time in 86 years in 2004, the New England Patriots win the Superbowl that same year, the Boston Celtics win the NBA Championship in 2008, and the Boston Bruins win the Stanley Cup in 2010-2011. Steve Jobs releases the first iPhone in 2007, followed by the first iPad in 2010. A subprime mortgage crisis sets off the worldwide Great Recession in December 2007. In 2008, Barack Obama is the first black man to be elected president of the United States. The Affordable Care Act is signed into law in 2010. By 2015, 98% of the world's cinemas have replaced film projectors with digital ones, transforming the consumption of movies. And in that same year, the Supreme Court rules that state-level bans on same-sex marriage are unconstitutional.

7

Same, Only Different

I couldn't wait to give my firstborn the gift of literacy. By four, he was reading and writing on his own. By six, he had become a self-taught writer and illustrator, composing long and elaborate stories. He entered school independent, cooperative, and creative. By the age of ten, his confidence had disintegrated. A highly imaginative youngster accustomed to learning on his own, he couldn't adjust to the product-orientated focus of school.

On the Defensive

Context

I have five very able children. My eldest son, Perry, is a computer technologist in Florida. Justin is a writer, teacher, and small business owner who auditioned successfully at eight for his first professional acting pursuit. Timothy is a chemist who earned all-American honors in track and field at age fifteen. Anna-Maria is an accomplished violinist/violist who soloed in Japan when she was twelve. My youngest son, Joshua, who acted professionally at four, earned all-state honors in soccer, and is a Reggae composer-singer.

From bottom left going clockwise: Justin, Perry, Henry, Marilyn, Anna-Maria, and Tim, c. 1985.

From bottom left to right: Tim, Henry, Anna-Maria, Marilyn, and Josh, c. 1990.

My children have been blessed with talent and accomplishment. Despite this fact, however, success did not come easily to them, especially Justin, who, by the age of four, had taught himself to read and write. Inexplicably, his talents went unnoticed in school. By the time he entered high school, his confidence was shattered. Sadly, he's not alone. Though I'm not sure if race played a factor, I suspect countless children of color struggle in school for reasons that have little connection to their abilities.

442

Following my graduation from college in 1966, with a master of education degree, I taught for two years, as teaching experience was a prerequisite for doctoral work in counseling. As I completed my second year in a suburban school, I decided to postpone my studies to join Vista, the domestic version of the Peace Corps. I expected to go to an Indian reservation or an urban tenement. Instead, I went to the U.S. Virgin Islands as a literacy worker. I found an apartment in a Spanish-speaking village with corrugated metal and cardboard shacks and children who broke bottles for play. Young men from other islands came to my apartment to tell stories and play dominoes. Many slept in doorways or under cardboard slats, lucky to know how to write their names.

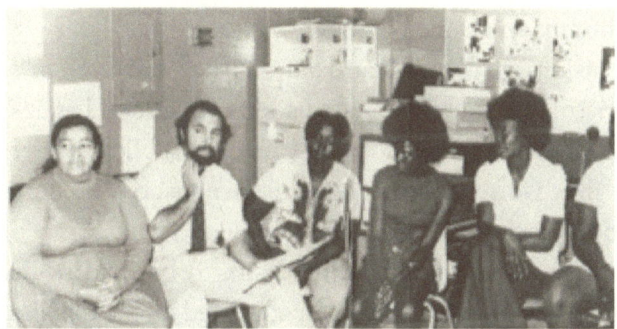

Working as VISTA member in St. Croix, U.S. Virgin Islands, ca. 1970

I helped them to read, write, and find work. A year later, I became the head of the Vista operation on Saint Croix, where I met my wife—an immigrant from Trinidad and Tobago—when she responded to a job ad I had placed in the local newspaper. She was a secretary who lived with her family and young son Perry.

When I married Marilyn, I knew nothing about parenting. A colleague who had just returned to Saint Croix with a master's degree in literacy discouraged me from teaching Perry to read. She believed

Marilyn and Perry

443

that children who learned to read at home became bored in school. "Instead," she advised, "concentrate on his social development and let the school teach him to read."

I was struck by her cynicism. On deeper reflection, though, I realized that teaching twenty children to read and write must be a great deal of work, and a child who was different might arouse suspicion. Besides, sending an unencumbered child to school agreed with the parenting philosophy in the 1946 classic *The Common Sense Book of Baby and Child Care.*[1]

Convinced that we were taking the right action, my wife and I did not teach our son to read, instead devoting evenings to simple pleasures, such as family swims. Weekends we set aside for picnics, hikes, beach outings, church, and Sunday school.

On occasion, we played board games, shared stories, or read aloud. Every Christmas, the child dictated a letter to Santa. I snuck in a word game once or twice to see how well he could follow patterns. When he turned five, we sent him to a church-sponsored kindergarten that focused on his social and moral development.

About this time, we left Saint Croix to become students at the University of Wisconsin. I had been admitted to the doctoral program and decided to study literacy rather than counseling. My wife pursued music. My son was excited about playing in the snow and making new friends. I was enthusiastic about his new school, to which many university people sent their children. A month later, I noticed that he was not waking up for school with his usual eagerness. Sensing something wrong, I spoke with his teacher. She told me that he was the only child in class who did not know the alphabet. She also said that he did not know nursery rhymes and became distracted when she read to the class.

I didn't think that we had neglected his education; in fact, I had expected my son to learn well—he was a happy child who attended a reputable school. Anxiety replaced optimism by the end of his first week in the first grade, when the teacher assigned him to the lowest reading group. For the next several months, he took turns reading aloud and copying sentences from his book. In January, he started taking weekly spelling tests. If he completed his work on time, he could go to the

"Treasure Box" for toy and candy prizes. If he didn't finish his work, he had to stay in at recess.

My son never made it to the Treasure Box. Copying sentences left him fatigued, and he couldn't spell. At home, I used read-along tapes to aid his fluency. Rather than follow along in the book, he skipped ahead to see what came next.

Perry in St. Croix, c. 1972, enjoying a carefree life.

Perry in Wisconsin, c. 1975, going to school.

445

I switched to story dictation, but he tired easily or forgot what he had just said. I tried word wheels and linguistic games, but he continued to stare out the kitchen window at his friends riding bikes. Determined to further his reading ability, I yelled as my father would have done, "You're going to learn whether you like it or not!" My son began to unravel.

In early October of his second-grade year, my son's principal asked me to stop by. I assumed that my mentor had recommended me for a consulting gig. The principal met me in the foyer, grim and steadfast. Skipping pleasantries, he got to the point. "Perry's teacher reports that he cannot read on grade level and rarely completes his seatwork. I asked my special education teacher to time his on-task behavior. Here are the results." Training my eyes on the report, I saw Perry reduced to dots on a graph. The principal concluded, "I recommend that he be moved back to the first grade."

I felt like a coal truck had just backed into me. I was aware that he wasn't reading on grade level, but I didn't think that he needed to go back to the first grade. I knew that teachers could accommodate differences in classrooms. My initial reaction was to fight back, but the principal's body language told me that he had made up his mind. His demeanor was not about dialogue but authority. I told him that I would sleep on it.[2]

On the walk home, I became angry with myself for not teaching my child to read before he entered school. Racked with guilt, I couldn't sleep that night. The next morning, I dug out his first-grade folder. In it were scores of commercial worksheets and workbook pages. The teacher had stamped each one: "Good Work." His writing folder consisted of copying exercises and spelling tests. I reread his report cards. His teacher had written that Perry was close to grade level and hoped that he would have a good second grade. I reread the only letter she had sent home, asking us to practice spelling with him.

Noticing a comment about missed recesses, I asked him why he couldn't complete his work. After much thought, he said, "My brother looked different to me." I knew he was referring to his brother's birth. He hadn't dared to come back to the delivery room because the baby's paleness frightened him. I also recalled my self-absorption with my work. As I had coached my wife in the delivery room, I had studied for a linguistics test. The child had suffered in secret, an afterthought at the time of his brother's birth. No wonder he couldn't concentrate on his schoolwork.

I retrieved a diagnostic reading test to see what else I could learn. The child's oral reading was at the second-grade level. He was able to quickly correct most of his mistakes, and his comprehension was perfect. His silent reading was on grade level too. I asked him to write a story about a day in the life of a sneaker. He wrote with great flair and humor. When we were finished he asked earnestly, "Did I do good?"

I said, "Sure!" and I meant it. Despite his slow start, he was becoming a reader and a writer. At the follow-up meeting with the principal, I recommended that he remain in the second grade because he was progressing nicely. I also shared information about his carefree childhood. All he needed, I suggested, was a little more time to catch up. I promised to do my part at home.

As I spoke, his teacher stared at me. When I finished, she said, "You want me to treat your son differently. I won't do that; it would be unfair to the other children."

I replied lamely, "The child's needs can be met without upsetting your routines. Just give him a little more time to complete his work."

Avoiding the issue, she said, "He belongs in the first grade."

This exchange signaled an important moment in my consciousness about the importance of the school climate for student learning. Stubborn refusal to change an opinion had just cast a shadow on my child's success as a student. I replied, "I'm afraid that I can't allow that to happen."

We adjourned in silence, each left to sort out the next step. I feared that my son's teacher would instruct him with no interest in his happiness. I was right. My heart broke as I watched him try to spell words that he couldn't read. As the year progressed, his interest eroded. Hoping for a miracle, I continued our father-and-son projects and outings. My wife was involved too. By the end of the second grade, my son avoided reading altogether.

By April, I had received three tenure-track teaching offers. I accepted the most prestigious one, from a distinguished university in the

South. We moved to Nashville on the day that Elvis died. I didn't fear the legacy of racism—I assumed that the university would safeguard us. My unease had more to do with keeping my job. Knowing how much effort I had to expend to write, I knew that keeping my job would be difficult. But I was determined not to fail.

Our son's new school sat on a tree-lined street amid single-family dwellings. It was a turn-of-the-century brick building with big, airy classrooms, much like the Adams School of my childhood. Unlike the Adams School, however, forced integration dictated bussing in nearly 40 percent of the student population from low-income projects near Meharry Medical College.

Like the Adams School and my son's school in Wisconsin, grades were self-contained. The child remained in the lowest reading group for the third year in a row. Two months later, his teacher sent home a request to place him in the Chapter I reading program. I declined, knowing that the research on pullout programs wasn't good. A few weeks later, I asked him how he was doing. He said, "I don't read anymore because I go to English class."

"English class? What English class?" I asked incredulously.

"A person asked me if I spoke another language. I said yes, because you always use Italian and Spanish words."

"Like mama mia?" I said with a wild edge in my voice.

"Yeah, and *que pasa*," he said, pleased with his pronunciation.

He was happy to be out of his reading group, but I was furious. I called the bilingual education office to find out why he had been put in an ESL class. The administrator said that the teachers asked all the children if they heard a second language at home, and the school placed those who said yes in the program. He assured me that this method was a cost-efficient way of screening children into English as a Second Language classes. I assured *him* that the child's only language was English.

I used my son's school as a practicum site for my course in developmental reading. During a visit, I stopped by to say hello to his teacher. My son's group was on the third story in his basal reader. The more advanced groups were further along. I wasn't surprised.[3]

I asked to meet with her. She told me that she didn't stay after school because she had a farm to run. Perhaps she sensed animus on my part. I flashed back to the unspoken words I'd had with my child's second-grade teacher. Me: "Everything you're suggesting doesn't work." Teacher: "Why are you disregarding me?"

I had a snowball's chance in hell of solving this crisis. The teacher's snub added to my frustration over the banal. The child had been defenseless against the ruthless pull of hollowness since he'd started school. Behind in letter knowledge and writing, he received bland materials, and teachers expected him to respond rapidly. Never skilled quite enough, he hid in the wings, his natural desires muted. At home, we reprimanded his carefree approach to life. Each year, he fell farther behind. His teachers compensated by lowering their expectations, shunning him, and trying to ship him out of the room, actions that only increased his helplessness and isolation. Socially, however, he had friends.

His downward spiral was uncomfortably similar to my father's school experiences. Despite Dewey's (1916) promise to make schools democratic and humane, little had changed since Parker's time. My child and his group sat and waited, while the accomplished children read with the teacher or worked enthusiastically on independent projects. The result was a deepening chasm between my son's ability and his accomplishments. Teachers needed to treat him as a reader, not an annoyance who spent his time in silence.

Adella and Andrew Gordon, Marilyn's parents and Perry's grandparents, in St. Croix. Adella didn't have a background in literacy, but she wanted to pass her passion for reading onto Perry.

We celebrated his ninth birthday with a trip to a restaurant. When school let out for summer, his grandparents sent for him. His grandmother, Adella Gordon, knew that he was struggling and understood exactly what he needed. When he arrived, she told him, "Perry, darling, I want to see you with a book in your hand. Carry one every place you go. Put it in your back pocket and read from it every day."

She didn't doubt Perry's ability. She loved reading herself and had passed on her passion to her ten children. She also knew that feelings mattered. Unlike me, she never raised her voice in ire. She made everyone around her feel important. She was a remarkable woman who embodied the quiet dignity, serenity, and intelligence of the Caribbean. Her love of learning was unyielding, and she wasn't going to let it slip away from her first grandchild.

Her own identity as a reader was uniquely cultural and social. Her mother had been the daughter of a Carib Indian—one of the last speakers of the Carib language and a Portuguese immigrant who had come to Saint Vincent in the late-nineteenth century as a sugar-cane cutter from Madeira. Her father had been a police constable in the service of the colonial government.

My wife's grandmother was a strikingly beautiful and defiant woman—hazel eyes; long, straight light hair; and a fair complexion. In a society that considered whiteness a sign of authority and disdained blackness, mixed-race women possessed stature. When she told her parents that she wanted to marry the local police officer, they were scandalized. He was ebony black, below her in status. In desperation, her parents pleaded with the village priest to talk her out of it. She stood her ground, even though her parents threatened to disown her. Unfazed, she left home for Saint Lucia with her new husband.

My wife's grandfather had been born and educated on the island of Antigua. He was a police officer, carpenter, avid reader of scripture, and a preacher. Although imposing at six foot four, he had a gentle demeanor and followed a simple rule: Never speak to children in anger. At night, he narrated stories about the islands he had visited as a young man. He also read stories from the Bible. He believed that character and achievement provide the only recourse in a racial society.

The family built a home on a hill that overlooked the high mountains and green valleys to the west and the deep blue Caribbean to the east. Theirs was a cohesive and self-reliant family, growing their own food, sewing their own clothes. Although buying books was impossible, reading was a very important part of their lives. Each child took turns reading aloud from the Bible at evening devotions.

My son's grandmother thrived in this environment. Quiet, unassuming, intelligent, and deeply religious, she learned to read and write at home and excelled in school. Books were her respite. After school and chores, she escaped to her secret place, a sea grape tree that faced the brilliant sea. There, on her windswept hill, she nuzzled into the boughs to read her Bible and dream.

My son obeyed his grandmother, whom he adored. He stuck a book in his back pocket when he went to the shops or to the beach for a swim. At night, he put it under his pillow. He read to himself and to his grandmother. After supper, he shared favorite parts with her. They talked in a conversational manner, without threat or tension.

Each day, he read better and better, and eventually, his desire to please his grandmother gave way to reading for himself. The more he read, the more easily he recognized words. He zipped across the pages, eager to find out what event would happen next. Patterns appeared; soon, he expected to see certain words. Storylines became just as predictable. He would anticipate which actions and occurrences would appear next and then read to see if he had guessed correctly. For example, if a baby were hungry, he expected to read about crying. His expectations pulled him from page to page. He was suddenly recognizing words that had stumped him only a few months earlier. Tentativeness gave way to confidence, pauses and skips to fluency.

On the day he returned home, he asked me to buy him Judy Blume's (1972) *Tales of a Fourth Grade Nothing*. I looked up from my newspaper, puzzled. This boy had avoided reading at all costs. I couldn't imagine why he had changed his mind. My mother-in-law wasn't a teacher or a reading expert, so she couldn't have "taught" him to read. Reading fluency depended on the automatic translation of symbols into thought. At least that's what my own education had taught me. My son's literacy jarred me. His grandmother's dictum to "read every day" had given him the impetus to read. His grandmother had made him a reader by making him *her* reader.

My son's learning gave me firsthand proof of the naturalistic learning that writers like Frank Smith (1995) had been advocating for so long, and Garrison Keillor (1985) humorously portrayed in *Lake Wobegon Days*. In the following passage, the narrator reminisces about his reading:

> It took me a long time to read. I was wrong about so
> many words. *Cat, can't. Tough, through, thought. Shinola.*
> It was like reading a cloud of mosquitoes. Donna in

the seat behind whispered right answers to me, and I learned to be a good guesser, but I didn't read well until Mrs. Meiers took me in hand.

One winter day she took me aside after recess and said she'd like me to stay after school and read to her. "You have such a nice voice," she said, "and I don't get to hear you read in school as much as I'd like."

No one had told me before that I had a nice voice. She told me many times over the next few months what a *wonderful* voice I had, as I sat in a chair by her desk, reading to her as she marked worksheets.

"The little duck was so happy. He ran to the barn and shouted, 'Come! Look! The ice is gone from the pond!' Finally it was spring."

"Oh, you read that so well. Read it again," she said. When Bill the janitor came in to mop, she said, "Listen to this. Doesn't this boy have a good voice?" He sat down and I read to them both. "The little duck climbed to the top of the big rock and looked down at the clear blue water. 'Now I am going to fly,' he said to himself. He waggled his wings and counted to three. 'One two three.' And he jumped and—"

I read in my clear blue voice. "I think you're right," Bill said. "I think he has a very good voice. I wouldn't mind sitting here all day and listening to him" (p.15).

Several years ago, I shared Perry's story with my youngest son, Josh, who was eight years old at the time. I wanted to see how a young child perceived the act of becoming a reader. His own reading had taken off in the second grade, when he started to read chapter books. In addition, he had just completed *Tales of a Fourth Grade Nothing*.

He told me, "If you like a book, you'll know it. If you like a book, you'll learn it. You have to have fun with a book. Fun helps you learn. If you know about it, you won't be bored. But if you read something that is boring, you won't be able to concentrate on it and say the words. Then you won't love it. Take *Tales of a Fourth Grade Nothing*. Perry's in the fourth grade and he has a little brother, so he says to himself, 'That's just like me. I have a little Peter.'"

Like my mother-in-law, Josh knew that the key to literacy is personal. If people read what they know, he reasoned, they'll concentrate on the words. I found his insight remarkably similar to those of Paulo Freire (1940/1970) and Krathwol, Bloom, and Masia (1964)—that desire triggers learning. In Perry's case, exercises that had done little more than take up time had suppressed his literacy. He found his way to books the same way that many of us do—on a journey of imagination with someone who matters.

The year was 1977, the height of psycholinguistic theory about language and literacy. Although I had embraced the "knowledge is innate" arguments of Plato (trans. 1992), Jean Piaget (1954), and Carol Chomsky (1970, 1971, 1972, 1976), deep down I still assumed that adults had to "give" children strategies and skills. I had totally underestimated the autonomy that children need to construct their own meaning. Perry's accidental literacies had set me straight.

Three weeks later, my excitement gave way to indignation when he returned to school. Teachers again assigned him to the lowest reading group, without any assessment of his progress. They based the decision on the recommendation of his previous teacher, and it was binding. My pleas went unheeded.

What loomed ahead was another year of the same dull, superfluous skill and drill that had already destroyed his school life. [4] Predictably, he came home filled with tears, anger, unwillingness, and resentment. Worse, he stopped reading at home because doing so counted for nothing. As writers like John Holt (1964) assert, some teachers are more interested in keeping order than in teaching children. My son could not shake his past.

Justin's Literacies

Justin, age five

Justin was born as Perry completed first grade. I decided to take an active role in his education, although at the time fathers weren't ordinarily partners in children's learning. After Perry's experience, however, I wasn't going to entrust Justin's literacy to strangers. Although I had never taught young children to read and write, I knew that literacy developed naturally under the right conditions.[5]

In graduate school, I had become aware of the critical issues in early reading. The question that intrigued researchers was "How early should teachers introduce literacy to children?" This was still the Thorndike era of using screening devices to determine who should begin instruction and who should not. Many tests assessed the auditory and visual discrimination of letters and sounds.

Durkin (1966) took a different tactic. She found a number of children who had learned to read at home and interviewed their parents to find out how they had facilitated learning. They had provided their children with abundant paper, pencils, and books and allowed them to learn spontaneously. The underlying constant was exposure to print. The children's natural curiosity about structure allowed them to discover how words work.

This era was also that of Sputnik and of blaming reading instruction for losing the space race to the Soviets. As Flesch (1955) argues in *Why Johnny Can't Read*, parents who don't want schools to mess up their children should follow his program of fifteen minutes a day of phonic exercises.

Durkin's (1966, 1970a & b) research appealed to educators and policymakers who wanted to improve reading performance by moving instruction back a year and not using phonics, per se. If children learned to read at home before the age of six, educators reasoned, they should be able to do so in school as well. Durkin's findings led to the introduction of reading instruction in kindergarten. Unfortunately, the prescribed curriculum of basal readers and workbooks was simply moved back a year.

Durkin (1974) also conducted a longitudinal study to see if a less formal approach might work better than basals. She trained a group of teachers to use the language-experience approach with kindergarten children. Her control group was a class of first graders assigned to basal readers. The kindergarten children learned to

Noam Chomsky
Aspects of the Theory of Syntax
1965

Noam Chomsky, (1928–) professor of linguistics at MIT, is considered one of the most important intellectuals alive. His theories of transformational grammar--words, phrases, and sentences correspond to abstract surface structures, which in turn correspond to deeper structures and universal grammar (i.e., learning language is innate)--undermined behavioral models of how the mind works. In the following passage Chomsky distinguishes between linguistic performance and linguistic competence—the knowledge of a language or, more narrowly, of a grammar, which makes those speech actions possible. A limited set of rules, he believes, allows the production of an infinite number of sentences. We thus make a fundamental distinction between competence (the speaker-hearer's knowledge of his language) and performance (the actual use of language in concrete situations). Only under the idealization set forth in the preceding paragraph is performance a direct reflection of competence. In actual fact, it obviously could not directly reflect competence. A record of natural speech will show numerous false starts, deviations from rules, changes of plan in mid-course, and so on. The problem for the linguist, as well as for the child learning the language, is to determine from the data of performance the underlying system of rules that has been mastered by the speaker-hearer and that he puts to use in actual performance.

read rapidly but lost their advantage to the basal readers by the fourth grade. Durkin speculated that young children who learn to read naturally do so without adult intervention or routine. The kindergarten readers in her study lost their advantage to conventional readers as soon as they came under the control of classroom protocols.

Another study caused me to question the advantages of early natural reading. Barr (1975) tracked a number of kindergarten children who came to school reading. The school retained one of them at the end of the year, because he had stopped reading. The child had given up when the teacher's insistence on correctness interfered with his inner search for meaning. Like Durkin's (1966, 1970a & b, 1974), Barr's work buttresses Dewey's (1910) assumption that many teachers spend more time on external matters, such as order, than on fostering the mental play of children.

Despite my reservations, I drew up a plan, starting with Krathwhol, Bloom, and Masia's (1964) dictum about print-rich environments. They write that children learn to read once they sense a reason to do so. It's important, therefore, to have diverse materials to trigger desire. Durkin's (1970a & b) emphasis on natural, spontaneous learning impressed me, too. Her idea about paper and pencil made sense. I would let Justin construct his own strategies. In addition, I would model fanciful storytelling and use lyrical prose, songs, puzzles, and educational toys, such as musical wheels and building blocks.

From Carol Chomsky (1976), I borrowed the notion of using predictable books in a read-along format, as well as magnetic letter activities. Like Durkin, she discovered that young children are curious about letters if adults present them naturally. I also accepted her point about accommodating children's spontaneous spelling.

Finally, I would encourage Justin to watch *Mr. Rogers' Neighborhood* (1968–2001) and *Captain Kangaroo* (1955–1984). I felt very good about the calm reassurance that Mr. Rogers communicated to children, and the kindness and humor of Captain and his gang. Both shows celebrated the innate goodness of children.

We had very little money, so Marilyn hunted for materials at garage and estate sales and buttressed those purchases with library books. We purchased inexpensive Golden Books, puzzles, pencils, paper, crayons, and posters. We collected pop-culture books and found cloth books that Justin could bring with him right into the bathtub.

A real advantage of purchasing inexpensive materials is that the children can mark them up, bring them outside, or even lose them without great monetary loss. I was impressed with the idea that children will naturally want to interact with these materials, so adults should not discourage youngsters from scribbling in them.

Building a library was inexpensive and fun. The hard part was finding time to be with Justin. My transition from graduate student to university professor had been difficult. I was putting in eighty-hour workweeks, leaving early in the morning and arriving home, exhausted, in the dark. I had five different course preparations, two in areas about which I knew little, so I had to learn new content and develop instructional activities. Moreover, two of my courses were field-based, so I had to be on the road three days a week. Because I believe in using writing as a tool for learning, I also had a constant stack of student papers to read. I took advising seriously, so I followed an open-door policy, even though department obligations required me to prepare for and attend weekly committee meetings. Working in my office was difficult, interrupted by student drop-ins and incessant telephone calls.

Worse, I had left Wisconsin with my dissertation half finished, which caused my new dean to immediately cut my salary by 10 percent. Being the son of a tough guy, I lowered the thermostat, stopped eating out, and worked like a robot. I ate supper and then helped Perry with his math homework. Next, I prepared Justin for bed and read to him. Once he fell asleep, I moved to the dining room table to pick up with my dissertation.

I rarely made it out of the boys' bedroom without falling asleep with a child's book in my hand. For one thing, stories that don't hold my interest put me to sleep. All I could think about was finishing them. Most of the time, I simply fell asleep because Justin didn't want me to leave.

I reminded myself that "read-alouds" were supposed to be fun, not painful. A change occurred a few months later, thanks to my review of notes about Carol Chomsky's (1972) study of syntax in older children. She discovered that parents who share books that they had enjoyed as youngsters read aloud in a more animated fashion.

I found a copy of Disney's *The Three Little Pigs* (1933), the TV version that I had adored as a child. Precious memories of my uncle building his house flashed before me. I even started to whistle "Who's Afraid of the Big Bad Wolf?" (1933). I couldn't wait to share my memories with Justin.

As soon as I started reading the book to him, something changed. My voice was alive with energy and affection. I dramatized the wolf blowing down the house, pausing with great exaggeration whenever he huffed and puffed. Justin was so caught up in my excitement that he ran around the bedroom in circles.

I hadn't wandered, lost my place, or dozed off. The next night, I turned reading into a multimedia event. With great fanfare, I pulled out of the closet a Disney album of favorite tunes, including "Who's Afraid of the Big Bad Wolf?" I put it on the record player, opened the album jacket, and showed him the illustrations. Together, we studied the pictures as we listened to the music. Other books followed.

Shortly after he turned two, Justin learned to print the alphabet. Marilyn had found a used easel at a garage sale and equipped it with newsprint, tempera paints, and brushes. As a children's record played, I printed a single letter in big, colorful strokes. Justin watched and then tried it himself. He liked the activity so much that he rapidly learned to paint and name each letter.

A year later, Marilyn dropped him off at my office on her way to music class. I was busy, so I gave him a pad of paper and a pencil. A few minutes later, he said that he had a present for me. It was a remarkable portrait of me with my pipe. With a few well-placed vertical and circular lines, he'd created a subtle figure with arms and legs attached to a head, body, and feet. This portrait wasn't scribbling or a generalized abstraction common to children of his age. He'd drawn me precisely in very little time.

I was astonished, as I hadn't seen him draw before. Nor had I taught him how, per children's art experts Kellogg and O'Dell's (1967) assertion that adults must teach children to draw. My only recollection of Justin's artwork had been his Magic Marker scribbles on the dining room walls, markings that I had washed off as soon he'd made them. As with Perry, Justin was helping me to break down conventional assumptions about how children learn.

I asked this self-taught artist if he liked to draw. He said, "Yes." I flashed back to my own memories of drawing on notepads that my dad brought home from the shipyard. "Make sure," I said to myself, "to have lots of paper in the house." I raced ahead to the future, relieved to know that this precocious observer would become an early reader.

At about this time, we purchased an older home across town, a "handyman's special" that an assistant professor with a growing family could afford. We asked the kids to choose their bedrooms. Justin chose a tiny space at the top of the second-floor landing. Perry chose the bigger room. I painted the walls, sanded and stained the floors, and stripped down and refinished a circular oak table and chairs for a workstation.

Marilyn purchased affordable furniture at auctions and stocked their rooms with paper, pencils, crayons, books, posters, globes, and record players. One Sunday after church, she surprised them with a box of used computer paper. Justin especially loved his room. It was a place of fantasy and imagination to be alone, look at picture books, listen to records, and draw.

When Justin turned three, we sent him to Mercy Montessori School, near campus. I had noted in class my desire to find him

Justin's drawing of me, age 5 a good preschool, and one of my students suggested Mercy, where she sent her children. Having just read Elkind's (1967) article "Piaget and Montessori," I was eager to learn about Montessori education. My student recommended a number of books, and I liked what I read.

Aside from fostering academic excellence in students, the Montessori approach emphasizes the emotional and spiritual well-being of children who exhibit concentration, attention, and spontaneous self-discipline.

Montessori believed that children are capable of learning virtues such as trustworthiness, compassion, courage, and patience. She also believed that students can learn to make positive contributions to their communities and societies by developing excellence in all areas. She emphasized the joy of learning, which creates a thirst for knowledge that brings more lasting results, rather than pass/fail tactics alone. Taken together, these guiding principles promote the education of the whole child (McClure's Magazine 1911).

The approach was compatible with then-current theories about intrinsic motivation and matched the values that were important to us. Moreover, Mercy practiced the European form of Montessori education, which keeps verbal praise to a minimum. Teachers demonstrate a task to the children, who watch and then perform it on their own. Later, they may elect to perform the task independently.

My only reservation about the school was the literacy component. Central to Montessori's teaching is the tracing of letter names and the tactile use of sandpaper letters to aid in the recognition of letter names and their corresponding sounds. Once students learn the two- and three-letter words, they sound them out as the teacher forms them. The professional literature of the time widely criticized this synthetic approach to phonics, popularized by the Public Broadcasting System on shows like *Sesame Street* (1969) and *The Electric Company* (1971/1977) because it decontextualized learning.

I, however, didn't mind the practice, because I knew that letter-sound information is essential to the invented spellings that young readers use in their writing. By chance, my linguistics professor had discovered that his young daughter's first spelling attempts, although lexically incorrect, were still phonemically justified. If she didn't know how to represent a sound in a word that she wanted to write, she used a letter that made a sound close to it. Thus, she spelled fish as "fes." The part of her method that intrigued me most was the letter-sound knowledge that she had to have to generate the approximations. How had this three-year-old girl acquired such knowledge? I found the answer indirectly in a footnote; John's daughter had attended the Montessori school in Cambridge.

During his first year at Mercy, Justin observed, traced his name using a template, and learned the sounds of letters. Although he liked to perform the life skill jobs after the teacher modeled them, he didn't initiate them on his own. His teacher knew, however, that he would reach that point when he was ready.

As the second year approached, I noticed Justin growing apprehensive about returning to school. To ease his tension, I made up whimsical stories during our commute. He and his two friends were heroic leaders who saved children from mean dragons. They also rescued Mickey Mouse from angry giants. The more exaggerated and melodramatic I became, the more excited he got. I was so carried away one morning that I ran through a traffic light. On another occasion, an officer pulled me over for speeding.

As soon as Justin arrived home, he rushed upstairs to draw stories. I joined him later, adding words. Soon he began to label the stories himself. I assembled blank booklets in case he wanted to generate his own stories. We usually played Mr. Rogers records when we worked together. Justin liked to listen to Popeye, as well. This character, perhaps the most familiar figure in pop culture, is a lovable little guy who believes that people should never be rude to one another. Justin also loved Practical Pig's messages about integrity, hard work, and honesty. His favorite lesson, however, was the power of positive thinking practiced by *Puff and Toot*.

Three Leaders Story (age four)

Justin's literature contributed to his philosophical disposition and cultivated his aesthetic sensibilities and understanding of others. As Isaiah Berlin (2002) might have suspected, however, these sensibilities would leave him defenseless against "people who regard philosophic principles with contempt, or awe, or suspicion according to their temperaments"

Justin was a four-year-old storyteller when his reading and writing exploded after we saw Altman's *Popeye*. Returning home, he turned on his record player and took out his Popeye book and record. Over the next two months, he expended tremendous amounts of concentration and energy drawing scores and scores of Popeye figures. His goal was to represent Popeye as the character appeared on the page. At first, Justin drew generalized features, especially head and arms. These portrayals were very abstract representations, but as he deduced features and combined lines into patterns, they became more like the image that he saw on the page. He created and recreated abstractions until he mastered the figure from many perspectives.

Justin's Popeye schema, developed over a six month period.

The drawings reflect an imaginative mind unencumbered by time and convention. He embellished them with various details, such as the pipe and tattoo. Each drawing built upon previous ones. Once he mastered one detail, he tackled another, moving from fixed patterns to organized scenes and proportion. By early spring, he began creating original drawings that exuberantly expressed his own version of the character.

Popeye had released Justin's creative energies. As the drawings progressed, words appeared in thought-bubbles. Soon, his reading and writing accelerated without any involvement on my part. He was learning graphic language as he had learned to speak and was figuring out how to make his stories look real. Capitals, periods, exclamation points, and calligraphy-like letters appeared spontaneously. More words followed, as he realized that pictures could not convey the full meaning. His plots became more sophisticated.

Drawing and writing became his medium of communication. Effort bypassed prizes, rewards, or contrived praise. His need to express himself motivated him. Once Justin discovered what Cazden (1972) refers to as "internal organization," his output exploded in competence and abstraction. As Smith (1966, 1972) foreshadowed, Justin had become literate without being taught.

Over the next three months, his storytelling, drawings, and reading increased at a breathtaking rate. Countless other characters inspired him: the Easter Bunny, the Fox and the Hound, and Condorman. He would meet a character in a movie or TV show, ask for the record, and focus on drawing comics about it. He never wrote about himself.

That fall, he used Mickey Mouse to reason about good and bad, matching the character to the core Montessori values of responsibility, truthfulness, cooperation, kindness, and respect. He was a charming character who solved problems without the bluster of his nemesis Donald Duck.

Justin's Mickey Mouse, age 5

Justin's wit, spontaneity, and self-confidence touched me deeply. We developed a fun, simple rhythm. I disguised my voice as one of his characters when I spoke with him on the telephone. We talked about the latest adventure or story that he was writing. He used his favorite toy, a plastic telephone, to carry on imaginary dialogues with me. He also loved to dress up as his favorite characters. Marilyn made sure that he had a Puff and Toot engineer outfit; Mickey Mouse pants and shoes; and a little professor shirt, tie, and corduroy jacket.

No Way Out

Organization Man

Two years after I arrived in Nashville, my college went bankrupt, and the university that took it over turned down my arts and sciences colleagues who went up for tenure. I was scheduled for my fourth-year review at a time of great personal triumph. My professional work had been validated, and Justin had just acquired powerful literacies that informed my research and teaching. My department chair presented his recommendation to my department:

> Professor Amoroso has not established a [publishing] record and it is unlikely he can in the next two years. Given his propensity toward teaching and service, Professor Amoroso will be better served if he works at an institution that values teaching over scholarship. He will also be more marketable if he searches for a job without the stigma of losing his tenure.

I had done everything that the department and university had asked of me. Over three years, I had developed and taught ten new courses, three at the doctoral level. Despite my heavy teaching and advising load, my teaching recommendations were superior. In fact, undergraduate students had just voted me "Favorite Professor." I also had a varied service record, including committee work, statewide and overseas consulting, leadership in the development of an off-campus master's program, and successful Peace Corp collaborations. In terms of scholarship, I had written grants, opened a Freirian line of inquiry into adult learning, adapted Cuban literacy techniques to American learners, presented research at one regional and two national conferences, and published three articles.

Wearing my liberalism on my sleeve hadn't helped. I had frequently criticized our teacher education program for placing students in all-white, middle-class schools instead of urban settings. The dean who had cut my pay had also turned down my proposal to make our campus an Upward Bound site. I was expendable; I didn't fit into his culture. Scapegoating foreshadowed what lay ahead for Justin.[6]

We moved to Maine in December and rented a cottage on the beach. The closest Montessori school was twenty miles away. We decided to send Justin to the local kindergarten because winter driving conditions were treacherous. I was disappointed, however, having become a staunch advocate of the Montessorian education that had encouraged my son's joy of learning. He was a happy, self-motivated youngster who loved school and constantly read and wrote stories.

A colleague who lived in the same town assured me that the local school honored the personal happiness of every child. I met with the building principal to tell him about Justin. He listened respectfully and welcomed us. Unfortunately, I learned quickly that the school was not a match for my son's needs. He was coloring sheets instead of creating stories. He also spent time cutting out and pasting figures and completing reading readiness worksheets. Justin didn't mind; he was happy to ride the bus to school and play with his new friends. Besides, his real literacy occurred at home.

My impulse was to overlook the wasted time. Still, I couldn't understand why his teacher was ignoring his lively and vital literacy. I worried too about the impact that this dismissal was having on his love of learning. Perhaps Durkin (1974), Barr (1975), and my colleague in the Virgin Islands had been right about young natural readers threatening the status quo of the classroom.

In the meantime, the junior high school tested Perry's intelligence without notifying us. Fed up, we moved to a different community, where maple trees framed white clapboard homes. Steepled churches, historic shops, and red brick architecture connoted order and tradition. Immaculate school buildings surrounded by tall pines and expansive fields gave form to the neighborhood for which I had longed as a child. This place seemed like the perfect community in which to raise my sons.

Two weeks later, we enrolled Justin in an art camp at my university. He came home excited about kids wanting to be his friends because he was "the best artist in camp." When a local TV crew shot a segment on children's art, the reporter highlighted Justin's remarkable drawing of a feather, noting his impressive artisanship: correctly aligned shapes, proper placement of the feather, and deftly understated linework. His teacher passed off the drawing as normal for his age.

Feather etching composed by Justin at age 7

As a courtesy, I telephoned the principal of the elementary school to introduce myself. His reply was chilling: "Don't bother to come by if your intention is to request a new or specific teacher for your child. We don't do that here." There wasn't much that I could say, given that he had completely misunderstood my intention. Apparently this Norman Rockwell lookalike town didn't take kindly to strangers. I knew something about New England candor, but this principal's demeanor went well beyond the norm. Subsequent inquiries confirmed my worst fears: Justin's new principal had a reputation for keeping kids in their place.

Perry's entry into junior high school was equally appalling. Bullies looking to gain or solidify their reputations waited after school to attack him—the only African American child in the school. When I told the principal about this issue, he responded accusatorily: "Perry must have done something to provoke the kids."

Vandals regularly kicked over our white picket fence. US Immigration Service agents entered our home on a tip that my wife was an "undocumented worker." I constantly had to pick up candy wrappers and empty soda cans from our lawn. When I went back to the school principal, he informed me that once students left school property, he was not responsible for their behavior. The police agreed.

Perry came home perplexed about his inability to jump as high as other kids. I laughed to myself, because he was on the heavy side. The source of his confusion, however, was not amusing. His science teacher had told the class that blacks are superior athletes to whites because they have double hamstring muscles.

As a teacher myself, I had never embraced radical notions about teacher incompetence. Nor had I assumed that racial prejudice was at the root of such a problem. Yet my children experienced harassment daily. No amount of training had prepared me for this circumstance. I had an obligation to find schools that wanted them.

I remembered visiting a private school during my Montessori search. Every teacher who had met Justin had been friendly and courteous. The principal, a graduate of the University of New Hampshire who had studied under Donald Graves, encouraged journal writing, children's art, and work suited to each child's level of development.

On this visit, I asked her about the students. She told me that most were from middle-income families who scraped together tuition dollars so that their children could experience a "child-centered" approach to learning. This type of environment is what Justin needed: friendly, knowledgeable teachers who shared a common vision about childhood and learning.

Justin went into a small, nongraded class of ten boys and one girl. Instead of relying on snapshot placement tests, his teacher experimented with a variety of curricular activities over a four-week period. She shared the results with us and listened to our recommendations for year-long goals.

Justin wrote daily in a journal that he then handed in to his teacher for spelling corrections. The teacher gave spelling tests and taught handwriting skills separately and instructed skill work via a third-grade basal. Justin recorded daily the number of pages he read from chapter books.

After school, he went straight to his bedroom to read and write. By this time, we were purchasing materials whenever we could afford them. He also went to gymnastics and took piano lessons with our next-door neighbor.

He abandoned Mickey and Popeye for Jen of *The Dark Crystal* (Kurtz, Hensen, Oz, & Odell 1982), listening to the story so often that he memorized it word for word. In Theroux's (1996) terminology, Justin owned the story.

Justin's illuminated story about The Dark Crystal *composed at age six*

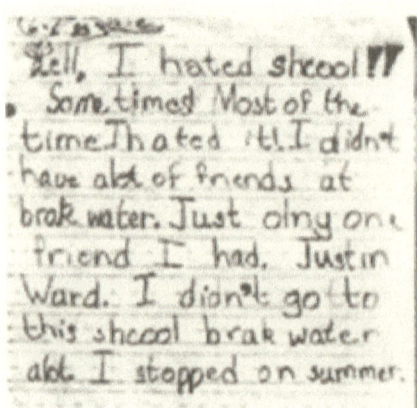

Justin's journal entry, first grade

Justin's prose became lyrical and virtuosic in length. Highly fanciful or supernatural characters dominated his fiction. His printing was exquisite and his mechanics appropriate.[7]

Despite his profuse literacies, we decided to send Justin to public school for the second grade. Our reasons were simple: Justin had a great capacity to notice people's moods. He often encouraged his classmates with praise, and when new children arrived at school, he was the first to befriend them. Yet he wasn't happy. He mentioned repeatedly that he didn't speak as well as the other children. I found a journal entry in which he lamented the fact that he had only one friend at school. The real culprit of our decision, however, was economic. We couldn't afford another year of private school.

On a drive back from apple picking in September, I heard Justin crying in the backseat. When I asked what was wrong, he answered with a question of his own: "Why am I different from the other kids?" He was ashamed because, to minimize his teacher's work, the reading specialist sent him from his classroom daily to another teacher. Although Justin read chapter books, this teacher put him in a third-grade basal so that he wouldn't jump too far ahead of the other children. I told the specialist about Justin's discomfort over leaving the room. He didn't respond.

The following week, he asked me to come to the school. "Justin," he said, "has a reading problem." I thought that he was playing a joke on me. "No," he responded, "Justin cannot segment vowels." I replied that the act in question probably didn't make sense to Justin because he had learned to read without segmenting vowels.

His teacher, who had been silent, now chided me for ignoring such an essential skill. When I disagreed with her pedagogy, she became hysterical, screaming, "You're arrogant, just like your other colleagues in the reading department." Her hysteria caught me off guard. Although I didn't cross swords with her, I remembered Barr's (1975) portrait of the boy who stopped reading. I wondered if I should speak with the principal, a school board member, or the superintendent. In the end, I concluded that no one would listen. Justin's education was a fait accompli in this pristine town of absurd pretensions. Like many parents before us, we took out a loan and sent him back to private school.

The Same Mistakes

The school had recently hired Justin's third-grade teacher for her expertise in special education. She was friendly and outgoing, with a good sense of humor. Justin liked her. In school and at home, he continued to produce compilations of inspired stories and artwork. Inexplicably, she rarely acknowledged his efforts.

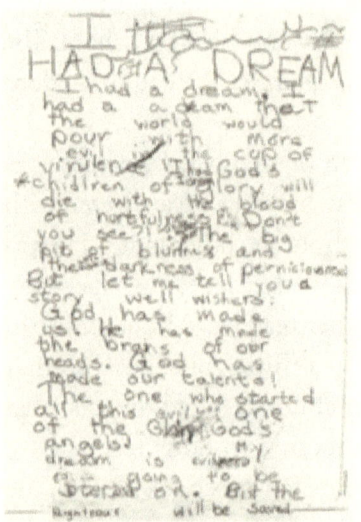

Justin's first draft of
"I Have a Dream"

One January afternoon, he told me that he wasn't a good writer. "Why?" I asked. As part of Martin Luther King Jr. Week, his teacher had played the "I Have a Dream" speech. For homework, she asked the children to write their own dream speech. Justin drafted one and then met with her. She asked him where he got the big words and questioned its "anti-Semitic" tone. She also told him to make it neat and coherent.

The teacher posted Justin's rewrite on the bulletin board, although he liked his first draft better. He said, "I tried to sound like Dr. King, so I spoke like him. I wanted to use words like he did, so I used a thesaurus." This "artist in residence" had captured the poetry, the grand theme, and the style of Dr. King's eloquence. In doing so, he had invented songlike prose, aesthetically pleasing in allegory and flow. Nevertheless, he did what the teacher instructed and toned down the writing. Another adult—yet again—had glided over his self-expression and feelings.

I had a dream. I had a dream that more evil will be coming to the wold. And the people of God will turn bad by the evil devil. You've got to change before its to late. Before it is to late to go in the evil pit of evil and unjustice. I had a dream that the evilness will be stepped on and if you change you'll be saved.

Revised draft of Justin's "I Have a Dream" speech

I begged Justin's teacher to understand his literacies. He wrote to comprehend the world. I used an entry from his home journal titled "The Interview of Tim" to demonstrate how he used dialogue to clarify his understanding of relativity:

"The Interview of Tim"

Gorge: Is light space? or space is light?

Tim: actually both

Gorge: how??

Tim: Think of it this way: light is in space, so space is half light, get it??

Gorge: NO!

Tim: light is in space right …

Gorge: Yes,

Tim: So half would be light. Wait heres a easier way of saying it, first space is whole but light is moving fast so there is a lot of light. Its both. Get it now??!

Gorge: Yes.

So now do you get it?

_____ (Y or N?)(If you don't understand ...
SPACE AND LIGHT SHARE!!!)

His teacher responded, "Justin chooses books that are too difficult for him to read. He's trying to impress me. There's obviously something wrong, since he chooses to read, not play, at recess." Later in the year, she paired him with a struggling reader in the hope that Justin's fluency would rub off on the boy. The opposite effect occurred. In a need to fit in, Justin started to mimic his partner's pauses and hesitations.

I was so desperate and frustrated that I shared Elkind's (1981) analysis of learned helplessness in *The Hurried Child: Growing up Too Fast Too Soon* with his principal. Justin was either too good or not quite good enough. Whatever the case, I didn't know how to stop the steady assault. Justin was metamorphosing into something closer to a failure than a truly literate person.

I recalled hearing in graduate school that if schools taught children to speak, they would turn out mute. I didn't want to believe that Justin's mis-education was willful, but I had to question why his teachers were turning his literacies into deficits. Had they been exposed to arcane training or misguided beliefs? Did they resent precocious children of color? Did they see him (or me) as a bit of an oddball? Whatever the cause or causes, their responses to him and his abilities were ripping Justin apart.

Chasing the American Dream

On his own, Justin auditioned for the musical *The Most Happy Fella* at the end of the first grade. His talent amazed the professional cast. The director wrote, "I consider Justin a superior talent. He is bright, imaginative, cooperative, and is genuinely interested in the quality of his work." He had the same results in community theater over the next two years. Shows included *Six Characters in Search of an Author,* *The King and I,* and *Scrooge.* Reviewers described him as "terrific," "very pleasing," "outstanding and appealing to the audience." His director in *Six Characters* also praised him: "expressive face, coupled with your dedication and concentration, made the part memorable and even now, days later, people are still talking to me about it."

At eight, he auditioned for and was cast in *Annie Get Your Gun* and *Oliver* at the Maine State Music Theater, one of Maine's only Actor's Equity group, held every summer on Bowdoin's campus in Brunswick. Directors continued to sing his praises. The head of the Portland Players stated that Justin was "disciplined and highly intelligent, creative, discerning and cooperative [with] an innate sense of his audience and how to reach them." Agents asked to represent him. Justin loved the idea of acting in movies. Auditions for commercials and films poured in.

Justin was ten when we decided to find a way to accommodate his busy schedule. The local private school that Judd Nelson and Liv Tyler had attended offered Justin a scholarship. The street in front of the admissions office was lined with Volvos, BMWs, Saabs, and Peugeots. I drove a Ford Escort. My anxiety was assuaged, however, when the admissions director told me that the school's "secondary teachers are graduates of the most prestigious universities in America. We hire scientists to teach the sciences, poets to teach poetry, historians to teach history. Our secondary teachers teach our middle schoolers, too, maintaining a writing intensive curriculum in all grades."

It was the mid-80s, when research on teaching reported impressive correlations between high verbal abilities of teachers and student achievement. Despite my reservations about our social fit at the school, the curriculum matched Justin's needs and abilities, so we enrolled him.

473

Justin's advisor and English teacher, a published author with a graduate degree in literature, asked him what he wanted to do. Justin said, "Write, produce, and direct my own play." His teacher agreed to help him. Titled *Wrights*, Justin drafted a script about a poor, misunderstood boy in turn-of-the-century America. His cast included imaginary and historical characters like Andrew Carnegie and Horatio Alger. He researched British and American history, scheduled auditions, designed costumes, worked up an elaborate storyboard, and planned a musical score.

The day before Thanksgiving, Justin's agent told us that the producer of *The Cosby Show* was flying east to meet with our son. I told her that Justin was the lead character in *Jungle Book*, a local production that opened the same day. He didn't have an understudy, so the show would close if he flew to New York City. She took care to point out that this was a once-in-a-lifetime offer. We declined and never heard from her again.

Justin as Mowgli in Jungle Book, 1985

A few weeks later, Justin's teacher told me that Justin seemed "unfocused." When I asked him to elaborate, he said that Justin had recently become "inattentive and preoccupied." He was concerned too that Justin was going to have difficulties with deadlines in middle school.[8] I asked for his insights. He thought that Justin's previous school had underprepared him for the "demands" of this one.

I suggested that Justin might be tired from recently beginning rehearsals on *Here's Love*, a musical adaptation of *Miracle on 34th Street*. I also suggested that his daydreaming might be related to his play production. Perhaps he was thinking about a new plot twist rather than completing his seatwork.

I asked Justin to tell me about school. It turned out that he spent most of the day completing worksheets. I then asked about his play, knowing how much time he had put into it. He responded that the teacher had canceled it because it was going to take too much of Justin's time to produce.

The great paradox in the teacher's concern about Justin's daydreaming was that a mix of depersonalized instruction and broken promises had negated his passions, but teachers pinned him with weaknesses he didn't have. More complaints followed. Justin's literature group had begun a unit of study on Russian folktales. The assignment was to write a two-page tale according to a timetable. Justin loved this kind of writing and, right or wrong, went into novelistic depth on a storyline inspired by our conversation of Dante's *Inferno*. He also illuminated the tale.

He missed the deadline. "What were you thinking?" I snapped. He told me tearfully that as he would complete one chapter, another idea would pop into his head. Engaged in the creative act, he lost track of time. This notion that he wasn't a clock watcher but an artist intent on creating meditations, essays, and parables escaped me. Ditto for his teacher. We failed to understand how Justin's insatiable need to know made him want to explore ideas in great depth.

Justin's educational problems escalated. His science teacher had assigned a group project for which Justin needed to look up scientific information, write a summary, and read it to a small group. He researched the physics of sound. Hearing "share it with a group," he chose an appropriate genre: A protagonist heard musical instruments in the desert.

SINGING SAND

"Oh, Sesame, I have a problem."

"Yes."

"When I was in the Mojave Desert in California where the sand was so soft I heard a tuba. When I looked around the desert there was no one but me. This scared

475

me so much I ran all the way back to Arabia to ask you what it was."

"Is that all?"

"Yes."

"I believe the tuba you heard was the sand."

"Yes. The sounds are produced when sand grains with certain characteristics like, ah ... extreme smoothness or roundness rub, rub, rub against each other in the wind or in a drift. You can only hear this when the weather is right. Oh, And another thing – you can hear this all over the world. Some of them are a sand mountain in ... ah ... Nevada that hums like a bass violan. Sounds on some beaches in the British Isles whistle like flutes.*ZZZZZZZZZZZZZZZZZZZZ*"

"Oh, thank you Sesame. Thank you, thank you." Bows to him.

His teacher's feedback follows:

"This is a fine piece of creative writing. Is it supposed to be a new article or what? Which assignment is this? Also, when you do write a summary, it needs to be straight meaning. Tell me about the article, or the animal, or the scientist. Please come see me if you have questions about this."

The remark, contemptuous in tone, shamed him into thinking that he was a bad writer. He had reached the same conclusion when his third-grade teacher had wreaked havoc on his Dr. Martin Luther King assignment. I asked him to tell me what had happened. He said, "We had to write reports and read them to our group. No one ever listens, though, because they're boring. I really wanted my group to understand my information, so I wrote it up in a humorous way."

I asked if he had succeeded. "Yes. They loved it." I also asked if he knew how to write a lab report. He said that he did.

The teacher's response seemed to have no other purpose than to shame him. He had comprehended difficult content and constructed an adventurous story based on his understanding of audience. "Singing Sand" was not only accurate in content but also correct in composition. As a matter of rhetoric, he had used the best means of persuasion available. Unfortunately, his teacher didn't share this interpretation.

Eager to discuss this point with her, I requested a conference. She said that if I wanted to meet with her, I would have to meet with the entire team. I agreed, hoping to explain to them Justin's unique approach to learning. I was greeted by a table full of file folders and grading books. No one asked me how I was or said anything positive about Justin's character, intelligence, artistic and musical talent, acting, or writing. Neither did they ask me how we might work together to make his year more productive. Instead, I got an earful about missed due dates.

For a moment, I flashed back to Cullum's (1971) *The Geranium on the Windowsill Just Died but Teacher You Went Right On*. I wanted to portray my son as the person he really was. I emphasized his origins, his intentions, and how he felt. I told them that a large part of him was the music he played, the clothes he chose, how he talked to friends. Then I explained why I had sent him to this school. I discussed his Montessori education; his self-taught literacies; his philosophical questioning; and his love of learning, literature, music, and acting. Justin was a cooperative, self-taught child of unusual ability who didn't learn well through drill. Children like him, I said, are never satisfied with their own products, so adults inflict damage when they call such learners procrastinators. I shared my concerns in an intellectual sense about his math curriculum, the play cancellation, and the "Singing Sand" debacle. My thesis was that he had not been assumptive but had simply tried to communicate in his own way.

When I finished, no one was looking at me. Perhaps they heard nothing. After all, there is no such thing as a "perfect" child. After a minute or so, the team leader signaled to me that she was ready to talk. Looking at her pen, she said, "Our school isn't the right place for your son." Her utter disregard for what I had just said floored me. Why would a child with extraordinary gifts not fit here? The school's curriculum guide spoke about developing the very attributes that Justin personified. We were talking about a gentle child whose self-consciousness was itself worthy of emulation. To say that he didn't belong was to blame him for the fact that they didn't know how to educate him.[9]

Absolutely nothing in her comment indicated how they could have helped Justin pass in his work on time. I wondered why. Was it fear of accountability or litigation? Tracking pressure? Her assessment made Justin's failure his fault. I left the meeting feeling mixed up and ignored, much as my son must have felt at school every day.

Deadlines

At about this time, Justin fell in love with the movie *Amadeus* (1984). Marilyn bought him a book of Mozart pieces for piano that included renditions from *Don Giovanni* (1787). He played them with boyish charm. A music professor friend of Marilyn's invited Justin to attend a Mozart concert in New Hampshire. Her first impression was Hobbsian-like. Children, she assumed, were too calculating to be taken seriously, but, as Justin spoke, she realized that his love of Mozart was real. She was so chagrined by her mistake in judgment that she wrote an essay about the pitfalls of underestimating children.

Justin practicing piano. After watching the film Amadeus, *he took up piano again, and took more joy in it. He would later say that piano became a "refuge."*

Although Justin had had exposure to musical notation at four years old, his instruction in Maine nearly strangled him. His teacher focused on inane TV commercials that turned playing into a

478

misery. She reacted by questioning his musicality. He stopped playing for a while.

Amadeus taught him that music is not about mastering material but communicating. Like Justin's other hero, Da Vinci, Mozart used art to express ethereal ideas. Empowered, Justin returned to the piano with purpose. Five years later, he earned a perfect score, playing with elegance and versatility Palmgren's *May Night* (1878) in the Maine Music Educator's Solo and Ensemble Festival.

I approached my son's sixth-grade year with trepidation. I had nothing to worry about, however, as his teachers were warm, supportive, and skilled. He especially adored his ancient history teacher. He built cities; made pottery; and learned about architecture, politics, and social history. Writing prompts allowed him to pretend that he was sending home letters from battlefields, conjuring myths, and researching topics that excited him. He also enjoyed English, during which he read literature, philosophy, and poetry, and the teacher encouraged him to imitate many types of persuasion. Here's an example:

> *Once upon a time, long, long ago when there was nothing but darkness and ignorance in the world, only a cold dull wind blowing about, the darkness was filled with the behavior of Hell and that is ignorance.*

To promote his identity as a writer, I took him to coffee shops and bookstores where writers hung out. His art approached boundaries that even adults couldn't grasp. He began a novel after reading by S. E. Hinton's *The Outsiders* (1967). Late in November, his agent set up two auditions, one for an off-Broadway musical and the other for a movie. He was a finalist in both. If either had accepted him, he would have had to leave school to live in New York. He was doing so well in school that we declined the offers.

His gains slipped over the next two years, however. Unhappiness and procrastination returned, due, in part, to technicist forms of teaching (Freire 1985). He was no longer learning from adults who understood him or who taught content that helped him adjust to the world. He turned to writing rather than his homework, a choice that displeased his teachers. Justin withdrew deeper into drafting a novel about intolerance. His advisor suggested that we take him to counseling. Justin's response was, "I'm not thinking about killing myself, and I don't take drugs." I supported his assessment.

Gradually, he drew away from the mores of school. Self-absorbed classmates, whose favorite put-down was "I'm better than you," contradicted his values.[10] He also abhorred the school's fixation on grades. His happiness came from self-expression, not competition.

Although Justin was an athletic dynamo, he chose to play B-level basketball. His bewildered coach said, "Justin wants to be a big fish in a little pond." The coach's moral judgment echoed an earlier teacher's concern that Justin was reading high-level books to impress her. The fact that his moral choices and behavior didn't include self-centeredness never dawned on either of them.

Justin was disturbed by children who considered themselves entitled, but many of their parents asked us to let Justin sleep over at their homes. "We want our kids to be like Justin," they said. He had an opposite reaction. Tired of being an object at art camp, in reading groups, on community sports teams, and at school, he started to read trashy novels, skip assignments, and spend all his money on the first day at camp. When I asked what he was up to, he told me, "I want to know how it feels to be like other kids."

Justin's greatest difficulty came with his transition to exposition. His linguistic output had been prolific from an early age. Philosophically speaking, he wrote to understand himself. Exposition, however, had a completely different epistemology and purpose: to collect, analyze, and interpret the ideas of others. With roots in science and law, it replaced imaginative constructs with arguments supported by logic and footnotes. Objective and impersonal, it didn't allow feelings to enter discourse. It was the definitive method of communication in academic circles.

Justin's teachers believed that sixth-grade students needed a heads-up on academic writing, which they introduced through a rigid algorithm that specified order and sequence. Children collected sources, developed a thesis, generated a draft outline, and composed a five-paragraph argument with a conclusion. Teachers passed out examples of plagiarism.

Two of my colleagues had first-year sons at Ivy League schools who had graduated in the top 10 percent of their high school classes and with high SATs. Every weekend, my friends edited their sons' writing from a distance. They did so in good conscience and with wonderful effect. I wanted to help my son write good academic papers too.

He had a four-page research paper due in his sixth-grade ancient history class. He liked Greece better than Rome because the Romans used Greeks as slaves. He wondered if slavery contributed to the decline of Roman civilization. Knowing that he was capable of seeing patterns, I also knew that he had a *Decline and Fall of the Roman Empire* (1776–1789) tome in him.

He couldn't find any information about slavery in his library, so we went to the university library. He was unsure about what texts he should search. Titles about decline? Roman society? Chapters in books about Rome? He was also unclear about proofs. Did providing evidence mean citing people who agreed with him? It took hours of searching, reading, and discussions to amass an annotated bibliography on three-by-five index cards.

Once he had his proofs, he was ready to outline. Predictably, he drafted a plot sequence. Formulaic sentences and proofs, he said, didn't work for him. I reminded him that his audience was his teacher, but this shift in writing purpose was so profound that he couldn't accomplish it. We spent hours debating the merits of formal, empirical sentences and outlining. He was reluctant to replace words that he had written. By the time he wrote his final draft, I had developed a good case of insomnia. His structures were clumsy and packed with malapropisms. Fortunately, his teacher understood his struggle so, rather than criticize him, she coached him. "Keep on trying until you find the right word."

His dread of exposition escalated throughout high school.[11] He began to put off assignments. Dishevelment set in. He captured his diffidence and tentativeness in this note to his ninth-grade history teacher:

I just wanted to give you a note of explanation and apology. A thousand excuses and apologizes for frustrating you to the point of intolerance. I do understand that I was not communicating to you very well and therefore I left you alone in an uncomfortable and unfamiliar territory. It was quite rude of me and I do beg for pardon. My explanation for all this mess is a poor one but my honest one. My problem was, my commitment to this paper in the beginning was a very insecure one. I did not take it seriously and my whole situation did not seem real to me until the deadline came close to me. My reason for this laziness is as follows. I was confused, I did not know where to start, what I was doing and I was not quite sure what my thesis was so I was unclear where and what to research. Of course, I have the reason of my procrastination. I had such a big topic I thought it gave me more reason to ignore this very important responsibility. In addition, I kept ignoring this paper until I was so behind I would need something that really pushed me. I am fine now and have learned my lesson. I must thank you for your incredible patience and tolerance with me. Again, a thousand apologies.

Formulaic instruction, threats, scoring rubrics, grade reductions, and tutoring had not worked. For Justin, writing was too personal to be objectified and rational. He needed to experience persuasive tactics consistent with his needs, which happened at Fordham when a friend, a senior in philosophy, shared a few of his personal musings. There was something magical in his writing. Sentences expressed complex propositions emotively and poetically, in the same way that Justin had written in the past. Armed with the realization that academic writing does not have to be rigid, Justin read as much of Plato, Aristotle, and, later, Montaigne as he could. By the end of his first year, his writing had smoothed out.

During his high school years, I had tried to respect his acting life. He hadn't auditioned for a local play in two years when I told him about an open audition at Brunswick. He declined. I suggested that we would return home if he felt uncomfortable at the audition. He agreed and received an important part in *Big River.* When that play ended, a local director offered him major parts in *Charlie Brown*, *Dirty Works*, and *1776*.

Justin Amoroso plays Ben Franklin in the Schoolhouse Arts Center's production of "1776" now playing at 8 p.m. at the theater. Routes 33/114 north, Sebago Lake. Tickets are $7/$5. Call 642-3743.

Reprinted with permission from the Portland Press Herald/Maine Sunday Telegram. Reproduction does not imply endorsement.

Justin continued to have difficulties in sports, although by high school he had become a premier athlete in three sports, and coaches told him that he had the potential to be the best soccer player in the state. He also made the varsity basketball team but declined the spot, assuming that his playing time would be minimal. He changed his mind but, as he had anticipated, played little. He had another reason for not wanting to join the varsity team. Diversity rhetoric disappeared in the locker room. "Justin," his teammates told him, "you're an Oreo, because you listen to Mozart instead of rap."

Reprinted with permission from the Portland Press Herald/Maine Sunday Telegram. Reproduction does not imply endorsement.

He understood this comment to mean that he was not worthy of their respect.

A sports injury revealed other burdens that he faced alone. In April of his sophomore year, he tore his ACL, sliding into third base. Diagnosed as a strain, the ER doctor wrapped his knee in ice and sent him home on a pair of crutches. The coach wrote in his report, "Justin needs to focus on coming to practice and paying attention or run risk of injury," blaming Justin for his own injury.

The coach's words were self-serving. Months before baseball season started, Justin had earned a scholarship to a Saturday morning art class. Without notice, the coach scheduled indoor Saturday practices before the season began. Justin informed him that he would have to miss two practices that interfered with his art classes. The coach told him to drop the class. "Justin," he said, "you need to set priorities and stick with your commitments."[12]

This advice was akin to poking out Justin's eyes and then telling him that he was blind. When I sat down to talk with the coach about commitment, I suggested that he should have acknowledged Justin's dilemma rather than blame him for something he didn't do. In the long run, the coach's actions didn't matter; Justin had already begun to tire of the man's bias. When the other players elected Justin captain, the coach decreased his playing time. In baseball, he moved Justin from the position that he'd held the previous two seasons. Disillusioned, my son quit basketball his senior year to concentrate on his college applications. During that time, he experienced a reprieve of sorts. One of the classes he took was chorus, and his teacher encouraged him to try out for the All-State Chorus. In addition to making the Maine All-State Team in soccer earlier in the year, he had now been accepted into the Maine All-State Chorus. Moreover, he auditioned for and was selected as the Tenor II to represent Maine in the All-Eastern Honor Choir to sing in Washington D.C. He felt especially honored when the choir director of the All-Eastern Choir singled him out for his voice and his playing on the piano.

For years I had fumbled along, trying to ascertain the process and progress of my children's education. Although I had much to say in my own classes about educational matters, I didn't know how to protect my sons. Part of the problem arose from the stigma of being a college professor at a state-sponsored university that expected me to leave unquestioned the decisions that schools or teachers made. When I voiced criticism, word inevitably got back to my dean. I was blacklisted. The pressure to be detached from my children's reality was so great that I was unable to sleep at night. Nothing had prepared me for dealing with the atmosphere that I began to call the ethos of schools.

At about this time, Claude Steele (1992) published an article in *Atlantic Monthly* on school failure among black students. In this work, he claims that the prestigious universities in the study failed black students at higher rates than white students with comparable academic backgrounds. Something other than academic preparation, he reasons, interfered with their achievement. Steele posits that many teachers are culturally conditioned to see the worst in black children, a negation that he calls stigma.[13] No matter how brilliant black children might be, educators may vastly under appreciate them. When this circumstance occurs, the students stop identifying with learning and fail.

Steele (1992) depicts an episode that struck home for me regarding the artwork of a young black child named Jerome:

> I have a good friend, the mother of three, who spends considerable time in the public school classrooms of Seattle, where she lives. In her son's third-grade room, managed by a teacher of unimpeccable good will and competence, she noticed over many visits that the extraordinary art work of a small black boy named Jerome was ignored—or, more accurately perhaps, its significance was ignored. As genuine art talent has a way of doing—even in the third grade—his stood out. Yet the teacher seemed hardly to notice. Moreover, Jerome's reputation, as it was passed along from one grade to the next, included only the slightest mention of his talent. Now, of course, being ignored like this could happen to anyone—such is the overload in our public schools. But my friend couldn't help wondering how

the school would have responded to this talent had the artist been one of her own, middle-class white children.

An "I Can Succeed" mind-set marked Justin's early school years. By the time he reached twelve, however, he had developed a self-defeating attitude and a negative self-image. As I reflected on his school experiences, a persistent pattern of devaluation and underappreciation emerged. He was usually the lone child of color in his classes, an easy target for name-calling, harassment, and resentment.

Perhaps "unfocused" is a polite way to label children who don't fit into the dominant culture. I shared Steele's (1992) hypothesis with the headmaster who, earlier in the year, had suggested counseling for Justin, saying, "Everyone needs help coping with life's pressures." I summarized Steele's thesis and showed him the coach's note blaming Justin for his injury. I also described other types of negation at school and concluded by saying that therapy did not address the root cause of the problem.

That summer, Charles Abbot, artistic director of the renamed Maine State Music Theater, formerly the Brunswick Music Theater, in which Justin had acted in as a child, cast him as one of the apostles in *Jesus Christ Superstar*. During the run, he socialized with Broadway veterans such as Stacey Robinson, Larry Raiken, and Bernard Wurger. He responded with a remarkable performance. When he returned to school, he made the honor roll. His advisor had never seen such a turnaround without the help of professional counseling. I tipped my hat to Justin's stage friends; he disagreed, saying that he simply wanted a new start.

His battles with institutional learning were not over, however. He came home confused by an assignment in creative writing class. He needed to write the next chapter to Wright's (1945) *Black Boy*, but he couldn't, he said, because it would distort the author's message. To Justin, writing was a moral act that should not be contrived. Tampering with a completed work was perverse; so doing subordinated the author's authority over it.

Assuming that his teacher had no ax to grind, I said, "Good point. Why don't you tell her this? I'm sure she'll understand."

He returned home the next day, chagrined.

"What happened?" I asked.

"She said that I'll lose a letter grade for every day I'm late."

I mumbled something like, "Well, okay. She doesn't want you to mess with the story; can't you just copy his technique?"

That night, he wrote the next chapter from the point of view of the protagonist, a black man who worked as a dishwasher and boarded at a restaurant in Chicago. One night, the boss's white daughter came into his room to seduce him. The father exploded in rage. Justin captured the man's loathing with the social knowledge that he had experienced. His teacher went out of her way to downgrade the paper because the seduction scene was too graphic.

In late August, his community theater director offered him the part of Tobias in *Sweeney Todd*, promising him that rehearsals would not interfere with schoolwork. Justin agreed. I thought ahead to his other responsibilities: serving as soccer captain, filling out college applications, and keeping up with demanding classes. He said that he could balance school and acting. He craved the camaraderie that he always found with cast members.

He arrived home after soccer practice, ate, drove to rehearsal, and then returned home at ten to study. Most of the time, he fell asleep at his desk. I begged him to drop the play. He insisted that he had given his word, so he couldn't quit. I asked him to alert his teachers about his predicament, but he was afraid to speak with them.

His first quarter grades arrived just before *Sweeney Todd* ended. Justin's teachers blamed his difficulties on a lack of commitment. I met with his advisor to tell him that I couldn't defend Justin's behavior. He suggested that Justin speak with his teachers. I pointed out that he was too sensitive to criticism to do so, but the man just reaffirmed Justin's need to speak with his teachers.

The following night, his principal attended the show—the first time that faculty or staff had seen Justin perform on stage. He was so impressed with Justin's talent and energy that he sent us a note. We appreciated his genuine and heartfelt sentiment; still, we needed to find a way for his teachers to see him in a different light.

I encouraged Justin to take a course at my university as one way to remove himself from the negativity at school. He did very well, but he had one final crisis to overcome: He had fallen behind on his gender studies project. His teacher had implied that he plagiarized a source, which was enough to make him feel like a fraud. He said that no one could question "sacred truths" in class without being called sexist. When I asked Justin what the teacher did when classmates attacked him, he said, "Nothing."

The state baseball tournament had just begun when I found out about these troubles. I told him that he couldn't play until he completed his work. He didn't disagree; he knew that he had to live up to his responsibilities. The coach was livid over losing his lead-off hitter and center fielder and had his assistant call repeatedly to ask me to let Justin play. He returned to the lineup as soon as he completed his project.

College and Beyond

Justin matched the admissions profiles of highly selective schools: intellectually curious and multitalented. With regard to personal qualities, he had few peers. His previous headmaster said that Justin "was one of the most mature, motivated, and honest students ever to attend the school." His current principal wrote that he was "a rare and talented young man." His Senior Male Sportsman of the Year announcement characterized him as a "quiet but intense leader ... who holds the value of good ethics as the basis of his style of play." Middle-school classmates had voted him the person who demonstrated the "greatest amount of daily cheerfulness, patience, and understanding in his relationships with other members of the school family." Past theater directors praised his dedication, concentration, and sense of audience.

Justin discovered quickly that Tier I institutions profile academic achievement, not talent or character. GPAs, SATs, academic awards, and teacher recommendations matter, nothing else. Artistic and athletic accomplishments are "extracurricular." Personal qualities like gentleness, discipline, and selflessness bear no relation to admission.

Justin's SAT scores were average; his GPA a solid B; and his awards prolific in voice, piano, leadership, and athletics. No one in his class had achieved so much in so many areas. Yet no teacher or staff member would give him an unconditional recommendation. As Steele (1992) might have posited, Justin was invisible. This lack of support caused further erosion to his confidence, as did Tier I provisos that he attend mandatory minority-student orientations and take reduced workloads and noncredit courses until he could prove his ability to successfully perform college work.

Justin matriculated at Fordham University, a Jesuit institution in New York City with a strong core curriculum. He dropped voice, stage work, and athletics to concentrate on academics. He did, however, study piano with a Julliard professor. He transferred to the uptown campus the following semester and, for the next three years, earned work-study, ran the university intramural sports program, and served as a resident counselor.

Free from pigeonholing, he excelled in the classroom. His writing portfolio satisfied his college writing requirement; in fact, one professor said that he had passed in the best analytical essay he had ever read. An interdisciplinary course in language and thinking introduced him to philosophy. His esprit is evident in a letter he sent home during his first semester:

> I discovered who my new idol is. Goethe. Why have you never told me about him dad? His play, "Faust," although I have not finished reading it, it is one of my all time favorite plays. I discovered Goethe through a viewing of an opera called "Mefistofele," which is based on "Faust." The man is who I want to be in every way. In [an essay] I read, [I learned] he was perhaps one of the most multitalented writers of all time. He made an anatomical discovery, proposed an important hypothesis in botany, worked out a theory of colors, directed a theater for 26 years, and his favorite composer was Mozart. Not only that, but his writing style is very innovative & creative and his ideas of God, heaven, and the meaning of life are very inspirational. I wish I had discovered him sooner.
>
> One more thing I wanted to tell you guys about. The highlight of my New York stay happened over last weekend. Friday night a friend of mine, Bobby, and I

went to a small jazz club in the village. It was incredible. There I met a famous actor. You know the coach of the Indians in the movie "Major League"? That's James Gannon. I met him, his wife, and his nephew, who was a trumpet player at the jazz club. We had a nice conversation. Jimmy still doesn't know exactly what my name is but refers to me as "Sox" because I wore my White Sox hat that night.

Anyway, Jim invited [me] and Bobby to see his new show "Simpatico," written and directed by Sam Shepherd at the Public Theater. The play also starred Beverly D'Angelo, Ed Harris, Fred Ward, James Gannon, and Marisa Jay Harden. The theater actually was pretty small and it resembled the Portland Stage Company. It was the final dress rehearsal for them, and Bobby and I got in for free. Can you imagine that? So there I was at the play, sitting next to Jim's wife and her nephew with Sam Shepherd sitting two rows directly behind me, and I just thought to myself, so this is New York City. It was quite an experience.

Four years later, Justin graduated with a degree in philosophy. For the next four years, he managed the Mozart Cafe in the Chelsea district of Manhattan, submitted screenplays for national review, started a graduate program in philosophy, and worked as a substitute teacher. He has compled graduate studies in philosophy and teaches philosophy at Southern Maine Commuity College.

A Different Kind of Student

Despite the stigma at school he was a grounded individual who understood his strengths, learned from his failures and deftly immersed himself in his art and writing; an innate creative thinker—luminous, sophisticated, emotionally intense. At home, he taught himself to read, write, and draw and later mastered classical piano, voice, acting, and athletics. Although intellectually and artistically precocious, the encouragement he received was intermittent.

Art was his first medium of communication. His early drawings, deftly executed, reveal intelligence far beyond his years. Piano, voice, and acting gave him additional channels of expression. His performances were uncommonly exceptional, winning the admiration of both audiences and critics. Even early on, he was a multitalented artist without an ounce of pretense.

Justin arrived at school full of wit and verve, in the tradition of Montessori learners, but schooling, both private and public, only offered him learning that was at odds with his self-directed predisposition. He found little value in the almost exclusive emphasis on systemized learning. No one wanted to hear about his digressions or discoveries. Unless he manufactured false conformity, he risked failure.

Throughout his journey, he remained principled and also steadfast in his literacies. He showed great courage and patience with those who ignored him; thus, it's hardly surprising that he rejected alcohol and drugs and never played the race card.

Justin continues to follow his muse, writing about social issues in contemporary life. In addition, he draws in his sketchbook, plays in pickup games, practices his piano, collects books, and reads incessantly. Metaphorically speaking, he is home again. When I first interviewed him for this chapter, he told me, "You're making too much out of my school experience. I was too ambitious. It was all part of growing up. Don't worry; I'm not a quitter."

Recently, he reflected on what went awry in his education:

> Here is why I shut down in high school and did better at college. Whenever education seemed to be for its own sake, whether it was my education as a four-year-old, in the sixth grade, or in college, I did well. I felt free from competition and prestige. When grades became an issue—receiving lower marks for earnest work—I shut down. I found a voice in philosophy, because ideas were not split into separate subjects but intertwined with moral questions.

This is the world I lost and recovered in philosophy. Why did the burden of prestige drop? I am not sure. Maybe the geographic split from home, maybe the encouragement to pursue a major not for financial gain but for the love of it, or maybe I was determined to prove to myself that I was not as stupid as I felt in high school. The point is, when my approach to education changed—to enjoy learning—things changed.

Indeed, Justin's life has been a footnote to his earliest literacies, reflecting the virtues of Rose and Adella. His talents, achievements, and goodness remind us not to leave out or give up on students who don't fit in.

Notes

1. Dr. Benjamin Spock, 1903–1998, personifies progressive thought in action. In his lifetime, his text *The Common Sense Book of Baby and Child Care*, first published in 1946, "would go through seven editions; be translated into 39 languages; and sell more than 50 million copies, making it second in sales only to the Bible" (Bright Knowledge 2011, para.23). His focus on the emotional aspects of childhood and family dynamics was revolutionary. He assured parents that cuddling babies and bestowing affection on children would only make them happier and more secure. Instead of adhering to strict, one-size-fits-all dictates on everything from discipline to toilet training, Spock urged parents to be flexible and see their children as individuals. Perhaps most revolutionary of all, he suggested that parenting could be fun, that mothers and fathers could actually enjoy their children and steer a course in which their own needs and wishes also were met …

   Dr. Benjamin Spock, 1903-1998 (2004). For a compilation of essays authored by Spock, see Stein (2001), *Dr. Spock's the First Two Years: The Emotional and Physical Needs of Children from Birth to Age Two*. To examine Spock's themes in the development of thinking about childhood, see Synnott (1983), "Little Angels, Little Devils: A Sociology of Children."

2. Perry's story mirrors the closed climate of schools prevalent in many twentieth-century social institutions. Crozier (1964) hypothesizes that autocratic institutions reflect the cultural values and traditions of society and serve to perpetuate them. Nachtscheim and Hoy (1976) believe that control ideology and authoritarianism in personality are directly related.

3. Researchers like Hadermann (1976) and Lefkowitz (1972) had been reporting for some time that grouping practices discriminate against children in the lowest "ability" groups. Children in the highest ability groups usually cover more content and work faster than those in low-ability groups. High-ability groups also receive more flexibility in procedures and assignments and more emphasis on comprehension than the lower ability groups, which usually engage in structured assignments on decoding skills.

4. Before 1776, instructional materials in reading stressed religious themes. By the 1840s, graded textbooks like the *McGuffey Eclectic Readers* replaced the Psalter and the Bible with stories that focused overtly on moral tales and religious tenants (Westeroff 1978; Murphy & Murphy 1984). By the end of the nineteenth century, the aim of basic readers had evolved to cultivating

a taste for literature. When educators and publishers discovered that many children were unable to read and write (Smith 1934/1965), they reduced words per page and switched content to factual, informative, or contemporary concerns. By the 1930s, reading further narrowed to a sequence of skills carefully organized around proficiency charts (Robinson 1977). Despite the scientific control of reading, Americans continued to crave the moral content of the nineteenth-century McGuffey readers (Bohning 1986).

5. Goodman's (1967) psycholinguistic theory posits that readers predict words in context. Frank Smith (1971) talks about spontaneous natural reading, as does Dolores Durkin (1970a, 1970b). Carol Chomsky (1970, 1971) offers insights into invented spellings and is convinced that writing precedes reading.

6. Sociologists and others social scientists have long argued that stigmatized groups are frequently blamed for their shortcomings by the very people who oppress them (Henslin 2003). Others (Sykes 1992; Dineen 1996) reject victimization as liberal bias that minimizes responsibility. They believe that the psychotherapeutic community and attorneys perpetuate a victim culture for their own financial and professional gain.

7. Justin was a quiet, discreet, and efficient learner in the constructivist tradition. He was entirely self-directed, as Piaget (1954), Smith (1966), and Taylor (1989) define it. His literacy learning effectively supported Chomsky's (1968) innate theory of learning. We avoided labeling him "gifted" because we didn't want to use him as a status symbol.

8. Time is an artifact invented in part by Frederick Taylor to increase profits in a commercial society (Accel Team Development 2008; Doray 1988). In contrast, some children stick to tasks until they perfect them and are indifferent to time and deadlines.

9. Delpit (1988, 1995) posits that schools dismiss the culture of the less powerful as inconsequential or deficient. To counter this predicament, she wants all students to learn the rules of power.

10. Graduates of prep schools tend to dominate the world of business and finance (Armstrong 1981). Cookson and Persell (1985) found that many prep school graduates assume that their effort gives them the right to be ahead of others. In another of their works, Persell and Cookson (1985) report that elite schools have limited impact on their students' commitment to service because many learners embrace their parents' pursuit of success, power, and money.

11. For a critique of expository writing, see Andrews (2003), "The End of the Essay?"

12. Increasing numbers of young children participate in adult-organized, community-based sports (MacPhail, Gorely, & Kirk 2003). Most parents believe that the goals of youth sports are fun, fair play, and development. Berlage (1982) found, however, that youth sports orient children to a corporate economy. Fathers believe that sports foster the importance of learning to be part of a team, and coaches emphasize the need for the child to totally commit to the team. This stress on dedication to the team is similar to corporate demands for total commitment. See Figler (1981), *Sport and Play in American Life: A Textbook in the Sociology of Sport* for a critical appraisal of sport as a political tool and method of socializing children to competition.

13. In the original study of Pygmalion effects, Rosenthal and Jacobson (1968) told teachers that several of their students had exceptional abilities. These students outperformed their peers, particularly in grades one and two. Thorndike (1968) counters that the study data are flawed. Brophy and Good (1970) investigated the relationship between teachers' perceptions of students' abilities and their manner of interacting with students in classroom settings by observing twelve first-graders and their teachers and recording their behaviors. Teachers consistently favored high-ability over low-ability students in demanding and reinforcing quality performance. Good's (1987) work takes a broader view, reviewing all the research documenting how teacher expectations affect individual students. Rosenthal (1987) also conducted a meta-analysis of the research on teacher expectations, concluding that "there is a phenomenon to be explained ... [and] that the phenomenon is nontrivial in magnitude" (p. 10). Wineburg (1987a, 1987b) counters, however, that the research does not prove the existence of self-fulfilling prophecies. In a more recent study of teacher expectations, Levering (2000) found that how teachers communicate disappointment to students can exacerbate the negative effects of their experiences.

References

Accel Team Development (2008). "Historical perspective on productivity improvement: Scientific management and Frederick Winslow Taylor." http://www.accelteam.com/scientific/ scientific_02.html.

Andrews, R. "The end of the essay?" *Teaching in Higher Education* 8, no. 1 (2003): 117–128.

Armstrong, C. F. Pathways to preeminence: A comparative study of graduates from American and British boarding schools. Paper presented at the North Central Sociological Association (NCSA) annual conference, Cleveland, Ohio, May 1981.

Barr, R. "Processes underlying the learning of printed words." *The Elementary School Journal* 75, no. 4 (1975): 258–268.

Berlage, C. I. "Are children's competitive team sports teaching corporate values?" *ARENA Review* 6, no. 1 (1982): 15–21.

Berlin, I. *The Power of Ideas.* Princeton, NJ: Princeton University Press, 2002.

Blume, J. *Tales of a Fourth Grade Nothing.* New York: Random House, 1972.

Bohning, G. "The McGuffey eclectic readers: 1836-1986." *The Reading Teacher* 40, no. 3 (1986): 263–269.

Brookfield, S. D. *Adult learners, adult education and the community.* Milton Keynes, UK: Open University Press, 1983.

Brophy, J. E. & T. L. Good (1970). "Teachers' communication of differential expectations for children's classroom performance: Some behavioral data." *Journal of Educational Psychology* 61, no. 5 (1970): 365–374.

Cazden, C. B. *Child language and education.* New York: Holt, Rinehart & Winston, 1972.

Chomsky, C. "Reading, writing, and phonology." *Harvard Educational Review* 40, no. 2 (1970): 287–309.

Chomsky, C. "Write first, read later." *Childhood Education* 47, no. 6 (1971): 296–299.

Chomsky, C. "Stages in language development and reading exposure." *Harvard Educational Review* 42, no. 1 (1972): 1–33.

Chomsky, C. "After decoding: What?" *Language Arts* 53, no. 5 (1976): 288–296, 314.

Chomsky, N. *Language and the mind*. New York: Harcourt Brace Jovanovich, 1968.

Cookson, P. W., Jr. & C. A. Persell. *Preparing for Power: America's Elite Boarding Schools*. New York: Basic Books, 1985.

Crozier, M. *The Bureaucratic Phenomenon*. Chicago: University of Chicago Press, 1964.

Cullum, A. *The Geranium on the Windowsill Just Died but Teacher You Went Right On*. Kingston, RI.: Harlin Quist, 1971.

Delpit, L. D. "The Silenced Dialogue: Power and pedagogy in educating other people's children." *Harvard Educational Review* 58, no. 3(1988): 280–298.

Delpit, L. D. *Other People's Children: Cultural conflict in the classroom*. New York: New Press, 1995.

Dewey, J. *How We Think*. Boston: D. C. Heath & Co., Publishers, 1910.

Dewey, J. *Democracy and Education: An introduction to the philosophy of education*. New York: Macmillan, 1916.

Dineen, T. *Manufacturing Victims: What the psychology industry is doing to people*. Westmount, Canada: Robert Davies Multimedia Publishing, 1996.

Doray, B. *From Taylorism to Fordism: A rational madness*. London: Free Association Books, 1988.

Durkin, D. "The achievement of pre-school readers—two longitudinal studies." *Reading Research Quarterly* 1 (1966): 5–36.

Durkin, D. "What does research say about the time to begin reading instruction?" *The Journal of Educational Research* 64, no. 2 (1970a): 52–56.

Durkin, D. "A language arts program for pre-first- grade children: Two-year achievement report." *Reading Research Quarterly* 5, no. 4 (1970b): 534–565.

Durkin, D. "A six year study of children who learned to read in school at the age of four." *Reading Research Quarterly* 10, no.1 (1974): 9–61.

Elkind, D. "Piaget and Montessori." *Harvard Educational Review* 37, no. 4 (1967): 535–545.

Elkind, D. *The Hurried Child: Growing up too fast too soon.* Reading, MA: Addison-Wesley, 1981.

"Famous doctors: Benjamin Spock." *Bright Knowledge*, 2011. http://www.brightknowledge.org/knowledge-bank/medicine-and-healthcare/famous-medicine/famous-doctors-benjamin-spock.

Flesch, R. *Why Johnny Can't Read—and What You Can Do About It.* New York: Harper & Row, 1955.

Figler, S. K. *Sport and Play in American life: A textbook in the sociology of sport.* Philadelphia: Saunders College Publishing, 1981.

Freire, P. *Pedagogy of the Oppressed.* Translated by M. B. Ramos. New York: Continuum, 1940/1970.

Freire, P. *The politics of education: Culture, power, and liberation.* Translated by D. Macedo. Westport, CT: Bergin and Garvey, 1985.

Gibbon, E. *The decline and fall of the Roman Empire* (vols. 1-6). London: Strahan & Cadell, 1776–1789.

Good, T. L. "Two decades of research on teacher expectations: Findings and future directions." *Journal of Teacher Education* 38, no. 4 (1987): 32–47.

Goodman, K. "Reading: A psycholinguistic guessing game." *Journal of the Reading Specialist* 6, no. 4 (1967): 126–135.

Hadermann, K. "Ability Grouping—Its Effect on Learners." *NASSP Bulletin* 60, no. 397 (1976): 85–89.

Henslin, J. M. *Essentials of Sociology: A down-to-earth approach* (5th ed.). Boston: Allyn & Bacon, 2003.

Hinton, S. E. *The Outsiders*. New York: Viking Press, 1967.

Holt, J. *How Children Fail*. New York: Putnam Publishing Company, 1964.

Keillor, G. *Lake Wobegon Days*. New York: Viking Penguin, Inc., 1985.

Kellogg, R. & S. O'Dell. *The psychology of children's art*. New York: CRM Inc./ Random House, 1967.

Krathwohl, D. R., B. S. Bloom,, & B. B. Masia. *Taxonomy of educational objectives: Handbook II: Affective domain*. New York: David McKay Company, Inc., 1964.

Kurtz, G. (Producer), Henson, J. & Oz, F. (Directors), & Odell, D. (Screenwriter). *The Dark Crystal* [Motion picture]. Britain: ITC Entertainment, 1982.

Lefkowitz, L. "Ability Grouping: De facto segregation in the classroom." *Clearing House* 46, no. 5 (1972): 293–297.

Levering, B. "Disappointment in teacher-student relationships." *Journal of Curriculum Studies* 32, no. 1 (2000): 65–74.

MacPhail, A., T. Gorely, & D. Kirk. "Young people's socialization into sport: A case study of an athletics club." *Sport, Education and Society* 8, no. 2 (2003): 251–267.

Murphy, A. M. & C. Murphy. "Onward, upward with McGuffey and those readers." *Smithsonian* 15, no. 8 (1984): 182–208.

Nachtscheim, N. & W. K. Hoy, "Authoritarian personality and control ideologies of teachers." *The Alberta Journal of Educational Research* 22, no. 2 (1976): 173–178.

Persell, C. H., & P. W. Cookson Jr. "Leadership training in elite American boarding schools: Reconciling the difference between what is taught and what is learned." *The International Journal of Sociology and Social Policy* 5, no. 4 (1985): 31–45.

Piaget, J. *Construction of reality in the child.* Translated by M. Cook. New York: Basic Books, 1954.

Plato. *Republic.* Translated by G. M. A. Grube. Indianapolis, IN: Hackett Publishing Company, Inc., 1992.

Robinson, H. A., ed. *Reading and Writing Instruction in the United States: Historical Trends.* Newark, DE: International Reading Association, 1977.

Rosenthal, R. & L. Jacobson. *Pygmalion in the Classroom: Teacher expectation and pupils' intellectual development.* New York: Holt, Rinehart and Winston, 1968.

Rosenthal, R. "'Pygmalion' effects: Existence, magnitude, and social importance." *Educational Researcher* 16, no. 9 (1987): 37–40.

Smith, F. "Phonology and Orthography: Reading and writing." *Elementary English* 49, no. 4 (1972): 1075– 1088.

Smith, F., ed. *Psycholinguistics and Reading.* New York: Holt, Rinehart and Winston, 1973.

Smith, F. *Reading without Nonsense.* New York: Teachers College Press, 1979.

Smith, F. *Insult to Intelligence: The bureaucratic invasion of our classrooms.* New York: Arbor House, 1986.

Smith, F. "Let's declare education a disaster and get on with our lives." *Phi Delta Kappan* 76, no. 8 (1995) 584–590.

Smith, F. *The book of learning and forgetting.* New York: Teachers College Press, 1998.

Smith, F. & K. S. Goodman. "On the psycholinguistic method of teaching reading." *Elementary School Journal* 71, no. 4 (1971): 177–181.

Smith, F. & G. A. Miller, eds. "The Genesis of Language: A psycholinguistic approach." Proceedings of a conference on language development in children. Cambridge, MA: MIT Press, 1966.

Smith, N. B. *American Reading Instruction*. Newark, DE: International Reading Association, 1934/1965.

Spock, B. *Dr. Spock*. http://www.drspock.com.

Spock, B. *Dr. Spock's Baby and Child Care* (9th ed.). Revised and updated by R. Needleman. New York: Pocket Books, 1945/2011.

Spock, B. *The Common Sense Book of Baby and Child Care*. New York: Duell, Sloan and Pearce, 1946.

Steele, C. M. "Race and the Schooling of Black Americans." *Atlantic Monthly* 269, no. 4 (1992): 67–78.

Stein, M., ed. *Dr. Spock's the first two years: The emotional and physical needs of children from birth to age two*. New York: Simon & Schuster, 2001.

Sykes, C. J. *A nation of victims: The decay of the American character*. New York: St. Martin's Press, 1992.

Synnott, A. "Little angels, little devils: A sociology of children." *The Canadian Review of Sociology* 20, no. 1 (1983): 79–95.

Taylor, D. "Toward a unified theory of literacy learning and instructional practices." *Phi Delta Kappan* 71, no. 3 (1989), 184–193.

Theroux, P. *My Other Life*. New York: Houghton Mifflin, 1996.

Thorndike, R. L. "Review of Pygmalion in the Classroom." *American Educational Research Journal* 5, no. 4 (1968): 708–711.

Westerhoff, J. H. *McGuffey and His Readers: Piety, morality, and education in nineteenth-century America*. Nashville, TN: Abingdon Press, 1978.

Wineburg, S. S. "Does research count in the lives of social scientists?" *Educational Researcher* 16, no. 9 (1987a): 42–44.

Wineburg, S. S. "The self-fulfillment of the self-fulfilling prophecy." *Educational Researcher* 16, no. 9 (1987b): 28–37.

PART II

CRITICAL ESSAYS ON THE CAUSES OF LITERACY FAILURE

8

Keeping History Alive

Chapter 8 uses my grandmother's story to argue for a critical interpretation of literacy. Rose represents the tens of thousands of illiterate immigrants who made it in America because they had the capacity to think for themselves. I explore the nature of her competence to learn from experience. I discuss the value in teacher training of studying the lives of past leaders who challenged traditional practices and beliefs.

Redefining Literacy and Intelligence

Lost Memories

Many Americans distance themselves from the past. Part of our disconnect relates to who we are as a people. We are a nation of immigrants each with our own language, traditions, culture, and aspirations. Nineteenth-century visionaries like Horace Mann (1796–1859) realized that in order for democracy to work newly arrived immigrants needed to speak a common language and share common values about democracy, freedom, and achievement. This need for sameness was rooted in the fear of thousands of uneducated illiterates in the streets. The priority became creating a common school experience aimed at making us one out of many.

Compulsory education, organized around the precepts of the Protestant work ethic, was enacted in Massachusetts in 1853. The development of sound moral character was the overarching goal.

Children acquired moral compasses by modeling their lives after famous Americans. We learned about the righteous Pilgrims who fled religious persecution to settle in New England. We learned about Washington's devotion to prayer before battle. Jefferson's extraordinary talents as an author, architect, and politician fired their imaginations. Ben Franklin taught us that a penny saved is a penny earned. Lincoln's devotion to reading by the candlelight inspired our literacies.

Our heroes taught us to be punctual and thrifty. We learned to face adversity with confidence and courage. We learned to value education, to seek truth, and to obey the law.

I entered the Adams School in Quincy, Massachusetts, in 1950. Most of my classmates were third-generation Italian and Irish Americans. The third largest group was Scottish. Our dads were firemen, electricians, and clerks. No one had a dad who was a doctor or a lawyer.

I had a classmate whose ancestors came to America on the Mayflower. She lived in a white antique house on a hill. I envied her because she was a real American. I used to steal a look at her as our teacher read stories about our founding fathers. She swelled with pride as she listened to how her ancestors had subjugated the fierce Indians of the Massachusetts Bay Colony. She knew she was more American than the rest of us. We treated her with great awe and reverence.

My American roots were less than fifty years old. Italian American heroes in my neighborhood weren't role models like the Pilgrims. They were tough men like Mario the Barber who took bets and allowed kids to look at pornography in the back of his barbershop. I resented him because he mocked America.

School kept my ethnic history locked away. Aside from knowing that an Italian had discovered America and another named it, I did not know anything about my ancestors except that their past was hunger, want, never enough work, and unhappiness. My parents were offended by the ethnic jokes they had to endure as youngsters. Their parents dressed in the old-fashioned way, spoke with an accent, and prepared odd food. They were kidded about their parents and their poverty. They grew up in crowded apartments without privacy. Talking about the past didn't put food on the table. Knowing anything about Italy did not make them smart at school.

Our ignorance was not unique. A large part of the immigrant experience was forgetting about the past. Most immigrants wanted to become Americans as quickly as possible.

Gradually, my notion of American history started to unravel as I learned that the Narragansett Indians saved the Pilgrims from starving and that Thomas Jefferson had fathered six children with one of his slaves. I also discovered that Franklin lauded virtue as long as it contributed to his wealth.

Despite my suspicions, something was lacking in my education. I was not proud of where I had come from. My heroes lived in books or on the screen. Italians were not players in the grand saga called American history. My bloodline was not a part of this story. I had not yet discovered the simple truth that Handlin (1951) found in his study of American immigration:

> Immigrants are American history. The immigrant condition is one of poverty. The immigrant easily stands for the America experience. He is not merely one of its founders but the first to feel the difficulty of the American Dream. In him played out it tensions and hopes, the prejudice of uprooting and cultural conflict.

Rose's Competence

Only later did I discover the meaning of these words. I grew up with a hero without knowing it. I was fortunate to be raised by my father's mother, Rose, who taught me to tie my shoes and to say my prayers. She took me on wonderful adventures to the city. She was a source of pride too. I knew that she had raised three young children alone after my grandfather died. I knew about the hard work she had done to feed and clothe them. Her courage and determination were extraordinary, but I never really connected to her in an emotional way. I did not appreciate what she meant to me until I wrote this book. Only then did I understand her significance.

When I was a youngster, she had been more of an annoyance than an inspiration. She always cut into my favorite TV shows so that she could watch the news. She was responsible for keeping the room hot because she was always cold. She was always trying teaching me Italian and getting me to eat Italian food when I wanted to be an American.

She aggravated my parents and relatives too. They were constantly arguing over whose turn it was to take her in. When she was close to seventy, they tried to put her in a nursing home. Instead, she moved in with a friend on Water Street. Every morning she put on her blue hat and walked to the city to shop. Although mentally strong, she was physically frail and frequently ended up lost or disoriented. Abhorring the thought of his mother wandering about the city, my father screamed, "Why can't you stay put?" She looked him in the eye and said, "Watch your mouth."

My grandmother lived outside our lives. She was a nuisance because we were self-absorbed in our own lives. This remarkable woman, who had sacrificed her happiness so that we might have a life, died alone in a nursing home. The tragedy, of course, lay in our abandonment and in our lack of respect for her past. Born poor and subjected to terrible events throughout out her life, she refused to give up. She fought back with single-mindedness and determination. We reacted selfishly, misjudging her doggedness as stubbornness and her authority as intrusiveness.

From a historical perspective, her intelligence and confidence put her in conflict with others. Although attractive, nobody wanted her. That is because her mother had taught her to need no one. When suitors came to the house, they were puzzled by her calm. Most women avoided men's looks. Rose looked them in the eye. They squirmed, knowing quite well when she uncovered their flaws. With downcast eyes, they searched for a way to retreat from the house.

Rose was content to bake, clean the house, embroider with friends, and go to church on Sunday. When she turned eighteen, she knew it was time to do something with her life. Three years later she arrived in America. Her convictions served her well in the harsh and obscene mills of Lawrence. One day a fellow Sicilian sent a love note to her. She said little, utterly indifferent to him. Unknown to her, her history made her susceptible. She gave her virginity to him but not her solitude. Her mother had taught her never to give her soul to a man. The marital advice backfired because it made Carmelo lonely and miserable. Her life was shortened by his tragic death. So deep was her pain she could not love again.

With three small children to raise, she spent the rest of her life working, paying bills, managing the household, taking care of the children, and passing on traditions and values. She was an authority figure who did not let up for a moment.

In researching her past, I discovered she had a brother who had left for Africa about the same time she immigrated to America. This thought about Africa fascinated me. I assumed all Sicilians had immigrated to the New World, but here was a relative who set off in the opposite direction. My father didn't know anything about him, so I turned to the library. I found out that late in the nineteenth century, the British began the huge task of repairing the Suez Canal. Sicilian masons were recruited to do the work. Antonio had left Sicily to work on the Suez Canal. He lived and worked in Egypt, one of the great civilizations of the ancient world. Through him, I was a part of this world and a participant in one of the greatest engineering feats of all time.

With blue eyes and fair hair, my grandmother looked different from the Italian Americans in my community. My father did not know why she looked different. I found a plausible answer in another book. Blue-eyed northern Europeans, called the Normans, had invaded Sicily at the turn of the first millennium. They brought with them plans for castles and their own religious practices. They also brought their gene pool. My grandmother tied me to this past.

When Mario Puzo (1969) described the Sicilian beauty Appolina in his masterpiece, *The Godfather*, I no longer felt suffocated. But Appolina was a fictional character. My grandmother was real. I wanted to know everything about her. Had she been in love as a young woman? My aunt told me that yes, she had loved a young man she had met harvesting the lemon crop.

Nothing had come of the romance because she wanted to leave Sicily. I wondered about their first eye contact as they worked together. I smelled the perfumed air, damp on the grass, as she told him she could not marry. I pictured her as she walked away, a red kerchief on her head. Her life in this ancient land, where Greeks had settled more than three thousand years ago, was over. Ahead was the unknown, across a cold sea that ended against the rocky shores of New England. Her love story turned my darkness into light.

I didn't know the details of Sicilian life or the specifics behind her departure. I had assumed a company had recruited her. This wasn't the way it happened. She approached her father with the idea of leaving. He turned her down, but she persisted. He finally gave in but only after setting up demanding conditions. This was a society in which the oppression of women had been legitimatized for generations. Why had she consented to his plan? Was it out of her desire to rid herself of the subservient role her culture had forced on her. A distant world was simply too preferable to domination. Her decision reflected her critical consciousness.

I have seen the pictures of immigrants departing from the ships in New York Harbor, fear etched across their faces. I imagined Rose's fears as she entered the harbor. I found out that it was rare for young women to travel alone. The more frequent pattern was for the girls much younger to be part of an entire family. In her case, she was twenty-two years old. She was also in charge of her younger brother. She was a very meticulous woman. How could she have withstood the loss of privacy and the physical examination? How did the change of climate affect her? What about the uncertainties of that first day? How did she get around? Did she have anyone to meet her? I assumed that boat contractors took care of her. I never realized the role friends and family played and the intelligence it took to face the unknown.

I knew she had worked as a seamstress in a factory but little else. I discovered that she lived in a moment of history that embodied horrible labor practices. Like other young female workers, she had to toil in a garment factory for long hours at low wages. Even more remarkable, she witnessed the most significant labor strike of the twentieth century. Her life was more interesting than anything I could have invented.

Writing my grandmother's history brought out an emotional truth in me. This tiny woman who died in solitude had been a moral force in my life. She was an intelligent and confident individual who refused to subjugate herself to anyone. She suffered great indignities, yet never felt sorry for herself. She adapted to this country, but she kept Old World traditions alive. One was to express her political judgments without shame. She was on the side of unions and against greed and selfishness. Although I didn't have an attic filled with dusty old copies of *National Geographic*, I developed a passion for history by watching her write letters in Italian, viewing pictures of her family, accompanying her to her mill, and studying maps of Sicily by her side. Her curiosity about the world—she watched the news nightly—got me reading newspapers. She loved Italian music but never put it before her prayers. I did the same. Her embroidery reflected complexity; in addition, she was a master seamstress who sewed practically all of her children's clothes. Her aesthetic sensibilities deepened my own.

Although I didn't follow her Mediterranean diet, I incorporated her sense of moderation into my life. Her stories shaped my values. She was the only person I knew who kept her promises. And although she had complex relationships in her life, her moral compass never spun out of control. Until her death, she lived humbly with a sense obligation to family and church.

Rose's spirit is embodied in our national character. We see it in Lincoln's duty to justice, in the bravery of the pioneers along the Oregon Trail, in Martin Luther King's promises. We celebrate it in the stories of our newest immigrants, the Jamaicans and Asians who are succeeding in school and in business. Conservatives bemoan the loss of personal responsibility. Movies like *Clueless* (1995) and *Bring It On* (2000) satirize the self-absorption of wealthy young people. For them, life is an endless round of having everything—cellular phones, expensive cars, and good grades without effort. Frequently, the most difficult problem they face is the choice of the perfect outfit for the day.

For many, today's heroes are professional athletes. We read about the millions they make and the way they live above the law. In the old days, we assumed that sports heroes sublimated their personal pleasures to train for fame and glory. We thought of them as team players, loyal to their fans. Today's athlete owes no allegiance to his team. The focus is on personal achievement through free agency. Market drives value. Ethics are tied to ego.

People like my grandmother rejected these values. They chose instead to shape the lives of others. They were humble, unassuming individuals who helped others succeed. Their personal characteristics were not property that was used when it was advantageous to them. They acted out of integrity and conviction. The fact she never pandered to her testimony reveals her character. I was proud of and humbled by her.

Philosophical Dichotomies

Americans like to celebrate the unique bond between teachers and pupils. Many teachers inspire us to express ourselves and take joy in learning. Good teachers tend to be funny, compassionate, and caring people who value hard work and discipline (Meers 1979). Many follow child-centered methods that have a spellbinding effect on learners. Their bottom line is to help children reach their potential.

Others are uncaring and cynical, filled with neurotic and hateful repressions. They are strict, unyielding taskmasters whose goal seems to be to keep children in their place (Brock and Grady 2007; Alexander and Winne 1997).

Conservatives blame student failure on skill and family deficiencies (Valencia 1997). Liberals find the causes of failure in traditional classroom settings (D'Angelo and Zemanick 2009). Hoffman and Burrello (2004) state that radical theorists find the root of the problem in goals designed to foster economic interests of the rich and powerful, advocating greater emphasis on critical analysis and real-world exposure in the curriculum. They also call on educators and administrators to acknowledge young people's need for an ethical framework upon which to build a good life. Nel Noddings (2005) said it best:

> Schooling, like other social institutions in our time, fails to care for people--that is, address their real needs and nourish their growth. Ruled by a "methodolatry" that values standardization over individuality, and by an "ideology of control" that sees young people as merely an economic resource, schools do not nurture students' diverse interests, talents, and abilities.

To quote Bond and Caust (2005), "Teachers vary considerably in their observational skills, their understanding of learning, their comfort with the ambiguous information, and their personal knowledge of students." Teachers also vary in their definitions of the world, as captured in this sixteenth-century saying: You cannot make silk purses from sows' ears. The aphorism means that it is impossible to turn something ugly or inferior into something attractive or of value. It is a negative viewpoint that is embedded in Puritan and Calvinistic doctrines about the depravity (sin) and predestination of the human race. We see it in today's teacher slogans like, "Don't smile until December" or "Follow the five-finger rule." (If a child makes more than five oral errors reading aloud, the page is too difficult for her/him to comprehend.) Both reveal keeping a steady hand on children.

The study of the humanities is the study of history, literature, and philosophy. The meaning behind this system of inquiry is positive and affirming. Grounded in ancient-world thinking, including Judeo-Christian claims about the basic dignity of every individual, humanists ask questions about the values embedded in society, ethics, and aesthetics. Humanistic inquiry requires an appreciation of the relationship between ideas.

Critical theory, associated with the New Left in American academia, uses Marxist thought to examine schools and society. Marx (1818–1883) had argued that conflicts within a society are based on the unjust exploitation of the lower classes, the proletariat, by the bourgeoisie, individuals with status and power. Applied to education, critical theorists examine how power determines relationships in schools. Power refers to the ways in which a dominant person or group exerts its influence over others (Foucault 1998). Hegemony relates to the processes by which a dominant culture maintains its dominant position. Writers like Habermas assert that schools breed dependency on authority and top-down communication (Ewert 1991).

Kent, McNergney and Herbert (1995) have written that many of the negative attributes of school have been identified and attacked by modern education reformers who are not Marxists but who nonetheless "recognize the debilitating effects of the status quo." Their goal is to use education and educational research to change the world. Theorists like

Apple, Giroux, and McLaren use critical pedagogy to question and challenge curriculum, testing, governance, teacher training, educational financing, and virtually any meaningful educational problem.

The Past as Prologue

The historical antecedents to today's debates about literacy and schooling trace back to the Enlightenment, a philosophical movement of the eighteenth century associated with individualism, rationalism, and optimism. In terms of political philosophy, Enlightenment thinkers contended that laws governing society would improve the human condition. This was counter to Hobbes's (1588–1679) opinion that human nature is so individualistic, warlike and desirous of power that society requires a sovereign, an absolutist, to maintain order (*Leviathan*, 1651). Enlightenment optimism resulted in the creation of the United States of America (Bailyn 1992).

Enlightenment philosophers also had a profound effect on American educational policy and practice. Noddings (1993) discussed the enduring role philosophy has had in educational discourse: "The role of philosophy as it is applied to education is not to dictate answers, but [promote] understanding of the [theoretical] issues underlying contemporary debates."

Just as Antonio states in *The Tempest*, "What's past is prologue," so too what was written prior to the eighteenth century set the stage for Enlightenment thinking. Erasmus (1466–1536), a Dutch Renaissance humanist, raised many of the same questions heard in debates about the meaning of education. He argued, for example, that the aim of education is the forming of an upright moral character. Montaigne (1533–1592), the inventor of the essay, argued there is no certainty anywhere, so a learned person questions everything. Comenius (1592–1670) disapproved of studying grammar and memorizing texts because they diminished student interest in learning. He also felt that all children were entitled to a full education.

Rationalists like Galileo, Newton, and Descartes ushered in the modern age with its emphasis on science, reason and mathematics. A study of the physical world, they argued, should replace religion as a primary source of knowledge. Spinoza (1632–1677) felt so strongly about the power of the mind to discern truth he judged the serenity of the mind as the only thing that matters in life.

Voltaire (1694–1778) wrote about the problem of evil. In *Candide* (1759), his most celebrated work, he attacked inhumane cruelty in all its forms. Rousseau (1712–1778) revolted against Descartes's cold intellectual rationality by celebrating subjectivity and introspection. Like Erasmus, he wanted teachers to develop a pupil's character and morality to protect them from the vices found in society. Later reformers Pestalozzi, Froebel, Montessori, Parker, and Dewey extended his idealism.

The Scientific Method

The scientific method, indebted to philosophers like Aristotle (384-322 BCE) who observed nature, medieval Muslim scholars like Ibn al-Haytham (965-1040) who devised experiments in optics, Roger Bacon (1214-1294) who promoted inductive reasoning, and Francis Bacon (1561-1626) who championed the scientific method as an improved way to determine facts over relying on religious dogma. Descartes's method of finding "clear and distinct ideas," pushed this idea into the mainstream. David Hume (1748), author of *Inquiry Concerning Human Understanding*, was one of the first to critique the inductive nature of the scientific method. By the nineteenth century, the scientific method yielded such great successes in the study of natural phenomena that Nietzsche (1887) thought scientists have become the new priests (*Genealogy of Morals*, third essay).

Toward the end of the century, sociology and economics adopted the scientific method. In psychology, science led to the formulation of behaviorism, the experiential study of human behavior. Education fell in love with this standard, feared by Heidegger (1933) as having the potential to "darken the world." Chomsky's 1959 critique of Skinner's *Verbal Behavior* and his 1966 publication *Cartesian Linguistics: A Chapter in the History of Rationalist Thought* espoused that innate abilities account for language learning. This shift in thinking from the observable to internal cognitive functions led to the demise of behavioral psychology. Others shattered its hold on educational practice by pointing out that studying only the observable is inappropriate to the study of children who possess free wills and imaginations (Kant 1790; Korsgaard 2009).

An Organic Intellectual

Are contemporary teachers more Hobbesian than Rousseauian in their beliefs and practices? Consider these journal entries, one from a former debt collector who was training to become a teacher, and the second from an experienced second-grade teacher:

Journal Entry One

I noticed one girl was practicing her cursive writing today. She was practicing writing the cursive letter "d" I believe, and I saw her erase it at least once, if not twice. This was kind of comical to watch because she was erasing her practice letters and trying to write them neater. This tells me that young students do not quite understand the concept of practice makes perfect yet. The idea was to keep practicing writing the letter d in cursive until they were good at it. This girl wanted to make sure that each letter she wrote was perfectly neat and legible. I think this also has a little bit to do with access to an eraser. Students this age are taught that if they make a mistake, erase it. Students see messy handwriting as a mistake, therefore they erase their writing every time it looks messy. My solution to this issue would be very simple. If students are working on a writing assignment that asks them to practice something until they get good at it (i.e. cursive writing), they should use pencils without erasers.

Journal Entry Two

The curriculum that is hidden in my classroom, but not always unintentional is that school is a warm, safe place where children are respected and encouraged to take risks in their learning. Children are respectful with materials and books. I have overheard students saying to one another, "Be careful with that, Miss ... bought that with her own money." Unintentionally I have let students know that I want the best for them, and the school is not always able to provide the materials I need in order to teach.

A key purpose of "Rose Speaks" was to remind readers that modern American education was forged in the clash of ideas over the nature of humanity. The story opened in the Sicily of 1883 and ended forty years later in Quincy, Massachusetts. Rose had to reconcile numerous conflicts: her father's provisos for leaving, the provincialism of her sister, Durmalo's presumptive thought, Marina's self-absorption, nativist sentiments in the mills, and Carmelo's gaiety. Her problem solving was active, not passive. She was focused and decisive, a useful contrast to the people around her. Although she was not formally educated, she intertwined reason and intuition with her sense of duty and obligation. Her special gift, called agency, parallels what good teachers do every day—ask questions, make choices, and act on those choices.

What is the connection in the dialogues between, say, Rose and John Dewey? They represent Voltaire's way of challenging intolerance. They showed how easy it is for some intellectuals to become arrogant (Tittle 2004). The dialogues spoke to Rose's concern that fairness should be at the center of life. Finally, they reestablished the purpose of literacy—giving voice to those who do not have it.

Many of the events in "Rose Speaks" were unbelievable but nevertheless true. The conventional picture of a turn-of-the-twentieth-century Italian immigrant was someone who was unskilled and inept. The misuse of science perpetuated this myth. Early IQ experts labeled immigrants pejoratively as idiots, imbeciles, or morons. Goddard (1917), for example, concluded after testing hundreds of immigrants on mental tests that 79 percent of Italian immigrants were feeble-minded. Psychologists like Thorndike (1874–1949) embraced eugenics, selective breeding to improve the human race, as way to rid society of undesirable individuals (Lynn 2001; Gould 1981).

On the other hand, reformers like Jane Addams and Emma Goldman knew poor and working people's intelligence and culture because they spoke with them and observed the ways they approached problem solving in the natural world. Their insights allowed them to assault the prevailing prejudices against the poor, just as reformers like Pestalozzi (1746–1827) and Parker (1837–1902) had done. Literary figures like George Bernard Shaw (1856–1950) also attacked eugenic ideology in dramatic writings like *Pygmalion*, even though he had come from the bourgeois class. That is because he believed in a society grounded in equality, not exploitation. Gramsci (1927) argued that men of letters were not the only intellectuals. He believed that working-class individuals had the capacity to think for themselves. He called them "organic intellectuals."

In Need of a Working-Class Intellectual

Most of great educational and social reformers of the past who came from the bourgeoisie class were prolific readers and writers, much versed in history. Christine Stansell (2001) pictured their homes filled with books because

> books attest to the serious and sustained immersion in the past. Prominently displayed with other appurtenances of status and self, books preside over living rooms and dens, announcing a gentlemanly devotion to learning and linking homes to an earlier age when gentleman scholars pored over thick tomes in gloomy well-appointed studies graced by dark, lustrous oil paints. (Christine Stansell, "Details, Details" [two books about Theodore Roosevelt—Review] in *The New Republic*, December 10, 2001).

Who among the reformers rose up from the lowest classes, the proletariat, without the "appurtenances" of status and wealth? We did not see the rise of working class intellectuals for long time. When they emerged, it was not without conflict. Dreiser (1871–1945) was one of the first American novelists who came out of poverty. The intellectuals of his time went after his manhood, his intellect, and his worth. By mid-twentieth century, working-class writers like Eric Hoffer (1902–1983) and Mario Puzo (1920–1999) faced demeaning labels that smacked of class distain. Pietro di Donato (1911–1992), a first-generation Italian American writer and former bricklayer with a limited education, produced one of the best novels of 1939, *Christ in Concrete*. Rather than celebrate his amazing accomplishment, one critic wrote that he had "beginners luck." My aunt Connie dealt with same prejudices, as evidenced in the newspaper reporting of her scholarship.

Eric Hoffer, called by many the first proletarian philosopher, was a self-educated worker and longshoreman. He learned to read very early in English and German, but the death of his mother and the loss of his eyesight forced him to stop attending school. When his vision returned as a teenager, he began to read at public libraries. Montaigne was one of his favorite writers. His extensive reading of Enlightenment thinkers led him to write after work in libraries. His ideal person was autonomous, at peace with himself, open-minded, humble, and critical of the elitism of the educated. He especially had it in for writers, scientists, philosophers, and other intellectuals who used the common man as raw material in their work and then discarded them.

He was right to criticize the bias (Hofstadter 1963) of the intellectual class as Benda (1928) had done a generation earlier in *The Treason of the Intellectuals*. Conflict, he argued, was class-based, the common man against effeminate snobs. Swift (1726) did the same thing in *Gulliver's Travels* two hundred years earlier, portraying the Lilliputians as sophists who lacked common sense and decency. It is a shame that Hoffer was chastised by the Left and is rarely read today. The shear brilliance of his self-taught literacies, not his politics, verified Gramsci's claim that the search for justice should come out of the poor and working classes.

Meritocracy Arguments

Disdain speaks to the arrogance of power; in this case, the use of rhetoric to subjugate the less educated. The historical context for this type of elitism originated with the Anglo-Protestant disdain for the emotionalism associated with the poor (Beck 1992).

Stephen Toulmin's thesis in his book *Cosmopolis* (1990) is that modernity actually began with Renaissance Humanism (for example with religious figures such as Martin Luther; philosophers like Montainge, Machiavelli, More, Pico, Bacon; writers like Shakespeare, Rabelais, Erasmus, Cervantes; scientists like Bruno, Galileo, Copernicus; artists like Botticelli, Leonardo, Michelangelo; travelers like Polo, Bartolomeo, Columbus).

Now, present-day fundamentalist Christians might cringe at the term "humanism" thinking it refers to what is antireligious, what is opposed to Christianity, and maybe even what is atheist. But Renaissance thinkers didn't think of themselves in these terms. Martin Luther, Erasmus, Montaigne saw themselves as good Christians. Erasmus may have mocked dogmatism in his *In Praise of Folly*, but he ultimately advocated for a simple Christian piety. Likewise, Montaigne in his *Essays* criticized theological certainty like Erasmus did, but he too considered himself to be a good Catholic. In fact, Renaissance Humanists lived within a European culture that was dominated by Christianity, and so were Christian. So, the Christian fundamentalist use of the term as what's antireligious is like a "bogeyman." But if this is so, how did Renaissance thinkers differ from Medieval thinkers, and why would Toulmin argue that the Humanists were the real starting point of modernity, rather than the figures of the scientific revolution during the seventeenth century?

Renaissance thinkers seemed to have a different attitude toward humanity than medieval scholars. For medieval scholars, the morsels in the diversity of human affairs didn't have a lot of import. Humanity's sinful, fallible ways made humans *less* interesting and gave these scholars reason to ignore them. But Renaissance thinkers began to see human foibles and failings as what made humans *more* interesting. Rather than ignore or condemn these, Renaissance Humanists celebrated the varieties of human fallibility. For them, humans could be "admirable and deplorable, noble and selfish, inspiring and laughable" (p. 27), and that's all good because both sides make us human.

The recovery of ancient history and literature only fueled the

Humanists' feeling for the many-hued diversity of human affairs, and their fascination with how those affairs depended on particular circumstances. And so, they embraced concrete experience; welcomed the variety of perspectives as intellectual *pro*fusion (rather than *con*fusion); respected the complexity of context; preferred empirical study (studying the "Book of Nature" became another way to know God) over abstract doctrine; they had a growing taste for the "exotic" and diversity of cultures since these added to the testament of human life and enlarged sympathy with all humans; and so they were nonjudgmental, and honest enough to understand that human intellectual power has limits—i.e., doctrines can never be absolute truths.

Speaking of "absolute truths" (read: dogmatism), Renaissance figures were especially wary of them. Against the background in which they were working was a growing conflict between these "new" Protestants and the Catholics. This conflict exploded in the Thirty Years War (1618-1648), the longest, deadliest religious war in European history, resulting in eight million casualties.

A "counter-Renaissance" arose during this war, according to Toulmin, as a reaction against Renaissance Humanism. In other words, Toulmin makes the controversial case that this "counter-Renaissance," wherein the scientific revolution took place, was in fact the "second" starting point of modernity. Renaissance tolerance of diversity no longer seemed to be a viable option during the bloody time of the Thirty Years War. In fact, one mathematician named Rene Descartes (1596-1650), inspired by the work Galileo Galilei (1564-1642) was doing in physics and by Michel de Montaigne's (1533-1592) claim that certainty was a chimera, offered Europe a new vision. This vision was different than the Renaissance one. And it would turn out to captivate the West for the next three or four centuries. Toulmin makes the case that we're still captivated by the vision to this day, and it has provided an intellectual underpinning for certain social dichotomies. This was Descartes's vision.

Descartes wanted to prove Montaigne wrong that certainty was a chimera by using the mathematical methods of Galileo. After all, mathematics and the sciences seemed to yield truths that were indubitable. Developing a universal method that sought "clear and distinct ideas," Descartes beat the bushes for *the* one absolutely certain truth that could serve as a new foundation for all knowledge—a foundation that would be so certain, it could be true for all time, all cultures, all humans (including both Protestants and Catholics).

Descartes's one certain thing? Rationality, our ability to think clearly and distinctly. In this discovery, he turned his back on the concrete and the particular and he privileged the abstract and the universal instead. For example, in Chapter 1 of his *Discourse on Method* (1637), Descartes says the study of history, poetry, letters have value like "travel"—these might be fun but "nothing solid can be built on such shifting foundations." Timely questions were less important for Descartes because they can lead to error. But the timelessness of number, for him, can lead to certainty. So, what was rational and apart from matter, then, was of a "higher" sort than what was irrational and of matter. In fact, mind and matter turned out to be so distinct from each other that Descartes wasn't sure how they could interact. Here's how this metaphysical dichotomy may have shaped modern social dichotomies. It has to do with Toulmin's word "cosmopolis."

The term "cosmopolis" comes from an ancient Greek idea that saw an Order of Nature (*cosmos*) on one hand, and an Order of Society (*polis*) on the other. Part of Toulmin's thesis is that the way we envision nature often influences the way we order ourselves socially. *Cosmos + polis = cosmopolis*. And so, Toulmin thinks Descartes' vision of the cosmos influenced the way we order ourselves socially to this day.

Again, in Descartes' vision, mind (rationality) was separate from and of a "higher" sort than matter. Forty-six years after Descartes published *Meditations on First Philosophy* in 1641, Sir Isaac Newton (1642-1726) published his *Principia Mathematica* in 1687. Newton's mathematical discoveries into how the universe worked seemed to corroborate Descartes's vision. That is, Newton's mathematical model of the universe seemed to be rationally ordered and stable. After the Thirty Years War, Europeans especially needed social order. The old feudal world had been crumbling, so Europeans didn't look to restore it. So, those who organized public schools, who had access to printing and publishing, and who preached to the congregations found Descartes's dream of universal rationality not only respectable but "official" (p. 119) and used it as their new social model. Here's how the "upper" and the "lower" classes in this new social world differed from the "upper" and the "lower" classes in the medieval class system.

In medieval feudalism, the social lines of division had been cut *vertically*. An artisan, for example, had a feudal duty to the "Master" above him. But after 1650, more persons were becoming "masterless," i.e., they no longer had feudal loyalties. As a result, people found themselves belonging side-by-side each other along the same *horizontal* level. The "upper," "middle" and "lower" classes were now placed on a spectrum where the "higher" order was on one end, and the "lower" orders on the other (p. 96-7).

What distinguished the "higher" sort from the "lower" sort in the "modern" social world? Rationality. The "higher" order was the rational order, the "lower" order was closer to "irrationality." The rational Order of Nature Descartes (and subsequently Newton) gave to Europe justified this "rational" Order of Society. Nation-states modeled themselves after this hierarchy of rationality: an "enlightened despot" who was now separate from the Church stood at the center of a nation-state, the way a Rational Sun keeps bits of irrational matter in the fringes within a stable "solar system." King Louis XIV (1638-1715), the "Sun King," was probably the most famous example of this new Order of Society.

This new Order of Society didn't stop with political organization. It extended to *all* things seen as either more or less rational. For example, on the irrational (material) side included: women, non-European cultures, non-European races, the "lower" classes, emotions, the arts and humanities (unless stringently rational), sex, nature. On the rational (mental) side included: men, European cultures, European races, the "upper" classes, reason, the sciences and mathematics, sexual constriction, civilization. This rationalistic vision had become so entrenched in this new "modern" culture that Toulmin calls it a "hidden agenda," something that "went without saying." And so the "Age of Reason" (or the Enlightenment) was ushered in, and along with it colonialism, the "divine right of kings" and the germs of nationalism.

The point is, in this new social order based on rationality was a dichotomy: the "upper" rational sorts on one side and the "lower" irrational sorts (emotional, libidinous) on the other. Just as the mind needed to "control" matter (and nature), so the rational social sorts needed to subordinate the irrational social sorts. Fortunately, some Enlightenment thinkers like Rousseau, Kant, Hume, Wollstonecraft worked within this framework to challenge these assumptions, and by doing so helped sow the seeds for the French Revolution.

The tensions between the "lower" orders and the "higher" orders erupted in the French revolution of 1789 and, according to Toulmin, it marked the beginning of a progression of "lower" orders resisting the subordination by the "higher" orders. After the social, political, and economical resistance of the French Revolution, the Romantic movement of the nineteenth century in the arts embraced emotion and the exotic. As for science, in 1859, Darwin published *On the Origin of Species*, challenging the notion that nature is inert, hierarchical, fixed. And in the early twentieth century, Einstein and Planck challenged the Newtonian model of a stable universe. Further in philosophy, twentieth-century philosophers like Martin Heidegger and John Dewey challenged the Cartesian quest for certainty.

What's more, tensions between nation-states and ideas of racism escalated into horrendous worldwide warfare between 1914-1918 and 1939-1945 in World War I and World War II. During these wars, non-European nations like India resisted their colonization. As a side note, during World War II, philosophers Theodor Adorno and Max Horkeheimer wrote the book *Dialectic of Enlightenment* (1947) that arguably inspired the Critical Social Theory school. In that book they asked how could Europe, the supposedly most rational civilization in the world, home of rational science, home of rational political concern for individual rights, how at its height of rationality could the most irrational barbarism develop? Their answer: when rationality is separated from nature, reason becomes instrumental, emptied of humanity. Instrumental reason divided from humanity has nothing of substance to say morally.

By the 1960s, feminists and civil rights leaders led resistances against the notion that their "orders" were somehow lower than. And the work continues today. As Adorno and Horkeheimer argued in *Dialectic of Enlightenment*, Toulmin points out that the value we've placed on rationality has, on the one hand, led to the incredible progress we've made in science and technology. But on the other, it has cast deep shadows on the human level. By applying rationalistic, mathematical methods to the social (read: human) realm, we act without humanity. Toulmin argues one way to redress this shadow is to recover the vision the Renaissance Humanists originally had, and to strike a balance between it and the great work scientists and mathematicians still do to this day. And of course, one area we still struggle with in how the "modern agenda" has been applied to the human realm is education.

In fact, Michael Young, a British politician, coined a term to satirize a practice in education that he saw as a mistake, "meritocracy." He took the Latin word for "earn," *mereō* and combined it with the Greek word for "power" *kratos*. His term "meritocracy" stood for a political philosophy that thought persons who passed intelligence exams should be the ones who hold political power. IQ + effort = merit = political power. But the practice of "meritocracy" itself could probably be traced further back in history to ancient China, where anyone--regardless of background, class, or political ties--could obtain a government position if he passed a difficult "civil service exam." There are also traces of meritocracy in Plato and Aristotle, except they never spoke about measuring intelligence through exams. But the term itself is relatively new as it first appeared in Young's 1958 novel.

In *The Rise of the Meritocracy*, Young envisioned a dystopian U.K. in the year 2034 where IQ-driven education had triumphed. The central dogma of society had become intelligence (or rationality). The elite class was comprised of those who earned their high status through effort and passing an intelligence test. The subjugated underclass who were ingrained "down there" to this lower social standing were seen as deserving to be there, either because they were genetically less intelligent, or because they were lazy. The main character, a sociologist, looks back at 160 years of British education and struggles to discover how this happened.

Fascinatingly, meritocratic arguments are still in vogue. I say "fascinatingly" because Young meant the term to be sarcastic, even derogatory. But today many use the term positively, thinking that deserving individuals should be rewarded (or punished) in kind. For example, many conservative analysts argue that merit is a good thing because it rewards efforts rather than a person's gender or race or class or political ties. They argue that a meritocracy is a mark of a true egalitarian society since everyone has a "fair" chance to "go up" the ladder.

But others disagree, believing that a meritocratic class perpetuates the status quo and its own selfish hold on power, social status, and privilege. For example, Young criticized meritocracy because there are so many different types of intelligence and merit. An IQ test will invariably miss other intelligences, gifts and talents a person might possess. After all, can creativity, imagination, initiative, good will be measured? And speaking of good will, as we saw with the shadows modernity has cast (and continues to cast), what good is intelligence without character? Can a standardized test measure a person's character? Therefore, not only is the "selection of one ... a rejection of many" (Michael Young, *The Rise of Meritocracy*, 1958, p. 15), but many gifted persons who could contribute much to a society might fall through the cracks and never develop these gifts as intelligence tests don't have the ability by their nature to recognize (or value) them.

Moreover, Chinese history is rife with examples of students, such as Hong Xiuquan (1814-1864), who passed a preliminary examination with the highest marks, but was unable to advance any further because he couldn't afford the education. So, there are economic circumstances (access to tutoring and education, material support, financial support) and even psychological circumstances (emotional support) that play a role in how well a person performs within a meritocratic system. How fair, equal, and egalitarian, then, is a meritocracy truly?

Finally, applying Toulmin's idea of cosmopolis to meritocratic arguments reveals another possible dark-side to meritocracy. If Darwin gave us an Order of Nature where nature evolves through a process of "Natural Selection," one might argue that a meritocratic argument uses Darwin as its justification. In other words, a common misinterpretation of Darwin's Natural Selection is as the "survival of the fittest"--a phrase, incidentally, coined by economist Herbert Spencer, not Darwin. In other words, in this misinterpretation species survive by competing against another, and this view of Darwin might be used as a justification of a meritocracy: it's the way nature works. But if underlying this meritocratic justification is a fallacious interpretation of Natural Selection, the reason it's false is because there's little biological evidence that individualistic competition is the driving force of survival. Darwin and other biologists have noted that cooperation and adaptation are what improve survival. Nature, in fact, is more like an "ecology" where organisms are interconnected, where they relate and interact with each other, and where they adapt to environments and change. The way of nature is flexible and ecological, not "meritocratic."

In contrast to the individualistic, out-for-myself, competitive premise underlying meritocracy is the idea of altruism. Altruism is the unselfish regard for the welfare of others. Deriving from the ethics of the world's great religions like Christianity, altruism posits that we are inclined to help, not compete against each other.

This might be why Elspeth Stuckey goes so far to argue in her book *The Violence of Literacy* (1990) that literacy issues are often used as an ideological platform to veil, maintain, and perpetuate inequality. Literacy must not be used as a way to perpetuate a "higher" order vs. a "lower" order. Literacy is literacy, a prerogative (and a gift open) for every person.

So, if more of our teachers spoke to students' intrinsic motivation to read, i.e., cultivated a joy for reading in itself, rather than motivate students extrinsically through rewards and punishments (making it into a chore), literacy might be more available to all. We would then approach education less through a meritocratic spirit and more with an altruistic one. And so those who might be deemed as belonging to the "lower" sort *and* those who might be deemed as belonging to the "privileged" sort would both benefit as co-equals.

Again, in nature species thrive when not "besting" each other to obtain more "good stars" than the other, but when they're interacting, adapting to change, and engaged in an activity for its own joy. If we adopted this kind of model for the classroom, we might do our part in challenging the false dichotomies inherent in the "Counter-Renaissance" tradition, and recover that humane approach inherent in the Renaissance tradition. Rather than a "meritocracy," perhaps then we could move closer to a "democracy."

Literacy Is Political and Historical, Not Neutral

"Rose Speaks" celebrates the altruism of the noncelebrated in life-story format, a record of personal experience. We commemorated her romantic moments with Carmelo, her sense of obligation to her parents, and her selflessness with her children. We also applauded her fight against overwhelming oppression at work and the severity of her widowhood. But "Rose Speaks" offers us more than a good story. Success in school grows out of habits of reading and comprehending. Rose did not have the chance to develop her own literacies. Nevertheless, she made her voice heard in plain language when she questioned the educational and moral theories Dewey and Goldman.

In the same way, literacy leaders need to express their agency against practices that turn learning into utilitarian competitions. When the NCLB laws were passed, politicians did not question their limits because the rhetoric was simple and authoritative. But if they had known then what they know now about how it has undermined confidence in schools (Wood 2008), they might have used cross-checking (theory triangulation) to verify the credibility of the claims. As Plato warned in the *Phaedo*, "The partisan, when he is engaged in a dispute, cares nothing about the rights of the question, but is anxious only to convince his hearers of his own assertions" (paragraph 91 in Jowett's translation).

In recent years school administrators have been using standardized tests to monitor how much teachers are helping children learn. Rees (2001) defines it this way:

> By requiring the use of multiple-choice, standardized testing for assessment purposes, the federal and state governments are intruding upon the prerogative of teachers to teach what they want in the manner they see fit. These requirements echo the attempts of Frederick Taylor and other practitioners of what Taylor called "scientific management" to control industrial workers around the turn of the Twentieth Century. Forcing teachers to address content that can be measured in standardized tests and to avoid more analytical material hinders learning. Doing so also devalues the profession of teaching in the same way that scientific management devalued the role of skilled craft workers in American factories.

The following excerpts from a middle-school teacher's journal capture Reese's words in practice. They also show the teacher's agency.

September 08

I've been back to school with kids, for 8 days as of last Friday. Next week I will be prepping my kids per order of our curriculum coordinator for the NECAP testing they will take. I know it's supposed to be a measure of what they know, but my district doesn't believe the kids know anything, so we're going to prep them beforehand and turn in our prep evidence to prove we did it. They don't trust us either. This week we will be giving all of our kids our new diagnostic, standardized testing, the first of three times we will do so. It's the NWEA, an online, 52-question test, whose report breaks kids into separate bands in order to give teachers a better idea on how to meet their needs. If you're in one band, I'm in the next, and Sally is in the next, you can't be instructed in the same group as Sally. That is because your needs are too different. I on the other hand can be in your or Sally's instructional group. We're doing this in reading, science writing, and math. I feel sorry for myself, but worse for my kids. Everything, everything is about test scores. The only thing that keeps the administration off of my back is my students' test scores. Ninety-four percent of my students for the last two years have met or exceeded state standards.

September 09

Today my principal—nice guy really, just misguided about literacy—came to our team meeting to take it over. He wanted to talk to us about the scheduling for our upcoming NWEA testing, and to let us know that we had one week more than previously thought to submit our NECAP test data. Therefore, we would have an extra week to prep kids. And he hoped we were all engaged in prepping our students. There were many distressed voices in the room. I responded that I was okay for the one-week movement forward but that I was not engaged in preparing my students for answering the constructed response questions. My plans called for 5-6 days of prep for the test and that's all I felt was needed. What he said next was that he would talk with me later about my plans, and since I "was a big part of the success that we had had," I don't remember his exact words, it was okay.

I pointed out that our 4–6 feeder school state scores for 6th grade—our current 7th grade students—were really better than previous results. Not one kid did not meet standards. Only a handful exceeded standards, 2-3 handfuls met standards, and a ton of them partially met standards. Their scores were terrible for the constructed response questions--only one score of a 4, not many 3's, mostly 1's and 2's with some 0's. The potential to move a multitude of kids into the meeting the standard category is tremendous.

In crunching my data from last year's state scores, I noticed that three of my 'special education kids' scores showed the letter "B" instead of the 0–4 scoring. I thought it must mean "Blank" and I was disappointed that these reluctant writers in my classroom prep chose to leave all three of the constructed response questions blank because all three students missed meeting the standards by only two points. So I went to my 8th grade Special Education person to tell her she needed to be aware that these three students were leaving the constructed response questions blank.

Then I accosted one of the three students when he came to my classroom after school to borrow some Manga, Japanese graphic novels. I told him he was "Skewing my data. Why did he leave those questions blank?" He was like, "What? What? We typed those on the computer in the Special Ed room." Alarms went off. I pointed this discrepancy to my curriculum coordinator who promised to contact Measured Progress yesterday. She still had not done so at noon today. Whatever the cause behind the "B" we didn't want it t repeated in the upcoming NECAP's.

All this from a guy who after putting me through the wringer when deciding to give me a continuing contract or not, who at the last possible minute—the night of the school board meeting to recommend or not--said to me, "In case you haven't heard, we're going to recommend you for a continuing contract, but perhaps you should get more on board with what the high school (a failing school that is struggling to AYP) is doing." I just said thank you and bit my tongue, but wanted to say that perhaps they should be getting on board with what I'm doing. I'm an outsider here; in philosophy and by virtue of not being born here.

Anyway, even an offhand acknowledgement is better than nothing. Henry, those three students; if I moved them from partially meets to meets would mean only two of my students did not meet or exceed standards for reading. I'm proud of that. I don't really value the prep for the constructed response, or the reason for engaging in it. I don't think it is my best writing instruction or makes my kids great writers. They will know how to answer the question according to what the scorers expect. There are many better opportunities to have kids write where the same kind of data can be gathered while producing real writers and writing that matters. Onward.

Although Gramsci is little known to teachers, what he said makes sense to any of us who have worked with students who are failing in school. Teachers need to listen to their hopes and concerns, their dreams and aspirations. Vast numbers fail in our schools not because they are unintelligent or neurologically impaired but because they are victimized by their social and moral contexts (Coles 2000). We need to know the environment from which they come. We need to know how they learn and how they were previously taught. Parents want the best for their children. That includes the poor, who do not always know how to advocate for their children.

G. Reid Lyon (1999) states that half of children who are placed in special education classes are there for reading difficulties. A NIH study shows that 95 percent of learning-impaired children who do not get it automatically can become effective readers if taught by scientifically proven methods (Staples 2002). While I agree that everyone who fails to read and write needs second chance, my experience tells me that the right pedagogy is not phonics (i.e., scientifically proven methods) but a generative approach that uses materials that are relevant to the lives of the reader, asks open-ended questions, and spends time helping children connect to literature. Likewise, there are plenty of examples of generative approaches for secondary classrooms. Guthrie et. al. (1996) described one that emphasizes self-direction, collaborative learning, and self-expression.

And yet these recommendations, idiomatically speaking, are on the ropes. Failing children are now regularly put into materials that focus solely on skills. As Zemelman, Daniels, and Bizar (1999) said it aptly in *60 Years of Reading Research, But Who's Listening?*

Personal author, compiler, or editor name(s); click on any author to run a new search on that name.,,,

> Yet 60 years of research and thousands of studies that resoundingly validate progressive approaches to literacy learning still haven't produced the strong consensus we might expect. In fact, many school people -- even progressive teachers themselves—act as though this information didn't exist at all or were somehow unreliable, inconclusive, or tainted. We witness this phenomenon every time the promoters of the latest "breakthrough study" seek to overturn decades of solid, workmanlike research with a faddish, mechanistic gimmick such as "decodable text." Curiously cowed by such dubious "evidence," many educators stand mute even as the preponderance of scientific proof shouts just the contrary. So what's up?

It takes great courage to challenge this thinking when it is defended as scientific and mandated by state and federal officials. One of the prevailing misconceptions is that politically driven mandates are grounded in valid assumptions about literacy. This is especially evident with two programs for children who struggle with literacy: the RTI (Response to Intervention) program and the Dynamic Indicators of Basic Early Literacy Skills (DIBELS). Both promise to reduce illiteracy through precise identification of students with learning disabilities and explicit basic skills instruction. DIBELS uses brief, timed measures such as reading nonsense words and oral reading of a passage to track student growth over time.

Kenneth Goodman (2006) mocks these claims, saying the "DIBELS [is] an absurd set of silly little one-minute tests that never get close to measuring what reading is really about—making sense of print." Critics like Nell Duke and P. David Pearson (2008/2009) point out there are compelling structural factors that are equally responsible for literacy failure. They include ineffective staff development, lack of leadership, hasty hiring, increased class size, overreliance on untrained helpers, and more rules and harsher punishments. Finally, a reading of Aristotle, Spinoza, Kant, Hume, Hegel, and Dewey and modern cognitive scientists reminds us that the imagination (mental imagery), essential to learning, is shortchanged in mechanistic practices.

In Need of Heroes and Heroines

Literacy difficulties are frequently misunderstood and misdiagnosed (Elliot 2009). Thomas Sowell (2001) says the problem is so great parents need help rescuing their children from school placements where they don't belong. "Rose Speaks" brought forth the drama of this statement. Was my grandfather constitutionally incapable of becoming a skilled mechanic, or was he a victim of discrimination? Was Rose's poverty self-inflicted or imposed by those above her? What made my father torture himself with failure—ADD or stress from losing his father? Did my troubles with written assignments relate to my rigid upbringing or a lack of reading? My son's literacy was improvisational, but his classroom instruction wasn't. Did this mean he was ADD or simply stigmatized?

Our stories show how eager some "experts" were to take control of our lives in smug, self-assured ways. Rose distrusted their prefabricated interpretations. They seemed to her to be dilettantes arguing in the abstract, whose only knowledge of the poor came from those who worked for them. Brian Myers, (2001) in a piece written for *Atlantic Monthly* called "A Reader's Manifesto," describes class differences this way:

> The American supermarket is presented as a haven of womblike contentment, a place where people go to satisfy deep emotional needs. . . . This sort of patronizing nonsense is typical of Consumerland writers; someone should break the news to them that the average shopper feels nothing in a supermarket but the strong urge to get out again. . . .
>
> This is the irony of Consumerland fiction: its fans are even more helpless in the presence of authoritative posturing, and even more terrified of saying "I don't understand," than the shoppers they feel superior to. . . .
>
> At the 1999 National Book Awards ceremony Oprah Winfrey told of calling Toni Morrison to say she had to puzzle over many of the latter's sentences. According to Oprah, Morrison's reply was "That, my dear, is called reading." Sorry, my dear Toni, but it's actually called bad writing. . . . This is what the cultural elite wants us to believe: if our writers don't make sense or bore us to tears, that can only mean that we're not worthy of them. . . . The old American scorn for pretension is bound to reassert itself someday, and dear God, let it be soon.

In Ivor Goodson's (1993) words, "Why it is that so much educational research has tended to be manifestly irrelevant to the teacher?" And why is academic writing "lifeless" (Nehring 2009) without any real texture of the poor and working class who fail in schools? Researchers with no history of sensitivity to poor people or working people may end up using children as objects, as stones in monuments to themselves. They may think they are progressives, but to me they are being exploitative. In contrast, the reflective narratives in "Rose Speaks" reveal details about the poor that do not appear in traditional data. And yet teachers of literacy do not find stories in remedial texts. Instead, they read about research that leaves out much. It is as if editors publish scholarship that inflates particular ideologies, especially in the area of assessment (Houston 2007). Broadfoot (2002) seemed to have seen the future when she wrote "assessment, far more than religion, has become the opiate of the people."

Texts on critical theory and pedagogy have their own problems reaching teachers, as evidenced by their sales rank on Amazon.com. For example, one of the most well-respected academic texts on caring and moral development was analyzed by readers this way:

Poorly written and extremely boring.

I was forced to read this book as part of my teacher education program. Virtually every other student I have spoken to shared sentiments similar to mine. Even the arguments that [the author] puts forth are at most argumentative. Most people would have a very tough time believing the argument that there should be no punishment in schools. And the basic theme in her book that woman are more caring than men is plain and simply sexist and without any factual basis.

... sad generalizations that are plain wrong ... the arguments are based on groundless opinions of a small minority of feminists in our society.

I was forced to read this piece of garbage for my ethics in education class, and I cannot believe anyone would publish this insipid trash. [The author's] arguments are weak and confusing and she brings nothing new or inspiring to the issue of morality.

The appeal to fair play should resonate with teachers who want to make a difference with children who have failed to read through traditional instruction. Many argue, however, that the questions critical theorists raise are in political conflict with their school districts (Goldstein 2008). Worse, there is a deep resentment when discourse takes the shape of blaming teachers as oppressors when they perceive themselves as enablers. Here is a sample of this thinking:

> This book is a poor attempt to criticize schools and those who work hard every day to help prepare students for life. If you are a teacher, administrator, or school official, do not waste your hard-earned time and money with this non-sense. It provides no appreciation to the dedication of those who care, no matter their race, ethnicity, or gender.

Given the mandated pressures they are under, teachers favor books that are inspiring and that give them a wealth of strategies and ideas. How, then, did progressive reformers like Dewey get heard? He should have been labeled un-American because he was a radical Platonic utopian who wanted education to create a new social order. He was heard because he attacked the status quo by appealing to good sense and was politically moderate in that he spoke about gradual change.

Many reformers could learn from him. Barry Kanpol (1988) says that teachers need to oppose prevailing institutional values through questioning and reasoning. That can only happen if we know the historical and ideological roots of our profession. What battles have reformers fought? What were the stakes? Who won? Who lost? Familiarity with the past also gives us way to understand why Daniel Tanner (1998) believes that "visible members of the social science research community have fallen in league with the political Right on issues of education policy." Deepening our awareness of the unsung heroes who challenged traditionalism, even though they could have been fired, exhorts us to continue the same fight.

Critical Interpretation of Literacy Research and Practice

At the time that Rose landed in America, schools were in trouble. Most Americans in rural settings attended school for only a few years. Their one-room schoolhouses were filled with children who ranged in ages from five to twenty-one. Teachers had little formal education. Instruction was assigning passages to memorize, drill, and recite.

In cities, urban schools could not adapt to the massive influx of immigrant children. Sixty thousand were turned away in New York City for lack of classroom space. Those who were admitted were placed in age-specific classrooms with desks bolted to floors. Grace Irwin (1922), a young New York City teacher, described her class this way:

> I look at my class today and sigh. There are forty-three in the room a few are absent. They are the offspring of two dozen and more nationalities not including Americans and American colored children. One girl is part Negro and part Indian—a rare combination for temperament. Thanks to the vigilance of the school nurse, they are not called dirty, although their clothes are often filthy arid ill smelling they do not leave home in the morning with a parental kiss, hut more often with a curse or a blow, and no breakfast. The district in which I have taught since I left my "Little Italy" has no picturesque or novel background of foreign peasantry, for it is merely ugly, sordid and commonplace. Literally speaking, such a section is only of passing moment to the rest of the country— for it lies about a railroad's coal yards. The world is forever passing through it, but, bent only on what lies beyond and its journey's end; it ignores its drab and hideous aspect.

The central question was what to do with so many unschooled immigrant children. The answer was to tie their education to the workplace. Superintendents quickly turned schools into Frederick-Taylor-like (1915) models of corporate efficiency, relying on extensive testing to weed out undesirables. Thorndike, mirroring Herbert Spenser's love of the scientific method, devised tests that reduced students to objects to be measured and quantified. William Bagley (1907) preached the same ideology in *Classroom Management*—classrooms should be run as business enterprises. Dewey (1916) fought back arguing that schools ought to Americanize immigrant children by teaching political and civic virtues. He also used Pestalozzi's and Parker's claims that child-centered pedagogy enhances the success of all children: "Experience has shown that when children have a chance at physical activities which bring their natural impulses into play, going to school is a joy, management is less of a burden, and learning is easier."

Debates over the aims and content of education have been waged for more than four hundred years. Traditionalists have held to the primacy of the mind, the development of reasoning powers, and the use of discipline to motivate. Progressives view children as intrinsically good, in no need of forced learning if properly motivated.

Those who have confronted harsh, inhumane teaching practices deserve our gratitude. Past voices we owe much to are Comenius and Rousseau, who asked us to trust children. Parker advocated for authenticity in curriculum, including the use of literature in reading instruction. He even took issue with teachers who spoke harshly to children. His colleague John Dewey attacked the laws of learning, testing, punishment, and control—the status quo in education—because he believed learning needs to build on the interests of the child, not the factory. Jean Piaget's (1896–1980) study of children's cognitive development undermined Locke's (1632–1704) and Skinner's (1904–1990) *tabula rasa* (blank slate) notion of the mind, with reward and punishment as key motivators to learning (Case 1999).

There are many others, little known or long forgotten, who fought for literacy reform. As we have done with Rose, we should acknowledge them. Gertrude Hildreth (1898–1984) drew attention to the scandal that was school failure in the 1930s. She approached the question of failure with care. She wrote about applying psychology to students' problems in school, although Goodman never mentioned her. although Goodman never mentioned her. John Holt (1923–1985) and Neal Postman (1931–2003) were two of first critics of contrived learning. Holt, a teacher and writer who minced no words with anyone who dared to use contrived learning in classroom, believed that school practices do not support children's actual thinking and learning. They are designed, instead, to train of factory workers.

Using Descartes's rationalistic method of inquiry, Chomsky (1928–) developed theory of human cognition and language learning that occurs naturally. Goodman (1967) applied his theory to literacy learning when he wrote in his landmark essay, *Reading: A Psycholinguistic Guessing Game*, "Reading is a selective process. It involves partial use of available minimal language cues selected from perceptual input on the basis of the reader's expectation. As this partial information is processed tentative decisions are made to be confirmed, rejected, or refined as reading progresses." Psycholinguist and author Frank Smith followed up with convincing books and articles that showed how children begin to read from the moment they become aware of print.

James Britton (1908–1994) was one of the first A brief narrative description of the journal article, document, or resource.writing researchers to discuss the importance of poems, stories, and active language to make practical and moral sense of the world. He felt that traditional teaching inhibited student creativity and fantasy. Writing as an act of producing art put the author in control of his creation. Teachers can't simply correct a story without embracing the writer's assumption he has just created something good. Britton argued that there is a perverse aspect to saying to a writer, "Make it his way." We are wrong to assume we are free to do anything with his art. Assessment is a full-fledged disaster that discriminates, stigmatizes, and disempowers individuals for life.

Richard S. Alm (1981) was one of the first researchers A brief narrative description of the journal article, document, or resource. totototototo show how educational practices can result in students' reading difficulties. Areas he considered problematic were classroom atmosphere, reading attitudes, parental reactions, dull or difficult reading materials, limited reading resources, teaching practices, overemphasis on skills, and the individual needs of students. Denny Taylor (1990), anticipating Smith's (1995) claim that "assessment is a full-fledged disaster that discriminates, stigmatizes, and disempowers individuals for life," exposed the harsh bureaucratic side of special education testing. Who will ever forget Patrick's story about being tested endlessly for a learning disability, despite substantial documentation of his intellectual growth and literacy? Finally, David Aronowitz (1997) has offered a cogent explanation for why a progressive curriculum has never become mainstream. He traces the cause to philosophical conflicts between child- centered teaching and traditional teaching.

There is a long tradition of humanistic-based psychologists who have fought the same fight. Notables include G. Stanley Hall, Abraham Maslow, Erik Erickson, Carl Rodgers, and Albert Bandura. More recently Robert Coles's (2003) advocacy of helping students develop morally and emotionally as well as cognitively draws attention to how children, through their stories, acquire literacy.

David Elkind, reflecting Vico's call for gripping exposition, has exposed the negative effects on learning and self-esteem when children are given developmentally inappropriate instruction, in his book *The Hurried Child*. His research as a clinician at Tufts University found that most "[c]hildren become withdrawn, listless and apathetic and retreat anything that has to do with reading." And Candy Lawson (2002), a clinical psychologist at the Center for Development and Learning, has discussed how certain thoughts and emotion can negatively affect in her article "The Connection between Emotions and Learning":

> Motivation is a drive or desire that compels us to do something. Often students don't seem to be motivated in school. They don't want to do homework or schoolwork and believe that they have no control over their grades. They believe that they are dumb or stupid. Even though they put out effort, they are never successful and fail to achieve their goals. As a result, they begin to feel stressed out by school and start to feel helpless and hopeless. In this situation, their thoughts affected or

caused their negative feelings. Other times students seem unmotivated because they are anxious or depressed. As a result, they have trouble concentrating in school and can't keep their mind on their work. They may think too much about personal problems and focus on the negative. In this situation, their emotions affected or caused their negative thoughts. In both situations, a lack of motivation prevents new learning; it "turns off the switch."

The debate over literacy methods goes back to the late 1800s with Parker's condemnation of phonics. The "look-say" reading method defined reading instruction from the early 1920s to about the 1950s. Beginning in the late '60s a back-to-basics movement using specialized phonics materials was reestablished. A constructivist method called Whole Language was popular from about 1980 to 1995. It was grounded in Chomsky's rationalist concept of language learning (Waters 2007) and Goodman's application of psycholinguistic theory and research to the reading process. Whole Language was also influenced by British and New Zealand developments in constructivist thinking (Goodman 1989). Whole Language paid attention to making meaning through a love of reading real literature. It became so popular with teachers it put several basal companies out of business and changed traditional language arts courses into courses that emphasized the writing process. Teachers reported great success with it, including the learning disabled (Martin, Martin, and Cavalho 2008).

About the same time, the publication *A Nation at Risk* (1983) linked poor economic indicators to our flawed education system, with its emphasis on progressive methodologies, including Whole Language. With conservatives in power, senators, representatives, and state legislatures passed laws related to standards for all students and accountability of teachers for student achievement.

In 1993, the Massachusetts Education Reform Act required a common curriculum and statewide tests (Massachusetts Comprehensive Assessment System). Other states followed Massachusetts's lead and implemented similar high-stakes testing programs. In 2001, President

George W. Bush signed the controversial No Child Left Behind act (NCLB). The law held schools accountable for student achievement levels, providing penalties for schools that did not make adequate yearly progress toward meeting the goals of NCLB. By 2004, H.R. 1350, the Individuals with Disabilities Improvement Act (IDEA 2004), reauthorized and modified IDEA. Changes, which took effect on July 1, 2005, included increased authority for school personnel in special education placement decisions and alignment of IDEA with the No Child Left Behind Act of 2001.

These alleged "scientifically superior" approaches (Strauss and Altwerger 2007)—code for direct instruction and phonics-only instruction—seemed to be in reprisal for years of progressive hegemony in educational practice. Basals returned to schools, prompted writing exercises replaced writing workshops, and fluency measurements returned. Despite what Michael W. Apple (2007) calls the "ideological successes" of the past ten years, the return to Taylor-like policies have proven to be inconclusive (Hoff 2009; Edmondson and D'Urso 2009; Zimmer, Gill, Razquin, Booker, and Lockwood 2007). Critics like Patrick Shannon and Patricia Crawford (2007), Kenneth Goodman (2005), Robert Coles (2003, 1989), Frank Smith (2003) and Richard Allington (2002), despairing at the damage caused by these efforts, continue to fight against "empiricist dogma" (Chomsky 1977) as bad science driven by ideological agendas.

Life Histories in Teacher Education

"Rose Speaks" taught us to stand up for principles. Many critical literacy theorists do this every day. Scholars like Joan Wink (1999), John Taylor Gatto (2000), Michael Rose (1989), Margaret Gallego and Sandra Hollingsworth (2000), David Hicks (2005), and Patricia Carini (2001), frustrated with the injustice and bias in the educational system, show how all teachers can be agents of change. Others advocate the use literacy histories in teacher-training programs, even though they have not become mainstream. It remains enigmatic why this is so. One reason may be the estrangement between empiricism and this type of research referred to an as auto-ethnography. Perhaps publishers and editors of educational materials, who still favor experimental data, judge histories to be subjective, narcissistic, or propagandistic.

And yet, "Rose Speaks" shows how personal literacy histories deepen awareness of unknown details about literacy development and also deepen personal ethnic, cultural, and class beliefs about teachers and the children they teach. In addition, it demonstrates the importance of social and cultural contexts in understanding literacy failure and sharpens the connection between history and the ethics teachers practice in schools and classrooms. Finally, "Rose Speaks" encourages political action on the part of educators. Is it possible that the call for research-driven data was nothing more than a tactic to silence debate about the complexities of learning and literacy?

Producing a family literacy history is a compelling way to redress imbalances in literacy research. Listening to relatives talk about their school experiences encourages everyone to talk openly about her or his feelings regarding learning and literacy. Students can lie low, as Studs Terkel (1967) does in reporting his histories, providing commentary in short introductions to each speaker's story. The histories can also be divided into sections: the culture and context individuals grew up in, what kind of lives and careers they had, what experiences they had in dealing with school, and documenting outside influences on their literacy development (Hull and Schultz 2001).

Some students will trace their love of learning to highly literate ancestors and members in their communities. Others will find that their literacies are grounded in stories of their forbearer's immigration to the New World, analyzing how they beat the odds against poverty. All will reveal ethnic, religious, cultural, and class issues in their own learning. In addition, the histories can be used to answer questions such as

(1) Are answers to failure found in the social context of literacy learning?

(2) Was your learning to read separated from feelings and emotion?

(3) What unlocking your imagination important in learning to read?

Students should also discuss the methods of self-reflection, interviews, field notes, and artifacts they used in writing their histories.

References

Alexander, P. and Winne P., eds. *Handbook of Educational Psychology*. New York: Routledge, 2006.

Allington, R. L. *Reading to Learn: Lessons from Exemplary Fourth-grade Classrooms*. New York: Guilford Press, 2002.

Alm, Richard S. "The Educational Causes of Reading Difficulties." *Journal of Research and Development in Education*, v. 14, no. 4 (Summer, 1981): 41-49.

Aronowitz, David. "A Different Perspective on Educational Inequality." In *Education and Cultural Studies: Toward a Performative Practice*. Edited by Henry A. Giroux and Patrick Shannon. New York: Routledge, 1997.

Apple, M. W. "Ideological successes, educational failure? On the politics of No Child Left Behind." *Journal of Teacher Education*, v. 58, no. 2 (2007): 108-116.

Bailyn, B. *The Ideological Origins of the American Revolution*. Cambridge: Belknap Press, 1992.

Bagley, W. C. *Classroom Management: Its Principle and Technique*. London: Macmillan, 1907.

Benda, J. *The Treason of Intellectuals*. Trans. Richard Aldington. New York: W. W. Norton, 1928.

Bond, T and Caust, M. "Silk purses from sows' ears? Making measures from teacher judgements." *Australian Association for Research in Education*, 2005. http://www.aare.edu.au/publications-database.php/4595/silk-purses-from-sows-ears-making-measures-from-teacher-judgements.

Broadfoot, P. "Assessment for Lifelong Learning: Challenges and choices." *Assessment in Education: Principles, Policy & Practice*, v. 9, no. 1, (2002): 5-7.

Brock B. L. and Grady M. L. *From First-Year to First-Rate*. Thousand Oaks: Crowen Press, 2007.

Carini, P. F. *Starting Strong: A Different Look at Children, Schools, and Standards*. New York: Teachers College Press, 2001.

Case, R. "Conceptual Development in the Child and in the Field: A Personal View of the Piagetian Legacy." In *Conceptual Development: Piaget's legacy.* Edited by E. K. Scholnick, K. Nelson, S. A. Gelman, and P. H. Miller. New York: Psychology Press, 1999.

Chomsky, N. *Language and Responsibility.* New York: Pantheon, 1977.

Chomsky, N. *Cartesian Linguistics: A Chapter in the History of Rationalist Thought.* New York: Harper & Row, 1966.

Coles, R. *The Call of Stories: Teaching and the Moral Imagination.* Boston: Houghton Mifflin, 1989.

Coles, R. *The Moral Life of Children.* New York: Atlantic Monthly Press, 2000.

Coles, R. *Children of Crisis. Children of Crisis: Selections from the Pulitzer Prize-Winning Five-Volume Children of Crisis Series.* Boston: Little, Brown and Company, 2003.

D'Angelo, F. and Zemanick, R. "The Twilight Academy: An Alternative Education Program That Works." *Preventing School Failure: Alternative Education for Children and Youth,* v. 52, no. 4, (2009): 211-218.

Descartes, R. *Discourse on Method.* In *Discourse on Method and The Meditations.* Translated by F. E. Sutcliffe. New York: Penguin Books, 1968.

Dewey, J. *Democracy and Education: An Introduction to the Philosophy of Education.* New York: Macmillan, 1916.

Duke, N. K. and Pearson, P. D. "Effective Practices for Developing Reading Comprehension." *The Journal of Education,* v. 189, no. 1/2, (2008/2009): 107-122.

Edmonson, J. and D'Urso, A. "Considering alternatives for federal education policy in the United States: a critical perspective on No Child Left Behind." *Critical Studies in Education,* v. 50, no. 1 (2009): 79-91.

Elkind, D. *The Hurried Child: Growing up too fast too soon.* Reading: Addison-Wesley, 1981.

Elliot, J. As cited by "Thousands of children wrongly diagnosed with dyslexia." *The Telegraph* (April 7 2009).

Ewert, G. (1991) "Habermas and Education: A Comprehensive Overview of the Influence of Habermas in Educational Literature." *Review of Educational Research*, v. 61, no. 3 (June 30, 2016): 345-378.

Foucault, M. Ethics: *Subjectivity and Truth: Essential Works of Foucault, 1954-1984, Vol. 1*. Translated by Robert Hurley. Edited by Rabinow, P. New York: The New Press, 1998.

Gallego, Margaret A., and Sandra Hollingsworth, "Introduction: The Idea of Multiple Literacies." In Gallego, Margaret A., and Sandra Hollingsworth, eds. *What counts as Literacy?: Challenging the school standard*. New York: Teachers College Press, 2000.

Gardner, D. P. et al. *A Nation At Risk: The Imperative For Educational Reform An Open Letter to the American People. A Report to the Nation and the Secretary of Education*. Washington D.C.: The Commission on Excellence in Education, 1983.

Gatto, J. T. *The underground history of American education: A schoolteacher's intimate investigation into the problem of modern schooling*. New York: Oxford Village (2000).

Goddard, H. H. "Mental tests and the immigrant." *Journal of Delinquency*, v. 2, no. 5 (1917): 243-277.

Goldstein, L. S. "Kindergarten Teachers Making "Street-Level" Education Policy in the Wake of No Child Left Behind." *Early Education and Development*, v. 19, no. 3 (2008): 448-478.

Goodman, K. S. "Reading: A psycholinguistic guessing game." *Journal of the Reading Specialist*, v. 6, no. 4 (1967): 126-135.

Goodman, K. S. "Whole-Language Research: Foundations and Development." *The Elementary School Journal*, v. 90, no. 2 (1989): 207-221.

Goodman, K. S. *What's Whole in Whole Language*. Berkeley: RDR Books, 2005.

Goodman, K. S. *The Truth About DIBELS: What It Is - What It Does*. Portsmouth: Heinemann, 2006.

Goodson, I. F. "The Devil's Bargain: Educational Research and the Teacher." *Education Policy Analysis Archives* [online serial], v. 1, no. 3 (March 5 1993). Available at: http://epaa.asu.edu/ojs/article/view/680/802.

Gould, S. J. *The Mismeasure of Man*. New York: W. W. Norton & Company, 1981.

Gramsci, A. *Prison Notebooks (Volumes 1, 2, & 3)*. Edited and translated by Joseph A. Buttigieg. New York: Columbia University Press, 1992-2007.

Handlin, O. (1951) *The Uprooted: The Epic Story of the Great Migrations That Made the American People*. Boston: Little, Brown and Company, 1951.

Heidegger, M. "The Self-Assertion of the German University." In *The Heidegger Controversy*. Edited and translated by R. Wolin. Cambridge: MIT Press, 1992. Also see: https://archive.org/stream/MartinHeidegger-TheSel fAssertionOfTheGermanUniversity 1933/HeideggerMartinTheSelf-assertionOfTheGermanUniversity_djvu.txt.

Hicks, D. V. *Norms and Nobility: A Treatise on Education*. Lanham: Rowman & Littlefield, 1991.

Hobbes, Thomas. *Leviathan*. Edited by Edwin Curley. Indianapolis: Hackett Publishing, 1994.

Hoff, D. "Schools Struggling to Meet Key Goal on Accountability: Number Failing to Make AYP Rises 28 Percent." *Education Week*, v. 28 no. 16 (January 2009): 14-15.

Hoffman L. P. and Burrello L. C. "A case study illustration of how a critical theorist and a consummate practitioner meet on common ground." *Educational Administration Quarterly*, v. 40, no. 2 (2004): 268-289.

Hofstadter, R. (1963). *Anti-intellectualism in American Life*. New York: Vintage Books, 1963.

Horkheimer M. and Adorno, T. W. *Dialectic of Enlightenment: Philosophical Fragments*. Edited by Gunzelin Schmid Noerr. Translated by Edmund Jephcott. Stanford: Stanford University Press, 2002.

Houston, D. "TQM and Higher Education: A Critical Systems Perspective on Fitness for Purpose." *Quality in Higher Education*, v. 13, no. 1 (2007): 3-17.

Hull G. and Schultz K. "Literacy and Learning Out of School: A Review of Theory and Research." *Review of Educational Research*, v. 71, no. 4 (December 1 2001): 575-611.

Irwin, G. "The Teacher and the Taught." *Harper's Monthly Magazine: Volume CXLIV, December 1921 – May 1922*. New York: Harper & Brothers, 1922.

Kanpol, B. "Teacher Work Tasks as Forms of Resistance and Accommodation to Structural Factors of Schooling." *Urban Education*, v. 23, no. 2 (Jul 1 1988): 173-187.

Kant, I. *Critique of Judgment*. Translated by James Creed Meredith. Oxford: Claredon Press, 1952.

Kent, T. W., Herbert J. M., and McNergney R. F. "Telecommunications in Teacher Education: Reflections on the First Virtual Team Case Competition." *Journal of Information Technology for Teacher Education*, v. 4, no. 2 (1995): 137-148.

Korsgaard, C. M. *Self-Constitution: Agency, Identity, and Integrity*. Oxford: Oxford University Press, 2009.

Lawson, C. (2002) "The Connections between Emotions and Learning." *The Center for Development and Learning* (January 1 2002). http://www.cdl.org/articles/the-connections-between-emotions-and-learning.

Lynn, R. *Eugenics: A Reassessment*. Westport: Praeger, 2001.

Lyon, G. R. "NICHD Research Program in Reading Development, Reading Disorders, and Reading Instruction: Workshop Summary and Map." *National Institute of Child Health and Human Development, National Institutes of Health U.S. Department of Health and Human Services, 1999*. https://www.nichd.nih.gov/publication/pubs/Documents/reading_ centers.pdf.

Martin D., Martin M., Cavalho K. "Reading and Learning-Disabled Children: Understanding the Problem." *The Clearing House: A Journal of Educational Strategies, Issues and Ideas*, v. 81, no. 3 (2008): 113-117.

Meers G. D. "Moving beyond Cynicism: The First Step Toward Effective Teaching." *VocEd*, v. 54, no. 3 (Mar 1979): 22-24.

Myers, B. R. "A Reader's Manifesto: An attack on the growing pretentiousness of American literary prose." *The Atlantic Monthly* (July/August 2001).

Nietzsche, F. *On the Genealogy of Morals* (Third Essay, Sections 23-28). In *On The Geneology of Morals and Ecce Homo*. Translated by Walter Kaufman and R. J. Hollingdale. New York, Vintage Books, 1989.

Nehring, C. "CORRESPONDENCE: Another Way to Honor Feminism." *New Republic* (September 21, 2009).

Noddings, N. *The Challenge to Care in Schools: An Alternative Approach to Education.* New York: Teachers College Press, 2005.

Noddings, N. *Educating for Intelligent Belief or Unbelief.* New York: Teachers College Press, 1993.

Plato. *Phaedo* (paragraph 91). Translated by Benjamin. Jowett. In *The Dialogues of Plato, Volume 1.* Oxford: Claredon Press, 1871.

Puzo, M. *The Godfather.* New York: New American Library, 1969.

Rees, J. "Frederick Taylor in the Classroom: Standardized Testing and Scientific Management." *Radical Pedagogy*, v. 3, no. 2 (2001): 1-8.

Rose, M. *Lives on the Boundary. The Struggles and Achievements of America's Underprepared.* New York: The Free Press, Macmillan, Inc., 1989.

Shannon, P. *Reading against democracy. The Broken Promises of Reading.* Portsmouth: Heinemann, 2007.

Shannon, P. and Crawford, P. "Manufacturing descent: Basal readers and the creation of reading failures." *Reading & Writing Quarterly*, v. 13, no. 33 (1997): 227-245.

Smith, F. *Between Hope and Havoc: Essays into Human Learning and Education.* Portsmouth: Heinemann, 1995.

Smith, F. *Unspeakable Acts, Unnatural Practices: Flaws and Fallacies in Scientific Reading Instruction*. Portsmouth: Heinemann, 2003.

Sowell, T. *The Einstein Syndrome: Bright Children Who Talk Late*. New York: Basic Books, 2001.

Stansell, C. *American Moderns: Bohemian New York and the Creation of a New Century*. New York: Henry Holt and Company, LLC, 2001.

Staples, B. "How the Clip 'N Snip's Owner Changed Special Education." *New York Times*, January 5, 2002.

Strauss, S. L., and Altwerger, B. "The logographic nature of English alphabetics and the fallacy of direct intensive phonics instruction." *Journal of Early Childhood Literacy*, v. 7, no. 3 (2007): 299-319.

Stuckey, J. E. *The Violence of Literacy*. Portsmouth: Heinemann, October 1990.

Swift, J. *Gulliver's Travels*. London: Benjamin Motte, 1726.

Tanner, D. "The social consequences of bad research." *Phi Delta Kappan*, v. 79, no. 5 (1998): 345-349.

Taylor, D. "Teaching without testing: Assessing the complexity of children's literacy learning." *English Education v.* 22, no. 1 (1990): 4-74.

Taylor, F. W. *The Principles of Scientific Management*. New York: Harper Brothers Publishers, 1915.

Terkel, S. *Division Street: America*. New York: Pantheon Books, 1967.

Tittle, C. R. "The arrogance of public sociology." *Social Forces*, v. 82, no. 4 (2004): 1639-1643.

Toulmin, S. *Cosmopolis: The Hidden Agenda of Modernity*. Chicago: University of Chicago Press, 1990.

Valencia, R. R., ed. *The Evolution of Deficit Thinking: Educational Thought and Practice*. Abingdon, Oxon UK: RoutledgeFalmer, 1997.

Waters, Lindsay. "Time for Reading." *Chronicle of Higher Education*, v. 53, no. 23 (2007): B6.

Wink, J. *Critical Pedagogy: Notes from the Real World (2nd Edition)*. Boston: Allyn & Bacon, 1999.

Wood, R. and Ashfield, J. "The use of the interactive whiteboard for creative teaching and learning in literacy and mathematics: a case study." *British journal of educational technology*, v. 39, no. 1 (2008): 84-96.

Young, M. *The Rise of the Meritocracy: 1870-2033*. London: Pelican Books, 1958.

Zemelman, S., Daniels, H., & Bizar, M. "Sixty years of reading research--but who's listening?" *Phi Delta Kappan*, v. 80, no. 7 (Mar 1999): 513.

Zimmer, R., Gill, B., Razquin, P., Booker, K. and Lockwood, J. R. "State and Local Implementation of the No Child Left Behind Act: Volume I— Title I School Choice, Supplemental Educational Services, and Student Achievement." *U.S. Department of Education* (2007).

9

The Role of Desire in Literacy

The material in this chapter connects with my father's story. It responds to the question, what would have kept him in school? The chapter revisits the old debates about central nervous system disorders and hyperactive deficits that can only be overcome with systematic instruction and stimulants. An alternative response to failure is to center instruction on what the student already knows. This approach, called dialogical teaching, is grounded in historical antecedents, and is supported by years of research including my own studies of prison inmates.

Simple Dualisms

Harmful Stereotypes

My father represents talented but troubled learners who give up on school. Historically, we have assigned them to special schools or classes intended to fix their behavioral problems and/or low levels of reading and writing (Shannon 1997). Toby was such a student. Remarkably, he learned to read and write without specialized instruction. He read because his tutor, Lee, gave him a reason to read. Some may assume that Toby's achievements are unproven or untested. Still others believe his literacies dramatize the inherent power of dialogical teaching to keep learners on track.

My father never thought of himself as a good student. He was retained several times in his school career. His mother could never get him to study. His typical complaint was "I can't do it, and don't ask me to try." He was never interested in school. The more he fell behind, the more he turned away from books. He was always in trouble. He took on the persona of a wise guy with a short fuse, much like Joe Pesci's character in *Goodfellas*.

He carried his school failure into his adult life, always self-conscious about making mistakes. He passed up buying a house because he was worried he would fall behind in the payments. When he had a chance to go into business, he turned it down. He never sought a promotion at work. He disclaimed interest in reading. When I gave him subscriptions to magazines like *Sports Illustrated*, he put them on his coffee table, unopened.

If Dad were a student today, what would we do with him? We could give him time to grow into his reading. This is a variation of the maturational argument that posits that learning will not take place until the learner is developmentally ready to learn. Elkind (1987) supports this approach because this is how his son learned to read and write. The danger in maturation theory is that time is running out for many students to find purposes on their own.

In contrast, there are the early intervention approaches advocated by reading disability proponents. If we used this approach with him, we would first decide if he qualified for something like the Chapter One program. He would because he is the son of a poor, single parent. Yet this approach, with its emphasis on skill instruction, might be unnecessary because my father knew how to read. His problem was that he didn't value reading.

We could look into special testing to see if he suffers from a neurological condition called attention deficit hyperactivity disorder (ADHD), which causes a marked inability to sustain concentration. That might explain why he avoids reading. If the diagnosis came back positive, we might medicate him on Ritalin, an amphetamine that can produce a powerful euphoric rush. Or we could treat him with play therapy, chiropractics, biofeedback, dietary supplements, or perceptual/motor training. I am afraid these plans would not improve his willingness to read or study. Why? There is no actual test that diagnoses ADHD, just APA guidelines. Besides, there is scant evidence to support the positive effects of chemical intervention (Breggin 1998) or the other treatments listed above.

What about ordering a learning disability diagnosis? We could justify it because there is a gap between his intelligence and his achievement. A positive diagnosis would allow him to take tests untimed and perhaps get him on a computer with a spellchecker. Recent research in this area recommends that the IQ-achievement discrepancy definition of this disorder be discarded (Vellutino, Scanlon, and Lyon 2000). Second, these interventions may not fit his problem. Dad can read and write. His problem is in not caring enough about school to study and achieve.

We might send him to a therapist to see if his problem is anxiety-related. Perhaps his resistance to school is a form of rebellion against the death of his father or the tyranny of his mother. Perhaps he received little or no encouragement in school or at home. A psychological variables (anxiety, depression) approach ignores the matter of drug intervention and who will pay for lengthy and expensive therapy.

How about private tutoring on the assumption that he needs undivided attention to catch up on his work? I am afraid that his mother would not be able to afford it.

There is not much left to try. We could retain him. Perhaps it might work this time—a third repeat would surely shake off his deadbeat attitude. We could also punish him with detentions or bribe him with lollipops, but I am afraid neither would work any better today than they did seventy years ago. My grandmother tried every punishment and praise tactic she could think of without success.

The sad fact is we are no closer today to helping him than we were all those years ago. He is a student who started out with dreams but lost his way and dropped out of school, his desire to please giving way to a vicious cycle of giving up and quitting.

Real Identities

My father's story is common to many American men who learn to read but who drop out never having excelled in school. Statistics show that men fail at greater numbers than females, are in the remedial classes more frequently, are drugged at higher rates, and drop out more than girls (Ansalone 2009, Flynn and Rahbar 1994). Why do we find it so difficult to educate boys like my father, and what can we do about it?

The gender explanation posits that boys have a more difficult time sitting and conforming because they have more energy to burn. The standard practice for the past sixty years has been to adjust the curriculum with more appropriate materials for them. A classic study done in 1940 showed how boys readily used materials that connected to their lives. The study was controversial because it challenged the concept of a common uniform curriculum for everyone. If affected, each child would only read material of interest to him.

Still, teachers who faced the imposing task of teaching unruly, unmotivated kids took to the idea. After all, it makes sense that a child will pay more attention to something he is interested in. Their enthusiasm led to the publication of high-interest low-readability materials popularized in the '50s. The demand for supplementary materials escalated in the '60s after the federal government funded the ESEA act for remedial reading programs. Publishers put out specialized library kits for boys. Teachers spent their own money to bring in magazines and newspapers—anything that would relate to the real lives of boys.

Despite the common sense that undergrids this approach, it offered no panacea. One summer years ago, one of my students who was an architectural major, took my summer reading course as an "easy" summer elective. The student signed on for the tutor a prisoner requirement. She asked to work with females. She was assigned to an Afro American drug user.

The tutor brought in magazines about black singers and athletes because she assumed her student would be interested in them. She underestimated her student. The student didn't open the magazines and barely spoke a word to the tutor. The tutor complained to me that she was going to receive a poor grade for the course.

I asked her to bring in materials that she had at home. She balked, claiming that her student could not possibly be interested in her personal books. Nevertheless, she collected a boxful of materials. One was a book about gnomes and fairies. The student picked it up and browsed through it. The next day she returned with several pages of poetry she had dictated to her cellmate.

I asked other prisoners what happened here (Amoroso 1984). One said, "She wasn't into music and sports." Another prisoner questioned the motives of the tutor:

> If you were a prisoner in a prison they would want to know your motive for wanting to come out here and wanting to teach them. And then there's this, you probably run into a lot of bitterness ... A lot of people in prison are bitter. And out of this bitterness ... like you said you had a student from New York City from the streets, right? And a well-educated, wealthy young lady from [college] teaching her and she probably had resentment ... you know, like this girl, what's her idea? She's got everything. What's she doing out here? Playing a role? Is she doing me some kind of favor?

The professional literature is full of examples of how being wrong about what students should read devalues them as individuals. One Mexican-American student, in writing about himself, talked about his teacher who had recommended him to the vocational track. He resented this pigeon-holing because he wanted to be a poet. The teacher cast him in a position of secondary importance because he assumed all that Mexican American children wanted nothing more in life than to work with their hands. He didn't know the student wanted to be a poet because he never asked the student what he wanted to do with his life.

I had another student who worked with a child who was reluctant to make up stories for her. Knowing the child liked to play football, she brought in football props to motivate him to make up a story about football. The child sat silently, not offering a sentence.

I suggested to her that she bring in a few things from home and merely ask the child to describe what he saw. She brought in a soda can and an egg carton. This time the child responded effortlessly. She wrote down his words and read them back. He reciprocated by reading the words on his own. The tutor succeeded in getting the child to talk and read his own words that had been written down because she offered him a starting place to communicate with her.

It is easy to stereotype learners who are unwilling to read and write. It is easy to blame them for being immature or slow or learning disabled. Their silence is interpreted as a deficit. A literacy teacher with a degree in economics from a very prestigious university once asked me for advice. She was getting no place with her adult student. No matter how many times she tried to get a story out of him, she failed. Her technique was to give him a prompt like, "Tell me about your favorite politician." The student's reply was usually, "I don't know nothing about that."

I asked her what she thought was going on. She said, matter-of-factly, that he had never gone on trips, stayed in hotels, participated in election campaigns, coached Little League, or volunteered at church. His only interest was watching TV.

I asked her what he did for a living. She told me that he loaded and unloaded fish on the Portland waterfront. I asked her why he came to her class. She said his wife had prodded him after seeing a commercial on TV. I asked her about his education: Did he like school? What had gone wrong? Who were his favorite teachers? If he had to do it again, what would he do differently? She didn't know because she hadn't asked him. I asked her about practical things like childhood friends and if he had to work as a youngster. I asked her about his family: Did he have children? What did he do with them? Once again, she didn't know.

My questions related to his life, not hers. No wonder he turned away in silence. There was no chance to tell his story. Learners need to realize that their likes and dislikes, their fears and aspirations are important subjects of study. This is especially true when they have not had the opportunity to talk freely about things that matter to them. I asked the tutor to find those things in her student's life that he cared about—places and stories that would bring feelings out in the open. She thought for a moment and said, "Teaching is supposed to be objective. What you are asking me to do is more than I bargained for." She did not accept the fact that teaching is a dialogue. She had to care about her learner getting an education for him to care about that education. We smiled at each other and departed.

Rationalizations and Excuses for Literacy Failure

Let Them Eat Cake

An example of objectivist thinking goes something like this: "It is unrealistic to think that all students have the ability to read and write and to be educated. Some kids are just not smart enough. Others are too lazy or undisciplined to work at it. Besides, not everyone needs an education. We should limit schooling to those can and want to learn." This view, gaining in popularity among conservatives in recent years, assumes the inevitability of winners and losers in schools and in society. Beneath its veneer of reasonableness is a deep-seated compulsion to keep the poor in their place.

The following interview was between a teacher and the chairman of the English Department at an integrated high school north of Nashville, Tennessee. African American students from Nashville's inner city had been bused to the school for several years.

> Chairman: The basic students we have are programmed. I emphasize that word programmed because the brain has a program in it for reading. And it's been devised for the student from the earliest moment of awareness. These students that have missed this programming, who missed the optical programming that is necessary for reading, can't make it up. You cannot reproduce the programming. It is just as if they are not aware of listening to any sort of speech patterns, they can never speak their language properly. If they are not aware of how to a see words and see signs and see symbols if they miss that part, then they will never become aware of it.

> Teacher: Well, if we can't do anything directly, other than to help what is already programmed, can we do anything in the areas of attitudes and motivation, do you think?

557

Chairman: Well, we can motivate and give them a certain attitude but if they don't have the equipment to do it, then it becomes frustrating for them.

Teacher: Well, this is the old argument in education that there are some people who cannot be made literate. Would you go along with that?

Chairman: Yes. And there are some people who don't need to be made literate. I don't think that you are an incomplete person if you are not able to read or write.

Teacher: Right, but—

Chairman: I think that perhaps our concepts about the purpose of life are entirely incorrect. We think that you have to be an extraordinary human being, being able to read and write and be social and all of this. Who says all this? Why do we have to be that way?

Teacher: Is the problem that we can't change our essential programming?

Chairman: The problem is that we were trained in a different period of time. We haven't changed; we won't see anything differently. We are trying to force people into the patterns that we were forced into when we were young.

The chairman's argument sounds convincing because he uses science to support it. It's a chilling example of fraud because no such neurological evidence exists. Worse, attaching it to a claim that society has made too big a thing out of literacy and education absolves him from teaching the disaffected. Is it any wonder that he asks in righteous indignation, "Who says you have to be literate?"

Both elitists and traditionalists, around for a long time in different disguises, have embraced this antidemocratic argument about literacy. It is the same put-down attributed to Marie Antoinette when she was informed of widespread suffering of the poor: "Let them eat cake."

Filled with the arrogance that the educated know what is best for the uneducated, it is as deeply flawed as the silly argument that slavery was a good thing because it fed Africans.

Slavery was good as long as you were not the slave.

The best way to test it out is to run it by previously illiterate adults. I have been doing this for many years with incarcerated individuals in the South and in New England. Here is a snapshot of what they have told me. One person remarked that he had never known what he had missed. All the news he wanted was off the radio, so why did he need to read? Once he started reading the newspaper, though, he discovered the other side to the story. He discovered literacy put him in charge of information. In his own words:

> My deal is, I felt good once I left because I never tried to read the paper, you know. Once I first come and see the clippings out of the paper for the president elections and stuff like that. Something important from the day before or something like that. She would bring back, and I would read it and I get me by reading the clippings she brought for me out of the paper would make me want to go back the next day and or after I leave here and get the paper and read it. Before then, I would just see the paper and see somebody else read it and I would be interested in what's on TV. I didn't care anything about the paper. After I started reading the paper along with her and out of certain books. That made me wants to go pick up a book and read it then. See I saw some things that I was missing by not trying to read it. So that helped me a whole lot.

Another inmate, a fifty-two-year-old male, who thought of himself as "slow working," spoke of literacy this way:

> There is one point about [reading] that a lot of people don't stress. It is not necessary to get a good job or the ability to carry on a good conversation, but it is a feeling inside a person of self-worth and self-gratification ... a satisfaction about "yes, I have an education; yes, I do know this, and yes, I can work this problem myself. I don't need you.

A forty-one-year-old woman from an Adult Basic Education class, who had worked since she was sixteen, saw coming to class as an opportunity "to start [her] life." She told me in a simple yet forceful way how it was to grow up illiterate: "Well, I found through school and also job-wise through working most of my life, a lack of communication because they want you to do your work and keep your mouth shut."

Others spoke of similar feelings of inadequacies brought on by their inability to read and write. One student told me:

> I was ashamed to ask people different things because I didn't want them to know how dumb I was and I knew they were going to laugh and make fun of me. I remember a time when I couldn't do it and like, I'd say, "Yeah, yeah, it's did" and "you know" and "I ain't did nothing" but just because I'm ashamed. I don't want to say, "I don't knows." I don't want to ask this man here and you put him over here because I don't want you all to think that I'm dumb. It's just like some kind of image that they instilled or you done seen or projected I don't need no help. I'm this, I'm that and really you don't know head from tail and then again you want to project the I know it all.

Like the learners interviewed by Eberle and Robinson (1980), adults I have worked with felt alienated and dependent. They needed to prove to themselves that they were capable of doing things on their own. Literacy symbolized a hope or a dream of self-worth and dignity.

This conception of literacy as a process of self-fulfillment is not consistent with the chairman's view or instrumental claims about literacy as an economic tool. Rather, most were striving to develop a better sense of who they were as individuals. They were people who never had learned to read and write, and as a result had been trapped in what Freire (1970) has labeled "a culture of silence," unable to overcome their sense of inadequacies with respect to other people.

The idea of literacy as an act of "becoming someone" strongly parallels Freirean concepts (1976, 199) he developed working with illiterates in the Third World. The adults he knew who worked were dispossessed peasants seeking to overturn aristocratic landlords or colonial domination. My interviewers were American citizens living in one of the most open and free and technologically advanced societies in the world. In light of this contrast, what could possibly be the sociocultural reality that linked them to their Third World equals?

Some clues are found in their school recollections. Most remembered school as oppressive place where teachers ignored them, telling them if they didn't like a subject to "just close the book and get out of class." Little personal attention was given to them, and what appeared to be attention was often inappropriate. As one adult recollected,

> A lot of teachers get to the stage where they don't really care. I've had them tell me you're going to the next grade, just get out of my face. Because I was a bad child, they didn't try to find out why I was a bad child. They just didn't try to work with me or nothing.

Another adult echoed the alienation that dominated him this way: "[School] used to be a place where you could never have an opinion. It was 'Shut up and do your work. You gonna have to sit and listen.'"

When I asked them how they dealt with the remoteness and authoritarian attitudes of their teachers, the answer was unequivocal: They lost all respect for them. School was clearly an unsafe place. Many reacted by skipping classes or daydreaming. All eventually dropped out of school, only to become underemployed, unwanted, and dependent on others.

In coming to terms with their scorn, the adults hid behind a wall

561

of self-deception and bravado. One put it this way: "Somebody would show me something and say 'Check this out.' And 1 looks at it and act like I know it. I'd say, 'Yeah, that's all right.' And don't even know what it was. And I really don't care that I don't know."

Others vented bitterly, as did this high school dropout who lived in a halfway house:

> Student: Don't waste my time, you know, with teachers I don't get anything out of them. I did it myself. I don't sit at their desk. What I have is inside my head. If a teacher asks me why I do not read, I just tell them something else just to not to let them know what is happening.

> Interviewer: How far did you get in school?

> Student: Went through the seventh. Then I quit. And ah, well actually I was expelled. At school, I had some friends; we were having midterms, you know, and fighting. The principal called us into the office. Started talking to us about everything. One thing led to another and a fight broke out there, so he expelled me. And I just never went back to school. Never, just joined street gangs and that's another story.

> Interviewer: I want you to read this little bit there. When it comes time to respond, are we are going to have problems?

> Student: I ain't gonna answer the question. I know it, but I ain't got to answer to you. You ain't my own momma or daddy. Really, the other kids here can't read. They said they were copping out. To make them look tough. I believe they were covering up.

Pedagogy of Communication

Transformations happened all the time in literacy programs I have been associated with in the Caribbean, Nashville, and in Maine. The most dramatic example was Toby, the young inmate I wrote about in the opening chapter. His tutor, Lee, unlocked Toby's literacy by making Toby a storyteller. Once he did, Toby's silence ended. Toby valued Lee because he listened to him and was sincerely interested in his life, someone who provided support. Lee cared about Toby's literacy not because he was illiterate but because he deserved it. Toby reciprocated because Lee was his friend, someone who understood his hurt and humor and was capable of teaching him the right things.

Authentic communication in literacy learning is the key finding in my prison research. Many learners talked about a two-way street for learning to take place. One writer captured Freire's (1985) dialogic concept poignantly:

> Usually teachers have a tendency—when I went to school and to college—they had a tendency to put themselves above you. I know it, and if you're gonna learn anything, you hafta learn it from me. Rather than coming down to our level and saying, "You know I have learned some things and I want to share this with you, and you can share with me." So, you know, it's no longer a teacher student thing, but it's people getting together and learning. And I think that's what they will say here—what we found out. We learned learning has to be a two way street. What happens in most schools is the one-way street. You're being taught and you're being taught and you're sitting back here and saying, "No." If you want to come down here, we'll learn, the doors are wide open. We can learn, you know, forever. If you're gonna teach me, then I probably won't stay very long to listen to this.

Communication means trusting the thoughts of others. When we distrust our learners' voices, they smell our phoniness. When they trust us, they reciprocate, as evidenced in this long section of an interview I had with writers who had just finished a literacy program:

> Henry: Let me just describe an experience again from my work in Nashville, Tennessee. I want to get your thoughts on this particular experience. We were working with a fella who was, at the time, eighteen. He had gone on to school to the eighth grade in public schools. He hadn't learned to read or write. He had been in what was called Special Ed classes, and in those classes they had tried to teach him to read, using pictures, for example rather than the word fish they would have a picture of a fish. He never learned to read, and he was in prison, and he came to our program, and the tutor didn't know an awful lot about teaching or tutoring, so this tutor was trying different things and nothing was working. One day he came into the session, and the tutor had a paperback novel that his girlfriend have given him, and it had an attractive cover, and the fellow in prison said, "What's that all about?" And so the tutor said. "Well, it's a story about a guy on a farm." And the fellow said, "Well, read something to me; read it to me.": So the tutor started reading it, and something clicked. The learner really related to this incident that was being described. There were two men fighting about this woman, and they were fighting, and the fella had to put his hand out on the line, and he got it chopped off or something, and the learner's saying, "I know why that guy did that. If I was in that situation, I would have done the same thing." He was really getting off on the story. I remember he was eighteen, and he had gone through life not knowing how to read or write, and this, I think, was one of the first times that anyone had ever read to him, and he was relating to it. He understood …

what was happening. And fortunately, the tutor said, "Hey, I know you have a story inside of you too that's probably just as good," and that's all it did; it clicked. And the guy went upstairs to the dorm, and he had a cellmate that could write, and the fellow just started talking, and the next session came back with about ten pages of experiences growing up in Mississippi. And one of the things that he said that his cellmate wrote down was, "All this is true because it's not a lie, because I can't lie on paper." You know, "it's true because I can't lie on paper," and within a short period of time he went from being a nonreader to being a very, very good reader. What's your thinking on what he said? "That all this I wrote is true because I can't lie on paper." What was he really telling us?

Writer 1: I think he was telling you, "I wrote this; read what I wrote."

Henry: Why was it important to say that?

Writer 2: Anytime somebody reads something I write, they're reading a part of me. [It] all comes from somewhere inside of you and either from what you wished happened or somebody else you know it threw it as something and it all comes from a part somewhere inside of you, and that's not a lie. That it exists; it can't be a lie.

Writer 4: When we started this course, when I first saw my first three pages typed out, I was hooked. I had to keep writing, had to complete, see something completed in my name that I knew that I wrote, and I knew that it was fairly, that I liked what I wrote.

565

Henry: Knowing someone else is gonna read it too. Right?

Writer 4: Everybody that's read what I've written—guys having coffee down stairs—anybody that's read it, has read it completely and hasn't just read three pages and stopped, has said, "You had me hooked from the first three pages on. I wanted to keep reading it. It's good."

Henry: A question: is what you wrote really you? It's not a lie?

Writers: Yes, yes, it is.

Henry: Why did you choose to reveal what you did? Why did you—

Writer 2: I knew about what I was writing about. You know I couldn't pick a story like *On the Other Side of the Mountain* and write about mountains because I didn't know too much about mountains. You know? If you describe scenery of the mountains or the winters, I could write about hitchhiking because I knew how to hitchhike. It came easier than trying to research a subject I didn't know.

Henry: Did you hold anything back?

Writer 5: My story is true. I don't feel embarrassed about writing what happened. This story started from the first grade, 'bout me and my buddy growing up and how I got in trouble and why How my parents—my father worked at night, and he bartended, and he slept days. He wasn't strict on us, just my mother took care of us. And just don't feel embarrassed about anything that happened in my story. I just hoping that it help out little kids get to it right. They'd read it in like the first, second, third grade—they'll know not to hang around. They'll listen to their parents 'cause maybe my story is about I should have listened to my father and mother. I should have really listened to them.

Henry: Obviously you could have written about a lot of things, but you wrote about that.

Writer 5: My tutor, he didn't tell me what to write just said to write anything, fictional or true.

Henry: Obviously, he could have turned you off. Once again, I'm back to knowing [your] reason for writing what you did.

Writer 5: I wasn't embarrassed. I realized it isn't gonna be the name of the person at the end of the paper [that matters]. It's what the person has to say and how different people are gonna be able to see that in different ways and get what they want out of it.

It is easy to strip away trust when we turn writing for new writers into contrived topics, sentence drills, or correction procedures. Britton (1982) pointed out years ago that corrections/revisions will only be made willingly if the writer is writing to be understood by others. When that happens, revisions are internally motivated. Unrehearsed drafts of new writers are intended for self. Since only the writer is reading them, there is no need to revise because she or he understands what was written. If corrections are forced, we end up alienating the writer, with many clamming up. Correction suggestions kick in once there is distance between the writer and what he has just written. This is called transactional writing intended to communicate thoughts or ideas to an audience. Listen to how this new literate put Britton's theory into his own words:

In a school you're taught the grammar, the sentence structure, how to choose your verb, the tense and stuff. Here we're allowed to write and then by writing you want to express yourself, and you want to do it clearly so you write. And then the tutor would say, "You know you aren't using the right verb tense again on your sentence that fits your topic?" For me if I had to learn to get back into writing everything for the rec room, it would be a really big drag and a let-down, but by being able to write and then to correct my writing because I wanted to write this thing, you know I had the story that I wanted to write. It was no longer a heavy burden to learn sentence structure and verb tenses, it was something that I wanted to do because I wanted to get this thing written.

One of the most frequent messages failing students hear is, "I am here. You know where I am if you want me to help you." In my experience, students will not solicit help because they don't know how to ask for it. They are afraid to ask because they do not think they matter. Communication has to be genuine, not superficial, in order to work. As an inmate in a maximum security prison told me, a pedagogy of communication is more about trust than it is about following a script.

I have noticed in a lot of cases that teachers say hey, I'm the teacher and you're to listen. Do the work I gave you. Then bring it up to me and if it's not right I will tell you and you can do it again. Don't go into your classrooms with the attitude of I'm the teacher, I'm the boss and the one you have to listen to. Use something that I have learned to use in this prison and program. I am going through empathy. Put yourself in that person's shoes and him in yours. See how you would feel if he comes in every day and says, I'm the boss listen to me and we are gonna do it this way, and you don't like it that way, then I'm sorry. If you don't know other ways to teach this person, then find the people to learn those ways so you can go back and say okay, I'm ready to listen to you. I'm ready to stop being the boss for a change and find out the views of yours. Learn to work on his views, work on your views and to put them both across at the same time can accomplish more. Put yourself as a football team he is the receiver and you are the quarterback. He is not gonna kick that ball unless he knows your playing. He is not gonna know you're playing unless he understands what your telling him. If he can't understand you, you may as well take the play back and don't use it. The way I see it, find out his views and learn to understand them; learn to help him understand you. You got your winning team all together.

A communication approach to literacy is translated into classroom practice whenever teachers treat students like Toby—respectfully because learning to write and read comes from the heart. Lee assumed that Toby did not choose to be a failure but responded to the messages he heard every day. Being called immature, irresponsible, or lazy and coupling it with Old Testament assumptions about sparing the rod and spoiling the child broke his will. Others tried to shame him into trying harder. Although his teachers used sharp words to motivate him, he heard silence. So, he gave up by putting his head on his desk.

The prison tapes are full of stories that give power to writers through choices. They were in control of the stories they wrote, the revisions they made, and the skills they practiced. Tutors did not dictate anything. They simply followed the writer's wishes as seen in this statement:

The prison tapes are also full of frightening stories. Whenever I asked men and women why the failed, they blamed teachers who didn't care about them. A twenty-two-year-old female who made it to the tenth grade before being expelled for striking a teacher said, "Anyone who wants to learn can learn by someone who cares."

This statement, however simple, affirms one of the most crucial ideas expressed by the adults I have interviewed over the years. All were unanimous in their insistence that literacy teachers be emotionally involved with them. Their concerns were entirely personal. They valued someone who would listen to them, someone who would be sincerely interested in their inner lives, someone who could provide moral support in times of stress and anxiety.

This need for teachers to be caring and supportive is central to the concept of literacy as an act of becoming someone. As pointed out earlier, many of the adults grew up unappreciated and misunderstood and frequently were treated as objects in dependent relationships. In this context, there was always a withdrawal from literacy because there was no one to motivate them or push them or discipline them. Their extreme alienation led many to believe they were incapable of producing a complete thought. In response, they wanted teachers who could transmit encouragement openly and freely. As a young adult told me, "Becoming literate depends on the teacher being true with the dude and letting him know I care about you. I care if you're going to get an education."

Most of the adults emphasized the importance of genuineness between teacher and learner. As one adult explained, "Teachers can't merely say, 'I'm interested in you.' They must care for this person not only because he is a student but because he is a person."

> Coming here, it's taught me more than just to learn how to read, but it's taught me respect for my teacher because instead of just bringing books in that she wants us to read, that could be easy for her to teach us on, she preys on what we want or what I want. She told me when I asked her why that she took the time out to get these books. She felt that if I weren't interested in the book she brought that I wouldn't read or couldn't get into the book. She said I feel that if the more interested you are in the book, the better you are going to do. And I would like to get the material that you would like. That surprised me. Another thing that surprised me was

the way teachers like to come here and teach people. It seems that there are hardly any people in the free world that want to come here to a prison with inmates and teach us. They have doubts about the people; they maybe have a little fear about the people. You have slightly fears about how I am gonna deal with this person, how are we gonna communicate. They show you when they come in that they are not looking at you as a con or inmate or whatever. They are looking at you as other people.

A powerful example of the importance of "realness" in the teacher-pupil relationship is found in this reaction to the following question:

Let me see how you analyze this situation: I worked with a teacher one time who came from a wealthy family and went to a well-known university. She came out to a prison to teach reading. Her first student was an eighteen-year- old woman from New York City. The teacher brought a lot of magazines, you know, *TV Guide*, *Sports Illustrated*. The student refused to look at the materials or talk with her. The teacher got frustrated and was ready to give the whole thing up. I suggested that they bring out other types of books. The next time she brought along books about architecture, poetry, and a children's book on fairies arid gnomes. The student browsed through the fairy book. The next session the student came back with six pages of poems she had written and asked the teacher to read them to her. After that, they got along just fine. What happened here? Why do you think the student connected with the fairy book?

Dialogical teaching is rarely cited in the literature. There is a conforming tendency in some teachers to teach the way they were taught. Traditional instruction reflects cultural values of discipline, competition, and achievement. A book is something to be mastered, a trophy manifesting individual effort. Illiteracy represents a moral shortcoming on the part of the student. In contrast, dialogic teaching defines a teacher as a coequal who serves students, not someone who controls them. This Rousseauian notion that puts learners before managing requires great empathy for the disaffected and a rejection of the ethos of blaming the victim.

Medical-Based Redux

Medical-based theories of failure have existed for a long time. The key assumption is that neurological wiring prevents certain children from concentrating on learning. We call these attention deficit disorders. We have other labels too, including dyslexia. We usually prescribe a drug called Ritalin that calms the child so that he can concentrate. Learning disabilities (LD) is not treated with drug therapy but by controlling the environment. More than thirty years ago, Schrag and Divoky (1975) warned, in *The Myth of the Hyperactive Child and other Means of Child Control*, about gimmicks for making unruly juveniles behave more submissively. They wrote, "The processes and apparatus of public education as epiphenomena of deeper forms of social oppression which it is the schools' function to support."

Although medical theories are very popular, millions of children, mostly boys, are currently being treated with Ritalin, their validity has never been proven. Gerald Coles (1987) for example, in *The Learning Mystique: A Critical Look at Learning Disabilities*, argues that neurological explanations of reading and learning problems have never been proven to exist. Alternative explanations reside within social constructs like the school ethos and home family life. More recently, Breggin (1998) has pointed out that numerous studies show that drugs have adverse effects on the brain and behavior, including "making children more docile and obedient, and more willing to comply with rote, boring tasks, such as classroom school work and homework." Drugs and gimmicks did not produce the literacy gains reported here. What did was working with tutors who gave the adults a real desire to read and write.

More on Learner-Centered Strategies

Generative Word Approaches

Efforts to reach alienated students holistically have received considerable attention since the publication of Paulo Freire's *Pedagogy of the Oppressed*. Freire (1970), a Brazilian Marxist philosopher, worked with adult learners in Latin America and elsewhere. He proposed a political context for articulating the general goals of literacy education. He decried the notion of literacy as simply a tool or possession that is tied to economic considerations. In his view, literacy is a means to free the learner from his sense of inferiority and powerlessness. It is a medium of freedom through which the learner can critically reflect on his own experiences and thus transform his reality.

Venceremos

Jonathan Kozol (1983) described, in *Children of the Revolution*, Cuba's application of Freire's philosophy of literacy. Ministry of Education officials wrote a primer titled *Vencermos* (Spanish for "we will overcome") that consisted of fifteen stories, each one somewhat more difficult and explicitly political than the one before it. Each story used "active" words, ones that bore associations of emotion—love, longing, ecstasy, or rage—among the learners. A photograph of Cuban life that served both to provoke discussion about the story and to clarify the main theme of the lesson preceded each (e.g., the land is ours, the right to a home).

A tutor and the learner read the story in unison until the learner was able to read it on her or his own. As a final step, the teacher and the learners dealt with practice exercises aimed at analyzing letter sound patterns, sight words, and so forth.

Organic Primers

I developed an organic primer approach (Amoroso 1985) that combined the central concepts of Freire's (1972) generative word approach with psycholinguistic notions about the reading process. Four major assumptions characterize the approach: (1) Literacy is a thinking-liberating process in which the learner is presented with recognizable situations that demonstrate the values of literacy; (2) Literacy instruction should be personal and dialogical; (3) Literacy instruction should immerse the learner in large amounts of print and should encourage the discovery of word recognition skills when the learner needs them; and (4) The model of literacy instruction should be easy for the teacher to implement. It should also be anthropological (observational) in design so that the teacher can develop an intellectual understanding of the way the reading process works.

Like *Venceremos*, an organic primer is a collection of teacher-generated storylines, each slightly more difficult than the proceeding one in terms of length and complexity. Each story is active-based, which means that learners are presented with content that provokes critical reflection of their own experiences. Similarly, organic primers use active-based stories in a fixed format and practice exercises.

Figure 5
The Construction and Use of Organic Primers

Stage One-Establishing the conditions for Learning

Goals

Construct an Organic Primer—one which will be filled with rewarding and satisfying stories.

Guidelines

- ¤ Use active-based or charged words to guide your writing
- ¤ Write stories with the recognizable situations.
- ¤ Explore basic themes.
- ¤ Use familiar sentence patterns.
- ¤ Use familiar vocabulary.
- ¤ Repeat new words.
- ¤ Select appropriate illustrations.
- ¤ Gradually increase sentence complexity and passage length.

Goals

Use the Organic Primer in the same way you would guide a direct reading activity

Guidelines

- ¤ Your goal during the Discussion Stage is to initiate a conversation in regard to the photograph
- ¤ Find out what the learner knows, thinks and feels about the topic.
- ¤ Clarify concepts.
- ¤ Critically examine ideas and themes.

- ¤ Then Read the Passage for him a few times. Follow this by unison reading. Once the learner is familiar with the passage, have him read it on his own.
- ¤ Follow up the oral reading with Strategy Exercises.
- ¤ Analyze constituent elements---patterns, generalizations, sight words—informally <u>and</u> only when the reader expresses an interest in letter – sound generalizations.
- ¤ Use journal writing and spelling- dictation exercises whenever possible.

<u>Goals</u>

Help the reader build a concept of what a good reader does.

<u>Guidelines</u>

- ¤ Provide spaced practice and review.
- ¤ Following the lesson, generate a discussion about reading and try to help the reader understand what he needs to do to improve his performance. Here are a few questions that may prove to be
- ¤ Did you feel your reading improved today?
- ¤ Did you concentrate any better today?
- ¤ Did you keep the ideas you were reading about straight in your head?
- ¤ Were there a lot of words in the story you did not know?

Several differences should be noted, however. First, the content in the primer is eclectic, not explicitly political, since the aim is to stimulate self-expression, not to provoke radical social change. Second, story difficulty is not based on conventional measures of readability, such as syllable count or sentence length. Instead, vocabulary and sentence structures are natural, familiar, and predictable. Learners feel more comfortable, and their remembering is facilitated because intuitively understood structures are used. Finally, practice exercises are not restricted to syllable drills. Rather, the activities are more varied and multileveled, emphasizing higher order syntactic and semantic strategies for figuring out how words work. They are used informally and only when learners express an interest in them.

Primers have been effective in helping learners who have had little success with other approaches to reading. They have proven to be especially suitable with learners who lack motivation or who have negative attitudes toward reading or themselves. Moreover, they have been successful with students who seem to lack a concept of what reading is, especially those who have had intensive phonics training, yet who have not learned to read fluently. They can be used with any learner who lacks confidence in his or her ability to learn or who does not know the value of reading.

Writing from the Heart

Dramatic improvements in the teaching of writing emerged in the early 1970s with the research of notables such as James Britton, Janet Emig, and James Tierney and development of the Bay Area Writing Project. This project, replicated at hundreds of colleges across the country, operated on a teacher-teaching-teachers model. It was process orientated in which teachers were taught to emphasize the reading/ writing connections and revisions in writing workshops. Donald Graves, William Murray, Nancy Atwell, and Thomas Newkirk added immensely to the process approach to writing.

With the passage of the NCLB legislation and standards best testing, collaborative efforts became institutionalized, with teachers being required to add formulaic procedures, rubrics, and assigned prompts required by statewide competency tests. Instruction for many returned to the study of parts of speech and sentence diagramming. What started out as a democratic process became more concerned with controlling (owning) children than fostering a reciprocal relationship between teacher and student (Kozol 1985).

I Know There Is Good Story Inside You

When Lee told Toby he had a good story inside him, Toby started to dictate stories to his cellmate and did not stop until he had filled scores of pages. Working off Lee's intuitive response—we all have stories to tell—I helped establish several writing programs in Maine and Canada. *Voices*, a student-written magazine published quarterly, gave new literates in adult literacy classes in Vancouver, BC, a chance to see their stories in print. Paid teachers followed writing-process guidelines. Students chose their own topics. All were about love, family life, school and work, immigration, and making a living. All stories were true and genuine. Revisions took place during one-on-one meetings with teachers and within their writing groups. Copies were sent to other adult programs in Canada to facilitate reading and writing. *Writers at Work*, the literacy component of the Casco Bay Project for Work Place Education (Martz and Clasby 1995) was a student-produced publication similar to *Voices*.

I also set up prison literacy programs. I usually worked with tutors who had minimal training in teaching and writing so as to replicate what the Cubans had done with middle-school tutors and with what volunteer literacy programs like Literacy Volunteers were doing. Students were recruited under the proviso that they had stories to tell that younger students would benefit from. I provided minimal training on the characteristics of adult learners, tips for initiating discussions, and Newkirk's "words saturated in meaning" correction strategies. Tutors kept detailed journals. I interviewed them and their students after the programs ended to discover motives and transformations.

The results have been consistent across time and place. Tutors who normally volunteered for the programs did so for personal reasons, like résumé building. Few spoke in personal terms, such as an opportunity to get to know someone they probably would have otherwise not met

(Rogers 1985). All tended to be apprehensive and fearful about meeting students. For many, success appeared to be measured by "how quickly the time went by." Many reacted negatively to the initial sessions by pointing out how angered they were because the students didn't know why they were there. The external manifestation of these feelings appeared in statements like "I left with a why am I doing this; it's not going to be easy."

All tutors immediately began correcting the first drafts their students wrote. The consequences were immediate. A tutor from Maine with a BS in psychology wrote:

> I pointed out some of the information was missing that made it unclear to the reader what was happening, but I also told him he had some good details, especially in describing the scenery. We made up an outline that we could follow in describing the sequence of events a few facts he should include so the reader will understand the story better. I also had him make a list of characters and explained that he should describe them so that the reader could get a better picture. He then began to do some writing but he found it difficult with me there.

Another tutor felt uncomfortable and confused by her failure to correct her student's first draft. As stated in her log: "When I suggested that I thought his opening paragraph was great, he countered with the fact that his grammar was bad and his spelling good.

Later, she tried to analyze what went wrong:

> I feel frustration myself with the various goals of the project. Everyone seems to have a different reason— Susan (consultant), Dr. A., the tutors, the inmates … I think it's important to see something written and then perfected and finished.

The tutors did not understand that their students were withdrawn or resistant because they were communicating an urgency to a correct their words. Greater tolerance emerged after a few sessions. Another Maine tutor reported how she learned to subordinate her function as the boss (owner) to one of a friend. She reports:

> She was thinking all of the time and did not always
> accept my suggestions by telling me she liked it better
> her way. I'm trying to let her follow her own instincts
> in forming the story. The majority of help I can give is
> to clarify and organize her thoughts.

After trust has been established, an explosion of writing and revisions took place. Statements about clock watching, prison politics, students not showing up on time, or poor structure to the program give way to more positive and involved reporting. Students began to bring pages of drafts to the sessions for comment and revision. Tutors learned how to suggest change and felt more comfortable speaking with their students. In addition, there was a growing perception that when students are allowed to write freely about themselves, profound things happen. They slowly discovered that self-expressive aspects of the writing process are legitimate and that their role needs to shift from a product focus (how many pages are being produced?) to an interactive function (how can I help you use your experience to write?). As a result, their initial fears about being incompetent (the authoritarian, expert role) and not knowing what to say (interpersonal) were transformed into more reciprocal, caring concerns.

This reorientation of the teaching function took on many forms. One tutor describing the impact of getting to know her student on a personal level stated: "I am becoming defensive of her work and protective of her work. I don't consider her a student but a comrade who enjoys writing stories for others to enjoy."

She also analyzes the social and personal implication of her instruction:

> Today was the first time she has given me permission to
> edit whatever needs to be done—she's quite flexible and
> has allowed me to add or subtract whatever I wish. A
> lot of socialization goes on between us and that centers

on her writing, which generates more writing for the next time!

Another writer captures the power of Newkirk's saturated in meaning strategy:

> What I like, my teacher was asking me about my school days from years ago. She asked me about some of the things I liked to do when I was going to school. What kind of subjects I liked to take up and games I liked to play and all that. Like football and basketball. She told me to write an autobiography on that. I did what I had given her she went home and she had one she wrote out of the same of what she thought it should have been like. I read it and it was almost perfect of what I had done and did. I read and reread it for about three days and going over and over it. I really liked it and some the things she did like bringing certain things and she figured out things for me to read. She asked me things I liked and I tell her and she would go home write it and she would bring it back and we would read it and then she would let me read it and what I don't know she was there to tell me the words.

This student, a middle-aged gentleman who did not know how to read or write, shows how he learned what to do when narrating his memory of a story aloud. His pathos is still touching after all these years because it's constructivism in its purest form.

> She used to ask me when I read over something and she would ask me if I remember what I read. I turn the paper upside down and try to relate back to her what I read and not look at the papers. If I could remember and all that. I think that helped a lot cause you see I found out that you have to remember what you read. You don't

remember, you can read it all day long and it's not gonna
do you any good.

I learned years ago not to fall into the silly trap of warring against
phonics categorically, especially the structured linguistic kind. That
is because I have seen too many learners, aged five to sixty, benefit
from them. My son Tim is a good example. Although he had been
read to for years and had been dictating stories and writing his own
with invented spellings, he started school unable to read. Within two
weeks of being placed in a linguistic reader, he was reading fluently.
He needed a quick way to figure out sound-spelling patterns. This
adult discusses how simple syllable lessons put him on the same path to
reading independence:

> First she, I didn't know the [word barrel] and how to
> catch the sounds in words and she came down and break
> the words down to me. Whatever to break down and
> two pause, three pause or what and she would just sit
> there just like a dictionary. She would have her words
> written down or just write down words and we would
> sit down and she would take her pencil and put a mark
> between the words to break it down and help me to
> pronounce that word. She did that a lot till I got use to
> it. Now I can, I still might not know exactly what a word
> is but I can break that word down. I might take half of
> it and the rest of it and if I keep working with it I can
> figure it out myself. I don't need anybody to tell me.

Another example of the transformation from a product focus to a
more interactive one is worth noting. Initially, a tutor spoke in terms
of needing an "attack" and more direction so he could "accomplish
something." In his first log entry, he described himself as a "results-
oriented person" who finds it "difficult not to analyze the text." Gradually,
however, his feelings of defenselessness changed to confidence and
commitment as he began see his student "put to paper what seems to
be a pretty good story" (an autobiography about alcohol dependency).

Remarkably, as he continued to support his student's writing—"it's good medicine for him"—he found himself wanting to extend his time in the program. In his own words, "Speaking of commitment, I have pretty much decided to carry this project on beyond the end of the class."

This reorientation of the teaching function took on many forms. One tutor, describing the impact of getting to know her student on a personal level, stated, "I am becoming defensive of her work and protective of her work. I don't consider her a student but a comrade who enjoys writing stories for others to enjoy."

She also analyzed the social and personal implication of her instruction:

> Today was the first time she has given me permission to edit whatever needs to be done—she's quite flexible and has allowed me to add or subtract whatever I wish. A lot of socialization goes on between us and that centers on her writing, which generates more writing for the next time!

It is also worth mentioning that some tutors became entrenched. A middle-school teacher never accepted the fact that she did not own her student's story. She seemed to be confused when the student resisted her correction attempts, never recovering from the feeling that "I didn't really help him; all he really wanted was someone to type and correct spelling and grammar. Of the ten suggestions made for clarity, all were rejected."

Another tutor, who worked with a nonreader by collecting his oral history on tape, felt confusion and annoyance with his student's "ramblings" and "wrong use of tense." He remained critical throughout his program, failing to engage the learner in any kind of meaningful discourse. He even criticized the learner's story as empty and uneventful. Unlike the others, he failed to see his student as an individual and, as a result, became detached and passive with regard to his role and function.

Finally, a middle-school teacher in Nashville became entrenched in the critic's role, never accepting the reality that her student's needs were not to publish but to simply put on paper his life story. She also seemed angry when her student resisted her correction attempts, never recovering from her product focus (how many pages are being produced?) to an interactive one (how can I help you use your experience to write?). As a result, their initial fears about being incompetent (the authoritarian, expert role) and not knowing what to say (interpersonal) were transformed into more reciprocal, caring concerns.

Epiphanies

In one of my programs, I printed and shared the prison stories with forty-three certified teachers in two of my university classes. Their job was to evaluate the stories on a holistic rating scale: clearness, emotional appeal, and empathetic appeal. I chose these criteria because good narrative succeeds when readers understand what happened, feel emotions, and respond empathetically to the message in the story (Coe 1981). The raters were also asked to record their personal comments about any story or poem they read.

Mean scores were extremely high with clearness attaining the highest. The writers were less successful in eliciting emotional or empathetic responses from the readers. As often happens in writing to persuade, writers may not provide enough emotional appeal to fully communicate what they were trying to say. At the same time, real communication, as Rodgers points out, occurs only when the expressed views and attitudes of characters are seen from that character's point of view.

While I did not interview the raters to determine the reasons behind their scores, their written comments offered a lot of insight. The two stories, which received the lowest scores for emotional appeal and empathy, were "Pony Business" and "On My Father's Farm." "Pony Business" was a realistic story about the struggle of a rural family to make ends meet. Based on a true event, the story depicts how a poor but close-knit family moves from fair to fair with their daughter's pony for hire. The success of the venture changes the father's mind about keeping the animal. In the end, he finds full-time employment selling pony rides. "On My Father's Farm" is the author's attempt to recall his impressions of life as a youngster on the family farm. Writing in the first person, the author gives a sympathetic account of rural life and its meaning. His longing for the family relationships and responsibilities of an earlier time give insight into his longing to be free.

An analysis of the raters' comments reveals that only one person empathized with "Pony Business." His comment: "A quiet intelligent story about learning to make a living while avoiding corporate oppression." As with any narrative, the power of "Pony Business" has to come from the reader and his or her ability to connect the experience to a larger audience. The next comment reveals how distant and judgmental one rater felt: "If this is the way the author brought up his children, it sounded very unstable."

Lacking was any understanding of the author's use of irony to show how wrong he was to have doubted his daughter's love of her pony. The reader's response also gave insight into her personal values. As Richards pointed out years ago, how easy it is for raters to put on "mental blinders and take another man's words in the ways in which we can put him down."

Responses to "On My Father's Farm" point to the same disconnect between raters and the author. One rater trivialized the story by suggesting that it added nothing to the farm literature genre. Another saw it as a description of farm life. Others reduced the piece to a story for children, suggesting that its style was "childish." Three raters viewed it favorably but without comment. Only one saw it as a metaphor about longing for a life of freedom and independence.

What do these comments suggest? The absence of a match between what was intended and what was understood in "Pony Business" and "On My Father's Farm" is partly attributable to detached and superficial reading. It also reveals the readers' lack of empathy with another's life experience. Without such a frame of reference, one has no viable way to judge someone else's writing except through spelling or grammar or punctuation.

Is it any wonder why so much of writing instruction is dishonest? My years of teaching literacy courses and running writing programs reinforce Freire's (1972) point that many teachers do not connect to the lives of their learners. Is it any wonder why so many students resist or reject their criticisms, however constructive? How easy it is to turn a new writer into a demoralized one.

Back to Dad

We should care about the students we work with, mediating with kind words, if we want them to set aside doubts and fears. We don't need advanced degrees in literacy to do this. After all, young middle-school children in Cuba taught thousands of adults to read. The same with the tutors who have worked with me. The key is less assessment and more attention to creating a desire to read and write. Linda Gubbe (1998) adds that we should also "assess the quality of [our] interactions [and our] aware[ness] of the cultural histories and socialization experiences students bring with them."

Dialogic teaching is serendipitous, meaning you cannot always plan for it because you are following the lead of the learner. It also requires freedom. Many teachers do not have that freedom because the curriculum is set, books are assigned, and administrators judge us on the results we produce. At the same time, results will happen, so document them. Second, dialogic teaching requires intrinsic motivation. I know it sounds trite, but Shoeless Joe Jackson's words in *Field of Dreams* are applicable: "If you build it, he will come." As psychologist Albert Bandura argued in *Self-Efficacy* (1997), the pleasure students get from improving self-efficacy or confidence in performing, will lead to greater learning. Finally, their success will depend on your own love of the written word. Without being a reader yourself, you may not be able communicate your own joy of the written word. Books about the love of reading include Anna Quindlen, *How Reading Changed My life*; Anne Fadiman, *Ex Libris*; Lynne Sharon Schwartz, *Ruined by Reading: A Life in Books*; Tom Raabe, *Biblioholism The Literary Addiction*; and Earl Lovelace, *A Brief Conversation*.

References

Amoroso, H. C. "On Becoming Literate: Professional Perspectives." Presented at the Annual Meeting of the American Educational Research Association (68th, New Orleans, LZ, April 23-27, 1984).

Amoroso, H. C. "Organic Primers for Basic Literacy Instruction." *Journal of Reading*, v. 28, no. 5 (February 1985): 398-401.

Ansalone, G. E. *Exploring Unequal Achievement in the Schools: The Social Construction of Failure.* Lanham: Lexington Books, 2009.

Bandura, Albert. *Self-Efficacy: The Exercise of Control.* New York: W.H. Freeman and Company, 1997.

Breggin, P. R. *Talking Back to Ritalin: What Doctors Aren't Telling You About Stimulants and ADHD.* Cambridge: Da Capo Press, 1998.

Britton, B. K. "Effects of prior knowledge on use of cognitive capacity in three complex cognitive tasks." *Journal of Verbal Learning and Verbal Behavior*, v. 21, no. 4 (August 1982): 421-436.

Coe, Richard M. and Gutierrez, K. "Using Problem-Solving Procedures and Process Analysis to Help Students with Writing Problems." *College Composition and Communication*, v. 32, no. 3 (October 1981): 262-271.

Coles G. *The Learning Mystique: A Critical Look at Learning Disabilities.* New York: Ballantine Books, 1987.

Eberle, A. and Robinson, S. *The Adult Illiterate Speaks Out: Personal Perspectives on Learning to Read and Write. Washington, D.C.:* National Institute of Education, U.S. Department of Education, 1980.

Elkind, D. "Viewpoint 1. Superbaby Syndrome Can Lead to Elementary School Burnout." *Young Children*, v. 42, no. 3 (March 1987): 14.

Fadiman, A. *Ex Libris: Confessions of a Common Reader.* New York: Farrar, Strauss and Grioux, 1998.

Flynn, J. M. and Rahbar, M. H. "Prevalence of reading failure in boys compared with girls." *Psychology in the Schools*, v. 31, no. 1 (January 1994): 66–71.

Freire, P. *Pedagogy of the Oppressed.* Translated by M. B. Ramos. New York: Continuum, 1970.

Freire, P. "Education: Domestication or Liberation?" *Prospects*, v. 2, no. 2 (Summer 1972): 173-181.

Freire, P. "Literacy and the Possible Dream." *Prospects*, v. 6, no. 1 (1976): 68-71, 76.

Freire, P. *The Politics of Education: Culture, power and liberation.* Translated by D. Macedo. New Haven: Bergin & Garvey, 1985.

Kozol, J. *Children of the Revolution: A Yankee Teacher in the Cuban Schools.* New York: Delacorte Press, 1981.

Kozol, J. *Illiterate America.* New York: Anchor Press, 1985.

Lovelace, E. *A Brief Conversation and Other Stories.* New York: Persea, 2003.

Gubbe, L. M. "Impact of the Hidden Curriculum and Student Resistance on Attrition in Developmental Education Courses." *Research and Teaching in Developmental Education*, v. 15, no. 2 (Spring 1999): 37-45.

Martz N. B., and Clasby, M. "Casco Bay Partnership for Workplace Education. Final Performance Report [and] Final Evaluation Report." *University of Southern Maine, Gorham* (1995).

Quindlen, A. *How Reading Changed My life.* New York: Ballantine Books, 1998.

Raabe, T. *Biblioholism: The Literary Addiciton.* Golden: Fulcrum Publishing, 1991.

Rogers, Carl R. "Toward a More Human Science of the Person." *Journal of Humanistic Psychology*, v. 25, no. 4 Spring (1985): 7-24.

Schrag, P. and Divoky, D. *The Myth of the Hyperactive Child: And Other Means of Child Control.* New York: Pantheon, 1975.

Schwartz, L. S. *Ruined by Reading: A Life in Books*. Boston: Beacon Press, 1996.

Vellutino, F. R., D. M. Scanlon, and G. R. Lyon. "Differentiating between difficult-to-remediate and readily remediated poor readers: More evidence against the IQ-achievement discrepancy definition of reading disability." *Journal of Learning Disabilities*, v. 33, no. 3 (2000): 223-238.

10

Reclaiming the Past

This chapter makes clear the social and political meaning of literacy. It focuses on the link between my story and that of the fictitious child Felia portrayed in chapters 2 and 3. We were obedient children who did what we were told. In school, we were neither moody nor irritable, merely passive—that is, until friends showed us how literature could free us from deception and manipulation.

Theories of Motivation

I remember the first question I asked as a doctoral student at the University of Wisconsin. It happened in an introductory course that met weekly in a large lecture hall. No one asked questions in this class; instead, we took notes as the distinguished professor covered the content in lecture format.

During the session on remedial reading, he analyzed the theoretical concepts behind several popular instructional approaches. The approaches were based on the assumption that instruction is needed in unmastered skills. I listened intently because I wanted to know what could be done for older learners who did not know how to read. After all, I had just spent the past five years of my life as a literacy worker in the Caribbean trying to answer this question. Although I had taught a few adults to read, most of my students had resisted instruction. Few seemed to be interested in books.

As he neared the completion of his lecture, my hand shot up. I asked him why he thought children would pay attention to instruction they had resisted in the past. He responded with a deep sigh and said that in his experience, the essential question in reading was motivation, that teachers should reject force, bribery, or manipulation as ways to get children to open a book. As to a foolproof "technique," he could not offer one. I was impressed with his candor.

That exchange took place thirty-five years ago. Since then, literature reading has dropped dramatically, with fewer than half of American adults now reading literary works (Bradshaw and Nichols 2004). The worst decline has been with the youngest age groups. Overcoming aversion to print is hard to do if students think literature discussions are a right and wrong guessing game. Consider the following:

> By high school, I was fed up with the idea at having to speculate an author's meaning. When faced with questions like, "What did the author mean by the phrase ...?" or "How do you think the author felt about ... I felt as though we were invading the author's privacy by even attempting to answer these questions. I never believed that there was one right answer to these types of questions, as our teachers would have had us believe. By this point, I called myself a reader but did not have a great motivation to do so. It had become such a chore that I did not even read assignments; these were perfectly good and interesting novels that I may very well have picked up to read all on my own. I did not, however, read them as assigned. What a terrible result of someone who started her literacy career so strongly.

Those who fail run away from books or postpone assignments until the last minute. Others forget assignments, compensate by drawing or doodling, or simply complain. Fed up with the same negative messages they have heard for years, numerous students decide they do not need to be literate and so give up trying. For them, failure is so absolute, they drop out of school.

We see in my father's story resistance and defiance of school. We also see people who admired his resiliency, helping him to make his way—the theater owner who gave him a job; the stranger who sent him to summer camp; the nun who gave him an orange every day in the coatroom; and Salvation Army friends who offered him clothing and food.

I represent students who inherited a lot from relatives—honesty from my grandmother and strength from my father. I also inherited inhibitions that kept me from sharing my feelings with others. Dad's screaming gave me a feeling of being small and unimportant. He so distracted me I couldn't concentrate on anything, and so I withdrew into television, as he had into movies. Many students do the same thing today with gaming and the Internet—classic avoidance behaviors (Hazlett-Stevens 2008). I was also determined to prove that I was smart. Even though I tried to learn fancy words, I still spoke with a blue-collar accent. No one knew or cared if I did not read at home. After all, I got good grades because school was about memorization. Not having read anything that gripped my imagination, I wasted my time daydreaming, in denial, hating books. Threats to have me removed from sports teams unless I submitted weekly book reports did not work. They only made me more resistant to authority figures telling me what to do.

These are the same problems that many students face today. Who admits their problem? Part of our indifference is hidden in what Popkewitz (1985) calls our instrumental culture. We are quick to judge talent and brilliance that comes with achievement and scorn those who fail. Jane Addams, Emma Goldman, and Antonio Gramsci fought against the same bias a hundred years ago. Still, conventional assumptions about success and failure restrict learning. One is the inevitability argument— why help students who choose to fail? Brilliant hard workers deserve praise and attention. Let the others find their own way.

Deep down I had interests and ability. I stumbled onto books through friends like Richard's brother, Hans, and Jon, who recommended that I read. Thank goodness school is not the only place to read real books because aliteracy is a needless waste of time. Teachers of youth need to take a more aggressive approach to understanding why many students turn their backs on books. They need to help them find a reason to read and to overcome their inhibitions about taking risks. Students, who are fearful of making mistake or a committing to long pages of prose, need dialogue, not judgment.

It is generally accepted that dialogic teaching (Freire 1993) is time-consuming, complicated, and counter to traditional instruction. Let's face it: dialogic conversations with students are counter to authoritative teaching (Scott, Mortimer, and Aguiar 2006). The political complexion of leadership is another factor that inhibits students from thinking and talking in classrooms. The line that separates dialogue from submissive listening has less to do with student unwillingness to think critically than it does with those who enforce conformity from away.

Too many people believe students choose to be alliterate (*a person who is able to read but rarely chooses to do so*) Some sound like out-of-control talk-radio hosts who strip complexity down to oversimplifications. These same individuals abhor watered-down standards. The problem with half-baked thinking is that it is insulting, shallow ineffectual, and, in the end, harmful to children.

Building Confidence to Read and Write

Over the years many explanations about motivation have appeared in psychological literature. The basic premise is that the beliefs a student holds about himself affect his success or failure in school (Pajares, Britner, and Valiante 2000). Self-esteem studies based on the research of luminaries such as Maslow and Rodgers were very popular in the '40s through the '70s. In humanistic psychology, confidence became the precondition of all learning. Children who fail, it was felt, developed a mind-set against trying. The role of the teacher was to reestablish confidence.

Self-esteem recommendations included taking long walks with students, pep talks, breathing exercises, sharing positive attitudes, and talking a respectful manner. It also meant avoiding or minimizing tasks that threatened self-esteem. This meant putting students into materials that were not too difficult. Others tried to boost student self-esteem through challenging activities like Upward Bound—environmental education and rock climbing. Here, the assumption was that conquering a difficult task leads to renewed confidence in tackling new tasks. This concept of challenge was very popular with radical thinkers like John Gatto.

Ravitch (2000) argued in her *Left Back: A Century of Failed School Reforms* that progressive reforms had bad consequences on school curriculum. Self-esteem strategies suffered when similar critics charged they had become too permissive. Some called them social worker talk because they postponed academic teaching until confidence was regained. Research also found little correlation between self-esteem and achievement. This development led to the rejection of nurturing the emotional health of children in school. In its place the back-to-basics movement argued that using particular instructional materials improved academic learning.

Needing a Reason to Read

Behind my decision to read on my own was discovering a starting point. I had to have a reason to read. Mario Puzo, a highly successful novelist, was an unlikely candidate to become a great writer. His parents were Sicilian and illiterate. He lived in a crowded and treeless neighborhood. His father came home too tired to be involved in the life of his kids. His mother disciplined them, as Rose did, with flying pans. He had no goal other than to become a clerk. He did not look to his relatives for help because, in his own words, they were "contemptible, course, vulgar, and insulting folk." His neighbors were always angry, shouting at each other, quick to quarrel. His friends stole and thought that only sissies read. Puzo hated his life.

Puzo went to the local Boys' Club in his neighborhood. There, he found people who looked out for him. He also went on trips to New Hampshire that offered him an alternative to his chaotic urban family life. He also had time on his hands. In the summer, he played outside and stole all the time. Winter was a different matter. There was nothing to do, no entertainment, just constant quarreling and bickering.

At a very early age, he found that reading books took him out of this chaos. Luckily, he had access to books at the Boys' Club, and he could walk to the local library. There, he became friends with the librarian. He read about Indians. He discovered Doc Savage and the Shadow.

Adventure stories satisfied his need for heroes. At fifteen he discovered Dostoevsky. In doing so, "I understood for the first time what was happening to me and the people around me. I believed in art."

Books offered Puzo a way to understand his life. His dream—actually, his need—was to describe his experience. He knew this meant becoming a writer. When he told his mother he wanted to become an artist, she laughed. In her upbringing, artists were rich people. Puzo didn't care. Not even his dear mother could distract him from following his dream. He went in the service, where he continued to read. When he returned from duty he enrolled in the Writers Project at Columbia. He wrote about what he knew best—the people who had surrounded him as a child.

Many people have written about the power of literacy to explain their existence. The ability of literacy study experience is easily misunderstood. We may make it the end when, in fact, it is the beginning. We may make it to the end when, in fact, it is the beginning. The reward in reading great literature is in reading great literature. But often we manipulate learning with prizes, pizza parties, the possibility of getting good jobs, even through coercion. This may work in the short-term but it crushes the joy and the intrinsic desire to read and write in the long term. This is unfortunate. Reading gives us the right purpose and perspective. It gives us the confidence to be life long learners. Let's not try to manipulate learning with prizes or pizza parties or coercion.

None of these techniques satisfy the human need to know. Motivation has to come from within or else it cannot sustain the effort it takes to learn.

This is what happened to me. Reading became such a chore, because it was done for a gold star, that I escaped into television in my free-time rather than read. My parents' reading was limited to the newspaper. We could not afford to purchase books, my school did not have a library, and the public one was inaccessible. Without resources and encouragement, reading became a stumbling over words, so I avoided it. Thank goodness I did not give up on books entirely. Three very important events reminded me how important they were.

Expectation

Certain people in my life communicated the importance of reading. My neighbor Mrs. Andrews gave me a book early in my life. Although it was too hard to read, I treasured it because I looked up to her. She was my idea of what it meant to be an American. Her sons had graduated from high school, and dressed liked successful Americans. Her daughter babysat me when I was younger. She used to talk about her school experiences, especially the dances she attended. Mrs. Andrews's home had an attic and a fireplace—I had never seen either of these before because I lived in a multifamily apartment building. Her attic was full of clothes, like varsity sweaters her children had worn in high school. It was also packed with mementoes from the First World War. On summer days, she would invite me over to play in the attic.

The second time I received a book was when I went through my Catholic confirmation in the fifth grade. The True sisters gave me a book about sports heroes. I was ready for it. The passages were short and easy to read and were accompanied by illustrations. The stories were about great men and women I had heard about since I was a young kid, playing catch with my father and Gus, our next-door neighbor, on long summer evenings in front of our house. This gift gave me a chance to find out why athletes were so important to the men in my neighborhood. I learned how Jim Thorpe had won Olympic medals, how Jessie Owens had stumped Hitler, and how Jessie Paddock overcame a physical handicap to become a world-class sprinter. Their stories were inspirational. I would return to them many times over the years, fascinated by the heroism and determination. This gift opened me to the joys of biography.

The third person was my eighth-grade English teacher at South Junior High School. The school was in a rundown section of the city. Most of my classmates were third-generation Italian Americans. Our fathers worked as mechanics or semi-skilled laborers. Few drove new cars or owned second homes. We came from working-class backgrounds that stressed obedience and following rules.

Yet I repudiated my teacher's demands to read because that

represented high-status values. My teacher's telling me I had to wear a tie in a family play was as if she was telling me there was something wrong with my father and my uncles. She seemed to be conceited. I did not appreciate however, that if I was going to make it, I had to read.

Comic-book reading bridged television watching to literature. This was reading where I wouldn't get evaluated on, so it wasn't a chore—it was fun.

I could never find a good library book to read. They all seemed long, boring, and contrived. Comic books were different. They were packed with clever comedy situations, lively dialogue, gags, and strong humor. The plots and settings were exciting too. Stories took place in exotic locales and foreign countries. I went on an African safari to the Congo, visited the Australian Outback, learned the story of *The Odyssey* and the Midas touch, the mines of King Solomon, and the ancient Egyptians who guarded the ancient treasures of King Tut. The Mayans taught me about the difficult and dangerous pursuit of archeology and the reason why their civilization collapsed. Comics were historical fiction without being didactic or sentimental.

Imagination

I lived my early years without mental images of faraway places. I relied on the stories my father told me about relatives and on television shows to create metaphors of sadness, courage, or adventure. I liked especially James Cagney movies when he spoke like the tough guys in my neighborhood: "You dirty rat." On occasion I drew warships, made tents in the living room, played with toy soldiers or trains, and built snow forts with friends. That was it. My room contained no books to escape into.

At some point real literature kicked in. It was in the seventh grade with a required reading of Longfellow's *Evangeline.* Dactylic hexameter opened me to a tragic tale of how beautiful Evangeline searched for years for her phantom lover, Gabriel, only to find him, old and near death. In a scene I could get not get out of my head, Gabriel died in her arms.

I had stumbled into art (Green 1983). Longfellow helped me find myself through lyrical, picture-making, historical context and a profound sense of what love and grief feel like. I was an adolescent kid, mired in self-doubt questions like, "Who am I?" or "Am I normal? What am I going to become?" I was trapped because I didn't feel free to talk with anyone about these questions, nor did I know that stories answered these questions. I was what McCarthy (1998) calls "complainant and myopic." I finally discovered, "It is what you read when you don't have to that determines what you will be [like]" (Wilde).

Apply These Insights to Instruction in Schools

Literacy is about understanding our inner secrets. Since literacy is personal, it cannot be prescribed. Rosemary Bowler and Carolyn Olivier (1996) make an obvious point—let the young decide what they read. At the same time, teachers of reluctant readers need to be librarians, metaphorically speaking, recommending stories that will fire up their students' imaginations.

Many children were especially vulnerable to today's pressures, exposed to busy lives and a culture that celebrates violence. Others hear mixed messages about reading as a waste of time. It is hard to break the aliteracy habit when a child has never had his imagination stimulated by words. We have to push them into new experiences. A story about pets may be perfect for a child who has a cat. But the same story may have a deeper meaning, in this case, about loss of a loved one. We need to match and push reluctant readers to think about multiple meanings in stories.

References

Bowler, R. and Olivier, C. *Learning to Learn*. New York: Fireside, 1996.

Bradshaw, T. and Nichols, B. "Reading At Risk: A Survey of Literary Reading in America." *National Endowment for the Arts,* Report #46 (June 2004): 47 pages.

Freire, P. *A Critical Encounter*. New York: Routledge, 1993.

Green D. R. "A Survey of Probability Concepts in 3000 Pupils Age 11-16 Years." *Proceedings of the Second International Conference on Teaching Statistics*. Edited by D. R. Grey, P. Holmes, V. Barnett, and G. M. Constable (1983): 766-783.

Hazlett-Stevens, H. *Psychological Approaches to Generalized Anxiety Disorder: A Clinician's Guide to Assessment and Treatment*. New York: Springer, 2008.

McCarthy, T. J. *From This Clay: Gifts, surprises, and questions from the spiritual quest*. Lanham: Lexington Books, 2006.

McCarthy, T. J. *Relationships of Sympathy: The Writer and the Reader in British Romanticism*. Leicester: Scolar Press, 1998.

Pajares, F., Britner, S. L. and Valiante, G. "Relation between Achievement Goals and Self-Beliefs of Middle School Students in Writing and Science." *Contemporary Educational Psychology,* v. 25, no. 24 (October 2000): 406-422.

Popkewitz, T. S. "Ideology and social formation in teacher education." *Journal of Teaching and Teacher Education*, v. 1, no. 2 (1985): 91-107.

Ravitch, D. *Left Back: A Century of Failed School Reforms*. New York: Simon & Schuster, 2000.

Scott, P. H., Mortimer, E. F. and Aguiar, O. G. "The tension between authoritative and dialogic discourse: A fundamental characteristic of meaning making interactions in high school science lessons." *Science Education*, v. 90, no. 4 (July 2006): 605–631.

11

Power and Pedagogy

Justin's story demonstrates how some schools stifle the human spirit. It is about a child who went to school reading and writing; someone who constructed knowledge on his own; someone who had a purpose and a goal in mind. He was not accommodated. His talents were seriously misread, unappreciated, and devalued. He learned to doubt himself. He ended up an underachiever because the right questions were not asked about him.

Young, Gifted, and Biracial

Why should we be concerned with Justin's story? Some will say, "Get over it. Life is unfair." Others will argue that his literacy history is nothing more than a rite of passage many gifted children go through. Still others will declare that setbacks teach bright children to be humble. To back up such a claim, Rozycki (2004) points out that the ancients believed "we grow through facing adversity." Add to this mix the assertion that this is a family dynamic of no concern to others.

There are many reasons why we should care about what happened to him. His failings have less to do with rites of passage or family dynamics than with the ethos of schools. Words matter. Silence matters. Low teacher expectations can change lives tragically (Arcilla 1992). The expectations he suffered still affect him two decades later. Beyond all this, Justin's dumbing down (Gatto 1992) raises questions about how institutional racism contributes to failure.

Family Dynamics

Why did schools get it so wrong? I believe that part of it was due to the poor quality of training teachers receive with respect to children who teach themselves to read and write. Part of it was racially motivated by the bilingual stigma that was placed on him. Part was due to inflexible school rules and regulations. There was also a long-standing belief that a worried child is symptomatic of family dynamics.

To be frank, I was apprehensive about Justin's passage from home to school. As a student of literacy research, I knew how easily children like him can fall prey to errors in judgment. I imagined him sitting alone in a corner with pages of worksheets to do because his teachers did not know what to do with him. I also imagined teachers ignoring his precociousness (Moore, Ford, and Milner 2005) because he was the only child of color in their school.

In trying to shield him from real and imagined threats, I may have overreacted. Case in point. Justin started to play organized sports in the second grade. His first experience was winter basketball at the YMCA in Portland. He was small but very quick, able to steal the ball effortlessly. His forte—fast breaks—allowed him to dominate games. I shared my excitement with him on rides home.

Now that I think about it, my enthusiasm may have backfired. Too much praise, as Shannon Zentall and Bradley Morris (2010) argue in their article "Good job, you're so smart," may have made him self-conscious about performing the following week. As a self-taught reader and writer and student of Montessori education, he was not used to verbal praise (Whitescarver and Cossentino 2008). His motivation came from the internal satisfaction of learning on his own. From Alfie Kohn's (1993) perspective, my excitement could have disrupted his calm. Is it any wonder why he had me take him to a gym before the next game to practice?

Lillard (2005) makes the case this way:

> Incentives undermine intrinsic interest cognitive performance, creativity, prosocial behavior, and a host

of other good outcomes in children. In other words, the use of extrinsic rewards, may well contribute to children coming to dislike school and to poorer performance than many children would otherwise achieve.

The following spring he wanted to try out for Little League. I discouraged him because he had only started to play T-ball the year before. I figured he might get hit by an errant pitch or yelled at by a coach because he really did not know the rules. Frankly speaking, I didn't think he would make the cut. Nevertheless, he wanted to try out, so I agreed. He made the team and rapidly improved because he was playing with older, more skilled players.

I soured the following season when he did not get much playing time. A select group of town kids got the breaks, playing the most coveted positions and getting the most innings. Justin got a token inning or two per game in right field. The less playing time he got, the less he developed. I also saw a slip in his confidence. I became moody after games, complaining aloud about the politics of sport.

By the sixth grade, he did not want me to attend his games. It became more pronounced in middle school. I was devastated because I got so much pleasure out of watching him play. I asked him if I made him nervous. He asked me not to talk about it and said he would come to me, not me to him. Another time he told me, "Dad, you make me nervous because you want me to play perfectly." By high school I had to sneak into games to watch him. I finally stopped attending.

Many parents push their children too hard, wanting them to live up to their (the parents') dreams. I didn't think of myself as a pushy, competitive dad, yelling at him, arguing with coaches, filming him, or criticizing him after games. In fact, I perceived myself as affirming and supportive. I now realize that my fervor may have made him anxious. As Anthony E. Wolf in his book *The Secret of Parenting* (2000) has pointed out, kids pick up on everything parents say and do, including our disappointments.

Stigma

Perry needed a break with respect to his school failure. His seventh-grade social studies teacher gave him one by preparing easy-to-read materials, which allowed him to participate in classroom discussions. Denny Taylor's (1990) story about Patrick in *Learning Denied* underscores the problem of failing children who need just and caring accommodations like Perry's social studies teacher and his grandmother had given him.

Justin had to deal with different issues. Although a precocious piano player, he never played in public. I remember relatives saying intuitively that he was a sensitive child who lacked self-confidence. Elliot and Dweck (2005), in fact, show that many bright children lack confidence to tackle ordinary things because they have been told for too long they are extra-intelligent. Justin was greatly inspired by Renaissance masters who spoke in the language of music and art. Since music was a new language, he had to learn its underlying structure. This is why he studied and practiced so hard. Music was not about entertaining others or securing awards but a way to unlock his inner voice. As Victor Hugo wrote in his book on art *William Shakespeare* (1864), "Music expresses that which cannot be put into words and that which cannot remain silent" (Part I, Book II, Chapter IV).

Justin's prolific ability in the visual arts went unacknowledged. At art camp he produced an exceptional sketch of a feather. He received no recognition from his teacher, who merely checked it off as another assignment done on time. Did she resent his talent because all the campers wanted to sit next to him?

His artistic and musical abilities were more appreciated in the community than at school. He won a scholarship in middle school to attend an art institute. He was also one of eight students selected to represent Maine in Washington, DC, at the All-Eastern Chorus. The director singled him out for his musical ability.

Biracialism

Reverend Herbert D. Daughtry, Sr. (2001) uses harsh words to describe the world of mixed-race couples: "In the world we live in, people stare and talk under their breath as biracial couples walk past. In this world, biracial couples have the added pressure of being ostracized and hated." Things are no better for their children. Henry Harris (2002) reports that biracial children experience more academic problems than whites, and they are not genuinely accepted. Francis Wardle (1988) lists the difficulties that hinder educators' abilities to respond to biracial children.

The following story captures the reality of a biracial child in school. I changed the name of the child to Chris to protect his identity. About ten years ago I got a call from a frantic parent whose biracial son was having behavioral problems at school. She told me that he was reading real literature at home but cried every day before going to school. She had attempted to tell the school he was gifted and needed stimulation. The school disagreed, saying he had behavioral problems. The administration agreed to let me visit the school to observe Chris and to evaluate his vast assessment file. Every imaginable test was in there, including occupational therapy screening results. Missing was a report that analyzed everything. I did locate an account of his three-day visit to the gifted class. Although the writer acknowledged Chris's great success, he did not recommend a permanent placement because the child's regular classroom behavior had disqualified him.

I went to observe Chris. He sat alone in the corner with his basal unopened. The teacher said she placed him there because he was highly distractible. The fire alarm went off, so I walked outside with the class. As we returned, a teacher pulled Chris out of line and scolded him for not having his shoelaces tied. A second teacher did the same thing as he neared his room. I noticed that several other boys with untied sneakers were not reprimanded.

Chris had been labeled disruptive because he didn't finish his work. His teacher added, "His sloppiness sets a bad example for the other children." Meanwhile, the evidence showed that he had a strong love of learning by doing, a reliable sign of intelligence (Skererjian 1990). It wasn't for the lack of information that Chris was in trouble. All the signs were evident. In my one-on-one session with him, he came across as highly literate, intelligent, engaged, and responsive. In his gifted audition, he was alive and energetic. In his regular classroom, he was passive, cut off, and ignored. If the school had embraced his gifts, he would have been a lot happier. That was impossible because minds were made up. It was as if Harper Lee's (1960) *To Kill a Mockingbird* was being written all over again. People who failed to judge Chris from his own perspective crushed him, just as the jury had done to Tom Robinson, the black farmhand accused of rape.

The Social Construction of Literacy Failure

Academic achievement is socially constructed. Schools become dangerous places when they ignore this fact. Albert Cullum's (1971) *The Geranium on the Window Sill Just Died, but Teacher, You Went Right On* dramatizes this point from a child's perspective. Although written close to forty years ago, its critique of insensitive teaching is still relevant today. As a commentator wrote, "My school experience was hellish and emotionally damaging. I went to school and hated it."

Progressive reformers continue to plead with teachers to assess their relationships with children. For one thing, there is evidence that positive relationships foster achievement. Elizabeth Moje (1996) found that the relationships she established with her students motivated them to engage in literacy activities. On the other end, rogue teachers (Colón 2006; Brendgen, et al. 2006) who neglect or ignore children send them on a downward spiral. Perhaps the stresses of teaching can lead to cynical or uncaring behavior. The point is we need to think about who we are, the words we use, why we teach, and what is behind our judgments. We also need to think about consequences and be accountable for our actions.

Charging schools with malfeasance seems harsh and one-sided. Yet education critics like Paul Goodman (1964) and, more recently, John Gatto (2000, 1997) and Alfie Kohn (2004) have exposed ideologically driven prejudices that harm children. There are no happy endings for bright, gifted biracial children when their talents are misappropriated. Ivor Goodson and Andy Hargreaves (1996) predicted that educational restructuring would move teachers away from a moral responsibility to a narrow technical competence prescribed by the new state and federal laws. He was right. Many continue to ignore the students they should care about, citing as their excuse, "We are not paid to be social workers" (Amoroso 1995).

If teachers are responsible for the moral education of all students, what is behind their opposition to this goal? Kozol (2007) thinks it could be an institutional political resistance. In simpler terms, it is easier to support institutional values than to take them on. Consider the journal entry of a graduate student teacher at an urban school in the northeast:

> I saw kids every day that came to school excited to be there, saying their good mornings to their friends and their teachers and many teachers didn't give them the time of day. All these kids wanted was someone to talk to, someone to tell them about their night or what they did over the weekend and the teachers wouldn't give them two seconds; rather they would say things like "Joseph hang up your coat and eat breakfast so we can begin morning meeting on time." What message are we sending to these kids when we do this to them? Too often students tell us things and our only response is wow, that's good or how exciting; it's almost like it is preset in us.
>
> There are very few teachers in this school who truly take the time to get to know their students and are able to meet their needs and make learning fun and successful for all. To tell you the truth, not to be conceited or anything but I was able to make connections with a few students that were considered to be very difficult that no other teacher had been able to make and to be honest I saw the kids' faces and attitudes change when I took the time to sit down and talk to them one on one and tell them that I was their friend too and to give them a hug (not that you can do that in all school systems).
>
> The teacher-administration relationship was the worst of all. Never, at any time, the whole time I was there did I see the teachers or administration on the same page or supportive of one another. The administration didn't care to listen, they didn't care to help, they didn't

care to make any sort of difference, they didn't care to get involved in anything. They always put things on the back burner and had no plan for anything. Actually, the principal, word for word, said, "I don't like having plans, plans don't work."

School is a place where decisions about children determine what they think about themselves. Lee Galda et al (1995) presents convincing evidence that student perceptions can have a pronounced effect on performance. Children see others rewarded unfairly (Babad 1995). Children see favoritism all the time. They see it in sports, in music, in the classroom. Unfairness poisons them, and they may grow up passing on the poison to their children.

Favoritism degrades all of us when we only reward those who look like us. We need to get back to a time when we cared about all children. Biracial children, especially, need to be free from stigma, prejudice, and the contradictions that fill their lives.

The core problem is that a teacher's job is, by nature, judgmental. Teaching requires compassion and practicality, virtues that seem to be in short order lately. Some teachers are burned out, trying to meet the high expectations for test scores. Others seem to start with a conclusion: make my work as easy as possible so that I can maximize my rewards without an effort. Commitment to every child in my classroom is damaging to my personal life. I want the biggest return for the least amount of effort.

To be sure, teacher unhappiness can be affected by many factors. Regardless of the cause or causes, we become spiritually bankrupt when we reduce teaching to punching a timecard. Maria Montessori rejected selfishness. Her yardstick was, what can I do to improve the lives of all children, especially those from poor and working-class families? All great educational reformers taught the same thing. If we work in a moral vacuum, where egoism (pursuit of one's welfare) drives us, we do not give children any real consciousness about who they are. Instead of empowering them with a passion for learning, we teach them to hate school and give up.

Teacher Expectations

How is it that Justin's work could have been so overlooked? Part of the answer is found in the concept of stigma, endemic devaluation of black accomplishment. When you look at blacks in good colleges, most start valuing achievement highly. Yet 98 percent collect C+ averages, while only 34 percent of the whites do. Claude Steele (1997) believes that if you are treated as a valued person and your efforts are reaffirmed, you become confident. On the other hand, if you are not accepted or if you are not appreciated, you begin to see the worst in yourself. Without appreciation, you become vulnerable to failure. Failure is defined as a feeling of isolation. Students have to work extra hard when their achievement is overlooked. Evelyn Hanssen (1998) reinforces Steele's thesis by listing unintentional forms of racism in schools. They include underrepresentation of black authors in the curriculum, lack of faculty diversity, and a persistently "white" school ethos.

Social science researchers have been investigating the concept of teacher expectations for more than forty years. Teachers' beliefs have definite consequences on student achievement (Benner and Mistry 2007; Rubie-Davies 2005). High expectations lead to high performance and vice versa. How many of Justin's school problems were connected to low teacher expectations? None of his teachers looked at this possibility. Was their silence due to their failure to recognize it? We give teachers workshops in identifying drug usage and domestic violence. We create noncredit classes and place low achievers in the lower tracks. It seems more difficult to reflect on our relationships with students than it is to add deficit-orientated programs.

I asked Justin's teachers to allow him to read and write on his own. As with Perry's teachers, I ran into a buzz saw of acrimony that turned into finger pointing. All children, I was reminded contentiously, need to cover all the skills laid out in the curriculum. No exceptions. Ironically, his writing surpassed their benchmarks for his age and stage of reading and writing. For example, he packed stories with dialogue that captured the way people actually spoke. He also used gags, paradox and irony beyond his years. His writing reflected an intelligent observer of his environment.

Asking his teacher to allow him to read materials at his reading level was not unreasonable. Yet the teacher and her reading specialist retaliated by looking for weaknesses in his phonics and then sending him to remedial reading for segmentation drills. Their hidden agenda shut off communication. Forget about sharing what we know about young natural readers. Not even common sense would work. I was face-to-face with bias, racial or otherwise, in this pristine New England town that kept everyone in his or her place. The king had ordered conformity, and his bishops were enforcing it.

Not knowing how to push back, I enrolled Justin in an independent school, the language arts curriculum of which was based on the work of Donald Graves. The principal embraced Justin's strengths as a reader, storyteller, and artist. But at the classroom level, he was put in a basal, required to keep a daily journal for correction purposes, and assigned a reading buddy who could not read. When I mentioned using real *literature* for instruction, his teacher struck back with the same recriminatory tone I had faced in Wisconsin, Tennessee, and now Maine. She told me it was wrong for Justin to stay in at recess to read.

This reminded me of Emperor Joseph II telling Mozart in *Amadeus*, "My dear young man, don't take it too hard. Your work is ingenious. It's quality work. And there are simply too many notes, that's all. Just cut a few and it will be perfect." Hurt and angered, Mozart replies in a petulant manner, "Which few did you have in mind, Majesty?" A betrayed Mozart then turns to court composer Salieri, who says, "My dear Mozart, there are only so many notes that the ear can hear at any one time!"

So, there you have it—the amateur, Emperor Joseph, and the composer's nemesis, Salieri, telling Mozart that his opera is second-rate because it has too many notes. Talk about blindsided hubris. In a similar vein, villagers on Saint Croix used to tell me that too much reading leads to bad eyesight. Porter (1998), by the way, gives examples of anti-book comments made by the apostles, the Greeks, Erasmus, Gutenberg, and others.

But back to the teacher who said it was wrong for Justin to stay in at recess. She was also the same teacher who misconstrued Justin's Dr. Martin Luther King's "I Have a Dream" speech. His intention was to emulate the rhetorical style of the great Dr. King, so he used a thesaurus and a Bible to set words to the rhythm of Dr. King's speech. Incredibly she told him to rewrite the story in simple English with no biblical references. It was an infuriating response, more one-track than bearing witness to Justin's ability to tackle a new genre. Why did she reject his inspired elocution? Perhaps her professional training taught her to focus on one specific item to the exclusion of everything else. Whatever the reason, I believe, as Harrison Crenshaw II, David Thompson and Janet Leighman (1994) reported, she would have benefitted from reading about classroom climate and student achievement. No wonder there is so much cynicism about schools. Rather than celebrate ingenuity, we hunt for imperfection. If Plato is right about how we understand, we must look for the good first, or we misunderstand. So, it's important as teachers that we look for the good in our students, in addition to how we can help our students improve. Otherwise we can misunderstand and destroy. Emerson (1847) wrote touchingly in "The Rhodora": "In May when sea winds pierced our solitudes, I found the fresh Rhodora in the woods." Emerson is telling us that he never thought to ask where this common flower came from. Teachers, too, may not always recognize the genesis of talent, but that should not justify ignoring it.

Constructivism

A key conflict in Justin's education was the way he learned and how his teachers taught. Justin taught himself to read and write by figuring out how words and how stories are structured. This is called constructivist learning. In contrast, traditional teaching emphasizes knowledge through skill packets, practice exercises, repetition, and tests. Teachers assign an exercise and correct for errors. It does not require depth or breadth of knowledge to make a decision. You add up the correct answers to get a percentage score.

Constructivism works on a different set of assumptions. Learning is by doing; in this case, detecting patterns and rules. In searching, the child asks, "What is this? Why does it work? How can I learn to do that?" He comes up with a thesis and tests it out. If it works, fine; if not, try again. If a child wants to punctuate a story correctly, he or she examines how it is done in real text. Learning is active because the child is generating hypotheses. What is learned and when depends on what the child needs to know at that moment. There is no scope and sequence. And there is no guarantee that hunches will be correct. A self-taught reader or writer will keep on hunting until he or she has learned what is desired.

Benchmarks are very different for children who are self-taught and those who are taught in traditional ways. In reading, the child who is a natural reader constructs meaning by asking, Does this make sense? Errors or miscues that produce phrasing or sentences that don't sound right are self-corrected. If errors sound right and are understandable, they may not be corrected because they do not disrupt meaning. An example is saying Bill for Billy. In writing, teachers look for a child's willingness to revise, elaborate, or add new information. Spellings are invented until the child begins to write for an audience, which triggers the need to use correct orthographic spellings. Studying printed text teaches mechanics. The natural writer does not need a paint-by-numbers rubric to guide his work because he has already constructed a mental model of what good writing looks like.

Traditional teaching dictates what is to be learned, when it has to be learned, and how it is to be learned. It is objective, rational, precise, and linear. Assignments and due dates are clear and posted. Rubrics take the guesswork out of the structural elements of good writing. Students know exactly what is needed to get a good grade—following directions and being on time with assignments. Since learning can turn into a game called "Pleasing the Teacher," students learn to conform to what has to be done to get good grades. Others need to be paid to study.

The Hidden Curriculum

The hidden curriculum is the centerpiece of all schooling. Every school and classroom has a hidden or implicit curriculum—behaviors, attitudes, and knowledge—that unintentionally teach morality to students. Lawrence Kohlberg (1975) put it this way in his article "Moral Education for a Society in Moral Transition":

> The guts of the hidden curriculum are the praise, the teacher's use of rewards or punishments; the crowd or the life in a crowded group; and the teacher's power. Our episode of the teacher blaming kids for not putting their books away is the natural exercise of teacher power, the natural use of praise or blame in a crowded setting where order is a necessary preoccupation. To the teacher it is not moral education, it is a natural reaction to the classroom situation. To my son, however, it was moral education or miseducation. It defined the good boys and the bad. That is what I meant by claiming that the school or teacher's methods of classroom management, the unstudied or hidden curriculum, should be approached from a theory of moral education. This implies that not only did we need to study the hidden curriculum, but to take a moral position on it.

Since it is impossible to observe what is hidden, one must ask, "In addition to my goals and the school's stated learning outcomes, what else are students learning?" The three dimensions of school life where students receive moral lessons are (1) organizational: time, facilities, materials; (2) interpersonal: teacher-student, teacher-administrator, teacher-parent, student-students; and (3) institutional: policies, routine procedures, rituals, social structure, extracurricular activities available to the student and the community.

Students are learning moral lessons about competition, individuality, and achievement and other deeply held cultural values, including hierarchy, conformity, success, control, and punctuality. Justin was an engaged and independent child who loved learning. That was lost on the school because their mission was to place him in school board-purchased materials and be graded. The moral message was, if you do what we say, good. If you don't, you don't belong here. This message was communicated incessantly. No one picked up on the fear and confusion it created in Justin.

A growing number of parents seek out independent schools. One reason might be that, according to education consultant Dave Bergman (2014), college counselors in public schools typically spend only 23% of their time on helping students navigate the college admissions process as compared with college counselors in private schools who spend about 53%. Moreover, roughly 95% of private high school graduates attend college, while 49% of public school graduates do.

Yet on the other hand, while many public schools in the United States might be in a dilapidated condition, many others also offer amenities that are on par with private schools. Many public schools also offer credentialed, dedicated instructors, and a bounty of AP courses. Finally, attending a private school surrounded by fellow academic superstars could have a negative, cutthroat impact on a student's experience, and furthermore can have a negative effect on admissions to an elite college. For example, a student who scores 1300 on the SATs at a public school where the average SAT is 1000 will look more attractive to an admission committee than a student who scored 1300 at a private school where the average SAT score is 1300. When it gets down to it, if a student can finish well at a solid public school and enlist the help of a college counselor, being a "big flower in a small greenhouse" could actually be advantageous.

But what exactly are the pedagogical practices of teachers who work in high-achieving independent schools? Is it visionary instruction that promotes reflective thinking and empathy? Or is it traditionalist with high levels of expectations, considerable amounts of homework, and limitations on high grades? Do they assume there is a subject to be mastered, and it is the responsibility of the student to learn it? Do they assume their students need to master high levels of competence? Is their verbal encouragement minimal?

Ann Mullen (2009) reports that class stratification remains deeply entrenched in gaining admission to elite Ivy League schools. Caroline Persell and Peter Cookson (1985) found that teachers see school through the prism of winners/losers and effort/merit, where the fittest survive. Students are sorted into two groups: winners and losers, or those who think and those who do not. High achievers consist of those students with strong intellectual skills. Many are elected to the special societies and receive book awards. They have the smallest classes and the best teachers. For many, this breeds superiority.

In schools where the high competitiveness is the norm, do high-status achievers make other groups hostile? If so, does meritocracy breed alienation? Our representative form of government requires us to be cooperative, not competitive. The world is a place where we have to learn how to get along with others. The workplace is becoming less competitive and more cooperative. The real challenge in preparing students for the future has less to do with competitiveness than it does with character. We need to be mutually respectful of others. We cannot forget Dewey's notion that we are all important and all interdependent.

Hidden Curriculum and School Athletics

E. M. Swift (1991) argues that participation in school athletics prepares students for the future because society consists of winners and losers, where rules are either obeyed or broken. Like life, there are no compromises, interpretations, or extenuating circumstances in a game. When there's violation, a price is paid. Athletic games teach lessons in accountability.

The value of an individual to a team has little to do with his or her natural talent or ability. Character is more important than points scored or assists made. Is the athlete ready when he/she is called upon? Does the athlete try? Does he/she care about the team? Is he/she dependable? The real value in playing school sports is in learning the shared responsibility of teamwork.

Swift argues for an accept-the-rules attitude, in which everyone tries his or her best and is dependable. Games are fair and objective because effort and teamwork are rewarded. Players can trust their coaches because they build character through athletic competition.

The sad fact is that some team members are more equal than others. Players with less ability frequently learn that they are inferior, that they don't count, and that they are destined to be subordinates. Some players and coaches do not play to win and excel. What about the child who tries her hardest, makes an effort, but plays with teammates who do not work as hard or share in team responsibilities? If she complains to the coach, she might be told that the goal of the game is not to win but to have fun. This student athlete might end up feeling guilty about trying her best.

And what about the way some student athletes treat others? There are countless examples of name-calling, harassment, and cliques. Some players feel they are elite and deserve special treatment because they are better than others. What about coaches who do nothing about peer harassment? What about school athletes who drink alcohol? Engage in sexual harassment or domestic violence? Denigrate the award of sportsmanship? Favoritism? Steroid use? Playing the coaches favorites ahead of others? Winning at all costs?

If there is a dark side to school sports, why do so many young people participate in them? Perhaps they join teams because they want to have fun. Others may crave glory, fame, and future earnings. Some kids (and their parents) may have motives that are selfish and undermine the goals of team play and sportsmanship. Many times I have heard selfish players only talk about their minutes or statistics.

Coaching school sports involves dealing with the students' self-esteem and enthusiasm. It also involves encounters with parents who could become overly involved in a game. Are coaches sensitive to the alienation that develops among players? What about sexual abuse of students by some sports coaches? Do team rules or codes of conduct reflect the core values of the school and of the community? Are there disciplinary situations in sports that are cruel or destructive? What are the psychological consequences of reducing playing time? Is the superior social position of some athletics justified because they earned it and thus deserve it?

Procrastination and Perfectionism

Procrastination is putting off until tomorrow what one should do today. It is a motivational problem related to fear of failure. Many college students are procrastinators. Perfectionism is related to procrastination. Many gifted students have perfectionist tendencies because they try to perform constantly without flaw. Perfectionism leads to procrastination when we think our best efforts won't matter. Working with children who are perfectionists is often difficult. It's like singing the tune "Don't Worry, Be Happy" to someone who is depressed.

How do we explain the school's response to Justin's difficulties with deadlines? The most popular policy in schools and colleges today is the old Skinnerian/Thorndike holdover called operant conditioning that assigns penalties for missing deadlines and bonus credits for early completion of material. Spot quizzes are part of this behavioral package, aimed at forcing students to study out of fear of bad grades.

Operant conditioning reflects teacher dominion over student learning. It also ignores much about what we know about learning. Students need to be confident to meet deadlines. Most would agree that writers are more comfortable if the topic interests them. Students can become paralyzed by contrived prompts and time demands that interfere with the expression of their thoughts.

There are other theories about why good students miss deadlines. One is that ADD students cannot manage time. Another comes from the learning styles/multiple intelligences camps. Visual spatial thinkers, it is posited, do not have a concept of time because they think in pictures and images. They are driven by the need to observe the world around them, noticing subtleties and details. They become so engrossed in producing internal scripts they lose awareness of time. Similar to ADD students, it is argued, it is unfair for them to lose credit on late tests and assignments.

Two other theories are worth mentioning. A number of psychologists argue that procrastination is a sign of an obsessive-compulsive personality. Then there is the time-flies hypothesis. Two cases from ancient times illustrate this point. The first is about Rava, a Jewish Talmudist from Babylon, who was famous for debating Jewish law. One time he became so immersed in a debate he did not attend to a wound on his hand. Socrates had the same problem whenever he became engrossed in debates at Aristole's school.

Tied to constructivist principles, engrossment is considered a virtue, not a vice (Wright and Blackwell 2009). Peter Jarvis (1987) describes it this way in his book *Adult Learning in the Social Context*:

There are situations where the self is not self-conscious in taken for granted situations. For instance, people driving a car along an open empty road listening to the radio may be so engrossed either in the radio program or in the journey that they are not conscious of the process of driving.

Justin's Montessori education encouraged deep engagement by offering him jobs to do without deadlines. He could stay on one as long as he liked. His self-directed learning carried over to his literacies. He would become so engaged in writing or reading or drawing he would lose all concept of time. In school, his deep concentration got him into trouble because he would fall behind on his other work. He was tagged in middle school as "unfocused," unable to compartmentalize his time. This would not have happened if someone had known him as an individual.

Multitasking is necessary during the school day. Children need to listen to teacher's talk, participate in small-group work, take notes, take tests, check out library books, finish assignments, edit a colleague's writing in writer's workshop, check e-mail, do volunteer work with younger children, change for gym, eat lunch in a hurry, and remember lines in the class play, all while listening and remembering to how to subtract fractions. Multitasking develops in students a hurry-up-and-get-the-task-completed attitude. They seem less concerned with the quality of their work than with how fast they can finish it. The same get-it-done attitude exists in the workplace. If we drift, our manager is going to think we are wasting time.

It is rare in school and in the workplace to stay focused on one project in order to do it well. That is because we punish late work with reduced grades. In contrast, handcrafting a beautiful piece of furniture requires great skill and a great deal of attention to detail. The artisan also needs plenty of time to produce a high-quality unique piece of art.

Studies of natural learners show that they approach learning as artisans, carefully constructing a story or a project through study, observation, experiment, refinement, and more refinement. Schools seem to have replaced the old Yankee way of doing a job right with the mass production of test scores.

The child in Chaim Potok's (1972), *My Name Is Asher Lev*, reveals the inner workings of the artisan's mind. Asher is a five-year-old boy who was born with a gift for drawing. He tells us, "I have no recollection of when I began to use that gift. But I can remember, at the age of four, holding my pencil in the firm grip of a child and transferring the world around me to pieces of paper."

He draws his memories in his room, often altering a sketch. He describes the drawing of his father this way: "I drew him often during these very early years. I drew him as he sat evenings with my mother, reading or talking. I drew him drinking coffee with my mother at the kitchen table. I drew my memory of him praying in our synagogue." Asher is not practicing a skill as part of an automaticity drill he might have to do in school but is using art to interpret his world.

He also shows us how he learns complex drawing concepts using prior knowledge and motivation. The following scene, abridged because of its length, depicts how he hit upon shading:

> One Sunday afternoon I brought my pencil and pad into the living room and drew my mother sitting on the sofa ... I was having trouble with her face. The cheek on the left side of her face dropped sharply into a concave plane from the high ridge of bone. I could not do the shading with the pencil ... I used the eraser ... Then I tried it again and used the eraser again ... the drawing felt incomplete ... I saw the ashtray ... filled with my mother's smoke out cigarettes ... I looked at the dark ends of the cigarettes ... I used the burnt end of the cigarette onto my mother face ... the contours of her body began to come alive.
>
> I realized my father was in the room watching me ... That night as my father helped me out of my clothes, he said quietly, " I wish you would spend all your time playing with pencils and crayons, Asher. ... Who showed you to use cigarettes that way?" I thought

of it myself. Once I used sand in a drawing and I thought of it myself, too.

As he matures, he tells us, "I would put all the world into light and shade to bring life to all the wide and tired world. It did not seem an impossible thing to do." In school, he falls behind in mathematics, aloof to the subject. His father, one of leaders of the Ladover Hasidic community, expresses his anger. "He said to me once, gazing at one of my drawings, 'You have nothing better to do with your time Asher. Your grandfather wouldn't like you to waste time so much time with foolishness.'" Asher replies, "A drawing is not foolishness." Asher cannot stop drawing or only draw pretty things as his mother desires because he draws to understand the world he is in.

Frank Smith's articles and books are classics in literacy and learning. His 2001 article "Just a Matter of Time" is a passionate defense of the time-flies concept:

> Struggling readers are often victimized by time constraints--arbitrarily imposed timetables for mastering material and meeting standards. People learn best from experience, not by information acquisition, skill development, rote memorization, or assessment. Any type of learning he believes requires student participation in relaxed settings.

Let me finish with two related anecdotes. I use several short stories in class to put a human face on research. One is Margo Rabb's (1998) "My Mother's First Lover," a short story about a summer-school assignment for students who had failed English. The class is to write a story about true love. Mia, whose mom has just passed away, struggles with the assignment, unable to find any true love in her parents' relationship. Turmoil keeps intruding on her thoughts.

Ms. Poletti assigned the story from her love of Robert Browning's romantic poetry. She justifies it by saying, "Love is beauty," with a big sigh. She is continually critical of Mia's writing, including her style of detachment from emotional subjects, even though she knows about the death of the girl's mother. Her only acknowledgement is to say, "I know that other things have been going on in your life." She says that she will pass Mia if she only writes one piece that fulfills the assignment. Mia submits nothing and fails.

Most of my students, from beginning level teachers to experienced ones, agree that Ms. Poletti doesn't show any real caring for Mia's emotional state, nor any flexibility in her teaching. Many point out that she could have asked Mia if there was another topic that she would feel more comfortable writing about or if she could have asked her to write about her feelings of loss.

Juxtapose Ms. Poletti's lack of empathy with a high school English teacher who took a summer class from me years ago. He regularly took me to task for espousing liberal views. His position was that late assignments should be punished because that is how the real world works. A week later he asked me for an extension on his paper, claiming outside responsibilities had prevented him from passing it on time.

I asked him if he saw any contradictions in his request. He said, "No. I have special privileges teens do not have." Narcissistic thinking leads to a culture of silence in classrooms. I call it teaching without a conscience. His moral beliefs do not apply to his unequals. Compare his ethos to Michelle's, one of the tutors in my prison work:

> My tutor was sincere in wanting to help me. She got that point across just like that. The first five minutes she was here she was telling the truth. She's always been here. She listens really good and if she had something to tell me or if she thought I had a problem with something, then she would tell me without making me feel like I was an inferior woman in prison—an inmate type of thing.

References

Arcilla, R. V. "Tragic Absolutism in Education." *Educational Theory*, v. 42, no. 4 (1992): 473–481.

Babad, E. "The 'teacher's pet' phenomenon, students' perceptions of teachers' differential behavior, and students' morale." *Journal of Educational Psychology*, v. 87, no. 3 (1995): 361-374.

Benner, A. D. and Mistry, R. S. "Congruence of mother and teacher educational expectations and low-income youth's academic competence." *Journal of Educational Psychology*, v. 99, no. 1 (2007): 140-153.

Bergman, D. "Is There a Private School Advantage in College Admissions?" *College Transitions: Expert Planning for College Admission* and *Success*. Posted March 29, 2014. https://www.collegetransitions.com/blog/private-vs-public-hs.

Brendgen M., et al. "Examining genetic and environmental effects on reactive versus proactive aggression." *Developmental Psychology*, v. 42, no. 6 (2006): 1299-1312.

Colón, E. P., and Kranzler, J.H. (2006). "Effect of instructions on curriculum-based measurement of reading." *Journal of Psychoeducational Assessment*, v. 24, no. 4 (2006): 318-328.

Crenshaw II, H. M., Thompson, D. and Leighman, J. "Research on Climate and Test Scores in Rayburn Middle School." *NASSP Bulletin*, v. 78, no. 562 (1994): 99-102.

Cullen. A. *The Geranium on the Window Sill Just Died, but Teacher You Went Right On*. New York: Harlin Quist Books, 1971.

Daughtry. H. *My Beloved Community: Sermons, Speeches, and Lectures*. Trenton: Africa World Press, 2001.

Dweck C. S. and Elliot A. J., eds. *Handbook of Competence and Motivation*. New York: The Guilford Press, 2005.

Galda, L., Pellegrini, A. D., Shockley, B. and Stahl, S. "The nexus of social and literacy experiences at home and school: implications for primary school oral language and literacy." *British Journal of Educational Psychology*, v. 65, no. 3 (1995): 273–285.

Gatto, J. T. *Dumbing Us Down: The Hidden Curriculum of Compulsory Schooling*. Vancouver: New Society Publishers, 1992.

Gatto, J. T. *A Different Kind of Teacher: Solving the Crisis of American Schooling*. Berkeley: Berkeley Hills Books, 2000.

Gatto, J. T. Interview by Jerry Brown. *We the People*. Radio Transcription. March 25, 1997. Retrieved from: http://www.wtp.org/archive/transcripts/john_taylor_gatto.html.

Goodman, P. *Compulsory Miseducation*. New York: Horizon Press, 1964.

Goodson, I. F. and Hargreaves, A. "Teachers' Professional Lives: Aspirations and Actualities." In Goodson, I. F. and Hargreaves, A., eds. *Teachers' Professional Lives*. London: Falmer Press, 1996.

Hanssen, E. "A White Teacher Reflects on Institutional Racism." *Phi Delta Kappan*, v. 79, no. 9 (1998): 694-698.

Harris, H. L. "School Counselors' Perceptions of Biracial Children: A Pilot Study." *Professional School Counseling*, v. 6, no. 2 (December 2002): 120-129.

Hugo, Victor. *William Shakespeare*. Translated by A. Baillot. Saint Peter Port: Hauteville House, 1864.

Jarvis, P. *Adult Learning in the Social Context*. New York: Croom Helm, 1987.

Kohn, A. *Punished by Rewards: The Trouble with Gold Stars, Incentive Plans, A's, Praise, and Other Bribes*. Boston: Houghton Mifflin, 1993.

Kohn, A. *What Does It Mean To Be Well Educated? And More Essays on Standards, Grading, and Other Follies*. Boston: Beacon Press, 2004.

Kohlberg, L. "Moral Education for a Society in Moral Transition." *Educational Leadership*, v. 33, no. 1 (1975): 46-54.

Kozol, J. *Letters to a Young Teacher*. New York: Random House, 2007.

Lee, H. *To Kill a Mockingbird*. Philadelphia: J. B. Lippincott & Co., 1960.

Lillard, A.S. *Montessori: The Science Behind the Genius*. New York: Oxford University Press, 2005.

Moje, E. B. (1996). "I Teach Students, Not Subjects: Teacher-Student Relationships as Contexts for Secondary Literacy." *Reading research quarterly*, v. 31 no. 2 (1996), 172-195.

Mullen, A. L. "Elite Destinations: Pathways to Attending an Ivy League University." *British Journal of Sociology of Education*, v. 30, no. 1 (2009): 15-27.

Persell, C. H., & Cookson Jr, P. W. "Chartering and Bartering: Elite Education and Social Reproduction." *Social Problems*, v. 33, no. 2 (1985): 114-129.

Porter, R. "Reading is Bad for your Health." *History Today* [online serial], v. 48, no. 3 (March 1998): Available at: http://www.historytoday.com/roy-porter/reading-bad-your-health.

Potok, C. *My Name is Asher Lev*. New York: Knopf, 1972.

Rabb, M. "My Mother's First Lover." *The Atlantic Monthly*, v. 282, no. 5 (November 1998). See also: https://www.theatlantic.com/magazine/archive/1998/11/my-mothers-first-lover/377303.

Rozycki, E. G. "Hurt, Harm, and School Safety." *Educational Horizons*, v. 83, no. 1 (2004): 6-10.

Rubie-Davies, C. M. (2005). "Exploring class level teacher expectations and pedagogical beliefs." Paper presented at the New Zealand Association for Research in Education annual conference, Dunedin, New Zealand (2005).

Smith, F. "Just a Matter of Time." *Phi Delta Kappan*, v. 82, no. 8. (2001): 572-576.

Steele, C. M. "A Threat in the Air: How Stereotypes Shape Intellectual Identity and Performance." *American Psychologist*, v. 52, no. 6 (1997): 613-629.

Swift, E. M. "Sports in a school curriculum: Four postulates to play by." *Teachers College Record* 92, no. 3 (1991): 425–432.

Denny Taylor. *Learning denied*. Portsmouth: Heinemann, 1991.

Wardle, F. "'Who Am I?' Responding to the Child of Mixed Heritage." *PTA Today*, v. 13 no. 7 (1988): 7-10.

Whitescarver, K., & Cossentino, J. "Montessori and the Mainstream: A Century of Reform on the Margins." *Teachers College Record*, v. 110, no. 12 (2008): 2571-2600.

Wright, R. and Blackwell, D. "Cognitive Processing within Narrative-Centered Learning Environments." In *Proceedings of Society for Information Technology and Teacher Education International Conference 2009*. Edited by C. Crawford et al. Chesapeake: AACE, 2009.

Wolf, A. E. *The Secret of Parenting: How to be in Charge of Today's Kids—from Toddlers to Preteens—Without Threats or Punishments*. New York: Farrar, Straus and Giroux, 2000.

Zentall, S. R. and Morris, B. J. "'Good job, you're so smart': The effects of inconsistency of praise type on young children's motivation." *Journal of Experimental Child Psychology*, v. 107, no. 2 (2010): 155-163.

12

Rehumanizing Literacy Learning

If we are to fulfil the Jeffersonian ideal of an informed citizenry, changes in the way we think about literacy and education have to be made. A powerful starting point is to document our own literacy histories. The moral imperative is clear—literacy histories not only broaden our understanding of cultural norms that shaped our values, but they also balance our connections to families and communities. What's more, literacy histories make clear the level of our consciousness of the world. Some of us are rooted to the core value of competitive individualism; others to social and economic equality. Do we fully understand how our values and rules affect the way we teach and learn? In the final analysis, engaging the past provides a very powerful way to evaluate the basis of our decision-making.

Why do some students succeed in schools, while others fail? This question is central to both the training of educators and the ongoing analysis of schools and their ability to meet learner needs. It is a question that has been approached and studied from countless angles: the effects of biology on learning, poor attendance, lack of reading skills, and socio-cultural influences including the role of familial and classroom practices in children's academic achievement. The literature is replete with statistical analyses of factors and their relationship to success and failure. While all of the above shed light on what "makes it or breaks it" in school, they do not necessarily put a personal face on the issue of academic achievement, and so don't answer the question at its core.

Since the publication of Ivan Illich's *Deschooling Society* in 1970, critical pedagogy and anthropology have changed the way educators view classrooms, teachers, students, and learning itself. Classrooms are subcultures that promote official rules, curricular guidelines, and moral values for students to succeed or fail. Close attention to rules and guidelines shift the focus of failure from the child to probing what Max Van Manen (1997) calls the invisible life of school.

Gatto (1992) has argued that schools have a hidden curriculum that restricts thinking and learning. Public schooling, he argues, involves "dumbing children down" to the point where they are unable to use democratic machinery and traditions to defend themselves against a managed society. The high rate of illiteracy in the United States, he posits, is attributed to the methods by which reading has been taught since World War II. In his view, encouraging students to read real literature will ultimately improve the quality of education.

The language of critical pedagogy is laden with terms like outrage, social justice, invisible life, and liberatory pedagogy. Some find it offensive to be told that the goal of schooling is to liberate students from oppressive environments. They point out that contemporary schools provide children safe places and good teachers to mediate bad home environments. Peter Hlebowitsh (1994) has argued that John Dewey portrayed the hidden curriculum more positively than some of the ideologically laden interpretations in vogue today.

While critical pedagogy sheds light on what "makes it or breaks it" in school, it does not necessarily put a personal face on the issue of school failure. To understand what actually happens in schools and classrooms, we need to listen to the stories of students very carefully. Self-reported literacy and educational histories of teachers have been used to enhance teachers' voices and self-reflection (Stansell 1993; Wilson 1990; Goodson 1995), chronicle literacy development (Moorman, Blanton, and McLaughlin 1994), examine the relationship between teacher candidates' experiential roots and their education to be a teacher of literacy (Roe and Vukelich 1998), and to show the benefits of writing and exploring life experiences (Baghban 1997).

The stories in *Fighting Prosaic Messages* helped us look at school experience through the lives of real people. We met a vast array of individuals whose stories demonstrated how easily a teacher's words can bolster or break down a child's learning and how family troubles, social life, and just plain boredom can throw a student off track. The stories showed us how easily encouraging words can make all the difference in the world for a young learner.

The narratives also presented small glimpses into the lives of educators who made a difference in our lives, both good and bad. They provided no neat answers or prescriptions for change. My hope is that teachers, students of literacy education, or parents reflect about the inner and outer worlds of students and teachers and some of the myriad subtle influences that shape school success or failure.

Perhaps you will go on to create your own educational history and to look for the predominant influences therein. The value of literacy histories lies in their ability to put a face and spirit to students and their experiences, a practice that is essential education.

References

Baghban, M. "Past into Present: Literacy through Life Stories." *Paper presented at the Annual Spring Conference of the National Council of Teachers of English* (April 1997).

Gatto, J. T. *Dumbing Us Down: The Hidden Curriculum of Compulsory Schooling.* Gabriola Island: New Society Publishers, 1992.

Goodson, I. F. "The story so far: personal knowledge and the political." *International Journal of Qualitative Studies in Education*, v. 8, no. 1 (1995): 89-98.

Hlebowitsh, Peter S. "The Forgotten Hidden Curriculum." *Journal of Curriculum and Supervision*, v. 9, no. 4 (1994): 339-349.

Illich, I. *DeSchooling Society.* London: Marion Boyars Publishers, 1970.

Moorman, G., Blanton, W., & McLaughlin, T. "The Rhetoric of Whole Language." *Reading Research Quarterly*, v. 29, no. 4 (1994): 308-329.

Roe, M. F. & C. Vukelich "Literacy histories: Categories of influence." Reading Research and Instruction 37, no. 4. (1998): 281-295.

Stansell, J. C. "Reflection, Resistance and Research among Preservice Teachers Studying Their Literacy Histories: Lessons for Literacy Teacher Education." Distributed by ERIC Clearinghouse [Washington, D.C.] 1993. Available at: http://www.eric.ed.gov/contentdelivery/servlet/ERICServlet?accno=ED365950.

Van Manen, M. *Researching Lived Experience: Human Science for an Action Sensitive Pedagogy.* London: University of Western Ontario, 1997.

Wilson, S. M. "The secret garden of teacher education." *Phi Delta Kappan*, v. 72, no. 3 (1990): 204-209.

Afterword

In my foreword, I wrote about Plato's allegory of the cave. I based the cover on Plato's allegory, too. So, I was taken aback—no, more like amazed—when I discovered the email correspondence below between me and my dad. What spurred this book was a conversation we had about Plato's allegory. I was also surprised that he had saved it after all these years! But how I wish my dad had printed out his side of the conversation. In any event, I had been hunting for the original images for this book, as the ones he had scanned didn't have the right pixel dimensions. In the basement, I found a printout of my emails to him on that old computer paper with the multiple holes on each side. Here's a snippet of the conversation. At the time I was an 18-year-old freshman. So, please do excuse my typos:

Tuesday, January 31, 1995

One more quick thing I want to ask you. Did the Republic have a strong impact on who you are as a person? The reason I ask is you act exactly like the character Socrates. I think that's why mom gets so annoyed at you sometimes. She gets annoyed at the amount of questions you ask and how you pretend you really don't know anything. It was amazing. I'm reading the your first son Justin. Justin means justice and that is the entire question and argument Plato is exploring in this book. I don't know. It may sound stupid but it just struck me as being interesting as I was studying it. One more question, I promise. How is grandma. What's the status of that situation?

Thursday, February 2, 1995

So I was righ about Socrates, huh. I'm just starting realize the true meaning of the parable of the cave. That to me is just beautiful. You've told me about the cave but I didn't really understand it. Plato is really talking about the importance of education in this section, right? To Plato the quest for truth and justice cannot be accomplished without education. This is why education is so important to you, isn't it. Education allows the person to turn away from seeing only the shadow of the model of reality and aids them to leave the cave to be in the presence of the sun which is the truth that all human nature seeks to find. That is incredible. This is probably some of the most No, scratch that. It's amazing how much I'm learning about you in this. And me and about the meaning of life in general. This is probably some of the most fun I've had academically.

I've just realized how late it's getting. Wish me luck on my job. I'll talk to you later.

When I wrote the foreword in May and drafted the cover this past week in August, I chose Plato's allegory because it seemed most appropriate to my dad's message. I had forgotten it had also been the topic of the discussion we had that led him to writing this book. The conversation happened 20 years ago after all. Discovering this printout, I felt the book was making a full circle: the book began with me sharing my excitement with my dad over discovering Plato's allegory for the first time, and it ended with me writing about and drawing the allegory. I thought that was so cool, so I wanted to share it with you.

I also wanted to mention something else, as a comment on the chapter my dad wrote about me. I wanted to comment on how my dad called me "gifted." Although it makes my day hearing him talk in that way about me, I was no more gifted than anyone else. And I think his only point was there seems to be three kinds of students that tend to "fail" school: one who feels they're too "dumb" and who gives up learning after leaving school; one who gets good grades but develops no voice; and one who might exhibit an artistic bent but may get lost in a system structured so much toward fact knowing. For him, I represented that third kind of student. But I think his real point was this: great teaching happens when we assume *every* student has a voice, and *every* student is capable.

Yes, you're right. There are some students who may "get" something quickly. They may have an "aha moment" (a kind of leap of *insight*) that allows them to grasp something faster than another. Another student might have to work more to get it. So, it's tempting to think there are some who are more capable than other students.

But I think one could also make the argument that the concept of "talent" is hogwash. The concept I'm referring to is the notion some persons are born with a talent and everyone else is average. I see two dangers in that notion. First, there's a doctrine of superiority written into it. Any doctrine of superiority has no scientific basis and can lead us to act unjustly toward each other. In education, specifically, it can lead to helping a few to succeed and leaving the majority to fail. Second, the notion seems to have this danger for a student: the student who thinks they're untalented won't even bother trying. They might think, "Oh, those 'talented' people? That's for them. Me? I could *never* do that. I wasn't born with any talent. Ah! Why even bother trying?" But the reality is, "talented" people have to work and learn like everyone else. If they don't, their talent becomes unrealized.

Let me say that last thought in another way. Even if some "get it" quickly, they still have work to do. And those who didn't "get it" right away can get there with work, too. In both cases, work—along with the desire to work and the belief that it's possible to "get it"—is needed. Teachers can help with a student's belief and desire to work by approaching every student as capable.

Again, there's a temptation to favor those who *appear* "talented." And students might look on the "talented" person as if they didn't have to work at it or be taught. They think they're just born fully formed out of the womb. Ridiculous! Even Beethoven had to learn composition and counterpoint (his composition teacher was Haydn). Thank goodness Mozart's father was a professional musician, because Mozart still had plenty of things to learn. Newton once said the only reason he saw further was because he stood on the shoulders of giants. Everyone has to *work* to develop a skill. How many talented persons never develop beyond the first inklings of their "gifts" because they didn't work at it? One who thinks talent "just happened" can also be "talented," if they worked at it. So, whether a student "gets" something right away or doesn't, it doesn't matter. Anything can be learned with practice. A teacher can help any student "get it" often by approaching them as ultimately capable.

"But what if a person wants to be a star?" someone might ask me. "How could they become a star if they didn't start off life by getting it quicker than others?" I'd reply, is the point of learning to become a star or is there value in the process of development in itself?

My dad mentioned my piano playing, but he left this part of the story out. I was so bad at piano that my first teacher (who had given me TV jingles to play) asked my mother to stop giving me lessons. But after watching *Amadeus*, I wanted to continue. I had this burning desire to play the music of Mozart. My mother took me to a professor of piano whom I expressed that desire to, and he agreed to take me on. Even though I couldn't have been an easy student as I had a lot of "ruff" to get through, at one point he said I was musical. I can't tell you how much those words got me through my struggle with piano. In high school, when I received a perfect score in the piano competition—my dad left this part of the story out as well—the judge was none other than my first piano teacher! She had thought I lacked talent in piano back then. But through work, I eventually "got" how to play Mozart. I don't care that I'm not a world-famous player or that piano still doesn't come easily to me. Piano has become one of my best friends. It's taught me how to listen, it gives my imagination freedom to play, it helps me find a center within emotions and an outlet for them. Plus, while learning how to master the beast, I've been learning how to master myself in the process. So, why must we learn something to become a star? Why can't we learn something for its joy and because it may help us to develop?

On the flipside, drawing came easier to me. What I "got" early on is looking for shapes, and "feeling" the lines. What an aha moment it was to discover that all you needed to do to draw Mickey Mouse was to draw circles! And how I enjoyed losing myself in the activity. You know when you watch clouds in the sky and see different shapes in them? That's what the feeling of drawing was like. Add to that the feeling you get when, entering the present moment, the heaviness of time dissipates. I could draw for hours. However, when drawing became about a performance, I began to lose the joy. I became nervous. "What if this drawing turns out to be bad?" I would think to myself. "What if no one thinks I'm talented anymore?" Once the desire for "glory" (or the fear of losing it) tinged the activity, I stopped drawing—for a long time. A few years ago (thanks to my dad thinking I had a "gift" and to a book called *Drawing on the Right Side of the Brain*), I picked up a pencil again, and it was with difficulty. I had to consciously put the "artist hero" muck aside and allow myself to make mistakes and do a lot of bad drawings. I still struggle with freeing myself from the concept of "talent," but I'm back to learning the skill of drawing. And drawing is slowly becoming a joyful activity again for me—when I forget about performance and do it for the joy of it.

Please allow me give one last example. This entire book is an example of putting the notion of "talent" aside. My dad would always say about himself "I can't write." The times I encouraged him to, he would say he couldn't: "writing is for people like Hemingway or Steinbeck," he'd say. "I have no talent." But once he learned that the writers he admired (like Paul Theroux) had to work hard to write well (and it didn't come easily even to them), I think he began to put this notion of "the talented" aside and worked to write this thing anyway. One of the joys I've had in going through the book was hearing my dad's voice in it. Seriously. Reading this was like having a conversation with him again even though he's no longer here. He found and captured his voice. By working on this book over and over again (he worked on this book from 1995-2010), giving it to people to read, taking their feedback, his writing kept improving. Now, the message of his life's work—how vital care is to teaching—can be remembered.

Anyway, that's why I think the concept of "talent" can do more harm than good. It seems to miss the point that all of us are a diamond within. "Talent" is really about insight. Any student can have insight. Education is the process that helps students come to insight, whatever stage of ruff they might be in.

My dad used to say the secret to great teaching is care. Maybe what he meant is seeing *every* student as capable of having insight. I know his care helped me. Through "care" we can give more patience to students. We would take responsibility rather than blame or condemn or pigeonhole students. We would include imagination in classrooms to create a desire and love of learning within a student rather than resort to rewards and punishments. We would create an environment that strengthens a student's belief rather than destroy it—there's enough of destroying each other outside the classroom. No student would be too "dumb." Those students who do well in school would be given a way to find their voice. And the artists and dreamers who show early signs of having a voice might not go unrecognized and untaught.

That passage from *The Republic* I read those years ago excited me so much I had to email my dad. It excited me to hear Plato say education was key to moving closer toward a more just society. Maybe that's why John Dewey thought education was so important to democracy, too. By utilizing the Socratic assumption that every student is capable, maybe we teachers can help more students want, and believe they can, "wake up." Like I said in my preface, if the measure of a society's health is in how many develop, then helping more students succeed in school may help us evolve to that next, higher level.

Let's take care in our teaching.

Justin Amoroso
August 2017

Index

P

R

S

About the Author

Here's the obituary I wrote for my dad. I wanted to publish it here to keep alive the memory of kind of man he was, and what kind of life he led.

-Justin Amoroso

Henry C. Amoroso, Jr. was born in Quincy, Massachusetts and pursued his career in education for more than 40 years—first as a third and fourth grade teacher, second as a Vista director and volunteer in the U.S. Virgin Islands, then as an Assistant Professor at Vanderbilt University. He finished his career as an Associate Professor at the University of Southern Maine.

Professor Amoroso had been with USM since 1982. He pursued his career first and foremost as a teacher. He modeled his educational philosophy after the Socratic view that answers were within the student and the teacher was more a midwife who helped students discover answers on their own. In his own words he once wrote, "students enjoy being treated as intellectuals."

During his tenure at Vanderbilt, he worked with illiterate prisoners teaching them to read by helping them write their stories in their own voices. His work with prisoners inspired the foundation of *Voices*, a journal in Canada about adult literacy. He also served as a consultant in developing a Vista program in Africa. At the end of his tenure at Vanderbilt he was voted "Favorite Teacher" by the students at Peabody College for Teachers.

At USM he served the university in various capacities, as member of the Faculty Senate, elected faculty representative on two presidential searches, director of the Core Curriculum, team member of USM's

Accreditation Committee, and several other standing committees. He founded the Casco Bay Partnership for Workplace Education, which provided educational opportunities to immigrant workers at Barber Foods, Hannaford Brothers, and American Tool.

His work with Cuba resulted in the formation of the Maine-Cuba connection. Its mission was to bring a Cuban perspective to U.S. education by taking to Cuba over 20 policy makers, including a former governor. This effort resulted in the creation of joint courses in comparative education and Cuban history and culture between USM and the Pedagogical Institute of Havana.

He developed many other courses at USM including the first course on the Internet, a course that blended art and story together called "Illuminated Autobiography," and "Poverty in America." His scholarship in the fields of literacy and education resulted in numerous journal articles, editorials, text reviews, and professional presentations.

His book *Fighting Prosaic Messages* about his grandmother's immigrant experience from Sicily to the U.S. traces her life as well as the lives of three generations of her family grappling with literacy in schools. Wanting to engage the imagination, he incorporated story-telling with scholarship. A critique of education and literacy, it's been described as "a signature piece." He worked on it even while fighting Leukemia, and completed it before he passed in 2010.

In addition to his passion for teaching, Henry loved to work with his hands. He took joy in building a beautiful Zen-like garden in his backyard. It was during its completion that he was diagnosed with leukemia. He also loved hiking and camping, especially in the White Mountains, reading, cooking, and spending time with his family. He kept a blog about his experiences with cancer that entertained, provoked thought, and lifted the heart. It was a picture of the way he taught and walked through life.

Professor Amoroso received his Bachelor's in English from St. Michael's College, his M.Ed in Elementary Education from Goucher College, and his Ph.D. in Curriculum and Instruction from the University of Wisconsin-Madison. The year before he passed, the University of Southern Maine conferred Emeritus status to him for his contributions to the University and community.